BASICS
OF
THE INTERNATIONAL SYSTEM OF CUSTOMS AND TARIFFS

G. Gregory Letterman

Transnational Publishers, Inc.
Ardsley, New York

Published and distributed by Transnational Publishers, Inc.
410 Saw Mill River Road
Ardsley, NY 10502, USA

Phone: 914-693-5100
Fax: 914-693-4430
E-mail: info@transnationalpubs.com
Web: www.transnationalpubs.com

Library of Congress Cataloging-in-Publication Data

Letterman, G. Gregory, 1943–
Basics of the international system of customs and tariffs / G. Gregory Letterman.
p. cm.
Includes index.
ISBN 1–57105–222–4
1. Tariff. 2. Customs administration. 3. Foreign trade regulation. 4. International trade. 5. World Trade Organization. 6. General Agreement on Tariffs and Trade (Organization) I. Title: International system of customs and tariffs. II. Title.

HF1713 .L475 2001
382'.7—dc21 2001033307

Manufactured in the United States of America

To my wife, Katherine Hawkins Letterman

CONTENTS

Foreword

International trade is big business, and that trade involves sending goods across national borders. When goods are to be introduced into the territory of a country other than their place of origin, that is an importation. Any importation of goods will involve the national customs and tariffs of the recipient country. Every exportation of goods is, by definition, an importation somewhere else. Although each country has its own government authority to deal with import customs and tariffs which operates in accordance with national laws, regulations, policies, and established practices, and although each country will differ (sometimes greatly) from every other country in this regard, there does exist an international system of customs and tariffs that provides a generally harmonious bridge among the different national systems.

It is the nature of this international system that permits international traders to regularize their many transactions travelling across a complex grid of source and recipient countries through application of a consistent, coherent methodology. A number of multilateral and regional organizations and bilateral arrangements are involved in creating this international system, and these operate under a number of agreements, conventions, treaties, and other accords and standards.

This book will explain what that international system of customs and tariffs is, will identify and describe those organizations and arrangements involved in creating it, and will analyze the institutional provisions and agreements which establish the details, enforcement mechanisms, and means of future development of that system. This will offer the reader more than simply a theoretical understanding of the international system. It will provide the reader with practical knowledge of the structure of the system under which national customs and tariffs systems operate and in accordance with which they are required to be established and administered. Such an understanding is fundamental to properly and effectively engaging in international trade or advising those who do so.

As another in a series on international commercial law topics to be published by Transnational Publishers, Inc. with G. Gregory

Letterman as author or co-author, this book follows the format and methodology of its predecessor and successors. All begin with the words "Basics of." The nature and degree of detail of their coverage is reflected in the common start of each of their titles. The full range of topics to be included in this series remains fluid. Consequently, those with suggestions for topics for subsequent books in the series are invited to contact Mr. Letterman through Transnational Publishers.

As is the case with all other books in the series, this book will not—and could not in its limited length—treat all aspects of its general topic; all the details of specific topics subsumed within its larger topic; or post-publication developments regarding the topic. The targeted reader of this book will be a practicing attorney, a law student, a scholar or academic or a person engaged in international commercial dealings. The book is intended to be—and should be used by the reader as—an introduction to the topic which will permit him or her both (a) to be informed regarding the basic issues involved regarding the international system of customs and tariffs and (b) to use that understanding to formulate informed questions for legal counsel, to engage in independent research on details and recent developments regarding particular aspects of customs and tariffs laws and practices, and to contact appropriate organizations with special relevance to customs and tariffs matters.

This book will not suffice as the reader's only guide to the law of the international system of customs and tariffs. It will serve as an effective large-scale map of the topic from which the reader may identify and understand the narrower areas of particular interest to him or her. Once the reader has oriented himself or herself in this manner, subsequent resort to the many and excellent information resources available on relevant detailed aspects of customs and tariffs is appropriate and should prove more efficient and fruitful for a reader who made preliminary use of this book before engaging in further inquiries.

G. Gregory Letterman
Kansas City, MO
March 15, 2001

Table of Abbreviations, Acronyms, and Shortened Names

AAD	WTO Agreement's Agreement on Antidumping Duties
AAg	WTO Agreement's Agreement on Agriculture
ACP countries	Seventy-one countries of Africa, the Caribbean, and the Pacific which had generally been colonies of or are currently territories of France, The Netherlands, the UK, or Belgium, and which are granted special trade terms by the EU under what are often called the "Lomé Conventions"
AD	Antidumping Duty (when describing NAFTA)
Amsterdam Treaty	A recent foundation treaty of the EU
Andean Pact/ANCOM	A trading bloc of some countries lying along the South American Andes Mountains which aspires to create an "Andean Common Market"
ANSI	American National Standards Institute
Anti-Nontariff Barriers to Trade	GATT principle that requires the substitution (except in limited circumstances) of tariffs for technical barriers to importation
APEC	Asia-Pacific Economic Cooperation Council
ASCM	WTO Agreement's Agreement on Subsidies and Countervailing Measures
ASEAN	Association of Southeast Asian Nations
ATA	*Admission Temporaire*/Temporary Admission, the program providing carnet temporary customs admission for goods

ATI	US Andean Trade Initiative
Auto Pact	Agreement Concerning Automotive Products between the Government of the United States and the Government of Canada (with annexes) of January 16, 1965
Benelux	Collectively, Belgium, the Netherlands, and Luxembourg, that have traditionally —and still do to a lesser degree under the EU—cooperate and harmonize their laws regarding various matters
BITD	International Customs Tariffs Bureau/ *Bureau International des Tarifs Douaniers*
BTI	EU's Binding Tariff Information
Cairns Group	Group, named for the Australian city where it was formed, of thirteen (Argentina, Australia, Brazil, Canada, Chile, Colombia, Hungary, Indonesia, Malaysia, New Zealand, the Philippines, Thailand, and Uruguay) countries for which agricultural trade is economically significant
CACOM	Central American Common Market
CAP	EU's Common Agricultural Policy
CARICOM	Caribbean Community and Common Market
CBI	US Caribbean Basin Initiative
CCC	Customs Cooperation Council (see also WCO)
CCC Nomenclature	CCC's nomenclature used to categorize types of goods for customs classification purposes, formerly known as the "Brussels Tariff Nomenclature, and made up of *The General Rules for the Interpretation of the Harmonized System* and the Section and Chapter Notes and the first six digits of the Harmonized System

CER or ANZERTA	The Australia-New Zealand Closer Economic Trade Agreement
CIS	Commonwealth of Independent States made up of 12 former republics of the now defunct USSR
CITES	Convention on International Trade in Endangered Species of Wild Fauna and Flora of 1973
Combined Nomenclature	EU's application of the Harmonized System
COs	NAFTA Certificates of Origin
CVD	Countervailing Duty (used when describing NAFTA)
COMESA	Common Market for Eastern and Southern Africa
DOC	US Department of Commerce
DRM	NAFTA Dispute Resolution Mechanism
DSB	WTO Agreement's Dispute Settlement Body
DSU	WTO Agreement's Understanding on Rules and Procedures Governing the Settlement of Disputes
ECOWAS	Economic Community of West African States
EAEC	East Asian Economic Caucus
ECSC	European Coal and Steel Community
EFTA	European Free Trade Association
Escape Clause	GATT 1947's Article XIX used when emergency action may be taken against imports that injure or threaten to injure domestic producers
EEA	European Economic Area made up of the EU and those European countries specially permitted and agreeing to partici-

	pate which establishes a regional trade bloc within their collective territories
EEC	European Economic Community, predecessor of the EU
EU	European Union
Euratom	European Atomic Energy Community
FTAA	Proposed Free Trade Area of the Americas
FTZ	Free Trade Zone
G-3	Free trade area to be created among Colombia, Mexico, and Venezuela
G-7	The Group of Seven (sometimes of Eight when the Russian Federation is granted honorary participation unjustified by economic statistics) made up of the seven countries with the largest national economies meeting regularly among themselves at ministerial and executive levels
G-77	The informally-organized group representing the poorer countries of the world, now more than the original seventy-seven.
GATS	WTO Agreement's General Agreement on Trade in Services
GATT	General Agreement on Tariffs and Trade administered by the WTO
GATT 1947	GATT prior to the conclusion of the Uruguay Round of GATT negotiations
GATT 1994	GATT portion of the WTO Agreement found at its Annex 1A
GDP	Gross Domestic Product
GSP	Generalized System of Preferences
GSTP	Global System of Trade Preferences

Harmonized Code Convention	The International Convention on the Harmonized Commodity Description and Coding System of June 14, 1983, with its Protocol of June 24, 1986
Harmonized System/ HTS	CCC's universal system for classifying imported items
HSC	The current CCC Harmonized System Committee
ICC	International Chamber of Commerce headquartered in Paris, France
ICSID	International Center for the Settlement of Investment Disputes
IEC	International Electrotechnical Commission
IMF	International Monetary Fund
IPEC	Independent Petroleum Exporting Countries
ISO	International Organization for Standardization
ITC	US International Trade Commission
ITO	The proposed International Trade Organization (never established because of US Senate rejection) under the Havana Charter that established GATT
ITU	International Telecommunications Union
Kyoto Convention	The revised International Convention on the Simplification and Harmonization of Customs Procedures of 1999
LAFTA	Latin American Free Trade Association replaced by LAIA/ALADI
LAIA/ALADI	Latin American Integration Association
MERCOSUR	Southern Cone Common Market (an acronym for *Mercado Comun del Sur* in Spanish or *Mercado Comùndel Cono Sul* in Portuguese), a trading bloc of some

	southern South American countries
MFA	The Multifiber Arrangement
MFN	Most-Favored-Nation GATT principle
MIGA	Multilateral Investment Guarantee Agency of the World Bank
Millennium Round	A tentative name for the upcoming round of WTO/GATT negotiations
NAFTA	North American Free Trade Agreement among Canada, Mexico, and the United States
National Treatment Principle	Under GATT, once imported items are admitted to the domestic market of a member they may not be treated differently than similar domestic products
Nice Agreement	A very recent and as yet unratified EU foundation document
NIST	US National Institute of Standards and Technology
Nordic Union	Denmark, Finland, Iceland, Norway, and Sweden and their associated territories of Greenland, the Faroe Islands, the Åland Islands, the Svålbård Islands, Bouvet Island, and Jan Mayen Island which cooperate on various matters of law and policy
OAPEC	Organization of Arab Petroleum Exporting Countries
OAS	Organization of American States
OAU	Organization of African Unity
OECD	Organization for Economic Cooperation and Development
OECS	Organization of East Caribbean States
OPEC	Organization of Petroleum Exporting Countries

PECAs Agreements	Protocols to the European Agreements on Conformity Assessment
Plurilateral Trade	WTO Agreement side agreements that are binding only on those countries that have signed them
PRC	People's Republic of China
ROs	Rules of Origin
RVC	NAFTA's Regional Value Content
SAARC	South Asian Association for Regional Cooperation
SAD	EU's Single Administrative Document for customs purposes
SADC	Southern Africa Development Community
SAFTA	Proposed South American Free Trade Association to be formed—at least initially—by joining together MERCOSUR and the Andean Pact
SEA	Single European Act of the EU
SITC	UN Standard International Trade Classification
Soviet Union/USSR	The former Union of Soviet Socialist Republics
TAMA	Israel's import tax "uplift"
TAFTA	The proposed Transatlantic Free Trade Area
TARIC	EU's Integrated Community Tariff
TEU	EU's Maastricht Agreement or the Treaty on European Union together with the Treaty Establishing the European Community
TPL	NAFTA's Treaty Preference Level
TPRB	WTO's Trade Policy Review Body
TPRM	WTO's Trade Policy Review Mechanism

Treaty of Rome	The European Economic Community Treaty of 1957, the principal founding document of the EU
TRIPs	WTO Agreement's Agreement on Trade-Related Aspects of Intellectual Property Rights
TRIMs	WTO Agreement's Agreement on Trade Related Investment Measures
UEMOA	West African Economic and Monetary Union
UK	United Kingdom of Great Britain and Northern Ireland (used sometimes here interchangeably with, but not actually identical to, "Britain" or Great Britain, which is made up of England, Scotland, and Wales)
UN	United Nations
UNCITRAL	UN Commission on International Trade Law
UNCTAD	UN Conference on Trade and Development
URAA	US Uruguay Round Agreements Act, Pub. L. No. 103-465, December 8, 1994, which implemented into US law the consequences of the completion in 1994 of the GATT/WTO Agreement
Uruguay Round	The GATT round of negotiations culminating in the WTO Agreement
US	United States of America
USCFTA	US-Canada Free Trade Agreement
USIFTA	US-Israel Free Trade Area
US Customs	US Customs Service
USTR	Office of the US Trade Representative
VAT	Valued-Added Tax

WCO	World Customs Organization (see also CCC)\WIPO World Intellectual Property Organization
WTO	World Trade Organization

Chapter I: National Systems of Customs and Tariffs

What are Customs and Tariffs?

Every country maintains systems under which it may monitor, control, and restrict the introduction of people, objects, and even ideas (even though often only in the sense of technology but sometimes including what is characterized as seditious or subversive material or even as material threatening the domestic "culture" through overwhelmingly attractive foreign influences) into its national territory. In the case of the introduction (into what is usually referred to as the national "customs territory") of goods, the system employed is known as "customs and tariffs." Tariffs are taxes or fees levied by a government on imports and exports. Only those on imports will be considered here. The money collected from tariffs is called a "customs duty."

While the above is a true general statement, the devil—as always—is in the details. Each country's formal systems of customs and tariffs will differ from that of every other country. Each country will certainly impose different tariff rates on the importation of different types of products and each of these rates may be different than that imposed on identical imported products by other countries. One country may define a type of product differently than does another country so that an importer may find it difficult to know into what category its imported product will fall and, consequently, to what tariff rate it will be subject. A country may make its assessment of a tariff based upon the monetary value, the weight, or the number of the imported product or through some combination of the above or on some other basis. Particularly regarding the determination of the monetary value of an imported product, the method by which that determination will be made is certain to be complex and is likely to differ greatly from country to country. Even in determining, e.g., the weight of an imported product, this will be done through the application of abstruse rules (e.g., is the weight of the container included or excluded). The rate at which tariffs will be imposed (and sometimes even whether or not an imported product will be admitted) will sometimes differ depending upon the country of origin of the intended import (and the rules for making a determination of that country of origin where more than one country had a hand in its creation vary from country to country and are invariably intricate and even nonsensical). Of course, some intended imports will be excluded entirely from importation or be subject to annual levels of importation and those exclusions and quotas will differ from country to country.

The process by which each country will administer its program of customs and tariffs will not be the same. No enumeration of these differences could ever be exhaustive. Some processes may involve the latest technologies while others are archaic in the extreme. The language in which forms will be completed and customs proceedings conducted and the currency in which any tariffs, fees, and penalties must be made will differ from country to country. The forms required to be used and the schedules by which procedural steps for importation are to be taken are unlikely to be the same in each country. There will similarly be different methods for challenging determinations made by the relevant authority and for seeking legal adjudication of any final decisions of that authority.

The practical implementation of any national scheme of customs and tariffs will be subject to great variation. Some customs authorities are models of probity and professionalism. Others are notoriously corrupt, hopelessly incompetent, and sometimes both. In some instances, authorities strictly follow their own formal, written, and widely-distributed rules while in others they almost seem to make up the rules as they go along. Some countries' customs authorities are independent of governmental efforts to influence their decisions while others regularly follow the special instructions of senior political figures regarding irregular implementation of their own rules. In some countries where the national administration of customs has proven to be so corrupt or chaotic as to threaten the essential economic interests of the country, some or all aspects of the administration of the national customs and tariffs schemes have been farmed out to private—often foreign—entities. Of course, once the judiciary becomes involved in resolving customs and tariffs disputes, the separate issues of the differences in national legal systems and the comparative efficiency, competence, and honesty of national judiciaries are raised.

Although the collection of tariffs is among the duties of a national agency that administers checks at national border-crossing points and places of entry (such as ports and airports), that is not all that such an agency will do. Some items intended for importation will be excluded from a country's customs territory categorically with no prospect of admission even with the payment of a tariff. Such exclusion may be predicated on many bases, including that the imported item is contraband, such as pornography, weapons, or addictive drugs; may violate domestic laws regarding intellectual property, health and safety, or national security; or may simply be excluded entirely or subject to a quota for protectionist purposes. For example, the US Customs Service ("US Customs") describes its activities as follows:

> US Customs ensures that all imports and exports comply with US laws and regulations. It collects and protects the revenue, guards against smuggling, and is responsible for the following:
>
> Assessing and collecting customs duties, excise taxes, fees, and penalties due on imported merchandise.
>
> Interdicting and seizing contraband, including narcotics and illegal drugs.
>
> Processing persons, baggage, cargo, and mail, and administering certain navigation laws.
>
> Detecting and apprehending persons engaged in fraudulent practices designed to circumvent customs and related laws.
>
> Protecting American business and labor and intellectual property rights by enforcing US laws intended to prevent illegal trade practices, including provisions related to quotas and the marking of imported merchandise; the Anti-Dumping Act; and, by providing Customs Recordations for copyrights, patents, and trademarks.
>
> Protecting the general welfare and security of the United States by enforcing import and export restrictions and prohibitions, including the export of critical technology used to develop weapons of mass destruction, and money laundering.
>
> Collecting accurate import and export data for compilation of international trade statistics.
>
> Enforcing well over 400 other provisions of law for at least 40 agencies. A number of these statutes are quality of life issues that relate to the environment, such as motor vehicle safety and emission controls, water pollution standards, pesticide controls, freon smuggling, and the protection of endangered wildlife. Other laws safeguard American agriculture, business and public health, and consumer safety.

Here we will consider as "customs and tariffs" all those charges and restrictions imposed on imported goods at the time of importation predicated at least in part on the essential fact that those goods are "imported."

Were the international system of customs and tariffs nothing but the different, incompatible, and idiosyncratic jumble of national systems of customs and tariffs, a description of it would consist of little more than the particular description of each—or at least the most important or representative of them—country's national system. Fortunately, that is not now entirely, and is increasingly less, the case. There is coming into existence a truly **international** system. It is that international system that will be described in the following chapters. It is the existence of this international system that permits international traders in goods to adopt a globally coherent, consistent approach to conducting their international trade as it relates to dealing with customs and tariffs.

It should always be remembered that every export is, by tautology, also an import. As a result, no exporter may act on the assumption that importing is someone else's problem. For an international trade to be completed and for payment to be made, the exporter must assure that its export will prove to be a successful import.

There are several global aspects of that international system, including the system of harmonized tariff classifications described in Chapter II and the general system imposed under the World Trade Organization ("WTO") and the General Agreement on Tariffs and Trade ("GATT"), a description of which constitutes much of the remainder of the book.

Of great practical interest must be the definition by any country of its national "customs territory" since many countries will include in such description territories seemingly not directly connected with it, or exclude territories seemingly a part of or associated with the country. Readers are urged to check for whether a relevant piece of real estate falls within or without a country's national customs territory where this would seem to be both germane and at issue.

There are also regional aspects to this international system. These will be described above, principally in Chapters IV and V. As an introduction to understanding these regional aspects, it is necessary to distinguish among the different types of regional efforts that may be, and are being, attempted. Essentially, these may constitute (a) free trade areas, (b) customs unions, (c) common markets, (d) economic communities, and (d) economic unions.

A free trade area is an arrangement between two or more countries under which they have agreed to permit some or all goods (and sometimes services) produced within one or some combination of the members to circulate within their territories free of all or most tariffs and other restrictions. A primary but extraordinarily complex issue in any free trade area agreement is the establishment of Rules of Origin ("ROs") that determine when a good is or is not deemed to be a product of the free trade area. Nonetheless, no agreement will have been reached with regards to a common tariff schedule for goods or services imported into any one of the members nor for the free movement of extra-regional imported goods from one country to another within the free trade area. In most cases, parties to free trade area agreements will not immediately implement a perfect free trade area within their joint territories but will engage in a phased, graduated move from the status quo into a free trade area arrangement.

A customs union involves a relationship between two or more (usually) contiguous states that creates common trade barriers for all participating states to the entry of goods (and sometimes services) from nonmember countries. In some instances, when one of the members is far stronger and more advanced economically than the other(s), that state may unilaterally establish the tariff schedules, administer the customs procedures, and collect the tariffs on imported goods for all of the members. In such instances, there is normally an allocation of costs of administration and a division of collected tariffs among the members according to some pre-agreed formula. In a "customs union," any product imported into the territory consisting of the collective territories of the members of the customs union will be subject to the same harmonized customs and tariffs charges and rules without regard to through what point in the territory importation is made. After such importation has been made, imported goods may be moved within the territory without the imposition of additional charges or restrictions. Despite the common customs and tariffs treatment of all imports into the customs union territory, however, products produced within the customs union territory need not be permitted to move freely within the territory and may be subject to tariffs and other impediments when they are moved across a national border.

A common market combines the properties of a free trade area and a customs union. This permits the importation of goods to be made at any point in the collective economic community territory on identical terms and further permits all imported and locally-produced goods to be moved, used, and sold anywhere within the economic community territory without being subject to further charges or restrictions when crossing a national border. It involves an agreement among two or more countries under which is established common tariff and import-related procedures for the importation of extra-regional goods and services and for the free trade within the common market of goods and services, whether locally-produced or imported, without the imposition of further tariffs or customs restraints. In addition, it will often permit some additional commercial liberalization within the common market and may provide for the free movement among participatory states of factors of production—principally capital, labor, and technology. Under a common market, customs and similar administrative costs and receipts are generally shared.

An economic community is an institutional arrangement among member countries under which all the characteristics of a common market are present and, in addition, there is an attempt to establish a degree of harmonization of essential national economic policies by participatory states. Essential national economic policies may include those regarding transportation, taxation, corporate structure and regulation, monetary matters, and regional economic preferences.

An "economic union" is an economic community where the national economic policies have been harmonized to the point that they are virtually the same. When the regional economic group has added to its collective functions those unrelated to commerce, such as foreign relations or defense and/or has adopted collective institutions, such as a legislature, a common passport, or a common currency, which are normally associated with a sovereign state, it is, for most intents and purposes, a federated nation state. Nonetheless, it has, for its own reasons, chosen to reject self-designation as a nation state even though it may act in that capacity in various of its domestic and international roles. There is currently only one example of such an "economic union." That is the European Union ("EU"). It was until recently an economic community. Whatever the EU now is, it is unique and is likely to remain so. A more detailed description of it is provided in Chapter IV.

Finally, some treaties may establish bilateral free trade areas or common markets between and within two countries. The differing relationships among a mother country and its colonial or semi-autonomous or otherwise associated parts may create complex and confusing customs and tariff relationships.

An Abbreviated History of Customs and Tariffs

Customs and tariffs have a long history. They are mentioned in the Code of Hammurabi, the first written laws of which we have a record. In Classical Greece, with its small city states, sea traders would dock their ships at ports with the equivalent of lesser import tariffs when selling to nearby customers in other city states even when the city state had its own port that was a shorter distance from those customers. Import tariffs and the levying of customs duties developed in Europe in medieval times and have continued uninterrupted to the present day.

The earliest justification for import tariffs was the government's (or ruler's) need for money. Imports were among the easiest sources for that money. All imports had, by definition, to arrive at the borders of a political territory. Since the political entity had to man and defend its border under any circumstances, requiring those importing goods across them entailed only instructing the border guards to identify, assess, and tax those goods. The importers were usually foreign merchants (so local sensibilities were not directly challenged) who carried cash or its equivalent in such things as gold and silver(so the collection of duties was more satisfactorily and easily collected than would have been the case when receiving payment in kind) and local consumers were largely unaware of—although far from unaffected by—the tariffs and were therefore indifferent to their collection or their rates. Such tariffs were very important sources of revenue for governments and have remained so. For example, until the United States imposed an income tax in 1913, import tariffs were the major source of income for the US Government. They remain the second largest source of US Government revenues even today. The US Government early recognized the importance to it of customs duties. The US Constitution deals with imports and customs duties in some detail (Article 1, Section 8, Clauses 1 and 3, and Section 10, Clause 2) and the second law ever passed by the US Congress after the adoption of the US Constitution was the Act of 1789 for laying duties on goods, wares, and merchandise imported into the United States.

When the sole reason to impose import tariffs was the generation of revenues for the government, the sole basis for the setting of rates and the imposition of tariffs was revenue maximization. Although initially without a basis in economic theory, those responsible for imposing tariffs undoubtedly learned through trial and error that setting the highest possible tariff did not necessarily generate the greatest possible revenues. This was true because raising the tariffs above a certain rate reduced consumption because of higher sales prices and thereby reduced the volume of imports. Secondarily, a sufficiently high tariff provided an incentive for smuggling, import substitution, and other devices intended to directly or indirectly avoid the payment of those tariffs. Nonetheless, during this period tariffs were set at the rates that would optimize revenues from their collection.

Later, governments learned that the imposition of tariffs, which imports were subject to tariffs, and the rates at which tariffs would be collected influenced other economic activities of their countries. When governments sought to engineer social and economic activities within their countries by encouraging favored activities and inhibiting disfavored activities, the process of imposing tariffs on imports also factored in the provision of effective incentives and disincentives to identified social and economic conduct. Further, based upon diplomatic relationships among countries and the foreign policy objectives of any one country, rates were regularly set differently by a country depending upon what country was the source of the import.

There are several economic theories or policies that have been implemented from time to time through the imposition of tariffs or the restriction of imports. Although they are no longer as enthusiastically espoused as they once were, support for them remains an unspoken factor in some countries and some industrial sectors.

One was "mercantilism." Mercantilism presumed that the optimum national economic policy regarding international trade was to maximize a country's trade surplus by selling more than it bought and to engineer the terms of that trade to limit imports to raw materials unobtainable locally and to make most exports finished goods incorporating the imported raw materials along with local materials and labor. Mercantilism is literally a "beggar thy neighbor" policy that assumes crossborder trade is a pie of fixed size. Consequently, the bigger some other country's slice, the smaller the slice for one's own country. Among the flaws in the theory of mercantilism—apart from the fact that it is based on an erroneous premise—is that when other countries are treated only as customers for a particular country's exports, two things may happen. The first is that the program is successful and mercantilism so impoverishes the customer countries that they are unable to continue purchasing the vendor's exports. The second (and this is why mercantilism was most popular when it could be imposed by a "mother country" on colonies unable to exercise independent discretion) is that the customer countries resist by buying the exports of other vending countries or by producing local products to replace the imported ones. Among other countries, Japan seems often to still operate on mercantilist principles even though it never overtly admits to doing so. A variation on mercantilism that until recently was popular among developing countries and those who advised them was so-called "import substitution" through which national policy was to encourage and direct local economic development—including by foreign investment in the country—to replace imported products and thereby reduce expenditures of scarce foreign currency and to insulate the national economy and national security from dependence on foreign sources of essential goods.

Also perennially popular—at least in some circles—is "protectionism." Protectionism is intended to insulate selected local producers or industrial sectors from foreign competition in their domestic markets by prohibiting the importation of competing foreign goods or by making their domestic prices noncompetitively dear because of the imposition of high tariffs on their importation. While most protectionist acts are overtly indefinite in duration (and virtually all turn out to be endless in practice), some are justified as being necessary to create "incubator industries" in a country which will be protected only until they are operating at internationally-competitive levels. Protectionism is in some ways related to mercantilism, but may be exercised on a more particularized basis and relies at heart less on any economic theory for justification than on the political responsiveness of politicians to special pleading by their constituents (and these are often constituents with money who are willing to provide some of it to politicians who cater to their demands). Domestic monopolists and oligopolists are not the only advocates of protectionism. Their employees and the labor unions which represent those employees, as well as communities which would be adversely affected by diminishment in the economic fortunes of the domestic monopolists and oligopolists, also are often advocates of selective protectionism. Advocates of protectionism are not misguided due to flawed economic analysis. They are often—but not always—correct in believing that protectionism would be good for them. What is irrelevant to them is that protectionism is always—see the paragraph below—always bad for the general population of a country and for the political entity itself. The reason that special pleaders for protectionism so often prevail and that governments and politicians so often—and sometimes even knowingly—act against the general public interest is that the benefits to those receiving trade protection are immediate and great while the detriments suffered by the general public from protectionism (both through higher consumer prices and through the inefficient allocation of limited domestic resources) are prospective and—for the individual citizens—limited in size. As a consequence, beneficiaries from protectionism know they would lose important benefits were protectionism to end while the average citizen places little importance on any vague claims that he or she would realize marginal future gains were protectionism to be eliminated. As a result, advocates of protectionism are fierce in its defense while the public demands for an end to protectionism are weak and ineffectual. Nonetheless, the long-term effects of protectionism are invariably disastrous because of the ever-increasing relative inefficiencies of protected domestic industries and the expansion of protectionism's scope as more and more domestic industrial sectors demand it. Argentina from the 1930s through the early 1990s is a demonstrative example of protectionism's terrible effects. When the right—or wrong—country turns protectionist, the results may be catastrophic for the world. Some economists believe that what should have been a relatively short and modest economic recession was turned into a prolonged, global, and cataclysmic economic depression in the 1930s by the US Smoot-Hawley Tariff Act of 1930 which overnight raised tariffs of US imports by more than 50% and began a cycle of vicious, world-wide protectionism and retaliation.

The last economic principle adopted through national, regional, and global trade and tariff policies—and clearly the one favored unreservedly by the author—is "free trade." The eighteenth century English economist David Ricardo articulated his theory of international trade in a clear, succinct, and persuasive manner and its truth has been demonstrable without fail ever since, both by its benefits where its prescriptions were implemented and by the dire consequences of ignoring it. His essential proposition is known as "comparative advantage." That means that every country may productively use its limited capital in the most efficient way (through placing capital where it incurs the lowest "opportunity costs") such as to realize the greatest economic benefit to the country and its citizenry and that, for every country, the most efficient use of its domestic capital will differ from that for every other country. Consequently, any country will be best served by making the most efficient use of its domestic capital to produce those things that it is best suited to make and permitting other countries with greater efficiencies in producing other things to make them and sell them (at cheaper prices) as imports to that country. While this system would work best—and result in the greatest prosperity for all the world—were all countries to mutually eliminate all barriers to international trade, any **one** country would be better off unilaterally adopting free trade even **failing** universal adoption of free trade by some or all other countries. To illustrate the point, Ricardo posited trade between Britain and Portugal in wine and cloth. Since Portugal was most efficient in producing the former and Britain the more efficient in producing the latter, both countries would be better off by trading British cloth for Portuguese wine. Iceland may serve as a more extreme—and therefore better illustrative—example. Iceland could—assuming sufficient expenditures of capital and the use of adequate technology—both catch and sell codfish and grow and sell bananas. It would be ill-advised to attempt to do both since it is an efficient codfishing country and a highly inefficient banana-growing country. For the best interests of Iceland and its citizens, it would exclusively devote its resources to catching cod while procuring all its bananas from tropical countries. A more personalized illustration is the answer to the question of why Tiger Woods pays someone else to mow his lawn. Undoubtedly Mr. Woods would be a competent law mower if he chose to try. Perhaps he could do it as well as anyone he might employ to do it. He does not mow his own lawn because he realizes much greater income from playing golf for the amount of time it would take him to mow his grass than he would spend hiring even the most expensive gardeners to mow the grass for him.

Free trade is now the most popular international trading principle of the day. It has unquestionably been the greatest contributor—exceeding even that of technology—to the improved economic circumstances of the world and its peoples at the start of the new millennium. Nonetheless, there are growing signs that its popularity and implementation have already reached their high-water marks and that advocates of protectionism (sometimes acting behind obfuscatory screens of purported environmentalism or labor rights concerns) are successfully reasserting this demonstrably failed practice. British historian Thomas Babington Macauley said in 1824 that free trade is one of the greatest blessings that a government can confer on people. But he added, "Unfortunately, it is in almost every country unpopular." Macauley's statement appears to remain true in its entirety even today.

There **are** justifiable reasons to be concerned about the consequences of imported goods. National security is only one among these legitimate concerns. The Organization of Petroleum Exporting Countries ("OPEC") has demonstrated, through its petroleum embargoes and effective—at least temporarily—ability to unilaterally establish the global price for crude oil, that making satisfaction of a country's energy requirements dependent upon foreign sources may be dangerous to the national welfare no matter how justifiable a policy it may be based on arguments for the most efficient allocation of capital resources. Notwithstanding such cases, past experience shows that such "exceptional circumstances," which should lead a country to ignore the conclusions of Mr. Ricardo, are usually urged by those who are merely attempting to mask the ugly face of protectionism behind a more presentable façade.

Operating within National Customs and Tariffs Systems

When operating within any national customs and tariffs system, there are some steps that a party should take that will be applicable in every case.

The first is to understand that—unless the party is seeking to frustrate another party's efforts to complete an importation—the national customs and tariffs authority is an adversary and not a friend. It may seem courteous, efficient, and willing to be helpful, and may actually be all these things. Nonetheless, nothing such an authority does provides a benefit to an importer that could not be better served—from the importer's standpoint—by the total elimination of the authority. The importer and a national customs service do not share a common goal. The purpose of such authorities is to extract money from the importer, to delay or place additional burdens on the importer, or to frustrate completely the importer's efforts to complete an importation. Not only is this a customs services' job, but that service acts with police powers and may draw upon all the resources and authority of the state to compel compliance. Customs officers are rewarded and promoted for maximizing revenues for the state and for strenuously detecting and prosecuting those in violation of customs law and regulations. As a result, minimize contacts with the importing administrative authority and understand that there is no such thing as a "courtesy" visit or inspection by that authority. Understand that, once an importer has been found by a national customs service to be in alleged violation of customs laws or regulations, the importer has lost without regard to whether it is later vindicated. Resolution will be slow and costly. Impounded goods will accrue storage charges in the customs shed while they deteriorate or go out of fashion.

Second, obtain access to the current national laws, regulations, and tariff schedules (by preference in your own language) relating to importing of the country into which significant imports will be made. The importer should become familiar with these and with official, informed, or even anecdotal information regarding the practical aspects of importing into such countries. Such information may be obtained from a number of sources, including through commercial sources, the embassy or agencies of the country into which importation is to be made, and appropriate agencies of the importer's own country. The International Customs Tariffs Bureau/*Bureau International des Tarifs Douaniers* ("BITD") has been, since 1890, the global multilateral organization responsible for providing current translated versions of the tariff schedules of its members (see http://www.bitd.org or obtain its *International Customs Journal* which contains listings of the world's tariffs by tariff classification listing. *Worldtariff* (see http://www.worldtariff.com) is a series of publications from a private publisher containing national tariff schedules in English. The US International Trade Administration's web site at http://www.ita.doc.gov/TTFrameset.html is a good source to check for non-US tariffs information. It provides a link to all non-US customs authorities' web sites and has on its site the EU tariff schedule. The following web sites contain specific national tariff schedules (most, but not all, are in English): Asia Pacific Economic Cooperation (US, Canada, Mexico, Chile, and many Asian/Australasian countries) member tariff schedules at http:///www.apectariff.org; Common Market of Eastern and Southern Africa (Angola, Burundi, Comoros, Democratic Republic of the Congo, Eritrea, Ethiopia, Kenya, Madagascar, Malawi, Mauritius, Namibia,

Rwanda, Seychelles, Sudan, Swaziland, Tanzania, Uganda, Zambia and Zimbabwe) member tariff schedules at htttp://www.comesa.int; Iceland at http://www.tollur.is; Jordan at http://www.customs.gov.jo; Malta at http://customs.business-line.com/Default.htm; Norway at http://www.toll.no; Niger at http://www.cotecna; Morocco at http://www.douane.gov.ma.tarif; Pakistan at http://www.cbr.gov.pk; Qatar at http://www.qatar.net.q./customs/gen-e.htm; Singapore at http://gov.sg/customs; South African Customs Union at http://www.rapidttp.com.za/cargo; and United Arab Emirates at http://www.dxbcustoms.gov.ae. The national customs administrations of member countries of the World Customs Organization may be contacted at http://www.wcoomd.org/frmpublic.htm. Many have English-version web sites and provide information about national customs procedures and may even have copies of their tariff schedules on-line.

Third, utilize the services of appropriate professionals skilled in importing into the country to which goods are directed where this is required or necessary. In some instances the use of such professionals is mandated by law while in other cases their use will simply reflect prudence and good business practice. These professionals may include, *inter alia*, attorneys and customhouse brokers.

Fourth, where practicable the importer should take every preliminary step possible to obtaining the practical confirmation that its understanding of the applicable tariff rate and other conditions for the prospective importation is correct. This may involve obtaining such written confirmation from the national customs authority in accordance with administratively prescribed procedures or may involve making a small initial importation prior to subsequent imports in volume. Never engage in an international marketing program without first determining with certainty the actual landed cost of the imported product, including customs, insurance, and transportation, and always include in a sales contract a favorable escape clause—which will differ depending upon whether it is written by the importer or exporter—permitting a desired latitude of action (including termination or renegotiation of the contract) in the event of currency exchange rate changes, exclusion of the goods from the customs territory of the recipient, or significantly changed treatment of the goods upon importation. Remember, once costs have been incurred for transporting goods to the place of importation and into the customs shed, it will be an expensive, lengthy, and sometimes virtually impossible proposition to terminate the importation and have the goods returned to the exporter's custody in the country from which they were shipped.

Fifth, do not be a passive importer. Game the system. Do not simply know what the tariff is on a particular import from a particular place to a particular country. It is sometimes possible to so design a product or to ship it in separate unassembled parts or in a package of its unassembled parts so as to reduce or eliminate the tariff rate. It is often possible to have a product made in a chosen country or to be imported into a free trade zone in the country of importation and there to be assembled or otherwise manipulated so as to reduce or eliminate the tariff rate. It is even possible in some countries to get quicker, easier, or even more favorable customs treatment by selecting on the basis of local customs practices a particular port of importation in a country—even if such a port is otherwise less conveniently located to the ultimate recipient.

Sixth, know the other rules and pitfalls to which an importation may be subject. Be sure the imported product is marked as required. Be sure the imported product does not infringe on locally-protected intellectual property; is consistent with mandatory local standards, e.g., for electrical safety; and is not otherwise subject to exclusions or special charges.

Seventh, before making an importation, the importer must understand not only its obligations and its rights but must also have a realistic appraisal of its prospects for fair and timely recourse in any resolution of disputes or claims made against it by the national customs service. Adjudication of import-related disputes is an arcane and often unsatisfactory affair. One judge of a court dealing with these matters called the process "Alice in Wonderland" because cases hinged on such issues as whether a tomato is a fruit or a vegetable or whether whale flesh is fish or meat. A British judge was called upon to determine if the character "Spock," a humanoid alien from the planet Vulcan, appearing in the television program *Star Trek* is a human or not. An EU import quota had been placed on nonhuman dolls from China but no quota was imposed on human dolls. The verdict, for your information, is that, although most other *Starship Enterprise* crewmembers (and their dolls) are human, Spock is not (at least for purposes of the quota).

Operating Within the International System

While the international system of customs and tariffs provides a generally harmonious framework within which a party may arrange and plan its international trade in goods, that international system only imposes obligations and rights on sovereign countries. The private individual operating within this system may, therefore, not directly avail himself or herself of a recourse to the mechanisms or particulars of that system and may certainly not effect changes in that system. That does not mean that the system may not be used by the private individual or that the system itself is not subject to modification beneficial to the individual. The system itself is subject to challenge and change through the agency of its member governments. The private individual may influence one or more individual governments to assert challenges or argue for changes to the system in a manner desired by the individual. More common, however, is the ability of the private individual to familiarize himself or herself with and to fully understand the system. Becoming well-versed in that system is the beginning step in the private individual's operating effectively within and under that system through the various national customs and tariff systems.

Chapter II: Global Uniformity in Customs Classification

Harmonizing National Tariff Schedules

In any national schedule of tariffs, a universe of possible imported items must be broken down into categories under at least one of which any conceivable import might fall and guidance must be provided regarding rules which direct the classification of such an item into only one of the possible categories. The importation of any item falling into such a category is then charged with the tariff calculated at the applicable rate on such entry category.

Where the system of categorization of imported items of each country is entirely different, the complexity of engaging in international trade is greatly magnified. Not only is it necessary to have a current copy of each country's tariff schedule (presumably in a translation into one's own language) on hand in order to determine into what category any item one may wish to ship there falls, but an exporter/importer must also be thoroughly familiar with the way in which administrators and courts have interpreted and applied the individual tariff entries. Obtaining the requisite information would be very difficult. Performing such a task on a global scale is, of course, impossible.

Further, there are many uses for the numerical categorization of universal categories for imported items in addition to moving goods through a customs shed. For example, export and shipping documents all require the identification by product category of goods being shipped.

The need for transnational harmonization of the national systems of product classification for customs and tariffs purposes is obvious. Although it was late in coming, such a harmonized classification system now exists and is described below.

The principal formulator and administrator of that system is the Customs Cooperation Council ("CCC")/World Customs Organization ("WCO"), but it is not alone. The Group of Seven major industrialized countries ("G-7"), the United Nations Conference on Trade and Development ("UNCTAD"), the Organization for Economic Cooperation and Development ("OECD"), and the International Chamber of Commerce based in Paris, ("ICC") are among the other multilateral and international organizations that play a part.

The Customs Cooperation Council and the Harmonized System

The CCC, which—for general operating purposes—changed its publicly-used designation to the WCO in 1994, is a multilateral organization with its Secretariat based in Brussels, and is the only global multilateral, intergovernmental organization with competence in customs matters. Its address is 30, Rue du Marché, B-1210 Brussels, Belgium. Its telephone number is 32.2.209.92.11 and its facsimile number is 32.2.209.92.92. Details of the CCC/WCO may be found at the CCC web site—http://www.wcoomd.org/frmpublic.htm.

The CCC—created in 1952—grew out of the European Customs Union Study Group that was established following World War II. It is responsible for promoting harmonized laws and procedures for simplifying and improving national customs practices, for coordinating international detection and prosecution of violations of customs laws, and for improved communication and cooperation among national customs authorities. The CCC formulated and continues to administer the International Convention on the Harmonized Commodity Description and Coding System of June 14, 1983, with its Protocol of June 24, 1986 (1035 UNTS 3; KAV 2260) (the "Harmonized Code Convention"). In addition, the CCC has been responsible for a number of other customs conventions, recommendations, and standards and is in the process of formulating others. In particular, the CCC created the revised International Convention on the Simplification and Harmonization of Customs Procedures of 1999 ("Kyoto Convention").

The G-7 countries have mutually acted to create simplified and harmonized customs procedures, particularly regarding the harmonious use of electronic filing technology, uniformity in (and reduction in the amount of) data requirements, and standardization of forms and filing methodologies used in importing. The G7 Customs Group has standardized the data and format for the most common customs procedures. For imports, this includes the Cargo Report (manifest report by the carrier), and the declarations required for the release of goods and/or the settlement of duties and taxes (reports filed by the importer or his agent). For exports, this includes the carrier's Export Cargo Report and the Declarations. Any customs administrations concerned may demand additional information whenever more information is required for compliance measurement reasons and/or concerns about fraud or noncompliance. The CCC has been instrumental in assisting G-7 in this process.

The CCC also cooperates closely with the WTO, UNCTAD and the ICC and operates the ATA carnet system for temporarily admitting certain imported goods free of duty.

The CCC created a universal system for classifying imported items. It is called the "Harmonized System" and is used as a base for the "CCC Nomenclature" (formerly known as the "Brussels Tariff Nomenclature"). In part, the Harmonized System is based on the United Nations' Standard International Trade Classification ("SITC"). Sixty countries, fourteen multilateral organizations, nine private international organizations, and two national trade facilitation organizations participated in the development of the Harmonized System. By far the majority (over 95%) of the world's trade in goods is conducted under the Harmonized System. CCC members included 151 countries and territories in early 2001, 102 countries were member states of the Harmonized Code Convention as of July 15, 2000, and several other countries and territories apply the Harmonized System. The United States adopted the Harmonized System in 1989.

The Harmonized System is divided into 21 sections (most of which group articles from similar branches of industry or commerce), with country members permitted to add at least one additional section to accommodate special national treatment. The sections, numbered respectively 1 through 21 in Roman numerals, are: I. Live Animals; Animal Products; II. Vegetable Products; III. Animal or Vegetable Fats and Oils and their Cleavage Products; Prepared Edible Fats; Animal or Vegetable Waxes; IV. Prepared Foodstuffs; Beverages, Spirits, and Vinegar; Tobacco and Manufactured Tobacco Substitutes; V. Mineral Products; VI. Products of the Chemical or Allied Industries; VII. Plastics and Articles Thereof; Rubber and Articles Thereof; VIII. Raw Hides and Skins, Leather, Furskins and Articles Thereof; Saddlery and Harness; Travel Goods, Handbags and Similar Containers; Articles of Animal Gut (Other than Silkworm Gut); IX. Wood and Articles of Wood; Wood Charcoal; Cork and Articles of Cork; Manufactures of Straw, of Esparto or of other Plaiting Materials; Basketware and Wickerwork; X. Pulp of Wood or of Other Fibrous Cellulosic Material; Waste and Scrap of Paper or Paperboard; Paper and Paperboard and Articles Thereof; XI. Textiles and Textile Articles; XII. Footwear, Headgear, Umbrellas, Sun Umbrellas, Walking Sticks, Seatsticks, Whips, Riding Crops and Parts Thereof; Prepared Feathers and Articles Made Therewith; Artificial Flowers; Articles of Human Hair; XIII. Articles of Stone, Plaster, Cement, Asbestos, Mica, or Similar Materials; Ceramic Products; Glass and Glassware; XIV. Natural or Cultured Pearls, Precious or Semiprecious Stones, Precious Metals, Metals Clad with Precious Metal and Articles Thereof; Imitation Jewelry; Coin; XV. Base Metals and Articles of Base Metal; XVI. Machinery and Mechanical Appliances; Electrical Equipment; Parts Thereof; Sound Recorders and Reproducers, Television Image and Sound Recorders and Reproducers, and Parts and Accessories of Such Articles; XVII. Vehicles, Aircraft, Vessels and Associated Transport Equipment; XVIII. Optical, Photographic, Cinematographic, Measuring, Checking, Precision, Medical or Surgical Instruments and Apparatus; Clocks and Watches; Musical Instruments; Parts and Accessories Thereof; XIX. Arms and Ammunition; Parts and Accessories Thereof; XX. Miscellaneous Manufactured Articles; and XXI. Works of Art, Collectors' Pieces and Antiques.

The 21 sections are divided into 96 international chapters (with two additional chapters permitted for national purposes), numbered from 1 to 97 (chapter 77 remains "reserved" and unused). Each of these deals with a subset of a section's coverage. The sections generally cover an industry and the chapters cover the various materials and products of the industry.

The 96 chapters contain around 5,000 headings and 9,500 subheadings that are article descriptions of items moving in international trade. These are described under four digit general headings and six digit subheadings. For importation and other purposes, a number is assigned to each category of products at the lowest level of classification. The first six digits are mandatory and universally used in each national Harmonized Tariff Schedule. Four additional digits are permitted to be used for their own purposes (and are used by different nations in different ways) by nations adopting the Harmonized System.

The six mandatory digits reflect, respectively, the Harmonized System chapter in which a product is categorized by the first two digits; the descriptive heading by the third and fourth digits (and these first four digits constitute a heading identification); and the descriptive subheading by the fifth and sixth digits. Some countries may add additional sub-subheadings through subsequent numbers. The United States adds an additional two numbers for sub-subheadings and two more numbers as statistical suffixes.

Rules of Interpretation for the Harmonized System

The General Rules for the Interpretation of the Harmonized System, the Section and Chapter Notes and the first six digits of the Harmonized System constitute the international nomenclature. The rules by which determinations are to be made regarding into what category any actual imported item properly falls are those of the *Explanatory Notes to the Harmonized System* prepared by the CCC. They provide a commentary on the scope of each heading of the Harmonized System and are thus useful in ascertaining the classification of merchandise under the system. *The Compendium of Classification Opinions of the CCC* also gives CCC classification decisions. The opinions constitute the official interpretation of the Harmonized System by the CCC. The above documents are amended from time to time to reflect changes in interpretation. The CCC has designated a distributor in each member country of its explanatory notes, their updates, and other compendia.

The six "General Rules of Interpretation," as printed in the US Harmonized Tariff Schedule, read as follows:

"Classification of goods in the tariff schedule shall be governed by the following principles:

1. The table of contents, alphabetical index, and titles of sections, chapters and sub-chapters are provided for ease of reference only; for legal purposes, classification shall be determined according to the terms of the headings and any relative section or chapter notes and, provided such heading or notes do not otherwise require, according to the following provisions:

2. (a) Any reference in a heading to an article shall be taken to include a reference to that article incomplete or unfinished, provided that, as entered, the incomplete or unfinished article has the essential character of the complete or finished article. It shall also include a reference to that article complete or finished (or failing to be classified as complete or finished by virtue of this rule), entered unassembled or disassembled.

   (b) Any reference in a heading to a material or substance shall be taken to include a reference to mixtures or combinations of that material or substance with other materials or substances. Any reference to goods of a given material or substance shall be taken to include a reference to goods consisting wholly or partly of such material or substance. The classification of goods consisting of more than one material or substance shall be according to the principles of Rule 3.

3. When, by application of Rule 2(b) or for any other reason, goods are, *prima facie*, classifiable under two or more headings, classification shall be effected as follows:

   (a) The heading which provides the most specific description shall be preferred to headings providing a more general description. However, when two or more headings each refer to part only of the materials or substances contained in mixed or composite goods or to part only of the items in a set put up for retail sale, those headings are to be regarded as equally specific in relation to those goods, even if one of them gives a more complete or precise description of the goods.

(b) Mixtures, composite goods consisting of different materials or made up of different components, and goods put up in sets for retail sale, which cannot be classified by reference to 3(a), shall be classified as if they consisted of the material or component which gives them their essential character, insofar as this criterion is applicable.

(c) When goods cannot be classified by reference to 3(a) or 3(b), they shall be classified under the heading which occurs last in numerical order among those which equally merit consideration.

4. Goods which cannot be classified in accordance with the above rules shall be classified under the heading appropriate to the goods to which they are most akin.

5. In addition to the foregoing provisions, the following rules shall apply in respect of the goods referred to therein:

   (a) Camera cases, musical instruments cases, gun cases, drawing instrument cases, necklace cases and similar containers, specially shaped or fitted to contain a specific article or set of articles, suitable for long-term use and entered with the articles for which they are intended, shall be classified with such articles when of a kind normally sold therewith. The rule does not, however, apply to containers which give the whole its essential character.

   (b) Subject to the provisions of Rule 5(a) above, packing materials and packing containers entered with the goods therein shall be classified with the goods if they are of a kind normally used for packing such goods. However, this provision does not apply when such packing materials or packing containers are clearly suitable for repetitive use.

6. For legal purposes, the classification of goods in the subheadings of a heading shall be determined according to the terms of those subheadings and any related subheading notes and, *mutatis mutandis*, to the above rules, on the understanding that only subheadings at the same level are comparable. For the purposes of this rule, the relative section, chapter and subchapter notes also apply, unless the context otherwise requires."

The Harmonized System Committee ("HSC"), the only active CCC committee of four in existence at one time or another (and, confusingly, three of these were called the "Harmonized System Committee"), has continuing responsibility for administering the Harmonized Code Convention.

The Compendium of Classification Opinions contains decisions of the HSC on the classification of different products in response to requests presented to the CCC.

The reports of the Nomenclature Committee (the committee responsible for administering the CCC Nomenclature) and other HSC committees, working documents of the Nomenclature and Classification Directorate of the CCC, and letters from the Secretariat of the CCC also bear—at least to some small degree—on these issues, as do classification decisions of various national customs services.

The Harmonized System Convention provides that classification disputes between member countries will be resolved by negotiations between them. If these fail, questions will be referred to the HSC. Failing success there, they are referred to the CCC for a recommendation as to settlement. Disputant parties must accept the recommendation or decision before the dispute is considered resolved.

Limitations on US and Other Nations' Deference to the CCC

The information below deals not only with this subtopic but provides, through quoted passages in official US customs materials, valuable background data on the Harmonized System as well.

Countries participating in the CCC do not necessarily provide legal recognition to the actions or decisions of the CCC nor may they consider themselves bound in matters of national customs and tariffs policy or practice to conform to all CCC standards as defined by the CCC. Although the United States will be considered in detail below in this regard, other nations may display their own variations from CCC standards. The reader is urged to examine any national practices closely for countries critical to an importation to determine if any variations from CCC positions exist and are relevant to an import transaction.

The US Government participates in semiannual HSC meetings. US Customs, the US International Trade Commission, and the US Bureau of Census prepare position papers (although these do not constitute the official position of these organizations) in preparation for such meetings.

The US Government has determined that Explanatory Notes to the Harmonized System and the Compendium of Classification Opinions (discussed above) are useful for guidance by US Customs but are **not themselves dispositive** on any issue. Other CCC documents and the interpretations, opinions, and practices of other countries with Harmonized Tariff Schedules regarding the Harmonized System are accorded little or no weight by US Customs.

For a statement of this US Customs policy, see "United States Customs Service, Guidance for Interpretation of Harmonized System," 54 Fed. Reg. 35127 (1989), which is reproduced below. This policy statement is of interest because of its bearing on US importation policy but may also be representative of other similar national policies and contains information regarding the history of and deliberations that went into the formulation of the Harmonized System.

> "Pursuant to section 1204 of Public Law 100-418, the Omnibus Trade and Competitiveness Act of 1988, the Harmonized Tariff Schedule of the United States (HTS) was implemented effective as to merchandise entered or withdrawn for consumption on or after January 1, 1989.
>
> Since the implementation of the HTS, Customs has been urged to take into consideration a host of documents as background documentation in the classification of goods. These have included, not only the Explanatory Notes to the Harmonized System (HS), but such documents as reports of the Nomenclature Committee (the committee that administered the Customs Cooperation Council Nomenclature), letters from the Secretariat of the Customs Cooperation Council (CCC) and rulings and regulations from other Customs administrations. All of these matters are urged on Customs as an indication of the intent of the Harmonized System Committee (HSC) in drafting the system, or, sometimes, on the grounds that Customs has an obligation to interpret the HTS in uniformity with the interpretation of the CCC or that of other Contracting Parties to the Convention on the Commodity Description and Coding System (the Convention).
>
> This notice explains Customs' position on the various documentation that is available and gives an overall assessment of the weight that should be accorded to the various documents.
>
> Uniformity in the interpretation of the international system, the HS, is not a function of Customs. Customs is charged with the administration and interpretation of the HTS, the tariff enacted by Congress. The function of maintaining the uniform application of the HS resides with the HSC per Article 7 of the Convention. It is fundamental that the United States did not give

up sovereignty when it acceded to the Convention. There is, as such, no obligation on Contracting Parties for the uniform application of the HS. There is, however, an obligation on Contract Parties to 'not modify the scope of the sections, chapters, headings or subheadings of the Harmonized System.' Consequently, Customs takes background documentation into consideration so that classification rulings do not modify the system.

The Committees

An understanding of the documentation issued by the CCC requires some background into the various committees that dealt with the HS. The HS was drafted by a committee known as the HSC. Unfortunately this is the same name as the committee formed under the Convention, and this has produced some confusion. Four committees have dealt with the HS: (1) The HSC which existed from 1973 to 1983; (2) the Interim HSC; (3) the HSC formed under the Convention; and (4) the Nomenclature Committee.

The drafting Harmonized System Committee: The HSC which was charged with drafting the HS met in 31 sessions from June 1973 to June 1983. Its reports are designated: Summary Record of the XX Session of the Harmonized System Committee and its Working Party.

The Interim Harmonized System Committee (HSC): This committee met in 9 sessions, jointly with the Nomenclature Committee, from 1983 until the Convention went into force on January 1, 1988. It drafted the HS Explanatory Notes and reviewed the Compendium of Classification Opinions. Although it had no particular legal standing, it did make proposals for amending the HS.

The Harmonized System Committee: The committee formed under the Convention. It is the committee currently charged with the administration of the Convention. It meets twice a year and held its first session in April 1988.

The Nomenclature Committee: The committee formed to administer the Customs Cooperation Council Nomenclature (CCCN) (first known as the Brussels Tariff Nomenclature), the nomenclature which is replaced by the HS. Because the Nomenclature Committee had agreed to amend the CCCN to conform to the HS, it reviewed the work of the HSC to see if it found it acceptable for purposes of the CCCN.

The Documents

Explanatory Notes

The status of the Explanatory Notes (ENs) to the HS is specifically addressed in the report of the Joint Committee on the Omnibus Trade and Competitiveness Act of 1988. It is there stated:

The Explanatory Notes constitute the Customs Cooperation Council's official interpretation of the Harmonized System. They provide a commentary on the scope of each heading of the Harmonized System and are thus useful in ascertaining the classification of merchandise under the system.

The Explanatory Notes were drafted subsequent to the preparation of the Harmonized System nomenclature itself, and will be modified from time to time by the CCC's Harmonized System Committee. Although generally indicative of proper interpretation of the various provisions of the Convention, the Explanatory Notes, like other similar publications of the Council, are not legally binding on contracting parties to the Convention. Thus, while they should be consulted for guidance, the Explanatory Notes should not be treated as dispositive.

This is a clear statement of the intent of Congress in adopting the HS as a basis for the US Tariff. The status outlined by the Joint Committee of Congress applies only to the ENs and 'similar publications of the Council.' In that connection, Customs would point out that the only similar publication of the Council is the Compendium of Classification Opinions.

Among the international conventions administered by the CCC, the HS is a replacement for the former CCCN. There were ENs to the CCCN and they are sometimes cited in requests for rulings. The CCCN ENs have no value in interpreting the HS. They are the ENs to a different system; one which is now virtually nonexistent since most nations have adopted the HS.

It should also be noted that the ENs are a dynamic instrument reflecting the intent of the Contracting Parties on the application and interpretation of the HS. They will be amended from time to time and may thus reflect a change in interpretation. Customs believes they should always be consulted.

Classification Opinions

The CCC publishes a Compendium of Classification Opinions. These opinions represent decisions by the HSC on the classification of various products that were presented by the HSC on the classification of various products that were presented to the HSC for consideration. When a classification question is presented to the HSC, the Committee will frequently draft an opinion to be published in the Compendium. However, that is not always the case. Sometimes the decision of the HSC is converted into an amendment to the ENs, and sometimes it is merely reported in the report of the session of the HSC when the decision was made. The decision is included in the Compendium when it is thought to be instructive.

When a decision of the HSC is published in the Compendium it should receive the same weight as ENs. They constitute the official interpretation of the HS in consideration of a particular issue placed before the HSC.

There was also a Compendium of Classification Opinions under the CCCN. The Interim HSC reviewed that Compendium and adopted into the HS Compendium a number of the CCCN opinions. Approximately 20 percent of the CCCN opinions were carried over to the HS. The remainder were discarded, some because they were outdated, some because their substance had been incorporated into the HS ENs and some because they were thought to be erroneous under the HS. Opinions reported in the CCCN Compendium have no validity under the HS for the same reasons the CCCN ENs are not valid under the HS.

HSC Reports Prior to July 1983

The HSC prior to 1983 was tasked with drafting the HS. This required numerous decisions and these are reported in the Summary Records of the HSC sessions. The Summary Records of HSC sessions are a resource in ascertaining the intent of the Committee in the drafting of any particular text. Because the sessions were long and rather involved, the deliberations of the Committee are reported only in summary form. The Summary Records do contain reports on a number of decisions of the HSC. When such decisions are clearly reported they constitute history for the text concerned. The Summary Records are available to the public through the Department of Commerce National Technical Information Service. While these documents do not carry the weight of the ENs or the Compendium of Classification Opinions, they are frequently guides to the intention of the HSC.

Interim HSC Reports

The IHSC drafted the ENs and reviewed the CCCN Compendium of Classification Opinions. The reports of this Committee have the same relationship to those documents as do the Summary Records of the HSC to the legal texts of the HS. Since the ENs have no legal standing, these reports are not considered history for the HS. Customs considers them to be instructive in some instances.

The IHSC also considered a number of amendments to the HS. Because the IHSC had not defined standing, all of the IHSC decisions on amendments were referred to the HSC when the Convention came into force. Therefore, for some of the proposed amendments to the HS, background information can be found in the reports of the IHSC.

Reports of the HSC after 1/1/88

The Convention went into force on January 1, 1988, and sessions thereafter are reported in Reports of the Harmonized System Committee. The first session was held in April 1988. Decisions of this committee are advice and guides to the interpretation of the HS. None of these decisions are binding, but Customs considers that they often provide valuable insight into how the HSC views certain provisions.

In rendering its decisions, the HSC also usually decides whether the decision merits an amendment to the ENs, the issuance of a classification opinion to be added to the Compendium, or to merely report the decision in the report of the session. If the decision results in amendment of the EN or goes into the Compendium, it, then, should receive considerable weight. As Congress made clear, however, the decision should not be treated as dispositive.

Decisions of the HSC that are merely given in the report should be given little weight.

Decisions to amend the HS itself need to go through the amendment procedure provided in the Convention. They require domestic legislation to go into effect in the United States.

Nomenclature Committee Reports

Customs is frequently asked to consider reports of the Nomenclature Committee. They carry virtually no weight. Decisions of the Nomenclature Committee cannot imply an intent on the HSC. They are two separate committees, differently constituted, and set up for different purposes.

Normally, the HSC received reports from the Nomenclature Committee without comment. When the HSC adopted an opinion or decision of the Nomenclature Committee it was specifically noted in the Summary Record.

When the HS was drafted it was decided to prepare an entirely new convention to implement it. It was the intention of the HSC to start anew; to have a new convention unencumbered by the many years of action by the Nomenclature Committee. Although the HS is primarily based on the CCCN, it is a new and different nomenclature with a convention that provides for substantial difference in its voting membership. Customs finds that there is no reason to believe that questions decided by the Nomenclature Committee would produce the same result in the HSC.

Working Documents

Customs calls 'working documents' those documents issued by the Nomenclature and Classification Directorate of the CCC. These are the documents that form the basis for discussion in HSC sessions. They carry virtually no weight in interpreting the system. Working documents usually consist of commentary by delegations on questions before the Committee, commentary by the Secretariat on the comments made by delegations, and other material designed to frame the question the HSC is to discuss and to stimulate the discussion. Because it is preliminary material, none of it reflects the intent of the HSC.

The working documents are sometimes interesting because they contain more detailed descriptions of the goods under consideration and they sometimes contain the rationale for certain positions.

Rulings of Other Countries

The General Rules for the Interpretation of the Harmonized System, the Section and Chapter Notes and the first six digits of the Harmonized System constitute the international nomenclature. Therefore, in principle, all Contracting Parties to the Convention should give the same classification to identical merchandise through the six-digit subheading level. In this regard, classification rulings from other Customs administrations are sometimes submitted to Customs with a ruling request as evidence of how similar merchandise has been classified under the HS by that country.

Customs is not bound to abide by another country's rulings. The foreign ruling may have been subject to political realities or domestic regulations which are different from our own. The merchandise at issue in our ruling may not be identical to that in the foreign ruling. In either case, the foreign ruling is unlikely to describe fully the context in which it was issued. Therefore, at best, the foreign ruling is merely instructive of how others may classify like goods.

Position Papers

Prior to each session of the HSC, Customs, the International Trade Commission, and the Bureau of the Census prepare position papers to reflect the position to be taken by the US delegation at the session. These documents in no way reflect the position of Customs in the interpretation of the HTS. Position papers are guides for the delegation in the context of the HSC session; they are essentially negotiating positions. They are mentioned here because some position papers have received some circulation and have been cited in support of a classification; they have no value whatever for such purposes.

Summary

Customs is charged with the interpretation of the HTS and not, as such of the HS.

Customs' concern in looking at documents is to find the scope of headings and subheadings of the HTS.

As indicated by Congress, Customs will give considerable weight to Explanatory Notes and the Compendium of Classification Opinions because they are the official interpretation of the HS, but they shall not be treated as dispositive.

When it is necessary to determine the intent of the HSC, Customs will look to the Reports and Summary Records of the HSC.

Other documentation may be consulted for information purposes only.

In addition to the General Rules of the Interpretation of the Harmonized System, the US has added to its national Harmonized Tariff Schedule "Additional US Rules of Interpretation." These continued certain US pre-Harmonized Tariff rules of interpretation, were said to clarify or supplement the General Rules, but may be in conflict with the General Rules or may have equal or superior authority when compared with the General Rules. Those US "additional rules" read as follows:

"Additional U.S. Rules of Interpretation

1. In the absence of special language or context which otherwise requires

(a) a tariff classification controlled by use (other than actual use) is to be determined in accordance with the use in the United States at, or immediately prior to, the date of importation, of goods of that class or kind to which the imported goods belong, and the controlling use is the principal use;

(b) a tariff classification controlled by the actual use to which the imported goods are put in the United States is satisfied only if such use is intended at the time of importation, the goods are so used and proof thereof is furnished within 3 years after the date the goods are entered;

(c) a provision for parts of an article covers products solely or principally used as a part of such articles but a provision for 'parts' or 'parts and accessories' shall not prevail over a specific provision for such part or accessory; and

(d) the principles of section XI regarding mixtures of two or more textile materials shall apply to the classification of goods in any provision in which a textile material is named."

Chapter III: WTO/GATT—Administrator of the Global Customs and Tariffs System

The Global Customs and Tariffs System

The global customs and tariffs system has formally existed since soon after the end of World War II. It exists because the US wanted it. What the US wanted immediately following World War II it generally got because it was the sole remaining industrial economy not devastated by destruction from the conflict and was the sole source of funding for the reconstruction of the industrialized countries that had been devastated. While other countries acquiesced to US preferences, that acquiescence was often begrudging and was sometimes given in defiance of the real, contrary policies and preferences of the acquiescing government. The US officially favored increased liberalization in international trade and, in theory, advocated free trade (although the US was far from pure in its own domestic customs and tariff practices). The informal and voluntary international trading system that had prevailed before World War II under the overwhelming influence on global trade of the UK had been fatally crippled by the combined consequences of World War I and the great global economic Depression of the 1930s.

While GATT—and later the WTO—were and are the leading fora at which the details of that global system are formulated and articulated and through which they are administered, there are other multilateral and international organizations that play a role. Some were described in the previous chapter. An enumeration of customs conventions with on-line sources of their texts may be found at http://www.wcoomd.org/frmpublic_en.htm.

Another is the World Intellectual Property Organization ("WIPO") which has assumed responsibility for an Information Technology Agreement completed at Singapore on December 13, 1996, under a WTO Ministerial Declaration and which appears in WTO Document WT/MIN(96)/DEC, December 18, 1996. The Agreement on Implementation of the Ministerial Declaration on Trade in Information Products was completed on March 26, 1997, and appears in additional WTO Documents G/L/159 and G/L/160 of April 2, 1997. The WTO Information Technology Agreement liberalized the trade in information technology products under 25 national tariff schedules (Australia; Canada;

the Czech Republic; Costa Rica; Estonia; the EU; Hong Kong; Iceland; India; Indonesia; Israel; Japan; Korea; Macau; Malaysia; New Zealand; Norway; Romania; the separate customs territory of Taiwan, Penghu, Kinmen and Matsu; Singapore; Slovakia; Switzerland (and on behalf of Liechtenstein which participates with Switzerland in a customs union); Thailand; Turkey; and the United States—Panama and Poland belatedly submitted documents that would make those countries participants upon the acceptance of their documents and other countries may become participants upon their application and the approval of their participation terms) representing approximately 92% of world trade in those products. Elimination of customs duties and other charges on these products was envisaged by January 2000. The schedule of concessions under the Ministerial Declaration and Implementation Agreement were released, appropriately, through the Internet for most participating countries. The Implementation Agreement and Ministerial Declaration may be found at 36 International Legal Materials 375 (1997). The Ministerial Declaration contained a list of the WTO members and their agreement on the expansion of world trade in information technology products and the declaration that the parties' trade regimes should evolve to enhance market access opportunities for information technology products in addition to the specific elimination of duties and charges with respect to those products included in Attachments A and B to the Declaration. The Annex dealt with modalities and products coverage. Attachment A dealt with covered Harmonized System headings or parts thereof and Attachment B dealt with specific products to be covered by the Agreement without regard to where they are classified under the Harmonized System. The Implementation Agreement dealt with acceding WTO members, further implementation of the Declaration, compliance with criteria established in the Declaration Annex, establishment of a Committee of Participants on the Expansion of Trade in Information Technology Products, processes for monitoring implementation and consultations on and review of product coverage, and the GATT 1994 Article XXVIII procedures for proposed modifications or withdrawals of concessions. The Annex to the Declaration was incorporated into the Implementation Agreement. The Declaration stipulated that participants representing approximately 90% of world trade would have to notify their acceptance of the ITA by April 1, 1997. This occurred and the agreement entered into force with the first staged reduction in tariffs occurring on July 1, 1997.

History of GATT

GATT is a treaty. It is, with its associated agreements, the world's only multilateral instrument that establishes agreed rules for international trade.

GATT was first negotiated in 1947. Its liberalizing measures were strengthened through repeated negotiating rounds. Ultimately, "GATT 1947" consisted of over 200 agreements, protocols, understandings, and similar documents. It was transformed in 1994 by the successful conclusion of the lengthy Uruguay Round of negotiations. A new, successor undertaking ("GATT 1994" under the WTO Agreement) of the GATT 1947 regime was the result.

GATT 1947 had 126 states as parties. At least 20 more are expected to join under the WTO Agreement. GATT 1947's members included all market economy industrialized countries, about a hundred developing nations, and several former Communist countries. Some other countries, *e.g.*, the Republic of China on Taiwan, applied the rules of GATT 1947 on a *de facto* basis. Cumulatively, GATT 1947 members accounted for well over 90% of the world's trade. Members of GATT 1947 at the time the WTO Agreement entered into force [with the EU counted as a single member but with votes equal to the number of its member states] became members of the WTO Agreement. Accession of new members will be permitted only on terms specially established in each case. Among those countries currently seeking to become members are important trading nations, such as the People's Republic of China ("PRC"). Admission is not automatic. It generally requires a demonstration that a country's global and domestic trading is largely based on free market practices and that the country is truly committed to liberalized access to its national markets by the world's goods and services. Ultimately, a candidate member country must negotiate the terms of its admission that include tariff schedules and limitations on nontariff import restrictions.

The basic aim of GATT/the WTO Agreement has always been to liberalize and make secure the terms of world trade. GATT 1947 did a remarkably good job of reforming what had, at its inception, been a very protectionist world of international commerce. Average tariffs in industrial countries fell from an average of 40% in 1947 to 5% in 1988 while the volume of international trade in manufactured goods multiplied twenty-fold.

Nonetheless, over time GATT 1947's rules were increasingly subverted or ignored. US use of Section 301 proceedings under the 1974 Trade Act, 19 USCS §2411(a), as amended, and US refusal to operate through GATT 1947 procedures and dispute resolution channels elicited many complaints. They contributed to the decline in the authority of GATT 1947. Furthermore, large sectors of international trade, *e.g.*, agriculture; services—which constitute nearly 30% of all world trade; and textiles and clothing—though the Multifiber Arrangement ("MFA") which is a very lightly-veiled abandonment of GATT principles—were effectively beyond the regulation of GATT 1947. Between September 1986 and September 1987, the number of nontariff restrictions identified by GATT 1947 rose from 93 to 135—allegedly affecting half of all world trade. The US and the EU were largely responsible for the rise. More than two-thirds of GATT 1947's members were developing countries, many of whom paid—and were only required to pay—little more than lip service to GATT principles. It was the common view that, if it were not "fixed," GATT 1947 would soon become irrelevant.

GATT 1947 was negotiated in 1947. It entered into force in January 1948. The 23 signatories were simultaneously drawing up the charter—called "the Havana Charter"—for a proposed International Trade Organization ("ITO").

The Havana Charter was a comprehensive code governing the conduct of world trade. It contained both general statements of principle and specific commitments of national policy dealing primarily with national barriers to trade. It covered all types of restrictions on trade, *e.g.*, tariffs, preferences, and internal taxation and regulation (such as quantitative restrictions and related exchange matters); labor and employment; economic development and reconstruction; subsidies; state trading and related matters; general commercial provisions on freedom of transit; antidumping and countervailing duties; special provisions for free trade areas and customs unions; restrictive business practices; and intergovernmental commodity agreements.

GATT 1947 was largely based on parts of the Havana Charter. It had the limited purpose of cutting tariffs as a bridging measure pending approval of the Havana Charter. It was to be effected with minimal institutional arrangements because responsibility for trade liberalization was expected to soon be assumed by the ITO. Plans for the ITO were abandoned, however, when it became clear that the Havana Charter would not be ratified by the US Senate. GATT 1947 was, consequently, a treaty without its planned administering organization and which covered only a part of its originally intended scope.

GATT 1947 had 38 Articles. Part One, Article I, was the key article. It guaranteed "Most-Favored-Nation" ("MFN") treatment among all members. Article II provided for the actual tariff reductions agreed to under it. These were listed in annexed schedules that were integrated into it. Part Two stated that GATT 1947 was to be applied "provisionally" and that each member was required to apply the rules in Part Two only "to the fullest extent not inconsistent with" its own legislation which existed when it joined GATT 1947. Article III provided for national treatment of imports and prohibited internal taxes or regulations that discriminated against imports. Articles IV (cinematograph films), V (freedom of transit), VI (antidumping and countervailing duties), VII (customs valuation), VIII (fees and formalities), IX (marks and origin), and X (trade regulations) were the "technical articles" designed to prevent or control possible substitutes for tariffs. Articles XI to XIV dealt with quantitative restrictions. Article XI generally prohibited them. Article XII specified how they might be used for balance-of-payments reasons. Article XIII required that they be used without discrimination. Article XIV listed exceptions to Article XIII. Article XV concerned GATT 1947's cooperation with the International Monetary Fund ("IMF"). Article XVI called for the elimination of export subsidies. Article XVII required state-trading enterprises not to discriminate in their foreign trade. Article XVIII recognized that developing countries might need tariff flexibility and should be able to apply some quantitative restrictions to conserve foreign exchange. Article XIX (the "Escape Clause") prescribed when emergency action could be taken against imports that injure or threaten to injure domestic producers. Articles XX and XXI specified, respectively, general and security exceptions to GATT 1947 (*e.g.*, to protect public health). Article XXII dealt with consultations and Article XXIII with the settlement of disputes. Part Three, Article XXIV, regulated how customs unions and free trade areas might constitute exceptions to the MFN rule. Article XXV provided for action by member governments (including the granting of waivers). Articles XXVI to XXXV were operating rules for GATT 1947. They dealt with its acceptance and entry into force (XXVI), withdrawal of tariff concessions from former members (XXVII), rules for tariff negotiations and changes in tariff schedules (XXVIII), the relationship between GATT 1947 and the still-born ITO (XXIX), amendment of GATT 1947 (XXX), withdrawal from GATT 1947 (XXXI), the definition of "Contracting Parties" (*i.e.*, members) (XXXII), accession to GATT 1947 (XXXIII), the annexes to GATT 1947 (XXXIV), and nonapplication of GATT 1947's rules among particular members (XXXV). Part Four, Articles XXXVI to XXXVIII, was added in 1965. It concerned the special needs of the developing countries. Article XXXVI set out GATT 1947's principles and objectives in meeting these needs. Article XXXVII stated commitments which members undertook to this end. Article XXXVIII provided for joint action by developing countries.

The highest body of GATT 1947 was the Session of Contracting Parties. It met annually. GATT decisions were usually arrived at by consensus and not by vote. When voting took place, each member country had one vote. Most decisions by vote required a simple majority. Two-thirds of the votes cast, with the majority comprising more than half the member countries, were needed for "waivers" (authorizations, in particular cases, to depart from specific obligations under GATT

1947). Between Sessions of the Contracting Parties, the Council of Representatives (made up of representatives of all members and referred to as "the GATT Council") was authorized to act on both routine and urgent matters. It usually met once a month. Major GATT 1947 standing committees or councils were the Committee on Trade and Development (concerned with issues of special interest to developing countries), the Textiles Committee (made up of MFA signatories), and others concerned with the Tokyo Round agreements. *Ad hoc* committees dealt with specific transitory questions, such as requests for accession to GATT 1947, verification that agreements concluded by members conformed to GATT 1947, or the study of issues on which members might later make a joint decision. Panels of Conciliation were often empaneled to investigate disputes between particular members.

The GATT Secretariat consisted of about 350 people, headed by its Director-General. Its headquarters was in Geneva, Switzerland.

In eight successive multilateral negotiations, GATT 1947's rules were refined and obstacles to trade were progressively reduced. The negotiating "rounds" were those of 1947 (Geneva), 1949 (Annecy, France), 1951 (Torquay, England), 1956 (Geneva, Switzerland), 1960-61 ("the Dillon Round"), 1964-67 ("the Kennedy Round"), 1973-79 ("the Tokyo Round"), and 1986-1994 ("the Uruguay Round"—from the country where the round was first proposed).

The first six rounds were largely concerned with mutually negotiated tariff reductions. The Tokyo Round produced, as well as important tariff reductions, a series of new agreements covering nontariff measures; new arrangements applying to trade in dairy products, bovine meat and civil aircraft; and an improved legal framework for the conduct of world trade. Special and more favorable treatment for the trade of developing countries formed an important part of both the liberalizing and rule-improving aspects of the Tokyo Round results. These new agreements modified and added to GATT 1947's provisions.

Except for four agreements in the "Text prepared by Group Framework," Tokyo Round agreements did not automatically bind all members. Members were only bound by the codes they chose to sign.

The four "Framework Agreements" were: (1) Differential and More Favorable Treatment, Reciprocity, and Fuller Participation of Developing Countries; (2) Declaration on Trade Measures Taken for Balance of Payments Purposes; (3) Safeguard Actions for Development Purposes; and (4) Understanding Regarding Notification, Consultation, Dispute Settlement, and Surveillance.

Those codes which only bound those countries which had specially agreed to be bound by one, some, or all of them were: (1) Agreement on the Interpretation of Articles VI, XVI, and XXIII of the General Agreement (the Subsidies and Countervailing Duties Code); (2) Agreement on Implementation of Article VI of the General Agreement (the revised Antidumping Code); (3) Agreement on Technical Barriers to Trade (the Standards Code); (4) Agreement on Implementation of Article VII of the General Agreement (the Code on Customs Valuation); (5) Agreement on Import Licensing Procedures (the Import Licensing Code); (6) Agreement on Government Procurement (the Government Procurement Code); (7) Agreement on Trade in Civil Aircraft; (8) Arrangement on Bovine Meat; and (9) International Dairy Arrangement.

Both GATT 1947 and the WTO Agreement operated or operate according to the following four essential principles:

(1) **MFN TREATMENT PRINCIPLE**—The primary principle is that trade must be conducted on the basis of nondiscrimination. All Contracting Parties are bound to grant each other treatment as favorable as they give to any country in the application and administration of import and export duties and charges and other covered matters ("MFN" or "Most-Favored-Nation Treatment"). Thus, no member is to give special trading advantages to another or to discriminate against it. For goods, this is applicable to "like products" which are defined as directly competitive or substitutable products and are largely determined through uniform tariff classification. All are treated equally and all immediately partake in the benefits of any moves toward lower trade barriers. Members maintaining state trading enterprises must ensure that the imports and exports of these enterprises are administered in a nondiscriminatory manner.

Exceptions to this basic rule are allowed only under very special circumstances (there is concern that the WTO Agreement's treatment of services deviates from complete adherence to the MFN principle). Those exceptions are: (a) unspecified preferential arrangements (to be registered with GATT/WTO by members and whose "margins of preference" are frozen); (b) customs unions or free trade areas (in a free trade area, each member maintains its own commercial policy, including its tariff, towards nonmembers; a customs union adopts a unified customs tariff towards nonmembers) (GATT/the WTO Agreement permits this MFN exception only among developing nations or when certain strict criteria are met, *i.e.*, duties and other barriers to substantially all trade between countries in the group are required to be removed and duties or other regulations affecting the trade of members of the group with nonmembers are required to be no more restrictive than those preexisting establishment of the group); and (c) products originating in developing countries (including preferential tariffs under the "Generalized System of Preferences" or "GSP;" preferential nontariff barriers; regional or global arrangements between or among developing countries; and special preference for least developed countries). Developing countries are expected to "graduate" into regular member status as their economies improve.

(2) **NATIONAL TREATMENT PRINCIPLE**—Once imported items are admitted to the domestic market of a member, they may not be treated differently than similar domestic products ("National Treatment"), *e.g.*, imported items from members may not be subjected to more onerous internal taxes or regulations than are like domestic products (which include regulations covering the ownership of goods, vessels, or other means of transport).

(3) **ANTI-NONTARIFF BARRIERS PRINCIPLE**—A third principle is that, where protection is given to domestic industry, it should be extended exclusively (subject to very limited exceptions) through customs tariffs and not through other commercial measures. Among other things, the aim of this rule is to make the extent of protection clear and quantifiable. Fees and charges other than tariffs must be limited to the approximate cost of the services. Treatment given to marks of origin must not be discriminatory and should be consistent with protection of the consumer.

The "Escape Clause" exception permits the imposition of tariffs and nontariff barriers where, as a result of unforeseen developments, any product is being imported into the territory of a Contracting Party in such increased quantities and under conditions as to cause or threaten serious injury to domestic producers in its territory of like or directly competitive products. These may be imposed only to the extent and for such a time as is necessary to prevent or remedy the injury. Exceptions also exist for national security, public morals, short supply or domestic price stabilization, health, and other valid public policy reasons.

(4) **TARIFF CONCESSION PRINCIPLE**—Standard GATT/WTO operating practice is for a country wishing to become a party to submit negotiated tariff concession schedules (including lists of non-GATT-complying nontariff trade restrictions). These are sometimes referred to as "bindings." They may include sched-

ules of tariff reductions or the elimination of specified nontariff trade restrictions. These tariff concession schedules have been negotiated with other members collectively. They constitute the "high water" mark for that country for its tariffs and nontariff trade restrictions as long as it remains a member. Thereafter, tariffs and other trade restrictions may only (with certain exceptions that invite retaliatory action by other members) be reduced or eliminated through scheduled, unilateral, or mutually-negotiated further trade liberalization. They may not be increased.

This final principle is a curious, albeit practical, one since Ricardo's theories regarding free trade assert that any one country unilaterally adopting free trade would be better off even if no other country were to follow its lead. The Tariff Concession Principle operates on the implicit assumption that any one country is inflicting an injury upon itself by reducing its tariffs and doing so can only be justified by a negotiated and mutual reduction in the tariffs of other countries. Undoubtedly this disconnect between economic theory and the implicit assumptions of GATT negotiations is due to the fact that the guiding powers behind GATT negotiations are politicians and not economists.

History of the WTO

A new negotiating round, called the Uruguay Round, was announced in September 1986. It was the most ambitious trade negotiation ever held. The United States insisted on enlarging the scope of GATT 1947 to incorporate things never previously covered by it, *e.g.*, international investments, intellectual property, and the international trade in services.

There were almost 150 nations and territories participating directly or indirectly in negotiations. These included both developed and developing countries. During the course of negotiations the Soviet Union (also called the "USSR," perhaps now "the USSWere") collapsed and fragmented. Its former republics and satellite states repudiated Communism, attempted to institute market economies, and sought to participate in GATT/WTO and general global commerce.

Uruguay Round negotiations were so slow, so uncertain, and so marked by bitter negotiations that a common quip at the time was that "GATT" stood for "General Agreement to Talk and Talk."

Negotiations almost foundered, *inter alia*, on the issue of liberalized trade in agricultural products. The strongest overt opposition came from the EU. Japan was also firmly, if more quietly, opposed. Negotiations were essentially successfully concluded in 1993.

The success of the Uruguay Round was, until the very last minute, in jeopardy. The US Congress appeared poised to prevent US participation in the WTO Agreement. Fortunately, this calamity did not occur. US acceptance of the Uruguay Round was under the Uruguay Round Agreements Act ("URAA"), Pub. L. No. 103-465, December 8, 1994. The Act authorized the President to accept the Uruguay Round Agreements and implement the WTO Agreement. It denied treaty status to the WTO Agreement and domestic legal effect to the Uruguay Round Agreements as such. It excluded private actions under those Agreements. It made sometimes extensive changes to US laws to bring them into conformance with the requirements of the WTO Agreement.

Some issues that one or more countries had established as objectives of the Uruguay Round were not addressed at all, such as the international trade in motion pictures. Others were dealt with only in part or inadequately, such as the treatment of transportation services under the rules on the international trade in services. Some critical aspects and implementing measures of the WTO Agreement had yet to be finally negotiated. The WTO Agreement itself contemplates further negotiations to both liberalize trade under its present terms and to broaden its scope of coverage of international commercial issues.

GATT 1947 studies estimated that the successful conclusion of the Uruguay Round would generate substantial annual increases in global income and trade. Nonetheless, each commercial sector and each country is certain to realize different—sometimes disparate—benefits from the completion of the Uruguay Round. At least some developing countries may experience net detriments from it.

In December 1993, the Trade Negotiations Committee of the Uruguay Round adopted by consensus the texts in the Final Act embodying the results of the Uruguay Round. The Final Act consists of the Final Act itself [33 International Legal Materials 11-12 (1994)]; the Agreement establishing the WTO (referred to in the Final Act as the Multilateral Trade Organization or "MTO") [33 International Legal Materials 13-23 (1994)] and agreements annexed to it; and additional ministerial decisions, declarations, understandings, recommendations, and side agreements (including the Marrakech Protocol, which was the final document completing the Uruguay Round). Although a great accomplishment, it falls short of the intended coverage of the earlier, unimplemented, Havana Charter.

The WTO Agreement provides a new legal basis for the international trade in goods and services, the protection of intellectual property rights, and—to a lesser extent—trade-related investments; furnishes a common organizational and institutional framework for the conduct of trade relations among its members; and serves as a forum for negotiations on further trade liberalization and additional legal disciplines. In addition, mutual reductions in tariffs and nontariff barriers regarding the global trade in goods were negotiated.

The basic principles of the WTO Agreement remain the same as those of GATT 1947. An important difference between GATT 1947 and the WTO Agreement is that the latter is a "single undertaking" which integrates many Uruguay Round and earlier GATT 1947 agreements into a single legal framework. This helps solve four problems of GATT 1947. First, by integrating most of the agreements, all WTO members will be bound by the multilateral agreements, including the integrated dispute settlement system and surveillance under the Trade Policy Review Mechanism. Many of GATT 1947's codes and agreements were binding only on those members that had specifically bound themselves by them. Second, such integration, coupled with the increased responsibilities of developing countries, reduces GATT 1947's problem of "free riders," *i.e.*, developing countries that effectively and indefinitely delayed adherence to GATT 1947's standards while enjoying the full benefits of membership. The WTO Agreement may provide developing countries longer transition periods in which to assume new obligations, but ultimately they are required to perform obligations just as are developed countries. Although waivers of obligations may be available, especially for least-developed countries, they are subject to supermajority votes of members and must be specifically limited in duration. Third, almost all countries have participated in the Uruguay Round and are expected to join the WTO. Thus, the WTO Agreement is likely to be more nearly universal than was GATT 1947. Fourth, GATT 1947's "provisional" basis, with its "grandfathered" protection of certain nonconforming measures, was for long a contentious issue although its significance had diminished over time. The Final Act requires a definitive application of the Uruguay Round.

WTO/GATT is envisioned as a continuing process and not as a final and fixed result. Consequently, interim negotiations and adjustments have been continuously engaged in since the end of the Uruguay Round and a new round of negotiations, tentatively called the Millennium Round, will soon begin and the parameters of those negotiations are the subject of present intense exchanges and meetings.

The Structure of the WTO and the WTO Agreement

The WTO Agreement established the WTO as the common institutional framework for the conduct of trade regulations among members in matters related to the agreements and associated legal instruments included in the annexes to the WTO Agreement. The WTO Agreement has four annexes. The agreements in Annexes 1-3 (called the "Multilateral Trade Agreements") are integral parts of the WTO Agreement and are binding on all members. Annex 4 is made up of agreements (so-called "Plurilateral Trade Agreements") which are binding only on those members that have accepted them.

Annex 1 includes substantive agreements on trade in goods ("GATT 1994" in Annex 1A); the new General Agreement on Trade in Services ("GATS" in Annex 1B), and the new Agreement on Trade-Related Aspects of Intellectual Property Rights ("TRIPs" in Annex 1C).

GATT 1994 is essentially GATT 1947 and associated legal instruments in their final form prior to the adoption of the WTO Agreement but with some—and sometimes significant—modifications plus several new agreements, *e.g.*, those dealing with agriculture and textiles. Other interpretative understandings arrived at in connection with GATT 1994 were: (a) Understanding on the Interpretation of Article II:1(b); (b) Understanding on the Interpretation of Article XVII; (c) Understanding on Balance-of-Payments Provisions; (d) Understanding on the Interpretation of Article XXIV; (e) Understanding in respect of Waivers of Obligations; (f) Understanding on the Interpretation of Article XXVIII; and (g) Understanding on the Interpretation of Article XXXV.

Annex 2 consists of the Understanding on Rules and Procedures Governing the Settlement of Disputes. It provides detailed rules and deadlines for the settlement of disputes under the WTO Agreement and/or any of the agreements found in the Annexes. The Understanding will be administered by a Dispute Settlement Body ("DSB") which will make decisions solely by consensus.

Annex 3 provides for the Trade Policy Review Mechanism ("TPRM") which establishes a process for the multilateral surveillance of national trade policies. It is a modified version of a 1989 GATT 1947 decision. Trade policies and practices of members are to be reviewed by the Trade Policy Review Body ("TPRB") on the basis of reports by members and a report drawn up by the Secretariat. The TPRB also conducts an annual overview of developments in the international trading environment.

Annex 4 is made up of agreements (so-called "Plurilateral Trade Agreements") which are binding only on those members that have accepted them. The Plurilateral Trade Agreements are the Agreement on Trade in Civil Aircraft; the Agreement on Government Procurement; the International Dairy Agreement; and the International Bovine Meat Agreement. These are essentially pre-existing non-framework agreements that were created under GATT 1947 in 1979, although the Agreement on Government Procurement has been greatly expanded. The WTO Agreement has rules for adding or deleting agreements to or from Annex 4.

The WTO has the tasks of implementing the WTO Agreement and the Multilateral Trade Agreements; providing the framework for implementation of the Plurilateral Trade Agreements; providing the forum for negotiations among members concerning matters dealt with in the attached agreements; providing a forum for other negotiations (although members may hold future rounds of multilateral trade negotiations on further trade liberalization measures and additional legal disciplines outside the auspices of the WTO); and cooperating as appropriate with the World Bank, the IMF, and regional multilateral banks.

The WTO Agreement provides for a Secretariat, headed by a Director-General appointed by the Ministerial Conference. The Director-General is responsible for appointing members of the staff of the Secretariat. To the extent practicable, the Secretariat of GATT 1947 was carried over to the WTO. The WTO is headquartered in Geneva, Switzerland. It is accorded the normal privileges and immunities necessary to carry out its functions.

There is a Ministerial Conference with overarching authority. This is the principal organ of the WTO and is composed of representatives of all members. It is required to meet at least once every two years.

The Ministerial Conference has also established a Committee on Trade and Development; a Committee on Balance of Payments Restrictions for both GATT 1994 and GATS; and a Committee on Budget, Finance, and Administration.

During the periods between meetings of the Ministerial Conference, the Ministerial Conference's functions are carried out by the General Council (which also performs specific functions, such as approval of the budget and financial regulations). The General Council is the direct descendant of the GATT Council of GATT 1947. Like the GATT Council, it is made up of representatives of all members.

Under the General Council are three separate subcouncils: (a) the Council for Trade in Goods, (b) the Council for Trade in Services, and (c) the Council for Trade-Related Aspects of Intellectual Property Rights. Membership in each of these committees is open to representatives of all members. Each oversees the functioning of the relevant agreement at Annex 1A, 1B, or 1C and each may create subordinate subsidiary bodies.

The General Council also is charged with convening, on an *ad hoc* basis, the DSB, as provided for in the Dispute Settlement Understanding at Annex 2, and the TPRB, as provided for in the TPRM at Annex 3.

Rules of procedure for the existing standing committees on Trade and Development; Balance-of-Payments Restrictions; Trade and the Environment; and Budget, Finance, and Administration, as well as for any other standing committees the Ministerial Conference may create, are to be established by the General Council.

GATT 1947 practice with respect to decision-making, with a preference for "consensus" decisions, reflected through the absence of objections, is carried over into the WTO. In the event of an inability to form a consensus on critical matters, each WTO member has one vote in the Ministerial Conference and in the General Council. The WTO Agreement specifies that the MFN provision in the WTO Agreement, GATS, and TRIPS, and the WTO Agreement's amendments provisions may be amended only upon acceptance by all members. Special majorities of two-thirds or three-fourths are required for certain measures. Particular attention has been paid to safeguards regarding the adoption of binding interpretations of the WTO Agreement or the Multilateral Trade Agreements, waivers of obligations, and amendments. In the settlement of disputes, the ability of a single member to prevent implementation of the recommendations of dispute settlement fora through its effective veto over the creation of a consensus has been eliminated. This has been achieved through the automatic adoption of those recommendations unless there is a consensus **against** adoption —a methodology referred to as "reverse consensus."

GATT and the Global Trade in Goods

For the purposes of GATT, a "good" may be thought of as a tangible item that may be owned, bought, and sold. "Goods" include manufactured items, textiles and clothing, raw materials (such as unprocessed timber and mineral ores), and processed and unprocessed agricultural products.

GATT 1947 dealt exclusively with the global trade in goods. It excluded entirely from its coverage the global trade in services. No effort was made to deal under its terms with such commercial issues as intellectual property and foreign investments. Even many "goods," such as unprocessed agricultural products and textiles, were themselves not subject to the international liberalization in the conditions of trade prescribed by GATT 1947 or became removed from GATT 1947's coverage over time through the actions of various GATT members.

The principal means by which nations impeded the free international trade in goods at the time of the creation of GATT 1947 was through protectionist monetary tariffs. These were assessed against imported goods when they passed through a country's customs barriers before they entered the domestic market of that country. A secondary means by which the importation of goods was frustrated was through the application against imported goods of certain nontariff barriers to entry. Among these were absolute prohibitions against the importation of named items; annual quotas for the importation of named items (sometimes based upon country of origin); required import licenses; necessary certifications regarding the nature or quality of the imported product; customs examinations which were intentionally administered in ways which added delay, cost, and inconvenience to the importation of goods; and the creation and enforcement of arbitrary or unjustifiable product standards. In some countries, imported goods were made subject to special and discriminatory treatment, such as special taxation, even after they had passed through national customs barriers and entered the local market.

The means by which GATT 1947 sought to reduce these barriers to the trade in goods was through: (a) the requirement that each member reduce to writing and file with GATT 1947 the level of tariffs it imposed on the importation of any and all items, with such filings being incorporated into and made part of GATT 1947 (these tariff levels could not be unilaterally established by a country but had to be negotiated with all other members and the tariff filing might include specific country commitments to reduce or eliminate such tariffs by prescribed amounts and in accordance with a stipulated schedule of reductions); (b) the restriction on the ability of any country to ever again raise any or all of its tariffs higher than those stipulated in its filings except under very limited conditions whose use would subject the country to possible retaliatory trade penalties by other members; (c) the contemplation within GATT 1947's provisions of further mutually-negotiated tariff reductions; (d) the elimination of all nontariff trade barriers except those required for legitimate public policy purposes and their replacement with tariffs which were to be the exclusive permitted means for protecting domestic markets; (e) the requirement that each country prepare and file with GATT 1947 (which then became incorporated into and a part of GATT 1947) a listing of those nontariff barriers to trade which it planned to retain, including its justification for their retention and any schedule for reducing or eliminating one, some, or all of those nontariff barriers to trade; (f) the obligation of each member to treat the importation of goods from any other member as favorably as the treatment it accorded like goods from any other country (the so-called "Most-Favored-Nation Treatment" or "MFN" principle); and (g) the application of the same rules and exactions on goods imported from other members—once those goods entered the domestic market—as were applied to like locally-produced products (the so-called "National Treatment" principle). There were limited (but, with time, troublesome) exceptions to certain of the above rules, *e.g.*, of some applications of the rules by developing countries.

Distortion of the market for the free international trade in goods was also created through subsidized exports; through various subsidies provided to domestic producers whose products competed with imported goods; and through the operation of state-owned producers, importers, and exporters of goods. GATT 1947 sought to limit the use of such subsidies and to restrict discriminatory and nonmarket practices of state-owned entities.

Agreement among important trading nations was reached on a number of issues concerning the international trade in goods in the Tokyo Round but without general agreement by all members on those issues. Consequently, certain "side-agreements" were added to GATT 1947 that were not applicable to all GATT members. Each side-agreement applied only to those countries that specifically became signatories to it. There were nine of these agreements. Only five are of relevance here. The first was the Agreement on the Interpretation of Articles VI, XVI, and XXIII of the General Agreement ("the Subsidies and Countervailing Duties Code"). It sought to ensure that any use of subsidies by any signatory did not harm the trading interests of other signatories; that countervailing measures did not unjustifiably impede international trade; and that these measures were only to be applied where it could be shown that the subsidized imports in question were in fact responsible for causing material injury, or threatening such injury, to the domestic industry which had lodged the complaint. The second was the Agreement on Implementation of Article VI of the General Agreement ("the revised Antidumping Code"). It broadly defined "dumped" goods as imports that are sold at prices below those charged by the producer in its domestic market. It resulted in the general international standardization of national antidumping practices as well as in the increased acceptance of one nation's antidumping actions by other signatories. The third was the Agreement on Technical Barriers to Trade ("the Standards Code"). It required signatories to assure that —when governments or other bodies adopted technical regulations or standards for reasons of safety, health, consumer or environmental protection, or other purposes—these regulations or standards, and the testing and certification schemes related to them, did not create unnecessary obstacles to trade. The fourth was the Agreement on Implementation of Article VII of the General Agreement ("the Code on Customs Valuation"). It established what was meant to be a fair, uniform, and neutral system for the valuation of goods for customs purposes. The fifth was the Agreement on Import Licensing Procedures ("the Import Licensing Code"). It provided that import licensing procedures might be of administrative value but must be neutral in application and must be administered in a fair and equitable manner.

GATT 1947 was very successful in reducing average global tariffs on the importation of goods. It did so through a series of negotiating rounds that resulted in mutual reductions of tariffs by all members. GATT 1947 also achieved very significant gains in the global reduction in nontariff barriers to trade. The end result was the gradual creation of a much liberalized international trade order for goods. There were consequent significant increases in levels of the global trade in goods and in the general prosperity of GATT members.

Nonetheless, by 1986 problems concerning the international trade in goods that had been incipient in GATT 1947 or had developed through its implementation and exceptions taken to it came to overshadow GATT 1947's successes.

Agricultural products, which were originally intended to be covered under GATT 1947, were effectively removed from its coverage through a GATT waiver of US import protection statutes and the creation of the EU, one of whose fundamental institutions was a Common Agricultural Policy ("CAP") incompatible with GATT requirements. Other members, observing the world's two largest trading powers effectively excluding matters concerning the importation, exportation, and subsidization of agricultural products from their GATT obligations, tended to behave similarly. Although GATT 1947's standards regarding agricultural trade were sometimes made applicable to and enforced against such other countries, this happened only rarely and its patent unfairness tempered the regular use of such measures. In 1955, Article XVI:2-5 was added to GATT 1947. It was intended to discourage the use of agricultural export subsidies. It did not.

Textiles and clothing were also effectively removed from GATT 1947's coverage through the MFA—a "temporary" and "voluntary" export restraint agreement between importing developed countries and many textile and clothing exporters (all save Japan developing countries). MFA restricted quantities of these items permitted to be sent from certain exporting to certain importing countries. Exporting countries "volunteered" to join MFA only under extreme pressure from the importing countries. MFA's "temporary" measures continued and expanded for decades.

Similar bilateral or multilateral "voluntary" restrictive arrangements existed regarding other goods.

Certain bilateral arrangements, such as the US-Japan Semiconductor Arrangement, contained targeted "set-asides" of one party's domestic market for imports of products from the other party in seeming violation of MFN requirements.

Developing countries, through various GATT 1947 measures, increasingly became "free riders," *i.e.*, parties with all the benefits of but with few or none of the obligations arising from that membership.

The proliferation of customs unions and free trade areas with special, preferential trading terms among their members also added confusion to the MFN requirements of GATT 1947, as did the existence of the Tokyo Round side-agreements which were not universally applicable to all GATT members.

Antidumping and countervailing duty measures, which had been included in GATT 1947 at US insistence, were used effectively as "GATT-authorized" protectionist measures by the United States. Increasingly, other countries saw their potential. They enacted and enforced their own similar statutory measures and began to use them regularly for the same protectionist ends that the United States had pioneered.

The Uruguay Round of negotiations attempted to deal with many, if not all, the above problems of GATT 1947. It did so imperfectly but it did so to a surprisingly effective degree. The GATT agreement formulated as a result of the successful completion of the Uruguay Round by the WTO Agreement was not a mere marginal improvement on GATT 1947. It was a new agreement that replaced GATT 1947. GATT 1947 had dealt exclusively with the international trade in goods. The WTO Agreement dealt with many additional subjects that had little or nothing to do with the international trade in goods. This fact has misled some to overlook the fact that the WTO Agreement principally deals, as GATT 1947 dealt, with the international trade in *goods*. The WTO Agreement's coverage of other subjects is still sometimes rudimentary and of uncertain real significance.

The WTO Agreement created GATT 1994 under its Annex 1A, Multilateral Agreements on Trade in Goods. GATT 1994 is essentially GATT 1947 and its associated legal instruments in their final form, but with sometimes major modifications and additions, prior to the adoption of the WTO Agreement. These legal instruments include the protocols of accession; the protocols and certifications relating to tariff concessions; decisions on waivers granted under Article XXV of GATT 1947 and still in force; and other decisions of the Contracting Parties to GATT 1947. New understandings made part of GATT 1994 are: (a) the Understanding on Article II:1(b); (b) the Understanding on Article XVII; (c) the Understanding on Balance-of-Payments Provisions (including the 1979 Declaration); (d) the Understanding on Article XXIV; (e) the Understanding in Respect of Waivers; and (f) the Understanding on Article XXXVIII. GATT 1994 has incorporated into itself five Tokyo Round "side agreements" [the Agreements on Subsidies and Countervailing Measures or "ASCM" (which includes as Annex 1, an "Illustrative List of Subsidies"), Antidumping or "AAD," Standards, Customs Valuation, and Import Licensing], again sometimes only after substantial additions and improvements—thereby making them applicable to all WTO Agreement members. It has added other agreements to GATT 1994 which deal with the international trade in goods, most notably by providing for the scheduled reapplication of GATT's terms to the global trade in agricultural products, textiles, and clothing, and some other formerly effectively excluded goods. Those Agreements are: (a) the Marrakech Protocol; (b) the Agreement on Agriculture ("AAg"); (c) the Agreement on the Application of Sanitary and Phytosanitary Measures; (d) the Agreement on Textiles and Clothing; (e) the Agreement on Trade-Related Investment Measures ("TRIMs"); (f) the Agreement on Preshipment Inspection; (g) the Agreement on Rules of Origin; and (h) the Agreement on Safeguards.

Also of relevance to the trade in goods are the following ministerial decisions and declarations: (a) Decision on Measures in Favor of Least-Developed Countries; (b) Decision on Measures Concerning the Possible Negative Effects of the Reform Program on Least-Developed and Net Food-Importing Developing Countries; (c) Decision on Notification of First Integration under Article 2.6 of the Agreement on Textiles and Clothing; (d) Decisions Relating to the Agreement on Technical Barriers to Trade; (e) Decisions and Declaration Relating to the Agreement on Implementation of Article VI of GATT 1994; and (f) Decision Relating to the Agreement on Implementation of Article VII of

GATT 1994. The Plurilateral Agreements are also germane to the international trade in goods.

Under Uruguay Round auspices, new mutual tariff reductions were negotiated which are estimated to have resulted in an overall decrease of 38% in average developed country tariffs (from 6.3% to 3.9%). The number of industrial products receiving duty-free treatment in developed countries was increased from 20% to 43% of the total. The increase in the number of tariff lines "bound" under GATT 1947's Article II were raised—in the case of developed countries from 78% to 99%; in the case of developing countries from 22% to 72%; and in the case of countries in transition from controlled to market economies from 73% to 98%.

Some of the Multilateral Agreements on Trade in Goods are substantially those developed under GATT 1947. The Agreement on the Application of Sanitary and Phytosanitary Measures may generally be treated as ancillary to the AAg. Particular attention will be given in this or later chapters to the trade in agricultural goods, to the trade in textiles and clothing, to certain changes in GATT's treatment of subsidies and antidumping and countervailing duty measures, to preshipment inspection, and to ROs.

Private companies operating under contracts have in recent years performed preshipment inspections of products to be exported prior to their exportation as a legal requirement imposed by an (usually undeveloped) importing country. The purpose of the preshipment inspection is the elimination of false export/import documents, collusive evasion of tariffs and other imports duties owed, and the violation of national currency exchange laws. Although none have questioned the legitimacy of the purpose of the preshipment inspections, many exporters have complained of the administrative irregularities with which they are conducted and the inconveniences imposed on exporters by the inspections. The Agreement on Preshipment Inspection seeks to balance the conflicting interests of exporters and the importing country.

"Rules of Origin" ("ROs") are the rules used to determine the country of origin of a product. Such a determination is no longer simple now that a final product may incorporate parts and components from many countries and a single item may have undergone transformations in several countries. The Agreement on Rules of Origin established basic rules applicable to the WTO Agreement and GATT 1994 pending completion of a harmonization of nonpreferential rules undertaken by the WTO Committee on Rules of Origin and the Customs Cooperation Council.

During the Uruguay Round, agriculture was a major topic of negotiations. Pushing these negotiations was the so-called "Cairns Group" (named for the Australian city where it was formed) of thirteen countries (Argentina, Australia, Brazil, Canada, Chile, Colombia, Hungary, Indonesia, Malaysia, New Zealand, the Philippines, Thailand, and Uruguay) for which agricultural trade was economically significant. The United States was generally supportive of the Cairns Group. General agreement had been achieved as early as April 1989 to cut tariffs on tropical products, such as pineapples and bananas. This was an issue of particular interest to developing countries.

Nevertheless, the Uruguay Round nearly foundered on the refusal of the EU—because of the refusal of France—to make reasonable accommodation of the desire of other countries to liberalize the international trade in agricultural products and to subject that trade to GATT's rules. The US and the EU reached eleventh hour agreement on the matter. The result was less liberal than had been proposed in the so-called "Dunkel Draft" and than was sought by the Cairns Group. It was, nonetheless, generally accepted (although with some bitter murmurs from agricultural exporting countries that the big boys had cut their own deal and then offered it to the rest of the world on a "take it or leave it" basis).

In the AAg, GATT 1994's application to agricultural products was to be phased in over time with differing time schedules of implementation for developed and developing members.

Nontariff import restrictions on agricultural products are to be converted to tariffs. Such restrictions are not to be used in the future except pursuant to GATT 1994's special safeguards provisions and certain other exceptions. Quotas are no longer to be used to protect agricultural markets. Current market access is to be maintained and certain minimum market access is to be provided if current access is less than three percent of domestic production (rising to five percent over the implementation period).

Initial tariffs have been set to approximate the current level of protection. This means they are often very high—several hundred percent in some cases—and may even be higher than preexisting tariff levels. Tariffs were to be reduced by 36% over a six-year period (24% over 10 years for developing countries and least-developed countries are exempt) with developing countries making a minimum 15% reduction on every tariff line over a six year period.

Although the ASCM bans the use of export subsidies, it is explicitly made subject to the AAg. AAg Article 13 provides that, if certain conditions are met, agricultural subsidies will be exempt from actions otherwise authorized by ASCM. The types of export subsidies subject to reduction are enumerated and no other forms are permitted. Separate commitments are made on the basis of eighteen different commodity groupings which prevent switching subsidy supports from one group to another.

Export subsidies for agricultural products were to be reduced over the implementation period, compared to a 1986-1990 base period, under "bindings" submitted by each country by 35% in terms of value and by 21% in respect of volume of exports benefiting from them (24% and 14%, respectively, over a ten year period for developing countries and least-developed countries are exempt).

Domestic subsidies, which are responsible for much distortion in global agricultural trade, are to be reduced through "bindings" submitted by each member. Developed members are to cut certain specified domestic subsidies by 20% over the implementation period. Domestic subsidies for agriculture that provide income support for farmers without promoting production or distorting trade flows are favored.

The alleged justifications for the MFA were the low wages paid to textile workers in developing countries and the high level of government intervention in the introduction and promotion of the textile and clothing exporting sector in many countries. These were argued to be both ills in and of themselves and, through imports of textiles and related products resulting from them, disruptive of markets in importing countries. The market disruption of greatest concern was the threatened precipitous unemployment of importing country textile workers and the bankruptcy of their employers.

The first such voluntary export restraint on textiles was in 1936. The practice expanded to include ever more importing countries, exporting countries, and exported textiles and related products. The first actual MFA was signed in 1974 but it was a natural son of the voluntary export restraint agreements on textiles that had preceded it. The MFA and its predecessors were always billed as being "temporary," but the term seemed to be misused in this case.

The method used by the MFA to control imports of textiles and clothing was to establish annual quotas of imports of specific items from one member country to another. The allocation of visas authorizing utilization under a quota were administered by the exporting country.

The Agreement on Textiles and Clothing provides for the gradual reintegration of textile and clothing products into GATT 1994.

The first step required that each member, upon the entry into force of the WTO Agreement, integrate into GATT 1994's coverage products which accounted for not less than 16% of the total volume of the member's 1990 imports of the products in the Annex in terms of tariff lines or categories. The products to be integrated must encompass products from each of the following four groups: tops and yarns, fabrics, made-up textile products, and clothing. An additional 17% had to be reintegrated at the beginning of the fourth year; 18% at the beginning of the eighth year; and the rest (49%) at the beginning of the eleventh year. Remaining MFA quotas were to be expanded faster than had been agreed upon under the MFA.

There are special transitional safeguard measures, but once textiles and clothing have been fully reintegrated into GATT 1994 the Escape Clause of Article XIX is the applicable safeguard provision.

Despite these measures, normal tariffs of developed countries on textiles and clothing are generally much higher than average tariffs, *e.g.*, 1979 US trade-weighted average tariffs for industrial products, textiles, and apparel were, respectively, 5%, 10.5%, and 19.8%.

GATT 1947 as originally written contained provisions dealing with antidumping and countervailing duties. These were fleshed out in 1967 with an Agreement on Interpretation of Article VI ("the Antidumping Code"). The Tokyo Round Subsidies and Countervailing Duties Code of 1979 addressed countervail issues. The 1967 Antidumping Code was made to conform to its analogues in the Subsidies and Countervailing Duties Code. Export subsidies had been restricted by GATT 1947 since its inception. Relevant Uruguay Round agreements significantly modified the Antidumping and Subsidies and Countervailing Duties Codes and transferred most authority over agricultural subsidies to the AAg.

In the Uruguay Round, the US and the EU were concerned about gaining GATT acceptance of the use of certain devices to prevent the circumvention of antidumping duties and in regulating more closely the procedures used in antidumping actions because of the increased use by developing countries of antidumping measures. Countries commonly targeted under antidumping laws wanted substantive changes in the rules in order to reduce the use of antidumping statutes as protectionist devices. A compromise was achieved. The procedural rules were tightened, as were (although to a much lesser degree) the substantive rules. No agreement was reached, however, on anticircumvention measures. Further negotiations on that subject are expected.

Those issues dealt with by the ASCM and the AAD and the modifications made to them under the Uruguay Round are too numerous and too complex to receive full consideration in this chapter. They will, therefore, be described here only in the broadest terms. Reference should be made to those Agreements, to national legislation enacted to implement them, and to Chapter X.

There is a difference between (a) obligations restraining the use of subsidies and (b) rules governing the use of countervailing duties by an importing nation. Even where a subsidy is not prohibited by GATT 1994's rules, GATT 1994 may permit it to be offset by countervailing duties. Similarly, a subsidy against which countervailing duties are ineffective, *e.g.*, export subsidies for third-country markets, may still justify claims of GATT 1994 violations.

There are essentially two types of subsidies: the domestic subsidy and the export subsidy. The domestic subsidy is granted to an industry on all of its production of a product, regardless of whether that production is exported. It is potentially disruptive of a domestic market for imported like products. An export subsidy, by contrast, is paid to an industry only on products that are exported. Consequently, with an export subsidy, goods tend to be sold abroad at a price below that charged for the same goods sold in the domestic market.

The ASCM established three categories of subsidies: prohibited, actionable, and nonactionable. The following subsidies are prohibited: (a) those contingent, in law or in fact, whether solely or as one of several other conditions, upon export performance; and (b) those contingent, whether solely or as one of several other conditions, upon the use of domestic over imported goods. "Actionable" subsidies are those which cause adverse effects to the interests of other signatories, *i.e.*, injury to the domestic industry of another signatory, nullification or impairment of benefits accruing directly or indirectly to other signatories under the General Agreement (in particular the benefits of bound tariff concessions), and serious prejudice to the interests of another member. "Non-actionable" subsidies, which could either be non-specific subsidies or specific subsidies, are those involving assistance to industrial research and precompetitive development activity, assistance to disadvantaged regions, or certain types of assistance for adapting existing facilities to new environment requirements imposed by law and/or regulations. Where another member believes that an otherwise nonactionable subsidy is resulting in serious adverse effects to a domestic industry, it may seek a determination and recommendation on the matter.

The ASCM significantly expands GATT discipline over domestic subsidies, provides guidance on what are "unfair" domestic subsidies, and favors GATT dispute resolution rather than unilateral countervailing measures. The ASCM contains a definition of subsidy and introduces the concept of a "specific" subsidy. The latter is generally a subsidy available only to an enterprise or industry or group of enterprises or industries within the jurisdiction of the authority granting the subsidy. Only specific subsidies would be subject to the disciplines set out in the ASCM. Article 8 of the ASCM, which deals with "non-actionable subsidies", contains the so-called "green light" provisions applicable to certain domestic subsidies. They create a safe harbor for government programs that are not targeted in the sense of the specificity test of Article 2 or that represent qualifying governmental aid for research and development, for disadvantaged regions, or for environmental improvements.

The ASCM recognizes that subsidies play an important role in economic development programs of developing countries and in the transformation of centrally-planned economies to market economies and grants such countries broader latitude in their use of subsidies.

Extensive revision was made to the ASCM and the AAD which will materially change the way in which national antidumping and countervailing duty proceedings will be conducted. Only a few issues covered by these revisions will be treated in this chapter.

Much of the ASCM and the AAD concerns the procedures that an importing nation must follow before imposing a countervailing duty on subsidized imported goods or an antidumping duty on dumped goods. The ASCM sets out disciplines on the initiation of countervailing cases, investigations by national authorities, and rules of evidence to ensure that all interested parties can present information and arguments. The AAD specifies in detail the information that the authorities must have before an investigation may be initiated and prescribes, *inter alia, de minimis* dumping levels, procedural rights of those accused of dumping, methodologies for computing dumping levels, and the termination of antidumping duty orders after a fixed period barring demonstration of its continuing utility.

Both the AAD (Article 3.3.) and the ASCM (Article 15.3.) permit cumulation. Cumulation is the cumulative addition of different countervailable subsidies or dumping practices to reach the ultimate level against which offsetting duties on imports are imposed. Cumulation is permitted only (a) as long as the extent of the unfair practice is not *de minimis* and (b) a "cumulative assessment of the effects of the imports is appropriate in light of the conditions of competition between imported products and the conditions of competition between imported products and the like domestic product".

Countervailing investigations are to be terminated immediately in cases where the amount of the subsidy is *de minimis* (the subsidy is less than 1% *ad valorem*) or where the volume of subsidized imports, actual or potential, or the injury is negligible.

As regards post-Uruguay Round tariffs, it should be noted that a recent OECD study has found two persisting problems: (a) that there has been far from uniform reductions across all product lines, with some types of products still subject to significant tariff burdens, and (b) so-called "tariff escalation." Tariff escalation occurs when zero or low tariffs are applied to imports of primary commodities with the duties increasing or "escalating" as the product experiences increased fabrication. Tariff escalation produces a trade bias against processed goods due to the higher import duties imposed on these items. The result is increased protection of value-added inputs which twists world-wide distribution of a product in a mercantilist manner along processing chains to the detriment of countries with relatively abundant supplies of raw materials.

Plurilateral Agreements

Under the WTO Agreement there are both so-called "Multilateral Agreements" and "Plurilateral Agreements." Those terms must be specially explained because the meanings of, and the differences between, the two terms are not clearly apparent from a mere reading of them.

All the agreements of the WTO Agreement and related agreements are multilateral agreements with the exception of four agreements found in Annex 4 of the WTO Agreement. A "multilateral agreement" is one to which each and every one of the signatories of the WTO Agreement is bound.

The four "plurilateral agreements" found in Annex 4 are: (1) the Agreement on Trade in Civil Aircraft, (2) the Agreement on Government Procurement, (3) the International Dairy Agreement, and (4) the International Bovine Meat Agreement. They are distinguishable from multilateral agreements because all WTO Agreement signatory members are not bound by them. A "plurilateral agreement" is one which binds (and creates rights and obligations among) only those parties which have specially become signatories to any one of them. Consequently, a WTO Agreement signatory might choose to become a signatory to no plurilateral agreement or to any one or more of them. Plurilateral agreements are effectively treaties separate from the WTO

Agreement but which were negotiated under the auspices of and will be administered by the WTO.

There are obviously troubling aspects of the concept of plurilateral agreements under the WTO Agreement. The most important is that special side agreements which bind some but not all WTO Agreement signatories do injury to the concept of MFN treatment. MFN treatment is a fundamental underpinning of the WTO Agreement. It requires that each WTO Agreement signatory extend to the products and services, *inter alia,* of every other signatory terms of access to its domestic market at least as favorable as those extended to any other country. There are exceptions to the mandatory provision of MFN treatment, such as those that permit more favorable treatment to the products and services of developing countries and of members of free trade areas and customs unions. Nonetheless, each exception has been only granted after much deliberation. Each had an unsettling effect on GATT 1947. Any exception to such a fundamental concept calls into question the immutability and universality of the concept itself.

This concern is moderated by the fact that there are not so many such exceptions under the WTO Agreement as there were under the final version of GATT 1947. The WTO Agreement does, however, also contemplate the creation of additional plurilateral agreements to be negotiated and added to Annex 4.

Despite legitimate concerns about the disruptive effects that plurilateral agreements may have on the multilateral WTO Agreement regime, empirical evidence indicates that plurilateral agreements may serve as an intermediate way station on the road to multilateral acceptance. Agreements to which only some countries would agree when they were negotiated may become, with time and a satisfactory operating history, agreements that can later be incorporated into the general, multilateral body of the WTO Agreement. Further, concepts relevant to the WTO Agreement's field of global economic liberalization which had never before been the subject of international agreement might find initial acceptance only as plurilateral agreements, thus permitting the WTO Agreement's scope and effectiveness to increase over time. Consequently, instead of jeopardizing the WTO Agreement and its theoretical foundations, plurilateral agreements may instead strengthen the WTO Agreement and buttress those foundations.

Three of the remaining plurilateral agreements under GATT 1947, the Agreement on Trade in Civil Aircraft, the Arrangement on Bovine Meat (now called "the International Bovine Meat Agreement"), and the International Dairy Arrangement (now called "the International Dairy Agreement"), are essentially unchanged in the WTO Agreement, although revision of the Agreement on Trade in Civil Aircraft is expected to be negotiated in the near future. The Agreement on Government Procurement [33 International Legal Materials 1141 (1994)] has been substantially revised, expanded, and strengthened under the WTO Agreement.

The International Bovine Meat Agreement and the International Dairy Agreement are relatively unimportant. They have few signatories (the United States is a signatory to the former but not to the latter). Neither actually establishes rules for the international trade in their covered goods. Both agreements essentially provide for the exchange of information (such as quantities produced in a particular year or season) among signatories regarding their covered goods. Both provide for the establishment of authorities to receive, process, and disseminate this information and to coordinate the activities of signatories regarding the covered goods.

Australia, Canada, the EU, Egypt, Japan, Norway, Romania, Sweden, Switzerland, and the United States had all, by December 31, 1992, acceded to the Agreement on Trade in Civil Aircraft negotiated under the Tokyo Round and additional members have joined since the completion of the Uruguay Round. The Agreement applies to civil aircraft; civil aircraft engines and their parts and components; other parts, components, and subassemblies of civil aircraft; and ground flight simulators and their parts and components. The essential elements of the Agreement were that (a) duties on such products were to be eliminated; (b) duties on repairs of aircraft were to be eliminated; and (c) airlines were to be free to select suppliers on the basis of commercial and technological factors. Also addressed in the agreement was government support of aircraft makers, *i.e.*, subsidies. Article 6(1) of the Agreement provides that (a) the former Subsidies Code (now incorporated into the WTO Agreement) applies to the trade in civil aircraft and (b) regarding government participation in civil aircraft programs, signatory governments will try and avoid adverse effects on trade in civil aircraft of the type addressed in Article 8.3 of the Subsidies Code. Pricing of civil aircraft must, according to Article 6(2), be based on a reasonable expectation of an eventual recovery of all costs.

The issues dealt with by the Agreement were not fully resolved by the Agreement. In particular, the United States and the EU have a long-standing dispute concerning aircraft manufacturing and exportation subsidies. The United States has complained of EU subsidies of the Airbus, a joint venture of several EU companies in as many EU countries. Airbus was developed and manufactured under a special EU quasi-corporate structure whose effect—if not its intent—was to effectively mask from outside view and analysis the costs of development and production, the existence or extent of subsidies, and the degree to which reasonable marketing projections of sales of the aircraft would give rise to a realistic expectation that the collective joint venture would ever recover all costs of development and production of the aircraft. Airbus is now changing to a more traditional corporate legal structure. The EU has questioned, in response, whether the US indirectly subsidizes the production of American civil aircraft through its procurement of military aircraft from the American manufacturers of civil aircraft. The EU and the US entered into a bilateral agreement on the application of the Agreement on the Trade in Civil Aircraft in 1992. That bilateral agreement interpreted the general principle that aircraft purchasers should be free to select suppliers on the basis of commercial and technological considerations and spells out in greater detail the prohibitions of the Agreement on the Trade in Civil Aircraft on government-directed procurement, government-mandated subcontracts, and government inducements to discriminate against other suppliers. The bilateral agreement also limited the subsidization through direct support of new civil aircraft with 100 or more passenger seats to only those cases where there is the expectation of recoupment of all costs within 17 years from the date of first disbursement of support. Overall support is limited to 33% of the program's total development costs. Parties are to ensure that indirect government support (which is not to exceed 3% of the annual turnover of the party's civil aircraft industry or 4% of one firm's turnover) does not confer an unfair advantage on a producer or distort the international trade in such aircraft. The bilateral agreement has not put to rest the US-EU dispute.

Attempts in the Uruguay Round to renegotiate the Agreement on the Trade in Civil Aircraft and to make it into a multilateral agreement failed. Civil aircraft were excluded from some provisions of the WTO Agreement's multilateral Agreement on Subsidies and Countervailing Duties in the expectation, which proved to be unfounded, that a new agreement on the trade in civil aircraft would be reached in the near term.

Among the plurilateral agreements, of greatest general significance, and the Tokyo Round side-agreement to have emerged from the Uruguay Round of negotiations most changed and strengthened was that dealing with government procurement. Nonetheless, it is not directly related to the issue of the international systems of customs and tariffs and will not be considered in detail in this book.

WTO International Trade Disputes

Dispute resolution procedures under GATT 1947 were widely thought to constitute one of GATT 1947's most serious shortcomings.

The principal complaints about the GATT 1947 dispute settlement procedures were: (1) disuse (a complaint partially allayed by markedly increased use—from 38 complaints from the combined 1960s and 1970s to 115 complaints in the 1980s—in the last years of GATT 1947); (2) delays in the establishment of panels; (3) delays in appointing panel members; (4) delays in the completion of panel reports; (5) uncertain quality and neutrality of panelists and panel reports; (6) blocked panel reports; and (7) non-implementation of panel reports. In addition, the remedies available when there had been an identified GATT 1947 violation were sometimes unsatisfactory. A typical order was for the offending party to cease its conduct in violation of GATT 1947. If it refused to do so, recourse under GATT 1947 was for retaliatory measures to be taken by the injured party. Where the injured party was a small or poor nation, the costs of preparing and prosecuting the GATT 1947 claim might be onerous. A threat to impose retaliatory trading measures by such a state against a larger and richer country that refused to correct its noncompliance with GATT 1947 was often risible.

The WTO Agreement devised dispute resolution methodologies significantly different from and more effective than those of GATT 1947.

Nonetheless, the dispute resolution methodologies of the WTO Agreement are not without their flaws and perils—a fact even those who negotiated their terms would readily admit. Their real efficacy is only demonstrable through their effective use. They have been often used but are, as yet, not fully tested. The real issue is whether those made the subject of adverse decisions will actually change to bring themselves into compliance with the adverse ruling.

There are a number of ways in which disputes could or may arise under either GATT 1947 or the WTO Agreement. They generally hinge on whether a member's laws or practices are in conflict with GATT 1947/the WTO Agreement and/or nullify or impair benefits arising under them.

GATT 1947's Article XXIII also permitted an action to be brought where the "attainment of an objective of the General Agreement is being impeded." No party ever attempted to do so and no one seems to know the intended meaning of this clause.

Although most successful cases required the demonstration that the respondent breached an obligation under GATT 1947, "nullification or impairment" of the reasonable expectation of benefits accruing from GATT agreements may be—and has been—successfully actionable even when no violation of GATT 1947 rules had taken place. A complaint in such a case prevailed only if the complained of consequence resulted from application of a measure by the respondent. GATT 1947's Article XXIII also included the right to bring an action where the nullification or impairment was the result of "the existence of any other situation." This is a vague phrase whose enforcement was never attempted.

There are four procedural issues that are of critical importance when resolving disputes under GATT 1947/the WTO Agreement. The first is "Who may allege a nonconforming circumstance?" The second is "Who decides on the merits of those allegations and any defense to them and how is that decision to be arrived at?" The third is "What remedial measures may the dispute resolution forum impose if a nonconforming circumstance is found to exist?" The fourth is "Must a party or the parties to the dispute accept and implement the remedial measures prescribed by the dispute resolution forum?" These questions will be answered below.

There were at least 19 clauses in GATT 1947 that obligated members to consult between or among themselves in specific instances. They covered such varied subjects as customs valuation and any invocation of the Escape Clause. There were also at least seven different provisions for compensatory withdrawal or suspension of concessions. Articles VI, XIX, and XXVIII permitted unilateral retaliatory action (of countervailing duties to a subsidy, compensatory import restraints to an escape clause action, and compensatory withdrawal of tariff bindings to a prior withdrawal) by the injured nation without obtaining the permission of any other entity or party. Article XXV contained two provisions, one authorizing joint action by the Contracting Parties to facilitate the objectives of GATT 1947 and another authorizing waivers of GATT 1947 obligations, that could be used to resolve or defuse disputes. Article XXII merely required consultations with the aggrieved country and sympathetic consideration of its complaints. Article XXIII was the principal provision for handling disputes arising under GATT 1947.

GATT 1947 prescribed few procedural rules for dispute settlement under Article XXIII. The parties had to improvise and develop the procedures through practice over the years. Initially, the Contracting Parties considered disputes at their regular meetings. In some cases, however, working parties—which essentially restricted their activities to mediation and conciliation—were used. A working party was understood in the GATT 1947 context to mean a body whose members are "nations," so that each nation could send a representative of its own choosing.

In the 1950s, it became the practice to use panels (usually of three panelists) to consider disputes. A panel was composed of individuals who were expert in international trade and who acted in their individual capacities and not as national representatives. Panel members had normally to be acceptable to each disputing party. Despite their obligation to act in their individual capacities, panel members were often chosen from available national representatives. Such persons so closely associated with national governments and their policies were thought to make their decisions, whether subconsciously or overtly, in furtherance of their respective countries' national objectives. As a result, private sector and academic individuals were increasingly chosen as panel members in recent years.

The GATT Council oversaw the operation of the GATT 1947 dispute settlement system. The procedures used for dispute resolution under GATT 1947 were codified in a 1979 Tokyo Round understanding. An important series of improvements were agreed upon at the 1988 Uruguay Round midterm review session and were adopted in 1989.

After hearing the parties and considering their briefs, a panel ruled on the merits of the dispute and typically recommended the termination of any GATT 1947 violation. Although precedent or *stare decisis* concepts had no official application to panel decisions, in practice panels frequently cited at length prior panel decisions that were considered to be well-reasoned and persuasive. The GATT Council normally adopted the panel's report and recommendation. Any member could block the adoption of panel reports by the GATT Council (or by committees dealing with the Tokyo Round Codes). Consequently, every member—including a member against which the panel had found—held a veto over the acceptance of panel reports and recommendations. Although Article XXIII allowed the Contracting Parties to authorize the suspension of concessions if the violation were not remedied, this happened only once, in 1955.

It was increasingly the practice in the late 1980s and the 1990s for parties subject to unfavorable panel reports to block—temporarily or sometimes permanently—adoption of the panels' reports and recommendations. It was also common practice for the losing party to defiantly and with impunity delay for prolonged periods or indefinitely implementation of panel reports that had been adopted by the GATT Council or appropriate Code committee. The US was among those most flagrant in this practice.

It was thought that only about 40% of disputes ultimately resulted in a panel report adopted by the GATT Council. Consequently, much of the GATT 1947 dispute resolution system operated according to informal procedures.

The DSU is the first fully integrated text of GATT dispute settlement procedures. For the first time, the use of GATT/WTO dispute resolution methodologies according to GATT/WTO procedures is a mandatory treaty obligation and not merely something encouraged by mere "interpretations" or "understandings of practice." The DSU sets forth a fairly comprehensive statement (but with significant gaps) of dispute settlement rules. Although it builds on past practices, it makes several fundamental changes.

Much of GATT 1947 was adopted as part of the WTO Agreement, although parts of it only after lesser or greater modifications. Consequently, some of those GATT 1947 dispute resolution issues and methodologies—particularly those dealt with outside Article XXIII—described above remain as part of the WTO Agreement. In addition, DSU's Article 13.1 provides that, "Members affirm their adherence to the principles for the management of disputes applied under Article XXII and XXIII of GATT 1947. . ."

WTO Agreement dispute settlement is administered by the DSB. The DSB is effectively the WTO General Council acting in a specialized role. The DSU will regulate dispute settlement under all covered Multilateral and Plurilateral Agreements, although under some agreements special rules and procedures (most of which are listed under DSU's Appendix 2) will be applicable. DSU Article 1.2 explicitly provides that the DSB Chair (a person selected by DSB members) may decide what rules and procedures to follow under a dispute.

There are several stages in a WTO Agreement dispute settlement proceeding.

The first is the attempt by parties to resolve their differences through consultations. The rules for such consultations are found in DSU's Article 4. Among them is the rule of Article 4.7. Under it, the complaining party may request the establishment of a panel if consultations fail to settle a dispute within 60 days after the request for consultations.

The second, failing success in the first, is the opportunity under DSU's Article 5 for parties to avail themselves of DSU's good offices and conciliation or mediation services.

Third, and following or as an alternative to the second step, a panel may be established to hear the dispute as a matter of right under DSU's Article 6.1 if consultations, good offices, conciliation, and/or mediation services fail. Following the time period for consultations described above without successful resolution, the DSB will establish a panel at the request of a complainant unless there is a consensus in the DSB to not establish a panel. "Consensus" in GATT/WTO terminology means "unanimity." There can be no such "negative consensus" since the complainant may, sitting on the DSB and acting alone, prevent its creation.

Fourth is the selection of panel members. The WTO Secretariat maintains a roster of qualified panelists and proposes panel members. The WTO Director-General selects panel members in consultation with the parties to the dispute. Where the parties cannot agree on panel members, to avoid delays he or she may, under DSU's Article 8.7, do so on his or her own authority in consultation with the chairs of the DSB and the relevant council or committee.

Fifth is the establishment of terms of reference, *i.e.*, what the panel is expected to decide. To avoid delays, DSU's Article 7.1 provides for the use of standard terms of reference absent timely agreement (within 20 days) by the parties to the contrary. The standard terms are, "To examine, in light of the relevant provisions in [name of the covered agreement(s) cited by the parties to the dispute], the matter referred to the DSB by (name of party) in document DS/............ and to make such findings as will assist the DSB in making the recommendations or in giving the rulings provided for in that/those agreement(s)."

The sixth step is when the panel hears all interested and/or disputing parties, reviews their written submissions, and issues its report. Other WTO members may intervene (with the permission of the respondent) and present arguments to the panel, although the panel only considers issues raised by the principal parties. Panel proceedings are not public. Under the DSU, Article 15, the panel submits its description of the dispute, the parties' arguments, and the panel's legal analysis to the parties for comment. DSU, Appendix 3, specifies time limits for implementation of the various stages in the panel's processes. These generally require a panel report to be issued within six to eight months of the establishment of the panel.

The seventh is DSB's consideration for adoption of the report. DSU's Article 16 prevents blockage of DSB's acceptance of a panel report by a single WTO member. The DSB will adopt a report unless there is a consensus **against** adoption—a methodology referred to as "reverse consensus". A panel report is adopted at the second meeting on which it appears on the DSB's agenda barring consensus against adoption. This fundamental change in procedure was reluctantly taken in the hope that strengthened dispute settlement procedures would deter the United States from its practice of taking unilateral actions in trade disputes. DSU's Article 23.1 requires WTO members to use the dispute settlement system exclusively if they "seek the redress of a violation of obligations or other nullification or impairment of benefits under the covered agreements" although DSU's Article 25 permits the parties to submit controversies to binding arbitration in lieu of the use of a panel and DSB and Appellate Body review.

Eighth, and a GATT novelty, is the opportunity for appeal by any party to the dispute to the Appellate Body. Under DSU's Article 17, the Appellate Body is a standing body of seven members. Each member is to be a nongovernmental individual of recognized authority, with demonstrated expertise in law, international trade, and the subject matter of covered agreements generally. Each is appointed for a four-year term and may be reappointed only once. The membership of the Appellate Body must be representative of WTO membership. The Appellate Body will hear appeals in panels of three (or five at the request of the parties). It is limited by DSU Article 17.6 to considering issues of law covered in the panel report and legal interpretations developed by the panel. Appellate proceedings are normally to take only 60 days. They may not, in any event, take more than 90 days. An Appellate Body's report is subject to the automatic adoption rules and reverse consensus applicable to panel reports. Adoption, absent a reverse consensus, must be within 30 days of its circulation to DSB members.

The ninth step is—if either a panel or Appellate Body report has been adopted—monitoring of the implementation of the recommendations. A typical panel recommendation is that the offending member cease its violation of WTO Agreement rules, such as by withdrawing the offending measure in its laws or practices. DSU's Article 21.3 requires a losing respondent to indicate within 30 days of the adoption of a panel report what actions it plans to take to implement the panel's recommendation within a reasonable period of time. A "reasonable period of time" may be that set by the offending member and approved by the DSB, agreed to by the contending parties, or—where no solution is found within 45 days—established by arbitration. The normal period is not to exceed 15 months.

If the recommendations are not implemented, a tenth step is possible. The prevailing party may seek negotiated compensation from the losing party. The prevailing party may, under DSU's Article 22.1, also seek (initially or if compensation negotiations fail) the withdrawal from the recalcitrant party of concessions previously made by the prevailing party. Suspension of concessions is authorized automatically under DSU's Article 22.6 in the absence of implementation or compensation absent a DSB contrary consensus. Specific procedures under DSU's Article 22.4 provide for determining the level of such suspension, which should be equivalent to the level of nullification or impairment, if no agreement can be reached. Withdrawal of a nonconforming measure is preferred to compensation or suspension of concessions (which are viewed as "temporary measures") under DSU's Article 22.1 and Article XVI:4 of GATT 1947.

Although agreements under the WTO Agreement may provide for dispute resolution methodologies separate and apart from those of Article XXIII, those of Article XXIII have served as a model for dispute settlement under those other agreements. The Agreement on Trade-Related Aspects of Intellectual Property Rights, Article 64, provides that complaints under Article XXIII:1(b) and (c) would be not permitted for five years. During that time, the DSB is to determine whether such complaints are to be allowed. The General Agreement on Trade in Services, Article XXIII:3, permits only certain such complaints. Under the WTO Agreement's Agreement on Antidumping Duties, Article 17.6, there are standards of review significantly different from those provided by the DSU. That Article provides:

"(i) in its assessment of the facts of the matter, the panel shall determine whether the [national antidumping] authorities establishment of the facts was proper and whether their evaluation of those facts was unbiased and objective. If the establishment of the facts was proper and the evaluation was unbiased and objective, even though the panel might have reached a different conclusion, the evaluation shall not be overturned.

(ii) the panel shall interpret the relevant provisions of the [Antidumping] Agreement in accordance with customary rules of interpretation of public international law. Where the panel finds that a relevant provision of the Agreement admits of more than one permissible interpretation, the panel shall find the authorities' measure to be in conformity with the Agreement if it rests upon one of those permissible interpretations."

A ministerial declaration adopted at the end of the Uruguay Round stated that the above standard of review would be reconsidered after three years with the purpose of determining whether it should have broader application under the WTO Agreement.

TPRM administered by the TPRB is found at Annex 2 to the WTO Agreement. Its purpose is to improve compliance by WTO members with their obligations under WTO Agreement Multilateral and applicable Plurilateral Agreements and to increase the transparency of the trade policies and practices of WTO members. The TPRB may not do so through the imposition of new policy commitments on countries nor may it enforce specific obligations under those Agreements. It is restricted to a review of national policy and practice on the basis of reports from WTO members and the WTO Secretariat and the making of a final report that it submits to the WTO Ministerial Conference. The TPRB also drafts an annual review of developments in the international trading environment.

When resolving disputes under GATT 1947/the WTO Agreement, there are—as stated above—four procedural issues that are of critical importance. How are these matters dealt with under the WTO Agreement? The first issue is, "Who may allege the existence of a GATT-nonconforming circumstance?" Only WTO member states may participate in WTO Agreement dispute resolution proceedings, whether as complainants, respondents, or interested parties. No provision has been made for the participation of individuals or the initiation of proceedings by the WTO Director-General, the DSB Chair, or the TPRB. Some have alleged this to be a serious failing. The second is, "Who decides on the merits of those allegations and any defense to them and how is that decision to be arrived at?" The adjudicative fora under the WTO Agreement are prescribed with some precision. Nonetheless, they operate under a blanket of "confidentiality" which prevents the details of their proceedings from being publicly known; panelists do not include "nontrade" persons, such as environmentalists and labor specialists; and some of the procedures of the WTO Agreement dispute resolution bodies regarding the actual conduct of their proceedings are not prescribed in detail. The standards for review of the measures taken by a WTO member to determine their compliance with its WTO Agreement obligations or the WTO Agreement consequences of its actions are largely unspecified. Where a developing country is the party, and particularly where a developed country is the respondent, special procedures under DSU Articles 3.12, 4.10, 8.10, 12.10, 21.7, and 24 will apply. The third is, "What remedial measures may the dispute resolution forum impose if a WTO Agreement-nonconforming circumstance is found to exist?" WTO Agreement panels are largely restricted to ordering parties not in compliance with the WTO Agreement to bring themselves into compliance. There are many instances in which an effective award for the resolution of a dispute might better include other measures, including specific performance or the payment of damages. The fourth is, "Must a party or the parties to the dispute accept and implement the remedial measures prescribed by the dispute resolution forum?" Where the complainant is a weak trading partner, the suspension of trading concessions—the only real retaliatory measure permitted against a party that has refused to bring itself back into compliance with the WTO Agreement— is a toothless deterrent. Moreover, the withdrawal of such concessions may often hurt the country that withdraws them as much as it does the country from which the concessions are withdrawn. No concerted action against an offending party, such as expulsion from the WTO or international sanctions, is permitted. Certain special provision has been made for dispute resolutions where a developing country is a party.

Most perilous to the effectiveness of the WTO Agreement, however, is the possibility that its dispute resolution provisions may be so exacting and unavoidable that a major WTO member, when backed to the wall, may defy them with uncertain but perhaps devastating consequences for the WTO Agreement. GATT 1947 largely operated on the popular consensus and support—however begrudging at times—of the major trading countries. It permitted them to avoid politically or economically unpalatable steps dictated by GATT 1947's terms through various devices. However much violence to GATT 1947's principles was caused through the use of those devices and however unfair to other members their use may have been, their use permitted vitally-important GATT 1947 members and GATT 1947 to avoid direct confrontations. This may no longer be the case. Under these new circumstances, it remains to be seen whether those WTO members will now defer to or openly defy the WTO where their WTO Agreement obligations are clear and enforceable.

Chapter IV: Regional Trade Blocs

Regional and Transregional Economic Groups Compared

There are a number of regional trade blocs in the various parts of the world. Their number continues to grow, although some that are currently in existence seem to be faltering. Some of these regional trade blocs are effectively operational and are economically important. Many others are frameworks in which participants meet and speak grandly of the big things they plan to do—but never quite seem to get around to doing them in any meaningful way. Yet others are mere names, without infrastructures or real support from members, which have existed in this skeletal format for decades. Membership in some regional trade blocs is open to all countries within a region (and sometimes even those from outside the region) upon their application and agreement to abide by the rules of the bloc while others are only open to those countries that have specially been accepted or have successfully negotiated the terms of their admission. Principal among the regional trade blocs are the EU, the North American Free Trade Agreement ("NAFTA"), and MERCOSUR. These will be considered in detail in this chapter. Others will be described in lesser detail or will be mentioned in passing. While there is much that may be said about a regional trade bloc, such as its its multifaceted legislative and policy programs, coverage of each regional trade bloc in this chapter and this book will be restricted (except for some essential description of its history, membership, institutions, and similar matters) to the specific legislation, policy, and practice of each regional trade bloc as regards only customs and tariff matters.

The reader should remember the significance for customs and tariffs purposes of regional trade blocs. Where they constitute free trade areas, this permits movement throughout the free trade area of goods produced within the free trade without being subjected to tariffs or other impediments. Where they constitute customs unions, this permits the importation into the customs union at any point under the same tariffs and terms of entry with the ability to move the imported goods through the customs union without further payments of tariffs. Where they constitute common markets, the attributes of both a free trade area and a customs union are combined and the flexibility permitted an importer and trader by this combination exceeds the mere sum of the parts of free trade area and customs union.

There are many unilateral commercial relationships established between one or more developed countries and groups of developing and/or least-developed countries. One or more parties to these relationships may themselves be regional trade groups. In such a relationship, the developed country (or countries) offers to the developing countries special commercial terms of trade which are not reciprocated directly or through any other commercial concession by the developing countries. This is simply a device by which the developed countries, for humanitarian reasons, offer special trading opportunities to developing countries in an effort to assist those developing countries to achieve acceptable levels of prosperity and development. Examples of such programs of unilaterally preferential terms of trade include those of the United States under GSP and the Caribbean Basin Initiative ("CBI"). Most developed countries offer similar preferential trade assistance to all developing countries under a program similar to GSP or specially to some such countries under programs such as Canada's Caribbean Canadian Common Market ("Caribcan") for most English-speaking Caribbean countries and territories or the EU's Lomé Conventions which assist 71 selected African, Caribbean, and Pacific ("ACP") countries—most of them former colonies of EU members. These relationships will be described under Chapter VI.

There continue to be some European "mother country" and non-European "colony" relationships. The United States also maintains a few similar relationships. Under these political relationships, unlike the past when colonies were operated largely for the commercial advantage of the mother country, underdeveloped economies are subsidized by the mother country and their exports are permitted unrestricted entry to mother country markets. Consequently, there are a number of small island territories (plus French Guiana on the South American mainland) around the world which are subsidized so as to maintain living standards comparable to those of the mother country but grossly exceeding those of surrounding territories. Further, some countries have less than full authority over some semi-autonomous territories and with which they have relationships that are specially limited and defined. These will be described in Chapter V.

There are numerous bilateral commercial treaties between countries from different regions. Each such treaty may be argued to create a sort of "economic group" of two. There are at least 600 bilateral investment treaties signed between OECD countries and developing countries. More than 60 were signed in 1993 alone. Some of these bilateral commercial treaties (which includes those to which the EU is one of the parties) establish even more clearly that they are economic groups because they create free trade associations or customs unions. These will be described in Chapter V.

Finally, there are proposals for further regional and even transregional trade blocs. These will be considered in this chapter.

Regional Trade Blocs Generally

It is important for legal practitioners and businesspersons who deal in international commerce to know of the existence of regional trade blocs and to understand their institutions, legal requirements, and authorizations. This is true principally because it is often possible to structure trade, investments, manufacturing, and marketing within a region most cost-effectively by capitalizing on the special economic interrelationships and legal authorizations granted among the members of the group. It is also true, however, that a regional trade bloc—especially the EU—may impose restrictions and requirements which must be obeyed under penalty of law. Compliance is necessary and prudent. In order to comply, a person must first know that the rules exist and then understand them.

Nevertheless, since regional trade blocs are constantly changing and are often not quite what they seem, an international trader must constantly monitor the business news and repeatedly take the "temperature" of any regional trade bloc group to find out whether it is growing more important or falling apart, which countries are joining and which countries are leaving it, which countries and which products are partially or completely exempt from the rules, how its rules are changing or have changed, and whether there is a disparity between what it says it does or will do and what it actually does or becomes. It must be borne in mind in addition that many of these regional trade blocs deal almost exclusively with changes in their tariff schedules while nontariff barriers to trade may constitute the most onerous burden on trading among or with the member countries. It is also the case that often one country will be a member of more than one regional trade bloc or arrangement. How these different memberships are coordinated, whether they are coordinated at all, and even whether they are in conflict are questions of interest to those planning to trade with or invest in those countries.

There are many such regional trade blocs and their number seems to increase daily. Nearly all of the WTO's 136 Members have notified the WTO of participation in at least one bilateral or multilateral preferential trading arrangement, although notifications may also refer to the accession of new parties to an agreement that already exists. In the period 1948-1994, GATT received 124 notifications of such arrangements relating to the trade in goods. Since WTO's creation, 90 additional arrangements covering trade in goods or services have been notified to the WTO. Not all trading arrangements notified to GATT/WTO in the past half century are still in force, but most of those that have been discontinued were replaced by new arrangements among the same signatories. Out of the total of 214 agreements or enlargements so far notified to the GATT/WTO, 134 are deemed to be currently in force. The impetus for the current enthusiasm for regional trade blocs stems largely from the successes and importance of what is now called the EU and fears of being excluded from markets through the creation of protectionist regional trading blocs—most particularly NAFTA.

Many constitute little more than political posturing and wishful thinking and are unlikely to ever achieve any significance. In part, the ineffectiveness of such groups arises from a lack of political will by the leaders of their members to actually liberalize international trade and to make such trade subject to established rules rather than to the *ad hoc* and often corrupt practices of the ruling national elites. In part, it is due to the fact that such regional trade blocs are often made up only of economically backward countries. In most such cases, all members principally produce competing products whose markets are outside the regional group. Also in most such cases, none of the members individually or collectively provide a significant market for goods produced within the regional bloc. Such circumstances do not create synergies for economic growth nor do they produce successes that engender local interest groups that lobby for the continuation or strengthening of the regional blocs. These failings are compounded by the fact that, in some instances, the members of such groups are made up—at least in part—of implacably hostile and sometimes warring states. Finally, the effectiveness of a customs union or free trade area assumes that the parties actually believe Ricardo's arguments that free trade is the ideal and that its approximation is an unquestioned benefit for all concerned. It would appear that many parties to some such arrangements are at least tepidly supportive, when not actually antagonistic, to those concepts.

GATT and Regional Trade Blocs

There would appear to be a direct conflict between membership in a regional trade bloc—under which special and preferential trading terms are accorded members—and membership in WTO/GATT that requires all members to provide MFN treatment to imported goods. Although the appearance of conflict between the two is not fully allayed by this fact, the contradiction is effectively eliminated as a matter of organizational rules by the existence in the WTO Agreement of the recognition and authorization of qualifying regional trade blocs.

A cardinal principle of WTO/GATT is "Most-Favored-Nation" or "MFN" treatment. This requires every member of WTO/GATT to treat the covered products and services of every other member at least as favorably as it treats the similar imported products and services from **any** other country.

Free trade is the absence of **all** restraints on imports from **any** country. Since absolute global free trade does not now exist, the more nearly trade restraints approximate free trade the more nearly such a world-wide trading system will produce the benefits promised by free trade.

MFN treatment is an important factor in multinational trade that serves to approximate free trade. Its absence creates a global trading system that differs appreciably from free trade.

Regional trade blocs exist only to provide specially-favored terms of trade among their members when compared with terms of trade with nonmembers. Consequently, it seems intuitively obvious that regional economic groups are incompatible with free trade principles and with the requirements of WTO/GATT. Nonetheless, regional economic groups have long existed without being declared in violation of the requirements of WTO/GATT. How is this possible? WTO/GATT has justified, or perhaps rationalized, the existence of regional trade blocs. WTO/GATT specifically provides for the existence of regional trade blocs, but such provision is subject to special restrictions. In the past, GATT has been very permissive in permitting the existence of regional trade blocs and liberal in finding, even when this is clearly not the case, that they satisfy the requisite special restrictions.

Most countries on all continents around the world are now members of regional trade agreements (customs unions, free trade areas or other preferential arrangements). More than 200 regional trade agreements have been notified to the GATT or WTO over time. Over 130 of them are currently in force. Most have been concluded since 1990. Between 1995 and 1999, 90 agreements covering trade in goods or services or both were notified to the WTO.

The WTO's Committee on Regional Trade Agreements was given responsibility for monitoring such developments and reviewing them for WTO Agreement/GATT compatability. In February 1996, the WTO General Council established the Commitee on Regional Trade Agreements. Its duties include examination of individual regional agreements and consideration of the systemic implications of the agreements for the multilateral trading system and the relationship between them. WTO members (as were earlier GATT Contracting Parties) are bound to notify the Committee of any regional trade agreements in which they participate.

Article XXIV of GATT 1947, as amended, is the GATT provision that principally recognizes and accepts customs unions and free trade areas (under which categories common markets, economic communities, and economic unions are subsumed). That article states, at paragraphs 4 through 11, that customs unions and free trade areas which seek to increase freedom of trade are desirable and compatible with GATT under prescribed circumstances.

Those circumstances are, for a customs union, that the duties and other regulations of commerce imposed at the institution of the customs union shall not, on the whole, be higher or more restrictive for nonmembers than the general incidence of the duties and regulations of commerce applicable in the constituent territories of the group prior to the formation of the customs union. In addition, in a customs union (a) duties and other restrictive regulations of commerce (except those specifically exempted by GATT) must be eliminated with respect to substantially all the trade between the constituent territories of the customs union or at least with respect to substantially all the trade in products originating in such territories and (b) substantially the same duties and other regulations of commerce must be applied by each of the members of the customs union to the trade with nonmembers.

Those circumstances are, for a free trade area, that the duties and other regulations of commerce maintained in each of the constituent territories and applicable at the formation of the free trade area to the trade of nonmembers may not be higher or more restrictive than the corresponding duties and other regulations of commerce existing in the same constituent territories prior to the formation of the free trade area. A free trade area is defined as a group of two or more customs territories in which the duties and other restrictive regulations of commerce (except those specifically exempted by GATT) are eliminated on substantially all the trade between the constituent territories in products originating in such territories.

WTO/GATT has the aim of global and equitable economic welfare. Is the existence of regional and other similar economic groups inconsistent with global welfare? Logically, a regional economic group improves global welfare only if it creates more trade than it diverts from extraregional suppliers to regional suppliers. Were the diversion only from a national to a regional supplier because of greater comparative advantage, there would be no decrease in global trade but there would be an increase in "global welfare." If the diversion is from an extraregional supplier with a greater comparative advantage to a regional supplier with a lesser comparative advantage, the volume of trade would be reduced and global welfare diminished because regional trade would be conducted at the expense of more efficient extraregional trade.

In every instance, a regional economic group both diverts national to regional trade and diverts extraregional to regional trade. There must be a balancing in each case regarding whether the overall effect has diminished or increased global welfare.

As a rule, the bigger the initial volume of trade within the region, the higher tariffs were before the creation of the regional economic group, and the lower the common external tariffs following creation of the group, the more likely it is that the group will create trade and enhance global economic welfare.

With regards to whether a regional economic group is likely to have the effect desired by its members of increasing intraregional trade, economic integration principally among developed countries is likely to result in increased intraregional trade because all members produce products readily saleable in each others' markets. Economic integration among only developing countries is unlikely to increase intraregional trade because most of their products are commodities that only have substantial markets in developed countries. With regards to the latter case, it is sometimes argued in their favor that – by increasing the size of the common regional market – regional economic groups among developing countries permit the efficiencies of scale necessary to allow industrialization and the creation of manufacturing industries producing for the regional market.

Further information may be obtained by going to the WTO web site, clicking on "Trade Topics" and there clicking on "Regionalism." The WTO/GATT texts dealing with such preferential trading arrangements are reproduced below.

GATT Article XXIV and Related Documents—the Texts

[***asterisks** below mark the portions of the text which should be read in conjunction with notes and supplementary provisions in Annex I to the Agreement.]

"Article XXIV
Territorial Application - Frontier Traffic - Customs Unions and Free-trade Areas

1. The provisions of this Agreement shall apply to the metropolitan customs territories of the contracting parties and to any other

customs territories in respect of which this Agreement has been accepted under Article XXVI or is being applied under Article XXXIII or pursuant to the Protocol of Provisional Application. Each such customs territory shall, exclusively for the purposes of the territorial application of this Agreement, be treated as though it were a contracting party; *Provided* that the provisions of this paragraph shall not be construed to create any rights or obligations as between two or more customs territories in respect of which this Agreement has been accepted under Article XXVI or is being applied under Article XXXIII or pursuant to the Protocol of Provisional Application by a single contracting party.

2. For the purposes of this Agreement a customs territory shall be understood to mean any territory with respect to which separate tariffs or other regulations of commerce are maintained for a substantial part of the trade of such territory with other territories.

3. The provisions of this Agreement shall not be construed to prevent:

(*a*) Advantages accorded by any contracting party to adjacent countries in order to facilitate frontier traffic;

(*b*) Advantages accorded to the trade with the Free Territory of Trieste by countries contiguous to that territory, provided that such advantages are not in conflict with the Treaties of Peace arising out of the Second World War.

4. The contracting parties recognize the desirability of increasing freedom of trade by the development, through voluntary agreements, of closer integration between the economies of the countries parties to such agreements. They also recognize that the purpose of a customs union or of a free-trade area should be to facilitate trade between the constituent territories and not to raise barriers to the trade of other contracting parties with such territories.

5. Accordingly, the provisions of this Agreement shall not prevent, as between the territories of contracting parties, the formation of a customs union or of a free-trade area or the adoption of an interim agreement necessary for the formation of a customs union or of a free-trade area; *Provided* that:

(*a*) with respect to a customs union, or an interim agreement leading to a formation of a customs union, the duties and other regulations of commerce imposed at the institution of any such union or interim agreement in respect of trade with contracting parties not parties to such union or agreement shall not on the whole be higher or more restrictive than the general incidence of the duties and regulations of commerce applicable in the constituent territories prior to the formation of such union or the adoption of such interim agreement, as the case may be;

(*b*) with respect to a free-trade area, or an interim agreement leading to the formation of a free-trade area, the duties and other regulations of commerce maintained in each if the constituent territories and applicable at the formation of such free-trade area or the adoption of such interim agreement to the trade of contracting parties not included in such area or not parties to such agreement shall not be higher or more restrictive than the corresponding duties and other regulations of commerce existing in the same constituent territories prior to the formation of the free-trade area, or interim agreement as the case may be; and

(*c*) any interim agreement referred to in sub-paragraphs (*a*) and (*b*) shall include a plan and schedule for the formation of such a customs union or of such a free-trade area within a reasonable length of time.

6. If, in fulfilling the requirements of sub-paragraph 5 (*a*), a contracting party proposes to increase any rate of duty inconsistently with the provisions of Article II, the procedure set forth in Article XXVIII shall apply. In providing for compensatory adjustment, due account shall be taken of the compensation already afforded by the reduction brought about in the corresponding duty of the other constituents of the union.

7.

(*a*) Any contracting party deciding to enter into a customs union or free-trade area, or an interim agreement leading to the formation of such a union or area, shall promptly notify the CONTRACTING PARTIES and shall make available to them such information regarding the proposed union or area as will enable them to make such reports and recommendations to contracting parties as they may deem appropriate.

(*b*) If, after having studied the plan and schedule included in an interim agreement referred to in paragraph 5 in consultation with the parties to that agreement and taking due account of the information made available in accordance with the provisions of sub-paragraph (*a*), the CONTRACTING PARTIES find that such agreement is not likely to result in the formation of a customs union or of a free-trade area within the period contemplated by the parties to the agreement or that such period is not a reasonable one, the CONTRACTING PARTIES shall make recommendations to the parties to the agreement. The parties shall not maintain or put into force, as the case may be, such agreement if they are not prepared to modify it in accordance with these recommendations.

(*c*) Any substantial change in the plan or schedule referred to in paragraph 5 (*c*) shall be communicated to the CONTRACTING PARTIES, which may request the contracting parties concerned to consult with them if the change seems likely to jeopardize or delay unduly the formation of the customs union or of the free-trade area.

8. For the purposes of this Agreement:

(*a*) A customs union shall be understood to mean the substitution of a single customs territory for two or more customs territories, so that

(i) duties and other restrictive regulations of commerce (except, where necessary, those permitted under Articles XI, XII, XIII, XIV, XV and XX) are eliminated with respect to substantially all the trade between the constituent territories of the union or at least with respect to substantially all the trade in products originating in such territories, and,

(ii) subject to the provisions of paragraph 9, substantially the same duties and other regulations of commerce are applied by each of the members of the union to the trade of territories not included in the union;

(*b*) A free-trade area shall be understood to mean a group of two or more customs territories in which the duties and other restrictive regulations of commerce (except, where necessary, those permitted under Articles XI, XII, XIII, XIV, XV and XX) are eliminated on substantially all the trade between the constituent territories in products originating in such territories.

9. The preferences referred to in paragraph 2 of Article I shall not be affected by the formation of a customs union or of a free-trade area but may be eliminated or adjusted by means of negotiations with contracting parties affected.* This procedure of negotiations with affected contracting parties shall, in particular, apply to the elimination of preferences required to conform with the provisions of paragraph 8 (*a*)(i) and paragraph 8 (*b*).

10. The CONTRACTING PARTIES may by a two-thirds majority approve proposals which do not fully comply with the requirements of paragraphs 5 to 9 inclusive, provided that such proposals lead to the formation of a customs union or a free-trade area in the sense of this Article.

11. Taking into account the exceptional circumstances arising out of the establishment of India and Pakistan as independent States and recognizing the fact that they have long constituted an economic unit, the contracting parties agree that the provisions of this Agreement shall not prevent the two countries from entering into special arrangements with respect to the trade between them, pending the establishment of their mutual trade relations on a definitive basis.*

12. Each contracting party shall take such reasonable measures as may be available to it to ensure observance of the provisions of this Agreement by the regional and local governments and authorities within its territories."

"Ad Article XXIV

Paragraph 9

It is understood that the provisions of Article I would require that, when a product which has been imported into the territory of a member of a customs union or free-trade area at a preferential rate of duty is re-exported to the territory of another member of such union or area, the latter member should collect a duty equal to the difference between the duty already paid and any higher duty that would be payable if the product were being imported directly into its territory.

Paragraph 11

Measures adopted by India and Pakistan in order to carry out definitive trade arrangements between them, once they have been agreed upon, might depart from particular provisions of this Agreement, but these measures would in general be consistent with the objectives of the Agreement."

"UNDERSTANDING ON THE INTERPRETATION OF ARTICLE XXIV OF THE GENERAL AGREEMENT ON TARIFFS AND TRADE 1994

Members,

Having regard to the provisions of Article XXIV of GATT 1994;

Recognizing that customs unions and free trade areas have greatly increased in number and importance since the establishment of GATT 1947 and today cover a significant proportion of world trade;

Recognizing the contribution to the expansion of world trade that may be made by closer integration between the economies of the parties to such agreements;

Recognizing also that such contribution is increased if the elimination between the constituent territories of duties and other restrictive regulations of commerce extends to all trade, and diminished if any major sector of trade is excluded;

Reaffirming that the purpose of such agreements should be to facilitate trade between the constituent territories and not to raise barriers to the trade of other Members with such territories; and that in their formation or enlargement the parties to them should to the greatest possible extent avoid creating adverse effects on the trade of other Members;

Convinced also of the need to reinforce the effectiveness of the role of the Council for Trade in Goods in reviewing agreements notified under Article XXIV, by clarifying the criteria and procedures for the assessment of new or enlarged agreements, and improving the transparency of all Article XXIV agreements;

Recognizing the need for a common understanding of the obligations of Members under paragraph 12 of Article XXIV;

Hereby agree as follows:

1. Customs unions, free-trade areas, and interim agreements leading to the formation of a customs union or free-trade area, to be consistent with Article XXIV, must satisfy, *inter alia*, the provisions of paragraphs 5, 6, 7 and 8 of that Article.

I. Article XXIV:5

2. The evaluation under paragraph 5(a) of Article XXIV of the general incidence of the duties and other regulations of commerce applicable before and after the formation of a customs union shall in respect of duties and charges be based upon an overall assessment of weighted average tariff rates and of customs duties collected. This assessment shall be based on import statistics for a previous representative period to be supplied by the customs union, on a tariff-line basis and in values and quantities, broken down by WTO country of origin. The Secretariat shall compute the weighted average tariff rates and customs duties collected in accordance with the methodology used in the assessment of tariff offers in the Uruguay Round of Multilateral Trade Negotiations. For this purpose, the duties and charges to be taken into consideration shall be the applied rates of duty. It is recognized that for the purpose of the overall assessment of the incidence of other regulations of commerce for which quantification and aggregation are difficult, the examination of individual measures, regulations, products covered and trade flows affected may be required.

3. The 'reasonable length of time' referred to in paragraph 5(c) of Article XXIV should exceed 10 years only in exceptional cases. In cases where Members parties to an interim agreement believe that 10 years would be insufficient they shall provide a full explanation to the Council for Trade in Goods of the need for a longer period.

II. Article XXIV:6

4. Paragraph 6 of Article XXIV establishes the procedure to be followed when a Member forming a customs union proposes to increase a bound rate of duty. In this regard Members reaffirm that the procedure set forth in Article XXVIII, as elaborated in the guidelines adopted on 10 November 1980 (BISD 27S/26-28) and in the Understanding on the Interpretation of Article XXVIII of GATT 1994, must be commenced before tariff concessions are modified or withdrawn upon the formation of a customs union or an interim agreement leading to the formation of a customs union.

5. These negotiations will be entered into in good faith with a view to achieving mutually satisfactory compensatory adjustment. In such negotiations, as required by paragraph 6 of Article XXIV, due account shall be taken of reductions of duties on the same tariff line made by other constituents of the customs union upon its formation. Should such reductions not be sufficient to provide the necessary compensatory adjustment, the customs union would offer compensation, which may take the form of reductions of duties on other tariff lines. Such an offer shall be taken into consideration by the Members having negotiating rights in the binding being modified or withdrawn. Should the compensatory adjustment remain unacceptable, negotiations should be continued. Where, despite such efforts, agreement in negotiations on compensatory adjustment under Article XXVIII as elaborated by the Understanding on the Interpretation of Article XXVIII of GATT 1994 cannot be reached within a reasonable period from the initiation of negotiations, the customs union shall, nevertheless, be free to modify or withdraw the concessions; affected Members shall then be free to withdraw substantially equivalent concessions in accordance with Article XXVIII.

6. GATT 1994 imposes no obligation on Members benefiting from a reduction of duties consequent upon the formation of a customs union, or an interim agreement leading to the formation of a customs union, to provide compensatory adjustment to its constituents.

III. Review of Customs Unions and Free-Trade Areas

7. All notifications made under paragraph 7(a) of Article XXIV shall be examined by a working party in the light of the relevant provisions of GATT 1994 and of paragraph 1 of this Understanding. The working party shall submit a report to the Council for Trade in Goods on its findings in this regard. The Council for Trade in Goods may make such recommendations to Members as it deems appropriate.

8. In regard to interim agreements, the working party may in its report make appropriate recommendations on the proposed time-frame and on measures required to complete the formation of the customs union or free-trade area. It may if necessary provide for further review of the agreement.

9. Members parties to an interim agreement shall notify substantial changes in the plan and schedule included in that agreement to the Council for Trade in Goods and, if so requested, the Council shall examine the changes.

10. Should an interim agreement notified under paragraph 7(a) of Article XXIV not include a plan and schedule, contrary to paragraph 5(c) of

Article XXIV, the working party shall in its report recommend such a plan and schedule. The parties shall not maintain or put into force, as the case may be, such agreement if they are not prepared to modify it in accordance with these recommendations. Provision shall be made for subsequent review of the implementation of the recommendations.

11. Customs unions and constituents of free-trade areas shall report periodically to the Council for Trade in Goods, as envisaged by the CONTRACTING PARTIES to GATT 1947 in their instruction to the GATT 1947 Council concerning reports on regional agreements (BISD 18S/38), on the operation of the relevant agreement. Any significant changes and/or developments in the agreements should be reported as they occur.

IV. Dispute Settlement

12. The provisions of Articles XXII and XXIII of GATT 1994 as elaborated and applied by the Dispute Settlement Understanding may be invoked with respect to any matters arising from the application of those provisions of Article XXIV relating to customs unions, free-trade areas or interim agreements leading to the formation of a customs union or free-trade area.

V. Article XXIV:12

13. Each Member is fully responsible under GATT 1994 for the observance of all provisions of GATT 1994, and shall take such reasonable measures as may be available to it to ensure such observance by regional and local governments and authorities within its territory.

14. The provisions of Articles XXII and XXIII of GATT 1994 as elaborated and applied by the Dispute Settlement Understanding may be invoked in respect of measures affecting its observance taken by regional or local governments or authorities within the territory of a Member. When the Dispute Settlement Body has ruled that a provision of GATT 1994 has not been observed, the responsible Member shall take such reasonable measures as may be available to it to ensure its observance. The provisions relating to compensation and suspension of concessions or other obligations apply in cases where it has not been possible to secure such observance.

15. Each Member undertakes to accord sympathetic consideration to and afford adequate opportunity for consultation regarding any representations made by another Member concerning measures affecting the operation of GATT 1994 taken within the territory of the former."

Professor Jagdish Bhagwati of Columbia University argues that free trade areas permitted by WTO/GATT should be required to establish a customs union (*i.e.*, common tariffs) and that the common tariff for any item should be set equal to the lowest tariff applied to that good by any member before the free trade area was formed instead of GATT approving them—as is now the case—if the members set "duties and other regulations of commerce" that are not "higher or more restrictive" with respect to outsiders than the average of ones previously in effect. He also urges that the permitted WTO/GATT standards for antidumping actions and voluntary export restraints should be made more restrictive because, as global tariffs have fallen, when imposed as protectionist measures by a regional economic group these permit regional economic integration to become a path to regional protectionism. *The Economist* adds the suggestion that WTO/GATT require regional trade bloc members to notify the WTO before signing their agreements so that working parties could deliberate before the agreements come into force and provide for the continuous monitoring of regional trade blocs to assure that they **remain** in compliance with WTO/GATT requirements.

As a separate case, developing countries have been permitted to enter into regional trade blocs preferentially without fully satisfying the restrictions of WTO/GATT. "The GATT Contracting Parties Decision of November 28, 1979, on Differential and More Favorable Treatment, Reciprocity and Fuller Participation of Developing Countries [GATT, 26th Supp., BISD 203 (1980)]" states, in paragraph 2(c), that special and more favorable treatment may be accorded to developing countries with regards to, *inter alia*, "regional or global arrangements entered into amongst less-developed contracting parties for the mutual reduction or elimination of tariffs and, in accordance with criteria or conditions which may be prescribed by the Contracting Parties, for the mutual reduction or elimination of non-tariff measures, on products imported from one another."

That "Enabling Clause" is reproduced in its entirety below.

"DIFFERENTIAL AND MORE FAVOURABLE TREATMENT, RECIPROCITY AND FULLER PARTICIPATION OF DEVELOPING COUNTRIES

Decision of 28 November 1979 (L/4903)

Following negotiations within the framework of the Multilateral Trade Negotiations, the CONTRACTING PARTIES *decide* as follows:

1. Notwithstanding the provisions of Article I of the General Agreement, contracting parties may accord differential and more favourable treatment to developing countries [AND DEVELOPING TERRITORIES], without according such treatment to other contracting parties.

2. The provisions of paragraph 1 apply to the following [WHICH DOES NOT PRECLUDE ADOPTION OF FURTHER *AD HOC* MEASURES BY THE CONTRACTING PARTIES]:

(a) Preferential tariff treatment accorded by developed contracting parties to products originating in developing countries in accordance

with the Generalized System of Preferences [AS DESCRIBED IN THE DECISION OF THE CONTRACTING PARTIES OF 25 JUNE 1971, AS RELATING TO THE ESTABLISHMENT OF "GENERALIZED, NON-RECIPROCAL AND NONDISCRIMINATORY PREFERENCES BENEFICIAL TO THE DEVELOPING COUNTRIES (BISD 185/24)],

(b) Differential and more favourable treatment with respect to the provisions of the General Agreement concerning non-tariff measures governed by the provisions of instruments multilaterally negotiated under the auspices of the GATT;

(c) Regional or global arrangements entered into amongst less-developed contracting parties for the mutual reduction or elimination of tariffs and, in accordance with criteria or conditions which may be prescribed by the CONTRACTING PARTIES, for the mutual reduction or elimination of non-tariff measures, on products imported from one another;

(d) Special treatment on the least developed among the developing countries in the context of any general or specific measures in favour of developing countries.

3. Any differential and more favourable treatment provided under this clause:

(a) shall be designed to facilitate and promote the trade of developing countries and not to raise barriers to or create undue difficulties for the trade of any other contracting parties;

(b) shall not constitute an impediment to the reduction or elimination of tariffs and other restrictions to trade on a most-favoured-nation basis;

(c) shall in the case of such treatment accorded by developed contracting parties to developing countries be designed and, if necessary, modified, to respond positively to the development, financial and trade needs of developing countries.

4. Any contracting party taking action to introduce an arrangement pursuant to paragraphs 1, 2 and 3 above or subsequently taking action to introduce modification or withdrawal of the differential and more favourable treatment so provided shall [NOTHING IN THESE PROVISIONS SHALL AFFECT THE RIGHTS OF CONTRACTING PARTIES UNDER THE GENERAL AGREEMENT]:

(a) notify the CONTRACTING PARTIES and furnish them with all the information they may deem appropriate relating to such action;

(b) afford adequate opportunity for prompt consultations at the request of any interested contracting party with respect to any difficulty or matter that may arise. The CONTRACTING PARTIES shall, if requested to do so by such contracting party, consult with all contracting parties concerned with respect to the matter with a view to reaching solutions satisfactory to all such contracting parties.

5. The developed countries do not expect reciprocity for commitments made by them in trade negotiations to reduce or remove tariffs and other barriers to the trade of developing countries, i.e., the developed coun-

tries do not expect the developing countries, in the course of trade negotiations, to make contributions which are inconsistent with their individual development, financial and trade needs. Developed contracting parties shall therefore not seek, neither shall less-developed contracting parties be required to make, concessions that are inconsistent with the latter's development, financial and trade needs.

6. Having regard to the special economic difficulties and the particular development, financial and trade needs of the least-developed countries, the developed countries shall exercise the utmost restraint in seeking any concessions or contributions for commitments made by them to reduce or remove tariffs and other barriers to the trade of such countries, and the least-developed countries shall not be expected to make concessions or contributions that are inconsistent with the recognition of their particular situation and problems.

7. The concessions and contributions made and the obligations assumed by developed and less-developed contracting parties under the provisions of the General Agreement should promote the basic objectives of the Agreement, including those embodied in the Preamble and in Article XXXVI. Less-developed contracting parties expect that their capacity to make contributions or negotiated concessions or take other mutually agreed action under the provisions and procedures of the General Agreement would improve with the progressive development of their economies and improvement in their trade situation and they would accordingly expect to participate more fully in the framework of rights and obligations under the General Agreement.

8. Particular account shall be taken of the serious difficulty of the least-developed countries in making concessions and contributions in view of their special economic situation and their development, financial and trade needs.

9. The contracting parties will collaborate in arrangements for review of the operation of these provisions, bearing in mind the need for individual and joint efforts by contracting parties to meet the development needs of developing countries and the objectives of the General Agreement."

The World's Most Important Regional Trade Bloc— The European Union

SOURCES FOR INFORMATION ON THE EU Of course, direct contact with the EU and its relevant agencies and institutions is the primary source of information on the EU and may be the only source for the most recent materials or for insights into policies and proposals not yet reduced to official documents and releases. Direct contact with the EU may be made through its offices in Brussels, Belgium (with telephone or postal contact made with the particular office or institution responsible for the issue in question), the representative delegation of the EU in one's own country, or through the EU's web site at http://www.europa.int, which provides both on-line information and E-mail communications. The EU has established information points at universities and other designated locations around the world which are provided with extensive and updated materials, often in computerized form, on the EU. Each EU delegation (the equivalent of an embassy) in a non-EU country may also be the source of timely and extensive information, as may the appropriate agencies of one's own government which monitor or interact with the EU. In addition to numerous unofficial web sites devoted to or dealing in part with the EU, there are many official EU web sites that may prove valuable. Among them are: http://europa.eu.int/comm/internal_market/en, http://europa.eu.int/scadplus/leg/en/s06020.htm, http://europa.eu.int/eur-lex/en/lif/reg/en-register-1720.html, or http://www.eurunion.org.

A HISTORY OF THE EU The EU was formerly known as the European Common Market and the European Economic Community ("EEC"). It now exerts a dominating influence over Western and Central Europe's commercial and political life, even of those countries that are not members of it.

It had its inception in 1958 following World War II. Its initial advocates were enthusiasts for European political integration. At the time of the origins of the EU, two world wars had demonstrated the perils of European political rivalries and had virtually destroyed the economies of Western Europe.

France and West Germany were the two pillars upon which the EU was built. France was anxious, and Germany seemingly agreed with this analysis of its national character, to firmly anchor West Germany within the community of Western Europe lest Germany revive its nationalistic and militaristic practices of the past. Economic factors also played a large part. As *The Economist* expressed it, the EU was "born from an exchange of enlightened selfishness: France opened its market to West German goods and in exchange West Germany subsidized France's poor farmers."

The EU was really three treaty organizations whose institutions were fused. These are the European Coal and Steel Community ("ECSC")—now defunct, the European Atomic Energy Community ("Euratom"), and the EEC. It is the EEC, as created by the Treaty of Rome (subsequently much amended) which principally defines the current EU.

Until the mid-1980s, the precursors of the EU played only a minor role in the lives and perceptions of Western Europeans. Efforts to integrate the members' economies had had very limited success. The resulting economic doldrums were sometimes referred to as

"Eurosclerosis." The EEC in 1985 declared its goal of achieving a barrier-free EEC internal market by 1992 through passage of the Single European Act ("SEA"). As the EEC took dramatic measures—under the charismatic and persuasive leadership of Commission President Jacques Delors—to actually implement that goal, great enthusiasm was generated both among Western Europeans and among foreigners seeking to participate in the EEC market. This was sometimes referred to as "Europhoria."

Although a Single European Market was not completely realized by the stipulated date of December 23, 1992, and although some actual implementation differed greatly from that originally envisioned, what was accomplished was very impressive. The EEC virtually completed development and implementation of 282 directives and regulations necessary to fully integrate the goods, services, and capital markets of the EEC. It eliminated an estimated 95% of the nontariff barriers operated by member states. It caught the attention of European and foreign businesses that began to deal with an "EEC" market rather than with segmented national markets in Western Europe. It focused the eyes of all Europeans on Brussels and the policies and proposals of the EEC.

In an act of audacity following its seeming great success in achieving the 1992 European Single Market, the EEC in 1993 took the possibly imprudent subsequent step that changed the EEC to the EU. This was the Treaty on European Union together with the Treaty Establishing the European Community ("TEU" and often called the "Maastricht Agreement" for the city in the Netherlands where it was adopted). It substantially modified the Treaty of Rome and incorporated into one document all three formative EU treaties. It was an agreement formulated by bureaucrats for bureaucrats. TEU was adopted by politicians behind closed doors. It was intended to create a more important bureaucracy in Brussels, to increase the monies coming into Brussels (much of which would be channeled to the poorer EU countries as hush money to keep them in line with other EU policies), to create a common currency and economic policy for the EU, to initiate a program of making the EU a political and defensive union rather than a mere commercial common market, and to fiddle with the political mechanics of EU decision-making without making it any more democratic. It was very unpopular with at least half the citizenry of most EU countries, few of whom were permitted to express their opinions through popular votes. The British and the Danes only accepted it under specially-negotiated terms which provide them "opt outs" for various of its requirements. In the face of this opposition, the Brussels EU *nomenklatura* waffled by redefining downwards the powers granted to it by the TEU and by lopping off some of the revenue transfers to Brussels that were previously budgeted.

The next major institutional change in the EU was implemented through the so-called "Amsterdam Treaty" of 1997. The aim of the negotiations was said to be the creation of the political and institutional conditions which would enable the EU to meet the challenges of the future such as the rapid evolution of the international situation, the globalization of the economy and its impact on jobs, the fight against terrorism, international crime and drug trafficking, ecological problems and threats to public health. Most changes were procedural and institutional, including the composition of the EU Commission and the weighting of votes in the EU Council.

Drafted but not yet ratified in 2001, the so-called "Nice Agreement" sought to accommodate the EU for enlargement by dealing with the prospective allocation of seats in EU institutions, procedural matters in those institutions, the official use of "EU" languages, the continuation and availability to newer members of existing programs —particularly of the Common Agricultural Policy ("CAP") and subsidy programs for poorer members, and similar matters. In a sense, the Nice Treaty was intended to deal with the tough issues that could not be resolved during negotiation of the Amsterdam Treaty. The contents of this Agreement fell far short of what was sought and, in the minds of many, fell far short of what was needed. Approval of the Agreement by the EU Parliament was, at the time of this writing, far from assured.

The EU's institutional income and budgetary requirements are now principally derived from the common external tariff, agricultural levies on imports, a small but growing portion of the value-added tax ("VAT") collected in every member state, and an assessment based on the Gross Domestic Product ("GDP") of each of the member states.

Increasingly a Single European Market that was intended to create a genuinely free market within Western Europe has been surreptitiously captured by bureaucrats whose model is that of the traditional French bureaucrat. That model operates on the premises (a) that the bureaucrat is better fitted than the parties involved to make economic and other decisions and (b) that anything that has not been formally sanctioned by the bureaucrat should be forbidden. This threatens to result in red tape that strangles, rather than frees, the EU's market. Also at issue is the claim that the British are trying to build a single internal market for consumers, the French one for producers.

Scheduled plans to create a common EU economic policy to be implemented by the members and to create a common EU currency and central bank were achieved but without the full participation of all members. This participation of some but not all EU members results in an effective differentiation among members by separate classes of EU membership. Bosnia and the general mess in what was formerly Yugoslavia demonstrated the inability of the EU to formulate sensible common foreign policies and its thorough ineffectiveness in making any decision regarding the commitment of military forces in support of such common foreign policies. This demonstrable failure has not deterred the EU from attempting to engage in further common foreign policy efforts and the formation of a "European" military force. Whether either of these attempts will get off the ground or be successful in their implementation remains uncertain.

Nonetheless, the EU is a great world economic power and must be credited as an institutional success. It is a prosperous single market with 370 million consumers (the largest in the industrialized world) and is scheduled to grow even larger. That has greatly contributed to the economic strength of the EU, which is now the biggest trading bloc in the world. It accounts for about a sixth of total global trade in goods (even excluding intra-EU trade). This is more than its main partners and competitors, the United States and Japan. Its total economic resources, annual production, and internal and external trade are vast and growing (even if sometimes more slowly than that of the US and more slowly than EU politicians and members would prefer).

EU MEMBERSHIP AND ECONOMIC RELATIONSHIPS WITH OTHER STATES Current membership of the EU is France, Germany, Belgium, the Netherlands, Luxembourg, and Italy (the earliest members); Ireland, UK, and Denmark (which joined in 1973); Greece (which joined in 1981); Spain and Portugal (which joined in 1986); and Austria, Sweden, and Finland (which became members as of January 1, 1995).

The Norwegian Government has twice sought and been offered membership only to have the Norwegian people each time repudiate EU membership in national referenda. The Swiss Government similarly sought and then rejected—because of opposition reflected in national referenda—EU membership and has even spurned participation in the European Economic Area. It is unclear whether those countries will, or can, maintain their isolated positions. Greenland, which became part of the EU along with Denmark, withdrew from the EU in 1983 out of pique with the EU Common Fisheries Policy. The German Democratic Republic (East Germany) was made part of the EU under existing West German membership through negotiated terms upon its reunification with the Federal Republic of Germany.

Each member country has separately negotiated its own entry into the EU under an accession treaty that may specify special terms and conditions of entry. Under those treaties, there are certain parts or quasiparts of the above member countries, *e.g.*, the Isle of Man, the Channel Islands, and the Faroe Islands, which are not fully part of the EU. Similarly, some member countries may deem territories outside Europe, such as enclaves in North Africa or island possessions in the South Pacific, the Indian Ocean, or the Caribbean, to be part of their "metropolitan territories," but they are not so treated by the EU.

The EU maintains special trading relationships with the so-called "ACP" countries of Africa, the Caribbean, and the Pacific that had been colonies of or are currently territories of the French, Dutch, British, and Belgians under the Lomé Conventions, with a number of underdeveloped "Mediterranean countries," and with underdeveloped countries generally under a GSP program. It also has numerous bilateral special trade arrangements with other countries, including free trade area agreements, customs cooperation agreements, and special agreements for participation in the EU customs union.

There is much controversy over the admission of other new members. The controversy is expressed in terms of whether to make the EU "wider"—that is, to add more members—or "deeper," that is, to maintain the present membership until popular identification with the EU and its institutions is more firmly entrenched in the minds of current residents. There are further administrative problems created by the procedures of the institutions of the EU which in many cases grant equal powers (and votes) to every member and require extensive translations into all EU languages. With an increase in EU membership, the level of difficulties created by these matters increases exponentially. In addition, permitting new, poorer, and agrarian members to participate in the CAP and the program of subsidization of poorer by richer EU countries would bankrupt the EU and greatly diminish the payments received by those current members most fully benefiting from them.

The EU has generally absorbed into its membership all economically-significant Western European countries. Only Switzerland and Norway remain outside the EU. A European Economic Area ("EEA") has been created that permits most European nonmembers to participate in largely free industrial trade with the EU's Single European Market. Non-EU members of the EEA are, however, denied the full opportunity to engage in making the rules that govern the Single European Market and are excluded from both the CAP and the system under which richer EU countries subsidize the poorer EU countries. Consequently, there is much clamor for the expansion of the EU to include Eastern European countries and various countries of the Balkans and Mediterranean as well as Turkey. Such expansion of the EU is very controversial, although the EU has recently agreed to it occurring—at least in theory and to a degree—at some date in the near future.

Turkey, Cyprus, and Malta have all previously sought EU membership and have received assurances (which are less than iron-clad) that such membership will be granted "some time." Some countries have "associate" EU membership or some other treaty status that grants them current special access to EU markets and at least some claim to a right to future admission to full EU membership. Title VII, Article O, of the TEU restricts membership to countries in Europe. An application for membership by Morocco was rejected as not satisfying that requirement. Why Turkey would satisfy the geographic requirement, and whether its Islamic religion and Middle Eastern culture would create problems of integration, are obvious questions that have seemingly been intentionally ignored. Some of the Central European countries formerly part of Yugoslavia or former Soviet satellites are also desperately seeking membership and some have made formal application to join. Accession of a country to EU membership requires the consent of the EU Parliament and the unanimous consent of existing EU members.

The process of EU enlargement was launched in March 1998. Negotiations are currently being held with the following twelve applicants: Bulgaria, Cyprus, the Czech Republic, Estonia, Hungary, Latvia, Lithuania, Malta, Poland, Romania, Slovakia and Slovenia. The basic principle of the negotiations is that all the applicant countries must accept existing EU law. None were expected to become a member before 2002 and many observers expressed doubt that there would be any new EU members before 2005.

THE FORMATIVE TREATIES OF THE EU There are three formative treaties creating the three organizations which are the basis for the EU. These are the ECSC, Euratom, and the EEC. They were each formed, respectively, under a treaty: the European Coal and Steel Community Treaty of 1951, 261 U.N.T.S. 140 (commonly called "The Treaty of Paris") which expires by its own terms in 2002; The European Atomic Energy Community Treaty of 1957, 298 U.N.T.S. 167; and the European Economic Community Treaty of 1957, which is usually referred to as "The Treaty of Rome."

The most important of the above treaties is the Treaty of Rome. Whereas the ECSC and Euratom were formed under treaties containing codes of rules that are to be implemented by the parties or institutions established under the treaties, the Treaty of Rome may be characterized as an "outline treaty." Aside from specific provisions regarding the dismantling of member state tariffs and quotas, the Treaty of Rome describes only in the most general terms the policies to be implemented under the Treaty.

The Merger Treaty of 1965, while not actually merging the above treaties, merged the institutions under which the three treaty communities operate.

The SEA [15 International Legal Materials 506 (1986)] and the TEU are of great importance. Both principally amended and fused the three formative treaties, particularly the Treaty of Rome. Some aspects of both the TEU and the SEA, however, lie outside the official structure of the EU and the purview of the EU Court of Justice and constitute separate multilateral agreements. Such a "side agreement" in the SEA is that concerning common foreign policy. In the TEU, these "side agreements" include those on common foreign and security policy and cooperation regarding justice and home affairs.

The SEA was essential to authorize and enable the EU to initiate its 1992 program to create a community without frontiers. It provided for voting procedures by a "qualified majority" rather than a unanimous vote in the EU Council. A very important SEA policy change was that of "mutual recognition" which required each EU state to recognize as valid and sufficient within its own territory those product standards and certifications and similar qualifying standards approved for the purpose by every other EU member state. The EU Court of Justice was authorized to establish a subordinate court of first instance. Other provisions were intended to increase member state cooperation and coordination in the fields of economic and monetary policy, social policy, economic and social cohesion, research and technological development, and protection of the environment. The EU member states also agreed to cooperate in setting foreign policy.

The most important TEU amendments to the Treaty of Rome concern the perhaps critical—but certainly ambiguous—principle of "subsidiarity" which permits the EU to assert its authority only over those issues which cannot be administered at a lower level (which principally means by an EU member state) and the economic and monetary integration of the EU according to a prescribed schedule for the convergence of national economies and the creation of a common currency. "Qualified majority" voting in the EU Council was extended to additional matters. Also significant were amendments to give the EU Parliament (a) a limited veto over legislation and EU international agreements, (b) the power to conduct inquiries into EU maladministration, and (c) the right to reject appointments of EU commissioners and new member state applicants.

The Amsterdam Treaty guarantees protection to fundamental rights within the EU, such as equality between men and women, non-discrimination, and data privacy. It also deals with freedom of movement within the EU and the inclusion in the Treaty of Rome of a new title on visas, asylum, immigration, and other policies linked to the free movement of persons. The EU was explicitly authorized to extend the scope of the common commercial policy to include international agreements on services and intellectual property rights. The EU Parliament was granted "codecision" power to strengthen its role. Weighting of votes in the EU Council and the extension of qualified majority voting were also approved. Aside from other institutional and procedural changes, the Treaty provided for consolidation of the subsidiarity principle through the inclusion of a protocol containing legally binding guidelines.

The Nice Treaty was only submitted for ratification in February 2001 and the process is likely to take up to 18 months (with some saying that ultimate adoption is far from certain, largely because the Treaty does too little although there are some who complain that it tried to do too much). Its principal focus was on a resolution of institutional issues that had not be resolved under the Amsterdam Treaty. Because which countries will become EU members and when any one will become a member are questions without answers, the Nice Treaty attempted to define the distribution of seats in the EU Parliament, the new composition of the EU Commission, and a new definition of "qualified majority" within the EU Council based upon a membership of 15 but adjustable to serve an enlarged membership. A number of procedural and policy changes were also made. The Treaty, through its Protocol on Enlargement and Attached Declarations, also establishes a "common position" to be adopted by current member states when negotiating accession to membership of applicant countries.

Also of importance are the EU accession treaties of each member state and those EU treaties establishing special trading relationships with other countries and territories. For some commercial undertakings with particular countries and territories, such relevant treaties should be reviewed before entering into final arrangements.

EU INSTITUTIONS There has been a common set of institutions for the ECSC, Euratom, and the EEC since 1967 although these institutions must follow different rules depending on whether they are acting for the ECSC, Euratom, or the EEC.

The principal institutions of the EU are the EU Council, the EU Commission, the EU Parliament, and the EU Court of Justice (to which a Court of First Instance was attached in 1989 and which is supported by the EU Court of Auditors). EU institutions have been given the mandate under the Treaty of Rome to devise the actual terms and conditions of the implementation of those policies generally described in the Treaty.

Under the TEU, the EU created a number of new—and extensively developed some existing—institutions. Their names are as follows: European Monetary Institute; European Environmental Agency; European Agency for the Evaluation of Medicinal Products; Office for Harmonization in the Internal Market (Trademark Office); Agency for Health and Safety at Work; European Training Foundation; European Monitoring Center for Drugs and Drug Addiction; Europol Drug Unit; Common Appeal Court for Community Patents; Center for Vocational Training; Institute for Prospective Technology Studies; and Office for Veterinary and Phytosanitary Inspection and Control.

THE EU COUNCIL The EU Council is the dominant institution in EU affairs. It meets in Brussels (and occasionally in Luxembourg). It is made up of representatives of the governments of all member states. Consequently, since there are now 15 members, there are now 15 representatives. Who those individual representatives are is constantly in a state of flux, depending on the issue being considered.

There is an EU Council that consists of the heads of state or government of the member countries. EU Council meetings where heads of state are in attendance are held at least twice a year at various locations. The Presidency of the EU Council rotates among the member governments every six months.

There is an EU Council of Ministers which is the EU Council when national governmental heads are absent. A member country's foreign minister is generally considered to be its main representative in the EU Council of Ministers, but EU Council agendas dealing with specific topics within the competence of other national ministries will usually result in EU Council attendance and representation by the relevant national ministers.

Sometimes several EU Council sessions—constituted of differing member representatives—will be in simultaneous session. EU Councils attended by governmental heads and by foreign ministers and the functions of the European Political Committee (staffed by junior foreign service members) function outside the Treaty of Rome and its various policy-making mandates and voting procedures, including consultation, cooperation, or codecision with the EU Parliament, although the EU Commission is normally represented at all such meetings.

The Permanent Representative Committee (known by its French acronym of *COREPER*) is made up of the Permanent Representatives (the equivalent of ambassadors of the members to the EU) of all members and is an important adjunct of the EU Council. *COREPER* consists of high-ranking national civil servants. It sits in permanent session in Brussels and coordinates the preparatory work for EU Council meetings. It thereby establishes the priorities of issues to be considered by the EU Council. *COREPER* may also reach unanimous agreement on technical points that the EU Council will in practice automatically adopt.

The role of the EU Council is to decide on principal EU policies. Any measure of general application or of a prescribed level of importance must be enacted by the EU Council, but (except in rare and prescribed instances) the EU Council may not initiate measures. Almost all policies on which the EU Council decides are submitted to it in the form of proposals by the EU Commission. Although the EU Council may accept the proposals of the EU Commission by a majority vote and may refuse to enact the proposals if a majority is lacking, the EU Council may only amend the proposals of the EU Commission or adopt contrary proposals by a unanimous vote.

Although unanimous consent may sometimes be demanded for EU Council decisions if so prescribed by the TEU, voting in the EU Council is almost always based on a weighted vote count (a so-called "qualified majority") which is broadly proportionate to the members' populations (10 votes each for France, Germany, Italy and the United Kingdom, 8 votes for Spain, 5 votes each for Belgium, the Netherlands, Portugal, and Greece, 4 votes each for Austria and Sweden, 3 votes each for Ireland, Finland, and Denmark, and 2 votes for Luxembourg for a total of 87—but these numbers will change if the Nice Agreement is adopted). To adopt legislation or otherwise proceed by a qualified majority vote, at least 62 (pending adoption of the Nice Agreement) affirmative votes must be cast. Where unanimous voting is required, each member has an effective veto over legislation. When the EU Council is not acting upon an EU Commission proposal, ten member states (pending adoption of the Nice Agreement) must participate in the majority. Consequently, legislation may be thwarted if all the "little" members vote as a bloc or if "big" members with a majority vote fail to enlist the support of some "little" members.

Designating the basis for EU legislation is frequently a contentious issue since this will determine whether a unanimous or qualified majority vote is required (and whether EU parliamentary participation is necessary). Under the so-called "Luxembourg Accord" of the mid-1960s, unanimous voting was required notwithstanding the Treaty of Rome's authorization of a qualified majority vote where "very important interests" were at stake. The TEU has virtually ended this practice, although in the case of such matters great efforts will be expended in seeking unanimous consensus before a qualified majority vote will prevail.

THE EU COMMISSION The EU Commission is made up of 20 commissioners (pending adoption of the Nice Agreement). EU Commission decisions are taken collegially, but simple majority votes prevail. Nonetheless, the commissioner in charge of the directorate-general with responsibility for the legislative or other proposal under review will usually be given considerable deference. The EU Commission is divided into 23 Directorates-General (departments), each with a specific allocation of administrative, legislative drafting, and law enforcement duties; each with a large staff; and each with a commissioner responsible for its work. Each commissioner also supervises a substantial personal staff, known as a cabinet. The EU Commission sits in Brussels. Its administrative staff (one-third of which is employed on linguistic work to assure equal recognition of the many EU languages) is located principally in Brussels with some staff located in Luxembourg.

Each commissioner, including the President of the EU Commission, is appointed by the member states acting in common accord for four-year renewable terms. In practice, each member state has at least one of its citizens as a commissioner and the larger states have two (pending adoption of the Nice Agreement). The commissioners are chosen on the basis of their competence. Each acts in his or her individual capacity independent of the government of his or her country and only in the interests of the EU. They may be compelled to resign as a body through the censure of the EU Parliament.

The duties of the EU Commission are generally those of an EU executive institution.

The EU Commission has the critically important function of proposing to the EU Council all legislative measures for the advancement of EU policies and serves as the advocate of EU interests to the EU Council.

Under the ECSC and Euratom, the EU Commission has extensive direct regulatory powers, respectively, over coal and steel, and over nuclear energy.

Under the Treaty of Rome, the EU Commission has direct rule-making powers regarding the establishment of a customs union in accordance with the Treaty of Rome's timetable. In other cases, particularly regarding common agricultural policies and competition law, the EU Commission acts under a mandate from the EU Council to conduct specified activities through the issuance of implementing regulations and decisions but only after compulsory consultation with various committees. Under Article 90 of the Treaty of Rome, the EU Commission may, on its own initiative, issue directives addressed to member states regarding public enterprises and thereby avoid the normal EU legislative process. The EU budget and funds of the EU common programs are administered by the EU Commission. The EU Commission publishes annually a general (and a series of specific) reports. It is also responsible for negotiating the EU's international trade and other agreements.

A principal one of its functions is the exercise of prosecutorial powers against individuals and enterprises for breaches of EU law. The EU Commission has the responsibility of ensuring that EU rules and principles are respected through adherence to formative EU treaties and the correct application of EU institutional decisions. It may itself conduct investigations and impose fines on individuals (particularly in competition law cases).

The EU Commission may also decide on requests by member states to implement safeguard clauses and authorize temporary waivers, called derogations, from the requirements of the EU's formative treaties.

THE EU SOCIAL AND ECONOMIC COMMITTEE For EU and Euratom matters, the EU Council and EU Commission are assisted by the Social and Economic Committee which is made up of representatives of three groups—employers, workers and "various interests," *e.g.*, consumer groups, academicians, farmers, and the self-employed. It meets once a month in Brussels. That Committee must be consulted before many decisions may be made and may also submit opinions on its own initiative.

THE COMMITTEE OF THE REGIONS The Committee of the Regions was created by the TEU. It is composed of representatives of regional and local bodies throughout the EU. It must be consulted on certain types of EU action and may render its opinions without being requested to do so. Its creation is seemingly an attempt to bring local officials into the regional legislative and decision-making processes and to recognize regional (as distinguished from national) rights and interests.

THE EU PARLIAMENT The EU Parliament (originally called "The Assembly") now has a total of 626 members, 25 each from Belgium, Greece, and Portugal; 16 each from Denmark and Finland; 87 each from France, the United Kingdom, and Italy; 31 from the Netherlands; 99 from Germany; 15 from Ireland; 6 from Luxembourg; 64 from Spain; 21 from Austria; and 22 from Sweden. These numbers will change if the Nice Agreement is adopted and admission of new EU members will obviously alter the allocation of votes. Members of the EU Parliament are directly elected every five years by their nation's citizens through universal suffrage. The number of parliamentary seats awarded to each member country is generally proportionate to its population (although Germany is significantly under-represented), with election of members made from geographical districts within member countries. Groupings of Members of the EU Parliament are by political association and not by national origin.

The EU Parliament has a large civil service (called its Secretariat) based in Luxembourg and an Office of the Ombudsman. Numerous parliamentary committees, most of which meet in Brussels, concentrate on particular areas of parliamentary interest. Plenary and public sessions of the EU Parliament are held in Strasbourg, France.

The EU Parliament does not have the legislative power typical of national legislative assemblies, although its powers have been significantly strengthened in recent years and there is pressure—particularly from Germany—to make it into a traditional legislative body. By custom, it has a right to be consulted and to give an "opinion" as part of the EU's legislative process, although such opinion is not binding upon the EU Commission or Council. It supervises the EU Commission and Council and may, and does, through individual members, address written and oral questions to those bodies to which they are required to respond. It has the power to remove the entire EU Commission by a two-thirds majority vote of censure. It may initiate litigation against the EU Commission or Council for failure to act and regarding the legality of the acts of the EU Commission or Council where its legislative process rights are at issue. It can intervene in litigation as an interested party. A "conciliation procedure" has been used since 1977 whenever the EU Council departs from an opinion of the EU Parliament on proposed legislation of importance to the EU's income or expenses.

The SEA granted new powers to the EU Parliament. It now has the right of "second reading" under the so-called "cooperation procedure" (which the EU Parliament must exercise within three months from communication to it by the EU Council of the legislative proposal) of Article 189C of the TEU. The cooperation procedure applied to nearly all "1992 internal market measures" and applies only to measures under TEU Articles 7, 49, 54(2), 56(2), 57, 118A, 130E, and 130Q(2). An EU Council decision through a qualified majority vote ("common position") on legislation proposed by the EU Commission is no longer final but is only preliminary. The EU Parliament may accept it, reject it, or amend it. Where the EU Parliament proposes amendments or rejects the common position, the EU Council must then cast a unanimous vote to overrule the decision of the EU Parliament but may ratify that decision with only a majority vote.

Under the changes of the TEU, the EU Parliament has virtual veto power over selected matters (EU single market, educational, cultural, health, consumer protection, environmental, transportation, and research matters) if conciliation through direct negotiations with the EU Council are unavailing according to a so-called "codecision procedure." The EU Parliament's advice must be sought before a new EU Commission President is chosen and the EU Parliament has other means to influence the selection of EU Commissioners, including a right of veto over their nomination. The EU Parliament now also has the authority to review and approve EU treaties where those agreements touch on a codecisional area or have institutional or budgetary implications.

THE EU COURT OF JUSTICE The EU Court of Justice sits in Luxembourg and is composed of 15 judges, one from each member state (pending adoption of the Nice Agreement). Each judge is appointed by agreement among member governments for six years and may be reappointed. The judges are grouped in chambers of between three and five judges each, with cases brought before the EU Court normally heard in one of the chambers. Only unusual cases will be heard by the full EU Court. The judgements of the EU Court must be unanimous.

A subordinate EU Court of First Instance hears minor cases, *e.g.*, staff disputes among EU civil servants who are prevented from taking their complaints to any national court, and consists of 15 judges, sitting in Luxembourg in chambers of three or five judges.

The EU Court is distinct from and unconnected with the International Court of Justice in The Hague ("The World Court") and the European Court of Human Rights which sits in Strasbourg, France (although all EU countries have chosen to recognize the jurisdiction of this Court, which was established by the Council of Europe—of which all EU members are also members—and not by the EU, in human rights cases).

The judges are assisted by five advocates general. The advocates general do not participate in the discussions that lead to the EU Court's decisions, but may carry out their own personal examinations of cases, express their own opinions, and examine any related questions even when they were not brought forward by the parties.

The working language of the EU Court is French, although cases may be heard in any of the EU languages. The structure of the EU Court is derived from the French *Conseil d'Etat* and the French legal system. Decisions of the EU Court are precedential to the degree that they are persuasive in subsequent cases but are not categorically binding on future EU Court decisions.

The EU Court, through the cumulative consequences of its decisions in individual cases, has contributed to the creation of a law of the EU that is applicable to EU institutions, member states, and nationals of member states. The EU Court determines the law of the EU by reference to the objectives of the EU articulated in the formative treaties. The EU Court's judgement on issues of EU law is superior to any decision of a national court (the so-called "supremacy doctrine"). Decisions of the EU Court not only provide authoritative interpretations of the EU formative treaties and implementing regulations under them but also develop what is referred to in the formative EU treaties as the general principles of law common to the member states. The purpose of the EU Court is to ensure implementation of the Treaty of Rome and other formative treaties in accordance with the rule of law. It has been given or has assumed jurisdiction over various specific types of legal issues. The parties that may bring suit or otherwise appear before it are prescribed through treaties and rules of the EU Court. The EU Court has been authorized or has assumed the right to make various kinds of awards and to impose various fines and penalties. In addition, under the so-called "direct effects doctrine," litigants are assured of the right to raise many EU law issues in EU member national courts and tribunals. The EU Court may annul any measures taken by the EU Commission or Council or member states that are incompatible with the formative EU treaties at the request of an EU institution, a member state, or a directly concerned individual. The EU Court may also render a judgement, at the request of a national court, on the interpretation or validity of the provisions of EU law through interlocutory decision requests by lower courts and through ruling requests for decisions on a particular issue of law by the highest court of appeal of a national court. The EU Court may also be asked to give its opinion—which then becomes binding—on contemplated EU agreements with nonmember countries.

THE EUROPEAN COURT OF AUDITORS The EU Court of Auditors, based in Luxembourg, is made up of 12 members appointed by the unanimous decision of the EU Council after consultation with the EU Parliament. It audits the accounts of the EU and its institutions, determines whether revenues and expenditures have been properly and lawfully dealt with, assures that sound financial management has been used, and reports on its findings to EU institutions.

EU BANKING AND MONETARY AUTHORITIES A European Central Bank and the European System of Central Banks are governed by an executive board of six persons appointed by the member states and the governors of the national central banks. These institutions are independent of any other EU institution and free from member state influence. Their main functions are to: (a) define and implement EU monetary policy; (b) conduct foreign exchange operations; (c) hold and manage the foreign reserves of the member states; and (d) supervise the payments systems. The EU Central Bank has the exclusive right to authorize the issuance of bank notes within the EU and will set interest rates as the principal means to achieve price stability. A council of member finance ministers ("The Ecofin Council") works closely with the EU Central Bank and issues broad guidelines of EU economic policy and may recommend changes to a national government's policy, including budget cuts, when current national policy is inconsistent with EU economic policy. Where the recommended changes are not made, the Ecofin Council may require a government to disclose the information with its bond issues, block European Investment Bank credits, or levy fines and penalties.

EU LEGISLATION The Treaty of Rome presumes a regional government of limited or derived powers. It conveys no general power to create EU law. EU law-making power is either specifically authorized or implied generally or under Article 235 which permits action if "necessary to attain, in the course of the operation of the common market, one of the objectives of the Community and this Treaty has not provided the necessary powers." Under the TEU's principal of "subsidiarity," a higher level of EU Government should only assume responsibilities that cannot be effectively undertaken at a lower level. This seemingly expresses—and was intended to express—a "states' rights" doctrine for EU member nations.

The equivalents of statutory and regulatory acts under the authority of the EU consist of *regulations* (ECSC general decisions) which have the immediate force of law and which are applied directly; which are binding only on the member states, entities, or individuals to whom they are directed; and *directives* (ECSC recommendations) which constitute EU policy but which must be implemented (within time limits) by member states through national statutes, regulations, or executive or ministerial orders. It is the EU directive which most nearly approximates, but is not, an EU statute. EU regulations are very nearly the same as the typical administrative regulations of a nation state. The EU Council may sometimes act outside the constraints of EU procedures and may, through the implementation of its declarations and resolutions, thereby circumvent the EU's normal institutional processes.

EU CUSTOMS UNION The EU maintains a common tariff structure among its members and tariff-free trade among them. Any imported item may enter at any point in the EU and be subject to the same tariffs and the same import procedures and restrictions. A binding tariff classification system based upon mutual recognition of the classification decisions made by EU national customs authorities and the provision of "binding tariff information" or ("BTI") under Articles 11 and 12 of the Common Customs Code upon the request of an importer have reduced, if not eliminated, divergent tariff classifications at different EU ports and from different EU national customs authorities. After an item has been imported into the EU proper, it may be transported, marketed, or used throughout the EU without further impediments or levies at national borders. In order to make the EU customs union/free trade area fully workable, the harmonization of some other laws, such as national VAT laws, was required.

The EU Commission, through DG XXI—Directorate General for Taxation and Customs Union, is responsible for initiatives for the development of customs policy, for proposals for customs legislation, for aiding coordination between EU members' administrations, and for seeking advice and feedback from business and industry at the EU level. The national customs administrations are responsible for the day-to-day application of EU law: collecting customs duties, excise duties, and VAT on imported goods and applying all the other policies as well as maintaining contacts with their national local business communities.

The provisions of the Treaty of Rome which deal specifically with trade between the EU and other countries are found in Articles 110-115 and vest in the EU control over EU external commercial relations (what is called the EU "Common Commercial Policy"). Common Commercial Policy deals both with exports and with imports.

The EU Court of Justice has found (*Criel and Schou v. Procureur de la République* (1976) Eur.Comm. Rep.1921) that the EU is supreme in the field and that EU member states may not enact national external commercial policies without "specific authorization" from the EU (although the text of the decision was demonstrative that the decision was not as categorically definitive as its assertions would indicate).

Of primary importance to readers of this book and to the original purposes of the EU was the creation of a common EU customs union. It was not fully operative until 1968. The relevant provisions of the Treaty of Rome are found in Articles 9-29.

Until 1994, EU customs laws were dispersed among at least 30 different directives and regulations. In 1994, these were collected and further developed into what is now the EU Common Customs Code. The Code covers customs clearance procedures, customs warehouses and free trade zones, duty free entry for processing and reexport – known as "inward processing arrangements," duty free entry of components of EU origin that have been processed abroad – known as "outward processing arrangements," classification, valuation, ROs, payment, and customs' bonds. The Common Customs Code contains the rules for importing and exporting goods to and from the EU's customs territory. The basic regulation sets forth the general principles. The details on binding tariff information, ROs, valuation, customs clearance, transit, warehousing, free zones, drawback, payment of duties, and other aspects of customs procedures are in the implementing regulations.

The Code brings together the general rules and all the customs procedures applicable to goods traded between the EU and non-EU countries in a single, coherent body of law. It starts by stating its scope and some basic definitions. It sets out general provisions on people's rights and obligations with regard to customs legislation (right of representation, decisions, information, etc.). It then lists the factors on the basis of which import and export duties and other measures prescribed in respect of trade in goods are applied. These are the EU customs tariff and the tariff classification of goods, their origin (preferential or non-preferential), and their customs value. The Code lists the provisions applicable to goods brought into the EU customs territory until they are assigned a customs-approved treatment or use. It covers the entry of goods into the EU customs territory, presentation of goods to customs, summary declaration and unloading of goods, the obligation to assign them a customs-approved treatment or use, and their temporary storage. Special provisions apply to non-EU goods that are moved under a transit procedure. A major section of the Code covers customs-approved treatment or use. It sets out rules for placing goods under a customs procedure, release of goods for free circulation, suspensive and other arrangements and customs procedures with economic impact, export and internal transit. Special provisions cover the position of free zones and free warehouses (which are part of the EU customs territory but are separate from the rest of it) and the re-exportation, destruction, and abandonment of non-EU goods. The section on "privileged operations" sets out provisions for relief from duty, returned goods, and products of sea-fishing and other products taken from the sea. Another section on "customs debt" sets out rules on providing security for customs debt, specifies when the debt is incurred, and provides for its recovery.

The Code provides for a two-stage right of appeal: in the first instance to the customs authority, then to the national courts. It establishes a Customs Code Committee with responsibility for examining any matter relating to customs regulations. The Code also sets out the legal effects in an EU member state of measures taken, documents issued, and findings made in another EU member state. Judicial reviews of decisions of national customs authorities must be allowed by a national court capable of referring questions of EU law to the EU Court of Justice under Article 177 of the Treaty of Rome.

The Code and EU tariffs are applied and collected by EU member states, with revenues forwarded by the national customs authorities to the EU Commission less a 10% administrative charge.

There is a uniform, integrated EU tariff schedule, formerly called the "Common Customs Tariff" but now known as "TARIC." Average EU tariffs on manufactured goods have dropped precipitously in recent decades and are now at 4.1% or less. Goods in many sectors may be imported without the payment of any tariffs. The Combined Nomenclature makes two fundamental distinctions. If an import is defined as being "Autonomous" it is subject to the much higher EU tariff schedules of 1968 and essentially constitutes a determination that the source of the imports is not a country which the EU is legally-required to offer MFN rates nor is it one to which it chooses to offer such rates. In other words, these are rates imposed on goods from countries greatly out of political favor with the EU. Much more commonly, and required to be offered to imports from any WTO member, are the MFN rates provided for imports defined as being "Conventional."

The Single European Market abolished the role of customs collecting excise taxes and VAT between EU members. Before the Single Market, free circulation of goods within the EU was not the reality. Numerous customs border formalities still existed because, *inter alia*, of the way VAT and excise duties were collected and of information gathering for statistical purposes. Before 1993, all transporters were stopped at the internal EU national borders for "customs" and tax clearance and even for inspections. Long waits by trucks at customs posts hindered intra-EU trade and cost EU trading companies large amounts of time and money. Customs legislation, though already harmonized, was not applied in a uniform way. Despite the absence of customs duties in trade among EU members, there was little factual difference in administrative burden or appearance between intra-EU trade and trade with non-member countries. The same situation was essentially applicable to travelers as well. "Customs" clearance at the EU's internal frontiers was elaborate and time-consuming. The constant production of new EU and national laws, regulations, and standards for health and consumer protection, etc. was formerly enforced by the customs services at the internal national borders. The first step in achieving a real Single European Market was the replacement of "customs" formalities at internal frontiers by new fiscal, statistical, and other control systems that required no control or documentation at the moment that the goods crossed the internal borders. On January 1, 1993, all "customs" checks at the EU internal borders were abolished for the movement of goods. Spot checks still occur for drugs and immigration, but routine internal border checks have disappeared.

While the free circulation of goods within the EU is the internal aspect of the customs union, the common customs tariff is its external aspect. It applies to imports of goods across the EU's external borders. The Common Commercial Policy fixes the tariff rates for customs charges due on goods imported into the EU and also specifies exceptions to these charges as well as prohibitions and restrictions on imports. The common customs tariff is common to all EU members, but the rates of duty differ from one kind of import to another depending on what they are and where they come from. Rates depend on the economic sensitivity of products and are a said to be a means of protecting the EU's economic interests. Raw materials and semi-manufactured goods, for which there is often no EU source and which the EU needs to produce goods, usually benefit from low duty rates. There are also temporary or permanent duty suspensions available if EU manufacturers have to use materials or components from outside to manufacture EU exports. This makes cheap raw materials and semi-finished goods available to EU manufacturers on the same terms available to non-EU processing companies. The duty relief systems are called "inward processing" or "duty suspension" depending on the one used. In some economic sectors it is thought to be necessary to stimulate competition by low tariffs. All these are, in general, adopted by the EU Council of Ministers and are approved by the EU Parliament on the basis of proposals made by the EU Commission. Subsidiary law, often called implementation provisions, is adopted by the EU Commission in strictly delimited circumstances and then usually only after approval by EU members' authorities as expressed in the Customs Code Committee for Customs Law or another committee where other legislation is concerned.

EU customs policy is fundamental to the EU and an essential element in the functioning of the Single Market. These common rules go beyond the customs union as such—with its common tariff—and extend to all aspects of trade policy, such as preferential trade, health and environmental controls, the common agricultural and fisheries policies, the protection of EU economic interests by non-tariff means, and external relations policy measures. Import controls are enforced concerning health risks in foodstuffs such as meat, poultry, milk, eggs, vegetables, fruit and wine imported from third countries; radioactive material; the environment (control of imported waste and dangerous goods, control of products which could endanger the ozone layer); and surveillance of or prevention of international trade in endangered species of wild fauna and flora (under the Washington "CITES" Convention of 1983). Under national legislation, controls are also imposed to prevent illicit trade in narcotics, firearms and ammunition, and pornographic material.

Customs legislation exceeding that essential to a customs union was progressively created in order to ensure that, wherever goods were imported into the EU, they were not only subject to the same tariff rules but also to the same customs provisions to ensure that the tariff was applied in the same way everywhere. One culminating step was the Single Administrative Document ("SAD"). In 1988, SAD was established as a declaration form that replaced 150 separate documents previously used by the customs administrations in the EU member states.

Almost all tariffs are levied on an *ad valorem* basis determined by the normal or arm's length transaction price plus freight, insurance, commissions, and all other charges and expenses incidental to the sale and delivery of the goods to the point of entry into the customs territory. Nonetheless, the EU application of the WTO's valuation standards may differ from those of other countries. For example, US and EU implementation differ regarding international freight and insurance charges (the EU includes these charges as part of the import value against which tariffs are levied). Purchasing agents' commissions, export permit or quota charges, weighing charges, and separately invoiced intro-EU transportation charges are not levied against, although computer software as part of the value of imported goods may be (*see Brown Boveri & CIE AG v Hauptzollamt Mannheim* (1991)

Eur.Comm.Rep. 1884 (Case C-79-89) and Article 167, EU Commission Regulation 2913/92). Also see Article 32(1)(c) of the Common Customs Code regarding whether licensing fees are includable in determining the valuation of imported goods for tariff calculation purposes. The EU tariff schedule is based on the Harmonized System (referred to in the EU as the "Combined Nomenclature") and the national origin of goods are generally determined in accordance with the Kyoto Convention. Special rules of origin exist for some products.

The EU's "Basic Customs Instruments" are provided on the EU's EUR-Lex website in the EU *Directory of Community Legislation in Force*. Due to length, annexes and tables are generally omitted from these sources. The full texts are available for purchase through EUDOR, the EU's electronic online document delivery service. TARIC may be purchased from Bernan Associates or European Document Research. The EU Taxation and Customs Union Directorate General recently has placed TARIF on its web site along with related databases. The *Official Journal* can be consulted at EU depository libraries in the United States. Subscriptions to the *Official Journal* are available from Bernan Associates and—on microfiche—are available from Norman Ross Publishing. Also refer to Chapter I for other on-line sources of EU tariff schedules and customs information.

The EU's basic customs rules are: Council Regulation (EEC) No. 2913/92 of 12 October 1992 establishing the Community Customs Code, in *Official Journal* L 302 of 1992; Parliament and Council Regulation (EC) No. 82/97 of 19 December 1996 amending Regulation (EEC) No 2913/92, in *Official Journal* L 17 of 1997; Council Regulation (EC) No 515/97 of 13 March 1997 on mutual assistance between the administrative authorities of the Member States and cooperation between the latter and the Commission to ensure the correct application of the law on customs and agricultural matters *Official Journal* L 82 of 22 March 1997; "Corrigendum to Council Regulation 2913/92/EEC of 12 October 1992 establishing the Community Customs Code," in *Official Journal* L 152 of June 11, 1997, p. 34; Communication pursuant to Article 12, paragraph 5, point b). of Council Regulation 2913/92EEC relating to information given by the customs authorities of the Member States on matters of classification of goods in the customs nomenclature *Official Journal* C 44 17 February 2000; Parliament and Council Regulation 955/99/EC of 13 April 1999 amending Regulation 2913/92/EEC with regard to the external transit procedure, in *Official Journal* L 119 of May 7, 1999, p. 1; and Commission Regulation 1602/2000 amending Regulation 2454/93 laying down provisions for the implementation of Council Regulation 2913/92 establishing the Community Customs Code.

The implementing EU customs rules are: Commission Regulation (EEC) No 2454/93 of 2 July 1993 laying down provisions for the implementation of Council Regulation (EEC) No. 2913/92 establishing the Community Customs Code, in *Official Journal* L 253 of 1993; Commission Regulation (EC) No. 89/97 of 19 December 1996 amending Regulation (EEC) No 2454/93, in *Official Journal* L 17 of 1997; Commission Regulation 1427/97/EC of 23 July 1997 amending Regulation 2454/93/EEC laying down provisions for the implementation of Council Regulation 2913/92/EEC establishing the Community Customs Code, in *Official Journal* L 196 of July 24, 1997, pp. 31-38; Commission Decision 98/405/EC of 16 June 1998 concerning the validity of certain tariff information *Official Journal* L 178, 23 June 1998; Commission Regulation 502/1999/EC of 12 February 1999 amending Regulation 2454/93/EEC, in *Official Journal* L 65 of 1999, pp. 1-49; and Commission Regulation 1662/1999/EC of 28 July 1999 amending Regulation 2454/93/EEC, in *Official Journal* L 197 of 29 July 1999, pp. 25-26.

These have been amended by: Commission Regulation (EC) No. 3665/93 of 21 December 1993, in *Official Journal* L 335 of 1993; Commission Regulation (EC) No. 655/94 of 24 March 1994, in *Official Journal* L 82 of 1994; Council Regulation (EC) No. 1500/94 of 21 June 1994, in *Official Journal* L 162 of 1994; Commission Regulation (EC) No. 2193/94 of 8 September 1994, in *Official Journal* L 235 of 1994; Commission Regulation (EC) No. 3254/94 of 19 December 1994, in *Official Journal* L 346 of 1994; Commission Regulation (EC) No. 1762/95 of 19 July 1995, in *Official Journal* L 171 of 1995; Commission Regulation (EC) No. 482/96 of 19 March 1996, in *Official Journal* L 70 of 1996; Commission Regulation (EC) No. 1676/96 of 30 July 1996, in *Official Journal* L 218 of 1996; Commission Regulation 2153/96 of 25 October 1996, in *Official Journal* L 289 of 1996; Commission Regulation (EC) No. 12/97 of 18 December 1996, in *Official Journal* L 9 of 1997; Commission Regulation 1427/97 of 24 July 1997, in *Official Journal* L 196 of 1997; Commission Regulation 1713/97 of 3 September 1997, in *Official Journal* L 242 of 1997; Commission Regulation 1714/97 of 3 September 1997, in *Official Journal* L 242 of 1997; Commission Regulation 1715/97 of 3 September 1997, in *Official Journal* L 242 of 1997; Commission Regulation 75/98 of 12 January 1998, in *Official Journal* L 7 of 1998; On 3 June 1998 the Commission adopted a proposal for a European Parliament and Council Regulation (EC) amending Council Regulation (EEC) No 2913/92 establishing the Community Customs Code COM(98) 226 final/II *Official Journal* C 228 21 July 1998; Commission Regulation 1677/98 of 29 July 1998, in *Official Journal* L 212 of 1998; Commission Regulation 46/1999 of 8 January 1999, in *Official Journal* L 10 of 1999; and Commission Regulation

1602/2000 amending Regulation 2454/93 laying down provisions for the implementation of Council Regulation 2913/92 establishing the Community Customs Code.

Also see Commission Decisions on the adoption of specific measures to temporarily prohibit the use of the comprehensive guarantee for certain external Community transit operators: Decision 95/521/EC in *Official Journal* L 299, 12 December 1995; Decision 96/37/EC in *Official Journal* L 10 13 January 1996; Decision 96/743/EC in *Official Journal* L 338 28 December 1996; Decision 97/583/EC in *Official Journal* L 237 28 August 1997; Decision 98/7/EC in *Official Journal* L 2 6 January 1998; and Decision 98/697/EC in *Official Journal* L 332 8 December 1998 (this decision renews the ban imposed by Decision 96/743/EC) **as well as** Commission Report on the Community Customs Code [COM(98)226/I final—not published in the *Official Journal.*

THE EU TARIFF SCHEDULES The rates of duties on products entering the EU's customs territory under the standard import regime have been published in *Official Journal* L 264 of 18 October 2000. This schedule incorporates the first rounds of reductions from the Uruguay Round of WTO/GATT negotiations and tarification of agricultural levies. Further reductions in specific sectors can be found in: Council Decision 97/359/EC of 24 March 1997, concerning the elimination of duties on information technology products, in *Official Journal* L 155 of 1997 (*OJ* L 155 also includes Agreement on trade in information technology products); Council Decision 97/360/EC of 24 March 1997, concerning the elimination of duties on certain spirituous beverages, in *Official Journal* L 155 of 1997 (*OJ* L 155 also includes the Agreement in the form of a memorandum of understanding between the European Community and the United States of America on spirituous beverages); Council Regulation 2216/97 of 3 November 1997 amending Regulation 2658/87 concerns the tariff and statistical nomenclature and Common Customs Tariff and autonomously suspends collection of Common Customs Tariff duties in respect of certain information technology products, in *Official Journal* L 305 of 1997, pp. 1-15; and Council Regulation 1110/1999/EC of 10 May 1999 providing for duty-free treatment of specified pharmaceutical active ingredients, in *Official Journal* L 135 of 1999, pp. 1-15. The US International Trade Administration's Trade Information Center offers the EU's 2001 Tariff Schedule on a special web site.

The integrated tariff or "TARIC" is designed to show the various rules applying to specific products when imported into the EU's customs territory or, in some cases, exported from it. Broken down to the 8-digit level, it has information on tariff suspensions, tariff quotas, preferential treatment, anti-dumping and countervailing duties, import prohibitions and restrictions, quantitative limits, export surveillance, licenses and certificates.

UNFAIR COMPETITION Unfair trade practices usually consist of dumping or paying illegal subsidies. Dumping exists when an exporter in a third country sells particular goods on the EU market more cheaply than on its domestic market. Sanctions can be introduced against subsidies when specific goods exported to the EU benefit from subsidies considered illegal under the terms of the WTO agreement. In both cases, the EU Commission can conduct detailed investigations in the suspect countries. Trade sanctions in the form of extra targeted duties (anti-dumping duties) or insistence upon importers agreeing a certain level of prices (price undertakings) can be applied to imports which cause significant economic difficulties to producers in the EU because of unfair trade practices. Sanctions are usually introduced after considering the request made by EU producers of a particular product about unfair competition. The measures the EU may take are those permitted under the WTO Agreement and are limited by the provisions of EU legislation. The nomenclature of the common customs tariff is used to define the products in question. The terms used are quite specific and provide for closely targeted protection. The scope of the measures that can be taken by the EU is limited to the level of dumping or subsidy or to what is necessary to eliminate negative economic effects suffered by EU industry, if such a level is lower than the dumping or subsidy. However, measures are only imposed when the investigation shows that they are in the EU's interest. The effects of such measures on the interests of users and consumers are thereby taken into account. Anti-dumping and countervailing duties are charged in addition to the rates of the Common Customs Tariff. The customs ROs determine whether the imported goods are considered to be from the suspect country.

RESTRICTIONS ON IMPORT QUANTITIES Imports of products originating in "low-cost" countries where the cost of production is unusually low can be subjected to import quantity limitations, or, as a first step, to surveillance to monitor the development of the situation. When quantitative restrictions are applied, the amount of designated products from designated sources allowed into the EU in a specified period (usually a year) will be limited and even those limited quantities will only be admitted once normal customs duties are paid. Restrictions on the quantity of imports of textiles and garments are now being phased out but are said by the EU to have allowed the EU textile and clothing industry to have the time to restructure production and to modernize its manufacturing processes in order to remain commercially competitive. The EU members' customs administrations implement surveillance and restriction measures under rules set by the EU.

GOODS INFRINGING ON EU INTELLECTUAL PROPERTY To protect EU producers' and legitimate importers' commercial interests in the enforcement of intellectual property rights, goods may be excluded from importation into the EU which infringe those rights. The system allows the owners of rights to ask customs to intervene when suspect goods are under customs control. The goods can be held for a limited time while the owners of the intellectual property right can take the question to the national courts under national law to seek redress.

EU AGRICULTURAL AND FISHERY POLICIES The EU maintains a CAP. CAP has a comprehensive system of support and protection for its principal agricultural products, with price supports commonly set well above world market levels. High price levels are maintained with import protection and export subsidies to dispose of surpluses. During the period from the end of World War II to the late 1970s, the EU was a major importer of grains, beef, poultry, and sugar. It is now the world's second leading net grain exporter and is the world's largest exporter of sugar, poultry, and dairy products.

Import protection for agricultural products is provided by variable import quotas, import levies, sluice-gate prices, duties, and sanitary restrictions. Variable levies, calculated differently for different products and for the same products differently processed and changed frequently—sometimes daily—in order to provide a level of protection that will more than offset the difference between world prices and domestic prices, are the basic forms of agricultural import protection. The EU grants export subsidies on a wide range of agricultural products as well as on some manufactured food products. EU export "restitution" payments permit its exporters to sell agricultural products on the world market at prices usually much lower than internal EU prices and sometimes lower than prevailing world market prices. This policy has had devastating effects on the European environment, is subject to frequent abuse and fraud, has created gigantic surplus stocks of some commodities (referred to, *e.g.*, as EU "butter mountains" and "wine lakes"), has imposed prices on EU consumers greatly exceeding world market prices, and has had a ruinous effect on more efficient but unsubsidized agricultural exporters in other countries.

EU customs helps enforce the common agricultural and fishery policies and also contributes to their development and modernization. Discrepancies between low world market prices and higher EU prices could lead to massive imports into the EU or loss of EU export markets were not protections established to insulate the EU market from global competitive pricing. The EU agreed in the Uruguay Round to abolish the former specific agricultural "levies" on importations and to replace them by the more generally accepted instrument of customs duties. The agricultural customs duties are made up of a number of elements and have a variable component, a seasonal element, and also take into account the price paid at the time of importation. EU members' customs administrations control the import of these goods and collect the customs duties. Customs administrations also calculate and pay the "refunds" provided for exports to third countries. The level of customs duties and the refunds are fixed by means of common market organizations based on market stability, EU consumer requirements, EU domestic prices, and income generation for EU farmers and fishermen.

EFTA

The European Free Trade Association ("EFTA") was organized in 1959 by the UK and established by the Stockholm Convention of 1960. It generally included the fringe or traditionally neutral nations of Western Europe. The British intended it as a counterweight to the EU but one that did not encompass the integrationist ideas of the EU that the British found objectionable. Members were Austria, Denmark, Iceland, Finland, Ireland, Norway, Liechtenstein, Portugal, Sweden, Switzerland, and the UK. All but Iceland, Norway, Liechtenstein, and Switzerland have become members of the EU. Some Central and Eastern European nations considered first seeking EFTA membership as a stepping stone to full EU participation.

The EFTA Treaty was very limited in scope. It applied to the free trade in industrial goods. It sought to negotiate coordinated bilateral trade agreements between member states and the EU. It omitted coverage of agriculture, transport, labor, capital, technology, and services to mention only a few areas fully incorporated into the Treaty of Rome which established the EU. A single institution, the EFTA Council, was created. Since it normally followed a unanimous voting principle, each of the member states retained a veto over new policy developments within EFTA and any surrender of national sovereignty to a supranational EFTA was minimized.

Each EFTA member has a free trade agreement with the EU and all but Switzerland are part of the EEA. Switzerland's voters have at last agreed to permit Switzerland to become part of the EEA. The EFTA is now clearly moribund and, because of its loss of membership and preeminence to the EU, has little continuing independent importance as a regional economic group. Further information on EFTA may be found at http://www.scretariat.efta.int.

EEA

Negotiations between EFTA and the EU to integrate their economies short of EFTA country membership in the EU began in the mid-1980s and were concluded in late 1991. The resulting agreement was to create the EEA or European Economic Area. The EEA effectively permits EFTA and EU members (except for Switzerland, which has now been permitted by its voters to again seek EEA participation) virtually unrestricted access to each other's markets for most goods, services, and people but only under EU rules and standards which EFTA members must largely (about 80%) adopt but have little opportunity to dictate or influence.

The EEA constitutes a market of approximately 380 million consumers and accounts for almost 18% of world imports and 20 % of world exports, excluding intra-EEA trade (1997). Within the EEA there is free movement of goods, services, capital and persons. Citizens of all 18 countries have the right to move freely throughout the EEA—to live, work, set up business, invest or buy real estate, with a few minor limitations in certain sectors.

The Agreement on the European Economic Area extends the EU's Single Market to three out of the four EFTA countries, namely Norway, Iceland, and Liechtenstein. Switzerland, while being a member of EFTA and a party to a free trade agreement with the EU, is not an EEA member since it rejected EEA membership in December 1992.

The EEA Agreement unites the 15 EU member states and Iceland, Liechtenstein, and Norway into one single market governed by the same basic rules (*Acquis Communautaire*). These rules cover the so- called four freedoms (free movement of goods, capital, services and persons) and competition rules. Under the Agreement the EFTA EEA countries are able to contribute to this common legislation. The EEA Agreement does not cover the EU's Common Agricultural Policy or the Common Fisheries Policy but contains provisions on various aspects of trade in agricultural and fish products. Trade policy towards third countries remains outside the EEA's scope of cooperation. In addition to internal market legislation, the Agreement includes so-called "flanking and horizontal policies" intended to strengthen the internal market. These additional fields of co-operation include research and development, statistics, education, social policy, the environment, consumer protection, tourism, small and medium-sized enterprises, culture, information services and audio-visual services.

The EFTA EEA countries participate in EU programs regarding these areas and have a voice in developing and managing them through participation in their committees.

The EEA Agreement is made up of 129 articles as well as 22 annexes and 49 protocols. The annexes refer to the *Acquis Communautaire* applicable in the EEA, without fully reproducing these legal texts. The protocols include provisions on specific areas such as ROs, transition periods for the EFTA states in certain fields and simplified customs procedures. These matters are generally not based on EU legislation.

The EEA generally embraces EU law on the free movement of goods, services, persons, and capital. Integration on agricultural, fisheries, and tax policy is excluded. The EFTA nations will retain their own border controls, tariffs, currencies, and external trade policies. Antidumping measures, countervailing duties, and illicit commercial practices law will not be applied to EEA trade. Any aspects of a political or defense union are also excluded from the EEA agreement. A number of EU policies were adopted by the EFTA countries. These include EU law on competition (including mergers), government subsidies, state monopolies, public procurement, intellectual property rights, consumer protection, the environment, companies, and social affairs generally. The goal of this integration is to create equal competitive conditions in the EU and EFTA.

Because of their relative wealth and to smooth the transition, EFTA members also agreed to make substantial financial contributions to a special "cohesion fund" to benefit the poorer EU nations. This was effectively the ransom payment demanded by the poorer countries of the EU (Greece, Spain, Portugal, Ireland, and—at least regionally—Italy) before they would agree to the EEA.

The EEA agreement reached in October of 1991 envisioned the creation of a number of interregional organizations vested with law-making and dispute settlement powers. These included an EEA Council, an EEA Joint Committee (akin to the EU Committee of Permanent Representatives), an EEA Court of Justice and Court of First Instance, an EEA Joint Parliamentary Committee, an EEA Consultative Committee (akin to the EU Economic and Social Committee), and an EFTA Surveillance Authority (akin to the EU Commission) which focuses on EFTA application of EU competition law.

On legislation, EFTA gets extensive consultation rights but little real decision-making power. However, a right to "opt out" of new EU legislation is granted to each EFTA state but (if exercised) this has the effect of suspending the new law's benefits for all EFTA nations.

In late 1991, the EU Court of Justice issued an opinion that EEA courts were incompatible with the Treaty of Rome. A revised EEA agreement was concluded in early 1993 that satisfied the EU Court of Justice's objections by (a) creating an EFTA Court of Justice, (b) establishing a "Joint Committee" of EU and EFTA political representatives for reviewing conflicts between the EU and EFTA Courts of Justice, and (c) devising certain procedures to resolve such conflicts which largely grant supremacy to the EU Court of Justice but provide for recourse to binding arbitration under certain circumstances.

Swiss rejection of participation in the EEA in late 1992 through a popular referendum required additional renegotiation of the EEA agreement. This was concluded, the results ratified, and the EEA came into force on January 1, 1994.

Further information on the EEA may be found at http://www.secretariat.efta.int/euroeco.

The Benelux Countries

The Benelux countries (Belgium, the Netherlands, and Luxembourg, parts of each of whose names are joined to form the name of the group) signed a Customs Union Treaty in 1948. By the middle of the 1950s, the Benelux nations were close to agreement on a comprehensive economic union. The Treaty of Rome expressly permits, at Article 233, the existence and completion of the Benelux Union to the extent that its objectives are not attained through the EU. There are a number of common Benelux laws and institutions, most notably that dealing with common intellectual property protection laws and institutions.

The Schengen Group

The Benelux states, Germany, Italy, Spain, Greece, Portugal, and France agreed to remove their internal frontier controls on people under the so-called "Schengen Accord." This accord was the product of intergovernmental agreement, not EU legislation. The Schengen Accord covers such sensitive issues as visas, asylum, immigration, gun controls, extradition, and police rights of "hot pursuit." The main points of contention were cross-border traffic of immigrants and criminals, especially terrorists and drug dealers. Although the Schengen Accord was due to become operative in 1994, its implementation was repeatedly postponed because of concerns by one or more members about the uncontrolled transborder movement of illegal aliens, terrorists, and drugs. Now consisting of all EU members save the UK and Ireland and including Norway and Iceland, the terms of the Schengen Accord (as modified) have been adopted into the EU structure by the Treaty of Amsterdam. The Schengen Convention of 1990 laid down common rules for visas, the right of asylum, checks at the external borders, and cooperation between police forces and customs authorities to allow freedom of movement for individuals within the territories of the signatory countries without disturbing law and order. A reporting system has been set up for the exchange of data about the identity of individuals.

The Nordic Union

Although not formally a regional economic group, the Nordic Union is a loose but important organization composed of Denmark, Finland, Iceland, Norway, and Sweden. Membership provides mutual and reciprocal legal rights and obligations and common negotiating and regulatory institutions. The member countries of the Nordic Union feel a strong affinity for each other and share many common institutions and circumstances and much common history. Greenland, the Faroe Islands, the Åland Islands, the Svålbård Islands, Bouvet Island, and Jan Mayen Island are all associated with Nordic states but are not completely integrated into them and may be separately represented on the Nordic Council or institutional bodies. Except for the Finns and the Inuit of Greenland and the Lapps in the north, all are close kindred racially and linguistically. As a consequence, over the years and particularly since 1945 they have developed a number of shared means for mutually pursuing their common interests and have provided reciprocal privileges to one another's citizens in a number of respects. While the Nordic Union does not exist as a fixed political or institutional organization, the cumulative ties and reciprocal understandings within this community clearly constitute a phenomenon within the region that must be recognized and understood. Among the institutions and arrangements of the Nordic Union are cross-border employment under the Nordic Tax Treaty of 1990, which replaced earlier similar treaties, and the Nordic Social Security Convention of 1981. The Nordic Tax Treaty is a multilateral tax treaty for taxation of employment income between Denmark, the Faroe Islands, Finland, Iceland, Norway, and Sweden. The Treaty is applicable to individuals who are tax residents in the Nordic countries as defined by their own national laws. Double taxation of employment income is avoided through the exemption method or, less commonly, the credit method. The Nordic Social Security Convention determines in which country a person is ensured when working in more than one Nordic country. There is a Nordic Council. It was established in 1952. Its members meet at least every two years and seek to strengthen cooperation among member countries. There is also a Nordic Investment Bank. There are Nordic fishing treaties and arrangements. There is a Nordic Patent Law under which a patent applied for in any Nordic country is valid in any other Nordic country. Persons and entities from Nordic countries have special authorization to work and do business in each other's countries on preferential terms. There is a Nordic passport union. For the foreign visitor to the Nordic countries, a visit to any and all Nordic countries for combined stays exceeding 3 months may constitute residency within each of them for employment or residency purposes. There is considerable harmonization of the laws in many areas of the Nordic countries. Even implementation of the EEA was in many aspects undertaken jointly through Nordic institutions.

The Commonwealth of Independent States

The Commonwealth of Independent States ("CIS") is a group formed upon the breakup of the Soviet Union by the former Soviet Republics. It was an interim measure created to provide some continuity to those newly independent states of the former Soviet Union whose economies and economic structures had been so thoroughly integrated for so long. Belarus has recently asked to be virtually incorporated into the Russian Federation. The Baltic states have consistently, and Georgia initially, refused to cooperate. Azerbaijan has been in the past only a tepid member and sometimes denies its membership in the CIS entirely. Recently, however, economic deterioration in many of the CIS states and the exercise of some Russian muscle to compel reluctant states to toe the line have resulted in a newly strengthened CIS. Whether CIS will be at all effective, which countries will continue to participate in it, and whether it is a permanent group or merely transitional is difficult to determine. Also uncertain is whether it will be a mutually-beneficial organization made up of independent and equal members or a vehicle for the reassertion of Russian hegemony in the region, as feared (or even hoped) by many of the CIS states.

The purpose of CIS is to coordinate economic, monetary, defense, foreign, and similar policies, which is essential because of the closely integrated nature of their infrastructures and economies consequent to their long inclusion within a single empire.

On December 8, 1991, Belarus, the Russian Federation, and Ukraine signed the Minsk Agreement establishing the CIS. The agreement pledged cooperation in forming and developing the united economic area, common European and Eurasian markets, and common customs policy, among other things, and established the city of Minsk as the official location of the coordinating bodies of the CIS. On December 21, 1991, 11 former Soviet republics (all but Georgia and the Baltic states) signed the Alma-Ata Declaration dissolving the Soviet Union and recognizing a new form of alliance as independent countries under the CIS.

Since those agreements were signed, other agreements have been signed to establish the customs union, to coordinate defense policies (which in practice has meant conceding Russian control over CIS member border defenses), monetary policy (which has often meant a continued use of the Russian ruble), and to reaffirm the existence and continued support of the CIS concept. Copies of the text of some of these agreements may be found at 34 International Legal Materials 1, p. 38 (1992) for establishment of the CIS and 34 International Legal Materials 5, p. 1279, for the CIS Charter, and p. 1298, for the creation of the CIF Economic Union (1995). The CIS basic documents are not self-executing. They provide only guidelines which must be realized through specific national legislative acts.

As now constituted, the CIS provides for a customs union, a free trade area, a monetary union, and the free movement of capital and labor in addition to other political and defense coordination. In reality, few of these things are implemented in practice. Many side agreements are binding only on those party to them. Many CIS members have made significant reservations even to those agreements they have signed. Each CIS state has bilateral trading and other commercial treaties with each other CIS state.

CIS institutions consist of a Council of the Heads of State and Council of the Heads of Government, Councils of Ministers of Foreign Affairs and Defense Ministers, a Coordinating and Consultative Committee, an Economic Court, a Commission of Human Rights, an Interparliamentary Assembly, and other specialized bodies. An Inter-State Economic Committee for the coordination of economic and social policy has a right to adopt decisions that are binding on all signatories.

The Baltic Free Trade Area

The Baltic Free Trade Area is composed of the Baltic States of Estonia, Latvia, and Lithuania. It was formed in 1993. It was supplemented in June of this year by a side agreement providing for free trade in agricultural products.

In September 1991, the Baltic States seceded from the Soviet Union. The three Baltic countries are generally considered to be distinguishable from former republics of the Soviet Union—although each was in fact a Soviet Republic—in large part because they were each independent countries during the period from the Versailles Treaty to their military conquest (with the collusion of Nazi Germany) and subsequent annexation by the Soviet Union. National independence itself does not distinguish the Baltic republics from other former Soviet Republics. At one or more times, most or all the non-Russian Soviet republics were independent and few, if any, truly voluntarily joined the Soviet state. Regardless, the United States and other countries never recognized the Baltic States' loss of independence and never considered them to have been legally made part of the USSR.

Despite sharing this feature plus the fact of their contiguous location on the Baltic Sea coast, they have little else in common except their all being small and with traditional orientations towards Western rather than Eastern Europe.

CEFTA

The Central European Free Trade Agreement ("CEFTA") was signed in December 1992 following a meeting in Visegrad, Hungary, in 1991 from which town the group was given its former popular name. It was originally established with the intention of setting up a free trade zone among Poland, Hungary, Slovakia, and the Czech Republic by the year 2001. Almost all duties on products traded among them were to be eliminated by 1998 and that schedule has been accelerated. Slovenia subsequently joined CEFTA. Other countries may be accepted as members. Romania, Bulgaria, Lithuania, Latvia, and Estonia were thought to be considering membership applications.

Member countries have all been satellite states of the Soviet Union. Upon the collapse of the Soviet Union and the rejection of dictatorial Communist governments by the member countries, existing trading relationships of these countries deteriorated. Even among each other, bilateral trade plummeted. CEFTA was designed to restore trade volumes among member countries. Declines in trade volumes have ceased and intraregional trade is now generally increasing.

CEFTA consists of the Agreement, six annexes, and seven protocols. The details are all in the annexes and protocols. CEFTA may be found at 34 International Legal Materials 1, p. 3 (1995). Among other things, members have agreed to protect intellectual property rights on a nondiscriminatory basis. The annexes provide elaboration of certain of the provisions in the Agreement. Annexes 3 and 4 include the terms for the regulation of quantitative restrictions on products traded by the members. Protocols 1 through 6 contain the schedules for reduction on specific goods with different rules for different products. Protocol 7 deals with "rules of origin" or "origination products" which are subject to the preferential treatment of the free trade area. Six supplementary protocols went into effect on July 1, 1994. Members accelerated the schedules for tariff reductions, opened trade liberalization more fully to agricultural products, and permitted additional members to join CEFTA. Discussions are being held on opening CEFTA to liberalized trade in services and the movement of capital. All duties on some products have already been eliminated.

Members are also to cooperate to bring each of and all their regulations of trade closer to those of the EU. It is the desire of all the members to ultimately become EU members. Further information may be obtained from CEFTA'S official web site at http://www.cefta.org.

Economic Cooperation Organization

Azerbaijan, Kazakhstan, Kyrgyzstan, Tajikistan, Turkmenistan, and Uzbekistan—all of Islamic culture—joined with Afghanistan, Iran, Pakistan, and Turkey in 1992 to form the Economic Cooperation Organization (sometimes called the "Islamic Common Market") which is viewed as a step toward the creation of an Islamic free trade area. Members have agreed to reduce tariffs among themselves and to focus on economic cooperation. The organization is headquartered in Tehran, Iran. Iran—representing fundamentalist Islam—and Turkey—representing a secular state where Islam is the prevailing religion—strongly compete for the allegiances of the Central Asian states of the former Soviet Union.

Further information may be obtained from the Economic Cooperation Organization's official web site at http://www.eco secretariat.org.

Black Sea Economic Cooperation

At Turkey's invitation, Albania, Armenia, Azerbaijan, Bulgaria, Georgia, Greece, Moldova, Romania, Russia, Turkey, and Ukraine signed a declaration in June 1992 paving the way for a Black Sea pact to promote economic and trade cooperation. The agreement was short and the details were few. Little seems to have come of it since.

Further information may be obtained from the Black Sea Economic Cooperation section on the web site at http://www.iews.org/srd/bsec/nsf.

TAFTA

Intimations of a proposal for a "Transatlantic Free Trade Area" ("TAFTA") between the United States and the EU have been circulated. In November 1990, the EU and the US signed a "Transatlantic

Declaration" providing for twice-yearly presidential summits and a number of annual lesser meetings. The EU issued a July 1995 paper proposing a "transatlantic economic space" in preparation for a summit meeting in Madrid in late 1995. Trade between the EU and NAFTA countries is worth around $225 billion a year and constitutes about one fifth of each side's exports and imports. Whether TAFTA has any prospect of practical realization remains unclear, but it is supported by powerful political figures on both sides of the Atlantic Ocean.

NAFTA/USCFTA

HISTORY AND STRUCTURE OF NAFTA Information concerning NAFTA is available through many sources provided by participating member governments, through privately published materials and unofficial on-line sources, and through the web site http://www.nafta-sec-alena.org. Only that information on NAFTA and its predecessor agreement that underlies or is germane to customs and tariffs will be presented here.

The North American Free Trade Agreement (here "NAFTA" and sometimes elsewhere "Nafta"), built on the earlier US-Canada Free Trade Agreement ("USCFTA") of January 1, 1989, which in turn incorporated much of the "Agreement Concerning Automotive Products Between the Government of the United States and the Government of Canada (with annexes)" of January 16, 1965 (the so-called "Auto Pact"). Of course, NAFTA and all other trading relationships among the three NAFTA parties are conducted within, and limited by, the parameters of the GATT/WTO Agreement and other international agreements to which the parties are members, including environmental agreements.

NAFTA was entered into trilaterally among the US, Canada, and Mexico and went into force on January 1, 1994. It has over 1,000 pages of operative text plus about 2,000 pages of annexes and technical materials. It is lengthy, it is complex, and it is important to all doing business in and with any or all the three party countries. It does not take so many pages to formulate free trade. NAFTA is obviously something more, and something less, than merely the declaration of a free trade area. It attempted to cover topics rarely if ever covered in early multilateral agreements and was in many ways the trail blazer for much of the Uruguay Round's successful extension of the coverage of the GATT/WTO Agreement. In many instances, the applicable NAFTA-imposed commercial conditions—at least during the phase-in period— may differ regarding the US and Canada, the US and Mexico, and Canada and Mexico. In many instances, Mexico was called upon to take far greater market opening measures than the other parties because of its relatively greater closed markets. Implementing legislation—which may be of independent importance—was required in each country member.

NAFTA consists of 8 parts; 22 chapters; 290 articles; a number of annexes to chapters including 300-A—Trade and Investment in the Automotive Sector, 300-B—Textiles and Apparel Goods, and 401—Specific Rules of Origin; seven annexes to the general agreement regarding reservations and exceptions to investment, cross border trade in services, and financial services in chapters 11, 12, and 14, *i.e.*, Reservations for Existing Measures and Liberalizing Commitments (Chapters 11, 12, and 14), Reservations for Future Measures (Chapters 11, 12, and 14), Activities Reserved to the State (Chapter 11), Exceptions Most-Favored-Nation Treatment (Chapter 11), Quantitative Restrictions and Other Items (Chapter 12), Miscellaneous Commitments (Chapter 12), and Reservations, Specific Commitments, and Other Items (Chapter 14); notes; supplemental agreements regarding the North American Agreement on Environmental Cooperation and the North American Agreement on Labor Cooperation; and Understanding Between the Parties to the NAFTA Concerning Chapter Eight - Emergency Action. Specifically, it is organized as follows: PART ONE–GENERAL PART; Chapter 1–Objectives; Chapter 2–General Definitions; PART TWO–TRADE IN GOODS; Chapter 3–National Treatment and Market Access of Goods; Section A–National Treatment; Section B–Tariffs; Section C–Non-Tariff Measures; Section D–Consultations; Section E–Definitions; Chapter 4–Rules of Origin; Chapter 5–Customs Procedures; Section A–Certification of Origin; Section B–Administration and Enforcement; Section C–Advance Rulings; Section D–Review and Appeal of Origin Determinations and Advance Rulings; Section E–Uniform Regulations; and Section F–Cooperation; Chapter 6–Energy and Basic Petrochemicals; Chapter 7–Agricultural and Sanitary and Phytosanitary Measures; Section A–Agriculture; Section B–Sanitary and Phytosanitary Measures; Chapter 8–Emergency Action; PART 3–TECHNICAL BARRIERS TO TRADE; Chapter 9–Standards Related Measures; PART 4–GOVERNMENT PROCUREMENT; Chapter 10–Government Procurement; Section A–Scope and Coverage of National Treatment; Section B–Tendering Procedures; Section C–Bid Challenge; Section D–General Provisions; PART 5–INVESTMENT SERVICES AND RELATED MATTERS; Chapter 11–Investments; Section A–Investments; Section B–Settlement of Disputes between a Party and an Investor of Another Party; Section C–Definitions; Chapter 12–Cross Border Trade in Services; Chapter 13–Telecommunications; Chapter 14–Financial Services; Chapter 15–Competition Policy, Monopolies, and State Enterprises; Chapter 16–Temporary Entry for Business Purposes; PART 6–INTELLECTUAL PROPERTY; Chapter 17–Intellectual

Property; PART 7–ADMINISTRATIVE AND INSTITUTIONAL PROVISIONS; Chapter 18–Publication; Notification, and Administration of Laws; Chapter 19–Review and Dispute Settlement in Antidumping and Countervailing Duty Measures; Chapter 20–Institutional Arrangements and Dispute Settlement Procedures; Section A–Institutions; Section B–Dispute Settlement; Section C–Domestic Procedures and Private Commercial Dispute Settlement; PART 8–OTHER PROVISIONS; Chapter 21–Exceptions; and Chapter 22–Final Provisions.

In its broad outline, NAFTA is a free trade area agreement to be phased in over a period of up to 15 years and contains many instances of "special interest" provisions insisted on by one or more member countries or interest groups. NAFTA provides for progressive annual reductions in tariff duties on the trade among the three countries of most "NAFTA" products. It also eliminates certain barriers to investment, trade in services, and trade in goods; provides protection for intellectual property rights; and establishes procedures for the resolution of disputes that may arise under it. It contains detailed provisions covering issues as varied as customs administration, antitrust, temporary residency for business persons, emergency actions to protect industries adversely affected by surges in imports, government procurement, and review of antidumping ("AD") and countervailing duty ("CVD") actions. ROs under NAFTA are extremely complicated and are still evolving through practical application.

The member countries—at the insistence of the US that sought unsuccessfully thereby to mollify its domestic critics of NAFTA—have negotiated environmental and labor standards side agreements. The US has a job training program for US workers who lose their jobs as a result of NAFTA.

NAFTA'S MEMBERSHIP AND MODIFICATION Other countries may join NAFTA. Chile once attempted to do so, although it was frustrated in its efforts by a US Congress and President reluctant to endorse further trade liberalization. Canada and Chile have agreed to a bilateral free trade agreement accord as a means of expediting NAFTA membership for Chile. If Quebec secedes from Canada, under international law it would not automatically become a fourth NAFTA party but would have to apply for and successfully negotiate its membership.

NAFTA'S OBJECTIVES NAFTA formally established a free trade area with the stated objectives of eliminating barriers to trade in goods and services; promoting conditions of fair competition within the free trade area; increasing investment opportunities within the free trade area; effectively protecting and enforcing intellectual property rights; and creating a framework for further cooperation to enhance the benefits of the Agreement.

DEVELOPMENT OF COMMON RULES Under NAFTA, each country undertakes to ensure that its laws and regulations, including those of any state or province, conform to certain standards specified in the Agreement. If any federal, state, or provincial law or regulation of a NAFTA country does not conform to the obligations of NAFTA, it may not be enforced against persons from other NAFTA countries unless: (1) it falls into certain categories of "exceptions" (such as measures dealing with matters of taxation; national security; health, safety, and consumer protection; or balance of payments emergencies) or (2) it is included on a special listing in NAFTA of "reservations" of nonconforming laws or regulations.

NAFTA sets forth general principles and standards that each NAFTA country is required to observe in the treatment of goods, services, and investors from each other NAFTA country. In general, the applicable standard of treatment for goods is "national treatment" for goods from any NAFTA country (treatment no less favorable than a country accords to its own domestic goods), although there are exceptions. For services or investors, the applicable standard is generally the better of national treatment or MFN treatment.

Under NAFTA, duty drawback programs were eliminated over time on intra-NAFTA trade. Such drawback programs within NAFTA permitted non-NAFTA manufacturers to use one of the NAFTA countries as an export platform.

NAFTA's Annex 312 requires the parties to develop a common set of rules to govern marking requirements to designate the country of origin of imported goods. Labeling requirements for textiles and apparel goods are to be harmonized among the NAFTA parties.

Customs users fees between the US and Mexico and the US and Canada were eliminated.

A common external tariff will be applied by all three countries to computer products through a 5-year phased-in reduction beginning in 1999. At the end of 2004, each country will assess duties at a 3.9% rate for computers and CPUs and at a 3.7% rate for keyboards, displays, and related units. Once a duty has been paid on such goods imported into the NAFTA territory, they may move freely among the NAFTA countries without incurring additional duties. This is the only "customs union," as opposed to a "free trade area," aspect of NAFTA.

NAFTA calls upon parties to facilitate the judicial enforcement in their territories of arbitration awards obtained in another party's country.

NAFTA's Chapter 9 addresses technical standards and NAFTA's Chapter 7 governs sanitary and phytosanitary measures. The NAFTA parties have agreed not to use standards-related measures as obstacles to trade. NAFTA affirmed the right of each country to adopt and apply standards-related measures aimed at safeguarding human, animal, and plant health and in protecting the environment and consumers. Public notice to all NAFTA parties is required prior to the adoption or modification of technical standards by any NAFTA party. Any NAFTA party (and anyone interested in a particular proposed technical standard) will be allowed to comment on it and designated "inquiry points" will respond to questions and provide information regarding technical standards and measures. Where a new technical standard is necessary to address an urgent problem relating to safety, these procedures may be deferred until after implementation of the new standard. Risk assessments are those under which an importing NAFTA party determines the level of risk involved in goods and services imported from a NAFTA party. Conformity assessments are those under which an importing NAFTA party implements its established procedures to determine whether or not a technical regulation was followed with regards to goods or services imported from another NAFTA party. Both are permitted by NAFTA as long as they do not create an unnecessary obstacle to trade. Each NAFTA party must recognize every other NAFTA party's conformity assessment bodies on the same basis they accredit or otherwise recognize their own and must give sympathetic consideration to another NAFTA party's request to negotiate agreements for the mutual recognition of the results of the parties' conformity assessments. Under the Agreement, NAFTA countries agreed to work together to promote the goals sought by standards-related measures and to make compatible their respective technical standard measures. Each importing NAFTA party is required to treat technical standards adopted by an exporting NAFTA party as equivalent to its own where it is demonstrable that the exporting party's technical standards adequately fulfill the importing party's legitimate objectives. Each NAFTA party is required, upon request, to provide technical advice, information, and assistance to enhance the requesting NAFTA party's standards mechanisms. Each country committed, where possible, to using international standards for its standards-related measures (although it may provide a higher level of protection than the international standard calls for). A Committee on Standards-Related Measures was established to facilitate cooperation towards harmonization and compatibility of standards-related measures and practices among the NAFTA parties. A Committee on Sanitary and Phytosanitary Standards was created to oversee the creation of standards.

NAFTA's Chapter 15 addresses competition policy and monopoly concerns. The NAFTA parties generally commit to apply their domestic competition rules to prevent anticompetitive business practices; to cooperate and coordinate in enforcing these rules; and to use regulatory controls to assure that state enterprises or state-designated monopolies observe the NAFTA commitments of their governments (principally by not discriminating in favor of local suppliers or purchasers to the detriment of businesses established in their countries by investors from other NAFTA countries). Other restrictions are imposed on state enterprises and state-designated monopolies which generally compel them to act in accordance with commercial considerations, not to discriminate in buying or selling, and to not use monopoly advantage to engage in noncompetitive practices outside their monopolized market. Intellectual property protection is stated to not constitute a monopoly for purposes of NAFTA's antitrust provisions. Although a trilateral Working Group on Trade Competition was created under NAFTA, few concrete mechanisms were established to harmonize NAFTA parties' antitrust regimes. Controversies over competition policy or enforcement (but not regarding state enterprises or monopolies) are explicitly exempted from NAFTA's dispute settlement provisions.

NAFTA parties are also required to harmonize their individual applications of NAFTA's RO applications.

DISPUTE RESOLUTION UNDER NAFTA NAFTA's Chapter 20, Section B, contains the general provisions for the resolution of disputes. Other dispute resolution methodologies for specific types of disputes may be found in NAFTA's Chapters 11 and 19 as well as elsewhere in NAFTA. The dispute resolution mechanisms ("DRMs") of NAFTA are akin to but different than those of USCFTA. These changes were a result of the new trilateral arrangement and Canada's displeasure with aspects of dispute resolution under FTA. Several types of DRMs were created, each addressing particular concerns of one or more party. The substantive areas include investments, trade in goods, import and export restrictions on textile and apparel goods, worn clothing, country of origin markings, emergency actions triggering quantitative restrictions, rules of origin, and disputes concerning goods produced outside the free trade area. The environmental and labor standards side agreements establish their own commissions to resolve disputes.

Recourse to NAFTA's dispute settlement procedures under Chapter 20, Section B, may be had for all disputes between the parties regarding the interpretation or application of NAFTA and where a party considers that an actual or proposed measure of another party is or would be inconsistent with NAFTA's imposed obligations or cause nullification or impairment of NAFTA. Although only a government party (with a "significant interest") may avail itself of NAFTA's dispute resolution mechanisms, the US will automatically trigger panel reviews in response to the timely requests of qualified American private parties.

NAFTA's Article 2001 creates a Free Trade Commission and NAFTA's Article 2002 establishes a permanent trilateral Secretariat to assist the Commission. The Commission and the Secretariat oversee the implementation and operation of NAFTA and supervise all committees and working groups created under NAFTA, including the resolution of disputes. Where a dispute arises both under GATT and NAFTA, NAFTA's Article 2005 permits the complaining party to select the forum to make its complaint but, upon the objection of any other party regarding in specially excepted cases, the dispute must be heard pursuant to NAFTA.

Cooperation among disputant parties is strongly encouraged, consultation and negotiation among them is compelled. The good offices, conciliation and mediation services, and expert advice (particularly of Scientific Review Boards) of the Commission should be solicited when consultations are unsuccessful. The Commission will then render recommendations to assist the parties to reach a mutually satisfactory resolution. When all else fails, and following 30 days (or longer with mutual agreement) after convening of the Commission, arbitration (but not binding arbitration) may be resorted to under NAFTA's Article 2008.

Arbitrators are normally chosen from a roster of legal, trade, and other experts and may be nationals of non-NAFTA countries. A special roster of persons with expertise or experience in financial services law or practice will be appointed with 3 year terms from which to choose panelists for disputes involving a financial services company. Panels are composed of 5 members and parties must agree to a chairperson within 15 days or one of the parties will be chosen by lot to select the chairperson. Thereafter, each party chooses 2 panelists who are citizens of the other party. Separate panel selection rules exist for instances when there are more than two disputant parties. Parties must select panelists from another disputing party's roster of panelists. Any party may exercise a peremptory challenge against an individual not on the roster. The Commission has established Model Rules of Procedure for the panels. Ninety days after panel selection (or other period established in the Model Rules or by agreement of the parties), the panel must issue a confidential initial report to the parties. The parties then have 14 days in which to submit comments to the panel. A final report, which may not state which panelists decided with the majority or the minority, will then be sent to the Commission for publication (unless the Commission decides otherwise) within 15 days. Upon issuance of the final report, the parties are again to negotiate the dispute without resorting to compensation. Compensation is to be used only as a last resort and then only pursuant to narrow parameters. If the final resolution of the dispute involves a finding that a measure is inconsistent with the obligations of NAFTA or causes a nullification or impairment of a NAFTA benefit, the emphasis is placed on taking action by amending or removing the offending domestic law. An injured party may suspend benefits to the offending party in the sector or sectors affected by the measure, but only after a mutually acceptable resolution has not been arrived within 30 days following the issuance of the final report. NAFTA establishes the guidelines for determining what benefits may be suspended and empowers the Commission to establish a separate panel to determine whether the level of benefits is manifestly excessive.

The resolution of investment disputes is dealt with specially in NAFTA's Chapter 11, Section B, Article 1115, 11-11, and is unique in NAFTA for providing a cause of action to private parties. An investor of a NAFTA member may submit to arbitration (after first exhausting resolution through consultations and negotiations) a claim that another party has breached NAFTA as it pertains to investments and that the investor has incurred loss or damage as a result of the breach. An investor is precluded from making a claim if more than 3 years have elapsed from the date when the investor acquired knowledge of the alleged breach and the result loss or damage. Arbitration may take place under the World Bank's International Center for Settlement of Investment Disputes ("ICSID") or any other tribunal operating under the arbitration rules of the UN Commission for International Trade Law ("UNCITRAL"). NAFTA provides for investment dispute resolution before a tribunal made up of 3 arbitrators, with each disputant appointing one and the third, who will preside, to be appointed by mutual agreement of the disputants. If either or both parties fail to appoint an arbitrator and fail to agree on the third arbitrator, the Secretary General of ICSID will appoint them from a roster of prospective arbitrators established by the NAFTA parties at the time NAFTA entered into force. The tribunal may consolidate common claims of law or fact and provide for interim measures necessary for the protection of party interests. Resolution shall be based on NAFTA's terms and applicable rules of international law.

Awards may only be in the form of monetary damages or restitution of property (with the losing party able to elect to pay monetary damages and applicable interest in lieu of making restitution) and costs of litigation in accordance with applicable arbitration rules. Awards are binding on the parties, compliance should be expeditious, and enforcement is possible under the ICSID Convention, the New York Convention, or the Inter-American Convention.

Per NAFTA's Chapter 19, 3 member panels are assembled on a case-by-case basis from a permanent 75 person roster and these panels will substitute for domestic judicial review in cases where either the importing or the exporting country seeks review of a final AD or CVD determination. Panelists are, to the extent practicable, to be sitting or retired judges rather than lawyers. Each party involved is entitled to select a panelist and the third panelist is named by agreement of the two parties. If no agreement is reached, the parties decide the third panelist by lot. There are no time limits on seeking review. The binational panels are to apply the same standard of review and general legal principles as the domestic law of the importing country. Following a hearing, the panel will either uphold or remand the final determination. Panel review deadlines ensure that a final decision will be issued within 315 days of the request for review. In the case of remand, the responsible domestic agency is ordered to not act inconsistently with the panel decision. Panel decisions are binding on all parties, final decisions are not reviewable, and no NAFTA party may provide in its domestic legislation for an appeal to domestic courts from any panel decisions.

Appeals of panel decisions may be made to an *ad hoc* 3 member Extraordinary Challenge Committee, with each party choosing one member from a roster of 15 sitting or former judges and the third chosen from the same roster by a party selected by lot, under NAFTA's Article 1904. Panel decisions may be overturned only when extraordinary and explicitly enumerated circumstances are found to have existed.

A three-member Special Committee (chosen in the same manner and from the same roster as the Extraordinary Challenge Committee) may be invoked under NAFTA's Article 1905 where a NAFTA party's domestic laws (or the absence of necessary laws) frustrate NAFTA's panel review process. Where the Special Committee agrees that such frustration occurs from that cause, the parties are to resolve the dispute through consultation. When this proves impossible after 60 days, the complaining party may suspend the binational review process for decisions affecting the other party (which the other party may reciprocate) or may suspend against the other party such NAFTA benefits as are appropriate under the circumstances. The Special

Committee may be reconvened at any time by the party complained against to seek a determination of whether the suspension of benefits is manifestly excessive or if the party complained against has corrected the problem. Where the Special Committee determines the party complained against has corrected the problem, remedial actions taken by the complaining party must be terminated.

New amendments to a NAFTA party's AD/CVD statutes may be reviewed by a five-member panel to determine that the amendments are consistent with GATT and the objectives of NAFTA and do not operate to overturn a prior decision of a binational review panel. Where the panel sustains the complaint but the parties are unable to achieve a mutually satisfactory solution within a specified period, a complainant may enact similar legislative measures or terminate its NAFTA relationship with the defendant.

The Rules of Procedure for binational panels, for the Extraordinary Challenge Committees, and the Special Committees and the Code of Conduct for proceedings under NAFTA's Chapters 19 and 20 may be found in Federal Register Volume 59, Number 1, of Monday, January 3, 1994.

NAFTA's Article 2022 requires the Advisory Committee on Private Commercial Disputes to report and provide recommendations to the NAFTA Commission on general issues referred to it by the Commission respecting the availability, use, and effectiveness of arbitration and other procedures for the resolution of private international commercial disputes in the free trade area.

TARIFF AND NON-TARIFF BARRIER ELIMINATION NAFTA's Chapter 3 eliminates import duties on goods originating within NAFTA. What goods originate in NAFTA and are eligible for preferential NAFTA tariffs is determined by an application of NAFTA's ROs. NAFTA provides for the elimination, either immediately or over the course of phase-out periods of 5 to 15 years, of virtually all tariffs, quotas, export taxes, and licenses on goods exported from one NAFTA country to another. Each NAFTA country may reimpose or suspend the elimination of tariffs when particular industries are seriously threatened by import surges as described more completely below.

Duties were removed in 1994 on key categories of goods, including computers and most automobiles. Duties on other products will be or have been phased out over 5 (1998), 10 (2003), and 15 (2008) year intervals. Duties on 50% of the 9,000 items covered by NAFTA ended on NAFTA's effective date, January 1, 1994. Tariffs on 15% more of the items ended in 1998 and the rest will be phased out in the sixth through fifteenth years. Those items subject to the final stages of tariff elimination are generally import-sensitive items, particularly those that the members particularly wish to protect because they are produced by substantial domestic industries in every one of the member countries. Among the products subject to the 15-year period are sneakers, ceramic tiles, household glassware, and a range of agricultural items. NAFTA permits exceptions to and acceleration of duty removal with the agreement of all NAFTA parties and significant acceleration has in fact occurred.

The duty reduction regime put in place between Canada and the US by USCFTA continued as scheduled until completed on the first day of 1999. US goods will lose their CFFTA eligibility if subsequently subjected to processing in Mexico that raises their value by more than 7%.

Chapter 3, Article 309, also removes non-tariff import and export restrictions, such as import licenses and quotas, unless existing restrictions have been "grandfathered." Removal of some nontariff restrictions will be phased-in, sometimes over a period of up to 15 years. Mexico may retain import licensing requirements on a long list of manufactured items, including computers and disk drives, for up to 10 years.

No taxes are to be imposed on exported goods unless the goods are subject to the same tax if consumed locally.

Duty deferral programs include foreign trade zones, temporary importations under bond, bonded warehouses, Mexican in-bond assembly *maquiladoras*, and inward processing programs. NAFTA provides a new method for duty remission with respect to importations of goods under any of the above duty deferral programs that are subsequently exported to another NAFTA country. NAFTA parties must grant duty free temporary admission to certain classes of goods imported from another NAFTA country.

None of the NAFTA countries may assess customs duties on goods that are exported for repair or alteration in another NAFTA country pursuant to a warranty and then reimported, regardless of the origin of the goods or whether they could have been altered or repaired in the exporting country. A NAFTA country may, however, choose to assess customs duties on the value of the repairs or alterations performed in another NAFTA country that are not pursuant to a warranty.

Special import tariff and non-tariff barrier reductions exist for certain classes of goods, particularly agricultural products, textiles and apparel, and vehicles and automotive products. These special regimes are described in some detail below.

SAFEGUARDS, ANTIDUMPING, AND COUNTERVAILING DUTIES NAFTA's Chapter 8 establishes the ground rules for when a NAFTA party may temporarily halt tariff reductions once (and only once) during an initial 10 year transition period to protect an industry that is being threatened with serious injury by surges in imports resulting from reductions. In such a case, the importing member may either suspend further reductions or, within limits, raise the duty on the product. Specific procedures and limitations for bilateral emergency action are provided in NAFTA's Article 801. When multilateral emergency actions are taken under GATT's provisions, NAFTA requires that goods originating from NAFTA parties be excluded from the global action unless those goods contribute substantially to the import injury. A NAFTA party against which emergency action is taken is entitled to compensation from the acting NAFTA party for any adverse tariff treatment. NAFTA's Article 803 requires the consistent, impartial, and reasonable administration of each NAFTA party's respective laws, decisions, and rulings governing emergency action proceedings through a competent investigating authority and the existence or creation by each NAFTA party of equitable, timely, transparent, and effective procedures for emergency action proceedings. An "Understanding Concerning Chapter Eight - Emergency Acts" was negotiated by President Clinton under which a working party with a broad mandate is to consider Chapter 8 issues. Certain safeguards are specially provided for agricultural products and financial services.

Canada has opted out of NAFTA's Article 802 bilateral provision and has maintained a similar provision—Article 1101—of USCFTA regarding bilateral emergency actions affecting it and the US. Where "escape clause" or "safeguards" relief is provided by national laws for domestic industries which are seriously damaged by fairly traded imported goods, Canada and the US agreed on procedures for granting relief and agreed to submit any disputes over the application of these laws to binding arbitration. USCFTA safeguards provisions differ from those of NAFTA in at least two important ways: (a) under USCFTA no safeguard action may be maintained for more than 3 years while NAFTA permits the acting party to extend the period specially for an additional year if the action involves sensitive products for which the NAFTA tariff elimination is particularly long and (b) USCFTA provides that the rate of duty to imposed following the emergency action is that which would have been in effect but for the action while NAFTA provides for a minitransition period of several months for the rate to float down to the level that it would have been but for the action.

Both Mexico and Canada were displeased with US AD/CVD laws but were unable to obtain significant modification of those laws through NAFTA negotiations. Canadian Trade Minister Roy MacLaren in a May 31, 1994, interview with *The Wall Street Journal* said that there is no possible economic rationale for preserving antidumping in a free trade area because antidumping rules are designed to prevent goods from being sold at unfairly low prices in a foreign market, not hinder the movement of goods within a free, open market, such as NAFTA is supposed to be. Although each NAFTA party may continue to apply its own AD/CVD law, each must advise the others in advance of any statutory changes to be made in that law. NAFTA's Chapter 19 focuses almost exclusively on new procedures for the review of AD/CVD decisions rendered by the administrative bodies of each NAFTA party.

GOVERNMENT PROCUREMENT Requirements of openness, transparency, and competitive bidding have been imposed on the procurement activities of NAFTA parties' federal government agencies and government-owned enterprises. Major government purchases above designated values (with some products, services, and governmental agencies in each country explicitly exempted) would be open to firms from all three countries, with a 10 year phase-out of Mexican limits for government energy companies. NAFTA would only prevent discrimination against local subsidiaries of NAFTA parties offering goods that originate in a NAFTA party. Detailed rules were established that each NAFTA party must implement in conducting procurements and in reviewing protests by disappointed NAFTA country bidders. Effective implementation, particularly in Mexico, is expected to be difficult and even problematic.

SPECIAL RULES FOR THE MOTOR VEHICLE SECTOR The US and Canada, under the Auto Pact, created a virtually integrated bilateral market in automotive products. Automotive products were also the largest component of US-Mexican and Mexican-Canadian trade at the time NAFTA was signed. Mexican automotive trade with the US and Canada will be fully integrated into a single market by 2004, subject only to questions regarding the definition of that market because of restrictive NAFTA rules of origin. Applicable ROs for motor vehicles are described below.

Mexico immediately reduced tariffs on Canadian- and US-made passenger automobiles by 50% on NAFTA's effective date and will phase out remaining tariffs over a 10 year period. Canada gained immediate access into Mexico for medium and heavy duty trucks and buses.

Mexican and Canadian tariffs on most auto parts were removed within 5 years and those on all automotive products are to be terminated within 10 years under a common tariff elimination schedule. Mexican duties on 75% of US auto parts were eliminated within 5 years. Mexico requires automotive companies to export $2 of automotive products for every $1 of imports. This requirement is to be reduced in stages and eliminated by 2004. Mexico may require an enterprise to maintain value added of up to 20% of its total sales in order to be considered a national supplier (and independent *maquiladoras* may receive national supplier status) or autoparts industry enterprise. The permissible means by which Mexico may calculate national value are prescribed in NAFTA and will change over a 15 year NAFTA phase-in period. NAFTA party investors could immediately invest up to 100% in Mexican national suppliers of parts and up to 49%—gradually increased to 100% over 5 years—in other automotive enterprises. Mexico will phase-out its ban on US and Canadian used cars over a period of 10 years, based on the age of the car. Canada will eliminate prohibitions on the importation of used Mexican motor vehicles over a 10 year period. The US immediately eliminated tariffs on NAFTA passenger cars, reduced the NAFTA light truck tariff to 10% with a phase-out in 5 years, and will totally eliminate tariffs on all NAFTA vehicles within 10 years. The US definition of domestically-produced parts and components was changed by a modification of the fleet content definition in the Energy Policy and Conservation Act.

SPECIAL RULES FOR TEXTILES The special ROs for textiles are described below. NAFTA's provisions regarding the trade in textiles take precedence over other agreements between the NAFTA parties regarding textile products. Most US-Mexican tariffs on textiles will disappear after 6 years, the remainder in 10. US-Canada textile tariffs were phased out by 1999 under USCFTA's schedule. All US quotas on Mexican textile products and apparel were immediately eliminated. For all but the 14 products that do not satisfy NAFTA's ROs, a tariff quota is established with imports up to the quota level paying a preferential duty and the over-quota shipments paying the MFN rate. Canada will unilaterally cut many of its textile yarn and fabric quotas on an MFN basis. Canada and Mexico have a 10 year reciprocal tariff phase-out period for apparel and an 8 year period for most textile products.

THE ENERGY SECTOR NAFTA's Chapter 6 deals with energy. Energy was made subject to special conditions and far less trade and investment liberalization than other sectors, largely because of the Mexican Constitution (and the strong public sentiment and historical experience underpinning it) that reserves to the Mexican state all ownership of Mexico's basic energy resources.

"CULTURAL INDUSTRY" Although the "cultural industry," *i.e.*, the publication of books, magazines, and newspapers; motion pictures and video recordings; music recording; and radio, television, and cable television broadcasting, was essentially excluded from USCFTA's and NAFTA's coverage in recognition of Canada's concerns regarding the preservation of a distinctive Canadian culture, Canada's exercise of any exclusion from USCFTA's and NAFTA's coverage of these economic sectors in a manner inconsistent with USCFTA or NAFTA will create a right by the US Government to take measures with an equivalent commercial effect notwithstanding any other USCFTA restrictions.

AGRICULTURAL TRADE Agricultural trade (covered in NAFTA's Chapter 7, Subchapter A for cross border trade in agricultural products and Subchapter B for sanitary and phytosanitary measures that may affect trade) was the only subject where NAFTA did not involve a trilateral agreement (although provisions of Chapter 7 dealing, *inter alia*, with domestic support measures and export subsidies, apply to all NAFTA countries). There were two bilateral agreements instead: Mexico-US (Annex 703.2, Section A) and Mexico-Canada (Annex 703.2, Section B).

US-Canadian trade continues to be covered by USCFTA. USCFTA focused on harmonizing technical standards and eliminating nontariff barriers. Canadian supply management programs and US support and marketing order programs were largely unaffected by USCFTA. Both countries agreed to phase out all tariffs on agricultural products over a 10 year period. In the case of fresh fruits and vegetables, for 20 years either country may apply tariffs (called "snap-backs") up to 180 days each year under certain price and production conditions, although the tariffs may not exceed the MFN rate. Canadian import licenses for wheat, barley, oats, and related products will not be required for US products as soon as the support levels for these products are equal in both countries. Both countries have reserved the right to impose or reimpose import restrictions on particular grains if imports increase significantly as a result of a substantial change in either country's support program for any such grain. Both countries agreed to exempt each other from their respective meat import laws and Canada raised its global import quotas for poultry, eggs, and their products to the average annual level of actual shipments of the five years preceding USCFTA. The US agreed not to impose restrictions on products from Canada containing 10% or less of sugar by dry weight for purposes of restricting the sugar content of those products. Technical barriers, such as differences in health and sanitary regulations, which complicate or restrict bilateral trade in agricultural products, foods, and beverages were to be reduced through closer cooperation between the regulatory authorities of both countries. Both countries agreed not to use export subsidies for agricultural products sold to the other and agreed to consider the interests of the other when subsidizing agricultural exports to third country markets. The Canadian supply management farm marketing board system was unaffected by USCFTA and continues to control the supply of certain domestically produced agricultural products and limits the total volume of such imports to Canada.

Essentially free trade in agricultural products between the US and Mexico will be in place after a transitional period of 15 years, subject only to temporary safeguard measures and to the provisions of the countervailing duty and antidumping laws.

The US agreed to eliminate its barriers against a large variety of Mexican horticultural products and against sugar and cotton. Mexico agreed to end its restrictions on field crops, dry beans, pork, potatoes, apples, and dry milk. Tariffs covering 57% by value of US-Mexican farm trade were eliminated immediately. An additional 6% of US-Mexican agricultural trade will be liberalized over five years and 23% more over ten years. The remainder, principally for sugar, orange juice, and peanuts, will be converted to a tariff quota and be phased-out over 10 to 15 years. Almost all nontariff barriers were eliminated immediately, generally through a conversion to ordinary tariffs or to tariff-rate quotas under which a tariff kicks in only if imports exceed a given quota for the year. Liberalization of the NAFTA sugar trade will be at the expense of the quotas of other sugar producers, notably those in the Caribbean.

In the first 10 years, Mexico will charge Canadian imports with tariff rates paralleling the rate on imports from the US and both countries will maintain nontariff barriers on sensitive products, such as dairy, poultry, and eggs. Except for sensitive products, import licenses will be replaced with quotas.

NAFTA addresses the issues of domestic support, export subsidies, and agricultural marketing standards with a general view to moving toward liberalized trade and fewer restrictions. Regarding subsidies in particular, NAFTA parties must provide 3 days notice of the introduction of any new agricultural product export subsidy, consultation must be sought on any action against subsidized agricultural imports, and no export subsidy may be imposed to counter another NAFTA party's actions.

There are two types of safeguards for agriculture: a 10 year tariff quota for certain listed agricultural products and a 3 year "snap back" to the pre-NAFTA tariff rate for any agricultural product where imports are a substantial cause of serious injury to the domestic industry. The snap back provision under FTA was for certain fresh fruits and vegetables whose import prices fall below a certain percentage of the average monthly import price and the planted acreage of the agricultural product is within certain limits.

NAFTA's Chapter 7, Subchapter B, deals with the trade in agricultural products and with sanitary and phytosanitary measures. Its objectives are to eliminate nontariff barriers to agricultural trade; eliminate tariff barriers over a 10 year period (15 years for particularly sensitive products); encourage the NAFTA countries to eliminate export subsidies and to limit domestic support measure to those which do not distort trade; ensure common application of agricultural classification, grading, and marketing standards; and avoid trade barriers resulting from sanitary or phytosanitary measures which are not based on scientific principles, are unfairly applied, or are not necessary to provide a country's chosen level of protection. When either Mexico or the US applies a measure regarding the classification, grading, or marketing of a domestic agricultural good, it will provide no less favorable treatment to like products imported from the other country for processing.

CROSS-BORDER INVESTMENTS GENERALLY Chapter 11 of NAFTA deals with foreign investments. It provides to investors from one NAFTA party substantial rights to invest in the territory of another NAFTA party and substantial protections for their investments once they are made. Investment is generally defined to include equity and debt investments in any business enterprise, any tangible or intangible property used for business purposes, and certain loans.

CROSS-BORDER SERVICES NAFTA's Chapter 12 deals with services and provides that any service provider from a NAFTA party is entitled to the better of national or MFN treatment.

INTELLECTUAL PROPERTY RIGHTS Intellectual property is covered by NAFTA's Chapter 14 and parts of Chapter 17. Each NAFTA country must provide adequate and effective protection and enforce intellectual property rights granted by other NAFTA countries. Each country must treat foreign NAFTA-party applicants the same as their nationals and provide effective enforcement of their rights. Each country must give effect to the substantive provisions of several enumerated international intellectual property conventions.

THE TEMPORARY TRANSBORDER MOVEMENT OF PERSONS FOR PROFESSIONAL PURPOSES NAFTA parties have sought to simplify and expedite the process for temporary, business-related admissions of citizens of one party into the territory of another party. Nonetheless, the reciprocal rights between Canada and the US under USCFTA in this regard have been retained and only lesser and gradually phased-in transborder movement rights are available to Mexicans entering the US.

NAFTA AND THE ENVIRONMENT Standards set by international environmental treaties will take precedence over NAFTA, and NAFTA countries agree to work together to enhance safety, health, environmental, and consumer protection standards. NAFTA countries agree not to seek competitive advantage by maintaining lower environmental standards than other NAFTA countries. A supplemental agreement created a new trilateral Commission on Environmental Cooperation and other institutions to promote cooperation on the development, improvement, and effective enforcement of environmental laws and regulations.

NAFTA AND LABOR STANDARDS A supplemental agreement created a new trilateral Commission on Labor Cooperation and other institutions to promote and improve labor laws and standards and to provide for the effective enforcement of those laws and standards. The parties committed to a number of "labor principles" and sought to achieve three objectives. The first was collaboration, cooperation, and information exchange among the NAFTA parties. The second was to make explicit and highly visible each country's labor laws and their implementation. The last was the use of effective mechanisms to encourage the enforcement of national labor laws. Fines up to US$20 million may be imposed on NAFTA governments but not upon private parties.

NAFTA'S RULES OF ORIGIN (ROS)? NAFTA is not a customs union like the EU. NAFTA is in transition to becoming solely a free trade area under which goods and services of the region may move freely within the region with the imposition of no or little tariffs or impediments when crossing regional national borders. There is no common tariff (except on computers and related items) for NAFTA members so it is important to exclude from NAFTA benefits goods produced outside the region. Consequently, the question of what is, and is not, a "NAFTA" product assumes great importance. Whether goods moving across the common borders of the three countries will be given the special tariff and other treatment of NAFTA depends entirely on whether or not (or to what degree) they are deemed to be NAFTA products. ROs are what determine the answers to that question. There are no objective answers to this question. The question is answered only on the basis of negotiated standards as delineated in NAFTA. Because any standard will be of pecuniary value to one or more countries and/or interest groups while it will cause economic harm to others, the negotiation of those standards was contentious and very much subject to political concerns and to pressures from national constituencies. The result was a politically acceptable agreement for each country. It was not a simple, internally consistent, strictly logical, or universally-endorsed result.

Details of NAFTA's ROs also owe much to the often unhappy experience (particularly for Canada) of applying the ROs under USCFTA. The single most prominent problem to arise under the USCFTA ROs—the dispute over calculation of the Canadian content in Honda automobiles—appears to have been successfully resolved by NAFTA's adoption of alternative tests for measuring regional value content ("RVC").

Not all goods "made" in Canada, Mexico, and the US qualify for NAFTA benefits. NAFTA's Article 401 precludes goods from other countries from obtaining those benefits by merely passing through a NAFTA country. Goods may not "originate" in Canada, Mexico, or the US, as that term is defined in NAFTA, but still be an "article" of Canada, Mexico, or the US for country of origin marking, statistical, or other purposes.

Although GATT dealt with ROs and there was a separate Agreement on Rules of Origin in the WTO Agreement, international standards for ROs remain both rudimentary and newly-minted.

No specific domestic content is required in order for most products to qualify for NAFTA benefits. NAFTA thereby differs from other US preferential duty programs that require a specified percentage of value to be imparted in the country claiming the duty benefit. It also differs from US customs standards for determining origin in product, marking, quota compliance, or trade sanctions cases, under which origin is conferred on the country in which the last "substantial transformation" occurred.

A primary concern in NAFTA negotiations was to assure that Asian manufacturers could not gain NAFTA's duty free benefits without making significant investments in Mexico. ROs are the principal means of addressing these export platform concerns.

NAFTA's ROs apply only to goods. Establishing when service providers are offering genuinely NAFTA services may prove difficult. Qualifying services are from providers controlled by persons from NAFTA countries or—subject to challenge—that have substantial business activities in a NAFTA country.

A determination under NAFTA's ROs of a change in origin through the transformation of imported "nonoriginating" components, parts, or materials will largely be based on whether transformation has been sufficient to make the minimum required move of the designation of the item within the tariff schedule. As a consequence, it was of critical importance that each of the NAFTA countries had adopted the Harmonized System of Tariff Classifications. This permits NAFTA's administrators and each of the member countries' implementing statutes and regulations to make reference to a commonly used and understood basis for determining when those changes, which are similarly articulated in each of their national tariff schedules, have occurred. Also a consequence of NAFTA's deference to the Harmonized System is the increased importance of the decisions of the Harmonized System Committee under the Convention on the Harmonized Commodity Description and Coding System in Brussels, Belgium—the international body which interprets and amends that System.

NAFTA devotes 193 pages to the issue of ROs. It generally requires that the product be made of an "originating" product and sometimes that a minimum percentage of a product's components be made in NAFTA before the product may be shipped duty free among the NAFTA countries. Although NAFTA's ROs are complex, they essentially hinge on the issues of determining (a) if a product or material is NAFTA originating and (b) the calculation of RVC. The content requirement and determinations of whether items have been transformed into originating materials or goods vary from product to product. Special rules are applicable to motor vehicles and automotive products, textiles and apparel, and some electronic products.

BASIC RO RULES UNDER NAFTA'S CHAPTER 4

NAFTA's Chapter 4 establishes the rules for determining which goods originate in NAFTA and are therefore eligible for duty free treatment and other benefits under NAFTA. The negotiators adopted the same basic ROs as governed USCFTA, *i.e.*, goods not wholly obtained or produced within the free trade area must generally themselves (or a requisite percentage of their imported components, parts, and materials) undergo sufficient processing within NAFTA to result in a change in tariff classification. NAFTA's Annex 401 establishes specific ROs based on a change in tariff classification, an RVC, or both. NAFTA's ROs differ greatly from those used under other US trade agreements and US customs practices.

The rules for determining origin under NAFTA are complex, costly to administer, and subject to many exceptions and special provisions. It is important to bear in mind that items made from imported "nonoriginating" parts, components, or materials may be transformed into NAFTA "originating" items. Determining when this has and has not been done is one of the most challenging issues facing those wishing to avail themselves of NAFTA. A good may be produced partly in one NAFTA country and be completed in another and still qualify for NAFTA benefits. NAFTA origin for NAFTA benefits purposes is available under NAFTA's Article 401 to goods that:

(a) are wholly obtained or produced (*i.e.*, natural resources, agricultural goods, scrap, and waste, or goods produced in the NAFTA territory from the above goods or from their derivatives at any stage of production) in NAFTA territory;

(b) are not wholly obtained or produced (*i.e.*, some or all foreign materials/components are imported into NAFTA territory and become "originating" NAFTA goods through further processing or manufacturing such as to result in a requisite "tariff shift" or "tariff change") in NAFTA territory;

(c) are produced entirely in NAFTA territory from materials originating in NAFTA territory (*i.e.*, finished goods manufactured in NAFTA territory exclusively from either wholly originating goods or imported raw materials which have been further processed such as to have become "NAFTA originating" through a requisite "tariff shift" or "tariff change" into intermediate materials); or

(d) are unassembled/disassembled and non-originating and the parts provided for same [*i.e.*, the goods are imported as complete but unassembled or disassembled inventories of finished goods and/or the parts provided for such finished goods but do not undergo the tariff changes required by NAFTA's Annex 401 to be originating goods and are

(i) imported into the NAFTA territory in an unassembled or disassembled form but are classified as assembled goods pursuant to General Rule of Interpretation 2(a) of the Harmonized Tariff System or

(ii) the goods are produced using materials imported into a NAFTA country that are provided for as parts according to the HTS and those parts are classified in the same subheading or undivided heading as the finished goods],

but for such goods to obtain special NAFTA benefits they must satisfy an RVC requirement (60% using the transaction value method and 50% using the net cost method) and wearing apparel and textiles may never qualify for favorable NAFTA treatment under this category.

A "tariff shift" or "tariff change" results when the NAFTA-dictated necessary change in HTS tariff classification occurs, which may be to the two (chapter), four (heading), or six (subheading) digit level, depending on circumstances. A check for exceptions to the general rules regarding tariff shifts should always be made. When an RO is based on a change in tariff classification, each of nonoriginating material used in the production of the goods must undergo the applicable change as a result of production occurring entirely in the NAFTA region, *i.e.*, the nonoriginating materials are classified under one tariff provision prior to processing and classified under another upon completion of processing. Specific ROs in NAFTA's Annex 401 define exactly what change in tariff classification must occur for a good to be considered originating.

NAFTA's Annex 401.1 provides an extensive enumeration of the tariff changes required in order to confer NAFTA origin on products produced from non-NAFTA components. The tariff category listings on NAFTA's Annex 401.1 will, in most cases, indicate the operations required to meet the change of tariff test for each item. There is no minimum domestic content required for most products to qualify for NAFTA benefits. The determinative requirement is whether, after undergoing processing in NAFTA territory, the product falls into a new tariff category as specified in NAFTA's Annex 401.1. The cost, complexity, and investment required to achieve and document a tariff classification change will differ from product to product.

To make most of these determinations, a person must first know the HTS number of a good and the tariff numbers of all the non-NAFTA materials used to produce the good. NAFTA's Annex 401 gives the applicable RO opposite each HTS number. The only reliable method for a manufacturer to determine whether a product will qualify for NAFTA origin under NAFTA is to review carefully the governing customs rulings in the tariff classification for the categories at issue or to obtain an advance ruling under procedures established in NAFTA's Chapter 5.

"RVC" requires that a certain percentage of value be added in the NAFTA territory for the good to qualify. For many goods, only a tariff shift is required to qualify for NAFTA benefits and there is no RVC requirement. For many others, to qualify the goods may be subject to *either* a tariff shift or an RVC. For some, *only* an RVC will make the goods qualifying.

NAFTA's Article 402 creates two methods of calculating the RVC of a good:

(a) Dividing the "transaction value ("TV")," which is the price actually charged (adjusted to an F.O.B. basis) for the finished good, less the price paid for non-NAFTA-origin materials used in the production of the good ("VNM") by the transaction value and then multiplying the result by 100, *i.e.*,

RVC = [(TV - VNM)/TV] x 100, and

(b) Dividing the "net cost ("NC")," which is the net cost to the producer of producing the good (in arriving at the net cost, the producer may exclude the sales, marketing, servicing, royalty, shipping, and nonallowable costs but there is a limitation for allowable interest), less the price paid for non-NAFTA-origin materials used in the production of the good ("VNM"), by the net cost and then multiplying the result by 100, *i.e.*,

RVC = [(NC - VNM)/NC] x 100.

The exporter or producer may elect the method to be used for each item. The transaction value is usually simpler to use but sometimes cannot be used (such as when there is no transaction value, in some related party transactions, for certain motor vehicles and parts, and when a producer is accumulating regional value). Where the transaction value cannot be used or yields a less favorable result, the net cost method—respectively—must or may be used. The transaction value is calculated using the total price paid for the good with certain adjustments, as established under the principles of the GATT Customs Valuation Code, for packing and other items. Because the transaction value method permits the producer to count all of its costs and profits as territorial, the required percentage of RVC under this method is higher than under the net cost method.

An imported material may be transformed into a NAFTA originating material through inputs in the NAFTA territory. It may then be sold to parties that could use it as originating material in the calculation of RVCs when it is incorporated into a finished product. Without an additional rule, however, the party transforming the imported material into originating material could not itself use that transformed originating material in calculating RVC if it incorporated that material into a finished good. Such a result would be both unfair to the vertically integrated party and contrary to society's interest in cost-efficiency dictated economic practices. That necessary rule was one that established recognition of an intermediate material. The benefit of designating an intermediate material is that the producer may treat self-produced materials similarly to the way in which it would treat an originating material purchased at arm's length for purposes of determining the value of the nonoriginating materials of the final goods.

An intermediate material is a self-produced material which is designated by the producer, meets the ROs of NAFTA's Article 401, and is incorporated into the final good. NAFTA's Article 415 defines a "self-produced material" as a material produced by the same party that produced the final goods and which is used in the production of those final goods. For purposes of calculating the RVC of final goods, NAFTA's Article 402(10) allows a producer to designate as an intermediate material any self-produced, originating material used in the production of the final goods. As long as the intermediate material qualifies as an originating material, its entire value may be treated as originating in determining the RVC of the finished goods.

An intermediate material may be composed of originating and nonoriginating submaterials. After determining that an intermediate material satisfies the applicable RO under NAFTA's Article 401, the total cost to produce that intermediate material is treated as an originating cost and the value of the nonoriginating materials used to produce the intermediate materials would not be counted as part of the value of nonoriginating materials when calculating the RVC of the final goods. If the intermediate material must satisfy a minimum RVC to qualify as originating, the net cost method must be used to calculate that RVC. A producer may make any number of intermediate material designations provided that no material subject to an RVC requirement may be designated as an intermediate material if it contains submaterials also subject to an RVC requirement that were also designated as intermediate materials. Where a single producer designates intermediate materials that qualify as originating solely based on a tariff change, that is, without having to satisfy an RVC requirement, subsequent designations can be made with previously designated intermediate materials.

There are two methods for determining the value of an intermediate material:

(a) the total cost incurred with respect to all goods produced that can be reasonably allocated to that intermediate materials; or

(b) the aggregate of each cost that forms part of the total cost incurred with respect to that intermediate material that can be reasonably allocated to that intermediate material.

The two methods allow producers to select the one that best fits their production and accounting practices. The value of the intermediate material should be approximately the same using either method. However, the net cost method must be used for intermediate materials subject to an RVC requirement. NAFTA's Article 402(8) lists those costs which may not be included when calculating the RVC of the intermediate material using the net cost method: (a) sales promotion, including marketing and after-sales service costs; (b) royalties; (c) shipping and packing costs; and (d) non-allowable interest costs. Although these costs are excluded in the net cost calculation, they form part of the total material costs. Accordingly, costs such as royalties are excluded when calculating the net cost when determining whether the material satisfies an RVC requirement (and thus originates and can be designated as an originating material), but are included in the total value of the material once its origin has been determined. As noted above, the total value of an intermediate material may be counted as an originating cost.

When producers determine the RVC of goods, the entire value of the materials used in the production of the goods that they acquire from suppliers is considered as wholly originating or wholly nonoriginating, as appropriate. The accumulation provision allows a producer/exporter of goods to choose to include as part of the goods' RVC any regional value added by suppliers of nonoriginating materials used to produce the final goods. Accumulation reduces the value of the nonoriginating materials used in the production of the good by taking into account the NAFTA inputs incorporated into those nonoriginating materials. Thus, a producer unable to satisfy an RVC requirement based on (i) its own processing costs and (ii) the value of originating materials it uses to produce a good may use accumulation to include any regional value added in the NAFTA territory by other persons who produced nonoriginating materials subsequently incorporated into the final good.

Conditions for using accumulation are: (a) producers or exporters who choose to use accumulation must use the net cost method to calculate any RVC; (b) producers/exporters of goods must obtain information on net cost and the RVC of nonoriginating materials used to make their goods from the producers/suppliers of those materials (government authorities will not obtain this information for them); (c) all nonoriginating materials used in the production of the goods must undergo the tariff classification change set out in NAFTA's Annex 401 and the goods must satisfy any applicable RVC requirement entirely in the territory of one or more of the NAFTA countries; and (d) the goods must satisfy all other applicable requirements of the RO.

Although requiring a change in tariff classification is a very simple principle, it requires that *all* originating materials undergo the required change. A very low percentage of the materials may not undergo the tariff change, thus preventing the goods from originating. Therefore, NAFTA contains a *de minimis* provision that allows goods to qualify as originating provided such materials are not more than a certain percentage (7% in most cases) of the transaction value of the goods adjusted to an FOB basis or, in some cases, of the total cost of the goods. In addition, where failure of materials to undergo a required change in tariff classification triggers a requirement for a minimum RVC, the calculation of that RVC is waived if the value of *all* nonoriginating materials used in the production of the goods is not more than the specified *de minimis* amount. However, if after application of the *de minimis* allowance the goods must still meet an RVC requirement in order to qualify as originating (that is, if the value of all nonoriginating materials exceeds the applicable *de minimis* allowance), the value of all nonoriginating materials must be taken into account in calculating the RVC. For textile goods classified in HTS Chapters 50 through 63, the *de minimus* rule is applied by weight instead of by value to the component of the good that determines its tariff classification in accordance with the HTS General Rules of Interpretation. For agricultural products provided for in HTS's Chapters 1 through 27, NAFTA's Article 405 *de minimis* rule does not apply unless the nonoriginating materials are classified in subheadings different from the subheading in which the finished goods are classified. The *de minimus* amount for cigars, cheroots, cigarillos, and cigarettes are 9%, not 7%. *De minimis* rules do not apply to specially designated materials.

NAFTA's Article 415 specifies that fungible goods and materials are goods and materials that are interchangeable for commercial purposes and have essentially identical properties. When a producer mixes originating and nonoriginating fungible goods so that physical identification of originating goods is impossible, the producer may determine origin of those goods based on any of the standard inventory accounting methods, *e.g.*, FIFO or LIFO, specified in the Uniform Regulations.

ROS FOR ACCESSORIES, SPARE PARTS, AND TOOLS

Accessories, spare parts, and tools that are delivered with the goods and that form part of the goods' standard accessories, spare parts, or tools are considered originating if the goods originate. They are disregarded in determining whether all the nonoriginating materials fall under any NAFTA Annex 401 tariff change. This provision applies provided the accessories, spare parts, and tools are invoiced with the goods and the quantities and value are customary for the goods. However, if goods are subject to an RVC requirement, the value of the accessories, spare parts, and tools are to be accounted as originating or nonoriginating materials, as the case may be, in calculating the goods' RVC.

PACKAGING FOR RETAIL SALE AND ROS "Packaging" and "packing" are used in NAFTA in different contexts. "Packaging" refers to retail sales while "packing" is used for shipping purposes. Packaging materials and containers in which goods are packaged for retail sale, if classified with the goods, are disregarded in determining whether all the nonoriginating materials used in the production of the goods undergo the applicable change in tariff classification set out in NAFTA's Annex 401. However, if the goods are subject to an RVC requirement, the value of the retail packaging materials and containers is taken in to account as originating or nonoriginating materials, as the case may be, in calculating the RVC of the goods.

PACKING FOR SHIPMENT AND ROS Packing materials and containers in which goods are packed for shipment are disregarded in determining whether nonoriginating materials used in the production of the goods undergo an applicable change in tariff classification set out in NAFTA's Annex 401 and in determining whether the goods satisfy an RVC requirement.

TRANSSHIPMENT AND ROS Goods that qualify as originating will lose that status if they subsequently undergo any operation outside the NAFTA territory, other than unloading, reloading, or any other operation necessary to preserve them in good condition or to transport the goods to any of the NAFTA parties.

OPERATIONS THAT DO NOT CONFER ORIGIN NAFTA's Article 412 provides that goods shall not be considered to originate if they are merely diluted with water or another substance that does not materially alter the characteristic of the goods. Thus, mere dilution—even if it results in a change in tariff classification—is not sufficient to confer origin. However, dilution coupled with another process may be sufficient to materially alter the characteristic of the goods and thereby confer origin. The same Article also indicates that goods will not be considered to originate if a preponderance of the evidence establishes that any production or pricing practice has been used to circumvent the intent of the Chapter 4 ROs. The ROs are designed to ensure that the processing and costs incurred with respect to the products are commercially significant and appropriate to the goods, as defined by the tariff change rules and, when applicable, the RVC rules.

NAFTA'S SPECIAL ROS Special RO rules for automobiles and automotive products, textiles and fibers, and electronic products increase the percentage RVC required or otherwise specially modify origin and transformation NAFTA benefits qualification requirements.

AUTOMOTIVE ROS NAFTA's Article 403 creates special origin requirements for automotive goods claiming NAFTA benefits. NAFTA's ROs for automotive products are based on a tariff change alone or on a tariff change and RVC requirement (calculated using the net cost method). An allocation of sales and servicing costs may count as part of the RVC. Producers of automotive and components goods may elect to average their costs when calculating RVC under categories of costs designated in detail by NAFTA. Accumulation, fungible goods, and intermediate materials provisions may also be useful in integrating and rationalizing NAFTA region production processes.

"Tracing" is required by NAFTA for certain components enumerated in NAFTA's Annexes 403.1 and .2. Tracing ensures greater accuracy in calculating RVC by tracking the value of major automotive components and subassemblies imported into the NAFTA region. Nonoriginating value is reflected in the calculation of the RVC of the final products, limiting "roll-up" and "roll-down" that count the full value of goods as originating or nonoriginating even when a combination of the two. Any nonoriginating value remains so through all stages of assembly until RVC is calculated for components subject to tracing.

Passenger autos, light trucks, and engines must contain NAFTA content, calculated on net cost basis, of 50% until 1998 when the requirement rises to 56% and caps at 62.5% beginning in 2002. Other vehicles and parts must reach 50%, 55%, and 60% levels according to the same schedule and calculated on the same basis. Other tariff and nontariff barriers to the trade in motorized vehicles will be eliminated.

The US wanted to effectively bar foreign investors from utilizing NAFTA for automobile-related assembly. Mexico and Canada wanted to encourage foreign investors to invest in that industry under it. A compromise was reached. For new plants built to produce autos of a new "class, marque, or size and underbody," the NAFTA content requirement is reduced to 50% for the first five years of production. For refitted plants producing a new "class, marque, or size and underbody of car," the requirement is reduced to 50% for two years. The Suzuki-General Motors plant in Ingersoll, Ontario, Canada, was treated specially. Vehicles produced at this plant may enter the US, but not the Mexican, market at a preferred rate.

TEXTILE ROS Textiles are governed by a separate annex to Chapter 4. The *de minimis* amount for textiles is 7% by weight and not by value. The Chapter 4 criteria used for wool fabric (including blended materials with wool except for wool suits, an important Canadian export to the US) is chief value.

NAFTA's Chapter 4 establishes a "yarn forward" requirement for most products. Under this test, textiles and clothing produced in a NAFTA country must be produced from yarn (but not necessarily fiber) produced in a NAFTA country to be eligible for NAFTA benefits.

Easier ROs govern certain knitted underwear, brassieres, and shirts made from fabric in short supply in the NAFTA region and textile and apparel articles made of fabric not commonly produced in the NAFTA region. For example, silk and linen apparel articles follow a "single-transformation" instead of a "yarn-forward" rule which grants NAFTA benefits if nonoriginating fabric is cut and sewn in one or more NAFTA countries.

Cotton products and other fibers produced in abundance in the NAFTA region are subject to a "fiber forward" rule which requires that fibers must be made in a NAFTA country and subsequent processing must occur in a NAFTA country if the final product is to be eligible for NAFTA benefits.

Clothing and fabrics not qualifying under the above ROs may nonetheless benefit from reduced tariff rates under tariff preference levels ("TPLs") which establish tariff rate quotas. TPLs permit specified quantities of certain fibers, yarns, and fabrics that do not satisfy NAFTA's Article 401 ROs but which are still subject to significant processing in the NAFTA region to be eligible for NAFTA benefits. Imported quantities exceeding TPL levels are subject to Most-Favored-Nation tariffs.

ELECTRONIC PRODUCTS ROS ROs for a number of electronic products are based strictly on a tariff change structured to require that key subassemblies of the products are produced in the NAFTA region. Other electronic products may originate in one of two ways: (a) by satisfying a tariff change or by meeting a less substantial tariff change (usually transformation of parts into a finished good) and (b) by satisfying an RVC requirement.

VERIFICATION OF ORIGIN AND ADMINISTRATION UNDER NAFTA'S CHAPTER 5 NAFTA's Chapter 5 provides safeguards for ensuring that only goods satisfying NAFTA's ROs are accorded preferential tariff treatment. These include origin verifications and advance rulings. In addition, it provides for record keeping requirements and cooperation between the member countries on customs-related matters. NAFTA established a working group to address future Chapter 5 modifications.

CERTIFICATES OF ORIGIN A uniform certificate of origin ("CO") must be prepared and signed by the exporter for single or multiple (called a "blanket certificate" and valid if all transactions are completed within a 12 month period specified on the CO) importations of identical goods. It certifies that a good being exported from one NAFTA member into the territory of another qualifies as an "originating good." Only importers with a valid CO may claim preferential NAFTA treatment for their imported goods. COs are available in French, Spanish, or English and may, at the exporter's discretion, be completed in either the language of the exporting or the importing country. Importers may, upon request, be required to submit copies and/or translations of COs to their own customs administrations.

COs are not required for the commercial or noncommercial importation of goods worth no more than US$1,250. A NAFTA member may, however, demand that shipping invoices for commercial importations contain a statement that the goods qualify as originating goods.

A false statement by an exporter in a NAFTA country's territory to the effect that a good to be exported to the territory of another NAFTA country qualifies as an originating good has the same legal consequences as applies to an importer in the first country's territory with respect to making false statements. Where an exporter voluntarily corrects an erroneous CO, the exporter is not subject to penalties with respect to making the erroneous classification. Exporters or producers that complete a CO must notify all parties to which such CO was given of any change that would affect its accuracy or validity.

When claiming preferential tariff treatment for an imported product, an importer must declare that the product qualifies as an originating good. The importer must base this declaration on a valid CO. When an importer omits making a justifiable claim for preferential tariff treatment, the importer may, within one year of the date on which the good was imported, apply for a refund of any excess duties paid as a result of the good not having been accorded preferential tariff treatment.

VERIFICATION OF CLAIMS OF ORIGIN The customs administration of each NAFTA country may verify whether a good imported into its territory qualifies as an originating good. This is done, in part, either by submitting written questionnaires to the exporter or by visits to the premises of an exporter or producer in the territory of the exporting country. NAFTA provides elaborate rules that effectively preclude surprise verification visits into other countries. For example, an exporter must give written consent to a verification visit. However, should an exporter or producer not give its written consent to a proposed verification visit by the customs administration of another NAFTA country, that country may deny preferential tariff treatment to the good that would have been the subject of the verification visit. Confidential business information collected will be kept confidential within the importing country's customs administration. After the customs authority of the importing country establishes whether the good originates, it must issue a written determination to the exporter/producer of its findings. Such determinations may be reviewed and appealed in the importing country at the request of the exporter or producer.

ADVANCE RULINGS Importers, exporters, and producers may obtain advance rulings from the customs administration of the country into which the goods are to be imported on (a) whether NAFTA's Annex 401 changes to imported materials have been undergone in specific cases; (b) whether a good satisfies an RVC requirement; (c) the calculation of the transactional value or the net cost of the good or of the materials used in the production of a good to determine an RVC; (d) whether a good qualifies as an originating good; (e) whether a good that reenters its territory after the good has been exported from its territory to another NAFTA country for repair or alteration qualifies for NAFTA duty free treatment; (f) whether the proposed or actual marking satisfies country of origin marking under NAFTA's Annex 311; (g) whether an originating good qualifies as a good of a NAFTA country under NAFTA's Annexes 300-B or 302.2 or Chapter 7; and (h) whether a good is a qualifying good under Chapter 7. Each member country has established procedures for the issuance of advance rulings, including a detailed description of the information required to process an application. NAFTA countries are bound by the rulings they issue, but such rulings may be (in certain limited circumstances) modified or revoked.

REVIEW AND APPEAL A member country must give exporters and producers located in other member countries' territories substantially the same rights of review and appeal of its origin determinations, marking determinations, and advance rulings as it provides to importers in its own territory. This must include one level of administrative review independent of the official or office responsible for the appealed determination as well as judicial or quasijudicial review.

UNIFORMITY OF NATIONAL RO RULES Member countries must establish uniform regulations regarding the interpretation, application, and administration of the ROs. Each member country must notify the other member countries of any determination of origin issued as a result of an origin verification as well as any determination that is contrary to another member country's rulings. NAFTA members must also cooperate in customs-related matters, such as the collection and exchange of statistics and the harmonization of documentation used in trade.

RECORD KEEPING Exporters and importers must maintain records relating to COs for a period of five years (longer if one's NAFTA country requires it). The aim of this requirement is to facilitate verification of NAFTA origin by permitting customs officials to trace components to their ultimate origin and to determine with precision production costs and assists incurred in NAFTA manufacture. The records required to be maintained include those related to the purchase of, cost of, value of, and payment for the good that is exported and the materials used in the production of that good. Documentation requirements impose burdensome record keeping duties on companies required to verify that their goods contain the requisite NAFTA content. Tracing of component and production stage costs is particularly difficult for small- and medium-size businesses who normally do not maintain records in such detail. For products on which the import duties are low to begin with, the cost of additional record keeping may eliminate the savings realized from obtaining duty free NAFTA benefits. The record keeping burdens imposed by NAFTA are so onerous that many importers may choose to forego the benefits of duty free or reduced duty NAFTA origin claims.

OAS

The Organization of American States ("OAS," see http://www.oas.org) is based in Washington, DC, and has as members all countries of the Western Hemisphere except Cuba, which was expelled. It was founded in 1948. It is the principal forum for inter-American affairs. Under its auspices, many activities and programs are conducted, including the Inter-American Judicial Committee that sponsors Inter-American Specialized Conferences on Private Law which result in conventions that member states, including the United States, may sign and have signed as treaties and controlling national law. It has been assigned responsibility for coordinating and perhaps fusing some or all Western Hemispheric regional economic groups.

LAIA/ALADI

The Association of Latin American Integration, Reciprocal Payments, and Credits ("LAIA" or "ALADI," the latter is the Spanish acronym) is a regional trade association. It was established by the Treaty of Montevideo of 1980 to replace the Latin American Free Trade Association ("LAFTA") which required members to multilaterally grant annual tariff reductions to other members, with all tariffs on reciprocal imports to be eliminated by 1972. The more industrially developed members of LAFTA only wished to maintain the tariff preferences among members that the members had traditionally been granting for years to each other through the administration of exchange controls. They could no longer maintain those tariff preferences because, in part, of the opposition of the IMF. This basic dispute with the purposes of LAFTA and between rival blocs of its members resulted in LAFTA's dissolution in 1980.

LAIA's members are Argentina, Bolivia, Brazil, Chile, Colombia, The Dominican Republic, Ecuador, Mexico, Paraguay, Peru, Uruguay, and Venezuela. The ALADI Agreement governed the flow of funds between member countries by replacing the international payment mechanisms that had traditionally been utilized. These changes in procedure were intended to result in greater interregional trade by reducing the need for hard currency, *e.g.*, US dollars, and the risk of local currency inconvertibility. It also provided a mechanism for replacing cross-border foreign private bank risk with local central bank risk. The principle that other member nations must be treated preferentially when a member country is regulating the access of imports to its local markets was accepted in all the countries of LAIA. This principle was implemented in a number of ways, largely through the LAIA rules themselves.

With the rise in regional enthusiasm for open markets and free trade, LAIA has become the regional umbrella organization under which customs unions and free trade areas have been organized. Information concerning LAIA/ALADI may be found at the official web site at http://www.aladi.org and also at http://www.mercosur.org.

MERCOSUR

MERCOSUR (an acronym from the Spanish *Mercado Comun del Sur* and/or the Portuguese *Mercado Comùndel Cono Sul*, both of which mean "Southern Cone Market") consists of Argentina, Brazil, Paraguay, and Uruguay. It is a market of 200 million people with annual GDP of over US$1 trillion and including the two largest (Brazil and Argentina) economies in South America. MERCOSUR has signed agreements with Chile that makes Chile a part of MERCOSUR's free trade area but not its customs union. Bolivia hopes to do the same and Venezuela may follow.

Information regarding MERCOSUR may be found, inter alia, on the official web site at http://www.mercosur.org.

MERCOSUR has signed a framework agreement with the EU aimed at developing free trade among the two groups by 2005. Brazil hopes to merge MERCOSUR and the Andean Pact and from this enlarge the proposed South American Free Trade Area ("SAFTA") to include all South America (a trading bloc which would be dominated by Brazil, which is why Brazil is so deeply committed to the proposal). More likely is the prospect of incorporating MERCOSUR into the proposed Free Trade Area of the Americas ("FTAA") which would include NAFTA.

MERCOSUR began with a deal between Argentina and Brazil in 1986. Trade barriers among members were to be eliminated by 1996, although Brazil insisted on the exclusion of more than 300 and Argentina almost 400 products from the free trade list.

MERCOSUR itself was founded in Asunción, Paraguay, under a 1991 treaty. That treaty provides ultimately for the free circulation of goods, services, and labor within Argentina, Brazil, Paraguay, and Uruguay. It establishes a common import tariff for all of them. It has been cutting internal tariffs on an automatic schedule to avoid pressures for delay. The last ones went at the end of 1994. The aim was to create a customs union and, in time, the free movement of labor and capital. A 1994 agreement (the Protocol of Ouro Preto) fleshed out the details. The document providing for the institutional structure of MERCOSUR may be found at 34 International Legal Materials 5, p. 1244 (1995). The common external tariffs that came into effect in 1995 were within a modest range of zero to a maximum of 20% with an average of about 10%. There is no sign of a deal on either services or labor, although steps have been taken to liberalize capital movements and to protect foreign investment. The goal was to have at least 80% of all intraregional goods traded freely by 2005. In June 1996, MERCOSUR established democracy as a condition for membership. A new commission has been created to deal with unfair trade issues (such as dumping and countervailing duties) and common external tariff harmonization.

Intraregional trade growth has been spectacular, increasing at least four fold since MERCOSUR's creation. Deeper integration is also taking place, with component procurement for manufacturing now being conducted regionally rather than nationally.

Things have not always gone as smoothly as planned, however. Two hundred (299 for Paraguay) products which have been kept outside the free trade area and the customs union for years are scheduled to be become part of the common tariff schedule in 2001. Certain capital goods are finally to be subjected to the common tariff schedule in 2001 with a maximum tariff of 14%. Certain computers and technology goods will not be part of the common tariff schedule until 2006. The above capital and technology goods constitute about 15% of all MERCOSUR trade. Sugar and automobiles are still subject to internal quotas. Brazil periodically—although it sometimes claims it does so inadvertently—imposes prohibitive tariffs and restrictive quotas on such things as automobiles without exempting MERCOSUR members. This is both irritating and economically ruinous to Argentina. Argentina put a temporary surcharge or "statistical tax" of 10% on Brazil's cheaper goods in 1993. It took a similar step again in 1995. Capital equipment made in other MERCOSUR countries will have to have a local content of at least 80% to be let into Brazil duty free. Argentina will have to eventually raise its own capital goods and high technology tariffs to the common (Brazilian) level under the Agreement.

With currency exchange rate differentials between Argentina and Brazil exacerbated by Brazil's devaluation of its currency and Argentina's lock of its currency into a fixed exchange rate with the US dollar, trade flows between the two have radically changed to Argentina's disadvantage. It is unclear whether MERCOSUR can endure in view of the deteriorating trading conditions between its two major parties. There will be a strong temptation for at least Argentina to seek refuge in any offer to participate in an FTAA.

ANCOM

The Andean Common Market ("ANCOM") or the Andean Pact (*Pacto Andino*) is made up of Bolivia, Colombia, Ecuador, Peru, and Venezuela. It constitutes a population of 105 million with an annual GDP of about US$480 billion.

It was created by the Agreement of Cartagena in 1969 and was largely a reaction to the disappointing performance of the earlier LAFTA and was predicated on the belief that central planning is a precondition of balanced trade and equitable growth. Chile withdrew in 1977. The members granted negotiated trade preferences to all other members, created a high common external tariff, assigned production of certain items for ANCOM to certain countries, and took negative and restrictive policies towards foreign investment. The Andean Court of Justice, the Andean Development Bank, the Andean Reserve Fund, and the Andean Parliament were established under the Agreement. ANCOM favored protectionism, heavy regulation, and the exclusion of foreigners from its markets. The ANCOM countries all had significant economic and political problems, ANCOM rules were often not honored in practice, and the continued existence of ANCOM was in doubt.

In 1988, the five relaunched the group in a very different spirit. ANCOM reinvented itself to favor economic liberalization, open markets, and receptiveness to foreign participation in its markets. As a result, ANCOM and its constituent countries are all showing new and unexpected signs of vigor, although there have been—and continue to be—serious glitches in consistent economic improvements within the region and in each of its members. Within the group, this has brought almost free trade since late 1992 and no more export subsidies. Externally, there are lower common tariffs and a customs union. Generally, external tariffs are according to a four-part structure of 5, 10, 15, and 20% tariffs (Bolivia has a lower 5 and 10% tariff structure while Peru has a 15% tariff on most imported goods and a 25% tariff on some) A common market is to be established no later than 2005 per a 2000 decision of ANCOM members. There is uniform "national" treatment for foreign investors. Refer to the excellent http://www.comunidadandina.org for the text of a number of recent ANCOM "decisions"—the equivalent of EU directives—on such matters as intellectual property, dumping and subsidies, ROs, and export restrictions and for other information on ANCOM. The common external tariff was placed into operation belatedly and there are still many "special cases" subject to different, non-free trade treatment.

G–3

Mexico, Venezuela, and Colombia, a market of over 140 million people, have been formally linked in the free trade area known as the "Group of Three," *Grupo de los Tres*, or "G–3" since 1994. Its underlying agreement is extremely detailed and concerns a wide-variety of issues and is comparable in scope to NAFTA. It is intended to create a free trade area by 2005.

CACM

The Central American Common Market ("CACM") is composed of Costa Rica, El Salvador, Honduras, Guatemala, and Nicaragua. Panama and Belize are observers. Panama generally follows CACM practices voluntarily or based on bilateral treaties with member states. CACM consititutes a population of 31 million with an annual GDP of US$92.8 billion. CACM was formed in 1958. It was intended to establish common external tariffs and customs practices on most products, to give customs preference to many CACM products within the market, and to coordinate national economic and related policies. Although still in existence, it has largely foundered on political disputes among its members.

It was relaunched in 1993 with a new agreement that partakes of the new free market spirit. Even travel is passport free. It works well in the three northern countries, less so in the south. Costa Rica is worried about the free movement of labor. The integration protocol set out goals for monetary union and a single currency but established no timetables. There is a Secretariat for Central American Economic Integration in Guatemala. A Central American Court of Justice was established in Managua, Nicaragua, in 1994. Both Panama and Costa Rica have opted out of some CACM provisions. The common external tariff schedule establishes tariffs generally within a range of 5 to 20%. The United States provides preferential treatment of trade with CACM members through its Interim Trade Program, which parallels the similar Caribbean Basin Initiative for CARICOM. Information on CACA may be found at the official web sites of the Integration System of Central America ("SICA") at http://www.sicanet.org.sv. or of the Secretariat for Central America Integration ("SIECA") at http://www.sieca.org.gt.

CARICOM

The Caribbean Community and Common Market ("CARICOM") was founded in 1973 to replace the earlier Caribbean Free Trade Association. Its cohesion did not endure economic decline in the region and it waned into insignificance. It was, in the early 1990s, revived and enlarged. It has removed most restrictions to regional trade among its members. Its goals include a common market, foreign policy coordination, and functional cooperation in other areas. A common external tariff of maximums of 20% on nonagricultural products and 40% on agricultural products has been established. CARICOM common external tariffs have never been implemented by all members. Member states are permitted to retain their own import surcharges, licenses, quotas, and prohibitions and these are often significant deterents to importation. CARICOM members are Guyana, Barbados, Jamaica, Trinidad and Tobago, Belize, the Leeward Islands (Anguilla, Antiguaamd Barbuda, Montserrat, and St. Kitts "and Nevis) and the Windward Islands (Dominica, Grenada, St. Lucia, and St. Vincent and the Grenadines). The Bahamas is a member but does not participate in the common market arrangement. CARICOM has 6 million people and an annual GDP of US$28.6 billion. Information on CARICOM may be found at its web site at http://www.caricom.org.

The Association of Caribbean States is an extension of CARICOM. Since 1993, it has included both Cuba and mainland countries bordering on the Caribbean. It consists of Antigua and Barbuda, Aruba, the Bahamas, Barbados, Belize, Colombia, Costa Rica, Cuba, Dominica, the Dominican Republic, El Salvador, France, Grenada, Haiti, Honduras, Jamaica, Mexico, the Netherlands Antilles, Nicaragua, Panama, St. Kitts and Nevis, Saint Lucia, St. Vincent and the Grenadines, Suriname, Trinidad and Tobago, and Venezuela. Information on the Association of Caribbean States may be found at http://www.acs-aec.org.

Also in the Caribbean is the Organization of Eastern Caribbean States ("OECS") which serves as a common voice through which its members deal economically with other states on some issues. It is a subgroup of CARICOM which was organized in 1981 and superseded the West Indies Associated States organization. Dominica, Grenada, St. Lucia, St. Vincent and the Grenadines, Antigua and Barbuda, Montserrat, and St. Kitts and Nevis are its members. All members (plus Anguilla) have harmonized monetary systems and utilize as their national currencies the East Caribbean dollar which is pegged to the US dollar. The East Caribbean Common Market is made up of OECS states with its major feature an allocation of regional industries among the members.

Countries of the region are generally beneficiaries of preferential trade arrangements with the US under the Caribbean Basin Initiative and may be beneficiaries of preferential trade arrangements with the EU under the Lomé Conventions.

FTAA

Western Hemispheric heads of state in 1967 agreed to create hemispheric free trade by 1985. It did not happen.

In June 1990, US President George Bush launched a grandly named "Enterprise for the Americas" which was to establish free trade from "Alaska to Tierra del Fuego." In June 1995, 34 governments (all the countries of the Western Hemisphere except Cuba, which was not invited) committed themselves to completing negotiations by 2005. Every country agreed to be bound by all, not just some, future FTAA rules (although it is unlikely that there would be no derogations in practice). At a March 1996 meeting in Cartagena, Colombia, Brazil scuttled US plans to base FTAA on the NAFTA model and to build it by expanding NAFTA (Brazil favors its own plan to create a South American Free Trade Area or SAFTA which would exclude the United States, Canada, and Mexico and leave Brazil as the dominant economic power in the organization).

The idea of an FTAA has lain dormant for several years but there are now committees actively drafting its various provisions and the new US President George W. Bush seems highly interested in pursuing the FTAA proposal revived by his father. The various regional economic groups within the Americas are (but with what degree of confidence this can be expected is impossible to say) presumably still to be fused into a single FTAA by 2005.

More information may be obtained from FTAA's web site at http://www.ftaa-alca.org.

SAFTA

An idea for a South American Free Trade Association ("SAFTA") was launched by Brazil in 1993. SAFTA is to be created by expanding MERCOSUR and incorporating the Andean Pact. Brazil's MERCOSUR partners have formally endorsed the idea but it would be preempted by FTAA—a prospect which is very displeasing to the Brazilian Government and is a source of contention and rivalry between the US and Brazil.

APEC

The Asia-Pacific Economic Cooperation ("APEC") is an informal group of 18 countries. It includes the ASEAN organization, Australia, Canada, Japan, South Korea, New Zealand, and the United States (all of which joined in 1989); the PRC, Taiwan, and Hong Kong (which joined in 1991); Mexico and Papua New Guinea (which joined in 1993); and Chile (which joined in 1994). All have Pacific coastlines as their somewhat inconsequential and irrelevant common denominator. There is an annual APEC Summit and there is an APEC version of G–7 meetings. There is also an APEC-appointed committee, the Pacific Business Forum, composed entirely of businesspersons.

The 18 countries of APEC now account for a big and growing slice of world trade—46% of all world exports in 1993, up from 38% in 1983. Around 70% of their exports went to other APEC countries in 1993, up from 61% in 1983.

Malaysia's Prime Minister, Mahathir Mohamed, is opposed to the participation of non-Asian countries in APEC and wishes to limit participation to his proposed but yet unrealized organization, the East Asian Economic Caucus ("EAEC"), which would include Japan but exclude all Western countries. Other APEC members have refused to exclude non-Asian states but have agreed to create an EAEC that will be a "caucus within APEC," whatever that may mean.

APEC was formed in 1989 as a forum in which member nations could discuss common problems in the Pacific region. Its record in what is ostensibly its chief purpose—speeding up economic liberalization around the Pacific—has been disappointing.

At the APEC heads of state summit in 1993, agreement was reached on what the leaders chose to call a "vision" of free trade in the Pacific. In November 1994, the APEC heads of state met in Bogor, Indonesia. They decided, in the so-called "Bogor Declaration," that the creation of an APEC free trade area would begin to be implemented in the year 2000 with developed countries to have fully completed trade liberalization by 2010 and with the four newly developed countries to have finished the job by 2015. Every APEC member is to have eliminated intra-APEC barriers to trade and provided for "free and open trade and investment" by 2020. There is some doubt as to whether this schedule can be achieved and whether all APEC members even mean to try and achieve it. Japan and South Korea wished to exclude agricultural products from APEC discussion. Malaysia even got into the Declaration a stipulation that the 2020 completion date is not binding. With regards to the question of which are developed and which developing countries, there are some countries which argue that currently undeveloped countries should be "grandfathered" into that status without regards to the state of their economic development in 2010. A code of nonbinding investment principles was worked out in 1994.

In November 1995, the APEC leaders, meeting in Osaka, Japan, recommitted themselves to free trade and investment among themselves by the year 2020 (with the richer countries to achieve this goal by 2010). There is disagreement concerning whether the Osaka APEC meeting was productive or a regressive step. Japan's and South Korea's efforts to exclude agriculture from discussion were rejected. Agreements were reached on key trade facilitation issues, including customs harmonization and simplification, product standardization, and mutual recognition agreements for product testing and certification. Although *The Economist* called them vague, Mr. Fred Bergsten—a close observer of and participant in APEC economic liberalization efforts—said Osaka produced precise agreements on nine principles, agenda on 15 topics, and timetables that together will guide the process for implementing the free trade pledge. Actual liberalization began in January 1997.

The next summit was held in Manila, the Philippines, in November 1996. APEC members offered promises of liberalization but each felt free to propose only what it liked. This is said to be the "Asian way." There were no "tit-for-tat" concessions common to other trade talks. "APEC is not based on contracts and treaties," according to Katsuhisa Uchida, Japan's then ambassador for trade. APEC's members are now concentrating on measures such as standardizing customs procedures and computerizing documentation.

There are great differences of opinion as to whether APEC will be the next regional trade bloc titan or will end up being much noise with little substance. The unwillingness of members to engage in serious and binding negotiations and the vagueness of their promises lends credence to those of the latter view, but APEC has proved nay sayers wrong in the past and may yet do so again.

Further information may be obtained from APEC's official web site at http://www.apec.sec.org.sg.

ASEAN

Association of Southeast Asian Nations ("ASEAN") members are Brunei Darussalam, Indonesia, Malaysia, the Philippines, Singapore, Thailand, and Vietnam. The original five member states were present at the founding in 1967. Brunei Darussalam joined in 1984 soon after obtaining its independence. Vietnam joined in 1995. ASEAN has more recently admitted Laos, Cambodia, and Burma (Myanmar) to membership and Papua New Guinea is an observer.

ASEAN was officially founded in August 1967 with the signing of the Bangkok Declaration. It was created to strengthen regional cohesion and self-reliance through economic, social, and cultural cooperation in reaction to the threat posed by North Vietnam's military power and aggressive intentions and that country's Communist ideology which was antithetical to ASEAN members' political and economic systems. At the time of ASEAN's founding, North Vietnam was providing direct and indirect military and other support to a Communist insurgency in the Republic of Vietnam. North Vietnam and its Viet Cong allies were opposed by the United States and other countries (including ASEAN members Thailand and the Philippines) which provided military bases and forces in support of the beleaguered Government of South Vietnam. ASEAN nations declared their collective area to be a zone of peace, freedom, and neutrality ("ZOPFAN") in 1971.

Following the fall of the Republic of Vietnam in 1975, this declaration was formalized in the Bali Declaration of 1976 (known as the Declaration of ASEAN Accord) which also established an ASEAN Secretariat in Jakarta, Indonesia, and called for the coordination of ASEAN cooperative activities in promoting industry, trade, and other objectives. ASEAN security concerns became even more profound with the increased threat of Vietnamese hegemony in Southeast Asia following America's defeat in the Vietnamese War and the subsequent military occupation by Vietnam of Laos and Cambodia (Kampuchea) and the administration of those states by Vietnam as tributaries.

Principal organs of ASEAN in addition to the Secretariat and its associated specialized intergovernmental committees are Meetings of the ASEAN Foreign Ministers, the ASEAN Standing Committee, and the ASEAN Economic Ministers. There are now also usually annual summits by ASEAN heads of government. The "PMC" is the Postministerial Conference held each year since the mid-1970s after the ASEAN Foreign Ministers' Meeting. In the PMC, ASEAN countries and the foreign ministers of ASEAN's "Dialogue Partners" - the United States, the EU, Japan, Australia, New Zealand, Canada, and South Korea - hold discussions on economic and security issues. Also significant is the ASEAN Regional Forum ("ARF") which was inaugurated in 1994. It groups ASEAN with ten countries/groups, including the Dialogue Partners, Russia, and the PRC. It has as its goals improvement in Asian security and the creation of a forum through which to reduce tensions and resolve problems in the region.

Although born of the fear of external military threat, ASEAN is not a military pact or mutual defense association. The member states of ASEAN have little in common except their location in Southeast Asia and their initial antipathy to the ideological and military forces represented by the Government of Vietnam (which is now an ASEAN member). Economic cooperation and coordination among ASEAN states is improving and ASEAN plays an increasingly important and unified role in international political and diplomatic spheres.

ASEAN has formulated certain market allocations within the territory of all its members for rationalized regional production of certain industrial products, has established internal tariff preferences, and has fostered regional joint venture and industrial development projects. Nonetheless, the degree of economic integration among members to date has been slight and that integration which has been adopted in theory has often not been implemented in practice. Since 1976, however, ASEAN has developed new cohesiveness and significance and has entered into collective negotiations with all its major trading partners on behalf of its members.

In addition to its diplomatic and economic efforts (including playing a large role in obtaining Vietnamese withdrawal from Cambodia and in seeking a resolution to the Spratly Island disputes through encouraging participation by the PRC in post-ASEAN heads of state meetings), ASEAN is to be applauded for preserving peace among its members—some of which have fought or threatened others at various times since the end of World War II.

In early 1992, ASEAN members states agreed to further expand economic cooperation by forming an ASEAN Free Trade Area ("AFTA").

ASEAN prides itself on its "Asian" way of dealing with problems and obtaining agreement, encapsulated in the two Malay/Indonesian words *musyawarah* and *mufakat* or "consultation" and "consensus." The organizational structure of ASEAN is weak and decisions, such as they are, are always made through consensus. Such decisions are generally made informally and in an *ad hoc* fashion.

Because its members had so little which they shared and so much which divided them, ASEAN developed slowly during its first decade except as a common lobby and support group in the face of prospective Vietnamese ideological and military aggression.

Except for Singapore, ASEAN members have—until recently—been dependent on agricultural products and natural resources for many of their exports. They pursue common policies on commodities and other economic issues in international fora.

ASEAN has a commercial and cooperative agreement with the EU which permits easier access by ASEAN products to the EU market.

For some purposes, ASEAN-origin products are dealt with specially and preferably under US tariffs and customs. The ASEAN-US economic dialogue began in 1977 and subsequent dialogues have been held approximately every 18 months. An ASEAN-US Council for Business and Technology was established in 1979 to bring together US and ASEAN private-sector leaders to discuss common interests and the enhancement of trade and investment. Since 1979, a US-ASEAN Development Cooperation Program provides coordinated US funding to ASEAN countries through bilateral arrangements. Under the ASEAN-US Initiative of 1990, regular ministerial-level consultations are held to explore mechanisms for enhancing trade and investment relations. The Economic Coordinating Committee ("ECC") was established in 1977 and comprises senior ASEAN-nation embassy officials in Washington, D.C., and their counterparts in the United States as well as US and ASEAN private sector representatives. The ASEAN Washington Committee is composed of the ambassadors to the United States of each of the ASEAN countries. It meets periodically with US officials to discuss common issues.

Since most products of ASEAN members compete in world markets rather than complement each other in their domestic markets, in the past there has been little enthusiasm or logical rationale for integrating their economies or reducing intra-ASEAN barriers to trade. This is changing to a degree with the growth in manufacturing and service industries in the region.

The ASEAN region has been a recent success story in terms of agriculture, industry, and trade and is rich in a number of both depletable and renewable critical natural resources, including 72% of the world's exported rubber and the world's biggest source of tropical timber. The average growth rate for ASEAN countries in 1990 was 7.6%. ASEAN nations are all committed to market- and export-oriented economic growth strategies. Significant US and other foreign investment has been attracted to ASEAN countries by low labor costs, favorable investment climates and market-oriented economies, and abundant natural resources.

The ASEAN Preferential Trading Arrangement of the 1970s was intended to reduce tariffs on intra-ASEAN trade but only affected 3.2% of it. The Arrangement fell into disrepute when it became clear that most of the items on the list were put there because they were so little traded. Indonesia, for example, cut tariffs on snowplows by 10% and Malaysia granted preferential tariffs on a list of rubber products of which it was the only large ASEAN producer.

A third ASEAN summit of national leaders in 1987 gave new emphasis to reducing external trade barriers and establishing joint industrial projects as well as to closer coordination on economic issues.

Largely because foreign investors in manufacturing operations would find a single market of 400 million people for their products more attractive than that of a single ASEAN country, ASEAN foreign ministers in 1991—and in 1992 ASEAN heads of government—agreed to create the AFTA. It did not include coverage of raw agricultural goods, services, or investments. Intra-ASEAN trade (worth US$48 billion in 1990, 75% of which is from or passes through Singapore, much of it from or to parties outside ASEAN) constitutes less than 20% of total ASEAN trade. Any ASEAN member can opt out of any of the plan's areas it finds too economically painful and there are a broad range of exemptions based on religion, culture, or protected economic sectors.

Under Common Effective Preferential Tariffs, intra-ASEAN tariffs will be progressively reduced in two steps to 0-5% on all manufactured products and processed agricultural goods within 15 years. Most nontariff barriers to intra-ASEAN trade are also to be eliminated. The first tariff reductions were to be effective January 1, 1993, but implementation was delayed for a year. A list of 15 priority items were subject at that time to 5% ASEAN tariffs and are to be reduced to 0% by 2003. Those items are: (1) vegetable oils; (2) cement; (3) chemicals; (4) pharmaceuticals; (5) fertilizers; (6) plastics; (7) rubber products; (8) leather goods; (9) pulp; (10) textiles; (11) ceramic and glass products; (12) gems and jewelry; (13) copper cathodes; (14) electronics; and (15) wooden and rattan furniture. To be eligible for the lower tariffs, a product must have at least 40% of its content originating from an ASEAN member. Covered items constitute about two-thirds of current intra-ASEAN trade. However, each ASEAN country has the right to temporarily exclude certain products from tariff reductions. Some sensitive items, such as cars and components, will be allowed protection until at least 2010. Vietnam has already been exempted from the 2003 target date on the grounds of its extreme poverty. Laos, Cambodia, and Burma are certain to be accorded similarly lenient treatment for the same reason when they become ASEAN members. There is a cogent argument made that AFTA will not be successful because it concentrates on tariffs while ignoring non-tariff barriers to trade, such as endless form-filling, restrictions on foreign investment, and hygiene and safety regulations that vary from country to country and are the really significant impediments to trade with most ASEAN countries. For ongoing updates on AFTA, call the US Commerce Department's PACRIM HOTLINE at (202) 482-3875.

In 1995, Indonesia reneged on some of its AFTA obligations and called into question whether the AFTA target date can be met for 15 agricultural products, including rice, sugar, wheat flour, and cloves. At least in the case of cloves and wheat flour, withdrawn trade liberalization may be based on narrow "domestic political" reasons. President Suharto's youngest son headed Indonesia's clove-trading monopoly and a long-time Suharto financial backer dominated Indonesia's wheat flour trade. A compromise was reached under which the 15 commodities where shifted to a specially-devised temporary exclusion list of "unprocessed agricultural products," an obvious misidentification at least in the case of wheat flour. The volume of trade involved is small (in part because of high tariff barriers to trade) —US$40 million annually—when compared with total intra-ASEAN trade of US$111 billion in 1994.

ASEAN Industrial Projects ("AIP") are large-scale, capital-intensive projects in which ASEAN governments are joint shareholders. Goods produced by AIPs are given preferential trade treatment within ASEAN for five years after operations begin. The only two operational AIPs are ammonia/urea fertilizer plants in Indonesia and Malaysia. ASEAN Industrial Complementation ("AIC") projects are principally initiated and pursued by the private sector and were authorized by the 1981 Basic Agreement on ASEAN Industrial Complementation. None have yet been approved. Under AICs, each country is to produce designated component parts of a regional product that can be traded among the member states for eventual assembly into a completed product. Participants in AICs receive certain benefits, including trade preferences and exclusive rights to their assigned component. ASEAN Industrial Joint Ventures ("AIJVs"), operating through private-sector cooperation, were provided for in 1983 and given preferential trade treatment within the participating countries and by other ASEAN countries on an optional basis. Firms in only two ASEAN countries need participate and—since 1987—foreigners may own up to 60% (and even more under certain circumstances) of a joint venture. Approval by ASEAN foreign ministers of AIJVs is required.

Additional information may be obtained from ASEAN's official web sites at http://ww.asean.or.id or http://www.aseansec.org.

SAARC

The South Asian Association for Regional Cooperation ("SAARC") was formed in 1985 to promote regional cooperation. It has India, Bangladesh, Bhutan, the Maldives, Nepal, Pakistan, and Sri Lanka as members. It has accomplished little because of several factors which characterize regional political relations, including the hostility between Pakistan and India, the power and inertia of the bureaucracies in each country, the prevailing sympathy in the region for statism and protectionism, the weaknesses of the regional national economies and the fact that most produce similar competing goods rather than compatible goods which could be traded among neighbors, general xenophobia, and fear of Indian hegemony by its neighbors.

India dominates the region. India has much higher tariffs than other members. Pakistan allows the importation of only 577 specified goods from India. Bangladesh wants India to hand over an enclave called Tin Bigha which, by treaty, should have been returned in the early 1980s. India sees SAARC as a forum for making regional economic and social progress free of bilateral antagonisms. The others view SAARC as a forum where they may sometimes unite against India and thereby drive a more favorable bargain.

In May 1995, a preferential trade agreement was approved at the annual meeting in Delhi, India, of SAARC member heads. The seven countries exchanged lists of goods on which they will offer tariff preferences. India had the longest list (106 items), followed by Pakistan (35), Sri Lanka (31) and Bangladesh (12). Trade between countries of the region amounts to barely 3% of their total trade and the items covered by the deal are a small fraction of even this. The trade agreement came into force on December 8, 1995.

No significant regional economic cooperation exists nor may it be expected in the near term.

Additional information may be obtained from the official SAARC web site at http://www.saarc-sec.org.

CER/ANZERTA

The economic relationship between Australia and New Zealand has been made closer and more clearly encouraged by law under the

Closer Economic Relations Trade Agreement ("CER," also referred to as "ANZCERTA") of 1983 which superseded the New Zealand-Australia Free Trade Agreement of 1966.

CER creates a full free trade area (originally scheduled for 1995) and not a customs union. It was intended to liberalize comprehensively and automatically trade between the two countries through the progressive elimination of tariffs and quantitative restrictions on the trans-Tasman Sea trade of goods produced or manufactured within either country (*i.e.*, those with 50% Australian and/or New Zealand content and whose last process of manufacture took place in either country).

It contains 26 Articles together with a series of annexes and attachments dealing with specific industries, products, and goods.

Three protocols resulted from the 1988 review of the CER—the Acceleration of the Free Trade in Goods; Trade in Services; and Harmonization of Quarantine Administration Procedures. The services protocol stipulates "national treatment" and nondiscrimination.

Ports, telecommunications and broadcasting, and international airways services—and to a lesser degree investment and banking—are not fully incorporated into the protocol on services.

Further agreements have been concluded on the reach of customs policies and procedures, industry assistance, technical barriers to trade, trans-Tasman shipping, state government purchasing, and the harmonization of business laws.

Implementation of CER provisions was accelerated and came fully into effect in 1990. There are no longer tariff or quantitative restrictions on the trade in goods between the two countries.

The value of trade between the two countries has increased significantly since 1983, with a great shift in the balance of trade in New Zealand's favor so that trade between the two is now about balanced.

The CER may provide opportunities for foreign commercial parties to enter the markets of Australia and New Zealand where duties may otherwise be high or other restrictions imposed. It also permits a single operating entity to serve both national markets. To qualify, goods must comply with the conditions set out in the appropriate Australian and New Zealand regulations for the granting of preference.

South Pacific Forum

The South Pacific Forum was founded in 1971 and is largely an informal talk shop for the heads of government of its members: Australia, Cook Islands, Federated States of Micronesia, Fiji, Kiribati, Republic of the Marshall Islands, Nauru, New Zealand, Niue, Papua New Guinea, Solomon Islands, Tonga, Tuvalu, Vanuatu, and Western Samoa. Nonetheless, it engages in significant cooperative and regional activities and formulates some common policies for member states.

Most important has been the Forum Pacific Agency which has negotiated fishing agreements—most notably that with the United States for tuna fishing. The Forum Secretariat encourages joint economic and trade policies within the region and by outsiders dealing with the region. The South Pacific Regional Environment Program Convention provides for the protection of the regional environment and has been signed by a number of extraregional parties, including the United States. The Committee for Coordination of Joint Prospecting for Mineral Resources seeks to coordinate the exploitation of regional mineral resources to assure that their exploitation preserves the culture and environment of the region while producing for the region the maximum financial advantage.

Members of the South Pacific Forum have special access to the Australian and New Zealand markets through the South Pacific Regional Trade and Economic Cooperation Agreement ("SPARTECA").

Most members have entered into a South Pacific Fisheries Agreement or Accord with the United States and the US Tunaboat Association regarding tunafishing rights of US parties in their waters. This Agreement or Accord permits US fishers to take tuna in the waters of signatories in exchange for specified annual payments to signatories by the United States.

Further information may be obtained from the South Pacific Forum's official web sites at http://www.forumsec.org.fj or http://chacmool.sdnp.undp.org/pacific/forumsec/default1.htm.

UAE

The United Arab Emirates, a confederation of emirates on the Arabian Peninsula along the Persian Gulf, may readily be argued to be a regional trading bloc rather than a country since the individual emirate's customs, immigration, and other laws and policies often follow more the pattern of independent states with some common and shared interests and policies than they do that of members of even the loosest confederacy operating as a sovereign state.

GCC

The Arab States Gulf Cooperation Council ("GCC") has significant impact on crossborder trade, industrialization, and other business activities within its member states, which are the United Arab Emirates, State of Bahrain, Kingdom of Saudi Arabia, Sultanate of Oman, State of Qatar, and State of Kuwait.

The GCC was established by the Unified Economic Agreement of 1981. Its scope and importance to the business community are suggested by its chapter titles: trade exchange; movement of capital, citizens, and exercise of economic activities; coordination of development; technical cooperation; transport and communication; and financial and monetary cooperation.

Under the GCC import regime, preference is given to the products and services of other GCC states. The GCC is working gradually towards common standards and regulations in areas ranging from customs and ship registration to banking and environmental protection. A common external tariff and free trade within the GCC was scheduled for implementation by 1992. Most GCC countries require detailed labeling in Arabic on all food imports, but the level of enforcement varies greatly among GCC countries.

The GCC and the EU signed an initial framework for trade cooperation in June 1988. Negotiations for a GCC-EU free trade agreement and US-GCC trade liberalization have been held.

The GCC has its headquarters in Riyadh, Saudi Arabia. The principal GCC administrative organs are the Supreme Council, the Ministerial Council, and the Secretariat-General. Headquartered in Kuwait is the GCC's Gulf Investment Corporation that invests in the equity of regional companies operating in certain fields in order to promote their development.

The League of Arab States

The League of Arab States has as members all states of West Asia and North Africa where Arabic is the primary language, although political disputes periodically bar one or more countries from membership. The League of Arab States coordinates many aspects of foreign and commercial policy among its members through periodic meetings of government officials and leaders. Among the activities of the Arab League is the boycott of Israel.

The Arab League Trade and Payments Agreement of 1953 accords preferential tariff rates to specified products of Arab League members. Some countries in the region are party to an Arab Common

Market which was founded in 1965 by the Arab League under the Agreement of Arab Economic Unity and an Arab Cooperation Council which was formed in 1989 with the intention of forming a common market, but these are of little or no significance.

Export credit insurance is often available through the Inter-Arab Investment Guarantee Corporation, an association of 22 Arab countries.

A number of states in the region are petroleum exporting countries. Some are members of The Organization of Petroleum Exporting Countries, The Organization of Arab Petroleum Exporting Countries ("OAPEC"), and The Independent Petroleum Exporting Countries ("IPEC") Group.

The Arab Co-Operation Council

The Arab Co-Operation Council, with Egypt, Iraq, Jordan, and North Yemen as members (an organization with an unpromising future due to antagonisms among its members), was formed in 1989. It is of little consequence for commercial relations.

UMA

The Arab Maghreb Union (*Union Maghrébine Arabe* or "UMA") of Morocco, Algeria, Mauritania, Tunisia, and Libya was formed in 1989. It encompasses five North African countries that have strong historical, cultural, and language affinities. In 1992, the AMU's Secretariat General, was established permanently in Rabat, Morocco. As of May 1996, there have been a total of 37 Maghrebi conventions. The main objectives of the AMU Treaty are to strengthen all forms of ties among member states in order to ensure regional stability and enhance policy coordination, as well as to introduce gradually free circulation of goods, services, and factors of production among them. Common defense and non-interference in the domestic affairs of the partners are also key aspects of the Treaty. The agreement provides the possibility for other Arab and African countries to join the UMA at a later stage. Since 1990, the five countries have signed more than 30 multilateral agreements covering diverse economic, social, and cultural areas. Only five have been ratified by all AMU members. These include agreements on trade and tariffs (covering all industrial products); trade in agricultural products, investment guarantees; avoidance of double taxation; and phyto-sanitary standards. Further information may be found at the official UMA web site at http://www.uneca.org/links_home.htm.

OAU

The nations of the continent of Africa created the Organization of African Unity ("OAU") in 1993. It is headquartered in Addis Ababa, Ethiopia. It considers questions of mutual interest to its more than 50 members, generally at regular meetings of the leaders and government officials of its members.

OAU formed The African Economic Community under a treaty signed in Abuja, Nigeria, in 1991. Full economic integration of all African states is to be obtained in six stages over a maximum of 34 years. Details of the treaty forming the African Economic Community may be found at 30 International Legal Materials 5, p. 1241 (1991). Also formed under the auspices of the OAU was The African Regional Standards Organization to coordinate and assist with the establishment of product standards and certifications for Africa's regional organizations.

The African Development Bank, headquartered in Abidjan, the Ivory Coast (Côte d'Ivoire), is a regional development bank of which most African countries are members and from which they derive economic benefits. Information concerning the OAU may be found at its official web site at http://www.oau.ona.org.

United States of Africa

On March 2, 2001, African leaders declared that an African political and economic union would be created (but admitted that not all African countries had formally ratified the proposal). Created would be an African Central Bank, a Court of Justice, a common currency, and an African Parliament (although apparently the Parliament would not have the authority to enact laws). The union is expected to be largely symbolic and is another brainchild of Libyan leader Moammar Gadhafi.

East African Community

The East African Community of Uganda, Kenya, and Tanganyika (now Tanzania) was imposed by the departing British colonial power in an effort to create a larger and more viable commercial territory for these newly liberated states. It failed because of disagreements among the members regarding economic policies and common assets. Perhaps the principal failing was the disparate ideologies separating capitalist Kenya from socialist Tanzania and Uganda. The countries have recently agreed to revive the East African Community effective July 2001. There will be a common passport, a customs union, a common market, free movement and residence of people within the Community, a council of ministers, a court, and a legislature to preside over this community of 81 million.

The Rhodesias and Nyasaland

The attempted economic union of Malawi, Zambia, and Zimbabwe (at the time, Northern Rhodesia, Nyasaland and Southern Rhodesia) was imposed by the departing British colonial power in an effort to continue the economic integration of these territories that had developed under colonial rule. This economic union collapsed for a number of reasons, among them the increasingly isolated political status of Rhodesia, formerly Southern Rhodesia.

UDEAC

In Africa, several of the Francophone countries of Central Africa formed the Economic and Customs Union of Central Africa ("UDEAC") in order to establish a common customs union and a foreign investment code. UDEAC now languishes in relative inactivity and desuetude. For more information, contact the official UDEAC web site (in French) at http://www.socatel.intnet.cf/accueil1.html.

OCAM

The Organisation Commune Africain et Malgache ("OCAM") whose members are Senegal, Central African Republic, Congo, Madagascar, Mauritius, Zaire, Côte d'Ivoire, Benin, Burkina Faso, Niger, Rwanda, Chad, and Togo remains in existence and performs some common harmonization functions among its members.

ECOWAS

Six Francophone West African countries formed the West African Economic Community ("CEAO") in 1974, which now operates within the larger Economic Community of West African States ("ECOWAS") which was founded in 1975. CEAO and ECOWAS have achieved some success. ECOWAS was formed by the Treaty of ECOWAS and has a secretariat in Lagos (to be moved to Abuja), Nigeria. It was set up to enhance the economic and social development in the West African region and includes English- and French-speaking countries. It was intended to establish a customs union by 1990. Under its planned trade liberalization scheme, there were to be 25% annual reductions on duties on 25 imported products originating from member states until a zero rate was achieved.

The ECOWAS formative treaty, the Treaty of Lagos, was revised in 1993 and proposes an economic and monetary union of its sixteen members (Benin, Burkina Faso, Cape Verde, Côte d'Ivoire, the Gambia,

Ghana, Guinea, Guinea-Bissau, Liberia, Mali, Mauritania, Niger, Nigeria, Senegal, Sierra Leone, and Togo). Information concerning ECOWAS may be found at the official web site at http://www.cmf.org/external/NP/sec/decdo/ecowas.htm.

UEMOA

Of some importance is the West African Monetary Union ("UEMOA") with a common Central Bank headquartered in Dakar, Senegal, which administers the CFA (Franc of the African Financial Community) franc zone through which funds may be transferred freely within the union. CFA francs are underwritten by France and are convertible in unlimited quantities to French francs at a rate fixed at parity per treaty. Until the early 1990s the rate had been 100 CFA francs to 2FFr, but that exchange rate was and had long been unrealistic. France unilaterally changed the rate to 100 CFA francs to 1FFr in the face of protests by many African member states. Members include Benin, Burkina Faso, Côte d'Ivoire, Niger, Senegal, Togo, Chad, Mali, and Niger. UEMOA is committed to the creation of a common market. More information may be found regarding UEMOA at its official web site at http://www.imf.org/external/np/sec/decdo/waemu.htm.

CEPGAL

There was apparently once an Economic Community of the Great Lakes Countries ("CEPGAL"). Whatever its nature and accomplishments may have been, it seemingly now only survives as an entry on recondite lists of African regional economic and financial organizations.

Western African Countries

The Comoro Islands, Djibouti, Ethiopia, Kenya, Malawi, Mauritius, Somalia, Uganda and Zambia have initiated a preferential trade agreement but this is of uncertain commercial importance.

COMESA

The Common Market for East and Southern Africa ("COMESA"), has as members Angola, Burundi, Comoros, Democratic Republic of Congo, Djibouti, Egypt, Eritrea, Ethiopia, Kenya, Madagascar, Malawi, Mauritius, Namibia, Rwanda, Seychelles, Sudan, Swaziland, Tanzania, Uganda, Zambia and Zimbabwe. It constitutes a population of 385 million people. It was formed by treaty in Kampala, Uganda, in 1993. It provides a preferential trade area—to evolve over time into a common market—for members. COMESA institutions include a Council of Ministers, a Committee of Governors of Central

Banks, an Intergovernmental Committee, a Technical Committee, a Secretariat, a Secretary General, a Court of Justice, a Consultative Committee of the Business Community, and other groups. The Charter of COMESA may be found at 33 International Legal materials 5, p. 1067 (1994) and the Protocol to the COMESA Treaty on the Rules of Origin may be found at 34 International Legal Materials 4, p. 908 (1995). COMESA was preceded by a Preferential Trade Area for East and Southern Africa established in 1983 and consisting of 18 regional states. It was intended to be the first step towards a regional common market. In this regard, note an East and Southern African States Preferential Trade Area Charter on a Regime of Multinational Industrial Enterprises at 30 International Legal Materials 3, p. 696 (1991). More information on COMESA may be found on its official web site at http://www.comesa.int.

SADC

The Southern African Development Coordination Conference ("SADCC") was a regional organization consisting of 9 countries in Southern Africa. The original rationale for the creation of SADCC in 1980 was to reduce the member countries' dependence on neighboring South Africa with its pariah apartheid regime. The Southern African Development Community ("SADC") replaced SADCC under an agreement signed in 1992 in Windhoek, Namibia. With its change in regime, South Africa has been welcomed as a SADC member. Members are: Angola, Botswana, the Democratic Republic of the Congo, Lesotho, Malawi, Mauritius, Mozambique, Namibia, Seychelles, South Africa, Swaziland, Tanzania, Zambia, and Zimbabwe. SADC is headquartered in Gabarone, Botswana. SADC institutions are a regular Summit of the Heads of State or Government, a Tribunal whose decisions are final and binding, and a Council of Ministers. The organization has been successful in project harmonization on a sectoral basis. Member states increasingly focuse on the goal of regional economic integration and current trade protocol negotiations are expected to soon establish a SADC free trade area. The Declaration of the Establishment of SADC may be found at 32 International Legal Materials 1, p. 267 (1993). SADC constitutes a population of 199 million with an annual GDP of US$176 billion. More information may be found at its official web site at http://www.sadcreview.org.

SACU

A customs union, called the Southern African Customs Union ("SACU"), was formed in 1969 among Botswana, Lesotho, Namibia, South Africa, and Swaziland. The agreement was later renegotiated to be more favorable to the smaller countries. It provides for the unrestricted flow of goods produced within the customs union as well as a free flow of imports and exports through South African territory to the other SACU states (all land-locked except Namibia). The Common Monetary Area consists of the same states as the customs union except for Botswana and provides for free transfers of funds between the member countries, free access to South African capital markets, and similar exchange controls for each member country. Whether this customs and monetary union will survive the change in government in South Africa from the former apartheid regime is unclear, but it seems likely that it will.

Chapter V: Bilateral Free Trade Agreements and Similar Agreements

Bilateral Commercial Arrangements Generally

Bilateral commercial arrangements involve, by tautology, two parties—in this case two sovereign countries or semi-autonomous territories. Such arrangements may create a free trade area between the two parties (and these two are sometimes noncontiguous and widely-separated) or permit one to participate in the customs area of the other. Most simply provide agreed terms between the two regarding the ability of those under one of their jurisdictions to do business in or with the other. Some are between a dominant sovereign power and a semi-autonomous or otherwise junior or subordinate territory.

Both agreements (a) creating bilateral free trade areas or customs unions and (b) defining the relationship between dominant and subordinate territories will be described here to the extent information could be obtained. Some of the more important of them will be described in some detail. Other bilateral commercial arrangements not rising to the level of these two categories may sometimes be described in this chapter where these are of particular interest or importance. Nonetheless, please refer to the previous chapter, which enumerates the preferential trading relationships that exist and are regularly reported to the WTO Committee charged with assessing and monitoring them. Many of these are bilateral, whether (a) between two countries or a country and semi-autonomous territory or (b) between a regional trading bloc and another regional trading bloc or a country or semi-autonomous territory. Just on the basis of the most recent report (1999) of that WTO Committee, at least 50 such bilateral agreements rising to the level of preference sufficient to require reporting to and examination by the WTO were reported for that year. Clearly no complete enumeration of all such treaties could be offered here and staying current with them is beyond the capabilities of a bound book. Readers are advised to independently seek information on any relevant germane bilateral agreements from the WTO at its official web site by clicking on "Trade Topics" and from there clicking on "Regionalism" or by turning to possible relevant parties to any such agreement for their official listings of trade agreements between them or between one of them and other parties.

Where the bilateral relationship creates a free trade area, this will permit the shipment between the two territories of goods covered by the free trade agreement without the payment of tariffs. Where the bilateral relationship creates a customs union, this will permit importation to be made into either of the parties' territories at the same tariff rate and under the same terms and thereafter to be shipped to the other territory without the payment of additional tariffs. Where other special terms of trade are established between the two territories, these will be of importance in planning effective trading strategies or avoiding those which are uncompetitively costly or complicated.

EU Bilateral Trade Relationships

The EU is perhaps the globe's most assiduous developer of bilateral free trade area agreements. In part, such agreements were needed to implement the EEA and to prepare for the inclusion of new members into the EU as described in the previous chapter. Other such EU bilateral relationships have been adopted to maintain trading terms with specific countries equal to those such countries have with other major trading countries through bilateral agreements or common participation in regional trading blocs. Some EU trade agreements with major trading countries have had the purpose of cooperation among the parties in customs and tariff matters, particularly joint efforts to prevent customs fraud. Finally, some such agreements have been adopted purely to assist economically-challenged countries or as political payoffs or sops for some countries in which the EU has particular geo-political interests or which the EU has denied or indefinitely delayed membership in the EU.

SO-CALLED EU "ASSOCIATION AGREEMENTS" Association agreements signed by the EU are generally those which had formerly been signed with countries that were considered likely candidates for EU membership (Cyprus and Malta) or were thought in need of special economic relations with the EU (Israel).

EU-CYPRUS AGREEMENT There is an EU Association Agreement with Cyprus (*Official Journal* L/133, 21.5.73) which went into force in 1973 which established a common customs union (for industrial products only) in two stages.

EU-ISRAEL AGREEMENT There is an EU Association Agreement with Israel (*Official Journal* L/147, 21.6.00) which went into effect in 2000.

EU-MALTA AGREEMENT There is an EU Association Agreement with Malta (Official Journal L/61, 14.3.71) which went into force in 1971 which established a common customs union (for industrial products only) in two stages.

SO-CALLED EU "CO-OPERATIVE AGREEMENTS" EU co-operative agreements, now being phased out, were those entered into with underdeveloped countries bordering on the Mediterranean Sea. They were principally with Arabic/Islamic countries (and these are now being replaced with so-called European-Mediterranean Association Agreements—see the next chapter), but the same type of agreement was provided to the countries which once comprised the former state of Yugoslavia, although most of these countries have since become parties with the EU to so-called "European Agreements" (see the next chapter).

EU-ALGERIA AGREEMENT There is an EU Co-Operative Agreement (*Official Journal* L/263, 27.9.78) with Algeria which went into force into 1976 but it is to be replaced by a European-Mediterranean Association Agreement now being negotiated.

EU-EGYPT AGREEMENT There is an EU Co-Operative Agreement (*Official Journal* L/266, 27.9.78) with Egypt which went into force into 1977 but it is to be replaced by a European-Mediterranean Association Agreement now being negotiated.

EU- STATES OF FORMER YUGOSLAVIA AGREEMENT There is an EU Co-Operative Agreement with the former states of Yugoslavia which went into force into 1998 and provided non-reciprocal preferential access to the EU for the products for all the above states but is to be replaced by stability and association agreements now being negotiated.

EU-JORDAN AGREEMENT There is an EU Co-Operative Agreement (*Official Journal* L/268, 27.9.78) with Jordan which went into force into 1977 but it is to be replaced by a European-Mediterranean Association Agreement signed in 1997.

EU-LEBANON AGREEMENT There is an EU Co-Operative Agreement (*Official Journal* L/267, 27.9.78) with Lebanon which went into force into 1977 but it is to be replaced by a European-Mediterranean Association Agreement now being negotiated.

EU-MOROCCO AGREEMENT There is an EU Co-Operative Agreement (*Official Journal* L/70, 18.3.00) with Morocco which went into force into 2000 but it is to be replaced by a European-Mediterranean Association Agreement now being negotiated.

EU-SYRIA AGREEMENT There is an EU Co-Operative Agreement (*Official Journal* L/269, 27.9.78) with Syria which went into force into 1977 but it is to be replaced by a European-Mediterranean Association Agreement now being negotiated.

EU-TUNISIA AGREEMENT There is an EU Co-Operative Agreement (*Official Journal* L/97, 30.3.98) with Tunisia which went into force into 1998 but it is to be replaced by a European-Mediterranean Association Agreement now being negotiated.

EU-PALESTINIAN AUTHORITY AGREEMENT There is an EU Co-Operative Agreement (*Official Journal* L/187, 16.7.97) with the Palestinean Authority which went into force into 1997 but has been replaced by an interim European-Mediterranean Association Agreement.

EU CUSTOMS UNION PARTICIPATION AGREEMENTS EU customs participation agreements exist between small enclaves that are effectively part of the economic, but not the political, territory of some EU state or as preparation for the membership of the non-EU party (Turkey) in the EU (or perhaps as a sop for being rejected for such membership).

EU-ANDORRA AGREEMENT There is an EU agreement (an exchange of letters found in *Official Journal* L/374, 31.12.90) with Andorra which established a customs union between the EU and Andorra (for industrial products only) that went into force in 1991.

EU-SAN MARINO AGREEMENT There is an EU agreement (*Official Journal* L/359, 9.12.92) with San Marino which established a customs union between the EU and Andorra which went into force in 1992.

EU-TURKEY AGREEMENT There is a Decision of January 1995 of the EU-Turkey Association Council (*Official Journal* L/35, 13.2.95) which established the final phase of a customs union between Turkey and the EU (for industrial products only) which went into force in 1995.

SO-CALLED EU "EUROPEAN AGREEMENTS" EU European Agreements (see the next chapter) are those signed with Eastern European countries that had formerly been Baltic Soviet Republics or now independent parts of the former Yugoslavia or had been satellite states of the Soviet Union.

EU-BULGARIA AGREEMENT There is an EU European Agreement (Official Journal L/358, 31.12.94) with Bulgaria that went into effect in 1994.

EU-CZECH REPUBLIC AGREEMENT There is an EU European Agreement (*Official Journal* L/360, 31.12.94) with the Czech Republic that went into force in 1992.

EU-ESTONIA AGREEMENT There is an EU European Agreement (Official Journal L/68, 9.3.98) with Estonia that went into force in 1995.

EU-HUNGARY AGREEMENT There is an EU European Agreement (Official Journal L/347, 31.12.923) with Hungary that went into force in 1992.

EU-LATVIA AGREEMENT The is an EU European Agreement (Official Journal L/26, 2.2.98) with Latvia that went into effect in 1995.

EU-LITHUANIA AGREEMENT There is an EU European Agreement (Official Journal L/51, 20.2.98) with Lithuania that went into effect in 1995.

EU-POLAND AGREEMENT There is an EU European Agreement (Offficial Journal L/348, 31.12.93) with Poland that went into force in 1992.

EU-ROMANIA AGREEMENT There is an EU European Agreement (Official Journal L/357, 31.12.94) with Romania that went into effect in 1993.

EU-SLOVAKIA AGREEMENT There is an EU European Agreement (Official Journal L/359, 31.12.94) with Slovakia that went into force in 1992.

EU-SLOVENIA AGREEMENT There is an EU European Agreement (Official Journal L/51, 26.2.99) with Slovenia that went into force in 1997

EU FREE TRADE AGREEMENTS The EU increasingly is entering into free trade agreements with other countries. This is done in many instances as a precursor to or the near equivalent of the incorporation of free trade agreement parties into the EEA. In others, it is intended to place the EU on trade terms with the free trade agreement party very similar to those of its main trade rivals with which the non-EU free trade party has, or is likely to develop, preferential trading relations bilaterally or within a regional trade bloc. In the case of South Africa, the free trade agreement was intended to shore up the economic status of South Africa during its transition out of the former apartheid regime to the post-apartheid regime.

EU-CHILE AGREEMENT An EU-Chile Free Trade Agreement is now being negotiated.

EU-FAROE ISLANDS AGREEMENT There is an EU-Faroe Islands Free Trade Agreement (*Official Journal* L/53, 27.2.97) which went into force in 1997, replacing an agreement of 1991.

EU-ICELAND AGREEMENT There is an EU-Iceland Free Trade Agreement (*Official Journal* L/301, 31.12.72) which went into force in 1973 but has since been overtaken by Iceland's participation in the EEA.

EU-LIECHTENSTEIN AGREEMENT There is an EU-Liechtenstein Free Trade Agreement (*Official Journal* L/1, 3.1.94) that went into force in 1994.

EU-MERCOSUR AGREEMENT There is an EU-Mercosur Free Trade Agreement now being negotiated.

EU-MEXICO AGREEMENT There is an EU-Mexico Comprehensive/ Free Trade Agreement (*Official Journal* L/276, 28.10.00) which went into force in 2000, augmented by the Decision 2000 of the EU-Mexico Joint Council (*Official Journal* L/157, 30.6.00).

EU-NORWAY AGREEMENT There is an EU-Norway Free Trade Agreement (*Official Journal* L/171, 27.6.73) which came into force in 1973 but has been overtaken by Norway's participation in the EEA.

EU-SOUTH AFRICA AGREEMENT There is an EU-South Africa Trade Development and Cooperation Agreement (*Official Journal* L/ 311, 4.12.99) which went into force in 2000 which created a free trade area under an exchange of letters applied provisionally since January 1, 2000.

EU-SWITZERLAND AGREEMENT There is an EU Free Trade Agreement (*Official Journal* L/187, 31.12.93) with Switzerland (that also covered Liechtenstein), the only member of EFTA that did not join the EEA, which came into force in 1973.

EU CUSTOMS ADMINISTRATION AGREEMENTS The EU has entered into a number of bilateral customs arrangements which are designed to regularize cooperation on various customs aspect of mutual interest and benefit to both parties.

EU-CANADA CUSTOMS COOPERATION AND MUTUAL ADMINISTRATIVE ASSISTANCE AGREEMENT There is a Customs Cooperation and Mutual Administrative Assistance Agreement between the EU and Canada to work jointly against customs fraud.

EU-US CUSTOMS COOPERATION AND MUTUAL ADMINISTRATIVE ASSISTANCE AGREEMENT There is a Customs Cooperation and Mutual Administrative Assistance Agreement between the

EU and the US to work jointly against customs fraud.

EU-SOUTH KOREA CUSTOMS COOPERATION AND MUTUAL ADMINISTRATIVE ASSISTANCE AGREEMENT There is a Customs Cooperation and Mutual Administrative Assistance Agreement between the EU and the Republic of Korea ("South Korea") to work jointly against customs fraud.

EU-AUSTRALIA MUTUAL RECOGNITION AGREEMENT There is an EU-Australia Mutual Recognition in Relation to Conformity Assessment, Certifications, and Marking between the EU and Australia.

EU-CANADA MUTUAL RECOGNITION AGREEMENT There is an EU-Canada Mutual Recognition of Conformity Agreement of 1998.

EU STEEL AGREEMENTS There are steel agreements with Kazakhstan, Russia, Turkey, and Ukraine which provide for restraints on shipping steel to the EU in lieu of the establishment of EU quotas that are set to expire in 2001.

EFTA Bilateral Trade Agreements

Despite its tenuous status because of the abandonment of most of its former members for EU membership and the participation of its current members in the EEA under EU tutelage, EFTA—whose remaining members are Norway, Iceland, Liechtenstein, and Switzerland—continues to establish bilateral trade agreements with some countries. In many instances, these agreements are undertaken in compatible tandem with agreements with the same countries made by the EU. As of March 2001, EFTA had 16 bilateral free trade agreements and ten declarations on cooperation which are envisioned to be the first step towards free trade agreements. Such agreements include those with Croatia, Mexico, Hungary, Poland, Romania, Lithuania, Estonia, Latvia, Slovenia, and Israel.

Other Non-US Bilateral Free Trade Agreements

In mid-1996, Canada and Israel signed a trade agreement similar to that the US and EU have with Israel to, in early 1997, eliminate tariffs on most industrial goods and establish low or zero duties of various agricultural and fisheries products. Dairy, poultry, and egg products are not covered by the Agreement.

Canada has a free trade agreement with Chile that is symbolically important, as well as being meaningful in its own right, since it clearly represented Canada's pique with the United States for failing to successfully conclude negotiations with Chile which would permit Chile to have become a member of NAFTA as was anticipated when

NAFTA was first signed and which would have represented the first stage of integration of the other Western Hemispheric countries into NAFTA's scheme of economic liberalization and integration of national markets.

The United Arab Republic ("UAR") of Egypt and Syria sprang from an enthusiasm for "Pan-Arabism" but collapsed in the face of the personal rivalries and practical difficulties of fusing the two noncontiguous and dissimilar countries. Libya's subsequent repeated seriocomic efforts to politically and economically unite, initially with Egypt under a reconstituted UAR and subsequently with virtually every one of its Arab neighbors in the region, was doomed to failure because of the eccentric nature of the Libyan regime.

In mid-March 2001, the Syrian legislature was reported to have approved a free trade area agreement with Iraq. Whether Iraq, yesterday's pariah state against which sanctions have failed and are now fast eroding, also wants a free trade agreement with Syria was unclear. The two countries are the only ones in the world with Ba'athist Parties (based on a very obscurantist ideology) in control, but instead of uniting them in the past this fact seems to have made the two neighbors blood enemies. Neither has shown much enthusiasm for economic liberalization. Perhaps the Syrian legislature's move is merely demonstrative of "free trade" now serving, rather like "socialist democracy" did in the 1960s, as today's most popular name to use in political theater where it is used as a descriptive term for a reality that is its opposite.

Venezuela has a free trade agreement with CARICOM.

Other Bilateral Customs Unions

There are some bilateral customs unions relationships. These are largely the result of smaller contiguous countries adopting for convenience purposes the customs, tariffs, and customs administration of a larger and often economically-dominant neighboring country, with administrative costs and revenues shared between the countries according to some agreed ratio or calculation.

SWITZERLAND-LIECHTENSTEIN CUSTOMS UNION Switzerland and Liechtenstein are, for most purposes, operated as a single economic entity and market. Liechtenstein entered into a customs union with Switzerland in 1923 that made both Swiss customs legislation and the Swiss Federal Stamp Duty Act applicable in Liechtenstein. With the refusal of the Swiss to become a part of either the EU or the EEA, Liechtenstein must have found it inconvenient to continue in lock step with Switzerland in a common customs union as that is now constituted but Switzerland's free trade agreement with the EU and its anticipated negotiation of participation in the EEA should relieve such concerns.

CZECH REPUBLIC-SLOVAKIA CUSTOMS UNION The Czech Republic and Slovakia were joined in the country of Czechoslovakia from 1918 until 1993. To reduce the confusion and economic dislocation from dividing what had for years been a single country and a single economy, the two formed a customs union upon their separation.

SENEGAMBIA Senegal and the Gambia are combined in an economic and political union, called "Senegambia." The President of Senegal is the President of Senegambia and the President of Gambia is the Vice-President of Senegambia. The purposes of the confederation are to integrate the two nations' armies and security forces; to develop economic and monetary union; to coordinate foreign policies; and to coordinate commercial policies.

US Bilateral Trade Relationships

The United States has relatively few bilateral trade agreements providing for general or limited free trade between the US and a treaty partner. Nonetheless, there are some such agreements and there seem to be a rush of new ones on the way. The relationship between the United States and Canada, USCFTA, was described under NAFTA in the previous chapter. The free trade agreements the United States has completed with Israel and with Jordan are examined in some detail below. At the time of publication, US free trade agreements with Chile and with Singapore were said to be near completion, although the change in US administrations because of a presidential election have delayed the completion of those agreements largely because of the expectation that the Bush Administration's trade objectives and negotiating positions would be distinctly different than those of the Clinton Administration under which those negotiations were begun.

USIFTA

The relationship between the governments and peoples of the US and Israel has been both special and close since the creation of the State of Israel in 1948. A number of US statutes and regulations make special provision for Israel. The US was the first country to formally recognize the State of Israel and has maintained very warm ties to that beleaguered nation ever since.

The Governments of the US and Israel signed a free trade agreement between them, entitled the Agreement on Establishment of a

Free Trade Area Between the Government of the United States and the Government of Israel ("USIFTA"), in 1985. The text of USIFTA may be found in 24 International Legal Materials 3, page 653, of May 1985. USIFTA consists of a preamble, 23 separate articles, and four annexes. Annexes 1 and 2 provide the separate schedules of tariff reductions for Israel and the US. Annex 4 articulates USIFTA's rules of origin. Annex 4 is a letter expressing Israel's commitment to the reduction and elimination of its export subsidies. There is no termination date for USIFTA. Either party may terminate USIFTA 12 months after providing the required written notice to the other party.

In the US, USIFTA was authorized by the Tariff and Trade Act of 1984 and implemented by the US-Israel Free Trade Area Implementation Act of 1985, Pub. L. 99-47, 99 Stat. 82, codified at 19 USC.S. §2112, and Presidential Proclamation 5365 of August 30, 1985. It has since been modified through Public Law 104-234 of October 2, 1996, and a Presidential Proclamation of November 17, 1996, which extended geographical coverage of USIFTA to the West Bank, the Gaza Strip, or a "qualifying industrial zone." USIFTA has consistently but tacitly been read by the US to permit Israel to define the territory of Israel from which goods benefitting under USIFTA originate. This has meant that goods from East Jerusalem and the Golan Heights fall under USIFTA's effective coverage. A separate agreement, the US-Israel Agreement on Trade in Agricultural Products, was signed on November 4, 1996, to take effect within 30 days, and to expire by its own terms in 5 years. This agreement eliminated some tariffs on agricultural products and provided for reductions in tariffs on others.

USIFTA operates under Article XXIV of GATT 1947. It is to be read, according to USIFTA's own terms, in conjunction with GATT in the determination and interpretation of its provisions. GATT 1947's General Exceptions of Article XX and the Security Exceptions of Article XXI are explicitly incorporated into USIFTA. USIFTA was the first occasion the United States had become part of a free trade area.

When the US and Israel wished to establish a free trade area, accomplishing this aim presented a number of special challenges. These were in addition to the normal difficulties under a free trade area agreement of, for example, negotiating ROs which define what is and is not a free trade area good and eligible for its benefits. First among those special challenges was the fact that Israel administered a large occupied territory and population in East Jerusalem, the Golan Heights, the Gaza Strip, and the West Bank. To varying degrees, the Government of Israel asserted sovereign claims to some of these territories (but paradoxically not to their indigenous populations) which the US Government did not and does not recognize. Second was the heavy participation of the Government of Israel, Israeli political parties, and their quasi-official organizations in the economy of Israel and the extensive subsidies granted by the Government of Israel to some private, governmental, and quasi-governmental commercial enterprises. Statism and subsidization create virtually intractable difficulties in establishing freer international trade because they generate circumstances in which the domestic market of one of the traders is itself not free. Third was the highly regulated nature of the Israeli economy. Extensive and intrusive regulation gave ample scope to Israeli regulators and the administrators and enforcers of Israeli regulations to impose (whether as official policy or on an informal basis) impediments to the entry and sale of US goods. Fourth, Israel's free trade area agreements with the EU and with EFTA created the danger that goods from Europe could enter Israel free of duties and then be reexported to the US under USIFTA's provisions without the payment of US duties.

Under the terms of USIFTA, trade and commerce between the two countries are conducted according to special terms and conditions with the intention of stimulating trade between them. The principal purpose of USIFTA is to eliminate tariffs and other restrictive regulations that impede commerce between the two countries. This was accomplished on a phased-in basis. The elimination of these impediments to trade were completed January 1, 1995, and USIFTA's transition to a US-Israel free trade area is now complete. During the phase-in process under USIFTA, the US was regularly very unhappy with Israeli compliance with and implementation of the agreement. Reportedly, with full phase-in both parties are now satisfied with each others' adherence to the terms and spirit of USIFTA. US exports to Israel nearly tripled from US$1.68 billion in 1985 to an estimated US$4.8 billion in 1994.

Summary descriptions of some of the more important of USIFTA's articles and annexes are offered below.

No new trade restrictions Article 4 provides that no new trade restrictions will be imposed by either party on the imports of the other party.

Safeguards Article 5 addresses the application of the safeguard provision of GATT Article XXIX to bring the bilateral arrangement between the US and Israel into conformity with US law.

Restrictions on the importation of agricultural goods Article 6 permits either party to establish sanitary and phytosanitary restrictions on the importation of agricultural products and to impose —on the basis of national treatment—import restrictions based on religious dietary laws (with Jewish kosher rules obviously the focus of this provision).

Infant industries Article 10 put restrictions on Israel's right to apply protective measures to benefit infant industries during the phase-in period to the increase or reintroduction of duties on specific products. Such protections were completely eliminated in 1995.

Balance of payments Article 11 restricts the more liberal GATT standards by putting severe limitations on the use of quantitative restrictions and other temporary trade measures occasioned by balance of payments difficulties.

Import licensing Article 12 makes import licensing procedures more restrictive than those of GATT 1947's Code on Import Licensing Procedures.

Export requirements Article 13 imposed new disciplines on the use of export requirements as a condition for receiving government incentives.

Intellectual property Article 14 reaffirms existing obligations regarding the protection of intellectual property.

Services Article 16 states that both parties agree to develop means of cooperation pursuant to a separate declaration of services which commits them to work towards opening their markets to their respective service industries, including transportation, tourism, communications, banking, insurance, construction, engineering, accounting, education, law, management consulting, computer services and advertising. The resulting declaration was a terse, nonbinding statement of intent.

Dispute resolution Articles 17, 18, and 19 create a joint committee as a consultation mechanism, encourage cooperation, and reaffirm existing bilateral and multilateral trade commitments.

Specific duties Article 21 modifies and enhances the right of both parties to increase specific import duties to keep pace with changes in the respective value of their national currencies.

Government procurement The US and Israel agreed in Article 15 to a further elimination of government procurement related trade restrictions beyond those of GATT 1947's International Government Procurement Code by lowering the threshold to around US$50,000 (about 1/3 of that under the GATT Code) for nondiscriminatory bidding for government contracts by nationals of the two countries. Israel also agreed to eliminate buy-Israel restrictions for non-military products by its ministry of defense and to relax off-set requirements in regard to civilian agency procurement.

Annexes 1 and 2 contain the schedules of phased-in reductions in tariffs. These were to be completed in ten years, *i.e.*, by January 1, 1995. Duties on covered US and Israeli products were gradually phased out in accordance with established schedules and they are not now subject to any duties upon importation. Products covered include most tariff items listed in the US Harmonized Tariff Schedule. These items are identified by "IL" in the "Special" rate column in subheadings under the US tariff schedule and are subject to the rate of duty shown in such "Special" column in the subheading.

Annex 3 establishes the rules of origin to be applied in determining eligibility of products for USIFTA preferential tariff treatment. These rules are, like all rules of origin, complex in their interpretation and application. They are not, however, novel for those familiar with other US preferential trading regimes. They are based upon the rules of origin of the US Caribbean Basin Initiative and are only slightly modified versions of those rules.

Under **Annex 4**, Israel undertook within six years to eliminate its export subsidies programs on industrial goods and processed agricultural products. It has done so.

ROs Rules of origin apply equally to products of the two countries. Below a description of eligible products will be for those from Israel while the analog terms for those from the US will be in **[brackets and bold print]**. Eligible products are those which are the growth, product, or manufacture of Israel **[or the US]** or, if they contain imported components, are transformed in Israel **[or the US]** into new and different articles of commerce distinct from the articles from which they were transformed. The sum of their costs or the value of the materials produced in Israel **[or the US]** plus the direct costs of processing operations performed in Israel **[or the US]** may not be less than 35% of the appraised value—generally the price charged on exportation—of such articles at the time they are entered. Up to 15% of the appraised value of the product may originate in the importing country and be counted towards the minimum 35% free trade area value added requirement.

Free trade area value added may include: (a) Labor costs including fringe benefits, on the job training and quality control costs; (b) Costs of dies, molds, tooling, inspection and testing, and depreciation of equipment; and (c) Research and development and design costs related to the product. Profit and indirect costs, such as administration salaries, advertising, and sales costs are excluded in determining the value of items produced.

Products must usually be imported from the exporting country directly but may also be imported via another country provided the products do not enter into the commerce of the intermediate country.

A certificate of origin, signed by the exporter and certified by its local chamber of commerce, is required if tariff concessions under USIFTA are claimed. For Israeli commercial shipments entering the US under a USIFTA claim for duty free or reduced duty rates covered by a formal entry, the Harmonized Tariff Schedule subheading number must be prefixed with an "IL" on the Customs Form 7501 or Customs Form 7505 Customs entry documents, as appropriate.

Israeli tariffs and taxes for imports from the United States under USIFTA may be calculated by applying the following rules and formulae. US goods (excluding a few agricultural products) which meet USIFTA ROs qualify for zero duty. USIFTA ROs require that at least 35 percent of the product be American and/or Israeli origin. A USIFTA Certificate of Origin must be completed. Some products are subject to the import uplift ("TAMA"), which is imposed on a c.i.f. basis. The TAMA rate varies by product and is used to calculate the VAT and purchase tax. An Israeli purchase tax (different rates apply to different goods) is applied on c.i.f. value plus the TAMA, plus port fee (if applicable). A VAT of 17% is applied on the c.i.f. value, purchase tax, and port fee and other fees (if applicable). A port fee of 1.3% is assessed on goods shipped by sea but not charged on goods shipped by air. Other fees are imposed on certain products, such as fuel, alcoholic beverages, and tobacco. To arrive at the total tariffs and fees assessed by Israel on the importation of US goods qualifying under USIFTA, begin by making the calculation of: c.i.f. + tariff + (c.i.f. times port fee) = Z; using the result Z, calculate TAMA Y by making the calculation of: Z + Z times TAMA rate = Y; Y – which is the TAMA – is not payable but is used to calculate the base on which the purchase tax is levied by making the calculation of: Y times purchase tax rate = purchase tax payable. From the purchase tax payable, the total Israeli tariffs and taxes owed on an importation of USIFTA qualifying goods is determined by making the calculation of: c.i.f. + port fee + purchase tax + tariff + other fees + VAT = total tariffs and taxes payable.

US-Jordan Free Trade Agreement

The US and Jordan are not major trading partners and Jordan produces little besides phosphates to export to anyone. Nonetheless, the US-Jordan Free Trade Agreement was important for two reasons.

Because of (a) the recent death of Jordan's king who had been a voice of reason and accommodation in the Middle East and a man generally not antipathetic to the US and his replacement by his relatively inexperienced son and (b) the importance of Jordan to any prospect of peace in the area, the United States was anxious to provide any real help it could to Jordan's rather bleak economy and any demonstration it could of its commitment and support to Jordan and its current regime. Further, the Clinton Administration wished to make the Jordan Free Trade Agreement its first—several others were then in the works—showcase on how it could square the circle by making an agreement ostensibly dealing with free trade to serve also as what is effectively the imposition on a foreign trading partner of US preferences regarding the environment and labor.

The US-Jordan Free Trade Agreement signed on October 24, 2000, eliminates duties and commercial barriers to bilateral trade in goods and services originating in the United States and Jordan. The agreement also includes, for the first time ever in the text of a trade agreement, provisions addressing trade and environment, trade and labor, and electronic commerce. Other provisions address intellectual property rights protection, balance of payments, ROs, safeguards, and procedural matters such as consultations and dispute settlement. Virtually all tariffs on industrial goods and farm products will be eliminated within 10 years. There will be free trade in services with full access to all important service sectors. Because the United States already has a bilateral investment treaty with Jordan, the agreement does not include an investment chapter.

Special Bilateral Relationships Between a Country and a Semi-Autonomous Territory, an Enclave, or a Client State

SPECIAL BILATERAL RELATIONSHIPS BETWEEN AN EU COUNTRY AND A SEMI-AUTONOMOUS TERRITORY, RESIDUAL COLONIAL POSSESSION, OR ENCLAVE European countries, because of their complex histories and former possession of colonial empires, are often possessed of semi-autonomous territories or residual colonial holdings that do not fit easily into the general system of dealings among sovereign states. They may also enclose or abut upon tiny enclaves that, for historical reasons, maintain a formal but insubstantial (but highly important to the enclave) independence. When a country becomes a member of the EU, it is generally difficult to either totally include the territory of such semi-autonomous territory, enclave, or non-European residual colonial holding fully within the EU common market or the exclude such entities entirely from that market. In most instances, EU members have negotiated the special terms of access to the EU for those territories, enclaves, and possessions. The result has often been an idiosyncratic, complex, and confusing melange of terms and conditions which is only moderated by the fact that such territories, enclaves, and possessions are rarely of substantial importance for purposes of EU or international trade. The EU maintains a special policy towards these territories both in and out of Europe under its Overseas Lands and Territories arrangement.

Within Europe, the UK has special relations with three territories: the Channel Islands comprised of the Bailiwicks of Jersey and Guernsey (each bailiwick is independent of the other and their connection is not to the UK but to the British sovereign); the Isle of Man, another island with fealty to the British sovereign and not to the UK and Gibraltar, a British Crown Colony on the tip of the Iberian Peninsula with title to it disputed from time to time by Spain. Nonetheless, none are actually part of the UK, to none are all the laws of the UK automatically applicable, and none are fully incorporated into the EU under the same terms as is the UK. Consequently, it will be necessary to determine the precise economic and legal relationship between each of these entities and the UK (and those relationships are extremely complex) and the terms of accession by the UK to the EU with regards to each of these entities in order to determine the degree to which each participates with the UK and/or the EU as part of an economic group. Each of the first two is effectively within the EU free trade area but is not subject to the full range of EU rights and obligations in other areas. Gibraltar is a duty-free port and, although it became associated with the EU at the time the UK negotiated membership, it is not part of the EU common tariff and is seemingly effectively outside of any meaningful participation in EU practices or policies.

The "Kingdom" of Denmark consists of European Denmark, the Faroe Islands, and Greenland, although neither of the latter two is part of "Denmark." The Faroe Islands are semi-autonomous islands lying about mid-way between Iceland and Scotland. They are a self-governing part of the Kingdom of Denmark with flexibility in the application of Danish law and have an independent ability to enter into international agreements, *e.g.*, international fishing agreements. Greenland is the world's largest island and once, until 1985, was fully incorporated into the EU but withdrew because of dissatisfaction with EU fishing policies.

Finland has the Åland Islands which lie between Finland and Sweden in the Gulf of Bothnia. Those islands were admitted under special terms when Finland negotiated its membership in the EU.

France has Monaco, or maybe it does not have Monaco, depending on dynastic succession. If the present line of Monegasque princes ever fails, Monaco reverts to France. The laws are mostly French, the currency is French, by law the Minister of State (the equivalent of premier) must be a French citizen, and there has been a customs union between France and Monaco since 1864.

Italy surrounds San Marino—a tiny independent state—and Italy's capital, Rome, fully encloses the Holy See (also called Vatican City). Italy has established special treaty relations with the independent states of the Vatican (Holy See) and San Marino which make these territories part of the Italian customs area and lira currency bloc.

No independent examination may be offered here of all the varying relationships that exist between EU states and their non-European possessions. What will have to suffice is what is hoped to be a definitive enumeration of them.

France has St. Pierre et Miquelon off the Southern coast of Newfoundland; Mayotte—one of the Comoro Islands—and Reunion (and five small islands administered from Reunion but also claimed by Madagascar) in the Indian Ocean; the French South Atlantic Territories of Kerguelen Island, Crozet Island, and St. Paul Island near Antarctica; New Caledonia near Australia; French Polynesia and the Wallis and Futuna Islands in the South Pacific; St. Barthélemy (St. Barts), half the island of St. Martin, Martinique, and Guadeloupe in the Caribbean; and French Guiana on South America's northeastern rim. The UK has Saint Helena and its dependencies of Ascension Island, Tristan de Cunha, and Gough Islands in the Atlantic Ocean at some distance from the African coast; the Cayman Islands, Montserrat, the British Virgin Islands, Anguilla, the Turks and Caicos, and Bermuda in or near the Caribbean; Pitcairn Island in the South Pacific; the Falkland (Malvinas if you are Argentine) Islands and South Georgia (and related islands) in the South Atlantic; and the British Indian Ocean Territory in the Indian Ocean far off the South Asian coast. Spain has Ceuta and Melilla in Northern Morocco and Chafarinas, Vélex de la Gomera, and Alhucemas—three islands off Morocco's Northern Coast. The Netherlands has the Netherlands Antilles and Aruba in the Caribbean.

SIMILAR RELATIONSHIPS OTHER THAN THOSE WITH AN EU MEMBER OR THE US Norway, although not a member of the EU, has equally ambivalent legal and political relations with Bouvet Island (one of several claimed Norwegian overseas territories on or near Antarctica), Jan Mayen Island—halfway between Scandinavia and Iceland—and the Svålbård Islands (sometimes called

"Spitsbergen") which Norway has had as an overseas territory since 1925, which lie 700 miles north of the Scandinavian Peninsula, and which are home to an officially-resident group of Russian miners working in a Russian state-owned mine.

The PRC has special economic relationships individually with its semi-autonomous territories of Hong Kong and Macau.

New Zealand is in voluntary association with the South Pacific states of Niue and the Cook Islands and has a South Pacific dependency of Tokelau.

US SPECIAL RELATIONSHIPS WITH TERRITORIES OUTSIDE THE 50 STATES AND THE DISTRICT OF COLUMBIA The US has numerous special relationships with a number of territories presently or formerly politically associated with it but never among the US states. Guam, American Samoa, the US Virgin Islands, Wake Island, the Midway Islands, Kingman Reef, Johnston Island, the Baker and Howland Islands, Jarvis Island, Palmyra Island, and Navassa Island are deemed US possessions. Puerto Rico and the Commonwealth of the Northern Mariana Islands are commonwealths of the United States. The US Possession of Guam is now seeking commonwealth status. There are a number of other small, uninhabited islands and reefs in the Caribbean and the South Pacific claimed by the US.

A US possession is directly administered by the US. The US Office of Territorial and International Affairs ("OTIA") of the US Department of the Interior administers American Samoa, Guam, the US Virgin Islands, and the Commonwealth of the Northern Mariana Islands. Some possessions are "incorporated" or "unincorporated" and some are "organized" or "unorganized." Whether they are incorporated or unincorporated determines, respectively, whether all provisions of the US Constitution do or do not apply to them. Whether they are organized or unorganized is determined by whether the US Congress has provided them with organic acts which act as their constitutions (the US Congress has sometimes permitted locals to draft their own constitutions under which their governments function in the latter case).

Puerto Rico and the Commonwealth of the Northern Mariana Islands are US commonwealths. Commonwealth status provides full autonomy in domestic affairs, offers certain economic advantages—principally easier access to US markets—and allows the commonwealth to enact its own constitution—compatible with the US Constitution—whose institutions of self-government can not be unilaterally abrogated or amended by the US Congress.

In the Pacific, the Republic of the Marshall Islands, the Republic of Palau, and the Federated States of Micronesia are independent, sovereign countries countries but were formerly United Nations Trust Territories administered by the US. Each of them has a Free Association Arrangement with the US.

Chapter VI: Special Dispensations from the Global System of Customs and Tariffs

In General

Although this book consists of a description of an international system of customs and tariffs, it is nonetheless true that it is often quite possible to fall outside that system in international transactions. On occasion, falling outside the international system will occur unintentionally and with negative consequences for the international trader. More commonly, getting outside that system is sought by international traders in order to avoid payments or to increase operational flexibility.

To state the obvious, it often occurs that a deal falls outside the international system because some countries remain outside that system. WTO/GATT require that a member have a national economy that is based on markets and have the credible ability to live up to any commitments it makes upon joining the WTO. Russia, for example, falls so woefully short of qualifying that it has not even sought WTO membership. The PRC, by contrast, has assiduously sought WTO membership for several years and has nearly completed the process, but still it somehow continues to remain outside the international system because the PRC cannot seem to ever quite accept the fact that WTO membership will actually curtail its flexibility and prevent its favored practice of manipulating or frustrating free market mechanisms. Some countries are part of the system but act in flagrant contravention of it. Corruption is often the cause of this, but France is an example of a country whose police and other authorities regularly passively—or perhaps even supportively—watch as protesting Frenchmen stop trucks coming into France with Italian wine or lamb meat and then pour the wine onto the ground or render the lamb unsaleable. If the French authorities are willing to do this to the imported products of another member of the EU, imagine how readily they would acquiesce to equally illegal treatment of a product from a non-EU country!

There are several specific means by which the strictures imposed by national customs and tariffs or the limitations of the international system of customs and tariffs may be legally avoided. These consist of (a) the special treatment that is permitted developing and least-developed countries under GATT/WTO; (b) the use of free trade zones, bonded warehouses, and the like; (c) special treatment accorded to imports that are used to ship goods on or in them and which will be removed from the customs territory and for other sample goods, work tools, and similar wares that will be consumed but not sold within the customs territory or will be removed again from it within a short time period; (d) duty drawback and similar systems under which customs paid (and even some sales and other taxes paid) may be refunded totally or partially upon the reexportation of the imported goods or of domestically produced goods incorporating imported goods; and (e) implementation of the escape clause, balance-of-payments provision, and similar emergency relief measures under WTO/GATT.

Special Preferential Conditions Permitted for Imports From, and for Customs and Tariff Practices by, Underdeveloped Countries

GATT/WTO provides numerous instances of special treatment for underdeveloped countries (and even more favorable treatment for "least-developed" countries or "LDCs". These will not be described here in great detail. Suffice it to say that the GATT/WTO provisions that follow are only those that exclusively deal with preferential treatment for underdeveloped and least-developed countries. Many other provisions which focus on other matters contain articles or sentences giving similar deference to those countries. It must be said that such countries both (a) deserve our commiseration because of their poverty and may be proper beneficiaries of preferential treatment in at least a token expression of hope that they may rise above it and (b) are largely inconsequential trading nations in the world's economy so that special treatment accorded those countries hardly matters in the big picture of global trade. Their unenviable situation is circular. They are poor because they are not economically competitive and, to a degree, they are not economically competitive because they are poor.

Special terms for underdeveloped countries may permit three quite different things. First, they effectively permit developed WTO members to admit goods into their customs territories from underdeveloped countries at favorable rates in contravention of MFN standards, either under the general program of Generalized System of Preferences ("GSP") or under special programs negotiated between the developed and undeveloped countries that provides preferential tariff and customs status **unilaterally** for goods originating in an underdeveloped country entering the customs territory of the developed country. Each developed country implementing the GSP will implement it differently subject to varying exclusions and including differing lists of qualifying underdeveloped countries. Most developed countries have developed their own special negotiated arrangements with blocs of underdeveloped countries for trade development and other purposes. Second, they permit underdeveloped countries to receive special consideration in the application of GATT/WTO rules and requirements, including delayed adoption of the provisions of GATT/WTO adopted in the Uruguay Round and through other negotiations. Third, they permit underdeveloped countries to form regional trading blocs and similar free trade areas and customs unions without being compelled to meet the same WTO/GATT standards as are such blocs made up of developed countries.

What are offered immediately below are (a) the relevant principal GATT/WTO provisions dealing with underdeveloped countries and (b) general descriptions of some special developed country unilateral trade preference programs with selected underdeveloped countries.

GATT 1947 Provisions and Their Interpretations with Special Application to Underdeveloped Countries—the Texts

[***asterisks** below mark the portions of the text which should be read in conjunction with notes and supplementary provisions in Annex I to the Agreement.]

"Article XVIII*

Governmental Assistance to Economic Development

1. The contracting parties recognize that the attainment of the objectives of this Agreement will be facilitated by the progressive development of their economies, particularly of those contracting parties the economies of which can only support low standards of living* and are in the early stages of development.*

2. The contracting parties recognize further that it may be necessary for those contracting parties, in order to implement programmes and policies of economic development designed to raise the general standard of living of their people, to take protective or other measures affecting imports, and that such measures are justified in so far as they facilitate the attainment of the objectives of this Agreement. They agree, therefore, that those contracting parties should enjoy additional facilities to enable them (*a*) to maintain sufficient flexibility in their tariff structure to be able to grant the tariff protection required for the establishment of a particular industry* and (*b*) to apply quantitative restrictions for balance of payments purposes in a manner which takes full account of the continued high level of demand for imports likely to be generated by their programmes of economic development.

3. The contracting parties recognize finally that, with those additional facilities which are provided for in Sections A and B of this Article, the provisions of this Agreement would normally be sufficient to enable contracting parties to meet the requirements of their economic development. They agree, however, that there may be circumstances where no measure

consistent with those provisions is practicable to permit a contracting party in the process of economic development to grant the governmental assistance required to promote the establishment of particular industries* with a view to raising the general standard of living of its people. Special procedures are laid down in Sections C and D of this Article to deal with those cases.

4.

(*a*) Consequently, a contracting party, the economy of which can only support low standards of living* and is in the early stages of development,* shall be free to deviate temporarily from the provisions of the other Articles of this Agreement, as provided in Sections A, B and C of this Article.

(*b*) A contracting party, the economy of which is in the process of development, but which does not come within the scope of sub-paragraph (*a*) above, may submit applications to the CONTRACTING PARTIES under Section D of this Article.

5. The contracting parties recognize that the export earnings of contracting parties, the economies of which are of the type described in paragraph 4 (*a*) and (*b*) above and which depend on exports of a small number of primary commodities, may be seriously reduced by a decline in the sale of such commodities. Accordingly, when the exports of primary commodities by such a contracting party are seriously affected by measures taken by another contracting party, it may have resort to the consultation provisions of Article XXII of this Agreement.

6. The CONTRACTING PARTIES shall review annually all measures applied pursuant to the provisions of Sections C and D of this Article.

Section A

7.

(*a*) If a contracting party coming within the scope of paragraph 4 (*a*) of this Article considers it desirable, in order to promote the establishment of a particular industry* with a view to raising the general standard of living of its people, to modify or withdraw a concession included in the appropriate Schedule annexed to this Agreement, it shall notify the CONTRACTING PARTIES to this effect and enter into negotiations with any contracting party with which such concession was initially negotiated, and with any other contracting party determined by the CONTRACTING PARTIES to have a substantial interest therein. If agreement is reached between such contracting parties concerned, they shall be free to modify or withdraw concessions under the appropriate Schedules to this Agreement in order to give effect to such agreement, including any compensatory adjustments involved.

(*b*) If agreement is not reached within sixty days after the notification provided for in sub-paragraph (*a*) above, the contracting party which proposes to modify or withdraw the concession may refer the matter to the CONTRACTING PARTIES which shall promptly examine it. If they find that the contracting party which proposes to modify or withdraw the concession has made every effort to reach an agreement and that the compensatory adjustment offered by it is adequate, that contracting party shall be free to modify or withdraw the concession if, at the same time, it gives effect to the compensatory adjustment. If the CONTRACTING PARTIES do not find that the compensation offered by a contracting party proposing to modify or withdraw the concession is adequate, but find that it has made every reasonable effort to offer adequate compensation, that contracting party shall be free to proceed with such modification or withdrawal. If such action is taken, any other contracting party referred to in sub-paragraph (*a*) above shall be free to modify or withdraw substantially equivalent concessions initially negotiated with the contracting party which has taken the action.*

Section B

8. The contracting parties recognize that contracting parties coming within the scope of paragraph 4 (*a*) of this Article tend, when they are in rapid process of development, to experience balance of payments difficulties arising mainly from efforts to expand their internal markets as well as from the instability in their terms of trade.

9. In order to safeguard its external financial position and to ensure a level of reserves adequate for the implementation of its programme of economic development, a contracting party coming within the scope of paragraph 4 (*a*) of this Article may, subject to the provisions of paragraphs 10 to 12, control the general level of its imports by restricting the quantity or value of merchandise permitted to be imported; *Provided* that the import restrictions instituted, maintained or intensified shall not exceed those necessary:

(*a*) to forestall the threat of, or to stop, a serious decline in its monetary reserves, or

(*b*) in the case of a contracting party with inadequate monetary reserves, to achieve a reasonable rate of increase in its reserves.

Due regard shall be paid in either case to any special factors which may be affecting the reserves of the contracting party or its need for reserves, including, where special external credits or other resources are available to it, the need to provide for the appropriate use of such credits or resources.

10. In applying these restrictions, the contracting party may determine their incidence on imports of different products or classes of products in such a way as to give priority to the importation of those products which are more essential in the light of its policy of economic development; *Provided* that the restrictions are so applied as to avoid unnecessary damage to the commercial or economic interests of any other contracting party and not to prevent unreasonably the importation of any description of goods in minimum commercial quantities the exclusion of which would impair regular channels of trade; and *Provided* further that the restrictions are not so applied as to prevent the importation of commercial samples or to prevent compliance with patent, trade mark, copyright or similar procedures.

11. In carrying out its domestic policies, the contracting party concerned shall pay due regard to the need for restoring equilibrium in its balance of payments on a sound and lasting basis and to the desirability of assuring an economic employment of productive resources. It shall progressively relax any restrictions applied under this Section as conditions improve,

maintaining them only to the extent necessary under the terms of paragraph 9 of this Article and shall eliminate them when conditions no longer justify such maintenance; *Provided* that no contracting party shall be required to withdraw or modify restrictions on the ground that a change in its development policy would render unnecessary the restrictions which it is applying under this Section.*

12.

(*a*) Any contracting party applying new restrictions or raising the general level of its existing restrictions by a substantial intensification of the measures applied under this Section, shall immediately after instituting or intensifying such restrictions (or, in circumstances in which prior consultation is practicable, before doing so) consult with the CONTRACTING PARTIES as to the nature of its balance of payments difficulties, alternative corrective measures which may be available, and the possible effect of the restrictions on the economies of other contracting parties.

(*b*) On a date to be determined by them* the CONTRACTING PARTIES shall review all restrictions still applied under this Section on that date. Beginning two years after that date, contracting parties applying restrictions under this Section shall enter into consultations of the type provided for in sub-paragraph (*a*) above with the CONTRACTING PARTIES at intervals of approximately, but not less than, two years according to a programme to be drawn up each year by the CONTRACTING PARTIES; *Provided* that no consultation under this sub-paragraph shall take place within two years after the conclusion of a consultation of a general nature under any other provision of this paragraph.

(*c*)

(i) If, in the course of consultations with a contracting party under sub-paragraph (*a*) or (*b*) of this paragraph, the CONTRACTING PARTIES find that the restrictions are not consistent with the provisions of this Section or with those of Article XIII (subject to the provisions of Article XIV), they shall indicate the nature of the inconsistency and may advise that the restrictions be suitably modified.

(ii) If, however, as a result of the consultations, the CONTRACTING PARTIES determine that the restrictions are being applied in a manner involving an inconsistency of a serious nature with the provisions of this Section or with those of Article XIII (subject to the provisions of Article XIV) and that damage to the trade of any contracting party is caused or threatened thereby, they shall so inform the contracting party applying the restrictions and shall make appropriate recommendations for securing conformity with such provisions within a specified period. If such contracting party does not comply with these recommendations within the specified period, the CONTRACTING PARTIES may release any contracting party the trade of which is adversely affected by the restrictions from such obligations under this Agreement towards the contracting party applying the restrictions as they determine to be appropriate in the circumstances.

(*d*) The Contracting Parties shall invite any contracting party which is applying restrictions under this Section to enter into consultations with them at the request of any contracting party which can establish a *prima facie* case that the restrictions are inconsistent with the provisions of this Section or with those of Article XIII (subject to the provisions of Article XIV) and that its trade is adversely affected thereby. However, no such invitation shall be issued unless the Contracting Parties have ascertained that direct discussions between the contracting parties concerned have not been successful. If, as a result of the consultations with the Contracting Parties no agreement is reached and they determine that the restrictions are being applied inconsistently with such provisions, and that damage to the trade of the contracting party initiating the procedure is caused or threatened thereby, they shall recommend the withdrawal or modification of the restrictions. If the restrictions are not withdrawn or modified within such time as the Contracting Parties may prescribe, they may release the contracting party initiating the procedure from such obligations under this Agreement towards the contracting party applying the restrictions as they determine to be appropriate in the circumstances.

(*e*) If a contracting party against which action has been taken in accordance with the last sentence of sub-paragraph (*c*) (ii) or (*d*) of this paragraph, finds that the release of obligations authorized by the Contracting Parties adversely affects the operation of its programme and policy of economic development, it shall be free, not later than sixty days after such action is taken, to give written notice to the Executive Secretary [NOW THE DIRECTOR-GENERAL] to the Contracting Parties of its intention to withdraw from this Agreement and such withdrawal shall take effect on the sixtieth day following the day on which the notice is received by him.

(*f*) In proceeding under this paragraph, the Contracting Parties shall have due regard to the factors referred to in paragraph 2 of this Article. Determinations under this paragraph shall be rendered expeditiously and, if possible, within sixty days of the initiation of the consultations.

Section C

13. If a contracting party coming within the scope of paragraph 4 (*a*) of this Article finds that governmental assistance is required to promote the establishment of a particular industry* with a view to raising the general standard of living of its people, but that no measure consistent with the other provisions of this Agreement is practicable to achieve that objective, it may have recourse to the provisions and procedures set out in this Section.*

14. The contracting party concerned shall notify the Contracting Parties of the special difficulties which it meets in the achievement of the objective outlined in paragraph 13 of this Article and shall indicate the specific measure affecting imports which it proposes to introduce in order to remedy these difficulties. It shall not introduce that measure before the expiration of the time-limit laid down in paragraph 15 or 17, as the case may be, or if the

measure affects imports of a product which is the subject of a concession included in the appropriate Schedule annexed to this Agreement, unless it has secured the concurrence of the CONTRACTING PARTIES in accordance with provisions of paragraph 18; *Provided* that, if the industry receiving assistance has already started production, the contracting party may, after informing the CONTRACTING PARTIES, take such measures as may be necessary to prevent, during that period, imports of the product or products concerned from increasing substantially above a normal level.*

15. If, within thirty days of the notification of the measure, the CONTRACTING PARTIES do not request the contracting party concerned to consult with them,* that contracting party shall be free to deviate from the relevant provisions of the other Articles of this Agreement to the extent necessary to apply the proposed measure.

16. If it is requested by the CONTRACTING PARTIES to do so,* the contracting party concerned shall consult with them as to the purpose of the proposed measure, as to alternative measures which may be available under this Agreement, and as to the possible effect of the measure proposed on the commercial and economic interests of other contracting parties. If, as a result of such consultation, the CONTRACTING PARTIES agree that there is no measure consistent with the other provisions of this Agreement which is practicable in order to achieve the objective outlined in paragraph 13 of this Article, and concur* in the proposed measure, the contracting party concerned shall be released from its obligations under the relevant provisions of the other Articles of this Agreement to the extent necessary to apply that measure.

17. If, within ninety days after the date of the notification of the proposed measure under paragraph 14 of this Article, the CONTRACTING PARTIES have not concurred in such measure, the contracting party concerned may introduce the measure proposed after informing the CONTRACTING PARTIES.

18. If the proposed measure affects a product which is the subject of a concession included in the appropriate Schedule annexed to this Agreement, the contracting party concerned shall enter into consultations with any other contracting party with which the concession was initially negotiated, and with any other contracting party determined by the CONTRACTING PARTIES to have a substantial interest therein. The CONTRACTING PARTIES shall concur* in the measure if they agree that there is no measure consistent with the other provisions of this Agreement which is practicable in order to achieve the objective set forth in paragraph 13 of this Article, and if they are satisfied:

(*a*) that agreement has been reached with such other contracting parties as a result of the consultations referred to above, or

(*b*) if no such agreement has been reached within sixty days after the notification provided for in paragraph 14 has been received by the CONTRACTING PARTIES, that the contracting party having recourse to this Section has made all reasonable efforts to reach an agreement and that the interests of other contracting parties are adequately safeguarded.*

The contracting party having recourse to this Section shall thereupon be released from its obligations under the relevant provisions of the other Articles of this Agreement to the extent necessary to permit it to apply the measure.

19. If a proposed measure of the type described in paragraph 13 of this Article concerns an industry the establishment of which has in the initial period been facilitated by incidental protection afforded by restrictions imposed by the contracting party concerned for balance of payments purposes under the relevant provisions of this Agreement, that contracting party may resort to the provisions and procedures of this Section; *Provided* that it shall not apply the proposed measure without the concurrence* of the CONTRACTING PARTIES.*

*20. Nothing in the preceding paragraphs of this Section shall authorize any deviation from the provisions of Articles I, II and XIII of this Agreement. The provisos to paragraph 10 of this Article shall also be applicable to any restriction under this Section.

21. At any time while a measure is being applied under paragraph 17 of this Article any contracting party substantially affected by it may suspend the application to the trade of the contracting party having recourse to this Section of such substantially equivalent concessions or other obligations under this Agreement the suspension of which the CONTRACTING PARTIES do not disapprove; *Provided* that sixty days' notice of such suspension is given to the CONTRACTING PARTIES not later than six months after the measure has been introduced or changed substantially to the detriment of the contracting party affected. Any such contracting party shall afford adequate opportunity for consultation in accordance with the provisions of Article XXII of this Agreement.

Section D

22. A contracting party coming within the scope of sub-paragraph 4 (*b*) of this Article desiring, in the interest of the development of its economy, to introduce a measure of the type described in paragraph 13 of this Article in respect of the establishment of a particular industry* may apply to the CONTRACTING PARTIES for approval of such measure. The CONTRACTING PARTIES shall promptly consult with such contracting party and shall, in making their decision, be guided by the considerations set out in paragraph 16. If the CONTRACTING PARTIES concur* in the proposed measure the contracting party concerned shall be released from its obligations under the relevant provisions of the other Articles of this Agreement to the extent necessary to permit it to apply the measure. If the proposed measure affects a product which is the subject of a concession included in the appropriate Schedule annexed to this Agreement, the provisions of paragraph 18 shall apply.*

23. Any measure applied under this Section shall comply with the provisions of paragraph 20 of this Article."

"Ad ArticleXVIII

Throughout Articles XI, XII, XIII, XIV and XVIII, the terms 'import restrictions' or 'export restrictions' include restrictions made effective through state-trading operations."

"Ad Article XVIII

The CONTRACTING PARTIES and the contracting parties concerned shall preserve the utmost secrecy in respect of matters arising under this Article.

Paragraphs 1 and 4

1. When they consider whether the economy of a contracting party 'can only support low standards of living,' the CONTRACTING PARTIES shall take into consideration the normal position of that economy and shall not base their determination on exceptional circumstances such as those which may result from the temporary existence of exceptionally favourable conditions for the staple export product or products of such contracting party.

2. The phrase 'in the early stages of development' is not meant to apply only to contracting parties which have just started their economic development, but also to contracting parties the economies of which are undergoing a process of industrialization to correct an excessive dependence on primary production.

Paragraphs 2, 3, 7, 13 and 22

The reference to the establishment of particular industries shall apply not only to the establishment of a new industry, but also to the establishment of a new branch of production in an existing industry and to the substantial transformation of an existing industry, and to the substantial expansion of an existing industry supplying a relatively small proportion of the domestic demand. It shall also cover the reconstruction of an industry destroyed or substantially damaged as a result of hostilities or natural disasters.

Paragraph 7 (b)

A modification or withdrawal, pursuant to paragraph 7 (*b*), by a contracting party, other than the applicant contracting party, referred to in paragraph 7 (*a*), shall be made within six months of the day on which the action is taken by the applicant contracting party, and shall become effective on the thirtieth day following the day on which such modification or withdrawal has been notified to the CONTRACTING PARTIES.

Paragraph 11

The second sentence in paragraph 11 shall not be interpreted to mean that a contracting party is required to relax or remove restrictions if such relaxation or removal would thereupon produce conditions justifying the intensification or institution, respectively, of restrictions under paragraph 9 of Article XVIII.

Paragraph 12 (b)

The date referred to in paragraph 12 (*b*) shall be the date determined by the CONTRACTING PARTIES in accordance with the provisions of paragraph 4 (*b*) of Article XII of this Agreement.

Paragraphs 13 and 14

It is recognized that, before deciding on the introduction of a measure and notifying the CONTRACTING PARTIES in accordance with paragraph 14, a contracting party may need a reasonable period of time to assess the competitive position of the industry concerned.

Paragraphs 15 and 16

It is understood that the CONTRACTING PARTIES shall invite a contracting party proposing to apply a measure under Section C to consult with them pursuant to paragraph 16 if they are requested to do so by a contracting party the trade of which would be appreciably affected by the measure in question.

Paragraphs 16, 18, 19 and 22

1. It is understood that the CONTRACTING PARTIES may concur in a proposed measure subject to specific conditions or limitations. If the measure as applied does not conform to the terms of the concurrence it will to that extent be deemed a measure in which the CONTRACTING PARTIES have not concurred. In cases in which the CONTRACTING PARTIES have concurred in a measure for a specified period, the contracting party concerned, if it finds that the maintenance of the measure for a further period of time is required to achieve the objective for which the measure was originally taken, may apply to the CONTRACTING PARTIES for an extension of that period in accordance with the provisions and procedures of Section C or D, as the case may be.

2. It is expected that the CONTRACTING PARTIES will, as a rule, refrain from concurring in a measure which is likely to cause serious prejudice to exports of a commodity on which the economy of a contracting party is largely dependent.

Paragraph 18 and 22

The phrase 'that the interests of other contracting parties are adequately safeguarded' is meant to provide latitude sufficient to permit consideration in each case of the most appropriate method of safeguarding those interests. The appropriate method may, for instance, take the form of an additional concession to be applied by the contracting party having recourse to Section C or D during such time as the deviation from the other Articles of the Agreement would remain in force or of the temporary suspension by any other contracting party referred to in paragraph 18 of a concession substantially equivalent to the impairment due to the introduction of the measure in question. Such contracting party would have the right to safeguard its interests through such a temporary suspension of a concession; *Provided* that this right will not be exercised when, in the case of a measure imposed by a contracting party coming within the scope of paragraph 4 (*a*), the CONTRACTING PARTIES have determined that the extent of the compensatory concession proposed was adequate.

Paragraph 19

The provisions of paragraph 19 are intended to cover the cases where an industry has been in existence beyond the 'reasonable period of time' referred to in the note to paragraphs 13 and 14, and should not be so construed as to deprive a contracting party coming within the scope of paragraph 4 (*a*) of Article XVIII, of its right to resort to the other provisions of Section C, including paragraph 17, with regard to a newly established industry even though it has benefited from incidental protection afforded by balance of payments import restrictions.

<u>*Paragraph 21*</u>

Any measure taken pursuant to the provisions of paragraph 21 shall be withdrawn forthwith if the action taken in accordance with paragraph 17 is withdrawn or if the CONTRACTING PARTIES concur in the measure proposed after the expiration of the ninety-day time limit specified in paragraph 17."

"PART IV*
TRADE AND DEVELOPMENT

Article XXXVI
Principles and Objectives

1.* The contracting parties,

(*a*) recalling that the basic objectives of this Agreement include the raising of standards of living and the progressive development of the economies of all contracting parties, and considering that the attainment of these objectives is particularly urgent for less-developed contracting parties;

(*b*) considering that export earnings of the less-developed contracting parties can play a vital part in their economic development and that the extent of this contribution depends on the prices paid by the less-developed contracting parties for essential imports, the volume of their exports, and the prices received for these exports;

(*c*) noting, that there is a wide gap between standards of living in less-developed countries and in other countries;

(*d*) recognizing that individual and joint action is essential to further the development of the economies of less-developed contracting parties and to bring about a rapid advance in the standards of living in these countries;

(*e*) recognizing that international trade as a means of achieving economic and social advancement should be governed by such rules and procedures–and measures in conformity with such rules and procedures–as are consistent with the objectives set forth in this Article;

(*f*) noting that the CONTRACTING PARTIES may enable less-developed contracting parties to use special measures to promote their trade and development;

agree as follows.

2. There is need for a rapid and sustained expansion of the export earnings of the less-developed contracting parties.

3. There is need for positive efforts designed to ensure that less-developed contracting parties secure a share in the growth in international trade commensurate with the needs of their economic development.

4. Given the continued dependence of many less-developed contracting parties on the exportation of a limited range of primary products,* there is need to provide in the largest possible measure more favourable and acceptable conditions of access to world markets for these products, and wherever appropriate to devise measures designed to stabilize and improve conditions of world markets in these products, including in particular measures designed to attain stable, equitable and remunerative prices, thus permitting an expansion of world trade and demand and a dynamic and steady growth of the real export earnings of these countries so as to provide them with expanding resources for their economic development.

5. The rapid expansion of the economies of the less-developed contracting parties will be facilitated by a diversification* of the structure of their economies and the avoidance of an excessive dependence on the export of primary products. There is, therefore, need for increased access in the largest possible measure to markets under favourable conditions for processed and manufactured products currently or potentially of particular export interest to less-developed contracting parties.

6. Because of the chronic deficiency in the export proceeds and other foreign exchange earnings of less-developed contracting parties, there are important inter-relationships between trade and financial assistance to development. There is, therefore, need for close and continuing collaboration between the CONTRACTING PARTIES and the international lending agencies so that they can contribute most effectively to alleviating the burdens these less-developed contracting parties assume in the interest of their economic development.

7. There is need for appropriate collaboration between the CONTRACTING PARTIES, other intergovernmental bodies and the organs and agencies of the United Nations system, whose activities relate to the trade and economic development of less-developed countries.

8. The developed contracting parties do not expect reciprocity for commitments made by them in trade negotiations to reduce or remove tariffs and other barriers to the trade of less-developed contracting parties.*

9. The adoption of measures to give effect to these principles and objectives shall be a matter of conscious and purposeful effort on the part of the contracting parties both individually and jointly.

Article XXXVII

Commitments

1. The developed contracting parties shall to the fullest extent possible - that is, except when compelling reasons, which may include legal reasons, make it impossible - give effect to the following provisions:

(*a*) accord high priority to the reduction and elimination of barriers to products currently or potentially of particular export interest to less-developed contracting parties, including customs duties and other restrictions which differentiate unreasonably between such products in their primary and in their processed forms;*

(*b*) refrain from introducing, or increasing the incidence of, customs duties or non-tariff import barriers on products currently or potentially of particular export interest to less-developed contracting parties; and

(*c*)

(i) refrain from imposing new fiscal measures, and

(ii) in any adjustments of fiscal policy accord high priority to the reduction and elimination of fiscal measures, which would hamper, or which hamper, significantly the growth of consumption of primary products, in raw or processed form, wholly or mainly produced in the territories of less-developed contracting parties, and which are applied specifically to those products.

2.

(*a*) Whenever it is considered that effect is not being given to any of the provisions of sub-paragraph (*a*), (*b*) or (*c*) of paragraph 1, the matter shall be reported to the CONTRACTING PARTIES either by the contracting party not so giving effect to the relevant provisions or by any other interested contracting party.

(*b*)

(i) The CONTRACTING PARTIES shall, if requested so to do by any interested contracting party, and without prejudice to any bilateral consultations that may be undertaken, consult with the contracting party concerned and all interested contracting parties with respect to the matter with a view to reaching solutions satisfactory to all contracting parties concerned in order to further the objectives set forth in Article XXXVI. In the course of these consultations, the reasons given in cases where effect was not being given to the provisions of sub-paragraph (*a*), (*b*) or (*c*) of paragraph 1 shall be examined.

(ii) As the implementation of the provisions of sub-paragraph (*a*), (*b*) or (*c*) of paragraph 1 by individual contracting parties may in some cases be more readily achieved where action is taken jointly with other developed contracting parties, such consultation might, where appropriate, be directed towards this end.

(iii) The consultations by the CONTRACTING PARTIES might also, in appropriate cases, be directed towards agreement on joint action designed to further the objectives of this Agreement as envisaged in paragraph 1 of Article XXV.

3. The developed contracting parties shall:

(*a*) make every effort, in cases where a government directly or indirectly determines the resale price of products wholly or mainly produced in the territories of less-developed contracting parties, to maintain trade margins at equitable levels;

(*b*) give active consideration to the adoption of other measures* designed to provide greater scope for the development of imports from less-developed contracting parties and collaborate in appropriate international action to this end;

(*c*) have special regard to the trade interests of less-developed contracting parties when considering the application of other measures permitted under this Agreement to meet particular problems and explore all possibilities of constructive remedies before applying such measures where they would affect essential interests of those contracting parties.

4. Less-developed contracting parties agree to take appropriate action in implementation of the provisions of Part IV for the benefit of the trade of other less-developed contracting parties, in so far as such action is consistent with their individual present and future development, financial and trade needs taking into account past trade developments as well as the trade interests of less-developed contracting parties as a whole.

5. In the implementation of the commitments set forth in paragraph 1 to 4 each contracting party shall afford to any other interested contracting party or contracting parties full and prompt opportunity for consultations under the normal procedures of this Agreement with respect to any matter or difficulty which may arise.

Article XXXVIII
Joint Action

1. The contracting parties shall collaborate jointly, with the framework of this Agreement and elsewhere, as appropriate, to further the objectives set forth in Article XXXVI.

2. In particular, the CONTRACTING PARTIES shall:

(*a*) where appropriate, take action, including action through international arrangements, to provide improved and acceptable conditions of access to world markets for primary products of particular interest to less-developed contracting parties and to devise measures designed to stabilize and improve conditions of world markets in these products including measures designed to attain stable, equitable and remunerative prices for exports of such products;

(*b*) seek appropriate collaboration in matters of trade and development policy with the United Nations and its organs and agencies, including any institutions that may be created on the basis of recommendations by the United Nations Conference on Trade and Development;

(*c*) collaborate in analysing the development plans and policies of individual less-developed contracting parties and in examining trade and aid relationships with a view to devising concrete measures to promote the development of export potential and to facilitate access to export markets for the products of the industries thus developed and, in this connection, seek appropriate collaboration with governments and international organizations, and in particular with organizations having competence in relation to financial assistance for economic development, in systematic studies of trade and aid relationships in individual less-developed contracting parties aimed at obtaining a clear analysis of export potential, market prospects and any further action that may be required;

(*d*) keep under continuous review the development of world trade with special reference to the rate of growth of the trade of less-developed contracting parties and make such recommendations to contracting parties as may, in the circumstances, be deemed appropriate;

(*e*) collaborate in seeking feasible methods to expand trade for the purpose of economic development, through international harmonization and adjustment of national policies and regulations, through technical and commercial standards affecting production, transportation and marketing, and through export promotion by the establishment of facilities for the increased flow of trade information and the development of market research; and

(*f*) establish such institutional arrangements as may be necessary to further the objectives set forth in Article XXXVI and to give effect to the provision of this Part."

"Ad Part IV

The words 'developed contracting parties' and the words 'less-developed contracting parties' as used in Part IV are to be understood to refer to developed and less-developed countries which are parties to the General Agreement on Tariffs and Trade.

Ad Article XXXVI

Paragraph 1

This Article is based upon the objectives set forth in Article I as it will be amended by Section A of paragraph 1 of the Protocol Amending Part I and Articles XXIX and XXX when that Protocol enters into force [THIS PROTOCOL WAS ABANDONED ON 1 JANUARY 1968].

Paragraph 4

The term 'primary products' includes agricultural products, *vide* paragraph 2 of the note *ad* Article XVI, Section B.

Paragraph 5

A diversification programme would generally include the intensification of activities for the processing of primary products and the development of manufacturing industries, taking into account the situation of the particular contracting party and the world outlook for production and consumption of different commodities.

Paragraph 8

It is understood that the phrase 'do not expect reciprocity' means, in accordance with the objectives set forth in this Article, that the less-developed contracting parties should not be expected, in the course of trade negotiations, to make contributions which are inconsistent with their individual development, financial and trade needs, taking into consideration past trade developments.

This paragraph would apply in the event of action under Section A of Article XVIII, Article XXVIII, Article XXVIII *bis* (Article XXIX after the amendment set forth in Section A of paragraph 1 of the Protocol Amending Part I and Articles XXIX and XXX shall have become effective [THIS

PROTOCOL WAS ABANDONED ON 1 JANUARY 1968]), Article XXXIII, or any other procedure under this Agreement.

Ad Article XXXVII

Paragraph 1 (a)

This paragraph would apply in the event of negotiations for reduction or elimination of tariffs or other restrictive regulations of commerce under Articles XXVIII, XXVIII *bis* (XXIX after the amendment set forth in Section A of paragraph 1 of the Protocol Amending Part I and Articles XXIX and XXX shall have become effective [THIS PROTOCOL WAS ABANDONED ON 1 JANUARY 1968]), and Article XXXIII, as well as in connection with other action to effect such reduction or elimination which contracting parties may be able to undertake.

Paragraph 3 (b)

The other measures referred to in this paragraph might include steps to promote domestic structural changes, to encourage the consumption of particular products, or to introduce measures of trade promotion."

Decision on Measures in Favor of Least-Developed Countries—the Text

"DECISION ON MEASURES IN FAVOUR OF LEAST-DEVELOPED COUNTRIES

Ministers,

Recognizing the plight of the least-developed countries and the need to ensure their effective participation in the world trading system, and to take further measures to improve their trading opportunities;

Recognizing the specific needs of the least-developed countries in the area of market access where continued preferential access remains an essential means for improving their trading opportunities;

Reaffirming their commitment to implement fully the provisions concerning the least-developed countries contained in paragraphs 2(*d*), 6 and 8 of the Decision of 28 November 1979 on Differential and More Favourable Treatment, Reciprocity and Fuller Participation of Developing Countries;

Having regard to the commitment of the participants as set out in Section B (vii) of Part I of the Punta del Este Ministerial Declaration;

1. *Decide* that, if not already provided for in the instruments negotiated in the course of the Uruguay Round, notwithstanding their acceptance of these instruments, the least-developed countries, and for so long as they remain in that category, while complying with the general rules set out in the aforesaid instruments, will only be required to undertake commitments and concessions to the extent consistent with their individual development, financial and trade needs, or their administrative and institutional capabilities. The least-developed countries shall be given additional time of one year from 15 April 1994 to submit their schedules as required in Article XI of the

Agreement Establishing the World Trade Organization.

2. *Agree* that:

(i) Expeditious implementation of all special and differential measures taken in favour of least-developed countries including those taken within the context of the Uruguay Round shall be ensured through, *inter alia*, regular reviews.

(ii) To the extent possible, MFN concessions on tariff and non-tariff measures agreed in the Uruguay Round on products of export interest to the least-developed countries may be implemented autonomously, in advance and without staging. Consideration shall be given to further improve GSP and other schemes for products of particular export interest to least-developed countries.

(iii) The rules set out in the various agreements and instruments and the transitional provisions in the Uruguay Round should be applied in a flexible and supportive manner for the least-developed countries. To this effect, sympathetic consideration shall be given to specific and motivated concerns raised by the least-developed countries in the appropriate Councils and Committees.

(iv) In the application of import relief measures and other measures referred to in paragraph 3(*c*) of Article XXXVII of GATT 1947 and the corresponding provision of GATT 1994, special consideration shall be given to the export interests of least-developed countries.

(v) Least-developed countries shall be accorded substantially increased technical assistance in the development, strengthening and diversification of their production and export bases including those of services, as well as in trade promotion, to enable them to maximize the benefits from liberalized access to markets.

3. *Agree* to keep under review the specific needs of the least-developed countries and to continue to seek the adoption of positive measures which facilitate the expansion of trading opportunities in favour of these countries."

Decision on Measures Concerning the Possible Negative Effects of the ReformProgram on Least-Developed and Net Food Importing Developing Countries—the Text

"DECISION ON MEASURES CONCERNING THE POSSIBLE NEGATIVE EFFECTS OF THE REFORM PROGRAMME ON LEAST-DEVELOPED AND NET FOOD-IMPORTING DEVELOPING COUNTRIES

1. *Ministers recognize* that the progressive implementation of the results of the Uruguay Round as a whole will generate increasing opportunities for trade expansion and economic growth to the benefit of all participants.

2. *Ministers recognize* that during the reform programme leading

to greater liberalization of trade in agriculture least-developed and net food-importing developing countries may experience negative effects in terms of the availability of adequate supplies of basic foodstuffs from external sources on reasonable terms and conditions, including short-term difficulties in financing normal levels of commercial imports of basic foodstuffs.

3. *Ministers* accordingly *agree* to establish appropriate mechanisms to ensure that the implementation of the results of the Uruguay Round on trade in agriculture does not adversely affect the availability of food aid at a level which is sufficient to continue to provide assistance in meeting the food needs of developing countries, especially least-developed and net food-importing developing countries. To this end *Ministers agree*:

(i) to review the level of food aid established periodically by the Committee on Food Aid under the Food Aid Convention 1986 and to initiate negotiations in the appropriate forum to establish a level of food aid commitments sufficient to meet the legitimate needs of developing countries during the reform programme;

(ii) to adopt guidelines to ensure that an increasing proportion of basic foodstuffs is provided to least-developed and net food-importing developing countries in fully grant form and/or on appropriate concessional terms in line with Article IV of the Food Aid Convention 1986;

(iii) to give full consideration in the context of their aid programmes to requests for the provision of technical and financial assistance to least-developed and net food-importing developing countries to improve their agricultural productivity and infrastructure.

4. *Ministers* further *agree* to ensure that any agreement relating to agricultural export credits makes appropriate provision for differential treatment in favour of least-developed and net food-importing developing countries.

5. *Ministers recognize* that as a result of the Uruguay Round certain developing countries may experience short-term difficulties in financing normal levels of commercial imports and that these countries may be eligible to draw on the resources of international financial institutions under existing facilities, or such facilities as may be established, in the context of adjustment programmes, in order to address such financing difficulties. In this regard Ministers take note of paragraph 37 of the report of the Director-General to the CONTRACTING PARTIES to GATT 1947 on his consultations with the Managing Director of the International Monetary Fund and the President of the World Bank (MTN.GNG/NG14/W/35).

6. The provisions of this Decision will be subject to regular review by the Ministerial Conference, and the follow-up to this Decision shall be monitored, as appropriate, by the Committee on Agriculture."

The WTO does not define "developed" or "developing" countries. Members may define them for themselves. Doing so does not automatically provide rights under preference schemes such as GSP. Other members may challenge those determinations. Such challenges may then lead to clarifying negotiations. For countries that negotiated to join the WTO after 1995, their status depends on the terms agreed in the accessions negotiations. The WTO recognizes as LDCs those countries that have been designated as such by the UN. There were in 2001 48 on the UN list, 29 of which were then WTO members. The latter are: Angola, Bangladesh, Benin, Burkina Faso, Burundi, Central African Republic, Chad, Democratic Republic of Congo, Djibouti, Gambia, Guinea, Guinea Bissau, Haiti, Lesotho, Madagascar, Malawi, Maldives, Mali, Mauritania, Mozambique, Myanmar, Niger, Rwanda, Sierra Leone, Solomon Islands, Tanzania, Togo, Uganda, and Zambia. Seven additional LDCs were in the process of accession to the WTO. They are: Cambodia, Cape Verde, Laos, Nepal, Samoa, Sudan and Vanuatu. Bhutan, Ethiopia and Yemen are WTO Observers.

"The Decision on Differential and More Favourable Treatment, Reciprocity and Fuller Participation of Developing Countries" (see Chapter IV for full text) was adopted under GATT in 1979 and enables developed members to give differential and more favorable treatment to developing countries. It is the legal basis for the GSP and for the Global System of Trade Preferences ("GSTP"). Under GSP, developed countries offer non-reciprocal preferential treatment (such as zero or low duties on imports) to products originating in developing countries. Preference-giving countries unilaterally determine which countries and which products are included in their schemes. Under GSTP, developing countries which are members of so-called Group of 77 countries (see http://www.g77.org) may exchange trade concessions among themselves. UNCTAD provides technical assistance to beneficiaries and conducts analyses of the various schemes.

Special Developed Country Programs of Trade Preferences for Underdeveloped Countries

In this chapter, only the special programs of the US and the EU will be described and these will only be covered cursorily. Nonetheless, other developed countries have similar programs.

US PREFERENTIAL TRADE PROGRAMS The Caribbean Basin Initiative ("CBI") and the Andean Trade Initiative ("ATI") are the two principal programs under which the US offers unilateral trade preferences to specific blocs of underdeveloped countries, although recent legislation through the Trade and Development Act of 2000, Including the African Grown and Development Act and the United States-Caribbean Basic Partnership Trade Act, provides similar assistance to African countries and augments the CBI program. CBI and ATI have much in common. ATI was modeled closely on CBI and ATI sought to economically integrate the Andean and Caribbean regions. Both are unilateral trade benefit programs (*i.e.*, US goods are given no preferential entry into CBI/ATI beneficiary country markets) initiated by the US for which eligible beneficiary countries must apply and qualify. Despite many similarities, there are some important differences between the two programs.

CBI was the result of The Caribbean Basin Economic Recovery Act of 1983. ATI was principally created by the passage of The Andean Trade Preference Act. Creation by the US of both CBI and ATI was in part motivated by humanitarian concerns but was firmly grounded on US self-interest. CBI is a broad program to promote economic development through private sector initiative in the beneficiary Central and South American and Caribbean countries and to expand foreign and domestic investment in nontraditional sectors, thereby diversifying CBI country economies and expanding their exports. It seeks to alleviate the poverty of this region that exists in part because the region has been increasingly deprived of the critically-important US market for its largest traditional export, cane sugar. This region is of strategic importance to the United States because of its proximity to US territory and the sea lanes which pass through it. ATI was meant to create alternatives to coca leaf production in beneficiary countries. Widespread use of coca leaf narcotic derivatives, such as cocaine, constitute a major US social and health problem. Efforts to curtail coca leaf production in the Andean countries and prevent its importation into the US through penal measures have been ineffective. ATI provides economic incentives to persons in the region to divert their labors from coca leaf production to other encouraged pursuits. CBI is a permanent program. ATI expires on December 4, 2001.

Eligible beneficiary countries under both CBI and ATI are named and limited by their enabling legislation. Unless there are overriding considerations of national, economic, or security interests, the US President may not designate a country as beneficiary under CBI (and ATI where indicated by an asterisk or ATI **only** where indicated by a double asterisk) if the country is (a) * a communist country; (b) * fails to meet certain criteria regarding nationalization or expropriation of US property; (c) does not take adequate steps to cooperate with the US to prevent narcotic drugs from entering the US; (d) * fails to recognize arbitral awards to US citizens; (e) * provides preferential treatment to the products of another developed country which adversely affects trade with the US; (f) * has not entered into an extradition treaty with the US; (g) * has not or is not taking steps to afford internationally recognized workers' rights to workers in that country; and (h) ** permits government-owned entities to engage in the broadcast of copyrighted material belonging to US copyright owners without the consent of its owner. Designation as a CBI or an ATI beneficiary will also be made only after taking into account the following discretionary criteria: (a) an expressed desire by the country to be designated; (b) economic conditions in the country; (c) the extent to which the country is prepared to provide equitable and reasonable access to its markets and basic commodity resources; (d) the degree to which the country follows the accepted rules of international trade; (e) the degree to which such country uses export subsidies or imposes export performance requirements and local content requirements (inapplicable in the case of ATI); (f) the degree to which the trade policies of the country as related to other CBI/ATI beneficiaries are contributing to revitalization of the region; (g) the degree to which a country is undertaking self-help measures to promote is own economic development; (h) the extent to which such country prohibits its nationals from engaging in the broadcast of copyrighted material belonging to US copyright owners without their express consent; (i) the extent to which such country is prepared to cooperate with the US in administering the provisions of Title I of the CBI legislation/the ATI legislation; (j) (ATI only) workers rights in that country; (k) (ATI only) whether such country has met certain narcotics requirements set forth in US law; and (l) (ATI only) the extent which such country protects the intellectual property rights, including patents and trademarks, of foreign nationals.

Major elements of the CBI program available to all CBI beneficiaries are: (a) duty free entry to the US for a wide range of products grown and manufactured in CBI countries as an incentive for investment and expanded export production and other special tariff statuses; (b) a special access program (Guarantee Access Levels under the CBI Textile Program) for textiles and apparels that guarantees markets for apparel assembled from US-formed and -cut material; (c) national treatment (treatment equal to that accorded domestic US parties) for producers in CBI countries in bidding for certain types of US Government procurement opportunities (CBI Government Procurement); (d) exemption for CBI exports to the US from US Import Merchandising Processing Fees (a fee based on a percent of value-based customs duty surcharge levied on incoming goods to cover costs of US Customs operations); and (e) a wide range of US Government, state government, and private sector business development programs, including trade and investment financing, business missions, and technical assistance programs partially supported through US foreign economic assistance. For CBI beneficiary countries that have also signed a Tax Information Exchange Agreement with the US, CBI Convention Tourism Tax Credit (a deduction on US taxes for companies that hold business conventions in an eligible country) and Foreign Sales Corporation status (which enables the establishment of a specialized sales subsidiary of a US export company in a CBI country and allows the organizer to receive US tax benefits) are also available. Section 936 below market cost fund loans that were previously available to CBI beneficiaries which had signed a Tax Information Exchange Agreement were eliminated with an amendment to the US Tax Code. In contrast with CBI, ATI does not extend most non-tariff provisions of CBI, particularly separate cumulation for antidumping and countervailing duty investigations, scholarship assistance, and a pilot preclearance program. ATI particularly stresses free access of regional agricultural products to the US since growing such products is most likely to displace coca leaf production.

Not all products of CBI and ATI beneficiary countries are admitted to the US duty free. Excluded ATI products are most textiles and apparel; footwear except disposable items and footwear parts such as uppers; certain leather, rubber, and plastic gloves; luggage, handbags, and flat goods; certain leather wearing apparel; rum and tafia; and watches and watch parts, if any component originated in a non-US-most-favored-country. Tariff rates on leather-related ATI products (excluding footwear) were reduced in 1997. Rum and tafia are the only products excluded under ATI that are not excluded under CBI. Sugar remains subject to the two-tier tariff-rate quota system. CBI and ATI countries may export a previously designated "lower tier" amount duty free and any sugar imports above that allocation are subject to an "upper tier" tariff. Ethanol, beef, and veal may be eligible for duty free treatment, but special conditions apply. For CBI beneficiary countries, textile products made of silk blends or of vegetable fibers other than cotton may enter duty free and bilateral agreements may be negotiated to permit duty free entry of certain traditional hand-loomed, hand-sewn articles.

Certain duty free admitted products may still be subject to federal excise taxes. Products from CBI and ATI beneficiary countries must still comply with all applicable US laws, regulations, and standards.

Products are deemed eligible for CBI or ATI duty free treatment if the following conditions are met: (a) the merchandise is imported directly from a beneficiary country; (b) the merchandise is produced in a beneficiary country (satisfied when goods are wholly the growth, product, or manufacture of a beneficiary country or the goods have been substantially transformed); (c) at least 35% of the appraised value of the article imported into the US consists of the cost or value of materials produced in one or more beneficiary countries and/or the direct costs of processing operations performed in one or more beneficiary countries [Puerto Rico and the US Virgin Islands are defined as beneficiary countries for purposes of this requirement; the cost of value of materials produced in the US customs territory (other than Puerto Rico) may be counted, but only to a maximum of 15% of the appraised value of the imported article; articles not from CBI/ATI countries, Puerto Rico/US Virgin Islands, and the US customs territory may be counted in this calculation if they have been subject to double substantial transformation; and—for ATI calculations – any of the 23 CBI beneficiary countries may be deemed a beneficiary country]; and (e) [per special tariff statuses for articles manufactured, processed, or assembled in CBI countries which were added with the 1990 amendments] (i) the 35% value added and substantial transformation requirements do not apply to products manufactured or assembled wholly from US components (other than textiles and apparel and petroleum and certain products derived from petroleum) and ingredients (other than water) and (ii) the general value added and substantial transformation rule is also excluded in the case of products that are the growth, product, or manufacture of Puerto Rico that are subsequently processed or advanced in value in another CBI beneficiary country.

Items not wholly grown, produced, or manufactured in CBI/ATI beneficiary countries may still be included in establishing requisite regional content to satisfy duty free import eligibility requirements as long as they are "substantially transformed" in a CBI/ATI country into new and different articles of commerce which are substantially transformed a second time upon incorporation into the benefited article. This total process is known as "double substantial transformation". Although the US Customs Service makes substantial transformation determinations on a case-by-case basis, factors such as a change in tariff classification, value added, and complexity of the operations are important considerations.

Only direct costs of processing and the cost of materials produced in a beneficiary country may be counted towards the minimum regional content percentage. Direct processing costs include those directly incurred or reasonably allocated to the production of the article, such as the cost of labor directly involved in production; direct supervision of processing; rent for productive factory space; electricity directly used in processing; dies, molds, tooling and depreciation on them; research and development; and inspection and testing. Administrative expenses, profit, insurance, advertising, and salespersons' salaries are not direct processing costs. The cost of materials used to produce an article includes freight, insurance, packing, and all other costs incurred in transporting the materials to the manufacturer's plant as well as the actual cost of waste or spoilage (less the value of recoverable scrap) and taxes or duties (as long as these are not remitted upon exportation) imposed on the materials by the beneficiary country.

Advance rulings from US Customs are available to ascertain the eligibility of a product for CBI/ATI duty free treatment prior to actual production in the CBI/ATI country or shipment to the US. Requests for advance rulings must be in writing and detail the production process and the direct costs of processing used to meet the 35% value added requirement.

The 24 countries taking part in CBI are Antigua and Barbuda, Aruba, the Bahamas, Barbados, Belize, the British Virgin Islands, Costa Rica, Dominica, the Dominican Republic, El Salvador, Grenada, Guatemala, Guyana, Haiti, Honduras, Jamaica, Montserrat, the Netherlands Antilles, Nicaragua, Panama, St. Kitts ("Christopher") and Nevis, St. Lucia, St. Vincent and the Grenadines, and Trinidad and Tobago. Regional countries eligible for but not participating in CBI are Anguilla, the Cayman Islands, Suriname, and the Turks and Caicos Islands.

Barbados, Dominica, the Dominican Republic, Grenada, Jamaica, St. Lucia, Trinidad and Tobago, Costa Rica, Guyana, and Honduras are the CBI beneficiaries that have signed Tax Information Exchange Agreements with the US.

ATI eligible and beneficiary countries are Bolivia, Colombia, Ecuador, and Peru. Although Venezuela is also a member of the Andean Pact it is not an eligible country under ATI.

The Caribbean Basin Initiative Trade Enhancement Act provides duty-free, quota-free access for apparel assembled in CBI-beneficiary countries from US fabric and yarn. Duty-free treatment is also provided for apparel assembled from CBI regional fabric, subject to a quantitative limit that increases with time. Duty-free treatment is extended to other products previously excluded from CBI, such as canned tuna, petroleum and its derivatives, and certain footwear.

The African Growth and Opportunity Act provides sub-Saharan African countries with opportunities for market-led investment. Economic growth should be created through the elimination of US tariffs (with no cap or limit on import amounts for most items but on other items import amounts are limited to a fixed percentage of total US apparel imports with that percentage to increase annually) on most African apparel imports, which are often 15% to 20% of the value of such imports and this has the potential to spur economic development and job creation in a desperately poverty-stricken and economically-backward region. Some special opportunities are provided to least-developed countries in sub-Saharan Africa and also generally offers many trade and investment opportunities in a number of other sectors. The Act provides additional security for investors and traders in eligible African countries by ensuring GSP benefits for eight years.

EU SPECIAL UNILATERAL TRADE RELATIONSHIPS WITH UNDERDEVELOPED COUNTRIES The EU and the ACP states concluded negotiations on a Partnership Agreement, one in a series generally referred to as the "Lomé Conventions," on February 3, 2000, in Brussels aimed at the establishment of a new framework for their future relations. It, *inter alia*, regulates trade between these two groups of countries, as well as the political dimension of their relations, their development cooperation strategies, and their financial cooperation subsequent to the expiration of the fourth Lomé Convention on February 29, 2000. The trade regime provisions do not apply to one of the ACP countries, South Africa, whose trade relations with the EU are regulated by a separate agreement. The trade provisions provide for a preparatory period of 8 years. The parties' ultimate objective is to enable the ACP states to integrate successfully in the world economy within the multilateral trading system. The parties have, therefore, agreed to conclude by the end of the preparatory period new trading arrangements which will be fully compatible with their WTO obligations, under which they will progressively remove barriers to trade between them and enhance cooperation in all areas relevant to trade. During the preparatory period, products originating in the ACP states will be imported into the EU free of customs duties and of charges having equivalent effect. Regarding imports of agricultural products from the ACP states, the EU has undertaken to adopt the necessary measures allowing more favorable treatment than that granted to third countries benefiting from the MFN clause. The Banana Protocol attached to the Fourth Lomé Convention has not been renewed and there is now a second banana protocol which does not provide for trade preferences for bananas. Preferential access for bananas is granted in accordance with the general principles of the partnership agreement between the ACP countries and the EU within the context of the EU's new banana import regime. ACP members are granted duty free access to the EU for all industrial products and for most agricultural ones and benefits from the most liberal rules of origin available in order to make most use of the tariff reductions and countries can use each other's products to satisfy the origin rules' "cumulation" options.

For LDCs, the EU has announced an "everything but arms" free trade access for their products to the EU market. While duty and quota elimination for essentially all products took effect on March 5. 2001, the full liberalization of sugar, rice, and bananas will be phased in during a transition period. Duties on fresh bananas will be reduced by 20% annually starting on January 1, 2002, and will be eliminated at the latest on January 1, 2006. Duties on rice will be reduced by 20% on September 1, 2006, by 50% on September 1, 2007, by 80% on September 1, 2008, and be eliminated at the latest by September 1, 2009. Duties on sugar will be reduced by 20% on July 1, 2006, by 50% on July 1, 2007, by 80% on July 1, 2008, and be eliminated at the latest by July 1,2009. In order to compensate for the delay in liberalization for these products, the EU will offer immediate and real market access through the creation of duty-free quotas for sugar and rice, based initially on the best figures for those countries' exports during the 1990s plus 15%. These will increase by 15% each year during the interim period.

The EU also maintains a special program preferential trading program with Mediterranean countries, principally of Arabic ethnicity and Islamic culture, in North Africa and West Asia. EU members agreed at the end of 1995 that new agreements would be established between the EU and its Mediterranean partners linking Mediterranean countries to the EU in the same way as the ACP countries regarding liberal rules of origin.

The EU also maintains a special preferential trading program with formerly Communist countries in Central Europe and on the Baltic under so-called "European Agreements" that provide for very liberal rules of origin to permit the countries to pool their production through cumulation in order to qualify imported goods for preferential entry into the EU. The agreements, formally known as "Protocols to the European Agreements on Conformity Assessment" ("PECAs"), extend certain benefits of the EU's single market to EU candidate countries for the first time in all sectors where legislation is aligned. PECAs eliminate additional testing and certification requirements for candidate countries that have implemented EU legislation. They provide for reciprocal improvement in market access and eliminate technical barriers to trade with respect to industrial products.

Entering Goods Through Customs Duty-Free Under Carnets and Through Similar Programs

There are many provisions in national customs and tariffs and through international conventions to accommodate ships, airplanes, trucks, and trains (particularly railroad box cars) that carry goods in international trade and which will depart the country once they have been unloaded by permitting their entry into and exit from a customs territory free of tariffs (and often the fuel and other stores needed to operate them may also have duty-free status). Similarly, containers (see particularly the Customs Convention on Containers, May 18, 1956, [1969] 20 UST 301, TIAS No. 6634), palettes, and like materials and packaging that is reusable and arrives in a customs territory only to be emptied of goods and then used for subsequent international shipment from the customs territory will be permitted admission on a duty-free basis based on national practice or international convention. Goods transiting a customs territory without being offloaded, used, or sold within the customs territory are, per WTO/GATT terms, not made subject to tariffs and similar impediments to transit (see immediately below).

GATT 1947 Article V and its Annex I Notes and Supplementary Provisions—the Text

[***asterisks** below mark the portions of the text which should be read in conjunction with notes and supplementary provisions in Annex I to the Agreement.]

“**Article V**
Freedom of Transit

1. Goods (including baggage), and also vessels and other means of transport, shall be deemed to be in transit across the territory of a contracting party when the passage across such territory, with or without trans-shipment, warehousing, breaking bulk, or change in the mode of transport, is only a portion of a complete journey beginning and terminating beyond the frontier of the contracting party across whose territory the traffic passes. Traffic of this nature is termed in this article ‘traffic in transit.’

2. There shall be freedom of transit through the territory of each contracting party, via the routes most convenient for international transit, for traffic in transit to or from the territory of other contracting parties. No distinction shall be made which is based on the flag of vessels, the place of origin, departure, entry, exit or destination, or on any circumstances relating to the ownership of goods, of vessels or of other means of transport.

3. Any contracting party may require that traffic in transit through its territory be entered at the proper custom house, but, except in cases of failure to comply with applicable customs laws and regulations, such traffic coming from or going to the territory of other contracting parties shall not be subject to any unnecessary delays or restrictions and shall be exempt from customs duties and from all transit duties or other charges imposed in respect of transit, except charges for transportation or those commensurate with administrative expenses entailed by transit or with the cost of services rendered.

4. All charges and regulations imposed by contracting parties on traffic in transit to or from the territories of other contracting parties shall

be reasonable, having regard to the conditions of the traffic.

5. With respect to all charges, regulations and formalities in connection with transit, each contracting party shall accord to traffic in transit to or from the territory of any other contracting party treatment no less favourable than the treatment accorded to traffic in transit to or from any third country.*

6. Each contracting party shall accord to products which have been in transit through the territory of any other contracting party treatment no less favourable than that which would have been accorded to such products had they been transported from their place of origin to their destination without going through the territory of such other contracting party. Any contracting party shall, however, be free to maintain its requirements of direct consignment existing on the date of this Agreement, in respect of any goods in regard to which such direct consignment is a requisite condition of eligibility for entry of the goods at preferential rates of duty or has relation to the contracting party's prescribed method of valuation for duty purposes.

7. The provisions of this Article shall not apply to the operation of aircraft in transit, but shall apply to air transit of goods (including baggage)."

"**Ad *Article V***
Paragraph 5

With regard to transportation charges, the principle laid down in paragraph 5 refers to like products being transported on the same route under like conditions."

CARNETS Perhaps the most significant and useful international arrangement to avoid the payment of tariffs for transient goods in a customs territory is through the use of what is called a "Carnet." The need for such an arrangement is obvious when one considers the large volume of work tools (including the musical instruments of performers), sample goods, demonstration equipment, art works and other items for temporary display, and similar items that are regularly entered temporarily into a country which should not be subject to the normal tariffs and other administrative impediments imposed on permanent imports. The trick in specially permitting such temporary imports is to obtain assurance that the goods will be reexported within the prescribed time and that any tariffs and other taxes will be paid if that reexportation does not take place. Carnets provide national customs authorities with that assurance.

CCC/WCO adopted the Customs Convention on the ATA Carnet for the Temporary Admission of Goods ("ATA Convention") in 1961. The term "ATA" is a combination of the initial letters of the French words "*Admission temporaire*" and the English words "Temporary Admission." A number of other similar international conventions for specific types of goods were also established.

An effort was made to combine into a single international instrument all thirteen existing temporary admission facilities agreements. The Convention on Temporary Admission was drafted by CCC/WCO and was adopted in 1990 (the "Istanbul Convention"). Each annex to the Istanbul Convention authorizes the temporary admission of goods imported for a specific purpose. Goods imported duty-free may not remain indefinitely in the country of temporary importation and the period fixed for reexportation is laid down in each annex. Such goods must be re-exported in the same state as they entered and may not undergo any change during their stay in the country of temporary importation, except normal deterioration due to the use made of them. The ATA carnet system (the ATA Convention and the Istanbul Convention) is of great benefit to traders and travelers. An ATA carnet replaces national customs formalities for temporary admission or transit. Any duties and taxes that may later be found to be owing are guaranteed payment through the presentation of the carnet to and its acceptance by customs officials so there is no need to furnish additional cash deposits or other forms of security. The ATA carnet covers the transport of goods in customs transit while en route to or returning from a country of temporary importation and, where applicable, within that country. For the period of validity of the ATA carnet (normally one year), the goods can be temporarily imported under cover of the same carnet in the customs territories of as many contracting parties, and as often, as the carnet holder wishes. The seals affixed or the identification of the goods by a customs office of a contracting party are recognizable by the customs offices of other contracting parties through which the goods subsequently pass. This facilitates customs controls and saves the carnet holder time when the goods cross frontiers. The practical advantages of this system are reflected in the increasing number of contracting parties. The ATA Convention is currently applied by 61 and the Istanbul Convention by 34 contracting parties.

The ATA is a system that permits the free movement of goods across frontiers and their temporary admission into a customs territory with relief from duties and taxes. All covered goods subject to other temporary admission conventions (scientific equipment, pedagogic material, professional equipment, packings, goods for display at exhibitions, and samples), may be admitted under cover of a single document known as the ATA carnet that is secured by an international guarantee system. This results in considerable simplification of customs formalities, particularly regarding the security to be furnished for the temporary admission of goods. No import duties or taxes are collected for the temporary importation of goods covered by the system since internationally valid security against their payment is provided through the national associations issuing the ATA carnets which are recognized by national customs authorities and are affiliated through a system of guarantees administered by the International Bureau of Chambers of Commerce.

Free Trade Zones, Bonded Warehouses, In Bond Assembly, and Similar Defined Exclusions from a National Customs Territory

Some territories, such as Hong Kong, are essentially "duty-free areas" where customs duties, tariffs, and other fees payable to the state are not charged on almost all imported and exported goods and where few other non-tariff barriers to trade impede imports and exports. Unfortunately, there are few such places. Most territories and countries collect duties of greater or lesser significance on many or most imports as well as imposing various non-tariff import barriers and may also administer excises on and other impediments to exports.

Even those territories and countries which impose duties and other impediments on imports and/or exports realize that, by doing so, they have made themselves less attractive places in which to conduct a number of international trade and commerce activities. Rather than foregoing such activities on their national territories, they have established special areas operating under special rules where such activities may be competitively and profitably engaged in without the payment of duties or being subject to many other impediments. These special areas may be thought of as being inside the national territory but outside the customs territory of a country. The national rules established and the type of such special area utilized will determine the degree to which any utilizer will have freedom to conduct operations or business or may act without payment of customs duties and other impositions. Such special areas may be called free trade zones, free trade areas, transit zones (which is a port of entry in a coastal country that is established as a storage and distribution center for the convenience of a neighboring country lacking adequate port facilities or access to the sea and is administered so that goods in transit to and from the neighboring country are not subject to the customs duties, import controls, or many of the entry and exit formalities of the host country), duty free ports, in bond facilities, *maquiladoras*, bonded warehouses, or some other name. Over 300 free ports, free trade zones, and similar facilities are in operation in over 75 countries and these may be subdivided into a number of smaller sites scattered across a broad geographical area.

Such special areas were created by national governments with specific uses in mind, such as the transshipment of foreign goods through the national territory for ultimate consumption abroad. Users have often found uses for such special areas that are distinguishable from—and sometimes at odds with—the governments' original intended purposes.

There are a number of issues of interest to parties when determining whether or not to use such special areas or determining which such special area (within a particular national territory or among those available in different national territories) to select. Included among these issues are the degree to which goods and operations within such special areas are subject to or free of the laws—particularly those regarding immigration and labor—and courts, property taxes and other taxes, and any other limiting or costly rules or impositions of the national territory in which the special area is located and the degree to which these impinge on the desired use or compare with other available special areas. Further, the ease with which items from the national customs territory may be brought into the special area and be combined with imported items, the degree to and conditions under which goods may be taken from the special area into the customs territory, the types of manipulations of and work on items in the special area that may be performed, and the treatment of items from the special area under the laws of the national territory in which the special area is located and other national territories regarding country of origin designation and the assessment duties, among other matters.

In short, such special areas are established to permit parties authorized to operate within them to escape many of the costs and bureaucratic difficulties associated with normal international business operations within the customs territory of such a country. A party which might use such a special area will only be tempted to do so if the location, costs, permitted flexibility of activities, and operating conditions are satisfactory and cumulatively superior to all competing sites in the same country or other countries in which similar activities might be performed.

The US provisions for such facilities will be considered below as representative of those found in other countries.

US Foreign Trade Zones ("FTZs") are secured areas which are legally outside the US customs territory and located near ports of entry. FTZs are operated as public utilities by states, political subdivisions, or corporations chartered for that purpose. Charges are made for use of FTZ facilities. Sub-FTZs are special purpose facilities for companies unable to operate effectively at central FTZ sites and are permitted to be noncontiguous to the main FTZ. Sub-FTZs are usually located in the FTZ user's private facility. A Foreign Trade Zone Board acting under the authority of the Foreign Trade Zones Act of 1934 reviews and approves applications to establish, operate, and maintain US FTZs. The Foreign Trade Zones Board may—but rarely does—determine that an operation is not in the public interest. Foreign goods remaining exclusively in an FTZ are still subject to the jurisdiction of US courts.

Users of FTZs may:

(a) Take maximum advantage of inverted US tariffs which levy lower rates of duty on items manufactured in FTZs from nonprivileged imported items than would be levied on the imported component parts. Import duties are calculated by taking the value of the components, exclusive of the value added in the FTZ, times the tariff rate set for the finished product. Savings in shipping charges may also result from FTZ assembly. Substandard foods and drugs may, in certain cases, be reconditioned to meet the requirements of the Food, Drug, and Cosmetics Act. These uses of FTZs have made manufacturing the single most important aspect of FTZ activity, usually undertaken in sub-FTZs.

(b) Defer the payment of duties on goods in FTZs until they are entered for consumption, which may result in significant "cost of money" savings. Storing goods in an FTZ permits immediate delivery into US commerce when goods are needed or sold; and FTZ warehousing guarantees the availability of warehoused goods for a seasonal market, such as Christmas. The use of an FTZ allows goods to be held pending the reopening of quota allocations for those goods.

(c) Avoid quotas by converting imported items in FTZs to items not subject to quotas that may then be entered into US commerce. Merchandise may be re-marked or relabeled in the FTZ to conform to requirements for entry into the commerce of the United States if the product is otherwise up to standard.

(d) Avoid the payment of duties by exporting the goods from the FTZ or (if due to use, consumption, or destruction within the FTZ) never entering the goods into US commerce. Products shipped to the FTZ in bulk can be dried, sorted, graded, cleaned, bagged, or packed. This eliminates the payment of customs duties and taxes on removed moisture, dirt or culls, and discarded damaged packages or broken bottles. Where evaporation results during shipment or while goods are stored in the FTZ, the contents of barrels or other containers can be regauged and savings obtained, as no duties are payable on the portions lost or removed.

(e) Establish US country-of-origin by substantial transformation of imported materials within the FTZ to make the final product "Made in USA." If the imported products were from Category 2 countries, the substantially transformed end product may enter US commerce at Category 1 rates. Domestic articles may be taken into a FTZ and, providing their identity is maintained in accordance with regulations, may be returned to US customs territory free of quotas, duties, or taxes, even though while in the FTZ they may have been combined with or made part of foreign-origin articles. Domestic distilled spirits, wine, beer, and a limited number of other kinds of merchandise may generally not be processed while in an FTZ.

(f) Eliminate the costs associated with bonded warehouses, avoid paying the bond required on goods in bonded warehouses, and keep goods in the FTZ indefinitely or enter them into the US customs territory, reexport them, or destroy them when the user wishes as opposed to being bound by the five year statutory limit for bonded warehouses.

(g) Avoid the need to use drawback procedures, which require the loss of use of paid customs duties until they are returned under drawback; which involve significant administrative costs; and which result in the permanent loss of 1% of paid customs duties.

Merchandise lawfully brought into FTZs may be stored, sold, exhibited on permanent marketing display, broken up, repacked, assembled, distributed, sorted, graded, cleaned, mixed with foreign or domestic merchandise, or otherwise manipulated or manufactured or processed. The resulting merchandise may thereafter be either exported or transferred into US customs territory.

The owner of foreign merchandise that has not been manipulated or manufactured in any way that would effect a change in its US tariff classification had it been taken into US customs territory when first imported may, upon request to the district director, have its dutiable status fixed and liquidated. This dutiable status will apply irrespective of when the merchandise is entered into US customs territory and even though its condition or form may have been changed by processing in the FTZ. These goods so classified are called "foreign privileged merchandise." Those not so classified are called "foreign nonprivileged merchandise" and their rates of duty will be determined by their condition when removed from the FTZ. This latter status is preferable for assembled goods with lesser rates of duty than the components imported into the FTZ and for imported goods subject to quotas or Category 2 classification which do not apply when articles assembled or processed from them are removed from the FTZ.

"Privileged domestic merchandise" is that registered on application to US Customs as being US merchandise which may be withdrawn from an FTZ without the payment of duties. "Nonprivileged domestic merchandise" are US articles entered into an FTZ and not so classified. Such goods will be subject to normal rates of duty for imported items when they are removed from an FTZ. "Zone restricted merchandise" is merchandise taken into an FTZ from the US customs territory exclusively to be exported, destroyed, or stored. Articles entered into FTZs and accorded this status are considered exported for drawback, excise and other internal revenue tax rebates, and temporary export bond cancellation purposes.

When goods, in their condition at the time of entry into the FTZ or after processing there, are transferred into the US customs territory, they must be entered at the US customhouse. If entered for consumption, duties and taxes will be assessed on the entered articles according to their condition and privileged status.

Foreign merchandise in customs bonded warehouses may be transferred to an FTZ at any time before the limitation on its retention in the bonded warehouse expires, but such a transfer to an FTZ may be made only for the purpose of eventual exportation, destruction, or permanent storage. When foreign merchandise is transferred to an FTZ from customs bonded warehouses, the bond on the merchandise is cancelled and all obligations in regard to duty payment or as to the time when the merchandise must be reexported are terminated. Similarly, the owner of domestic merchandise stored in US Internal Revenue Service bonded warehouses may transfer goods to an FTZ and obtain cancellation of bonds.

Bonded warehouses are secured, US Customs-approved warehouse facilities in which imported goods may be stored or manipulated in specific ways, such as cleaning, sorting, or repacking. Duty at the rate in effect on the date of withdrawal in their manipulated condition (if applicable) is not paid until goods are withdrawn from the warehouse and entered for consumption. No duties are payable on goods timely exported from a bonded warehouse. Perishable goods, explosive substances, or prohibited importations may not be placed in a bonded warehouse. Certain restricted articles, though not allowed release from custody, may be warehoused.

The costs for the use of bonded warehouses may be less than the costs for FTZs. Bonded warehouses may be established on a user's facilities, often with fewer difficulties than are involved in establishing sub-FTZs. Goods may remain in the bonded warehouse for up to 5 years from the date of importation. At any time during that period, warehoused goods may be reexported or they may be withdrawn for consumption. If destroyed under US Customs supervision, no duty is payable. The permitted types of manipulation of goods in a bonded warehouse are more limited than those permitted in FTZs. Goods may not be displayed for sale or be so manipulated as to constitute manufacturing in a bonded warehouse.

Tariff and Other Import Duty Drawbacks and Similar Rebate Programs

Although every national program will differ, there are often opportunities for an importer or recover some or all import tariffs and other duties paid on imported items if those goods are subsequently reexported. This is true even—and perhaps even particularly—if the imported goods have been modified or incorporated into other goods in the country of importation. The country of importation is certain to favor exports of products made within its borders. If the country does not itself have all the resources—particularly of raw materials but also often of component parts requiring special technology or manufacturing—to produce the goods it wishes to export, it must import them. Unlike most imports, such raw material and component part imports are officially favored because they are essential to desired export economic activity within the country. As a consequence, any tariff rebates upon reexportation permit the country to effectively provide a semi-concealed simulacrum of an export subsidy. These must be carefully crafted to not fall outside the prohibitions on export subsidies of WTO/GATT, but this can usually be accomplished with little difficulty. Importers are urged to consider drawbacks and similar tax and tariff rebate programs well in advance of requesting the return of such monies upon reexportation. It is often a requirement under national programs that certain filings and claims be made at the time of importation if a complete or partial return of import payments is to be obtained when the imported goods are subsequently reexported.

The WTO Escape Clause and Other Authorized Temporary or Permanent Abandonments of MFN and Similar WTO/GATT Obligations

GATT 1947's Article XIX (the "Safeguards Agreement" and sometimes referred to as the "Escape Clause") prescribed when emergency action could be taken against imports which injured or threatened to injure domestic producers. Articles XX and XXI specified, respectively, general and security exceptions to GATT (*e.g.*, to protect public morals; to protect human, animal, and plant health and life;

gold and silver imports and exports; products of prison labor; to preserve national art treasures; conservation of natural resources, pursuant to approved commodity agreements, and to deal with short-supply situations). Several Article XX exceptions are limited by requirements of "necessity". Developing countries were authorized under GATT Articles XII and XVIII to establish quantitative restrictions or quotas against imports when faced with balance of payments difficulties.

Article XIX is an Agreement on Safeguards which permits a member to take action to protect a specific domestic industry from an unforeseen increase of imports of any product which is causing, or which is likely to cause, serious injury to the industry. A Safeguards Committee oversees operation of its provisions and is responsible for surveillance of its commitments. Safeguard measures may not be applicable to a product from a developing country member where its (or developing countries', collectively) share of the market are below prescribed levels. A prohibition was established against so-called "gray area" measures. No voluntary export restraint, orderly marketing arrangement, or similar measures regarding exports or imports may be sought or maintained (with a four-year phase out period for one permitted exception per member where the directly concerned member had so mutually agreed). "Sunset" clauses were proscribed for all safeguards actions (the earlier of 8 years from first application or 5 years after entry into force of the WTO Agreement for existing agreements and four years, extendable to a maximum of eight years subject to confirmation of continued necessity by the competent national authorities where evidence shows the affected industry to be adjusting). Measures imposed for greater than one year are to be progressively liberalized over their lifetimes. Limits were imposed on the reimposition of safeguards on products previously subject to them. Safeguards measures by developing countries may be extended for up to two years beyond the normal maximum and the reimposition by them of safeguards on the same product under more lenient conditions. Standards were established for safeguards investigations and provisional but limited safeguards measures which may be imposed only under critical circumstances. Safeguard measures must, in principle, be applied without regard to source and allocation and quota schemes are subject to limitations and time limits. Consultations for compensation and other countermeasures in response to safeguards actions are provided for.

The full text of GATT 1947, Article XVIII on Governmental Assistance to Economic Development, is provided earlier in this chapter.

For all reading of GATT 1947 Articles below, ***asterisks** mark the portions of the text which should be read in conjunction with notes and supplementary provisions in Annex I to the Agreement.

GATT 1947 Article XII and Its Interpretation—the Texts

"**Article XII***
Restrictions to Safeguard the Balance of Payments

1. Notwithstanding the provisions of paragraph 1 of Article XI, any contracting party, in order to safeguard its external financial position and its balance of payments, may restrict the quantity or value of merchandise permitted to be imported, subject to the provisions of the following paragraphs of this Article.

2.

(*a*) Import restrictions instituted, maintained or intensified by a contracting party under this Article shall not exceed those necessary:

(i) to forestall the imminent threat of, or to stop, a serious decline in its monetary reserves, or

(ii) in the case of a contracting party with very low monetary reserves, to achieve a reasonable rate of increase in its reserves.

Due regard shall be paid in either case to any special factors which may be affecting the reserves of such contracting party or its need for reserves, including, where special external credits or other resources are available to it, the need to provide for the appropriate use of such credits or resources.

(*b*) Contracting parties applying restrictions under sub-paragraph (*a*) of this paragraph shall progressively relax them as such conditions improve, maintaining them only to the extent that the conditions specified in that sub-paragraph still justify their application. They shall eliminate the restrictions when conditions would no longer justify their institution or maintenance under that sub-paragraph.

3.

(*a*) Contracting parties undertake, in carrying out their domestic policies, to pay due regard to the need for maintaining or restoring equilibrium in their balance of payments on a sound and lasting basis and to the desirability of avoiding an uneconomic employment of productive resources. They recognize that, in order to achieve these ends, it is desirable so far as possible to adopt measures which expand rather than contract international trade.

(*b*) Contracting parties applying restrictions under this Article may determine the incidence of the restrictions on imports of different products or classes of products in such a way as to give priority to the importation of those products which are more essential.

(*c*) Contracting parties applying restrictions under this Article undertake:

(i) to avoid unnecessary damage to the commercial or economic interests of any other contracting party;*

(ii) not to apply restrictions so as to prevent unreasonably the importation of any description of goods in minimum commercial quantities the exclusion of which would impair regular channels of trade; and

(iii) not to apply restrictions which would prevent the importations of commercial samples or prevent compliance with patent, trade mark, copyright, or similar procedures.

(*d*) The contracting parties recognize that, as a result of domestic policies directed towards the achievement and maintenance of full and productive employment or towards the development of economic resources, a contracting party may experience a high level of demand for imports involving a threat to its monetary reserves of the sort referred to in paragraph 2 (*a*) of this Article. Accordingly, a contracting party otherwise complying with the provisions of this Article shall not be required to withdraw or modify restrictions on the ground that a change in those policies would render unnecessary restrictions which it is applying under this Article.

4.

(*a*) Any contracting party applying new restrictions or raising the general level of its existing restrictions by a substantial intensification of the measures applied under this Article shall immediately after instituting or intensifying such restrictions (or, in circumstances in which prior consultation is practicable, before doing so) consult with the CONTRACTING PARTIES as to the nature of its balance of payments difficulties, alternative corrective measures which may be available, and the possible effect of the restrictions on the economies of other contracting parties.

(*b*) On a date to be determined by them,* the CONTRACTING PARTIES shall review all restrictions still applied under this Article on that date. Beginning one year after that date, contracting parties applying import restrictions under this Article shall enter into consultations of the type provided for in sub-paragraph (*a*) of this paragraph with the CONTRACTING PARTIES annually.

(*c*)

(i) If, in the course of consultations with a contracting party under sub-paragraph (*a*) or (*b*) above, the CONTRACTING PARTIES find that the restrictions are not consistent with provisions of this Article or with those of Article XIII (subject to the provisions of Article XIV), they shall indicate the nature of the inconsistency and may advise that the restrictions be suitably modified.

(ii) If, however, as a result of the consultations, the CONTRACTING PARTIES determine that the restrictions are being applied in a manner involving an inconsistency of a serious nature with the provisions of this Article or with those of Article XIII (subject to the provisions of Article XIV) and that damage to the trade of any contracting party is caused or threatened thereby, they shall so inform the contracting party applying the restrictions and shall make appropriate recommendations for securing conformity with such provisions within the specified period of time. If such contracting party does not comply with these recommendations within the specified period, the CONTRACTING PARTIES may release any contracting party the trade of which is adversely affected by the restrictions from such obligations under this Agreement towards the contracting party applying the restrictions as they determine to be appropriate in the circumstances.

(*d*) The CONTRACTING PARTIES shall invite any contracting party which is applying restrictions under this Article to enter into consultations with them at the request of any contracting party which can establish a *prima facie* case that the restrictions are inconsistent with the provisions of this Article or with those of Article XIII (subject to the provisions of Article XIV) and that its trade is adversely affected thereby. However, no such invitation shall be issued unless the CONTRACTING PARTIES have ascertained that direct discussions between the contracting parties concerned have not been successful. If, as a result of the consultations with the CONTRACTING PARTIES, no agreement is reached and they determine that the restrictions are being applied inconsistently with such provisions, and that damage to the trade of the contracting party initiating the procedure is caused or threatened thereby, they shall recommend the withdrawal or modification of the restrictions. If the restrictions are not withdrawn or modified within such time as the CONTRACTING PARTIES may prescribe, they may release the contracting party initiating the procedure from such obligations under this Agreement towards the contracting party applying the restrictions as they determine to be appropriate in the circumstances.

(*e*) In proceeding under this paragraph, the CONTRACTING PARTIES shall have due regard to any special external factors adversely affecting the export trade of the contracting party applying the restrictions.*

(*f*) Determinations under this paragraph shall be rendered expeditiously and, if possible, within sixty days of the initiation of the consultations.

5. If there is a persistent and widespread application of import restrictions under this Article, indicating the existence of a general disequilibrium which is restricting international trade, the CONTRACTING PARTIES shall initiate discussions to consider whether other measures might be taken, either by those contracting parties the balance of payments of which are under pressure or by those the balance of payments of which are tending to be exceptionally favourable, or by any appropriate intergovernmental organization, to remove the underlying causes of the disequilibrium. On the invitation of the CONTRACTING PARTIES, contracting parties shall participate in such discussions."

"Ad Article XII

Throughout Articles XI, XII, XIII, XIV and XVIII, the terms 'import restrictions' or 'export restrictions' include restrictions made effective through state-trading operations."

"Ad Article XII

The CONTRACTING PARTIES shall make provision for the utmost secrecy in the conduct of any consultation under the provisions of this Article.

Paragraph 3 (c)(i)

Contracting parties applying restrictions shall endeavour to avoid causing serious prejudice to exports of a commodity on which the economy of a contracting party is largely dependent.

Paragraph 4 (b)

It is agreed that the date shall be within ninety days after the entry into force of the amendments of this Article effected by the Protocol Amending the Preamble and Parts II and III of this Agreement. However, should the CONTRACTING PARTIES find that conditions were not suitable for the application of the provisions of this sub-paragraph at the time envisaged, they may determine a later date; *Provided* that such date is not more than thirty days after such time as the obligations of Article VIII, Sections 2, 3 and 4, of the Articles of Agreement of the International Monetary Fund become applicable to contracting parties, members of the Fund, the combined foreign trade of which constitutes at least fifty per centum of the aggregate foreign trade of all contracting parties.

Paragraph 4 (e)

It is agreed that paragraph 4 (*e*) does not add any new criteria for the imposition or maintenance of quantitative restrictions for balance of payments reasons. It is solely intended to ensure that all external factors such as changes in the terms of trade, quantitative restrictions, excessive tariffs and subsidies, which may be contributing to the balance of payments difficulties of the contracting party applying restrictions, will be fully taken into account."

GATT Article XIV and Its Interpretation—the Texts

"Article XIV*

Exceptions to the Rule of Non-discrimination

1. A contracting party which applies restrictions under Article XII or under Section B of Article XVIII may, in the application of such restrictions, deviate from the provisions of Article XIII in a manner having equivalent effect to restrictions on payments and transfers for current international transactions which that contracting party may at that time apply under Article VIII or XIV of the Articles of Agreement of the International Monetary Fund, or under analogous provisions of a special exchange agreement entered into pursuant to paragraph 6 of Article XV.*

2. A contracting party which is applying import restrictions under Article XII or under Section B of Article XVIII may, with the consent of the CONTRACTING PARTIES, temporarily deviate from the provisions of Article XIII in respect of a small part of its external trade where the benefits to the contracting party or contracting parties concerned substantially outweigh any injury which may result to the trade of other contracting parties.*

3. The provisions of Article XIII shall not preclude a group of

territories having a common quota in the International Monetary Fund from applying against imports from other countries, but not among themselves, restrictions in accordance with the provisions of Article XII or of Section B of Article XVIII on condition that such restrictions are in all other respects consistent with the provisions of Article XIII.

4. A contracting party applying import restrictions under Article XII or under Section B of Article XVIII shall not be precluded by Articles XI to XV or Section B of Article XVIII of this Agreement from applying measures to direct its exports in such a manner as to increase its earnings of currencies which it can use without deviation from the provisions of Article XIII.

5. A contracting party shall not be precluded by Articles XI to XV, inclusive, or by Section B of Article XVIII, of this Agreement from applying quantitative restrictions:

(*a*) having equivalent effect to exchange restrictions authorized under Section 3 (*b*) of Article VII of the Articles of Agreement of the International Monetary Fund, or

(*b*) under the preferential arrangements provided for in Annex A of this Agreement, pending the outcome of the negotiations referred to therein."

"**Ad Article XIV**

Throughout Articles XI, XII, XIII, XIV and XVIII, the terms 'import restrictions' or 'export restrictions' include restrictions made effective through state-trading operations."

"**Ad Article XIV**

Paragraph 1

The provisions of this paragraph shall not be so construed as to preclude full consideration by the CONTRACTING PARTIES, in the consultations provided for in paragraph 4 of Article XII and in paragraph 12 of Article XVIII, of the nature, effects and reasons for discrimination in the field of import restrictions.

Paragraph 2

One of the situations contemplated in paragraph 2 is that of a contracting party holding balances acquired as a result of current transactions which it finds itself unable to use without a measure of discrimination."

GATT Article XIX—the Text

"Article XIX
Emergency Action on Imports of Particular Products

1.

(*a*) If, as a result of unforeseen developments and of the effect of the obligations incurred by a contracting party under this Agreement, including tariff concessions, any product is being imported into the territory of that contracting party in such increased quantities and under such conditions as to cause or threaten serious injury to domestic producers in that territory of like or directly competitive products, the contracting party shall be free, in respect of such product, and to the extent and for such time as may be necessary to prevent or remedy such injury, to suspend the obligation in whole or in part or to withdraw or modify the concession.

(*b*) If any product, which is the subject of a concession with respect to a preference, is being imported into the territory of a contracting party in the circumstances set forth in sub-paragraph (*a*) of this paragraph, so as to cause or threaten serious injury to domestic producers of like or directly competitive products in the territory of a contracting party which receives or received such preference, the importing contracting party shall be free, if that other contracting party so requests, to suspend the relevant obligation in whole or in part or to withdraw or modify the concession in respect of the product, to the extent and for such time as may be necessary to prevent or remedy such injury.

2. Before any contracting party shall take action pursuant to the provisions of paragraph 1 of this Article, it shall give notice in writing to the CONTRACTING PARTIES as far in advance as may be practicable and shall afford the CONTRACTING PARTIES and those contracting parties having a substantial interest as exporters of the product concerned an opportunity to consult with it in respect of the proposed action. When such notice is given in relation to a concession with respect to a preference, the notice shall name the contracting party which has requested the action. In critical circumstances, where delay would cause damage which it would be difficult to repair, action under paragraph 1 of this Article may be taken provisionally without prior consultation, on the condition that consultation shall be effected immediately after taking such action.

3.

(*a*) If agreement among the interested contracting parties with respect to the action is not reached, the contracting party which proposes to take or continue the action shall, nevertheless, be free to do so, and if such action is taken or continued, the affected contracting parties shall then be free, not later than ninety days after such action is taken, to suspend, upon the expiration of thirty days from the day on which written notice of such suspension is received by the CONTRACTING PARTIES, the application to the trade of the contracting party taking such action, or, in the case envisaged in paragraph 1 (*b*) of this Article, to the trade of the contracting party requesting such action, of such substantially equivalent concessions or other obligations under this Agreement the suspension of which the CONTRACTING PARTIES do not disapprove.

(*b*) Notwithstanding the provisions of sub-paragraph (*a*) of this paragraph, where action is taken under paragraph 2 of this Article without prior consultation and causes or threatens serious injury in the territory of a contracting party to the domestic producers of products affected by the action, that contracting party shall, where delay would cause damage difficult to repair, be free to suspend, upon the taking of the action and throughout the period of consultation, such concessions or other obligations as may be necessary to prevent or remedy the injury."

GATT Article XX and Its Interpretation—the Text

"Article XX
General Exceptions

Subject to the requirement that such measures are not applied in a manner which would constitute a means of arbitrary or unjustifiable discrimination between countries where the same conditions prevail, or a disguised restriction on international trade, nothing in this Agreement shall be construed to prevent the adoption or enforcement by any contracting party of measures:

(*a*) necessary to protect public morals;

(*b*) necessary to protect human, animal or plant life or health;

(*c*) relating to the importations or exportations of gold or silver;

(*d*) necessary to secure compliance with laws or regulations which are not inconsistent with the provisions of this Agreement, including those relating to customs enforcement, the enforcement of monopolies operated under paragraph 4 of Article II and Article XVII, the protection of patents, trade marks and copyrights, and the prevention of deceptive practices;

(*e*) relating to the products of prison labour;

(*f*) imposed for the protection of national treasures of artistic, historic or archaeological value;

(*g*) relating to the conservation of exhaustible natural resources if such measures are made effective in conjunction with restrictions on domestic production or consumption;

(*h*) undertaken in pursuance of obligations under any intergovernmental commodity agreement which conforms to criteria submitted to the CONTRACTING PARTIES and not disapproved by them or which is itself so submitted and not so disapproved;*

(*i*) involving restrictions on exports of domestic materials necessary to ensure essential quantities of such materials to a domestic processing industry during periods when the domestic price of such materials is held below the world price as part of a governmental stabilization plan; *Provided* that such restrictions shall not operate to increase the exports of or the protection afforded to such domestic industry, and shall not depart from the provisions of this Agreement relating to non-discrimination;

(*j*) essential to the acquisition or distribution of products in general or local short supply; *Provided* that any such measures shall be consistent with the principle that all contracting parties are entitled to an equitable share of the international supply of such products, and that any such measures, which are inconsistent with the other provisions of the Agreement shall be discontinued as soon as the conditions giving rise to them have ceased to exist. The CONTRACTING PARTIES shall review the need for this sub-paragraph not later than 30 June 1960."

"**Ad** ***Article XX***
Sub-paragraph (h)

The exception provided for in this sub-paragraph extends to any commodity agreement which conforms to the principles approved by the Economic and Social Council in its resolution 30 (IV) of 28 March 1947."

GATT 1947 Article XXI—the Text

"**Article XXI**
Security Exceptions

Nothing in this Agreement shall be construed

(*a*) to require any contracting party to furnish any information the disclosure of which it considers contrary to its essential security interests; or

(*b*) to prevent any contracting party from taking any action which it considers necessary for the protection of its essential security interests

(i) relating to fissionable materials or the materials from which they are derived;

(ii) relating to the traffic in arms, ammunition and implements of war and to such traffic in other goods and materials as is carried on directly or indirectly for the purpose of supplying a military establishment;

(iii) taken in time of war or other emergency in international relations; or

(*c*) to prevent any contracting party from taking any action in pursuance of its obligations under the United Nations Charter for the maintenance of international peace and security."

GATT 1947 Article XXIII—the Text

"**Article XXIII**
Nullification or Impairment

1. If any contracting party should consider that any benefit accruing to it directly or indirectly under this Agreement is being nullified or impaired or that the attainment of any objective of the Agreement is being impeded as the result of

(*a*) the failure of another contracting party to carry out its obligations under this Agreement, or

(*b*) the application by another contracting party of any measure, whether or not it conflicts with the provisions of this Agreement, or

(*c*) the existence of any other situation,

the contracting party may, with a view to the satisfactory adjustment of the matter, make written representations or proposals to the other contracting party or parties which it considers to be concerned. Any contracting party thus approached shall give sympathetic consideration to the representations or proposals made to it.

2. If no satisfactory adjustment is effected between the

contracting parties concerned within a reasonable time, or if the difficulty is of the type described in paragraph 1 (*c*) of this Article, the matter may be referred to the CONTRACTING PARTIES. The CONTRACTING PARTIES shall promptly investigate any matter so referred to them and shall make appropriate recommendations to the contracting parties which they consider to be concerned, or give a ruling on the matter, as appropriate. The CONTRACTING PARTIES may consult with contracting parties, with the Economic and Social Council of the United Nations and with any appropriate inter-governmental organization in cases where they consider such consultation necessary. If the CONTRACTING PARTIES consider that the circumstances are serious enough to justify such action, they may authorize a contracting party or parties to suspend the application to any other contracting party or parties of such concessions or other obligations under this Agreement as they determine to be appropriate in the circumstances. If the application to any contracting party of any concession or other obligation is in fact suspended, that contracting party shall then be free, not later than sixty days after such action is taken, to give written notice to the Executive Secretary [NOW THE DIRECTOR-GENERAL] to the CONTRACTING PARTIES of its intention to withdraw from this Agreement and such withdrawal shall take effect upon the sixtieth day following the day on which such notice is received by him."

GATT 1947 Article XXVIII and Its Interpretation—the Text

"**Article XXVIII***
Modification of Schedules

1. On the first day of each three-year period, the first period beginning on 1 January 1958 (or on the first day of any other period* that may be specified by the CONTRACTING PARTIES by two-thirds of the votes cast) a contracting party (hereafter in this Article referred to as the 'applicant contracting party') may, by negotiation and agreement with any contracting party with which such concession was initially negotiated and with any other contracting party determined by the CONTRACTING PARTIES to have a principal supplying interest* (which two preceding categories of contracting parties, together with the applicant contracting party, are in this Article hereinafter referred to as the 'contracting parties primarily concerned'), and subject to consultation with any other contracting party determined by the CONTRACTING PARTIES to have a substantial interest* in such concession, modify or withdraw a concession* included in the appropriate schedule annexed to this Agreement.

2. In such negotiations and agreement, which may include provision for compensatory adjustment with respect to other products, the contracting parties concerned shall endeavour to maintain a general level of reciprocal and mutually advantageous concessions not less favourable to trade than that provided for in this Agreement prior to such negotiations.

3.

(*a*) If agreement between the contracting parties primarily concerned cannot be reached before 1 January 1958 or before the expiration of a period envisaged in paragraph 1 of this Article, the contracting party which proposes to modify or withdraw the concession shall, nevertheless, be free to do so and if such action is taken any contracting party with which such concession was initially negotiated, any contracting party determined under paragraph 1 to have a principal supplying interest and any contracting party determined under paragraph 1 to have a substantial interest shall then be free not later than six months after such action is taken, to withdraw, upon the expiration of thirty days from the day on which written notice of such withdrawal is received by the CONTRACTING PARTIES, substantially equivalent concessions initially negotiated with the applicant contracting party.

(*b*) If agreement between the contracting parties primarily concerned is reached but any other contracting party determined under paragraph 1 of this Article to have a substantial interest is not satisfied, such other contracting party shall be free, not later than six months after action under such agreement is taken, to withdraw, upon the expiration of thirty days from the day on which written notice of such withdrawal is received by the CONTRACTING PARTIES, substantially equivalent concessions initially negotiated with the applicant contracting party.

4. The CONTRACTING PARTIES may, at any time, in special circumstances, authorize* a contracting party to enter into negotiations for modification or withdrawal of a concession included in the appropriate Schedule annexed to this Agreement subject to the following procedures and conditions:

(*a*) Such negotiations* and any related consultations shall be conducted in accordance with the provisions of paragraph 1 and 2 of this Article.

(*b*) If agreement between the contracting parties primarily concerned is reached in the negotiations, the provisions of paragraph 3 (*b*) of this Article shall apply.

(*c*) If agreement between the contracting parties primarily concerned is not reached within a period of sixty days* after negotiations have been authorized, or within such longer period as the CONTRACTING PARTIES may have prescribed, the applicant contracting party may refer the matter to the CONTRACTING PARTIES.

(*d*) Upon such reference, the CONTRACTING PARTIES shall promptly examine the matter and submit their views to the contracting parties primarily concerned with the aim of achieving a settlement. If a settlement is reached, the provisions of paragraph 3 (*b*) shall apply as if agreement between the contracting parties primarily concerned had been reached. If no settlement is reached between the contracting parties primarily concerned, the applicant contracting party shall be free to modify or withdraw the concession, unless the CONTRACTING PARTIES determine that the applicant contracting party has unreasonably failed to offer adequate compensation.* If such action is taken, any contracting party with which the concession was initially negotiated, any contracting party determined under paragraph 4 (*a*) to have a principal supplying interest and any contracting party determined under paragraph 4 (*a*) to have a substantial interest, shall be free, not later than six months after such action is taken, to modify or withdraw, upon the expiration of thirty days from the day on which written notice of such withdrawal is received by the CONTRACTING PARTIES, substantially equivalent concessions initially negotiated with applicant contracting party.

5. Before 1 January 1958 and before the end of any period envisaged in paragraph 1 a contracting party may elect by notifying the CONTRACTING PARTIES to reserve the right, for the duration of the next period, to modify the appropriate Schedule in accordance with the procedures of paragraph 1 to 3. If a contracting party so elects, other contracting parties shall have the right, during the same period, to modify or withdraw, in accordance with the same procedures, concessions initially negotiated with that contracting party."

"Ad Article XXVIII

The CONTRACTING PARTIES and each contracting party concerned should arrange to conduct the negotiations and consultations with the greatest possible secrecy in order to avoid premature disclosure of details of prospective tariff changes. The CONTRACTING PARTIES shall be informed immediately of all changes in national tariffs resulting from recourse to this Article.

Paragraph 1

1. If the CONTRACTING PARTIES specify a period other than a three-year period, a contracting party may act pursuant to paragraph 1 or paragraph 3 of Article XXVIII on the first day following the expiration of such other period and, unless the CONTRACTING PARTIES have again specified another period, subsequent periods will be three-year periods following the expiration of such specified period.

2. The provision that on 1 January 1958, and on other days determined pursuant to paragraph 1, a contracting party 'may ... modify or withdraw a concession' means that on such day, and on the first day after the end of each period, the legal obligation of such contracting party under Article II is altered; it does not mean that the changes in its customs tariff should necessarily be made effective on that day. If a tariff change resulting from negotiations undertaken pursuant to this Article is delayed, the entry into force of any compensatory concessions may be similarly delayed.

3. Not earlier than six months, nor later than three months, prior to 1 January 1958, or to the termination date of any subsequent period, a contracting party wishing to modify or withdraw any concession embodied in the appropriate Schedule, should notify the CONTRACTING PARTIES to this effect. The CONTRACTING PARTIES shall then determine the contracting party or contracting parties with which the negotiations or consultations referred to in paragraph 1 shall take place. Any contracting party so determined shall participate in such negotiations or consultations with the applicant contracting party with the aim of reaching agreement before the end of the period. Any extension of the assured life of the Schedules shall relate to the Schedules as modified after such negotiations, in accordance with paragraphs 1, 2, and 3 of Article XXVIII. If the CONTRACTING PARTIES are arranging for multilateral tariff negotiations to take place within the period of six months before 1 January

1958, or before any other day determined pursuant to paragraph 1, they shall include in the arrangements for such negotiations suitable procedures for carrying out the negotiations referred to in this paragraph.

4. The object of providing for the participation in the negotiation of any contracting party with a principle supplying interest, in addition to any contracting party with which the concession was originally negotiated, is to ensure that a contracting party with a larger share in the trade affected by the concession than a contracting party with which the concession was originally negotiated shall have an effective opportunity to protect the contractual right which it enjoys under this Agreement.

On the other hand, it is not intended that the scope of the negotiations should be such as to make negotiations and agreement under Article XXVIII unduly difficult nor to create complications in the application of this Article in the future to concessions which result from negotiations thereunder. Accordingly, the CONTRACTING PARTIES should only determine that a contracting party has a principal supplying interest if that contracting party has had, over a reasonable period of time prior to the negotiations, a larger share in the market of the applicant contracting party than a contracting party with which the concession was initially negotiated or would, in the judgement of the CONTRACTING PARTIES, have had such a share in the absence of discriminatory quantitative restrictions maintained by the applicant contracting party. It would therefore not be appropriate for the CONTRACTING PARTIES to determine that more than one contracting party, or in those exceptional cases where there is near equality more than two contracting parties, had a principal supplying interest.

5. Notwithstanding the definition of a principal supplying interest in note 4 to paragraph 1, the CONTRACTING PARTIES may exceptionally determine that a contracting party has a principal supplying interest if the concession in question affects trade which constitutes a major part of the total exports of such contracting party.

6. It is not intended that provision for participation in the negotiations of any contracting party with a principal supplying interest, and for consultation with any contracting party having a substantial interest in the concession which the applicant contracting party is seeking to modify or withdraw, should have the effect that it should have to pay compensation or suffer retaliation greater than the withdrawal or modification sought, judged in the light of the conditions of trade at the time of the proposed withdrawal or modification, making allowance for any discriminatory quantitative restrictions maintained by the applicant contracting party.

7. The expression 'substantial interest' is not capable of a precise definition and accordingly may present difficulties for the CONTRACTING PARTIES. It is, however, intended to be construed to cover only those contracting parties which have, or in the absence of discriminatory quantitative restrictions affecting their exports could reasonably be expected to have, a significant share in the market of the contracting party seeking to modify or withdraw the concession.

Paragraph 4

1. Any request for authorization to enter into negotiations shall be accompanied by all relevant statistical and other data. A decision on such request shall be made within thirty days of its submission.

2. It is recognized that to permit certain contracting parties, depending in large measure on a relatively small number of primary commodities and relying on the tariff as an important aid for furthering diversification of their economies or as an important source of revenue, normally to negotiate for the modification or withdrawal of concessions only under paragraph 1 of Article XXVIII, might cause them at such time to make modifications or withdrawals which in the long run would prove unnecessary. To avoid such a situation the CONTRACTING PARTIES shall authorize any such contracting party, under paragraph 4, to enter into negotiations unless they consider this would result in, or contribute substantially towards, such an increase in tariff levels as to threaten the stability of the Schedules to this Agreement or lead to undue disturbance of international trade.

3. It is expected that negotiations authorized under paragraph 4 for modification or withdrawal of a single item, or a very small group of items, could normally be brought to a conclusion in sixty days. It is recognized, however, that such a period will be inadequate for cases involving negotiations for the modification or withdrawal of a larger number of items and in such cases, therefore, it would be appropriate for the CONTRACTING PARTIES to prescribe a longer period.

4. The determination referred to in paragraph 4 (*d*) shall be made by the CONTRACTING PARTIES within thirty days of the submission of the matter to them unless the applicant contracting party agrees to a longer period.

5. In determining under paragraph 4 (*d*) whether an applicant contracting party has unreasonably failed to offer adequate compensation, it is understood that the CONTRACTING PARTIES will take due account of the special position of a contracting party which has bound a high proportion of its tariffs at very low rates of duty and to this extent has less scope than other contracting parties to make compensatory adjustment."

Understanding on GATT Balance-of-Payments Provisions—the Text

"UNDERSTANDING ON THE BALANCE-OF-PAYMENTS PROVISIONS OF THE GENERAL AGREEMENT ON TARIFFS AND TRADE 1994

Members,

Recognizing the provisions of Articles XII and XVIII:B of GATT 1994 and of the Declaration on Trade Measures Taken for Balance-of-Payments Purposes adopted on 28 November 1979 (BISD 26S/205-209, referred to in this Understanding as the '1979 Declaration') and in order to clarify such provisions [NOTHING IN THIS UNDERSTANDING IS INTENDED TO MODIFY THE RIGHTS AND OBLIGATIONS OF MEMBERS UNDER ARTICLES XII OR XVIII:B OF GATT 1994. THE PROVISIONS OF ARTICLES XXII AND XXIII

OF GATT 1994 AS ELABORATED AND APPLIED BY THE DISPUTE SETTLEMENT UNDERSTANDING MAY BE INVOKED WITH RESPECT TO ANY MATTERS ARISING FROM THE APPLICATION OF RESTRICTIVE IMPORT MEASURES TAKEN FOR BALANCE-OF-PAYMENTS PURPOSES.];

Hereby agree as follows:

Application of Measures

1. Members confirm their commitment to announce publicly, as soon as possible, time-schedules for the removal of restrictive import measures taken for balance-of-payments purposes. It is understood that such time-schedules may be modified as appropriate to take into account changes in the balance-of-payments situation. Whenever a time-schedule is not publicly announced by a Member, that Member shall provide justification as to the reasons therefor.

2. Members confirm their commitment to give preference to those measures which have the least disruptive effect on trade. Such measures (referred to in this Understanding as 'price-based measures') shall be understood to include import surcharges, import deposit requirements or other equivalent trade measures with an impact on the price of imported goods. It is understood that, notwithstanding the provisions of Article II, price-based measures taken for balance-of-payments purposes may be applied by a Member in excess of the duties inscribed in the Schedule of that Member. Furthermore, that Member shall indicate the amount by which the price-based measure exceeds the bound duty clearly and separately under the notification procedures of this Understanding.

3. Members shall seek to avoid the imposition of new quantitative restrictions for balance-of-payments purposes unless, because of a critical balance-of-payments situation, price-based measures cannot arrest a sharp deterioration in the external payments position. In those cases in which a Member applies quantitative restrictions, it shall provide justification as to the reasons why price-based measures are not an adequate instrument to deal with the balance-of-payments situation. A Member maintaining quantitative restrictions shall indicate in successive consultations the progress made in significantly reducing the incidence and restrictive effect of such measures. It is understood that not more than one type of restrictive import measure taken for balance-of-payments purposes may be applied on the same product.

4. Members confirm that restrictive import measures taken for balance-of-payments purposes may only be applied to control the general level of imports and may not exceed what is necessary to address the balance-of-payments situation. In order to minimize any incidental protective effects, a Member shall administer restrictions in a transparent manner. The authorities of the importing Member shall provide adequate justification as to the criteria used to determine which products are subject to restriction. As provided in paragraph 3 of Article XII and paragraph 10 of Article XVIII, Members may, in the case of certain essential products, exclude or limit the application of surcharges applied across the board or other measures applied for balance-of-payments purposes. The term 'essential products' shall be understood to mean products which meet basic consumption needs or which contribute to the

Member's effort to improve its balance-of-payments situation, such as capital goods or inputs needed for production. In the administration of quantitative restrictions, a Member shall use discretionary licensing only when unavoidable and shall phase it out progressively. Appropriate justification shall be provided as to the criteria used to determine allowable import quantities or values.

Procedures for Balance-of-Payments Consultations

5. The Committee on Balance-of-Payments Restrictions (referred to in this Understanding as the 'Committee') shall carry out consultations in order to review all restrictive import measures taken for balance-of-payments purposes. The membership of the Committee is open to all Members indicating their wish to serve on it. The Committee shall follow the procedures for consultations on balance-of-payments restrictions approved on 28 April 1970 (BISD 18S/48-53, referred to in this Understanding as 'full consultation procedures'), subject to the provisions set out below.

6. A Member applying new restrictions or raising the general level of its existing restrictions by a substantial intensification of the measures shall enter into consultations with the Committee within four months of the adoption of such measures. The Member adopting such measures may request that a consultation be held under paragraph 4(a) of Article XII or paragraph 12(a) of Article XVIII as appropriate. If no such request has been made, the Chairman of the Committee shall invite the Member to hold such a consultation. Factors that may be examined in the consultation would include, inter alia, the introduction of new types of restrictive measures for balance-of-payments purposes, or an increase in the level or product coverage of restrictions.

7. All restrictions applied for balance-of-payments purposes shall be subject to periodic review in the Committee under paragraph 4(b) of Article XII or under paragraph 12(b) of Article XVIII, subject to the possibility of altering the periodicity of consultations in agreement with the consulting Member or pursuant to any specific review procedure that may be recommended by the General Council.

8. Consultations may be held under the simplified procedures approved on 19 December 1972 (BISD 20S/47-49, referred to in this Understanding as 'simplified consultation procedures') in the case of least-developed country Members or in the case of developing country Members which are pursuing liberalization efforts in conformity with the schedule presented to the Committee in previous consultations. Simplified consultation procedures may also be used when the Trade Policy Review of a developing country Member is scheduled for the same calendar year as the date fixed for the consultations. In such cases the decision as to whether full consultation procedures should be used will be made on the basis of the factors enumerated in paragraph 8 of the 1979 Declaration. Except in the case of least-developed country Members, no more than two successive consultations may be held under simplified consultation procedures.

Notification and Documentation

9. A Member shall notify to the General Council the introduction of or any changes in the application of restrictive import measures taken for

balance-of-payments purposes, as well as any modifications in time-schedules for the removal of such measures as announced under paragraph 1. Significant changes shall be notified to the General Council prior to or not later than 30 days after their announcement. On a yearly basis, each Member shall make available to the Secretariat a consolidated notification, including all changes in laws, regulations, policy statements or public notices, for examination by Members. Notifications shall include full information, as far as possible, at the tariff-line level, on the type of measures applied, the criteria used for their administration, product coverage and trade flows affected.

10. At the request of any Member, notifications may be reviewed by the Committee. Such reviews would be limited to the clarification of specific issues raised by a notification or examination of whether a consultation under paragraph 4(a) of Article XII or paragraph 12(a) of Article XVIII is required. Members which have reasons to believe that a restrictive import measure applied by another Member was taken for balance-of-payments purposes may bring the matter to the attention of the Committee. The Chairman of the Committee shall request information on the measure and make it available to all Members. Without prejudice to the right of any member of the Committee to seek appropriate clarifications in the course of consultations, questions may be submitted in advance for consideration by the consulting Member.

11. The consulting Member shall prepare a Basic Document for the consultations which, in addition to any other information considered to be relevant, should include: (a) an overview of the balance-of-payments situation and prospects, including a consideration of the internal and external factors having a bearing on the balance-of-payments situation and the domestic policy measures taken in order to restore equilibrium on a sound and lasting basis; (b) a full description of the restrictions applied for balance-of-payments purposes, their legal basis and steps taken to reduce incidental protective effects; (c) measures taken since the last consultation to liberalize import restrictions, in the light of the conclusions of the Committee; (d) a plan for the elimination and progressive relaxation of remaining restrictions. References may be made, when relevant, to the information provided in other notifications or reports made to the WTO. Under simplified consultation procedures, the consulting Member shall submit a written statement containing essential information on the elements covered by the Basic Document.

12. The Secretariat shall, with a view to facilitating the consultations in the Committee, prepare a factual background paper dealing with the different aspects of the plan for consultations. In the case of developing country Members, the Secretariat document shall include relevant background and analytical material on the incidence of the external trading environment on the balance-of-payments situation and prospects of the consulting Member. The technical assistance services of the Secretariat shall, at the request of a developing country Member, assist in preparing the documentation for the consultations.

Conclusions of Balance-of-Payments Consultations

13. The Committee shall report on its consultations to the General Council. When full consultation procedures have been used, the report should indicate the Committee's conclusions on the different elements of the plan for

consultations, as well as the facts and reasons on which they are based. The Committee shall endeavour to include in its conclusions proposals for recommendations aimed at promoting the implementation of Articles XII and XVIII:B, the 1979 Declaration and this Understanding. In those cases in which a time-schedule has been presented for the removal of restrictive measures taken for balance-of-payments purposes, the General Council may recommend that, in adhering to such a time-schedule, a Member shall be deemed to be in compliance with its GATT 1994 obligations. Whenever the General Council has made specific recommendations, the rights and obligations of Members shall be assessed in the light of such recommendations. In the absence of specific proposals for recommendations by the General Council, the Committee's conclusions should record the different views expressed in the Committee. When simplified consultation procedures have been used, the report shall include a summary of the main elements discussed in the Committee and a decision on whether full consultation procedures are required."

Understanding on the Interpretation of GATT Article XXVIII—the Text

"UNDERSTANDING ON THE INTERPRETATION OF ARTICLE XXVIII OF THE GENERAL AGREEMENT ON TARIFFS AND TRADE 1994

Members *hereby* agree *as follows:*

1. For the purposes of modification or withdrawal of a concession, the Member which has the highest ratio of exports affected by the concession (i.e. exports of the product to the market of the Member modifying or withdrawing the concession) to its total exports shall be deemed to have a principal supplying interest if it does not already have an initial negotiating right or a principal supplying interest as provided for in paragraph 1 of Article XXVIII. It is however agreed that this paragraph will be reviewed by the Council for Trade in Goods five years from the date of entry into force of the WTO Agreement with a view to deciding whether this criterion has worked satisfactorily in securing a redistribution of negotiating rights in favour of small and medium-sized exporting Members. If this is not the case, consideration will be given to possible improvements, including, in the light of the availability of adequate data, the adoption of a criterion based on the ratio of exports affected by the concession to exports to all markets of the product in question.

2. Where a Member considers that it has a principal supplying interest in terms of paragraph 1, it should communicate its claim in writing, with supporting evidence, to the Member proposing to modify or withdraw a concession, and at the same time inform the Secretariat. Paragraph 4 of the 'Procedures for Negotiations under Article XXVIII' adopted on 10 November 1980 (BISD 27S/26-28) shall apply in these cases.

3. In the determination of which Members have a principal supplying interest (whether as provided for in paragraph 1 above or in paragraph 1 of Article XXVIII) or substantial interest, only trade in the affected product which has taken place on an MFN basis shall be taken into

consideration. However, trade in the affected product which has taken place under non-contractual preferences shall also be taken into account if the trade in question has ceased to benefit from such preferential treatment, thus becoming MFN trade, at the time of the negotiation for the modification or withdrawal of the concession, or will do so by the conclusion of that negotiation.

4. When a tariff concession is modified or withdrawn on a new product (i.e. a product for which three years' trade statistics are not available) the Member possessing initial negotiating rights on the tariff line where the product is or was formerly classified shall be deemed to have an initial negotiating right in the concession in question. The determination of principal supplying and substantial interests and the calculation of compensation shall take into account, inter alia, production capacity and investment in the affected product in the exporting Member and estimates of export growth, as well as forecasts of demand for the product in the importing Member. For the purposes of this paragraph, 'new product' is understood to include a tariff item created by means of a breakout from an existing tariff line.

5. Where a Member considers that it has a principal supplying or a substantial interest in terms of paragraph 4, it should communicate its claim in writing, with supporting evidence, to the Member proposing to modify or withdraw a concession, and at the same time inform the Secretariat. Paragraph 4 of the above-mentioned 'Procedures for Negotiations under Article XXVIII' shall apply in these cases.

6. When an unlimited tariff concession is replaced by a tariff rate quota, the amount of compensation provided should exceed the amount of the trade actually affected by the modification of the concession. The basis for the calculation of compensation should be the amount by which future trade prospects exceed the level of the quota. It is understood that the calculation of future trade prospects should be based on the greater of:

(a) the average annual trade in the most recent representative three-year period, increased by the average annual growth rate of imports in that same period, or by 10 per cent, whichever is the greater; or

(b) trade in the most recent year increased by 10 per cent.

In no case shall a Member's liability for compensation exceed that which would be entailed by complete withdrawal of the concession.

7. Any Member having a principal supplying interest, whether as provided for in paragraph 1 above or in paragraph 1 of Article XXVIII, in a concession which is modified or withdrawn shall be accorded an initial negotiating right in the compensatory concessions, unless another form of compensation is agreed by the Members concerned."

Chapter VII: WTO/GATT Texts on Customs and Tariffs

Coverage of This Chapter

This chapter will deal with the limitations imposed upon WTO members regarding the tariffs that may be imposed upon imports into their customs territories. Such limitations are generally established by GATT 1994.

GATT 1994 is found in Annex 1A, Multilateral Agreements on Trade in Goods. GATT 1994 itself is essentially a short enumeration of its constituent parts followed by those parts, the first of which is GATT 1947 as modified through the Uruguay Round. Included legal instruments include the protocols of accession; the protocols and certifications relating to tariff concessions; decisions on waivers granted under Article XXV of GATT 1947 and still in force; and other decisions of the Contracting Parties to GATT 1947 which will not be reproduced below.

New understandings made part of GATT 1994 are: (a) the Understanding on Article II:1(b); (b) the Understanding on Article XVII; (c) the Understanding on Balance-of-Payments Provisions (including the 1979 Declaration); (d) the Understanding on Article XXIV; (e) the Understanding in Respect of Waivers; and (f) the Understanding on Article XXXVIII. GATT 1994 has incorporated into itself five former plurilateral agreements, ASCM, AAD, Customs Valuation, Standards, and Import Licensing.

Other agreements were added to GATT 1994 which deal with the international trade in goods, most notably by providing for the scheduled reapplication of GATT's terms to the global trade in agricultural products, textiles and clothing, and some other formerly effectively excluded goods. Those Agreements are: (a) the Marrakech Protocol; (b) AAg; (c) the Agreement on the Application of Sanitary and Phytosanitary Measures; (d) the Agreement on Textiles and Clothing; (e) TRIMs; (f) the Agreement on Preshipment Inspection; (g) the Agreement on ROs; and (h) the Agreement on Safeguards. TRIMs will not be reproduced below because it has no direct relevance to customs and tariffs.

Also of relevance to the trade in goods are the following ministerial decisions and declarations: (a) Decision on Measures in Favor of Least-Developed Countries; (b) Decision on Measures Concerning the Possible Negative Effects of the Reform Program on Least-Developed and Net Food-Importing Developing Countries; (c) Decision on Notification of First Integration under Article 2.6 of the Agreement on Textiles and Clothing; (d) Decisions Relating to the Agreement on Technical Barriers to Trade; (e) Decisions and Declaration Relating to the Agreement on Implementation of Article VI of GATT 1994; and (f) Decision Relating to the Agreement on Implementation of Article VII of GATT 1994. The Plurilateral Agreements are also germane to the international trade in goods but will not be reproduced below.

So that the reader may refer to the text of these documents, most have been produced in full below. In some instances, sections of GATT 1994 and other documents will be reproduced in other chapters and this will be indicated where those sections and documents would otherwise have been found.

GATT 1994—the Text

"ANNEX 1

ANNEX 1A

MULTILATERAL AGREEMENTS ON TRADE IN GOODS

General interpretative note to Annex 1A:

In the event of conflict between a provision of the General Agreement on Tariffs and Trade 1994 and a provision of another agreement in Annex 1A to the Agreement Establishing the World Trade Organization (referred to in the agreements in Annex 1A as the 'WTO Agreement'), the provision of the other agreement shall prevail to the extent of the conflict.

GENERAL AGREEMENT ON TARIFFS AND TRADE 1994

1. The General Agreement on Tariffs and Trade 1994 ('GATT 1994') shall consist of:

(a) the provisions in the General Agreement on Tariffs and Trade, dated 30 October 1947, annexed to the Final Act Adopted at the Conclusion of the Second Session of the Preparatory Committee of the United Nations Conference on Trade and Employment (excluding the Protocol of Provisional Application), as rectified, amended or modified by the terms of legal instruments which have entered into force before the date of entry into force of the WTO Agreement;

(b) the provisions of the legal instruments set forth below that have entered into force under the GATT 1947 before the date of entry into force of the WTO Agreement:

(i) protocols and certifications relating to tariff concessions;

(ii) protocols of accession (excluding the provisions (*a*) concerning provisional application and withdrawal of provisional application and (*b*) providing that Part II of GATT 1947 shall be applied provisionally to the fullest extent not inconsistent with legislation existing on the date of the Protocol);

(iii) decisions on waivers granted under Article XXV of GATT 1947 and still in force on the date of entry into force of the WTO Agreement [THE WAIVERS COVERED BY THIS PROVISION ARE LISTED IN FOOTNOTE 7 ON PAGES 11 AND 12 IN PART II OF DOCUMENT MTN/FA OF 15 DECEMBER 1993 AND IN MTN/FA/CORR.6 OF 21 MARCH 1994. THE MINISTERIAL CONFERENCE SHALL ESTABLISH AT ITS FIRST SESSION A REVISED LIST OF WAIVERS COVERED BY THIS PROVISION THAT ADDS ANY WAIVERS GRANTED UNDER GATT 1947 AFTER 15 DECEMBER 1993 AND BEFORE THE DATE OF ENTRY INTO FORCE OF THE WTO AGREEMENT, AND DELETES THE WAIVERS WHICH WILL HAVE EXPIRED BY THAT TIME.];

(iv) other decisions of the CONTRACTING PARTIES to GATT 1947;

(c) the Understandings set forth below:

(i) Understanding on the Interpretation of Article II:1(b) of the General Agreement on Tariffs and Trade 1994;

(ii) Understanding on the Interpretation of Article XVII of the General Agreement on Tariffs and Trade 1994;

(iii) Understanding on Balance-of-Payments Provisions of the General Agreement on Tariffs and Trade 1994;

(iv) Understanding on the Interpretation of Article XXIV of the General Agreement on Tariffs and Trade 1994;

(v) Understanding in Respect of Waivers of Obligations under the General Agreement on Tariffs and Trade 1994;

(vi) Understanding on the Interpretation of Article XXVIII of the General Agreement on Tariffs and Trade 1994; and

(d) the Marrakech Protocol to GATT 1994.

2. *Explanatory Notes*

(a) The references to 'contracting party' in the provisions of GATT 1994 shall be deemed to read 'Member.' The references to 'less-developed contracting party' and 'developed contracting party' shall be deemed to read 'developing country Member' and 'developed country Member.' The references to 'Executive Secretary' shall be deemed to read 'Director-General of the WTO.'

(b) The references to the CONTRACTING PARTIES acting jointly in Articles XV:1, XV:2, XV:8, XXXVIII and the Notes *Ad* Article XII and XVIII; and in the provisions on special exchange agreements in Articles XV:2, XV:3, XV:6, XV:7 and XV:9 of GATT 1994 shall be deemed to be references to the WTO. The other functions that the provisions of GATT 1994 assign to the CONTRACTING PARTIES acting jointly shall be allocated by the Ministerial Conference.

(c)

(i) The text of GATT 1994 shall be authentic in English, French and Spanish.

(ii) The text of GATT 1994 in the French language shall be subject to the rectifications of terms indicated in Annex A to document MTN.TNC/41.

(iii) The authentic text of GATT 1994 in the Spanish language shall be the text in Volume IV of the Basic Instruments and Selected Documents series, subject to the rectifications of terms indicated in Annex B to document MTN.TNC/41.

3.

(a) The provisions of Part II of GATT 1994 shall not apply to measures taken by a Member under specific mandatory legislation, enacted by that Member before it became a contracting party to GATT 1947, that prohibits the use, sale or lease of foreign-built or foreign-reconstructed vessels in commercial applications between points in national waters or the waters of an exclusive economic zone. This exemption applies to: (*a*) the continuation or prompt renewal of a non-conforming provision of such legislation; and (*b*) the amendment to a non-conforming provision of such legislation to the extent that the amendment does not decrease the conformity of the provision with Part II of GATT 1947. This exemption is limited to measures taken under legislation described above that is notified and specified prior to the date of entry into force of the WTO Agreement. If such legislation is subsequently modified to decrease its conformity with Part II of GATT 1994, it will no longer qualify for coverage under this paragraph.

(b) The Ministerial Conference shall review this exemption not later than five years after the date of entry into force of the WTO Agreement and thereafter every two years for as long as the exemption is in force for the purpose of examining whether the conditions which created the need for the exemption still prevail.

(c) A Member whose measures are covered by this exemption shall annually submit a detailed statistical notification consisting of a five-year moving average of actual and expected deliveries of relevant vessels as well as additional information on the use, sale, lease or repair of relevant vessels covered by this exemption.

(d) A Member that considers that this exemption operates in such a manner as to justify a reciprocal and proportionate limitation on the use, sale, lease or repair of vessels constructed in the territory of the Member invoking the exemption shall be free to introduce such a limitation subject to prior notification to the Ministerial Conference.

(e) This exemption is without prejudice to solutions concerning specific aspects of the legislation covered by this exemption negotiated in sectoral agreements or in other fora."

GATT 1947—the Text

[***asterisks** below mark the portions of the text which should be read in conjunction with notes and supplementary provisions in Annex I to the Agreement.]

THE GENERAL AGREEMENT ON TARIFFS AND TRADE

The [CONTRACTING STATES]:

Recognizing that their relations in the field of trade and economic endeavour should be conducted with a view to raising standards of living, ensuring full employment and a large and steadily growing volume of real income and effective demand, developing the full use of the resources of the world and expanding the production and exchange of goods,

Being desirous of contributing to these objectives by entering into reciprocal and mutually advantageous arrangements directed to the substantial reduction of tariffs and other barriers to trade and to the elimination of discriminatory treatment in international commerce,

Have through their Representatives agreed as follows:

PART I

Article I
General Most-Favoured-Nation Treatment

1. With respect to customs duties and charges of any kind imposed on or in connection with importation or exportation or imposed on the international transfer of payments for imports or exports, and with respect to the method of levying such duties and charges, and with respect to all rules and formalities in connection with importation and exportation, and with respect to all matters referred to in paragraphs 2 and 4 of Article III,* any advantage, favour, privilege or immunity granted by any contracting party to any product originating in or destined for any other country shall be accorded immediately and unconditionally to the like product originating in or destined for the territories of all other contracting parties.

2. The provisions of paragraph 1 of this Article shall not require the elimination of any preferences in respect of import duties or charges which do not exceed the levels provided for in paragraph 4 of this Article and which fall within the following descriptions:

(*a*) Preferences in force exclusively between two or more of the territories listed in Annex A, subject to the conditions set forth therein;

(*b*) Preferences in force exclusively between two or more territories which on July 1, 1939, were connected by common sovereignty or relations of protection or suzerainty and which are listed in Annexes B, C and D, subject to the conditions set forth therein;

(*c*) Preferences in force exclusively between the United States of America and the Republic of Cuba;

(*d*) Preferences in force exclusively between neighbouring countries listed in Annexes E and F.

3. The provisions of paragraph 1 shall not apply to preferences between the countries formerly a part of the Ottoman Empire and detached from it on July 24, 1923, provided such preferences are approved under paragraph 5 of Article XXV, which shall be applied in this respect in the light of paragraph 1 of Article XXIX.

4. The margin of preference* on any product in respect of which a preference is permitted under paragraph 2 of this Article but is not specifically set forth as a maximum margin of preference in the appropriate Schedule annexed to this Agreement shall not exceed:

(*a*) in respect of duties or charges on any product described in such Schedule, the difference between the most-favoured-nation and preferential rates provided for therein; if no preferential rate is provided for, the preferential rate shall for the purposes of this paragraph be taken to be that in force on April 10, 1947, and, if no most-favoured-nation rate is provided for, the margin shall not exceed the difference between the most-favoured-nation and preferential rates existing on April 10, 1947;

(*b*) in respect of duties or charges on any product not described in the appropriate Schedule, the difference between the most-favoured-nation and preferential rates existing on April 10, 1947.

In the case of the contracting parties named in Annex G, the date of April 10, 1947, referred to in sub-paragraph (*a*) and (*b*) of this paragraph shall be replaced by the respective dates set forth in that Annex.

Article II
Schedules of Concessions

1.

(*a*) Each contracting party shall accord to the commerce of the other contracting parties treatment no less favourable than that provided for in the appropriate Part of the appropriate Schedule annexed to this Agreement.

(*b*) The products described in Part I of the Schedule relating to any contracting party, which are the products of territories of other contracting parties, shall, on their importation into the territory to which the Schedule relates, and subject to the terms, conditions or qualifications set forth in that Schedule, be exempt from ordinary customs duties in excess of those set forth and provided therein. Such products shall also be exempt from all other duties or charges of any kind imposed on or in connection with the importation in excess of those imposed on the date of this Agreement or those directly and mandatorily required to be imposed thereafter by legislation in force in the importing territory on that date.

(*c*) The products described in Part II of the Schedule relating to any contracting party which are the products of territories entitled under Article I to receive preferential treatment upon importation into the territory to which the Schedule relates shall, on their importation into such territory, and subject to the terms, conditions or qualifications set forth in that Schedule, be exempt from ordinary customs duties in excess of those set forth and provided for in Part II of that Schedule.

Such products shall also be exempt from all other duties or charges of any kind imposed on or in connection with importation in excess of those imposed on the date of this Agreement or those directly or mandatorily required to be imposed thereafter by legislation in force in the importing territory on that date. Nothing in this Article shall prevent any contracting party from maintaining its requirements existing on the date of this Agreement as to the eligibility of goods for entry at preferential rates of duty.

2. Nothing in this Article shall prevent any contracting party from imposing at any time on the importation of any product:

(a) a charge equivalent to an internal tax imposed consistently with the provisions of paragraph 2 of Article III* in respect of the like domestic product or in respect of an article from which the imported product has been manufactured or produced in whole or in part;

(b) any anti-dumping or countervailing duty applied consistently with the provisions of Article VI;*

(c) fees or other charges commensurate with the cost of services rendered.

3. No contracting party shall alter its method of determining dutiable value or of converting currencies so as to impair the value of any of the concessions provided for in the appropriate Schedule annexed to this Agreement.

4. If any contracting party establishes, maintains or authorizes, formally or in effect, a monopoly of the importation of any product described in the appropriate Schedule annexed to this Agreement, such monopoly shall not, except as provided for in that Schedule or as otherwise agreed between the parties which initially negotiated the concession, operate so as to afford protection on the average in excess of the amount of protection provided for in that Schedule. The provisions of this paragraph shall not limit the use by contracting parties of any form of assistance to domestic producers permitted by other provisions of this Agreement.*

5. If any contracting party considers that a product is not receiving from another contracting party the treatment which the first contracting party believes to have been contemplated by a concession provided for in the appropriate Schedule annexed to this Agreement, it shall bring the matter directly to the attention of the other contracting party. If the latter agrees that the treatment contemplated was that claimed by the first contracting party, but declares that such treatment cannot be accorded because a court or other proper authority has ruled to the effect that the product involved cannot be classified under the tariff laws of such contracting party so as to permit the treatment contemplated in this Agreement, the two contracting parties, together with any other contracting parties substantially interested, shall enter promptly into further negotiations with a view to a compensatory adjustment of the matter.

6.

(a) The specific duties and charges included in the Schedules relating to contracting parties members of the International Monetary Fund, and margins of preference in specific duties and charges maintained by such contracting parties, are expressed in the

appropriate currency at the par value accepted or provisionally recognized by the Fund at the date of this Agreement. Accordingly, in case this par value is reduced consistently with the Articles of Agreement of the International Monetary Fund by more than twenty per centum, such specific duties and charges and margins of preference may be adjusted to take account of such reduction; *provided* that the CONTRACTING PARTIES (*i.e.*, the contracting parties acting jointly as provided for in Article XXV) concur that such adjustments will not impair the value of the concessions provided for in the appropriate Schedule or elsewhere in this Agreement, due account being taken of all factors which may influence the need for, or urgency of, such adjustments.

(*b*) Similar provisions shall apply to any contracting party not a member of the Fund, as from the date on which such contracting party becomes a member of the Fund or enters into a special exchange agreement in pursuance of Article XV.

7. The Schedules annexed to this Agreement are hereby made an integral part of Part I of this Agreement.

PART II

Article III*
National Treatment on Internal Taxation and Regulation
[FOUND IN CHAPTER X]

Article IV
Special Provisions relating to Cinematograph Films

If any contracting party establishes or maintains internal quantitative regulations relating to exposed cinematograph films, such regulations shall take the form of screen quotas which shall conform to the following requirements:

(*a*) Screen quotas may require the exhibition of cinematograph films of national origin during a specified minimum proportion of the total screen time actually utilized, over a specified period of not less than one year, in the commercial exhibition of all films of whatever origin, and shall be computed on the basis of screen time per theatre per year or the equivalent thereof;

(*b*) With the exception of screen time reserved for films of national origin under a screen quota, screen time including that released by administrative action from screen time reserved for films of national origin, shall not be allocated formally or in effect among sources of supply;

(*c*) Notwithstanding the provisions of sub-paragraph (*b*) of this Article, any contracting party may maintain screen quotas conforming to the requirements of sub-paragraph (*a*) of this Article which reserve a m

(*d*) Screen quotas shall be subject to negotiation for their limitation, liberalization or elimination.

Article V
Freedom of Transit
[FOUND IN CHAPTER VI]

Article VI
Anti-dumping and Countervailing Duties
[FOUND IN CHAPTER X]

Article VII
Valuation for Customs Purposes
[FOUND IN CHAPTER VIII]

Article VIII
*Fees and Formalities connected with Importation and Exportation**
[FOUND IN CHAPTER X]

Article IX
Marks of Origin
[FOUND IN CHAPTER IX]

Article X
Publication and Administration of Trade Regulations
[FOUND IN CHAPTER X]

Article XI*
General Elimination of Quantitative Restrictions
[FOUND IN CHAPTER IX]

Article XII*
Restrictions to Safeguard the Balance of Payments
[FOUND IN CHAPTER VI]

Article XIII*
Non-discriminatory Administration of Quantitative Restrictions

1. No prohibition or restriction shall be applied by any contracting party on the importation of any product of the territory of any other contracting party or on the exportation of any product destined for the territory of any other contracting party, unless the importation of the like product of all third countries or the exportation of the like product to all third countries is similarly prohibited or restricted.

2. In applying import restrictions to any product, contracting parties shall aim at a distribution of trade in such product approaching as closely as possible the shares which the various contracting parties might be expected to obtain in the absence of such restrictions and to this end shall observe the following provisions:

(*a*) Wherever practicable, quotas representing the total amount of permitted imports (whether allocated among supplying countries or not) shall be fixed, and notice given of their amount in accordance with paragraph 3 (*b*) of this Article;

(*b*) In cases in which quotas are not practicable, the restrictions may be applied by means of import licences or permits without a quota;

(*c*) Contracting parties shall not, except for purposes of operating quotas allocated in accordance with sub-paragraph (*d*) of this paragraph, require that import licences or permits be utilized for the importation of the product concerned from a particular country or source;

(*d*) In cases in which a quota is allocated among supplying countries the contracting party applying the restrictions may seek agreement with respect to the allocation of shares in the quota with all other contracting parties having a substantial interest in supplying the product concerned. In cases in which this method is not reasonably practicable, the contracting party concerned shall allot to contracting parties having a substantial interest in supplying the product shares based upon the proportions, supplied by such contracting parties during a previous representative period, of the total quantity or value of imports of the product, due account being taken of any special factors which may have affected or may be affecting the trade in the product. No conditions or formalities shall be imposed which would prevent any contracting party from utilizing fully the share of any such total quantity or value which has been allotted to it, subject to importation being made within any prescribed period to which the quota may relate.*

3.

(*a*) In cases in which import licences are issued in connection with import restrictions, the contracting party applying the restrictions shall provide, upon the request of any contracting party having an interest in the trade in the product concerned, all relevant information concerning the administration of the restrictions, the import licences granted over a recent period and the distribution of such licences among supplying countries; *Provided* that there shall be no obligation to supply information as to the names of importing or supplying enterprises.

(*b*) In the case of import restrictions involving the fixing of quotas, the contracting party applying the restrictions shall give public notice of the total quantity or value of the product or products which will be permitted to be imported during a specified future period and of any change in such quantity or value. Any supplies of the product in question which were *en route* at the time at which public notice was given shall not be excluded from entry; *Provided* that they may be counted so far as practicable, against the quantity permitted to be imported in the period in question, and also, where necessary, against the quantities permitted to be imported in the next following period or periods; and *Provided* further that if any contracting party customarily exempts from such restrictions products entered for consumption or withdrawn from warehouse for consumption during a period of thirty days after the day of such public notice, such practice shall be considered full compliance with this sub-paragraph.

(*c*) In the case of quotas allocated among supplying countries, the contracting party applying the restrictions shall promptly inform all other contracting parties having an interest in supplying the product concerned of the shares in the quota currently allocated, by quantity or value, to the various supplying countries and shall give public notice thereof.

4. With regard to restrictions applied in accordance with paragraph 2 (*d*) of this Article or under paragraph 2 (*c*) of Article XI, the selection of a representative period for any product and the appraisal of any special factors* affecting the trade in the product shall be made initially by the contracting party applying the restriction; *Provided* that such contracting party shall, upon the request of any other contracting party having a substantial interest in supplying that product or upon the request of the CONTRACTING PARTIES, consult promptly with the other contracting party or the CONTRACTING PARTIES regarding the need for an adjustment of the proportion determined or of the base period selected, or for the reappraisal of the special factors involved, or for the elimination of conditions, formalities or any other provisions established unilaterally relating to the allocation of an adequate quota or its unrestricted utilization.

5. The provisions of this Article shall apply to any tariff quota instituted or maintained by any contracting party, and, in so far as applicable, the principles of this Article shall also extend to export restrictions.

Article XIV*
Exceptions to the Rule of Non-discrimination
[FOUND IN CHAPTER VI]

Article XV
Exchange Arrangements

1. The CONTRACTING PARTIES shall seek co-operation with the International Monetary Fund to the end that the CONTRACTING PARTIES and the Fund may pursue a co-ordinated policy with regard to exchange questions within the jurisdiction of the Fund and questions of quantitative restrictions and other trade measures within the jurisdiction of the CONTRACTING PARTIES.

2. In all cases in which the CONTRACTING PARTIES are called upon to consider or deal with problems concerning monetary reserves, balances of payments or foreign exchange arrangements, they shall consult fully with the International Monetary Fund. In such consultations, the CONTRACTING PARTIES shall accept all findings of statistical and other facts presented by the Fund relating to foreign exchange, monetary reserves and balances of payments, and shall accept the determination of the Fund as to whether action by a contracting party in exchange matters is in accordance with the Articles of Agreement of the International Monetary Fund, or with the terms of a special exchange agreement between that contracting party and the CONTRACTING PARTIES. The CONTRACTING PARTIES in reaching their final decision in cases involving the criteria set forth in paragraph 2 (*a*) of Article XII or in paragraph 9 of Article XVIII, shall accept the determination of the Fund as to what constitutes a serious decline in the contracting party's monetary reserves, a very low level of its monetary reserves or a reasonable rate of increase in its monetary reserves, and as to the financial aspects of other matters covered in consultation in such cases.

3. The CONTRACTING PARTIES shall seek agreement with the Fund regarding procedures for consultation under paragraph 2 of this Article.

4. Contracting parties shall not, by exchange action, frustrate* the intent of the provisions of this Agreement, nor, by trade action, the intent of the provisions of the Articles of Agreement of the International Monetary Fund.

5. If the CONTRACTING PARTIES consider, at any time, that exchange restrictions on payments and transfers in connection with imports are being applied by a contracting party in a manner inconsistent with the exceptions provided for in this Agreement for quantitative restrictions, they shall report thereon to the Fund.

6. Any contracting party which is not a member of the Fund shall, within a time to be determined by the CONTRACTING PARTIES after consultation with the Fund, become a member of the Fund, or, failing that, enter into a special exchange agreement with the CONTRACTING PARTIES. A contracting party which ceases to be a member of the Fund shall forthwith enter into a special exchange agreement with the CONTRACTING PARTIES. Any special exchange agreement entered into by a contracting party under this paragraph shall thereupon become part of its obligations under this Agreement.

7.

(*a*) A special exchange agreement between a contracting party and the CONTRACTING PARTIES under paragraph 6 of this Article shall provide to the satisfaction of the CONTRACTING PARTIES that the objectives of this Agreement will not be frustrated as a result of action in exchange matters by the contracting party in question.

(*b*) The terms of any such agreement shall not impose obligations on the contracting party in exchange matters generally more restrictive than those imposed by the Articles of Agreement of the International Monetary Fund on members of the Fund.

8. A contracting party which is not a member of the Fund shall furnish such information within the general scope of section 5 of Article VIII of the Articles of Agreement of the International Monetary Fund as the CONTRACTING PARTIES may require in order to carry out their functions under this Agreement.

9. Nothing in this Agreement shall preclude:

(*a*) the use by a contracting party of exchange controls or exchange restrictions in accordance with the Articles of Agreement of the International Monetary Fund or with that contracting party's special exchange agreement with the CONTRACTING PARTIES, or

(*b*) the use by a contracting party of restrictions or controls in imports or exports, the sole effect of which, additional to the effects permitted under Articles XI, XII, XIII and XIV, is to make effective such exchange controls or exchange restrictions.

Article XVI*
Subsidies
[FOUND IN CHAPTER X]

Article XVII
State Trading Enterprises

1.*

(*a*) Each contracting party undertakes that if it establishes or maintains a State enterprise, wherever located, or grants to any enterprise, formally or in effect, exclusive or special privileges,* such enterprise shall, in its purchases or sales involving either imports or exports, act in a manner consistent with the general principles of non-discriminatory treatment prescribed in this Agreement for governmental measures affecting imports or exports by private traders.

(*b*) The provisions of sub-paragraph (*a*) of this paragraph shall be understood to require that such enterprises shall, having due regard to the other provisions of this Agreement, make any such purchases or sales solely in accordance with commercial considerations,* including price, quality, availability, marketability, transportation and other conditions of purchase or sale, and shall afford the enterprises of the other contracting parties adequate opportunity, in accordance with customary business practice, to compete for participation in such purchases or sales.

(*c*) No contracting party shall prevent any enterprise (whether or not an enterprise described in sub-paragraph (*a*) of this paragraph) under its jurisdiction from acting in accordance with the principles of sub-paragraphs (*a*) and (*b*) of this paragraph.

2. The provisions of paragraph 1 of this Article shall not apply to imports of products for immediate or ultimate consumption in governmental use and not otherwise for resale or use in the production of goods* for sale. With respect to such imports, each contracting party shall accord to the trade of the other contracting parties fair and equitable treatment.

3. The contracting parties recognize that enterprises of the kind described in paragraph 1 (*a*) of this Article might be operated so as to create serious obstacles to trade; thus negotiations on a reciprocal and mutually advantageous basis designed to limit or reduce such obstacles are of importance to the expansion of international trade.*

4.

(*a*) Contracting parties shall notify the CONTRACTING PARTIES of the products which are imported into or exported from their territories by enterprises of the kind described in paragraph 1 (*a*) of this Article.

(*b*) A contracting party establishing, maintaining or authorizing an import monopoly of a product, which is not the subject of a concession under Article II, shall, on the request of another contracting party having a substantial trade in the product concerned, inform the CONTRACTING PARTIES of the import mark-up* on the product during a recent representative period, or, when it is not possible to do so, of the price charged on the resale of the product.

(*c*) The CONTRACTING PARTIES may, at the request of a contracting party which has reason to believe that its interest under this Agreement are being adversely affected by the operations of an enterprise of the kind described in paragraph 1 (*a*), request the contracting party establishing, maintaining or authorizing such enterprise to supply information about its operations related to the carrying out of the provisions of this Agreement.

(*d*) The provisions of this paragraph shall not require any contracting party to disclose confidential information which would impede law enforcement or otherwise be contrary to the public interest or would prejudice the legitimate commercial interests of particular enterprises.

Article XVIII*
Governmental Assistance to Economic Development
[FOUND IN CHAPTER VI]

Article XIX
Emergency Action on Imports of Particular Products
[FOUND IN CHAPTER VI]

Article XX
General Exceptions
[FOUND IN CHAPTER VI]

Article XXI
Security Exceptions
[FOUND IN CHAPTER VI]

Article XXII
Consultation

1. Each contracting party shall accord sympathetic consideration to, and shall afford adequate opportunity for consultation regarding, such representations as may be made by another contracting party with respect to any matter affecting the operation of this Agreement.

2. The CONTRACTING PARTIES may, at the request of a contracting party, consult with any contracting party or parties in respect of any matter for which it has not been possible to find a satisfactory solution through consultation under paragraph 1.

Article XXIII
Nullification or Impairment
[FOUND IN CHAPTER VI]

PART III

Article XXIV
Territorial Application - Frontier Traffic - Customs Unions and Free-trade Areas
[FOUND IN CHAPTER IV]

Article XXV
Joint Action by the Contracting Parties

1. Representatives of the contracting parties shall meet from time to time for the purpose of giving effect to those provisions of this Agreement which involve joint action and, generally, with a view to facilitating the operation and furthering the objectives of this Agreement. Wherever reference is made in this Agreement to the contracting parties acting jointly they are designated as the CONTRACTING PARTIES.

2. The Secretary-General of the United Nations is requested to convene the first meeting of the CONTRACTING PARTIES, which shall take place

not later than March 1, 1948.

3. Each contracting party shall be entitled to have one vote at all meetings of the CONTRACTING PARTIES.

4. Except as otherwise provided for in this Agreement, decisions of the CONTRACTING PARTIES shall be taken by a majority of the votes cast.

5. In exceptional circumstances not elsewhere provided for in this Agreement, the CONTRACTING PARTIES may waive an obligation imposed upon a contracting party by this Agreement; *Provided* that any such decision shall be approved by a two-thirds majority of the votes cast and that such majority shall comprise more than half of the contracting parties. The CONTRACTING PARTIES may also by such a vote

(i) define certain categories of exceptional circumstances to which other voting requirements shall apply for the waiver of obligations, and

(ii) prescribe such criteria as may be necessary for the application of this paragraph.

Article XXVI

Acceptance, Entry into Force and Registration

1. The date of this Agreement shall be 30 October 1947.

2. This Agreement shall be open for acceptance by any contracting party which, on 1 March 1955, was a contracting party or was negotiating with a view to accession to this Agreement.

3. This Agreement, done in a single English original and a single French original, both texts authentic, shall be deposited with the Secretary-General of the United Nations, who shall furnish certified copies thereof to all interested governments.

4. Each government accepting this Agreement shall deposit an instrument of acceptance with the Executive Secretary [NOW THE DIRECTOR-GENERAL] to the CONTRACTING PARTIES, who will inform all interested governments of the date of deposit of each instrument of acceptance and of the day on which this Agreement enters into force under paragraph 6 of this Article.

5.

(*a*) Each government accepting this Agreement does so in respect of its metropolitan territory and of the other territories for which it has international responsibility, except such separate customs territories as it shall notify to the Executive Secretary [NOW THE DIRECTOR-GENERAL] to the CONTRACTING PARTIES at the time of its own acceptance.

(*b*) Any government, which has so notified the Executive Secretary [NOW THE DIRECTOR-GENERAL] under the exceptions in sub-paragraph (*a*) of this paragraph, may at any time give notice to the Executive Secretary [NOW THE DIRECTOR-GENERAL] that its acceptance shall be effective in respect of any separate customs territory or territories so excepted and such notice shall take effect on the thirtieth day following the day on which it is received by the Executive Secretary [NOW THE DIRECTOR-GENERAL].

(*c*) If any of the customs territories, in respect of which a contracting party has accepted this Agreement, possesses or acquires full autonomy in the conduct of its external commercial relations and of the other matters provided for in this Agreement, such territory shall, upon sponsorship through a declaration by the responsible contracting party establishing the above-mentioned fact, be deemed to be a contracting party.

6. This Agreement shall enter into force, as among the governments which have accepted it, on the thirtieth day following the day on which instruments of acceptance have been deposited with Executive Secretary [NOW THE DIRECTOR-GENERAL] to the CONTRACTING PARTIES on behalf of governments named in Annex H, the territories of which account for 85 per centum of the total external trade of the territories of such governments, computed in accordance with the applicable column of percentages set forth therein, The instrument of acceptance of each other government shall take effect on the thirtieth day following the day on which such instrument has been deposited.

7. The United Nations is authorized to effect registration of this Agreement as soon as it enters into force.

Article XXVII
Withholding or Withdrawal of Concessions

Any contracting party shall at any time be free to withhold or to withdraw in whole or in part any concession, provided for in the appropriate Schedule annexed to this Agreement, in respect of which such contracting party determines that it was initially negotiated with a government which has not become, or has ceased to be, a contracting party. A contracting party taking such action shall notify the CONTRACTING PARTIES and, upon request, consult with contracting parties which have a substantial interest in the product concerned.

Article XXVIII*
Modification of Schedules
[FOUND IN CHAPTER VI]

Article XXVIII *bis*
Tariff Negotiations

1. The contracting parties recognize that customs duties often constitute serious obstacles to trade; thus negotiations on a reciprocal and mutually advantageous basis, directed to the substantial reduction of the general level of tariffs and other charges on imports and exports and in particular to the reduction of such high tariffs as discourage the importation even of minimum quantities, and conducted with due regard to the objectives of this Agreement and the varying needs of individual contracting parties, are of great importance to the expansion of international trade. The CONTRACTING PARTIES may therefore sponsor such negotiations from time to time.

2.

(*a*) Negotiations under this Article may be carried out on a selective product-by-product basis or by the application of such multilateral procedures as may be accepted by the contracting parties concerned. Such negotiations may be directed towards the reduction of duties, the binding of duties at then existing levels or undertakings that individual duties or the average duties on specified categories of products shall not exceed specified levels. The binding against increase of low duties or of duty-free treatment shall, in principle, be recognized as a concession equivalent in value to the reduction of high duties.

(*b*) The contracting parties recognize that in general the success of multilateral negotiations would depend on the participation of all contracting parties which conduct a substantial proportion of their external trade with one another.

3. Negotiations shall be conducted on a basis which affords adequate opportunity to take into account:

(*a*) the needs of individual contracting parties and individual industries;

(*b*) the needs of less-developed countries for a more flexible use of tariff protection to assist their economic development and the special needs of these countries to maintain tariffs for revenue purposes; and

(*c*) all other relevant circumstances, including the fiscal,* developmental, strategic and other needs of the contracting parties concerned.

Article XXIX

The Relation of this Agreement to the Havana Charter

1. The contracting parties undertake to observe to the fullest extent of their executive authority the general principles of Chapters I to VI inclusive and of Chapter IX of the Havana Charter pending their acceptance of it in accordance with their constitutional procedures.*

2. Part II of this Agreement shall be suspended on the day on which the Havana Charter enters into force.

3. If by September 30, 1949, the Havana Charter has not entered into force, the contracting parties shall meet before December 31, 1949, to agree whether this Agreement shall be amended, supplemented or maintained.

4. If at any time the Havana Charter should cease to be in force, the CONTRACTING PARTIES shall meet as soon as practicable thereafter to agree whether this Agreement shall be supplemented, amended or maintained. Pending such agreement, Part II of this Agreement shall again enter into force; *Provided* that the provisions of Part II other than Article XXIII shall be replaced, *mutatis mutandis,* in the form in which they then appeared in the Havana Charter; and *Provided* further that no contracting party shall be bound by any provisions which did not bind it at the time when the Havana Charter ceased to be in force.

5. If any contracting party has not accepted the Havana Charter by the date upon which it enters into force, the CONTRACTING PARTIES shall confer to agree whether, and if so in what way, this Agreement in so far as it affects relations between such contracting party and other contracting parties, shall be supplemented or amended. Pending such agreement the provisions of Part II of this Agreement shall, notwithstanding the provisions of paragraph 2 of this Article, continue to apply as between such contracting party and other contracting parties.

6. Contracting parties which are Members of the International Trade Organization shall not invoke the provisions of this Agreement so as to prevent the operation of any provision of the Havana Charter. The application of the principle underlying this paragraph to any contracting party which is not a Member of the International Trade Organization shall be the subject of an agreement pursuant to paragraph 5 of this Article.

Article XXX
Amendments

1. Except where provision for modification is made elsewhere in this Agreement, amendments to the provisions of Part I of this Agreement or the provisions of Article XXIX or of this Article shall become effective upon acceptance by all the contracting parties, and other amendments to this Agreement shall become effective, in respect of those contracting parties which accept them, upon acceptance by two-thirds of the contracting parties and thereafter for each other contracting party upon acceptance by it.

2. Any contracting party accepting an amendment to this Agreement shall deposit an instrument of acceptance with the Secretary-General of the United Nations within such period as the CONTRACTING PARTIES may specify. The CONTRACTING PARTIES may decide that any amendment made effective under this Article is of such a nature that any contracting party which has not accepted it within a period specified by the CONTRACTING PARTIES shall be free to withdraw from this Agreement, or to remain a contracting party with the consent of the CONTRACTING PARTIES.

Article XXXI
Withdrawal

Without prejudice to the provisions of paragraph 12 of Article XVIII, of Article XXIII or of paragraph 2 of Article XXX, any contracting party may withdraw from this Agreement, or may separately withdraw on behalf of any of the separate customs territories for which it has international responsibility and which at the time possesses full autonomy in the conduct of its external commercial relations and of the other matters provided for in this Agreement. The withdrawal shall take effect upon the expiration of six months from the day on which written notice of withdrawal is received by the Secretary-General of the United Nations.

Article XXXII
Contracting Parties

1. The contracting parties to this Agreement shall be understood to mean those governments which are applying the provisions of this Agreement under Articles XXVI or XXXIII or pursuant to the Protocol of Provisional Application.

2. At any time after the entry into force of this Agreement pursuant to paragraph 6 of Article XXVI, those contracting parties which have accepted this Agreement pursuant to paragraph 4 of Article XXVI may decide that any contracting party which has not so accepted it shall cease to be a contracting party.

Article XXXIII
Accession

A government not party to this Agreement, or a government acting on behalf of a separate customs territory possessing full autonomy in the conduct of its external commercial relations and of the other matters provided for in this Agreement, may accede to this Agreement, on its own behalf or on behalf of that territory, on terms to be agreed between such government and the CONTRACTING PARTIES. Decisions of the CONTRACTING PARTIES under this paragraph shall be taken by a two-thirds majority.

Article XXXIV
Annexes

The annexes to this Agreement are hereby made an integral part of this Agreement.

Article XXXV
Non-application of the Agreement between Particular Contracting Parties

1. This Agreement, or alternatively Article II of this Agreement, shall not apply as between any contracting party and any other contracting party if:

(*a*) the two contracting parties have not entered into tariff negotiations with each other, and

(*b*) either of the contracting parties, at the time either becomes a contracting party, does not consent to such application.

2. The CONTRACTING PARTIES may review the operation of this Article in particular cases at the request of any contracting party and make appropriate recommendations.

PART IV*
TRADE AND DEVELOPMENT
[FOUND IN CHAPTER VI]

ANNEXES A THROUGH G

[ENUMERATED LISTS OF TERRITORIES REFERRED TO IN GATT 1947 AND OPERATING UNDER SPECIAL TERMS OR EXEMPTIONS UNDER GATT 1947]

ANNEX H

[A LIST OF PERCENTAGE SHARES OF TOTAL EXTERNAL TRADE TO BE USED FOR THE PURPOSE OF MAKING THE DETERMINATION REFERRED TO IN ARTICLE XXVI]

ANNEX I

NOTES AND SUPPLEMENTARY PROVISIONS

Ad Article I
Paragraph 1

The obligations incorporated in paragraph 1 of Article I by reference to paragraphs 2 and 4 of Article III and those incorporated in paragraph 2 (*b*) of Article II by reference to Article VI shall be considered as falling within Part II for the purposes of the Protocol of Provisional Application.

The cross-references, in the paragraph immediately above and in paragraph 1 of Article I, to paragraphs 2 and 4 of Article III shall only apply after Article III has been modified by the entry into force of the amendment provided for in the Protocol Modifying Part II and Article XXVI of the General Agreement on Tariffs and Trade, dated September 14, 1948 [THIS PROTOCOL ENTERED INTO FORCE ON 14 DECEMBER 1948].

Paragraph 4

The term 'margin of preference' means the absolute difference between the most-favoured-nation rate of duty and the preferential rate of duty for the like product, and not the proportionate relation between those rates. As examples:

(1) If the most-favoured-nation rate were 36 per cent *ad valorem* and the preferential rate were 24 per cent *ad valorem*, the margin of preference would be 12 per cent *ad valorem*, and not one-third of the most-favoured-nation rate;

(2) If the most-favoured-nation rate were 36 per cent *ad valorem* and the preferential rate were expressed as two-thirds of the most-favoured-nation rate, the margin of preference would be 12 per cent *ad valorem*;

(3) If the most-favoured-nation rate were 2 francs per kilogramme and the preferential rate were 1.50 francs per kilogramme, the margin of preference would be 0.50 franc per kilogramme.

The following kinds of customs action, taken in accordance with established uniform procedures, would not be contrary to a general binding of margins of preference:

(i) The re-application to an imported product of a tariff classification or rate of duty, properly applicable to such product, in cases in which the application of such classification or rate to such product was temporarily suspended or inoperative on April 10, 1947; and

(ii) The classification of a particular product under a tariff item other than that under which importations of that product were classified on April 10, 1947, in cases in which the tariff law clearly contemplates that such product may be classified under more than one tariff item.

Ad Article II
Paragraph 2 (a)

The cross-reference, in paragraph 2 (*a*) of Article II, to paragraph 2 of

Article III shall only apply after Article III has been modified by the entry into force of the amendment provided for in the Protocol Modifying Part II and Article XXVI of the General Agreement on Tariffs and Trade, dated September 14, 1948 [THIS PROTOCOL ENTERED INTO FORCE ON 14 DECEMBER 1948].

Paragraph 2 (b)

See the note relating to paragraph 1 of Article I.

Paragraph 4

Except where otherwise specifically agreed between the contracting parties which initially negotiated the concession, the provisions of this paragraph will be applied in the light of the provisions of Article 31 of the Havana Charter.

Ad Article III
[FOUND IN CHAPTER X]

Ad Article V
Paragraph 5
[FOUND IN CHAPTER VI]

Ad Article VI
[FOUND IN CHAPTER X]

Ad Article VII
[FOUND IN CHAPTER VIII]

Ad Article VIII
[FOUND IN CHAPTER X]

Ad Articles XI, XII, XIII, XIV and XVIII

Throughout Articles XI, XII, XIII, XIV and XVIII, the terms 'import restrictions' or 'export restrictions' include restrictions made effective through state-trading operations.

Ad Article XI
[FOUND IN CHAPTER IX]

Ad Article XII
[FOUND IN CHAPTER VI]

Ad Article XIII
Paragraph 2 (d)

No mention was made of 'commercial considerations' as a rule for the allocation of quotas because it was considered that its application by governmental authorities might not always be practicable. Moreover, in cases where it is practicable, a contracting party could apply these considerations in the process of seeking agreement, consistently with the general rule laid down in the opening sentence of paragraph 2.

Paragraph 4

See note relating to 'special factors' in connection with the last sub-paragraph of paragraph 2 of Article XI.

Ad Article XIV
[FOUND IN CHAPTER VI]

Ad Article XV
Paragraph 4

The word 'frustrate' is intended to indicate, for example, that infringements of the letter of any Article of this Agreement by exchange action shall not be regarded as a violation of that Article if, in practice, there is no appreciable departure from the intent of the Article. Thus, a contracting party which, as part of its exchange control operated in accordance with the Articles of Agreement of the International Monetary Fund, requires payment to be received for its exports in its own currency or in the currency of one or more members of the International Monetary Fund will not thereby be deemed to contravene Article XI or Article XIII. Another example would be that of a contracting party which specifies on an import licence the country from which the goods may be imported, for the purpose not of introducing any additional element of discrimination in its import licensing system but of enforcing permissible exchange controls.

Ad Article XVI
[FOUND IN CHAPTER X]

Ad Article XVII
Paragraph 1

The operations of Marketing Boards, which are established by contracting parties and are engaged in purchasing or selling, are subject to the provisions of sub-paragraphs (*a*) and (*b*).

The activities of Marketing Boards which are established by contracting parties and which do not purchase or sell but lay down regulations covering private trade are governed by the relevant Articles of this Agreement.

The charging by a state enterprise of different prices for its sales of a product in different markets is not precluded by the provisions of this Article, provided that such different prices are charged for commercial reasons, to meet conditions of supply and demand in export markets.

Paragraph 1 (a)

Governmental measures imposed to insure standards of quality and efficiency in the operation of external trade, or privileges granted for the exploitation of national natural resources but which do not empower the government to exercise control over the trading activities of the enterprise in question, do not constitute 'exclusive or special privileges.'

Paragraph 1 (b)

A country receiving a 'tied loan' is free to take this loan into account as a 'commercial consideration' when purchasing requirements abroad.

Paragraph 2

The term 'goods' is limited to products as understood in commercial practice, and is not intended to include the purchase or sale of services.

Paragraph 3

Negotiations which contracting parties agree to conduct under this paragraph may be directed towards the reduction of duties and other charges on imports and exports or towards the conclusion of any other mutually satisfactory arrangement consistent with the provisions of this Agreement. (See paragraph 4 of Article II and the note to that paragraph.)

Paragraph 4 (b)

The term 'import mark-up' in this paragraph shall represent the margin by which the price charged by the import monopoly for the imported product (exclusive of internal taxes within the purview of Article III, transportation, distribution, and other expenses incident to the purchase, sale or further processing, and a reasonable margin of profit) exceeds the landed cost.

Ad Article XVIII
[FOUND IN CHAPTER VI]

Ad Article XX
[FOUND IN CHAPTER VI]

Ad Article XXIV
[FOUND IN CHAPTER IV]

Ad Article XXVIII
[FOUND IN CHAPTER VI]

Ad Article XXVIII bis
Paragraph 3

It is understood that the reference to fiscal needs would include the revenues aspect of duties and particularly duties imposed primarily for revenue purpose, or duties imposed on products which can be substituted for products subject to revenue duties to prevent the avoidance of such duties.

Ad Article XXIX
Paragraph 1

Chapters VII and VIII of the Havana Charter have been excluded from paragraph 1 because they generally deal with the organization, functions and procedures of the International Trade Organization.

Ad Part IV
[FOUND IN CHAPTER VI]

PROTOCOL OF PROVISIONAL APPLICATION OF THE GENERAL AGREEMENT ON TARIFFS AND TRADE

1. The Governments of [NAMED COUNTRIES AND THEIR TERRITORIES] undertake, provided that this Protocol shall have been signed on behalf of all the foregoing Governments not later than 15 November 1947, to apply provisionally on and after 1 January 1948:

(*a*) Parts I and III of the General Agreement on Tariffs and Trade, and

(*b*) Part II of that Agreement to the fullest extent not inconsistent with existing legislation.

2. The foregoing Governments shall make effective such provisional application of the General Agreement, in respect of any of their territories other than their metropolitan territories, on or after 1 January 1948, upon the expiration of thirty days from the day on which notice of such application is received by the Secretary-General of the United Nations.

3. Any other government signatory to this Protocol shall make effective such provisional application of the General Agreement, on or after 1 January 1948, upon the expiration of thirty days from the day of signature of this Protocol on behalf of such Government.

4. This Protocol shall remain open for signature at the Headquarters of the United Nations (*a*) until 15 November 1947, on behalf of any government named in paragraph 1 of this Protocol which has not signed it on this day, and (*b*) until 30 June 1948, on behalf of any other Government signatory to the Final Act adopted at the conclusion of the Second Session of the Preparatory Committee of the United Nations Conference on Trade and Employment which has not signed it on this day.

5. Any government applying this Protocol shall be free to withdraw such application, and such withdrawal shall take effect upon the expiration of sixty days from the day on which written notice of such withdrawal is received by the Secretary-General of the United Nations.

6. The original of this Protocol shall be deposited with the Secretary-General of the United Nations, who will furnish certified copies thereof to all interested Governments.

In WITNESS WHEREOF the respective Representatives, after having communicated their full powers, found to be in good and due form, have signed the Protocol.

DONE at Geneva, in a single copy, in the English and the French languages, both texts authentic, this thirtieth day of October one thousand nine hundred and forty-seven.

APPENDIX

The first section of this Appendix gives the source (legal instruments) of the various provisions of the GATT, other than schedules, their effective date and their respective citations in the United Nations *Treaty Series* (UNTS) or in GATT publications.

The second section contains a key to the abbreviated titles used in the first section, together with their citations. Column 4 refers to provisions in

Part I of the General Agreement and indicates where they have been qualified, for instance, with regard to territorial application or the maintenance of preferences. Column 5 refers to provisions in Part II of the General Agreement, and indicates where they have been qualified, e.g. with regard to dates of application. Column 6 refers to different applicable dates with regard to paragraph 1 of Article II. Column 7 refers to different applicable dates with regard to Article V:6, Article VII:4 (*d*), Article X:3 (c). Column 8 refers to different termination periods for withdrawal from the Agreement."

UNDERSTANDING ON GATT ARTICLE II:1(B) INTERPRETATION [FOUND IN CHAPTER X]

Understanding on GATT Article XVII Interpretation—the Text

UNDERSTANDING ON THE INTERPRETATION OF ARTICLE XVII OF THE GENERAL AGREEMENT ON TARIFFS AND TRADE 1994

Members,

Noting that Article XVII provides for obligations on Members in respect of the activities of the state trading enterprises referred to in paragraph 1 of Article XVII, which are required to be consistent with the general principles of non-discriminatory treatment prescribed in GATT 1994 for governmental measures affecting imports or exports by private traders;

Noting further that Members are subject to their GATT 1994 obligations in respect of those governmental measures affecting state trading enterprises;

Recognizing that this Understanding is without prejudice to the substantive disciplines prescribed in Article XVII;

Hereby agree as follows:

1. In order to ensure the transparency of the activities of state trading enterprises, Members shall notify such enterprises to the Council for Trade in Goods, for review by the working party to be set up under paragraph 5, in accordance with the following working definition:

> 'Governmental and non-governmental enterprises, including marketing boards, which have been granted exclusive or special rights or privileges, including statutory or constitutional powers, in the exercise of which they influence through their purchases or sales the level or direction of imports or exports.'

This notification requirement does not apply to imports of products for immediate or ultimate consumption in governmental use or in use by an enterprise as specified above and not otherwise for resale or use in the production of goods for sale.

2. Each Member shall conduct a review of its policy with regard to the submission of notifications on state trading enterprises to the Council for Trade in Goods, taking account of the provisions of this Understanding. In carrying out such a review, each Member should have regard to the need to ensure the maximum transparency possible in its notifications so as to permit

a clear appreciation of the manner of operation of the enterprises notified and the effect of their operations on international trade.

3. Notifications shall be made in accordance with the questionnaire on state trading adopted on 24 May 1960 (BISD 9S/184-185), it being understood that Members shall notify the enterprises referred to in paragraph 1 whether or not imports or exports have in fact taken place.

4. Any Member which has reason to believe that another Member has not adequately met its notification obligation may raise the matter with the Member concerned. If the matter is not satisfactorily resolved it may make a counter-notification to the Council for Trade in Goods, for consideration by the working party set up under paragraph 5, simultaneously informing the Member concerned.

5. A working party shall be set up, on behalf of the Council for Trade in Goods, to review notifications and counter-notifications. In the light of this review and without prejudice to paragraph 4(c) of Article XVII, the Council for Trade in Goods may make recommendations with regard to the adequacy of notifications and the need for further information. The working party shall also review, in the light of the notifications received, the adequacy of the above-mentioned questionnaire on state trading and the coverage of state trading enterprises notified under paragraph 1. It shall also develop an illustrative list showing the kinds of relationships between governments and enterprises, and the kinds of activities, engaged in by these enterprises, which may be relevant for the purposes of Article XVII. It is understood that the Secretariat will provide a general background paper for the working party on the operations of state trading enterprises as they relate to international trade. Membership of the working party shall be open to all Members indicating their wish to serve on it. It shall meet within a year of the date of entry into force of the WTO Agreement and thereafter at least once a year. It shall report annually to the Council for Trade in Goods [THE ACTIVITIES OF THIS WORKING PARTY SHALL BE COORDINATED WITH THOSE OF THE WORKING GROUP PROVIDED FOR IN SECTION III OF THE MINISTERIAL DECISION ON NOTIFICATION PROCEDURES ADOPTED ON 15 APRIL 1994.]."

UNDERSTANDING ON GATT BALANCE-OF-PAYMENTS PROVISIONS [FOUND IN CHAPTER VI]

UNDERSTANDING ON INTERPRETATION OF GATT ARTICLE XXIV [FOUND IN CHAPTER IV]

UNDERSTANDING IN RESPECT OF GATT WAIVERS OF OBLIGATIONS [FOUND IN CHAPTER VI]

Marrakech Protocol to GATT—the Text

MARRAKESH PROTOCOL TO THE GENERAL AGREEMENT ON TARIFFS AND TRADE 1994

Members,

Having carried out negotiations within the framework of GATT 1947, pursuant to the Ministerial Declaration on the Uruguay Round,

Hereby *agree* as follows:

1. The schedule annexed to this Protocol relating to a Member shall become a Schedule to GATT 1994 relating to that Member on the day on which the WTO Agreement enters into force for that Member. Any schedule submitted in accordance with the Ministerial Decision on measures in favour of least-developed countries shall be deemed to be annexed to this Protocol.

2. The tariff reductions agreed upon by each Member shall be implemented in five equal rate reductions, except as may be otherwise specified in a Member's Schedule. The first such reduction shall be made effective on the date of entry into force of the WTO Agreement, each successive reduction shall be made effective on 1 January of each of the following years, and the final rate shall become effective no later than the date four years after the date of entry into force of the WTO Agreement, except as may be otherwise specified in that Member's Schedule. Unless otherwise specified in its Schedule, a Member that accepts the WTO Agreement after its entry into force shall, on the date that Agreement enters into force for it, make effective all rate reductions that have already taken place together with the reductions which it would under the preceding sentence have been obligated to make effective on 1 January of the year following, and shall make effective all remaining rate reductions on the schedule specified in the previous sentence. The reduced rate should in each stage be rounded off to the first decimal. For agricultural products, as defined in Article 2 of the Agreement on Agriculture, the staging of reductions shall be implemented as specified in the relevant parts of the schedules.

3. The implementation of the concessions and commitments contained in the schedules annexed to this Protocol shall, upon request, be subject to multilateral examination by the Members. This would be without prejudice to the rights and obligations of Members under Agreements in Annex 1A of the WTO Agreement.

4. After the schedule annexed to this Protocol relating to a Member has become a Schedule to GATT 1994 pursuant to the provisions of paragraph 1, such Member shall be free at any time to withhold or to withdraw in whole or in part the concession in such Schedule with respect to any product for which the principal supplier is any other Uruguay Round participant the schedule of which has not yet become a Schedule to GATT 1994. Such action can, however, only be taken after written notice of any such withholding or withdrawal of a concession has been given to the Council for Trade in Goods and after consultations have been held, upon request, with any Member, the relevant schedule relating to which has become a Schedule to GATT 1994 and which has a substantial interest in the product involved. Any concessions so withheld or withdrawn shall be applied on and after the day on which the

schedule of the Member which has the principal supplying interest becomes a Schedule to GATT 1994.

5.

(a) Without prejudice to the provisions of paragraph 2 of Article 4 of the Agreement on Agriculture, for the purpose of the reference in paragraphs 1:(b) and 1(c) of Article II of GATT 1994 to the date of that Agreement, the applicable date in respect of each product which is the subject of a concession provided for in a schedule of concessions annexed to this Protocol shall be the date of this Protocol.

(b) For the purpose of the reference in paragraph 6(a) of Article II of GATT 1994 to the date of that Agreement, the applicable date in respect of a schedule of concessions annexed to this Protocol shall be the date of this Protocol.

6. In cases of modification or withdrawal of concessions relating to non-tariff measures as contained in Part III of the schedules, the provisions of Article XXVIII of GATT 1994 and the 'Procedures for Negotiations under Article XXVIII' adopted on 10 November 1980 (BISD 27S/26-28) shall apply. This would be without prejudice to the rights and obligations of Members under GATT 1994.

7. In each case in which a schedule annexed to this Protocol results for any product in treatment less favourable than was provided for such product in the Schedules of GATT 1947 prior to the entry into force of the WTO Agreement, the Member to whom the schedule relates shall be deemed to have taken appropriate action as would have been otherwise necessary under the relevant provisions of Article XXVIII of GATT 1947 or 1994. The provisions of this paragraph shall apply only to Egypt, Peru, South Africa and Uruguay.

8. The Schedules annexed hereto are authentic in the English, French or Spanish language as specified in each Schedule.

9. The date of this Protocol is 15 April 1994.

[THE AGREED SCHEDULES OF PARTICIPANTS ARE ANNEXED TO THE MARRAKECH PROTOCOL IN THE TREATY COPY OF THE WTO AGREEMENT.]"

The Agreement on Agriculture—the Text

"AGREEMENT ON AGRICULTURE

Members,

Having decided to establish a basis for initiating a process of reform of trade in agriculture in line with the objectives of the negotiations as set out in the Punta del Este Declaration;

Recalling that their long-term objective as agreed at the Mid-Term Review of the Uruguay Round 'is to establish a fair and market-oriented agricultural trading system and that a reform process should be initiated through the negotiation of commitments on support and protection and through the establishment of strengthened and more operationally effective GATT rules and disciplines;'

Recalling further that 'the above-mentioned long-term objective is to provide for substantial progressive reductions in agricultural support and protection sustained over an agreed period of time, resulting in correcting and preventing restrictions and distortions in world agricultural markets';

Committed to achieving specific binding commitments in each of the following areas: market access; domestic support; export competition; and to reaching an agreement on sanitary and phytosanitary issues;

Having agreed that in implementing their commitments on market access, developed country Members would take fully into account the particular needs and conditions of developing country Members by providing for a greater improvement of opportunities and terms of access for agricultural products of particular interest to these Members, including the fullest liberalization of trade in tropical agricultural products as agreed at the Mid-Term Review, and for products of particular importance to the diversification of production from the growing of illicit narcotic crops;

Noting that commitments under the reform programme should be made in an equitable way among all Members, having regard to non-trade concerns, including food security and the need to protect the environment; having regard to the agreement that special and differential treatment for developing countries is an integral element of the negotiations, and taking into account the possible negative effects of the implementation of the reform programme on least-developed and net food-importing developing countries;

Hereby *agree* as follows:

Part I

Article 1
Definition of Terms

In this Agreement, unless the context otherwise requires:

(a) 'Aggregate Measurement of Support' and 'AMS' mean the annual level of support, expressed in monetary terms, provided for an agricultural product in favour of the producers of the basic agricultural product or non-product-specific support provided in favour of agricultural producers in general, other than support provided under programmes that qualify as exempt from reduction under Annex 2 to this Agreement, which is:

(i) with respect to support provided during the base period, specified in the relevant tables of supporting material incorporated by reference in Part IV of a Member's Schedule; and

(ii) with respect to support provided during any year of the implementation period and thereafter, calculated in accordance with the provisions of Annex 3 of this Agreement and taking into account the constituent data and methodology used in the tables of supporting material incorporated by reference in Part IV of the Member's Schedule;

(b) 'basic agricultural product' in relation to domestic support commitments is defined as the product as close as practicable to the point of first sale as specified in a Member's Schedule and in the related supporting material;

(c) 'budgetary outlays' or 'outlays' includes revenue foregone;

(d) 'Equivalent Measurement of Support' means the annual level of support, expressed in monetary terms, provided to producers of a basic agricultural product through the application of one or more measures, the calculation of which in accordance with the AMS methodology is impracticable, other than support provided under programmes that qualify as exempt from reduction under Annex 2 to this Agreement, and which is:

(i) with respect to support provided during the base period, specified in the relevant tables of supporting material incorporated by reference in Part IV of a Member's Schedule; and

(ii) with respect to support provided during any year of the implementation period and thereafter, calculated in accordance with the provisions of Annex 4 of this Agreement and taking into account the constituent data and methodology used in the tables of supporting material incorporated by reference in Part IV of the Member's Schedule;

(e) 'export subsidies' refers to subsidies contingent upon export performance, including the export subsidies listed in Article 9 of this Agreement;

(f) 'implementation period' means the six-year period commencing in the year 1995, except that, for the purposes of Article 13, it means the nine-year period commencing in 1995;

(g) 'market access concessions' includes all market access commitments undertaken pursuant to this Agreement;

(h) 'Total Aggregate Measurement of Support' and 'Total AMS' mean the sum of all domestic support provided in favour of agricultural producers, calculated as the sum of all aggregate measurements of support for basic agricultural products, all non-product-specific aggregate measurements of support and all equivalent measurements of support for agricultural products, and which is:

(i) with respect to support provided during the base period (*i.e.* the 'Base Total AMS') and the maximum support permitted to be provided during any year of the implementation period or thereafter (*i.e.* the 'Annual and Final Bound Commitment Levels'), as specified in Part IV of a Member's Schedule; and

(ii) with respect to the level of support actually provided during any year of the implementation period and thereafter (*i.e.* the 'Current Total AMS'), calculated in accordance with the provisions of this Agreement, including Article 6, and with the constituent data and methodology used in the tables of supporting material incorporated by reference in Part IV of the Member's Schedule;

(i) 'year' in paragraph (f) above and in relation to the specific commitments of a Member refers to the calendar, financial or marketing year specified in the Schedule relating to that Member.

Article 2
Product Coverage

This Agreement applies to the products listed in Annex 1 to this Agreement, hereinafter referred to as agricultural products.

Part II

Article 3
Incorporation of Concessions and Commitments

1. The domestic support and export subsidy commitments in Part IV of each Member's Schedule constitute commitments limiting subsidization and are hereby made an integral part of GATT 1994.

2. Subject to the provisions of Article 6, a Member shall not provide support in favour of domestic producers in excess of the commitment levels specified in Section I of Part IV of its Schedule.

3. Subject to the provisions of paragraphs 2(b) and 4 of Article 9, a Member shall not provide export subsidies listed in paragraph 1 of Article 9 in respect of the agricultural products or groups of products specified in Section II of Part IV of its Schedule in excess of the budgetary outlay and quantity commitment levels specified therein and shall not provide such subsidies in respect of any agricultural product not specified in that Section of its Schedule.

Part III

Article 4
Market Access

1. Market access concessions contained in Schedules relate to bindings and reductions of tariffs, and to other market access commitments as specified therein.

2. Members shall not maintain, resort to, or revert to any measures of the kind which have been required to be converted into ordinary customs duties [THESE MEASURES INCLUDE QUANTITATIVE IMPORT RESTRICTIONS, VARIABLE IMPORT LEVIES, MINIMUM IMPORT PRICES, DISCRETIONARY IMPORT LICENSING, NON-TARIFF MEASURES MAINTAINED THROUGH STATE-TRADING ENTERPRISES, VOLUNTARY EXPORT RESTRAINTS, AND SIMILAR BORDER MEASURES OTHER THAN ORDINARY CUSTOMS DUTIES, WHETHER OR NOT THE MEASURES ARE MAINTAINED UNDER COUNTRY-SPECIFIC DEROGATIONS FROM THE PROVISIONS OF GATT 1947, BUT NOT MEASURES MAINTAINED UNDER BALANCE-OF-PAYMENTS PROVISIONS OR UNDER OTHER GENERAL, NON-AGRICULTURE-SPECIFIC PROVISIONS OF GATT 1994 OR OF THE OTHER MULTILATERAL TRADE AGREEMENTS IN ANNEX 1A TO THE WTO AGREEMENT.], except as otherwise provided for in Article 5 and Annex 5.

Article 5
Special Safeguard Provisions

1. Notwithstanding the provisions of paragraph 1(b) of Article II of GATT 1994, any Member may take recourse to the provisions of paragraphs 4 and 5 below in connection with the importation of an agricultural product, in respect of which measures referred to in paragraph 2 of Article 4 of this Agreement have been converted into an ordinary customs duty and which is designated in its Schedule with the symbol 'SSG' as being the subject of a

concession in respect of which the provisions of this Article may be invoked, if:

(a) the volume of imports of that product entering the customs territory of the Member granting the concession during any year exceeds a trigger level which relates to the existing market access opportunity as set out in paragraph 4; or, but not concurrently:

(b) the price at which imports of that product may enter the customs territory of the Member granting the concession, as determined on the basis of the c.i.f. import price of the shipment concerned expressed in terms of its domestic currency, falls below a trigger price equal to the average 1986 to 1988 reference price [THE REFERENCE PRICE USED TO INVOKE THE PROVISIONS OF THIS SUBPARAGRAPH SHALL, IN GENERAL, BE THE AVERAGE C.I.F. UNIT VALUE OF THE PRODUCT CONCERNED, OR OTHERWISE SHALL BE AN APPROPRIATE PRICE IN TERMS OF THE QUALITY OF THE PRODUCT AND ITS STAGE OF PROCESSING. IT SHALL, FOLLOWING ITS INITIAL USE, BE PUBLICLY SPECIFIED AND AVAILABLE TO THE EXTENT NECESSARY TO ALLOW OTHER MEMBERS TO ASSESS THE ADDITIONAL DUTY THAT MAY BE LEVIED.] for the product concerned.

2. Imports under current and minimum access commitments established as part of a concession referred to in paragraph 1 above shall be counted for the purpose of determining the volume of imports required for invoking the provisions of subparagraph 1(a) and paragraph 4, but imports under such commitments shall not be affected by any additional duty imposed under either subparagraph 1(a) and paragraph 4 or subparagraph 1(b) and paragraph 5 below.

3. Any supplies of the product in question which were *en route* on the basis of a contract settled before the additional duty is imposed under subparagraph 1(a) and paragraph 4 shall be exempted from any such additional duty, provided that they may be counted in the volume of imports of the product in question during the following year for the purposes of triggering the provisions of subparagraph 1(a) in that year.

4. Any additional duty imposed under subparagraph 1(a) shall only be maintained until the end of the year in which it has been imposed, and may only be levied at a level which shall not exceed one third of the level of the ordinary customs duty in effect in the year in which the action is taken. The trigger level shall be set according to the following schedule based on market access opportunities defined as imports as a percentage of the corresponding domestic consumption [WHERE DOMESTIC CONSUMPTION IS NOT TAKEN INTO ACCOUNT, THE BASE TRIGGER LEVEL UNDER SUBPARAGRAPH 4(A) SHALL APPLY.] during the three preceding years for which data are available:

(a) where such market access opportunities for a product are less than or equal to 10 per cent, the base trigger level shall equal 125 per cent;

(b) where such market access opportunities for a product are greater than 10 per cent but less than or equal to 30 per cent, the base trigger level shall equal 110 per cent;

(c) where such market access opportunities for a product are greater than 30 per cent, the base trigger level shall equal 105 per cent.

In all cases the additional duty may be imposed in any year where the absolute volume of imports of the product concerned entering the customs territory of the Member granting the concession exceeds the sum of (*x*) the base trigger level set out above multiplied by the average quantity of imports during the three preceding years for which data are available and (*y*) the absolute volume change in domestic consumption of the product concerned in the most recent year for which data are available compared to the preceding year, provided that the trigger level shall not be less than 105 per cent of the average quantity of imports in (*x*) above.

5. The additional duty imposed under subparagraph 1(b) shall be set according to the following schedule:

(a) if the difference between the c.i.f. import price of the shipment expressed in terms of the domestic currency (hereinafter referred to as the 'import price') and the trigger price as defined under that subparagraph is less than or equal to 10 per cent of the trigger price, no additional duty shall be imposed;

(b) if the difference between the import price and the trigger price (hereinafter referred to as the 'difference') is greater than 10 per cent but less than or equal to 40 per cent of the trigger price, the additional duty shall equal 30 per cent of the amount by which the difference exceeds 10 per cent;

(c) if the difference is greater than 40 per cent but less than or equal to 60 per cent of the trigger price, the additional duty shall equal 50 per cent of the amount by which the difference exceeds 40 per cent, plus the additional duty allowed under (b);

(d) if the difference is greater than 60 per cent but less than or equal to 75 per cent, the additional duty shall equal 70 per cent of the amount by which the difference exceeds 60 per cent of the trigger price, plus the additional duties allowed under (b) and (c);

(e) if the difference is greater than 75 per cent of the trigger price, the additional duty shall equal 90 per cent of the amount by which the difference exceeds 75 per cent, plus the additional duties allowed under (b), (c) and (d).

6. For perishable and seasonal products, the conditions set out above shall be applied in such a manner as to take account of the specific characteristics of such products. In particular, shorter time periods under subparagraph 1(a) and paragraph 4 may be used in reference to the corresponding periods in the base period and different reference prices for different periods may be used under subparagraph 1(b).

7. The operation of the special safeguard shall be carried out in a transparent manner. Any Member taking action under subparagraph 1(a) above shall give notice in writing, including relevant data, to the Committee on Agriculture as far in advance as may be practicable and in any event within 10 days of the implementation of such action. In cases where changes in consumption volumes must be allocated to individual tariff lines subject to action under paragraph 4, relevant data shall include the information and methods used to allocate these changes. A Member taking action under

paragraph 4 shall afford any interested Members the opportunity to consult with it in respect of the conditions of application of such action. Any Member taking action under subparagraph 1(b) above shall give notice in writing, including relevant data, to the Committee on Agriculture within 10 days of the implementation of the first such action or, for perishable and seasonal products, the first action in any period. Members undertake, as far as practicable, not to take recourse to the provisions of subparagraph 1(b) where the volume of imports of the products concerned are declining. In either case a Member taking such action shall afford any interested Members the opportunity to consult with it in respect of the conditions of application of such action.

8. Where measures are taken in conformity with paragraphs 1 through 7 above, Members undertake not to have recourse, in respect of such measures, to the provisions of paragraphs 1(a) and 3 of Article XIX of GATT 1994 or paragraph 2 of Article 8 of the Agreement on Safeguards.

9. The provisions of this Article shall remain in force for the duration of the reform process as determined under Article 20.

Part IV

Article 6
Domestic Support Commitments

1. The domestic support reduction commitments of each Member contained in Part IV of its Schedule shall apply to all of its domestic support measures in favour of agricultural producers with the exception of domestic measures which are not subject to reduction in terms of the criteria set out in this Article and in Annex 2 to this Agreement. The commitments are expressed in terms of Total Aggregate Measurement of Support and 'Annual and Final Bound Commitment Levels.'

2. In accordance with the Mid-Term Review Agreement that government measures of assistance, whether direct or indirect, to encourage agricultural and rural development are an integral part of the development programmes of developing countries, investment subsidies which are generally available to agriculture in developing country Members and agricultural input subsidies generally available to low-income or resource-poor producers in developing country Members shall be exempt from domestic support reduction commitments that would otherwise be applicable to such measures, as shall domestic support to producers in developing country Members to encourage diversification from growing illicit narcotic crops. Domestic support meeting the criteria of this paragraph shall not be required to be included in a Member's calculation of its Current Total AMS.

3. A Member shall be considered to be in compliance with its domestic support reduction commitments in any year in which its domestic support in favour of agricultural producers expressed in terms of Current Total AMS does not exceed the corresponding annual or final bound commitment level specified in Part IV of the Member's Schedule.

4.

(a) A Member shall not be required to include in the calculation of its Current Total AMS and shall not be required to reduce:

(i) product-specific domestic support which would otherwise be required to be included in a Member's calculation of its Current AMS where such support does not exceed 5 per cent of that Member's total value of production of a basic agricultural product during the relevant year; and

(ii) non-product-specific domestic support which would otherwise be required to be included in a Member's calculation of its Current AMS where such support does not exceed 5 per cent of the value of that Member's total agricultural production.

(b) For developing country Members, the *de minimis* percentage under this paragraph shall be 10 per cent.

5.

(a) Direct payments under production-limiting programmes shall not be subject to the commitment to reduce domestic support if:

(i) such payments are based on fixed area and yields; or

(ii) such payments are made on 85 per cent or less of the base level of production; or

(iii) livestock payments are made on a fixed number of head.

(b) The exemption from the reduction commitment for direct payments meeting the above criteria shall be reflected by the exclusion of the value of those direct payments in a Member's calculation of its Current Total AMS.

Article 7
General Disciplines on Domestic Support

1. Each Member shall ensure that any domestic support measures in favour of agricultural producers which are not subject to reduction commitments because they qualify under the criteria set out in Annex 2 to this Agreement are maintained in conformity therewith.

2.

(a) Any domestic support measure in favour of agricultural producers, including any modification to such measure, and any measure that is subsequently introduced that cannot be shown to satisfy the criteria in Annex 2 to this Agreement or to be exempt from reduction by reason of any other provision of this Agreement shall be included in the Member's calculation of its Current Total AMS.

(b) Where no Total AMS commitment exists in Part IV of a Member's Schedule, the Member shall not provide support to agricultural producers in excess of the relevant *de minimis* level set out in paragraph 4 of Article 6.

Part V

Article 8
Export Competition Commitments

Each Member undertakes not to provide export subsidies otherwise than in conformity with this Agreement and with the commitments as specified in that Member's Schedule.

Article 9
Export Subsidy Commitments

1. The following export subsidies are subject to reduction commitments under this Agreement:

(a) the provision by governments or their agencies of direct subsidies, including payments-in-kind, to a firm, to an industry, to producers of an agricultural product, to a cooperative or other association of such producers, or to a marketing board, contingent on export performance;

(b) the sale or disposal for export by governments or their agencies of non-commercial stocks of agricultural products at a price lower than the comparable price charged for the like product to buyers in the domestic market;

(c) payments on the export of an agricultural product that are financed by virtue of governmental action, whether or not a charge on the public account is involved, including payments that are financed from the proceeds of a levy imposed on the agricultural product concerned or on an agricultural product from which the exported product is derived;

(d) the provision of subsidies to reduce the costs of marketing exports of agricultural products (other than widely available export promotion and advisory services) including handling, upgrading and other processing costs, and the costs of international transport and freight;

(e) internal transport and freight charges on export shipments, provided or mandated by governments, on terms more favourable than for domestic shipments;

(f) subsidies on agricultural products contingent on their incorporation in exported products.

2.

(a) Except as provided in subparagraph (b), the export subsidy commitment levels for each year of the implementation period, as specified in a Member's Schedule, represent with respect to the export subsidies listed in paragraph 1 of this Article:

(i) in the case of budgetary outlay reduction commitments, the maximum level of expenditure for such subsidies that may be allocated or incurred in that year in respect of the agricultural product, or group of products, concerned; and

(ii) in the case of export quantity reduction commitments, the maximum quantity of an agricultural product, or group of products, in respect of which such export subsidies may be granted in that year.

(b) In any of the second through fifth years of the implementation period, a Member may provide export subsidies listed in paragraph 1 above in a given year in excess of the corresponding annual commitment levels in respect of the products or groups of products specified in Part IV of the Member's Schedule, provided that:

(i) the cumulative amounts of budgetary outlays for such

subsidies, from the beginning of the implementation period through the year in question, does not exceed the cumulative amounts that would have resulted from full compliance with the relevant annual outlay commitment levels specified in the Member's Schedule by more than 3 per cent of the base period level of such budgetary outlays;

(ii) the cumulative quantities exported with the benefit of such export subsidies, from the beginning of the implementation period through the year in question, does not exceed the cumulative quantities that would have resulted from full compliance with the relevant annual quantity commitment levels specified in the Member's Schedule by more than 1.75 per cent of the base period quantities;

(iii) the total cumulative amounts of budgetary outlays for such export subsidies and the quantities benefiting from such export subsidies over the entire implementation period are no greater than the totals that would have resulted from full compliance with the relevant annual commitment levels specified in the Member's Schedule; and

(iv) the Member's budgetary outlays for export subsidies and the quantities benefiting from such subsidies, at the conclusion of the implementation period, are no greater than 64 per cent and 79 per cent of the 1986-1990 base period levels, respectively. For developing country Members these percentages shall be 76 and 86 per cent, respectively.

3. Commitments relating to limitations on the extension of the scope of export subsidization are as specified in Schedules.

4. During the implementation period, developing country Members shall not be required to undertake commitments in respect of the export subsidies listed in subparagraphs (d) and (e) of paragraph 1 above, provided that these are not applied in a manner that would circumvent reduction commitments.

Article 10
Prevention of Circumvention of Export Subsidy Commitments

1. Export subsidies not listed in paragraph 1 of Article 9 shall not be applied in a manner which results in, or which threatens to lead to, circumvention of export subsidy commitments; nor shall non-commercial transactions be used to circumvent such commitments.

2. Members undertake to work toward the development of internationally agreed disciplines to govern the provision of export credits, export credit guarantees or insurance programmes and, after agreement on such disciplines, to provide export credits, export credit guarantees or insurance programmes only in conformity therewith.

3. Any Member which claims that any quantity exported in excess of a reduction commitment level is not subsidized must establish that no export subsidy, whether listed in Article 9 or not, has been granted in respect of the quantity of exports in question.

4. Members donors of international food aid shall ensure:

(a) that the provision of international food aid is not tied directly or indirectly to commercial exports of agricultural products to recipient countries;

(b) that international food aid transactions, including bilateral food aid which is monetized, shall be carried out in accordance with the FAO 'Principles of Surplus Disposal and Consultative Obligations', including, where appropriate, the system of Usual Marketing Requirements (UMRs); and

(c) that such aid shall be provided to the extent possible in fully grant form or on terms no less concessional than those provided for in Article IV of the Food Aid Convention 1986.

Article 11
Incorporated Products

In no case may the per-unit subsidy paid on an incorporated agricultural primary product exceed the per-unit export subsidy that would be payable on exports of the primary product as such.

Part VI

Article 12
Disciplines on Export Prohibitions and Restrictions

1. Where any Member institutes any new export prohibition or restriction on foodstuffs in accordance with paragraph 2(a) of Article XI of GATT 1994, the Member shall observe the following provisions:

(a) the Member instituting the export prohibition or restriction shall give due consideration to the effects of such prohibition or restriction on importing Members' food security;

(b) before any Member institutes an export prohibition or restriction, it shall give notice in writing, as far in advance as practicable, to the Committee on Agriculture comprising such information as the nature and the duration of such measure, and shall consult, upon request, with any other Member having a substantial interest as an importer with respect to any matter related to the measure in question. The Member instituting such export prohibition or restriction shall provide, upon request, such a Member with necessary information.

2. The provisions of this Article shall not apply to any developing country Member, unless the measure is taken by a developing country Member which is a net-food exporter of the specific foodstuff concerned.

Part VII

Article 13
Due Restraint

During the implementation period, notwithstanding the provisions of GATT 1994 and the Agreement on Subsidies and Countervailing Measures (referred to in this Article as the 'Subsidies Agreement'):

(a) domestic support measures that conform fully to the provisions of Annex 2 to this Agreement shall be:

(i) non-actionable subsidies for purposes of countervailing duties ['COUNTERVAILING DUTIES' WHERE REFERRED TO IN THIS ARTICLE ARE THOSE COVERED BY ARTICLE VI OF GATT 1994 AND PART V OF THE AGREEMENT ON SUBSIDIES AND COUNTERVAILING MEASURES.];

(ii) exempt from actions based on Article XVI of GATT 1994 and Part III of the Subsidies Agreement; and

(iii) exempt from actions based on non-violation nullification or impairment of the benefits of tariff concessions accruing to another Member under Article II of GATT 1994, in the sense of paragraph 1(b) of Article XXIII of GATT 1994;

(b) domestic support measures that conform fully to the provisions of Article 6 of this Agreement including direct payments that conform to the requirements of paragraph 5 thereof, as reflected in each Member's Schedule, as well as domestic support within *de minimis* levels and in conformity with paragraph 2 of Article 6, shall be:

(i) exempt from the imposition of countervailing duties unless a determination of injury or threat thereof is made in accordance with Article VI of GATT 1994 and Part V of the Subsidies Agreement, and due restraint shall be shown in initiating any countervailing duty investigations;

(ii) exempt from actions based on paragraph 1 of Article XVI of GATT 1994 or Articles 5 and 6 of the Subsidies Agreement, provided that such measures do not grant support to a specific commodity in excess of that decided during the 1992 marketing year; and

(iii) exempt from actions based on non-violation nullification or impairment of the benefits of tariff concessions accruing to another Member under Article II of GATT 1994, in the sense of paragraph 1(b) of Article XXIII of GATT 1994, provided that such measures do not grant support to a specific commodity in excess of that decided during the 1992 marketing year;

(c) export subsidies that conform fully to the provisions of Part V of this Agreement, as reflected in each Member's Schedule, shall be:

(i) subject to countervailing duties only upon a determination of injury or threat thereof based on volume, effect on prices, or consequent impact in accordance with Article VI of GATT 1994 and Part V of the Subsidies Agreement, and due restraint shall be shown in initiating any countervailing duty investigations; and

(ii) exempt from actions based on Article XVI of GATT 1994 or Articles 3, 5 and 6 of the Subsidies Agreement.

Part VIII

Article 14
Sanitary and Phytosanitary Measures

Members agree to give effect to the Agreement on the Application of Sanitary and Phytosanitary Measures.

Part IX

Article 15
Special and Differential Treatment

1. In keeping with the recognition that differential and more favourable treatment for developing country Members is an integral part of the negotiation, special and differential treatment in respect of commitments shall be provided as set out in the relevant provisions of this Agreement and embodied in the Schedules of concessions and commitments.

2. Developing country Members shall have the flexibility to implement reduction commitments over a period of up to 10 years. Least-developed country Members shall not be required to undertake reduction commitments.

Part X

Article 16
Least-Developed and Net Food-Importing Developing Countries

1. Developed country Members shall take such action as is provided for within the framework of the Decision on Measures Concerning the Possible Negative Effects of the Reform Programme on Least-Developed and Net Food-Importing Developing Countries.

2. The Committee on Agriculture shall monitor, as appropriate, the follow-up to this Decision.

Part XI

Article 17
Committee on Agriculture

A Committee on Agriculture is hereby established.

Article 18
Review of the Implementation of Commitments

1. Progress in the implementation of commitments negotiated under the Uruguay Round reform programme shall be reviewed by the Committee on Agriculture.

2. The review process shall be undertaken on the basis of notifications submitted by Members in relation to such matters and at such intervals as shall be determined, as well as on the basis of such documentation as the Secretariat may be requested to prepare in order to facilitate the review process.

3. In addition to the notifications to be submitted under paragraph 2, any new domestic support measure, or modification of an existing measure, for which exemption from reduction is claimed shall be notified promptly. This notification shall contain details of the new or modified measure and its conformity with the agreed criteria as set out either in Article 6 or in Annex 2.

4. In the review process Members shall give due consideration to the influence of excessive rates of inflation on the ability of any Member to

abide by its domestic support commitments.

5. Members agree to consult annually in the Committee on Agriculture with respect to their participation in the normal growth of world trade in agricultural products within the framework of the commitments on export subsidies under this Agreement.

6. The review process shall provide an opportunity for Members to raise any matter relevant to the implementation of commitments under the reform programme as set out in this Agreement.

7. Any Member may bring to the attention of the Committee on Agriculture any measure which it considers ought to have been notified by another Member.

Article 19
Consultation and Dispute Settlement

The provisions of Articles XXII and XXIII of GATT 1994, as elaborated and applied by the Dispute Settlement Understanding, shall apply to consultations and the settlement of disputes under this Agreement.

Part XII

Article 20
Continuation of the Reform Process

Recognizing that the long-term objective of substantial progressive reductions in support and protection resulting in fundamental reform is an ongoing process, Members agree that negotiations for continuing the process will be initiated one year before the end of the implementation period, taking into account:

(a) the experience to that date from implementing the reduction commitments;

(b) the effects of the reduction commitments on world trade in agriculture;

(c) non-trade concerns, special and differential treatment to developing country Members, and the objective to establish a fair and market-oriented agricultural trading system, and the other objectives and concerns mentioned in the preamble to this Agreement; and

(d) what further commitments are necessary to achieve the above mentioned long-term objectives.

Part XIII

Article 21
Final Provisions

1. The provisions of GATT 1994 and of other Multilateral Trade Agreements in Annex 1A to the WTO Agreement shall apply subject to the provisions of this Agreement.

2. The Annexes to this Agreement are hereby made an integral part of this Agreement.

ANNEX 1

PRODUCT COVERAGE

1. This Agreement shall cover the following products: [PRODUCTS LISTED - The product descriptions in round brackets are not necessarily exhaustive.]

2. The foregoing shall not limit the product coverage of the Agreement on the Application of Sanitary and Phytosanitary Measures.

ANNEX 2

DOMESTIC SUPPORT: THE BASIS FOR EXEMPTION FROM THE REDUCTION COMMITMENTS

1. Domestic support measures for which exemption from the reduction commitments is claimed shall meet the fundamental requirement that they have no, or at most minimal, trade-distorting effects or effects on production. Accordingly, all measures for which exemption is claimed shall conform to the following basic criteria:

(a) the support in question shall be provided through a publicly-funded government programme (including government revenue foregone) not involving transfers from consumers; and,

(b) the support in question shall not have the effect of providing price support to producers;

plus policy-specific criteria and conditions as set out below.

Government Service Programmes

2. General services

Policies in this category involve expenditures (or revenue foregone) in relation to programmes which provide services or benefits to agriculture or the rural community. They shall not involve direct payments to producers or processors. Such programmes, which include but are not restricted to the following list, shall meet the general criteria in paragraph 1 above and policy-specific conditions where set out below:

(a) research, including general research, research in connection with environmental programmes, and research programmes relating to particular products;

(b) pest and disease control, including general and product-specific pest and disease control measures, such as early-warning systems, quarantine and eradication;

(c) training services, including both general and specialist training facilities;

(d) extension and advisory services, including the provision of means to facilitate the transfer of information and the results of research to producers and consumers;

(e) inspection services, including general inspection services and the inspection of particular products for health, safety, grading or standardization purposes;

(f) marketing and promotion services, including market information, advice and promotion relating to particular products but excluding expenditure for unspecified purposes that could be used by sellers to reduce their selling price or confer a direct economic benefit to purchasers; and

(g) infrastructural services, including: electricity reticulation, roads and other means of transport, market and port facilities, water supply facilities, dams and drainage schemes, and infrastructural works associated with environmental programmes. In all cases the expenditure shall be directed to the provision or construction of capital works only, and shall exclude the subsidized provision of on-farm facilities other than for the reticulation of generally available public utilities. It shall not include subsidies to inputs or operating costs, or preferential user charges.

3. Public stockholding for food security purposes [FOR THE PURPOSES OF PARAGRAPH 3 OF THIS ANNEX, GOVERNMENTAL STOCKHOLDING PROGRAMMES FOR FOOD SECURITY PURPOSES IN DEVELOPING COUNTRIES WHOSE OPERATION IS TRANSPARENT AND CONDUCTED IN ACCORDANCE WITH OFFICIALLY PUBLISHED OBJECTIVE CRITERIA OR GUIDELINES SHALL BE CONSIDERED TO BE IN CONFORMITY WITH THE PROVISIONS OF THIS PARAGRAPH, INCLUDING PROGRAMMES UNDER WHICH STOCKS OF FOODSTUFFS FOR FOOD SECURITY PURPOSES ARE ACQUIRED AND RELEASED AT ADMINISTERED PRICES, PROVIDED THAT THE DIFFERENCE BETWEEN THE ACQUISITION PRICE AND THE EXTERNAL REFERENCE PRICE IS ACCOUNTED FOR IN THE AMS.]

Expenditures (or revenue foregone) in relation to the accumulation and holding of stocks of products which form an integral part of a food security programme identified in national legislation. This may include government aid to private storage of products as part of such a programme.

The volume and accumulation of such stocks shall correspond to predetermined targets related solely to food security. The process of stock accumulation and disposal shall be financially transparent. Food purchases by the government shall be made at current market prices and sales from food security stocks shall be made at no less than the current domestic market price for the product and quality in question.

4. Domestic food aid [FOR THE PURPOSES OF PARAGRAPHS 3 AND 4 OF THIS ANNEX, THE PROVISION OF FOODSTUFFS AT SUBSIDIZED PRICES WITH THE OBJECTIVE OF MEETING FOOD REQUIREMENTS OF URBAN AND RURAL POOR IN DEVELOPING COUNTRIES ON A REGULAR BASIS AT REASONABLE PRICES SHALL BE CONSIDERED TO BE IN CONFORMITY WITH THE PROVISIONS OF THIS PARAGRAPH.]

Expenditures (or revenue foregone) in relation to the provision of domestic food aid to sections of the population in need.

Eligibility to receive the food aid shall be subject to clearly-defined criteria related to nutritional objectives. Such aid shall be in the form of direct provision of food to those concerned or the provision of means to allow eligible recipients to buy food either at market or at subsidized prices. Food purchases by the government shall be made at current market prices and the financing and administration of the aid shall be transparent.

5. Direct payments to producers

Support provided through direct payments (or revenue foregone, including payments in kind) to producers for which exemption from reduction commitments is claimed shall meet the basic criteria set out in paragraph 1 above, plus specific criteria applying to individual types of direct payment as set out in paragraphs 6 through 13 below. Where exemption from reduction is claimed for any existing or new type of direct payment other than those specified in paragraphs 6 through 13, it shall conform to criteria (b) through (e) in paragraph 6, in addition to the general criteria set out in paragraph 1.

6. Decoupled income support

(a) Eligibility for such payments shall be determined by clearly-defined criteria such as income, status as a producer or landowner, factor use or production level in a defined and fixed base period.

(b) The amount of such payments in any given year shall not be related to, or based on, the type or volume of production (including livestock units) undertaken by the producer in any year after the base period.

(c) The amount of such payments in any given year shall not be related to, or based on, the prices, domestic or international, applying to any production undertaken in any year after the base period.

(d) The amount of such payments in any given year shall not be related to, or based on, the factors of production employed in any year after the base period.

(e) No production shall be required in order to receive such payments.

7. Government financial participation in income insurance and income safety-net programmes

(a) Eligibility for such payments shall be determined by an income loss, taking into account only income derived from agriculture, which exceeds 30 per cent of average gross income or the equivalent in net income terms (excluding any payments from the same or similar schemes) in the preceding three-year period or a three-year average based on the preceding five-year period, excluding the highest and the lowest entry. Any producer meeting this condition shall be eligible to receive the payments.

(b) The amount of such payments shall compensate for less than 70 per cent of the producer's income loss in the year the producer becomes eligible to receive this assistance.

(c) The amount of any such payments shall relate solely to income; it shall not relate to the type or volume of production (including livestock units) undertaken by the producer; or to the prices, domestic or international, applying to such production; or to the factors of production employed.

(d) Where a producer receives in the same year payments under this paragraph and under paragraph 8 (relief from natural disasters), the total of such payments shall be less than 100 per cent of the producer's total loss.

8. Payments (made either directly or by way of government financial participation in crop insurance schemes) for relief from natural disasters

(a) Eligibility for such payments shall arise only following a formal recognition by government authorities that a natural or like disaster (including disease outbreaks, pest infestations, nuclear accidents, and war on the territory of the Member concerned) has occurred or is occurring; and shall be determined by a production loss which exceeds 30 per cent of the average of production in the preceding three-year period or a three-year average based on the preceding five-year period, excluding the highest and the lowest entry.

(b) Payments made following a disaster shall be applied only in respect of losses of income, livestock (including payments in connection with the veterinary treatment of animals), land or other production factors due to the natural disaster in question.

(c) Payments shall compensate for not more than the total cost of replacing such losses and shall not require or specify the type or quantity of future production.

(d) Payments made during a disaster shall not exceed the level required to prevent or alleviate further loss as defined in criterion (b) above.

(e) Where a producer receives in the same year payments under this paragraph and under paragraph 7 (income insurance and income safety-net programmes), the total of such payments shall be less than 100 per cent of the producer's total loss.

9. Structural adjustment assistance provided through producer retirement programmes

(a) Eligibility for such payments shall be determined by reference to clearly defined criteria in programmes designed to facilitate the retirement of persons engaged in marketable agricultural production, or their movement to non-agricultural activities.

(b) Payments shall be conditional upon the total and permanent retirement of the recipients from marketable agricultural production.

10. Structural adjustment assistance provided through resource retirement programmes

(a) Eligibility for such payments shall be determined by reference to clearly defined criteria in programmes designed to remove land or other resources, including livestock, from marketable agricultural production.

(b) Payments shall be conditional upon the retirement of land from marketable agricultural production for a minimum of three years, and in the case of livestock on its slaughter or definitive permanent disposal.

(c) Payments shall not require or specify any alternative use for such land or other resources which involves the production of marketable agricultural products.

(d) Payments shall not be related to either the type or quantity of production or to the prices, domestic or international, applying to production undertaken using the land or other resources remaining in production.

11. Structural adjustment assistance provided through investment aids

(a) Eligibility for such payments shall be determined by reference to clearly-defined criteria in government programmes designed to assist the financial or physical restructuring of a producer's operations in response to objectively demonstrated structural disadvantages. Eligibility for such programmes may also be based on a clearly-defined government programme for the reprivatization of agricultural land.

(b) The amount of such payments in any given year shall not be related to, or based on, the type or volume of production (including livestock units) undertaken by the producer in any year after the base period other than as provided for under criterion (e) below.

(c) The amount of such payments in any given year shall not be related to, or based on, the prices, domestic or international, applying to any production undertaken in any year after the base period.

(d) The payments shall be given only for the period of time necessary for the realization of the investment in respect of which they are provided.

(e) The payments shall not mandate or in any way designate the agricultural products to be produced by the recipients except to require them not to produce a particular product.

(f) The payments shall be limited to the amount required to compensate for the structural disadvantage.

12. Payments under environmental programmes

(a) Eligibility for such payments shall be determined as part of a clearly-defined government environmental or conservation programme and be dependent on the fulfilment of specific conditions under the government programme, including conditions related to production methods or inputs.

(b) The amount of payment shall be limited to the extra costs or loss of income involved in complying with the government programme.

13. Payments under regional assistance programmes

(a) Eligibility for such payments shall be limited to producers in disadvantaged regions. Each such region must be a clearly designated contiguous geographical area with a definable economic and administrative identity, considered as disadvantaged on the basis of neutral and objective criteria clearly spelt out in law or regulation and indicating that the region's difficulties arise out of more than temporary circumstances.

(b) The amount of such payments in any given year shall not be related to, or based on, the type or volume of production (including livestock units) undertaken by the producer in any year after the base period other than to reduce that production.

(c) The amount of such payments in any given year shall not be related to, or based on, the prices, domestic or international, applying to any production undertaken in any year after the base period.

(d) Payments shall be available only to producers in eligible regions, but generally available to all producers within such regions.

(e) Where related to production factors, payments shall be made at a degressive rate above a threshold level of the factor concerned.

(f) The payments shall be limited to the extra costs or loss of income involved in undertaking agricultural production in the prescribed area.

ANNEX 3

DOMESTIC SUPPORT: CALCULATION OF AGGREGATE MEASUREMENT OF SUPPORT

1. Subject to the provisions of Article 6, an Aggregate Measurement of Support (AMS) shall be calculated on a product-specific basis for each basic agricultural product receiving market price support, non-exempt direct payments, or any other subsidy not exempted from the reduction commitment ('other non-exempt policies'). Support which is non-product specific shall be totalled into one non-product-specific AMS in total monetary terms.

2. Subsidies under paragraph 1 shall include both budgetary outlays and revenue foregone by governments or their agents.

3. Support at both the national and sub-national level shall be included.

4. Specific agricultural levies or fees paid by producers shall be deducted from the AMS.

5. The AMS calculated as outlined below for the base period shall constitute the base level for the implementation of the reduction commitment on domestic support.

6. For each basic agricultural product, a specific AMS shall be established, expressed in total monetary value terms.

7. The AMS shall be calculated as close as practicable to the point of first sale of the basic agricultural product concerned. Measures directed at agricultural processors shall be included to the extent that such measures benefit the producers of the basic agricultural products.

8. Market price support: market price support shall be calculated using the gap between a fixed external reference price and the applied administered price multiplied by the quantity of production eligible to receive the applied administered price. Budgetary payments made to maintain this gap, such as buying-in or storage costs, shall not be included in the AMS.

9. The fixed external reference price shall be based on the years 1986 to 1988 and shall generally be the average f.o.b. unit value for the basic agricultural product concerned in a net exporting country and the average c.i.f. unit value for the basic agricultural product concerned in a net importing country in the base period. The fixed reference price may be adjusted for quality differences as necessary.

10. Non-exempt direct payments: non-exempt direct payments which are dependent on a price gap shall be calculated either using the gap between the fixed reference price and the applied administered price multiplied by the quantity of production eligible to receive the administered price, or using

budgetary outlays.

11. The fixed reference price shall be based on the years 1986 to 1988 and shall generally be the actual price used for determining payment rates.

12. Non-exempt direct payments which are based on factors other than price shall be measured using budgetary outlays.

13. Other non-exempt measures, including input subsidies and other measures such as marketing-cost reduction measures: the value of such measures shall be measured using government budgetary outlays or, where the use of budgetary outlays does not reflect the full extent of the subsidy concerned, the basis for calculating the subsidy shall be the gap between the price of the subsidized good or service and a representative market price for a similar good or service multiplied by the quantity of the good or service.

ANNEX 4

DOMESTIC SUPPORT: CALCULATION OF EQUIVALENT MEASUREMENT OF SUPPORT

1. Subject to the provisions of Article 6, equivalent measurements of support shall be calculated in respect of all basic agricultural products where market price support as defined in Annex 3 exists but for which calculation of this component of the AMS is not practicable. For such products the base level for implementation of the domestic support reduction commitments shall consist of a market price support component expressed in terms of equivalent measurements of support under paragraph 2 below, as well as any non-exempt direct payments and other non-exempt support, which shall be evaluated as provided for under paragraph 3 below. Support at both national and sub-national level shall be included.

2. The equivalent measurements of support provided for in paragraph 1 shall be calculated on a product-specific basis for all basic agricultural products as close as practicable to the point of first sale receiving market price support and for which the calculation of the market price support component of the AMS is not practicable. For those basic agricultural products, equivalent measurements of market price support shall be made using the applied administered price and the quantity of production eligible to receive that price or, where this is not practicable, on budgetary outlays used to maintain the producer price.

3. Where basic agricultural products falling under paragraph 1 are the subject of non-exempt direct payments or any other product-specific subsidy not exempted from the reduction commitment, the basis for equivalent measurements of support concerning these measures shall be calculations as for the corresponding AMS components (specified in paragraphs 10 through 13 of Annex 3).

4. Equivalent measurements of support shall be calculated on the amount of subsidy as close as practicable to the point of first sale of the basic agricultural product concerned. Measures directed at agricultural processors shall be included to the extent that such measures benefit the producers of the basic agricultural products. Specific agricultural levies or fees paid by producers shall reduce the equivalent measurements of support

by a corresponding amount.

ANNEX 5

SPECIAL TREATMENT WITH RESPECT TO PARAGRAPH 2 OF ARTICLE 4

Section A

1. The provisions of paragraph 2 of Article 4 shall not apply with effect from the entry into force of the WTO Agreement to any primary agricultural product and its worked and/or prepared products ('designated products') in respect of which the following conditions are complied with (hereinafter referred to as 'special treatment'):

(a) imports of the designated products comprised less than 3 per cent of corresponding domestic consumption in the base period 1986-1988 ('the base period');

(b) no export subsidies have been provided since the beginning of the base period for the designated products;

(c) effective production-restricting measures are applied to the primary agricultural product;

(d) such products are designated with the symbol 'ST-Annex 5' in Section I-B of Part I of a Member's Schedule annexed to the Marrakech Protocol, as being subject to special treatment reflecting factors of non-trade concerns, such as food security and environmental protection; and

(e) minimum access opportunities in respect of the designated products correspond, as specified in Section I-B of Part I of the Schedule of the Member concerned, to 4 per cent of base period domestic consumption of the designated products from the beginning of the first year of the implementation period and, thereafter, are increased by 0.8 per cent of corresponding domestic consumption in the base period per year for the remainder of the implementation period.

2. At the beginning of any year of the implementation period a Member may cease to apply special treatment in respect of the designated products by complying with the provisions of paragraph 6. In such a case, the Member concerned shall maintain the minimum access opportunities already in effect at such time and increase the minimum access opportunities by 0.4 per cent of corresponding domestic consumption in the base period per year for the remainder of the implementation period. Thereafter, the level of minimum access opportunities resulting from this formula in the final year of the implementation period shall be maintained in the Schedule of the Member concerned.

3. Any negotiation on the question of whether there can be a continuation of the special treatment as set out in paragraph 1 after the end of the implementation period shall be completed within the time-frame of the implementation period itself as a part of the negotiations set out in Article 20 of this Agreement, taking into account the factors of non-trade concerns.

4. If it is agreed as a result of the negotiation referred to in paragraph 3 that a Member may continue to apply the special treatment, such

Member shall confer additional and acceptable concessions as determined in that negotiation.

5. Where the special treatment is not to be continued at the end of the implementation period, the Member concerned shall implement the provisions of paragraph 6. In such a case, after the end of the implementation period the minimum access opportunities for the designated products shall be maintained at the level of 8 per cent of corresponding domestic consumption in the base period in the Schedule of the Member concerned.

6. Border measures other than ordinary customs duties maintained in respect of the designated products shall become subject to the provisions of paragraph 2 of Article 4 with effect from the beginning of the year in which the special treatment ceases to apply. Such products shall be subject to ordinary customs duties, which shall be bound in the Schedule of the Member concerned and applied, from the beginning of the year in which special treatment ceases and thereafter, at such rates as would have been applicable had a reduction of at least 15 per cent been implemented over the implementation period in equal annual instalments. These duties shall be established on the basis of tariff equivalents to be calculated in accordance with the guidelines prescribed in the attachment hereto.

Section B

7. The provisions of paragraph 2 of Article 4 shall also not apply with effect from the entry into force of the WTO Agreement to a primary agricultural product that is the predominant staple in the traditional diet of a developing country Member and in respect of which the following conditions, in addition to those specified in paragraph 1(a) through 1(d), as they apply to the products concerned, are complied with:

(a) minimum access opportunities in respect of the products concerned, as specified in Section I-B of Part I of the Schedule of the developing country Member concerned, correspond to 1 per cent of base period domestic consumption of the products concerned from the beginning of the first year of the implementation period and are increased in equal annual instalments to 2 per cent of corresponding domestic consumption in the base period at the beginning of the fifth year of the implementation period. From the beginning of the sixth year of the implementation period, minimum access opportunities in respect of the products concerned correspond to 2 per cent of corresponding domestic consumption in the base period and are increased in equal annual instalments to 4 per cent of corresponding domestic consumption in the base period until the beginning of the 10th year. Thereafter, the level of minimum access opportunities resulting from this formula in the 10th year shall be maintained in the Schedule of the developing country Member concerned;

(b) appropriate market access opportunities have been provided for in other products under this Agreement.

8. Any negotiation on the question of whether there can be a continuation of the special treatment as set out in paragraph 7 after the end of the 10th year following the beginning of the implementation period shall be initiated and completed within the time-frame of the 10th year itself following

the beginning of the implementation period.

9. If it is agreed as a result of the negotiation referred to in paragraph 8 that a Member may continue to apply the special treatment, such Member shall confer additional and acceptable concessions as determined in that negotiation.

10. In the event that special treatment under paragraph 7 is not to be continued beyond the 10th year following the beginning of the implementation period, the products concerned shall be subject to ordinary customs duties, established on the basis of a tariff equivalent to be calculated in accordance with the guidelines prescribed in the attachment hereto, which shall be bound in the Schedule of the Member concerned. In other respects, the provisions of paragraph 6 shall apply as modified by the relevant special and differential treatment accorded to developing country Members under this Agreement.

Attachment to Annex 5

Guidelines for the Calculation of Tariff Equivalents for the Specific Purpose Specified in Paragraphs 6 and 10 of this Annex

1. The calculation of the tariff equivalents, whether expressed as *ad valorem* or specific rates, shall be made using the actual difference between internal and external prices in a transparent manner. Data used shall be for the years 1986 to 1988. Tariff equivalents:

(a) shall primarily be established at the four-digit level of the HS;

(b) shall be established at the six-digit or a more detailed level of the HS wherever appropriate;

(c) shall generally be established for worked and/or prepared products by multiplying the specific tariff equivalent(s) for the primary agricultural product(s) by the proportion(s) in value terms or in physical terms as appropriate of the primary agricultural product(s) in the worked and/or prepared products, and take account, where necessary, of any additional elements currently providing protection to industry.

2. External prices shall be, in general, actual average c.i.f. unit values for the importing country. Where average c.i.f. unit values are not available or appropriate, external prices shall be either:

(a) appropriate average c.i.f. unit values of a near country; or

(b) estimated from average f.o.b. unit values of (an) appropriate major exporter(s) adjusted by adding an estimate of insurance, freight and other relevant costs to the importing country.

3. The external prices shall generally be converted to domestic currencies using the annual average market exchange rate for the same period as the price data.

4. The internal price shall generally be a representative wholesale price ruling in the domestic market or an estimate of that price where adequate data is not available.

5. The initial tariff equivalents may be adjusted, where necessary, to take account of differences in quality or variety using an appropriate coefficient.

6. Where a tariff equivalent resulting from these guidelines is

negative or lower than the current bound rate, the initial tariff equivalent may be established at the current bound rate or on the basis of national offers for that product.

7. Where an adjustment is made to the level of a tariff equivalent which would have resulted from the above guidelines, the Member concerned shall afford, on request, full opportunities for consultation with a view to negotiating appropriate solutions."

AGREEMENT ON SANITARY AND PHYTOSANITARY MEASURES [FOUND IN CHAPTER IX]

Agreement on Textiles and Clothing—the Text

"AGREEMENT ON TEXTILES AND CLOTHING

Members,

Recalling that Ministers agreed at Punta del Este that 'negotiations in the area of textiles and clothing shall aim to formulate modalities that would permit the eventual integration of this sector into GATT on the basis of strengthened GATT rules and disciplines, thereby also contributing to the objective of further liberalization of trade;'

Recalling also that in the April 1989 Decision of the Trade Negotiations Committee it was agreed that the process of integration should commence following the conclusion of the Uruguay Round of Multilateral Trade Negotiations and should be progressive in character;

Recalling further that it was agreed that special treatment should be accorded to the least-developed country Members;

Hereby *agree* as follows:

Article 1

1. This Agreement sets out provisions to be applied by Members during a transition period for the integration of the textiles and clothing sector into GATT 1994.

2. Members agree to use the provisions of paragraph 18 of Article 2 and paragraph 6(b) of Article 6 in such a way as to permit meaningful increases in access possibilities for small suppliers and the development of commercially significant trading opportunities for new entrants in the field of textiles and clothing trade [TO THE EXTENT POSSIBLE, EXPORTS FROM A LEAST-DEVELOPED COUNTRY MEMBER MAY ALSO BENEFIT FROM THIS PROVISION.].

3. Members shall have due regard to the situation of those Members which have not accepted the Protocols extending the Arrangement Regarding International Trade in Textiles (referred to in this Agreement as the 'MFA') since 1986 and, to the extent possible, shall afford them special treatment in applying the provisions of this Agreement.

4. Members agree that the particular interests of the cotton-producing exporting Members should, in consultation with them, be reflected in the implementation of the provisions of this Agreement.

5. In order to facilitate the integration of the textiles and clothing sector into GATT 1994, Members should allow for continuous autonomous industrial adjustment and increased competition in their markets.

6. Unless otherwise provided in this Agreement, its provisions shall not affect the rights and obligations of Members under the provisions of the WTO Agreement and the Multilateral Trade Agreements.

7. The textile and clothing products to which this Agreement applies are set out in the Annex.

Article 2

1. All quantitative restrictions within bilateral agreements maintained under Article 4 or notified under Article 7 or 8 of the MFA in force on the day before the entry into force of the WTO Agreement shall, within 60 days following such entry into force, be notified in detail, including the restraint levels, growth rates and flexibility provisions, by the Members maintaining such restrictions to the Textiles Monitoring Body provided for in Article 8 (referred to in this Agreement as the 'TMB'). Members agree that as of the date of entry into force of the WTO Agreement, all such restrictions maintained between GATT 1947 contracting parties, and in place on the day before such entry into force, shall be governed by the provisions of this Agreement.

2. The TMB shall circulate these notifications to all Members for their information. It is open to any Member to bring to the attention of the TMB, within 60 days of the circulation of the notifications, any observations it deems appropriate with regard to such notifications. Such observations shall be circulated to the other Members for their information. The TMB may make recommendations, as appropriate, to the Members concerned.

3. When the 12-month period of restrictions to be notified under paragraph 1 does not coincide with the 12-month period immediately preceding the date of entry into force of the WTO Agreement, the Members concerned should mutually agree on arrangements to bring the period of restrictions into line with the agreement year [THE 'AGREEMENT YEAR' IS DEFINED TO MEAN A 12-MONTH PERIOD BEGINNING FROM THE DATE OF ENTRY INTO FORCE OF THE WTO AGREEMENT AND AT THE SUBSEQUENT 12-MONTH INTERVALS..], and to establish notional base levels of such restrictions in order to implement the provisions of this Article. Concerned Members agree to enter into consultations promptly upon request with a view to reaching such mutual agreement. Any such arrangements shall take into account, *inter alia*, seasonal patterns of shipments in recent years. The results of these consultations shall be notified to the TMB, which shall make such recommendations as it deems appropriate to the Members concerned.

4. The restrictions notified under paragraph 1 shall be deemed to constitute the totality of such restrictions applied by the respective Members on the day before the entry into force of the WTO Agreement. No new restrictions in terms of products or Members shall be introduced except under the provisions of this Agreement or relevant GATT 1994 provisions [THE RELEVANT GATT 1994 PROVISIONS SHALL NOT INCLUDE ARTICLE XIX IN RESPECT OF PRODUCTS NOT YET INTEGRATED INTO GATT 1994, EXCEPT AS SPECIFICALLY PROVIDED IN PARAGRAPH 3 OF THE

ANNEX.]. Restrictions not notified within 60 days of the date of entry into force of the WTO Agreement shall be terminated forthwith.

5. Any unilateral measure taken under Article 3 of the MFA prior to the date of entry into force of the WTO Agreement may remain in effect for the duration specified therein, but not exceeding 12 months, if it has been reviewed by the Textiles Surveillance Body (referred to in this Agreement as the 'TSB') established under the MFA. Should the TSB not have had the opportunity to review any such unilateral measure, it shall be reviewed by the TMB in accordance with the rules and procedures governing Article 3 measures under the MFA. Any measure applied under an MFA Article 4 agreement prior to the date of entry into force of the WTO Agreement that is the subject of a dispute which the TSB has not had the opportunity to review shall also be reviewed by the TMB in accordance with the MFA rules and procedures applicable for such a review.

6. On the date of entry into force of the WTO Agreement, each Member shall integrate into GATT 1994 products which accounted for not less than 16 per cent of the total volume of the Member's 1990 imports of the products in the Annex, in terms of HS lines or categories. The products to be integrated shall encompass products from each of the following four groups: tops and yarns, fabrics, made-up textile products, and clothing.

7. Full details of the actions to be taken pursuant to paragraph 6 shall be notified by the Members concerned according to the following:

(a) Members maintaining restrictions falling under paragraph 1 undertake, notwithstanding the date of entry into force of the WTO Agreement, to notify such details to the GATT Secretariat not later than the date determined by the Ministerial Decision of 15 April 1994. The GATT Secretariat shall promptly circulate these notifications to the other participants for information. These notifications will be made available to the TMB, when established, for the purposes of paragraph 21;

(b) Members which have, pursuant to paragraph 1 of Article 6, retained the right to use the provisions of Article 6, shall notify such details to the TMB not later than 60 days following the date of entry into force of the WTO Agreement, or, in the case of those Members covered by paragraph 3 of Article 1, not later than at the end of the 12th month that the WTO Agreement is in effect. The TMB shall circulate these notifications to the other Members for information and review them as provided in paragraph 21.

8. The remaining products, i.e. the products not integrated into GATT 1994 under paragraph 6, shall be integrated, in terms of HS lines or categories, in three stages, as follows:

(a) on the first day of the 37th month that the WTO Agreement is in effect, products which accounted for not less than 17 per cent of the total volume of the Member's 1990 imports of the products in the Annex. The products to be integrated by the Members shall encompass products from each of the following four groups: tops and yarns, fabrics, made-up textile products, and clothing;

(b) on the first day of the 85th month that the WTO Agreement is in effect, products which accounted for not less than 18 per cent of the total volume of the Member's 1990 imports of the products in the Annex. The products to be integrated by the Members shall encompass products from each of the following four groups: tops and yarns, fabrics, made-up textile products, and clothing;

(c) on the first day of the 121st month that the WTO Agreement is in effect, the textiles and clothing sector shall stand integrated into GATT 1994, all restrictions under this Agreement having been eliminated.

9. Members which have notified, pursuant to paragraph 1 of Article 6, their intention not to retain the right to use the provisions of Article 6 shall, for the purposes of this Agreement, be deemed to have integrated their textiles and clothing products into GATT 1994. Such Members shall, therefore, be exempted from complying with the provisions of paragraphs 6 to 8 and 11.

10. Nothing in this Agreement shall prevent a Member which has submitted an integration programme pursuant to paragraph 6 or 8 from integrating products into GATT 1994 earlier than provided for in such a programme. However, any such integration of products shall take effect at the beginning of an agreement year, and details shall be notified to the TMB at least three months prior thereto for circulation to all Members.

11. The respective programmes of integration, in pursuance of paragraph 8, shall be notified in detail to the TMB at least 12 months before their coming into effect, and circulated by the TMB to all Members.

12. The base levels of the restrictions on the remaining products, mentioned in paragraph 8, shall be the restraint levels referred to in paragraph 1.

13. During Stage 1 of this Agreement (from the date of entry into force of the WTO Agreement to the 36th month that it is in effect, inclusive) the level of each restriction under MFA bilateral agreements in force for the 12-month period prior to the date of entry into force of the WTO Agreement shall be increased annually by not less than the growth rate established for the respective restrictions, increased by 16 per cent.

14. Except where the Council for Trade in Goods or the Dispute Settlement Body decides otherwise under paragraph 12 of Article 8, the level of each remaining restriction shall be increased annually during subsequent stages of this Agreement by not less than the following:

(a) for Stage 2 (from the 37th to the 84th month that the WTO Agreement is in effect, inclusive), the growth rate for the respective restrictions during Stage 1, increased by 25 per cent;

(b) for Stage 3 (from the 85th to the 120th month that the WTO Agreement is in effect, inclusive), the growth rate for the respective restrictions during Stage 2, increased by 27 per cent.

15. Nothing in this Agreement shall prevent a Member from eliminating any restriction maintained pursuant to this Article, effective at the beginning of any agreement year during the transition period, provided the exporting Member concerned and the TMB are notified at least three months prior to the elimination coming into effect. The period for prior notification may be shortened to 30 days with the agreement of the restrained Member. The TMB shall circulate such notifications to all Members. In considering the elimination of restrictions as envisaged in this paragraph, the Members

concerned shall take into account the treatment of similar exports from other Members.

16. Flexibility provisions, i.e. swing, carryover and carry forward, applicable to all restrictions maintained pursuant to this Article, shall be the same as those provided for in MFA bilateral agreements for the 12-month period prior to the entry into force of the WTO Agreement. No quantitative limits shall be placed or maintained on the combined use of swing, carryover and carry forward.

17. Administrative arrangements, as deemed necessary in relation to the implementation of any provision of this Article, shall be a matter for agreement between the Members concerned. Any such arrangements shall be notified to the TMB.

18. As regards those Members whose exports are subject to restrictions on the day before the entry into force of the WTO Agreement and whose restrictions represent 1.2 per cent or less of the total volume of the restrictions applied by an importing Member as of 31 December 1991 and notified under this Article, meaningful improvement in access for their exports shall be provided, at the entry into force of the WTO Agreement and for the duration of this Agreement, through advancement by one stage of the growth rates set out in paragraphs 13 and 14, or through at least equivalent changes as may be mutually agreed with respect to a different mix of base levels, growth and flexibility provisions. Such improvements shall be notified to the TMB.

19. In any case, during the duration of this Agreement, in which a safeguard measure is initiated by a Member under Article XIX of GATT 1994 in respect of a particular product during a period of one year immediately following the integration of that product into GATT 1994 in accordance with the provisions of this Article, the provisions of Article XIX, as interpreted by the Agreement on Safeguards, will apply, save as set out in paragraph 20.

20. Where such a measure is applied using non-tariff means, the importing Member concerned shall apply the measure in a manner as set forth in paragraph 2(d) of Article XIII of GATT 1994 at the request of any exporting Member whose exports of such products were subject to restrictions under this Agreement at any time in the one-year period immediately prior to the initiation of the safeguard measure. The exporting Member concerned shall administer such a measure. The applicable level shall not reduce the relevant exports below the level of a recent representative period, which shall normally be the average of exports from the Member concerned in the last three representative years for which statistics are available. Furthermore, when the safeguard measure is applied for more than one year, the applicable level shall be progressively liberalized at regular intervals during the period of application. In such cases the exporting Member concerned shall not exercise the right of suspending substantially equivalent concessions or other obligations under paragraph 3(a) of Article XIX of GATT 1994.

21. The TMB shall keep under review the implementation of this Article. It shall, at the request of any Member, review any particular matter with reference to the implementation of the provisions of this Article. It shall make appropriate recommendations or findings within 30 days to the Member or Members concerned, after inviting the participation of such Members.

Article 3

1. Within 60 days following the date of entry into force of the WTO Agreement, Members maintaining restrictions [RESTRICTIONS DENOTE ALL UNILATERAL QUANTITATIVE RESTRICTIONS, BILATERAL ARRANGEMENTS AND OTHER MEASURES HAVING A SIMILAR EFFECT.] on textile and clothing products (other than restrictions maintained under the MFA and covered by the provisions of Article 2), whether consistent with GATT 1994 or not, shall (*a*) notify them in detail to the TMB, or (*b*) provide to the TMB notifications with respect to them which have been submitted to any other WTO body. The notifications should, wherever applicable, provide information with respect to any GATT 1994 justification for the restrictions, including GATT 1994 provisions on which they are based.

2. Members maintaining restrictions falling under paragraph 1, except those justified under a GATT 1994 provision, shall either:

(a) bring them into conformity with GATT 1994 within one year following the entry into force of the WTO Agreement, and notify this action to the TMB for its information; or

(b) phase them out progressively according to a programme to be presented to the TMB by the Member maintaining the restrictions not later than six months after the date of entry into force of the WTO Agreement. This programme shall provide for all restrictions to be phased out within a period not exceeding the duration of this Agreement. The TMB may make recommendations to the Member concerned with respect to such a programme.

3. During the duration of this Agreement, Members shall provide to the TMB, for its information, notifications submitted to any other WTO bodies with respect to any new restrictions or changes in existing restrictions on textile and clothing products, taken under any GATT 1994 provision, within 60 days of their coming into effect.

4. It shall be open to any Member to make reverse notifications to the TMB, for its information, in regard to the GATT 1994 justification, or in regard to any restrictions that may not have been notified under the provisions of this Article. Actions with respect to such notifications may be pursued by any Member under relevant GATT 1994 provisions or procedures in the appropriate WTO body.

5. The TMB shall circulate the notifications made pursuant to this Article to all Members for their information.

Article 4

1. Restrictions referred to in Article 2, and those applied under Article 6, shall be administered by the exporting Members. Importing Members shall not be obliged to accept shipments in excess of the restrictions notified under Article 2, or of restrictions applied pursuant to Article 6.

2. Members agree that the introduction of changes, such as changes in practices, rules, procedures and categorization of textile and clothing products, including those changes relating to the Harmonized System, in the implementation or administration of those restrictions notified or applied under

this Agreement should not: upset the balance of rights and obligations between the Members concerned under this Agreement; adversely affect the access available to a Member; impede the full utilization of such access; or disrupt trade under this Agreement.

3. If a product which constitutes only part of a restriction is notified for integration pursuant to the provisions of Article 2, Members agree that any change in the level of that restriction shall not upset the balance of rights and obligations between the Members concerned under this Agreement.

4. When changes mentioned in paragraphs 2 and 3 are necessary, however, Members agree that the Member initiating such changes shall inform and, wherever possible, initiate consultations with the affected Member or Members prior to the implementation of such changes, with a view to reaching a mutually acceptable solution regarding appropriate and equitable adjustment. Members further agree that where consultation prior to implementation is not feasible, the Member initiating such changes will, at the request of the affected Member, consult, within 60 days if possible, with the Members concerned with a view to reaching a mutually satisfactory solution regarding appropriate and equitable adjustments. If a mutually satisfactory solution is not reached, any Member involved may refer the matter to the TMB for recommendations as provided in Article 8. Should the TSB not have had the opportunity to review a dispute concerning such changes introduced prior to the entry into force of the WTO Agreement, it shall be reviewed by the TMB in accordance with the rules and procedures of the MFA applicable for such a review.

Article 5

1. Members agree that circumvention by transshipment, re-routing, false declaration concerning country or place of origin, and falsification of official documents, frustrates the implementation of this Agreement to integrate the textiles and clothing sector into GATT 1994. Accordingly, Members should establish the necessary legal provisions and/or administrative procedures to address and take action against such circumvention. Members further agree that, consistent with their domestic laws and procedures, they will cooperate fully to address problems arising from circumvention.

2. Should any Member believe that this Agreement is being circumvented by transshipment, re-routing, false declaration concerning country or place of origin, or falsification of official documents, and that no, or inadequate, measures are being applied to address and/or to take action against such circumvention, that Member should consult with the Member or Members concerned with a view to seeking a mutually satisfactory solution. Such consultations should be held promptly, and within 30 days when possible. If a mutually satisfactory solution is not reached, the matter may be referred by any Member involved to the TMB for recommendations.

3. Members agree to take necessary action, consistent with their domestic laws and procedures, to prevent, to investigate and, where appropriate, to take legal and/or administrative action against circumvention practices within their territory. Members agree to cooperate fully, consistent with their domestic laws and procedures, in instances of circumvention or alleged circumvention of this Agreement, to establish the relevant facts in the places of import, export and, where applicable, transshipment. It is agreed that such

cooperation, consistent with domestic laws and procedures, will include: investigation of circumvention practices which increase restrained exports to the Member maintaining such restraints; exchange of documents, correspondence, reports and other relevant information to the extent available; and facilitation of plant visits and contacts, upon request and on a case-by-case basis. Members should endeavour to clarify the circumstances of any such instances of circumvention or alleged circumvention, including the respective roles of the exporters or importers involved.

4. Where, as a result of investigation, there is sufficient evidence that circumvention has occurred (*e.g.* where evidence is available concerning the country or place of true origin, and the circumstances of such circumvention), Members agree that appropriate action, to the extent necessary to address the problem, should be taken. Such action may include the denial of entry of goods or, where goods have entered, having due regard to the actual circumstances and the involvement of the country or place of true origin, the adjustment of charges to restraint levels to reflect the true country or place of origin. Also, where there is evidence of the involvement of the territories of the Members through which the goods have been transshipped, such action may include the introduction of restraints with respect to such Members. Any such actions, together with their timing and scope, may be taken after consultations held with a view to arriving at a mutually satisfactory solution between the concerned Members and shall be notified to the TMB with full justification. The Members concerned may agree on other remedies in consultation. Any such agreement shall also be notified to the TMB, and the TMB may make such recommendations to the Members concerned as it deems appropriate. If a mutually satisfactory solution is not reached, any Member concerned may refer the matter to the TMB for prompt review and recommendations.

5. Members note that some cases of circumvention may involve shipments transiting through countries or places with no changes or alterations made to the goods contained in such shipments in the places of transit. They note that it may not be generally practicable for such places of transit to exercise control over such shipments.

6. Members agree that false declaration concerning fibre content, quantities, description or classification of merchandise also frustrates the objective of this Agreement. Where there is evidence that any such false declaration has been made for purposes of circumvention, Members agree that appropriate measures, consistent with domestic laws and procedures, should be taken against the exporters or importers involved. Should any Member believe that this Agreement is being circumvented by such false declaration and that no, or inadequate, administrative measures are being applied to address and/or to take action against such circumvention, that Member should consult promptly with the Member involved with a view to seeking a mutually satisfactory solution. If such a solution is not reached, the matter may be referred by any Member involved to the TMB for recommendations. This provision is not intended to prevent Members from making technical adjustments when inadvertent errors in declarations have been made.

Article 6

1. Members recognize that during the transition period it may be necessary to apply a specific transitional safeguard mechanism (referred to in this Agreement as 'transitional safeguard'). The transitional safeguard may be applied by any Member to products covered by the Annex, except those integrated into GATT 1994 under the provisions of Article 2. Members not maintaining restrictions falling under Article 2 shall notify the TMB within 60 days following the date of entry into force of the WTO Agreement, as to whether or not they wish to retain the right to use the provisions of this Article. Members which have not accepted the Protocols extending the MFA since 1986 shall make such notification within 6 months following the entry into force of the WTO Agreement. The transitional safeguard should be applied as sparingly as possible, consistently with the provisions of this Article and the effective implementation of the integration process under this Agreement.

2. Safeguard action may be taken under this Article when, on the basis of a determination by a Member [A CUSTOMS UNION MAY APPLY A SAFEGUARD MEASURE AS A SINGLE UNIT OR ON BEHALF OF A MEMBER STATE. WHEN A CUSTOMS UNION APPLIES A SAFEGUARD MEASURE AS A SINGLE UNIT, ALL THE REQUIREMENTS FOR THE DETERMINATION OF SERIOUS DAMAGE OR ACTUAL THREAT THEREOF UNDER THIS AGREEMENT SHALL BE BASED ON THE CONDITIONS EXISTING IN THE CUSTOMS UNION AS A WHOLE. WHEN A SAFEGUARD MEASURE IS APPLIED ON BEHALF OF A MEMBER STATE, ALL THE REQUIREMENTS FOR THE DETERMINATION OF SERIOUS DAMAGE, OR ACTUAL THREAT THEREOF, SHALL BE BASED ON THE CONDITIONS EXISTING IN THAT MEMBER STATE AND THE MEASURE SHALL BE LIMITED TO THAT MEMBER STATE.], it is demonstrated that a particular product is being imported into its territory in such increased quantities as to cause serious damage, or actual threat thereof, to the domestic industry producing like and/or directly competitive products. Serious damage or actual threat thereof must demonstrably be caused by such increased quantities in total imports of that product and not by such other factors as technological changes or changes in consumer preference.

3. In making a determination of serious damage, or actual threat thereof, as referred to in paragraph 2, the Member shall examine the effect of those imports on the state of the particular industry, as reflected in changes in such relevant economic variables as output, productivity, utilization of capacity, inventories, market share, exports, wages, employment, domestic prices, profits and investment; none of which, either alone or combined with other factors, can necessarily give decisive guidance.

4. Any measure invoked pursuant to the provisions of this Article shall be applied on a Member-by-Member basis. The Member or Members to whom serious damage, or actual threat thereof, referred to in paragraphs 2 and 3, is attributed, shall be determined on the basis of a sharp and substantial increase in imports, actual or imminent [SUCH AN IMMINENT INCREASE SHALL BE A MEASURABLE ONE AND SHALL NOT BE DETERMINED TO EXIST ON THE BASIS OF ALLEGATION, CONJECTURE OR MERE POSSIBILITY ARISING, FOR EXAMPLE, FROM THE EXISTENCE OF

PRODUCTION CAPACITY IN THE EXPORTING MEMBERS.], from such a Member or Members individually, and on the basis of the level of imports as compared with imports from other sources, market share, and import and domestic prices at a comparable stage of commercial transaction; none of these factors, either alone or combined with other factors, can necessarily give decisive guidance. Such safeguard measure shall not be applied to the exports of any Member whose exports of the particular product are already under restraint under this Agreement.

5. The period of validity of a determination of serious damage or actual threat thereof for the purpose of invoking safeguard action shall not exceed 90 days from the date of initial notification as set forth in paragraph 7.

6. In the application of the transitional safeguard, particular account shall be taken of the interests of exporting Members as set out below:

(a) least-developed country Members shall be accorded treatment significantly more favourable than that provided to the other groups of Members referred to in this paragraph, preferably in all its elements but, at least, on overall terms;

(b) Members whose total volume of textile and clothing exports is small in comparison with the total volume of exports of other Members and who account for only a small percentage of total imports of that product into the importing Member shall be accorded differential and more favourable treatment in the fixing of the economic terms provided in paragraphs 8, 13 and 14. For those suppliers, due account will be taken, pursuant to paragraphs 2 and 3 of Article 1, of the future possibilities for the development of their trade and the need to allow commercial quantities of imports from them;

(c) with respect to wool products from wool-producing developing country Members whose economy and textiles and clothing trade are dependent on the wool sector, whose total textile and clothing exports consist almost exclusively of wool products, and whose volume of textiles and clothing trade is comparatively small in the markets of the importing Members, special consideration shall be given to the export needs of such Members when considering quota levels, growth rates and flexibility;

(d) more favourable treatment shall be accorded to re-imports by a Member of textile and clothing products which that Member has exported to another Member for processing and subsequent reimportation, as defined by the laws and practices of the importing Member, and subject to satisfactory control and certification procedures, when these products are imported from a Member for which this type of trade represents a significant proportion of its total exports of textiles and clothing.

7. The Member proposing to take safeguard action shall seek consultations with the Member or Members which would be affected by such action. The request for consultations shall be accompanied by specific and relevant factual information, as up-to-date as possible, particularly in regard to: (*a*) the factors, referred to in paragraph 3, on which the Member invoking the action has based its determination of the existence of serious damage or actual threat thereof; and (*b*) the factors, referred to in paragraph 4, on the

basis of which it proposes to invoke the safeguard action with respect to the Member or Members concerned. In respect of requests made under this paragraph, the information shall be related, as closely as possible, to identifiable segments of production and to the reference period set out in paragraph 8. The Member invoking the action shall also indicate the specific level at which imports of the product in question from the Member or Members concerned are proposed to be restrained; such level shall not be lower than the level referred to in paragraph 8. The Member seeking consultations shall, at the same time, communicate to the Chairman of the TMB the request for consultations, including all the relevant factual data outlined in paragraphs 3 and 4, together with the proposed restraint level. The Chairman shall inform the members of the TMB of the request for consultations, indicating the requesting Member, the product in question and the Member having received the request. The Member or Members concerned shall respond to this request promptly and the consultations shall be held without delay and normally be completed within 60 days of the date on which the request was received.

8. If, in the consultations, there is mutual understanding that the situation calls for restraint on the exports of the particular product from the Member or Members concerned, the level of such restraint shall be fixed at a level not lower than the actual level of exports or imports from the Member concerned during the 12-month period terminating two months preceding the month in which the request for consultation was made.

9. Details of the agreed restraint measure shall be communicated to the TMB within 60 days from the date of conclusion of the agreement. The TMB shall determine whether the agreement is justified in accordance with the provisions of this Article. In order to make its determination, the TMB shall have available to it the factual data provided to the Chairman of the TMB, referred to in paragraph 7, as well as any other relevant information provided by the Members concerned. The TMB may make such recommendations as it deems appropriate to the Members concerned.

10. If, however, after the expiry of the period of 60 days from the date on which the request for consultations was received, there has been no agreement between the Members, the Member which proposed to take safeguard action may apply the restraint by date of import or date of export, in accordance with the provisions of this Article, within 30 days following the 60-day period for consultations, and at the same time refer the matter to the TMB. It shall be open to either Member to refer the matter to the TMB before the expiry of the period of 60 days. In either case, the TMB shall promptly conduct an examination of the matter, including the determination of serious damage, or actual threat thereof, and its causes, and make appropriate recommendations to the Members concerned within 30 days. In order to conduct such examination, the TMB shall have available to it the factual data provided to the Chairman of the TMB, referred to in paragraph 7, as well as any other relevant information provided by the Members concerned.

11. In highly unusual and critical circumstances, where delay would cause damage which would be difficult to repair, action under paragraph 10 may be taken provisionally on the condition that the request for consultations and notification to the TMB shall be effected within no more than five working days after taking the action. In the case that consultations

do not produce agreement, the TMB shall be notified at the conclusion of consultations, but in any case no later than 60 days from the date of the implementation of the action. The TMB shall promptly conduct an examination of the matter, and make appropriate recommendations to the Members concerned within 30 days. In the case that consultations do produce agreement, Members shall notify the TMB upon conclusion but, in any case, no later than 90 days from the date of the implementation of the action. The TMB may make such recommendations as it deems appropriate to the Members concerned.

12. A Member may maintain measures invoked pursuant to the provisions of this Article: (*a*) for up to three years without extension, or (*b*) until the product is integrated into GATT 1994, whichever comes first.

13. Should the restraint measure remain in force for a period exceeding one year, the level for subsequent years shall be the level specified for the first year increased by a growth rate of not less than 6 per cent per annum, unless otherwise justified to the TMB. The restraint level for the product concerned may be exceeded in either year of any two subsequent years by carry forward and/or carryover of 10 per cent of which carry forward shall not represent more than 5 per cent. No quantitative limits shall be placed on the combined use of carryover, carry forward and the provision of paragraph 14.

14. When more than one product from another Member is placed under restraint under this Article by a Member, the level of restraint agreed, pursuant to the provisions of this Article, for each of these products may be exceeded by 7 per cent, provided that the total exports subject to restraint do not exceed the total of the levels for all products so restrained under this Article, on the basis of agreed common units. Where the periods of application of restraints of these products do not coincide with each other, this provision shall be applied to any overlapping period on a *pro rata* basis.

15. If a safeguard action is applied under this Article to a product for which a restraint was previously in place under the MFA during the 12-month period prior to the entry into force of the WTO Agreement, or pursuant to the provisions of Article 2 or 6, the level of the new restraint shall be the level provided for in paragraph 8 unless the new restraint comes into force within one year of:

(a) the date of notification referred to in paragraph 15 of Article 2 for the elimination of the previous restraint; or

(b) the date of removal of the previous restraint put in place pursuant to the provisions of this Article or of the MFA

in which case the level shall not be less than the higher of (*i*) the level of restraint for the last 12-month period during which the product was under restraint, or (*ii*) the level of restraint provided for in paragraph 8.

16. When a Member which is not maintaining a restraint under Article 2 decides to apply a restraint pursuant to the provisions of this Article, it shall establish appropriate arrangements which: (*a*) take full account of such factors as established tariff classification and quantitative units based on normal commercial practices in export and import transactions, both as regards fibre composition and in terms of competing for the same segment of its domestic market, and (*b*) avoid over-categorization. The request for consultations referred to in paragraphs 7 or 11 shall include full information on such arrangements.

Article 7

1. As part of the integration process and with reference to the specific commitments undertaken by the Members as a result of the Uruguay Round, all Members shall take such actions as may be necessary to abide by GATT 1994 rules and disciplines so as to:

(a) achieve improved access to markets for textile and clothing products through such measures as tariff reductions and bindings, reduction or elimination of non-tariff barriers, and facilitation of customs, administrative and licensing formalities;

(b) ensure the application of policies relating to fair and equitable trading conditions as regards textiles and clothing in such areas as dumping and anti-dumping rules and procedures, subsidies and countervailing measures, and protection of intellectual property rights; and

(c) avoid discrimination against imports in the textiles and clothing sector when taking measures for general trade policy reasons.

Such actions shall be without prejudice to the rights and obligations of Members under GATT 1994.

2. Members shall notify to the TMB the actions referred to in paragraph 1 which have a bearing on the implementation of this Agreement. To the extent that these have been notified to other WTO bodies, a summary, with reference to the original notification, shall be sufficient to fulfil the requirements under this paragraph. It shall be open to any Member to make reverse notifications to the TMB.

3. Where any Member considers that another Member has not taken the actions referred to in paragraph 1, and that the balance of rights and obligations under this Agreement has been upset, that Member may bring the matter before the relevant WTO bodies and inform the TMB. Any subsequent findings or conclusions by the WTO bodies concerned shall form a part of the TMB's comprehensive report.

Article 8

1. In order to supervise the implementation of this Agreement, to examine all measures taken under this Agreement and their conformity therewith, and to take the actions specifically required of it by this Agreement, the Textiles Monitoring Body ('TMB') is hereby established. The TMB shall consist of a Chairman and 10 members. Its membership shall be balanced and broadly representative of the Members and shall provide for rotation of its members at appropriate intervals. The members shall be appointed by Members designated by the Council for Trade in Goods to serve on the TMB, discharging their function on an *ad personam* basis.

2. The TMB shall develop its own working procedures. It is understood, however, that consensus within the TMB does not require the assent or concurrence of members appointed by Members involved in an unresolved issue under review by the TMB.

3. The TMB shall be considered as a standing body and shall meet as necessary to carry out the functions required of it under this Agreement. It shall rely on notifications and information supplied by the Members under the relevant Articles of this Agreement, supplemented by any additional information or necessary details they may submit or it may decide to seek from them. It may also rely on notifications to and reports from other WTO bodies and from such other sources as it may deem appropriate.

4. Members shall afford to each other adequate opportunity for consultations with respect to any matters affecting the operation of this Agreement.

5. In the absence of any mutually agreed solution in the bilateral consultations provided for in this Agreement, the TMB shall, at the request of either Member, and following a thorough and prompt consideration of the matter, make recommendations to the Members concerned.

6. At the request of any Member, the TMB shall review promptly any particular matter which that Member considers to be detrimental to its interests under this Agreement and where consultations between it and the Member or Members concerned have failed to produce a mutually satisfactory solution. On such matters, the TMB may make such observations as it deems appropriate to the Members concerned and for the purposes of the review provided for in paragraph 11.

7. Before formulating its recommendations or observations, the TMB shall invite participation of such Members as may be directly affected by the matter in question.

8. Whenever the TMB is called upon to make recommendations or findings, it shall do so, preferably within a period of 30 days, unless a different time period is specified in this Agreement. All such recommendations or findings shall be communicated to the Members directly concerned. All such recommendations or findings shall also be communicated to the Council for Trade in Goods for its information.

9. The Members shall endeavour to accept in full the recommendations of the TMB, which shall exercise proper surveillance of the implementation of such recommendations.

10. If a Member considers itself unable to conform with the recommendations of the TMB, it shall provide the TMB with the reasons therefor not later than one month after receipt of such recommendations. Following thorough consideration of the reasons given, the TMB shall issue any further recommendations it considers appropriate forthwith. If, after such further recommendations, the matter remains unresolved, either Member may bring the matter before the Dispute Settlement Body and invoke paragraph 2 of Article XXIII of GATT 1994 and the relevant provisions of the Dispute Settlement Understanding.

11. In order to oversee the implementation of this Agreement, the Council for Trade in Goods shall conduct a major review before the end of each stage of the integration process. To assist in this review, the TMB shall, at least five months before the end of each stage, transmit to the Council for Trade in Goods a comprehensive report on the implementation of this Agreement during the stage under review, in particular in matters with regard to the integration process, the application of the transitional safeguard mechanism, and relating to the application of GATT 1994 rules and disciplines as defined in Articles 2, 3, 6 and 7 respectively. The TMB's comprehensive report may include any recommendation as deemed appropriate by the TMB to the Council for Trade in Goods.

12. In the light of its review the Council for Trade in Goods shall by consensus take such decisions as it deems appropriate to ensure that the balance of rights and obligations embodied in this Agreement is not being

impaired. For the resolution of any disputes that may arise with respect to matters referred to in Article 7, the Dispute Settlement Body may authorize, without prejudice to the final date set out under Article 9, an adjustment to paragraph 14 of Article 2, for the stage subsequent to the review, with respect to any Member found not to be complying with its obligations under this Agreement.

Article 9

This Agreement and all restrictions thereunder shall stand terminated on the first day of the 121st month that the WTO Agreement is in effect, on which date the textiles and clothing sector shall be fully integrated into GATT 1994. There shall be no extension of this Agreement.

ANNEX

LIST OF PRODUCTS COVERED BY THIS AGREEMENT

1. This Annex lists textile and clothing products defined by Harmonized Commodity Description and Coding System (HS) codes at the six-digit level.

2. Actions under the safeguard provisions in Article 6 will be taken with respect to particular textile and clothing products and not on the basis of the HS lines *per se*.

3. Actions under the safeguard provisions in Article 6 of this Agreement shall not apply to:

(a) developing country Members' exports of handloom fabrics of the cottage industry, or hand-made cottage industry products made of such handloom fabrics, or traditional folklore handicraft textile and clothing products, provided that such products are properly certified under arrangements established between the Members concerned;

(b) historically traded textile products which were internationally traded in commercially significant quantities prior to 1982, such as bags, sacks, carpetbacking, cordage, luggage, mats, mattings and carpets typically made from fibres such as jute, coir, sisal, abaca, maguey and henequen;

(c) products made of pure silk.

For such products, the provisions of Article XIX of GATT 1994, as interpreted by the Agreement on Safeguards, shall be applicable.

PRODUCTS WITHIN SECTION XI (TEXTILES AND TEXTILE ARTICLES) OF THE HARMONIZED COMMODITY DESCRIPTION AND CODING SYSTEM (HS) NOMENCLATURE

[A LIST FOLLOWS]"

AGREEMENT ON TECHNICAL BARRIERS TO TRADE
[FOUND IN CHAPTER IX]

AGREEMENT ON IMPLEMENTATION OF GATT ARTICLE VI
[FOUND IN CHAPTER X]

AGREEMENT ON IMPLEMENTATION OF GATT ARTICLE VIII

[FOUND IN CHAPTER VIII]

AGREEMENT ON PRESHIPMENT INSPECTION
[FOUND IN CHAPTER IX]

AGREEMENT ON RULES OF ORIGIN
[FOUND IN CHAPTER IX]

AGREEMENT ON IMPORT LICENSING PROCEDURES
[FOUND IN CHAPTER IX]

AGREEMENT ON SUBSIDIES AND COUNTERVAILING MEASURES
[FOUND IN CHAPTER X]

DECISION ON MEASURES IN FAVOR OF LEAST-DEVELOPED COUNTRIES
[FOUND IN CHAPTER VI]

Decision on Notification Procedures—the Text

DECISION ON NOTIFICATION PROCEDURES

Ministers decide to recommend adoption by the Ministerial Conference of the decision on improvement and review of notification procedures set out below.

Members,

Desiring to improve the operation of notification procedures under the Agreement Establishing the World Trade Organization (hereinafter referred to as the 'WTO Agreement'), and thereby to contribute to the transparency of Members' trade policies and to the effectiveness of surveillance arrangements established to that end;

Recalling obligations under the WTO Agreement to publish and notify, including obligations assumed under the terms of specific protocols of accession, waivers, and other agreements entered into by Members;

Agree as follows:

I. *General obligation to notify*

Members affirm their commitment to obligations under the Multilateral Trade Agreements and, where applicable, the Plurilateral Trade Agreements, regarding publication and notification.

Members recall their undertakings set out in the Understanding Regarding Notification, Consultation, Dispute Settlement and Surveillance adopted on 28 November 1979 (BISD 26S/210). With regard to their undertaking therein to notify, to the maximum extent possible, their adoption of trade measures affecting the operation of GATT 1994, such notification itself being without prejudice to views on the consistency of measures with or their relevance to rights and obligations under the Multilateral Trade Agreements and, where applicable, the Plurilateral Trade Agreements, Members agree to be guided, as appropriate, by the annexed list of measures. Members therefore agree that the introduction or modification of such measures is subject to the notification requirements of the 1979 Understanding.

II. *Central registry of notifications*

A central registry of notifications shall be established under the responsibility of the Secretariat. While Members will continue to follow existing notification procedures, the Secretariat shall ensure that the central registry records such elements of the information provided on the measure by the Member concerned as its purpose, its trade coverage, and the requirement under which it has been notified. The central registry shall cross-reference its records of notifications by Member and obligation.

The central registry shall inform each Member annually of the regular notification obligations to which that Member will be expected to respond in the course of the following year.

The central registry shall draw the attention of individual Members to regular notification requirements which remain unfulfilled.

Information in the central registry regarding individual notifications shall be made available on request to any Member entitled to receive the notification concerned.

III. *Review of notification obligations and procedures*

The Council for Trade in Goods will undertake a review of notification obligations and procedures under the Agreements in Annex 1A of the WTO Agreement. The review will be carried out by a working group, membership in which will be open to all Members. The group will be established immediately after the date of entry into force of the WTO Agreement.

The terms of reference of the working group will be:

— to undertake a thorough review of all existing notification obligations of Members established under the Agreements in Annex 1A of the WTO Agreement, with a view to simplifying, standardizing and consolidating these obligations to the greatest extent practicable, as well as to improving compliance with these obligations, bearing in mind the overall objective of improving the transparency of the trade policies of Members and the effectiveness of surveillance arrangements established to this end, and also bearing in mind the possible need of some developing country Members for assistance in meeting their notification obligations;

— to make recommendations to the Council for Trade in Goods not later than two years after the entry into force of the WTO Agreement.

ANNEX

INDICATIVE LIST [THIS LIST DOES NOT ALTER EXISTING NOTIFICATION REQUIREMENTS IN THE MULTILATERAL TRADE AGREEMENTS IN ANNEX 1A TO THE WTO AGREEMENT OR, WHERE APPLICABLE, THE PLURILATERAL TRADE AGREEMENTS IN ANNEX 4

OF THE WTO AGREEMENT.] **OF NOTIFIABLE MEASURES**

Tariffs (including range and scope of bindings, GSP provisions, rates applied to members of free-trade areas/customs unions, other preferences)

Tariff quotas and surcharges

Quantitative restrictions, including voluntary export restraints and orderly marketing arrangements affecting imports

Other non-tariff measures such as licensing and mixing requirements; variable levies

Customs valuation

Rules of origin

Government procurement

Technical barriers

Safeguard actions

Anti-dumping actions

Countervailing actions

Export taxes

Export subsidies, tax exemptions and concessionary export financing

Free-trade zones, including in-bond manufacturing

Export restrictions, including voluntary export restraints and orderly marketing arrangements

Other government assistance, including subsidies, tax exemptions

Role of state-trading enterprises

Foreign exchange controls related to imports and exports

Government-mandated countertrade

Any other measure covered by the Multilateral Trade Agreements in Annex 1A to the WTO Agreement"

DECISION ON MEASURES CONCERNING THE POSSIBLE NEGATIVE EFFECTS OF THE REFORM PROGRAMME ON LEAST-DEVELOPED AND NET FOOD IMPORTING DEVELOPING COUNTRIES

[FOUND IN CHAPTER VI]

Decision on Notification of First Integration Under Article 2.6 of the Agreement on Textiles and Clothing—the Text

"DECISION ON NOTIFICATION OF FIRST INTEGRATION UNDER ARTICLE 2.6 OF THE AGREEMENT ON TEXTILES AND CLOTHING

Ministers agree that the participants maintaining restrictions falling under paragraph 1 of Article 2 of the Agreement on Textiles and Clothing shall notify full details of the actions to be taken pursuant to paragraph 6 of Article 2 of that Agreement to the GATT Secretariat not later than 1 October 1994. The GATT Secretariat shall promptly circulate these notifications to the other participants for information. These notifications will be made available to the Textiles Monitoring Body, when established, for the purposes of paragraph 21 of Article 2 of the Agreement on Textiles and Clothing."

DECISION ON PROPOSED UNDERSTANDING ON WTO-ISO STANDARDS INFORMATION SYSTEM [FOUND IN CHAPTER IX]

DECISION ON ANTI-CIRCUMVENTION [FOUND IN CHAPTER X]

DECISION ON REVIEW OF THE ISO/IEC INFORMATION CENTRE PUBLICATION [FOUND IN CHAPTER IX]

DECISION ON REVIEW OF ARTICLE 17.6 OF THE AGREEMENT ON IMPLEMENTATION OF GATT'S ARTICLE VI [FOUND IN CHAPTER X]

Declaration on Dispute Settlement Pursuant to Agreement on Implementation of GATT's Article Part V of ASCD—the Text

"DECLARATION ON DISPUTE SETTLEMENT PURSUANT TO THE AGREEMENT ON IMPLEMENTATION OF ARTICLE VI OF THE GENERAL AGREEMENT ON TARIFFS AND TRADE 1994 OR PART V OF THE AGREEMENT

ON SUBSIDIES AND COUNTERVAILING MEASURES

Ministers recognize, with respect to dispute settlement pursuant to the Agreement on Implementation of Article VI of GATT 1994 or Part V of the Agreement on Subsidies and Countervailing Measures, the need for the consistent resolution of disputes arising from anti-dumping and countervailing duty measures."

DECISION REGARDING CASES WHERE CUSTOMS ADMINISTRATIONS HAVE REASONS TO DOUBT THE TRUTH OR ACCURACY OF THE DECLARED VALUE [FOUND IN CHAPTER VIII]

DECISION ON TEXTS RELATING TO MINIMUM VALUES AND IMPORTS BY SOLE AGENTS, SOLE DISTRIBUTORS AND SOLE CONCESSIONAIRES [FOUND IN CHAPTER VIII]

Decision on the Application and Review of the Understanding on Rules and Procedures Governing the Settlement of Disputes—the Text

"DECISION ON THE APPLICATION AND REVIEW OF THE UNDERSTANDING ON RULES AND PROCEDURES GOVERNING THE SETTLEMENT OF DISPUTES

Ministers,

Recalling the Decision of 22 February 1994 that existing rules and procedures of GATT 1947 in the field of dispute settlement shall remain in effect until the date of entry into force of the Agreement Establishing the World Trade Organization,

Invite the relevant Councils and Committees to decide that they shall remain in operation for the purpose of dealing with any dispute for which the request for consultation was made before that date;

Invite the Ministerial Conference to complete a full review of dispute settlement rules and procedures under the World Trade Organization within four years after the entry into force of the Agreement Establishing the World Trade Organization, and to take a decision on the occasion of its first meeting after the completion of the review, whether to continue, modify or terminate such dispute settlement rules and procedures."

Chapter VIII: WTO/GATT Prescribed Methods of Customs Valuation

Valuation and Tariffs

For importers, the process of estimating the value of a product entering customs is equally as critical to what they must ultimately pay upon importation as is the tariff duty rate levied by customs. Almost all import duties are assessed based on *ad valorem* or compound rates of duty. Customs officers must, in all such cases, first determine the value of imported merchandise if they are to levy tariffs on it. That valuation determines the level of import duties assessed. The customs value on imported goods is also an essential element for trade statistics, for monitoring quantitative restrictions, for tariff preferences, and for collecting internal national taxes, *inter alia*.

What importers want is a standard method of customs valuation that is fair, uniform, and neutral while reflecting commercial realities and which does not permit the use of arbitrary or fictitious customs values. Determining such values is often difficult, even when accurate and fair valuations are sought. There are many possible factors that may be included as part of the cumulative valuation, such as packing, transportation costs, agents' fees and commissions, etc.; these may be only determinable in foreign currencies which must then be translated into a national currency using any number of methods or rates of conversion; and the methods for making the valuation may include inferential or subjective determinations and other methodologies subject to challenge for lack of definitiveness and objectivity and also subject to abusive implementation by some customs officers or by the customs service generally.

Moreover, countries frequently do not really wish to arrive at objectively correct valuations. On the contrary, they may wish to maintain the maximum flexibility in establishing a valuation—and thereby in determining an applicable level of tariffs—in order to perpetuate those policies of protectionism and discrimination among importers and imports that GATT is intended to eliminate. As part of that effort, they may also make the regulations articulating their valuation methodologies so vague or unclear as to be opaque or may—in part or in whole—restrict the public availability of such regulations so that importers may not readily calculate, before making an importation, the applicable tariff levels nor may those who would challenge the objectivity of the methodologies cite the regulations in support of their challenges.

In addition, the difficulty of making any valuation is increased because of the desire of the importer to reduce its liability for import tariffs by reducing the importer's professed value of the imported item. It is not unknown for importers and their agents to structure an import transaction so as to reduce the calculable value of the imported item or to obscure the existence or worth of the various inputs that go into such calculation. Of course, some importers simply lie to customs officials about the value of imports or their inputs. In many cases, assertions of valuation for the same product will differ from place to place and from filing to filing so as to maximize benefits and reduce liabilities for the importer and/or other parties under various taxes, duties, and fees. This practice is particularly prevalent where the importer, the foreign provider, and/or other providers of the product are in some manner related entities.

Multilateral Institutions Involved in Valuation Standards

A new valuation code was one of the major products of the 1969 Tokyo Round of negotiations under GATT 1947. It essentially designated acceptable valuation methodologies, established a hierarchy of use preference among them, and specified how currency conversions were to be made. This valuation code was not imposed upon all GATT 1947 members but only upon those which had become specially signatories to the valuation code. GATT 1994 largely adopted whole the Tokyo Round Valuation Code Plurilateral Agreement as part of the WTO Agreement's multilateral system in its Article VII.

The implementation agreement of Article VII established a Committee on Customs Valuation composed of a representative from each WTO member so they could consult on matters relating to the administration of the customs valuation system and the furtherance of WTO Agreement objectives relating to valuation. The implementation agreement also established a Technical Committee on Customs Valuation under the auspices of the WCO with a view to ensuring, at the technical level, uniformity in interpretation and application of the implementation agreement's valuation provisions. The responsibilities of the Technical Committee include advising on specific technical matters as requested by WTO members or by a panel in a dispute. Its decisions are issued in the form of Advisory Opinions, Commentaries, Case Studies, Studies, *etc.*, which are published in the *Compendium of Customs Valuation*. CCC/WCO provides service to the WTO Technical Committee on Customs Valuation by organizing meetings, preparing working documents and reports, etc.; conducts technical assistance missions, such as training courses, workshops, seminars, and expert missions; prepares and offers to the publics publications relevant to customs valuation; provides technical advice upon request on specific valuation questions to WTO members' customs administrations; and develops specific projects within the mandate of the WTO Agreement and the WCO customs/business relationship.

The ICC which has sat on the Technical Committee since 1979 as an observer, explains to the committee specific aspects of commercial practice as well as offering its views and advice on specific technical issues. In May 2000, the WCO and ICC issued a joint statement promoting global application of the WTO Customs Valuation Agreement.

GATT/WTO Valuation Methods

The WTO Agreement provides a set of valuation rules, to a degree expanding on and giving greater precision to the provisions on customs valuation in GATT 1947's plurilateral Valuation Code. It does so under GATT Article VII and notes to that article, an agreement on implementation of that article, and some other understandings and documents whose full text is reproduced below. A related Uruguay Round ministerial decision gives customs administrations the right to request further information in cases where they have reason to doubt the accuracy of the declared value of imported goods. If the administration maintains a reasonable doubt, despite any additional information, it may be deemed that the customs value of the imported goods cannot be determined on the basis of the declared value.

Customs duties can be designated in either specific or *ad valorem* terms or as a mix of the two. With a specific duty, a specified sum is charged for a quantitative description of the good, such as per item or per ton, and the customs value of the good does not need to be determined since the duty is not based on the value of the good but on other criteria. In this case, no rules on customs valuation are needed and WTO's valuation rules are inapplicable. In contrast, an *ad valorem* duty depends on the value of a good. Under this system, the customs valuation is multiplied by an *ad valorem* percentage rate of duty in order to arrive at the amount of duty payable on an imported item.

Customs valuation is the customs procedure applied to determine the customs value of imported goods. If the rate of duty is *ad valorem*, the customs value is essential to determine the duty to be paid on an imported good. GATT 1947's Article VII established the general principles for an international system of customs valuation. It stipulated that the value for customs purposes of imported merchandise should be based on the actual value of the imported merchandise on which duty is assessed, or of like merchandise, and should not be based on the value of merchandise of national origin or on arbitrary or fictitious values. Although Article VII also contained a definition of "actual value," it still permitted the use of widely differing methods of valuing goods. In addition, "grandfather clauses" permitted continuation of old standards that fell below even the very general new standard.

GATT 1994's revision of the Tokyo Round Valuation Code does not contain obligations concerning valuation for purposes of determining export duties or quota administration based on the value of goods, nor does it lay down conditions for the valuation of goods for internal taxation or foreign exchange control. It does prescribe that customs valuation must, except in specified circumstances, be based on the actual price of the goods to be valued. That value is generally shown on the invoice. This price, plus adjustments for certain elements listed in Article 8, equals the transaction value, which constitutes the first and most important method of valuation referred to in the Article VII. When no transaction value exists or where the transaction value is not acceptable as the customs value because the price has been distorted as a result of certain conditions, the implementing agreement lays down five other methods of customs valuation, to be applied in the prescribed hierarchical order. The sequence of methods 4 and 5 below can be switched at the request of the importer but not at the discretion of the customs officer. These six methods are described briefly below.

METHOD 1—TRANSACTION VALUE The price actually paid or payable is the total payment made or to be made by the buyer to or for the benefit of the seller for the imported goods, and includes all payments made as a condition of sale of the imported goods by the buyer to the seller, or by the buyer to a third party to satisfy an obligation of the seller. The customs value is the transaction value if all of the following conditions have been fulfilled: (a) there must be evidence of a sale for export to the country of importation (*i.e.*, commercial invoices, contracts, purchase orders, etc.); (b) there must be no restriction on the disposition or use of the goods by the buyer, other than restrictions which (i) are imposed or required by law in the country of importation, (ii) are limited to the geographic area in which the goods may be resold, or (iii) do not substantially affect the value of the goods; (c) the sale or price must not be subject to conditions or considerations for which a value cannot be determined with respect to the goods being valued (examples are given in the implementing agreement's Annex I, Note to Article 1:1(b)), *e.g.*, (i) the seller establishes the price of the imported goods on the condition that the buyer will also buy other goods in specified quantities, (ii) the price of the imported goods is dependent upon the price or prices at which the buyer sells other goods to the seller, or (iii) the price is established on the basis of a form of payment extraneous to the imported goods; (d) no part of the proceeds of any subsequent resale, disposal or use of the goods by the buyer may accrue directly or indirectly to the seller, unless adjustment can be made in accordance with provisions in the implementing agreement's Article 8; (e) sufficient information is available to enable the specific adjustments to be made under the implementing agreement's Article 8 to the price paid or payable such as (i) commissions and brokerage, except buying commissions, (ii) packing and container costs and charges, (iii) assists, (iv) royalties and license fees, (v) subsequent proceeds, and (vi) the cost of transport, insurance and related charges up to the place of importation if the member bases evaluation on a c.i.f. basis, **but not** (vi) costs incurred after importation (*e.g.*, duties, transport, construction or assembly; see the implementing agreement's Annex I, Note 3 to Article 1); and (f) the buyer and seller are not related, but even if so, the use of the transaction value is acceptable if the importer demonstrates that (i) the relationship did not influence the price, or (ii) the transaction value closely approximates a test value.

The definition of related persons is found in the implementing agreement's Article 15. It says that persons are to be deemed to be related only if (i) they are officers or directors of one another's businesses, (ii) they are legally recognized partners in business, (iii) they are employer and employee, (iv) any person directly or indirectly owns, controls or holds 5% or more of the outstanding voting stock or shares of both of them, (v) one of them directly or indirectly controls the other (the Interpretative Note to Article 15 of the implementing agreement provides that one person shall be deemed to control another when the former is legally or operationally in a position to exercise restraint or direction over the latter and further states that "persons" includes legal persons, where this is appropriate), (vi) both of them are directly or indirectly controlled by a third person, or (vii) they are members of the same family.

Customs valuation based on the transaction value method is largely based on documentary input from the importer. Article 17 of the implementing agreement confirms that customs administrations have the right to "satisfy themselves as to the truth or accuracy of any statement, document or declaration." A "Decision Regarding Cases Where Customs Administrations Have Reasons to Doubt the Truth or Accuracy of the Declared Value" taken by the Committee on Customs

Valuation pursuant to a Ministerial Decision at Marrakech spells out the procedures to be observed in such cases. As a first step, customs may ask the importer to provide further explanation that the declared value represents the total amount actually paid or payable for the imported goods. If the reasonable doubt still exists after reception of further information (or in absence of a response), customs may decide that the value cannot be determined according to the transaction value method. Before a final decision is taken, customs must communicate its reasoning to the importer, who, in turn, must be given reasonable time to respond. In addition, the reasoning of the final decision must be communicated to the importer in writing.

METHOD—2: TRANSACTION VALUE OF IDENTICAL GOODS The transaction value is calculated in the same manner on identical goods if the goods are (i) the same in all respects including physical characteristics, quality, and reputation, (ii) produced in the same country as the goods being valued, and (iii) produced by the producer of the goods being valued. For this method to be used, the goods must be sold for export to the same country of importation as the goods being valued. The goods must also be exported at or about the same time as the goods being valued. Some exceptions to the above are accepted. Specifically, prescribed exceptions may be applied in the following cases (i) where there are no identical goods produced by the same person in the country of production of the goods being valued, identical goods produced by a different person in the same country may be taken into account, and (ii) where minor differences in appearance would not preclude goods which otherwise conform to the definitions from being regarded as identical, they may deemed to be identical. The definition excludes imported goods which incorporate engineering, artwork etc., provided by the buyer to the producer of goods free of charge or at a reduced cost, undertaken in the country of importation for which no adjustment has been made under the implementing agreement's Article 8.

METHOD 3—TRANSACTION VALUE OF SIMILAR GOODS The transaction value is calculated in the same manner on similar goods which are (i) goods closely resembling the goods being valued in terms of component materials and characteristics, (ii) goods capable of performing the same functions and are commercially interchangeable with the goods being valued, and (iii) goods produced in the same country as and by the producer of the goods being valued. For this method to be used, the goods must be sold to the same country of importation as the goods being valued and the goods must be exported at or about the same time as the goods being valued.

METHOD 4—DEDUCTIVE VALUE The implementing agreement provides that when customs value cannot be determined on the basis of the transaction value of the imported goods or identical or similar goods, it will be determined on the basis of the unit price at which the imported goods or identical or similar goods are sold to an unrelated buyer in the greatest aggregate quantity in the country of importation. The buyer and the seller in the importing country must not be related and the sale must take place at or about the time of importation of the goods being valued. If no sale took place at or about the time of importation, it is permitted to use sales up to 90 days after importation of the goods being valued. Under the implementing agreement's Article 5.1, the unit price at which the imported goods or identical or similar imported goods are sold in the greatest aggregate quantity is to be the basis for establishing the customs value. The greatest aggregate quantity is, according to the Interpretative Note to that Article, the price at which the greatest number of units is sold to unrelated persons at the first commercial level after importation at which such sales take place. To determine the greatest aggregate quantity all sales at a given price are taken together and the sum of all the units of goods sold at that price is compared to the sum of all the units of goods sold at any other price. The greatest number of units sold at one price represents the greatest aggregate quantity.

Since the starting point in calculating deductive value is the sale price in the country of importation, various deductions are necessary to reduce that price to the relevant customs value. They are (a) commissions usually paid or agreed to be paid, the sum of profits and general expenses added in connection with sales must also be deducted, (b) the usual transport costs and corresponding insurance are to be deducted from the price of the goods when these costs are usually incurred within the country of importation, (c) the customs duties and other national taxes payable in the country of importation by reason of the importation or sale of the goods are also to be deducted, and (d) value added by assembly or further processing, when applicable.

METHOD 5—COMPUTED VALUE Computed value is the most difficult and rarely used method. It determines the customs value on the basis of the cost of production of the goods being valued, plus an amount for profit and general expenses usually reflected in sales from the country of exportation to the country of importation of goods of the same class or kind. Computed value is the total of each of a number of elements. Each is described below.

The first element is the cost or value of materials and fabrication or other processing employed in producing the imported goods. Materials might include raw materials, costs to get the raw materials to the place of production; subassemblies, and prefabricated components that will eventually be assembled. Fabrication would include the costs for labor, any costs for assembly when there is an assembly operation instead of manufacturing process, and indirect costs such as factory supervision, plant maintenance, and overtime. Cost or value is to be determined on the basis of information relating to the production of the goods being valued, supplied by or on behalf of the producer. If not otherwise included, packing costs and charges, assists, engineering work, artwork, etc. undertaken in the country of importation are to be added.

The second element is profit and general expenses usually reflected in export sales to the country of importation by producers in the country of exportation (on the basis of information supplied by the producer) of goods of the same class or kind. The latter phrase means goods which fall within a group or range of goods produced by a particular industry or industry sector and includes identical or similar goods. The amount of profit and general expenses has to be taken as a whole (*i.e.*, the sum of the two). General expenses would include but not be limited to rent, electricity, water, and legal fees.

The final element is for other expenses that should be added to the price. These could include such things as the cost of transport of the imported goods to the port or place of importation; loading, unloading and handling charges associated with the transport of the imported goods to the port or place of importation; and the cost of insurance.

METHOD 6—REASONABLE MEANS OR "FALL-BACK" METHOD Customs value determinations may be based on "reasonable means consistent with the principles and general provisions of the Agreement, Article VII GATT and on the basis of available data" in the country of importation when attempts to apply all other methods of determination are unavailing. To the degree possible, this method should be based on previously determined values and methods with a reasonable degree of flexibility in their application. Under the fall-back method, the customs value must not be based on (a) the selling price of goods in the country of importation, *i.e.*, the sale price of goods manufactured in the importing country; (b) a system which provides for the acceptance for customs purposes of the higher of two alternative values since it is the lowest of these that should be used); (c) the price of goods on the domestic market of the country of exportation since valuation on this basis would go against the principle stated in the Preamble to the implementation agreement that "valuation procedures should not be used to combat dumping"; (d) the cost of production other than computed values which have been determined for identical or similar goods since valuation must be arrived at on the basis of data available in the country of importation; (e) the price of goods for export to a third country since two export markets are always to be treated as separate and the price to one should not control the customs value in the other; (f) minimum customs value unless a developing country has taken the exception which allows for use of minimum values; or (g) arbitrary or fictitious values because the valuation system is intended to eliminate just such practices.

SPECIAL DISPENSATIONS FOR UNDERDEVELOPED COUNTRIES Implementing agreement Article 20.1 allows developing country members who were not parties to the Tokyo Round Valuation Code to delay application of the provisions of the implementing agreement for a period of five years from the date of entry into force of the WTO Agreement for the member concerned. Article 20.2 allows such members to delay application of the computed value method for a period not exceeding three years following their application of all other provisions of the implementing agreement, effectively permitting those members to delay implementing the computed value method a total of 8 years. Paragraph 1 of Annex III of the implementing agreement allows developing country members for whom the five-year delay in the application of the provisions of the implementing agreement provided for in Article 20.1 is insufficient to request, before the end of the five-year period, an extension of such a period and it was understood that other members will give sympathetic consideration to such a request in cases where the developing country member in question can show good cause for that extended delay. Paragraph 2 of Annex III of the implementing agreement provides that developing country members may make a reservation to retain an already-existing system of officially established minimum values on a limited and transitional basis under such terms and conditions as may be agreed to by the Committee on Customs Valuation even though minimum prices are prohibited under the implementing agreement. Paragraph 3 of Annex III of the implementing agreement allows developing country members the right to make a reservation permitting them to refuse the request of importers, which importers may do under Article 4 of the implementing agreement, to reverse the order of the deductive and computed value methods. Paragraph 4 of Annex III of the implementing agreement allows developing country members the right to value the goods under the deductive method even if the goods have undergone further processing in the country of importation, whether or not the importer so requests. Under Article 20.3, developed country members must furnish, on mutually agreed terms, technical assistance to developing country members that so request it. On this basis, developed country members must draw up programs of technical assistance which may include, *inter alia*, training of personnel, assistance in preparing implementation measures, access to sources of information regarding customs valuation methodology, and advice on the application of the provisions of the implementing agreement.

The GATT/WTO Valuation Provisions

The earlier GATT 1947 separate Valuation Code was fully integrated into GATT 1994 and made an obligation of all GATT 1994 participants. Although developing countries may significantly delay implementation of the GATT valuation code and may to a degree permanently evade some of its requirements, GATT 1994's inclusion of the valuation code as an obligation of all GATT members has great importance as a device to insure the fair and transparent determination of valuation of goods for customs purposes by virtually all the nations of the world and particularly by almost all its major industrial and trading countries. The original Valuation Code of 1969 and its more general implementation in 1994 will eliminate or have eliminated most of the protectionist and subjective valuation methods used by some countries. For certain items—such as shipping containers—special international provisions and conventions may apply.

GATT 1947 Article VII (Valuation for Customs Purposes) and its Annex I Notes and Supplementary Provisions—the Texts

[***asterisks** below mark the portions of the text which should be read in conjunction with notes and supplementary provisions in Annex I to the Agreement.]

"Article VII
Valuation for Customs Purposes

1. The contracting parties recognize the validity of the general principles of valuation set forth in the following paragraphs of this Article, and they undertake to give effect to such principles, in respect of all products subject to duties or other charges* or restrictions on importation and exportation based upon or regulated in any manner by value. Moreover, they shall, upon a request by another contracting party review the operation of any of their laws or regulations relating to value for customs purposes in the light of these principles. The CONTRACTING PARTIES may request from contracting parties reports on steps taken by them in pursuance of the provisions of this Article.

2.

(*a*) The value for customs purposes of imported merchandise should be based on the actual value of the imported merchandise on which duty is assessed, or of like merchandise, and should not be based on the value of merchandise of national origin or on arbitrary or fictitious values.*

(*b*) 'Actual value' should be the price at which, at a time and place determined by the legislation of the country of importation, such or like merchandise is sold or offered for sale in the ordinary course of trade under fully competitive conditions. To the extent to which the price of such or like merchandise is governed by the quantity in a particular transaction, the price to be considered should uniformly be related to either (i) comparable quantities, or (ii) quantities not less favourable to importers than those in which the greater volume of the merchandise is sold in the trade between the countries of exportation and importation.*

(*c*) When the actual value is not ascertainable in accordance with sub-paragraph (*b*) of this paragraph, the value for customs purposes should be based on the nearest ascertainable equivalent of such value.*

3. The value for customs purposes of any imported product should not include the amount of any internal tax, applicable within the country of origin or export, from which the imported product has been exempted or has been or will be relieved by means of refund.

4.

(*a*) Except as otherwise provided for in this paragraph, where it is necessary for the purposes of paragraph 2 of this Article for a contracting party to convert into its own currency a price expressed in the currency of another country, the conversion rate of exchange to be used shall be based, for each currency involved, on the par value as established pursuant to the Articles of Agreement of the International Monetary Fund or on the rate of exchange recognized by the Fund, or on the par value established in accordance with a special exchange agreement entered into pursuant to Article XV of this Agreement.

(*b*) Where no such established par value and no such recognized rate of exchange exist, the conversion rate shall reflect effectively the current value of such currency in commercial transactions.

(*c*) The CONTRACTING PARTIES, in agreement with the International Monetary Fund, shall formulate rules governing the conversion by contracting parties of any foreign currency in respect of which multiple rates of exchange are maintained consistently with the Articles of Agreement of the International Monetary Fund. Any contracting party may apply such rules in respect of such foreign currencies for the purposes of paragraph 2 of this Article as an alternative to the use of par values. Until such rules are adopted by the CONTRACTING PARTIES, any contracting party may employ, in respect of any such foreign currency, rules of conversion for the purposes of paragraph 2 of this Article which are designed to reflect effectively the value of such foreign currency in commercial transactions.

(*d*) Nothing in this paragraph shall be construed to require any contracting party to alter the method of converting currencies for customs purposes which is applicable in its territory on the date of this Agreement, if such alteration would have the effect of increasing generally the amounts of duty payable.

5. The bases and methods for determining the value of products subject to duties or other charges or restrictions based upon or regulated in any manner by value should be stable and should be given sufficient publicity

to enable traders to estimate, with a reasonable degree of certainty, the value for customs purposes."

"**Ad Article VII**
Paragraph 1

The expression 'or other charges' is not to be regarded as including internal taxes or equivalent charges imposed on or in connection with imported products.

Paragraph 2

1. It would be in conformity with Article VII to presume that 'actual value' may be represented by the invoice price, plus any non-included charges for legitimate costs which are proper elements of 'actual value' and plus any abnormal discount or other reduction from the ordinary competitive price.

2. It would be in conformity with Article VII, paragraph 2 (*b*), for a contracting party to construe the phrase 'in the ordinary course of trade ... under fully competitive conditions,' as excluding any transaction wherein the buyer and seller are not independent of each other and price is not the sole consideration.

3. The standard of 'fully competitive conditions' permits a contracting party to exclude from consideration prices involving special discounts limited to exclusive agents.

4. The wording of sub-paragraphs (*a*) and (*b*) permits a contracting party to determine the value for customs purposes uniformly either (1) on the basis of a particular exporter's prices of the imported merchandise, or (2) on the basis of the general price level of like merchandise."

Agreement on Implementation of GATT Article VII—the Text

"AGREEMENT ON IMPLEMENTATION OF ARTICLE VII OF THE GENERAL AGREEMENT ON TARIFFS AND TRADE 1994

GENERAL INTRODUCTORY COMMENTARY

1. The primary basis for customs value under this Agreement is 'transaction value' as defined in Article 1. Article 1 is to be read together with Article 8 which provides, *inter alia*, for adjustments to the price actually paid or payable in cases where certain specific elements which are considered to form a part of the value for customs purposes are incurred by the buyer but are not included in the price actually paid or payable for the imported goods. Article 8 also provides for the inclusion in the transaction value of certain considerations which may pass from the buyer to the seller in the form of specified goods or services rather than in the form of money. Articles 2 through 7 provide methods of determining the customs value whenever it cannot be determined under the provisions of Article 1.

2. Where the customs value cannot be determined under the provisions of Article 1 there should normally be a process of consultation

between the customs administration and importer with a view to arriving at a basis of value under the provisions of Article 2 or 3. It may occur, for example, that the importer has information about the customs value of identical or similar imported goods which is not immediately available to the customs administration in the port of importation. On the other hand, the customs administration may have information about the customs value of identical or similar imported goods which is not readily available to the importer. A process of consultation between the two parties will enable information to be exchanged, subject to the requirements of commercial confidentiality, with a view to determining a proper basis of value for customs purposes.

3. Articles 5 and 6 provide two bases for determining the customs value where it cannot be determined on the basis of the transaction value of the imported goods or of identical or similar imported goods. Under paragraph 1 of Article 5 the customs value is determined on the basis of the price at which the goods are sold in the condition as imported to an unrelated buyer in the country of importation. The importer also has the right to have goods which are further processed after importation valued under the provisions of Article 5 if the importer so requests. Under Article 6 the customs value is determined on the basis of the computed value. Both these methods present certain difficulties and because of this the importer is given the right, under the provisions of Article 4, to choose the order of application of the two methods.

4. Article 7 sets out how to determine the customs value in cases where it cannot be determined under the provisions of any of the preceding Articles.

Members,

Having regard to the Multilateral Trade Negotiations;

Desiring to further the objectives of GATT 1994 and to secure additional benefits for the international trade of developing countries;

Recognizing the importance of the provisions of Article VII of GATT 1994 and desiring to elaborate rules for their application in order to provide greater uniformity and certainty in their implementation;

Recognizing the need for a fair, uniform and neutral system for the valuation of goods for customs purposes that precludes the use of arbitrary or fictitious customs values;

Recognizing that the basis for valuation of goods for customs purposes should, to the greatest extent possible, be the transaction value of the goods being valued;

Recognizing that customs value should be based on simple and equitable criteria consistent with commercial practices and that valuation procedures should be of general application without distinction between sources of supply;

Recognizing that valuation procedures should not be used to combat dumping;

Hereby *agree* as follows:

PART I

RULES ON CUSTOMS VALUATION

Article 1

1. The customs value of imported goods shall be the transaction value, that is the price actually paid or payable for the goods when sold for export to the country of importation adjusted in accordance with the provisions of Article 8, provided:

(a) that there are no restrictions as to the disposition or use of the goods by the buyer other than restrictions which:

(i) are imposed or required by law or by the public authorities in the country of importation;

(ii) limit the geographical area in which the goods may be resold; or

(iii) do not substantially affect the value of the goods;

(b) that the sale or price is not subject to some condition or consideration for which a value cannot be determined with respect to the goods being valued;

(c) that no part of the proceeds of any subsequent resale, disposal or use of the goods by the buyer will accrue directly or indirectly to the seller, unless an appropriate adjustment can be made in accordance with the provisions of Article 8; and

(d) that the buyer and seller are not related, or where the buyer and seller are related, that the transaction value is acceptable for customs purposes under the provisions of paragraph 2.

2. (a) In determining whether the transaction value is acceptable for the purposes of paragraph 1, the fact that the buyer and the seller are related within the meaning of Article 15 shall not in itself be grounds for regarding the transaction value as unacceptable. In such case the circumstances surrounding the sale shall be examined and the transaction value shall be accepted provided that the relationship did not influence the price. If, in the light of information provided by the importer or otherwise, the customs administration has grounds for considering that the relationship influenced the price, it shall communicate its grounds to the importer and the importer shall be given a reasonable opportunity to respond. If the importer so requests, the communication of the grounds shall be in writing.

(b) In a sale between related persons, the transaction value shall be accepted and the goods valued in accordance with the provisions of paragraph 1 whenever the importer demonstrates that such value closely approximates to one of the following occurring at or about the same time:

(i) the transaction value in sales to unrelated buyers of identical or similar goods for export to the same country of importation;

(ii) the customs value of identical or similar goods as determined under the provisions of Article 5;

(iii) the customs value of identical or similar goods as determined under the provisions of Article 6;

In applying the foregoing tests, due account shall be taken of demonstrated differences in commercial levels, quantity levels, the elements enumerated in Article 8 and costs incurred by the seller in sales in which the seller and the buyer are not related that are not incurred by the seller in sales in which the seller and the buyer are related.

(c) The tests set forth in paragraph 2(b) are to be used at the initiative of the importer and only for comparison purposes. Substitute values may not be established under the provisions of paragraph 2(b).

Article 2

1.

(a) If the customs value of the imported goods cannot be determined under the provisions of Article 1, the customs value shall be the transaction value of identical goods sold for export to the same country of importation and exported at or about the same time as the goods being valued.

(b) In applying this Article, the transaction value of identical goods in a sale at the same commercial level and in substantially the same quantity as the goods being valued shall be used to determine the customs value. Where no such sale is found, the transaction value of identical goods sold at a different commercial level and/or in different quantities, adjusted to take account of differences attributable to commercial level and/or to quantity, shall be used, provided that such adjustments can be made on the basis of demonstrated evidence which clearly establishes the reasonableness and accuracy of the adjustment, whether the adjustment leads to an increase or a decrease in the value.

2. Where the costs and charges referred to in paragraph 2 of Article 8 are included in the transaction value, an adjustment shall be made to take account of significant differences in such costs and charges between the imported goods and the identical goods in question arising from differences in distances and modes of transport.

3. If, in applying this Article, more than one transaction value of identical goods is found, the lowest such value shall be used to determine the customs value of the imported goods.

Article 3

1.

(a) If the customs value of the imported goods cannot be determined under the provisions of Articles 1 and 2, the customs value shall be the transaction value of similar goods sold for export to the same country of importation and exported at or about the same time as the goods being valued.

(b) In applying this Article, the transaction value of similar goods in a sale at the same commercial level and in substantially the same quantity as the goods being valued shall be used to determine the customs value. Where no such sale is found, the transaction value of similar goods sold at a different commercial level and/or in different quantities, adjusted to take account of differences attributable to commercial level and/or to quantity, shall be used, provided that such adjustments can be made on the basis of demonstrated evidence which clearly establishes the reasonableness and accuracy of the adjustment, whether the adjustment leads to an increase or a decrease in the value.

2. Where the costs and charges referred to in paragraph 2 of Article 8 are included in the transaction value, an adjustment shall be made to take account of significant differences in such costs and charges between the imported goods and the similar goods in question arising from differences in distances and modes of transport.

3. If, in applying this Article, more than one transaction value of similar goods is found, the lowest such value shall be used to determine the customs value of the imported goods.

Article 4

If the customs value of the imported goods cannot be determined under the provisions of Articles 1, 2 and 3, the customs value shall be determined under the provisions of Article 5 or, when the customs value cannot be determined under that Article, under the provisions of Article 6 except that, at the request of the importer, the order of application of Articles 5 and 6 shall be reversed.

Article 5

1.

(a) If the imported goods or identical or similar imported goods are sold in the country of importation in the condition as imported, the customs value of the imported goods under the provisions of this Article shall be based on the unit price at which the imported goods or identical or similar imported goods are so sold in the greatest aggregate quantity, at or about the time of the importation of the goods being valued, to persons who are not related to the persons from whom they buy such goods, subject to deductions for the following:

(i) either the commissions usually paid or agreed to be paid or the additions usually made for profit and general expenses in connection with sales in such country of imported goods of the same class or kind;

(ii) the usual costs of transport and insurance and associated costs incurred within the country of importation;

(iii) where appropriate, the costs and charges referred to in paragraph 2 of Article 8; and

(iv) the customs duties and other national taxes payable in the country of importation by reason of the importation or sale of the goods.

(b) If neither the imported goods nor identical nor similar imported goods are sold at or about the time of importation of the goods being valued, the customs value shall, subject otherwise to the provisions of paragraph 1(a), be based on the unit price at which the imported goods or identical or similar imported goods are sold in the country of importation in the condition as imported at the earliest date after the importation of the goods being valued but before the expiration of 90 days after such importation.

2. If neither the imported goods nor identical nor similar imported goods are sold in the country of importation in the condition as imported, then, if the importer so requests, the customs value shall be based on the unit price at which the imported goods, after further processing, are sold in the greatest aggregate quantity to persons in the country of importation who are not related to the persons from whom they buy such goods, due allowance being made for the value added by such processing and the deductions provided for in paragraph 1(a).

Article 6

1. The customs value of imported goods under the provisions of this Article shall be based on a computed value. Computed value shall consist of the sum of:

(a) the cost or value of materials and fabrication or other processing employed in producing the imported goods;

(b) an amount for profit and general expenses equal to that usually reflected in sales of goods of the same class or kind as the goods being valued which are made by producers in the country of exportation for export to the country of importation;

(c) the cost or value of all other expenses necessary to reflect the valuation option chosen by the Member under paragraph 2 of Article 8.

2. No Member may require or compel any person not resident in its own territory to produce for examination, or to allow access to, any account or other record for the purposes of determining a computed value. However, information supplied by the producer of the goods for the purposes of determining the customs value under the provisions of this Article may be verified in another country by the authorities of the country of importation with the agreement of the producer and provided they give sufficient advance notice to the government of the country in question and the latter does not object to the investigation.

Article 7

1. If the customs value of the imported goods cannot be determined under the provisions of Articles 1 through 6, inclusive, the customs value shall be determined using reasonable means consistent with the principles and general provisions of this Agreement and of Article VII of GATT 1994 and on the basis of data available in the country of importation.

2. No customs value shall be determined under the provisions of this Article on the basis of:

(a) the selling price in the country of importation of goods produced in such country;

(b) a system which provides for the acceptance for customs purposes of the higher of two alternative values;

(c) the price of goods on the domestic market of the country of exportation;

(d) the cost of production other than computed values which have been determined for identical or similar goods in accordance with the provisions of Article 6;

(e) the price of the goods for export to a country other than the country of importation;

(f) minimum customs values; or

(g) arbitrary or fictitious values.

3. If the importer so requests, the importer shall be informed in writing of the customs value determined under the provisions of this Article and the method used to determine such value.

Article 8

1. In determining the customs value under the provisions of Article 1, there shall be added to the price actually paid or payable for the imported goods:

(a) the following, to the extent that they are incurred by the buyer but are not included in the price actually paid or payable for the goods:

(i) commissions and brokerage, except buying commissions;

(ii) the cost of containers which are treated as being one for customs purposes with the goods in question;

(iii) the cost of packing whether for labour or materials;

(b) the value, apportioned as appropriate, of the following goods and services where supplied directly or indirectly by the buyer free of charge or at reduced cost for use in connection with the production and sale for export of the imported goods, to the extent that such value has not been included in the price actually paid or payable:

(i) materials, components, parts and similar items incorporated in the imported goods;

(ii) tools, dies, moulds and similar items used in the production of the imported goods;

(iii) materials consumed in the production of the imported goods;

(iv) engineering, development, artwork, design work, and plans and sketches undertaken elsewhere than in the country of importation and necessary for the production of the imported goods;

(c) royalties and licence fees related to the goods being valued that the buyer must pay, either directly or indirectly, as a condition of sale of the goods being valued, to the extent that such royalties and fees are not included in the price actually paid or payable;

(d) the value of any part of the proceeds of any subsequent resale, disposal or use of the imported goods that accrues directly or indirectly to the seller.

2. In framing its legislation, each Member shall provide for the inclusion in or the exclusion from the customs value, in whole or in part, of the following:

(a) the cost of transport of the imported goods to the port or place of importation;

(b) loading, unloading and handling charges associated with the transport of the imported goods to the port or place of importation; and

(c) the cost of insurance.

3. Additions to the price actually paid or payable shall be made under this Article only on the basis of objective and quantifiable data.

4. No additions shall be made to the price actually paid or payable in determining the customs value except as provided in this Article.

Article 9

1. Where the conversion of currency is necessary for the determination of the customs value, the rate of exchange to be used shall be that duly published by the competent authorities of the country of importation concerned and shall reflect as effectively as possible, in respect of the period covered by each such document of publication, the current value of such currency in commercial transactions in terms of the currency of the country of importation.

2. The conversion rate to be used shall be that in effect at the time of exportation or the time of importation, as provided by each Member.

Article 10

All information which is by nature confidential or which is provided on a confidential basis for the purposes of customs valuation shall be treated as strictly confidential by the authorities concerned who shall not disclose it without the specific permission of the person or government providing such information, except to the extent that it may be required to be disclosed in the context of judicial proceedings.

Article 11

1. The legislation of each Member shall provide in regard to a determination of customs value for the right of appeal, without penalty, by the importer or any other person liable for the payment of the duty.

2. An initial right of appeal without penalty may be to an authority within the customs administration or to an independent body, but the legislation of each Member shall provide for the right of appeal without penalty to a judicial authority.

3. Notice of the decision on appeal shall be given to the appellant and the reasons for such decision shall be provided in writing. The appellant shall also be informed of any rights of further appeal.

Article 12

Laws, regulations, judicial decisions and administrative rulings of general application giving effect to this Agreement shall be published in conformity with Article X of GATT 1994 by the country of importation concerned.

Article 13

If, in the course of determining the customs value of imported goods, it becomes necessary to delay the final determination of such customs value, the importer of the goods shall nevertheless be able to withdraw them from customs if, where so required, the importer provides sufficient guarantee in the form of a surety, a deposit or some other appropriate instrument, covering the ultimate payment of customs duties for which the goods may be liable. The legislation of each Member shall make provisions for such circumstances.

Article 14

The notes at Annex I to this Agreement form an integral part of this Agreement and the Articles of this Agreement are to be read and applied in conjunction with their respective notes. Annexes II and III also form an integral part of this Agreement.

Article 15

1. In this Agreement:

(a) 'customs value of imported goods' means the value of goods for the purposes of levying *ad valorem* duties of customs on imported goods;

(b) 'country of importation' means country or customs territory of importation; and

(c) 'produced' includes grown, manufactured and mined.

2. In this Agreement:

(a) 'identical goods' means goods which are the same in all respects, including physical characteristics, quality and reputation. Minor differences in appearance would not preclude goods otherwise conforming to the definition from being regarded as identical;

(b) 'similar goods' means goods which, although not alike in all respects, have like characteristics and like component materials which enable them to perform the same functions and to be commercially interchangeable. The quality of the goods, their reputation and the existence of a trademark are among the factors to be considered in determining whether goods are similar;

(c) the terms 'identical goods' and 'similar goods' do not include, as the case may be, goods which incorporate or reflect engineering, development, artwork, design work, and plans and sketches for which no adjustment has been made under paragraph 1(b)(iv) of Article 8 because such elements were undertaken in the country of importation;

(d) goods shall not be regarded as 'identical goods' or 'similar goods' unless they were produced in the same country as the goods being valued;

(e) goods produced by a different person shall be taken into account only when there are no identical goods or similar goods, as the case may be, produced by the same person as the goods being valued.

3. In this Agreement 'goods of the same class or kind' means goods which fall within a group or range of goods produced by a particular industry or industry sector, and includes identical or similar goods.

4. For the purposes of this Agreement, persons shall be deemed to be related only if:

(a) they are officers or directors of one another's businesses;

(b) they are legally recognized partners in business;

(c) they are employer and employee;

(d) any person directly or indirectly owns, controls or holds 5 per cent or more of the outstanding voting stock or shares of both of them;

(e) one of them directly or indirectly controls the other;

(f) both of them are directly or indirectly controlled by a third person;

(g) together they directly or indirectly control a third person; or

(h) they are members of the same family.

5. Persons who are associated in business with one another in that one is the sole agent, sole distributor or sole concessionaire, however described, of the other shall be deemed to be related for the purposes of this Agreement if they fall within the criteria of paragraph

Article 16

Upon written request, the importer shall have the right to an explanation in writing from the customs administration of the country of importation as to how the customs value of the importer's goods was determined.

Article 17

Nothing in this Agreement shall be construed as restricting or calling into question the rights of customs administrations to satisfy themselves as to the truth or accuracy of any statement, document or declaration presented for customs valuation purposes.

PART II

ADMINISTRATION, CONSULTATIONS AND DISPUTE SETTLEMENT

Article 18
Institutions

1. There is hereby established a Committee on Customs Valuation (referred to in this Agreement as 'the Committee') composed of representatives from each of the Members. The Committee shall elect its own Chairman and shall normally meet once a year, or as is otherwise envisaged by the relevant provisions of this Agreement, for the purpose of affording Members the opportunity to consult on matters relating to the administration of the customs valuation system by any Member as it might affect the operation of this Agreement or the furtherance of its objectives and carrying out such other responsibilities as may be assigned to it by the Members. The WTO Secretariat shall act as the secretariat to the Committee.

2. There shall be established a Technical Committee on Customs Valuation (referred to in this Agreement as 'the Technical Committee') under the auspices of the Customs Co-operation Council (referred to in this Agreement as 'the CCC'), which shall carry out the responsibilities described in Annex II to this Agreement and shall operate in accordance with the rules of procedure contained therein.

Article 19
Consultations and Dispute Settlement

1. Except as otherwise provided herein, the Dispute Settlement Understanding is applicable to consultations and the settlement of disputes

under this Agreement.

2. If any Member considers that any benefit accruing to it, directly or indirectly, under this Agreement is being nullified or impaired, or that the achievement of any objective of this Agreement is being impeded, as a result of the actions of another Member or of other Members, it may, with a view to reaching a mutually satisfactory solution of this matter, request consultations with the Member or Members in question. Each Member shall afford sympathetic consideration to any request from another Member for consultations.

3. The Technical Committee shall provide, upon request, advice and assistance to Members engaged in consultations.

4. At the request of a party to the dispute, or on its own initiative, a panel established to examine a dispute relating to the provisions of this Agreement may request the Technical Committee to carry out an examination of any questions requiring technical consideration. The panel shall determine the terms of reference of the Technical Committee for the particular dispute and set a time period for receipt of the report of the Technical Committee. The panel shall take into consideration the report of the Technical Committee. In the event that the Technical Committee is unable to reach consensus on a matter referred to it pursuant to this paragraph, the panel should afford the parties to the dispute an opportunity to present their views on the matter to the panel.

5. Confidential information provided to the panel shall not be disclosed without formal authorization from the person, body or authority providing such information. Where such information is requested from the panel but release of such information by the panel is not authorized, a non-confidential summary of this information, authorized by the person, body or authority providing the information, shall be provided.

PART III

SPECIAL AND DIFFERENTIAL TREATMENT

Article 20

1. Developing country Members not party to the Agreement on Implementation of Article VII of the General Agreement on Tariffs and Trade done on 12 April 1979 may delay application of the provisions of this Agreement for a period not exceeding five years from the date of entry into force of the WTO Agreement for such Members. Developing country Members who choose to delay application of this Agreement shall notify the Director-General of the WTO accordingly.

2. In addition to paragraph 1, developing country Members not party to the Agreement on Implementation of Article VII of the General Agreement on Tariffs and Trade done on 12 April 1979 may delay application of paragraph 2(b)(iii) of Article 1 and Article 6 for a period not exceeding three years following their application of all other provisions of this Agreement. Developing country Members that choose to delay application of the provisions specified in this paragraph shall notify the Director-General of the WTO accordingly.

3. Developed country Members shall furnish, on mutually agreed

terms, technical assistance to developing country Members that so request. On this basis developed country Members shall draw up programmes of technical assistance which may include, *inter alia,* training of personnel, assistance in preparing implementation measures, access to sources of information regarding customs valuation methodology, and advice on the application of the provisions of this Agreement.

PART IV

FINAL PROVISIONS

Article 21
Reservations

Reservations may not be entered in respect of any of the provisions of this Agreement without the consent of the other Members.

Article 22
National Legislation

1. Each Member shall ensure, not later than the date of application of the provisions of this Agreement for it, the conformity of its laws, regulations and administrative procedures with the provisions of this Agreement.

2. Each Member shall inform the Committee of any changes in its laws and regulations relevant to this Agreement and in the administration of such laws and regulations.

Article 23
Review

The Committee shall review annually the implementation and operation of this Agreement taking into account the objectives thereof. The Committee shall annually inform the Council for Trade in Goods of developments during the period covered by such reviews.

Article 24
Secretariat

This Agreement shall be serviced by the WTO Secretariat except in regard to those responsibilities specifically assigned to the Technical Committee, which will be serviced by the CCC Secretariat.

ANNEX I

INTERPRETATIVE NOTES

General Note

Sequential Application of Valuation Methods

1. Articles 1 through 7 define how the customs value of imported goods is to be determined under the provisions of this Agreement. The methods of valuation are set out in a sequential order of application. The primary method for customs valuation is defined in Article 1 and imported goods are to be

valued in accordance with the provisions of this Article whenever the conditions prescribed therein are fulfilled.

2. Where the customs value cannot be determined under the provisions of Article 1, it is to be determined by proceeding sequentially through the succeeding Articles to the first such Article under which the customs value can be determined. Except as provided in Article 4, it is only when the customs value cannot be determined under the provisions of a particular Article that the provisions of the next Article in the sequence can be used.

3. If the importer does not request that the order of Articles 5 and 6 be reversed, the normal order of the sequence is to be followed. If the importer does so request but it then proves impossible to determine the customs value under the provisions of Article 6, the customs value is to be determined under the provisions of Article 5, if it can be so determined.

4. Where the customs value cannot be determined under the provisions of Articles 1 through 6 it is to be determined under the provisions of Article 7.

Use of Generally Accepted Accounting Principles

1. 'Generally accepted accounting principles' refers to the recognized consensus or substantial authoritative support within a country at a particular time as to which economic resources and obligations should be recorded as assets and liabilities, which changes in assets and liabilities should be recorded, how the assets and liabilities and changes in them should be measured, what information should be disclosed and how it should be disclosed, and which financial statements should be prepared. These standards may be broad guidelines of general application as well as detailed practices and procedures.

2. For the purposes of this Agreement, the customs administration of each Member shall utilize information prepared in a manner consistent with generally accepted accounting principles in the country which is appropriate for the Article in question. For example, the determination of usual profit and general expenses under the provisions of Article 5 would be carried out utilizing information prepared in a manner consistent with generally accepted accounting principles of the country of importation. On the other hand, the determination of usual profit and general expenses under the provisions of Article 6 would be carried out utilizing information prepared in a manner consistent with generally accepted accounting principles of the country of production. As a further example, the determination of an element provided for in paragraph 1(b)(ii) of Article 8 undertaken in the country of importation would be carried out utilizing information in a manner consistent with the generally accepted accounting principles of that country.

Note to Article 1

Price Actually Paid or Payable

1. The price actually paid or payable is the total payment made or to be made by the buyer to or for the benefit of the seller for the imported goods. The payment need not necessarily take the form of a transfer of money. Payment may be made by way of letters of credit or negotiable instruments.

Payment may be made directly or indirectly. An example of an indirect payment would be the settlement by the buyer, whether in whole or in part, of a debt owed by the seller.

2. Activities undertaken by the buyer on the buyer's own account, other than those for which an adjustment is provided in Article 8, are not considered to be an indirect payment to the seller, even though they might be regarded as of benefit to the seller. The costs of such activities shall not, therefore, be added to the price actually paid or payable in determining the customs value.

3. The customs value shall not include the following charges or costs, provided that they are distinguished from the price actually paid or payable for the imported goods:

(a) charges for construction, erection, assembly, maintenance or technical assistance, undertaken after importation on imported goods such as industrial plant, machinery or equipment;

(b) the cost of transport after importation;

(c) duties and taxes of the country of importation.

4. The price actually paid or payable refers to the price for the imported goods. Thus the flow of dividends or other payments from the buyer to the seller that do not relate to the imported goods are not part of the customs value.

Paragraph 1(a)(iii)

Among restrictions which would not render a price actually paid or payable unacceptable are restrictions which do not substantially affect the value of the goods. An example of such restrictions would be the case where a seller requires a buyer of automobiles not to sell or exhibit them prior to a fixed date which represents the beginning of a model year.

Paragraph 1(b)

1. If the sale or price is subject to some condition or consideration for which a value cannot be determined with respect to the goods being valued, the transaction value shall not be acceptable for customs purposes. Some examples of this include:

(a) the seller establishes the price of the imported goods on condition that the buyer will also buy other goods in specified quantities;

(b) the price of the imported goods is dependent upon the price or prices at which the buyer of the imported goods sells other goods to the seller of the imported goods;

(c) the price is established on the basis of a form of payment extraneous to the imported goods, such as where the imported goods are semi-finished goods which have been provided by the seller on condition that the seller will receive a specified quantity of the finished goods.

2. However, conditions or considerations relating to the production or marketing of the imported goods shall not result in rejection of the transaction value. For example, the fact that the buyer furnishes the seller with engineering and plans undertaken in the country of importation shall not result in rejection of the transaction value for the purposes of Article 1.

Likewise, if the buyer undertakes on the buyer's own account, even though by agreement with the seller, activities relating to the marketing of the imported goods, the value of these activities is not part of the customs value nor shall such activities result in rejection of the transaction value.

Paragraph 2

1. Paragraphs 2(a) and 2(b) provide different means of establishing the acceptability of a transaction value.

2. Paragraph 2(a) provides that where the buyer and the seller are related, the circumstances surrounding the sale shall be examined and the transaction value shall be accepted as the customs value provided that the relationship did not influence the price. It is not intended that there should be an examination of the circumstances in all cases where the buyer and the seller are related. Such examination will only be required where there are doubts about the acceptability of the price. Where the customs administration have no doubts about the acceptability of the price, it should be accepted without requesting further information from the importer. For example, the customs administration may have previously examined the relationship, or it may already have detailed information concerning the buyer and the seller, and may already be satisfied from such examination or information that the relationship did not influence the price.

3. Where the customs administration is unable to accept the transaction value without further inquiry, it should give the importer an opportunity to supply such further detailed information as may be necessary to enable it to examine the circumstances surrounding the sale. In this context, the customs administration should be prepared to examine relevant aspects of the transaction, including the way in which the buyer and seller organize their commercial relations and the way in which the price in question was arrived at, in order to determine whether the relationship influenced the price. Where it can be shown that the buyer and seller, although related under the provisions of Article 15, buy from and sell to each other as if they were not related, this would demonstrate that the price had not been influenced by the relationship. As an example of this, if the price had been settled in a manner consistent with the normal pricing practices of the industry in question or with the way the seller settles prices for sales to buyers who are not related to the seller, this would demonstrate that the price had not been influenced by the relationship. As a further example, where it is shown that the price is adequate to ensure recovery of all costs plus a profit which is representative of the firm's overall profit realized over a representative period of time (e.g. on an annual basis) in sales of goods of the same class or kind, this would demonstrate that the price had not been influenced.

4. Paragraph 2(b) provides an opportunity for the importer to demonstrate that the transaction value closely approximates to a 'test' value previously accepted by the customs administration and is therefore acceptable under the provisions of Article 1. Where a test under paragraph 2(b) is met, it is not necessary to examine the question of influence under paragraph 2(a). If the customs administration has already sufficient information to be satisfied, without further detailed inquiries, that one of the tests provided in paragraph 2(b) has been met, there is no reason for it to require the importer to demonstrate

that the test can be met. In paragraph 2(b) the term 'unrelated buyers' means buyers who are not related to the seller in any particular case.

Paragraph 2(b)

A number of factors must be taken into consideration in determining whether one value 'closely approximates' to another value. These factors include the nature of the imported goods, the nature of the industry itself, the season in which the goods are imported, and, whether the difference in values is commercially significant. Since these factors may vary from case to case, it would be impossible to apply a uniform standard such as a fixed percentage, in each case. For example, a small difference in value in a case involving one type of goods could be unacceptable while a large difference in a case involving another type of goods might be acceptable in determining whether the transaction value closely approximates to the 'test' values set forth in paragraph 2(b) of Article 1.

Note to Article 2

1. In applying Article 2, the customs administration shall, wherever possible, use a sale of identical goods at the same commercial level and in substantially the same quantities as the goods being valued. Where no such sale is found, a sale of identical goods that takes place under any one of the following three conditions may be used:

(a) a sale at the same commercial level but in different quantities;

(b) a sale at a different commercial level but in substantially the same quantities; or

(c) a sale at a different commercial level and in different quantities.

2. Having found a sale under any one of these three conditions adjustments will then be made, as the case may be, for:

(a) quantity factors only;

(b) commercial level factors only; or

(c) both commercial level and quantity factors.

3. The expression 'and/or' allows the flexibility to use the sales and make the necessary adjustments in any one of the three conditions described above.

4. For the purposes of Article 2, the transaction value of identical imported goods means a customs value, adjusted as provided for in paragraphs 1(b) and 2, which has already been accepted under Article 1.

5. A condition for adjustment because of different commercial levels or different quantities is that such adjustment, whether it leads to an increase or a decrease in the value, be made only on the basis of demonstrated evidence that clearly establishes the reasonableness and accuracy of the adjustments, *e.g.* valid price lists containing prices referring to different levels or different quantities. As an example of this, if the imported goods being valued consist of a shipment of 10 units and the only identical imported goods for which a transaction value exists involved a sale of 500 units, and it is recognized that the seller grants quantity discounts, the required adjustment may be accomplished by resorting to the seller's price list and using that price applicable to a sale of 10 units. This does not require that a sale had to have

been made in quantities of 10 as long as the price list has been established as being bona fide through sales at other quantities. In the absence of such an objective measure, however, the determination of a customs value under the provisions of Article 2 is not appropriate.

Note to Article 3

1. In applying Article 3, the customs administration shall, wherever possible, use a sale of similar goods at the same commercial level and in substantially the same quantities as the goods being valued. Where no such sale is found, a sale of similar goods that takes place under any one of the following three conditions may be used:

(a) a sale at the same commercial level but in different quantities;

(b) a sale at a different commercial level but in substantially the same quantities; or

(c) a sale at a different commercial level and in different quantities.

2. Having found a sale under any one of these three conditions adjustments will then be made, as the case may be, for:

(a) quantity factors only;

(b) commercial level factors only; or

(c) both commercial level and quantity factors.

3. The expression 'and/or' allows the flexibility to use the sales and make the necessary adjustments in any one of the three conditions described above.

4. For the purpose of Article 3, the transaction value of similar imported goods means a customs value, adjusted as provided for in paragraphs 1(b) and 2, which has already been accepted under Article 1.

5. A condition for adjustment because of different commercial levels or different quantities is that such adjustment, whether it leads to an increase or a decrease in the value, be made only on the basis of demonstrated evidence that clearly establishes the reasonableness and accuracy of the adjustment, e.g. valid price lists containing prices referring to different levels or different quantities. As an example of this, if the imported goods being valued consist of a shipment of 10 units and the only similar imported goods for which a transaction value exists involved a sale of 500 units, and it is recognized that the seller grants quantity discounts, the required adjustment may be accomplished by resorting to the seller's price list and using that price applicable to a sale of 10 units. This does not require that a sale had to have been made in quantities of 10 as long as the price list has been established as being bona fide through sales at other quantities. In the absence of such an objective measure, however, the determination of a customs value under the provisions of Article 3 is not appropriate.

Note to Article 5

1. The term 'unit price at which ... goods are sold in the greatest aggregate quantity' means the price at which the greatest number of units is sold in sales to persons who are not related to the persons from whom they buy such goods at the first commercial level after importation at which such sales take place.

2. As an example of this, goods are sold from a price list which grants favourable unit prices for purchases made in larger quantities.

Sale quantity	*Unit price*	*Number of sales*	*Total quantity sold at each price*
1-10 units	100	10 sales of 5 units 5 sales of 3 units	65
11-25 units	95	5 sales of 11 units	55
over 25 units	90	1 sale of 30 units 1 sale of 50 units	80

The greatest number of units sold at a price is 80; therefore, the unit price in the greatest aggregate quantity is 90.

3. As another example of this, two sales occur. In the first sale 500 units are sold at a price of 95 currency units each. In the second sale 400 units are sold at a price of 90 currency units each. In this example, the greatest number of units sold at a particular price is 500; therefore, the unit price in the greatest aggregate quantity is 95.

4. A third example would be the following situation where various quantities are sold at various prices.

(a) Sales

Sale quantity	*Unit price*
40 units	100
30 units	90
15 units	100
50 units	95
25 units	105
35 units	90
5 units	100

(b) Totals

Total quantity sold	*Unit price*
65	90
50	95
60	100
25	105

In this example, the greatest number of units sold at a particular price is 65; therefore, the unit price in the greatest aggregate quantity is 90.

5. Any sale in the importing country, as described in paragraph 1 above, to a person who supplies directly or indirectly free of charge or at reduced cost for use in connection with the production and sale for export of the imported goods any of the elements specified in paragraph 1(b) of Article 8, should not be taken into account in establishing the unit price for the purposes of Article 5.

6. It should be noted that 'profit and general expenses' referred to in paragraph 1 of Article 5 should be taken as a whole. The figure for the purposes of this deduction should be determined on the basis of information supplied by or on behalf of the importer unless the importer's figures are inconsistent with those obtained in sales in the country of importation of imported goods of the same class or kind. Where the importer's figures are inconsistent with such figures, the amount for profit and general expenses may be based upon relevant information other than that supplied by or on behalf of the importer.

7. The 'general expenses' include the direct and indirect costs of marketing the goods in question.

8. Local taxes payable by reason of the sale of the goods for which a deduction is not made under the provisions of paragraph 1(a)(iv) of Article 5 shall be deducted under the provisions of paragraph 1(a)(i) of Article 5.

9. In determining either the commissions or the usual profits and general expenses under the provisions of paragraph 1 of Article 5, the question whether certain goods are 'of the same class or kind' as other goods must be determined on a case-by-case basis by reference to the circumstances involved. Sales in the country of importation of the narrowest group or range of imported goods of the same class or kind, which includes the goods being valued, for which the necessary information can be provided, should be examined. For the purposes of Article 5, 'goods of the same class or kind' includes goods imported from the same country as the goods being valued as well as goods imported from other countries.

10. For the purposes of paragraph 1(b) of Article 5, the 'earliest date' shall be the date by which sales of the imported goods or of identical or similar imported goods are made in sufficient quantity to establish the unit price.

11. Where the method in paragraph 2 of Article 5 is used, deductions made for the value added by further processing shall be based on objective and quantifiable data relating to the cost of such work. Accepted industry formulas, recipes, methods of construction, and other industry practices would form the basis of the calculations.

12. It is recognized that the method of valuation provided for in paragraph 2 of Article 5 would normally not be applicable when, as a result of the further processing, the imported goods lose their identity. However, there can be instances where, although the identity of the imported goods is lost, the value added by the processing can be determined accurately without unreasonable difficulty. On the other hand, there can also be instances where the imported goods maintain their identity but form such a minor element in the goods sold in the country of importation that the use of this valuation method would be unjustified. In view of the above, each situation of this type

must be considered on a case-by-case basis.

Note to Article 6

1. As a general rule, customs value is determined under this Agreement on the basis of information readily available in the country of importation. In order to determine a computed value, however, it may be necessary to examine the costs of producing the goods being valued and other information which has to be obtained from outside the country of importation. Furthermore, in most cases the producer of the goods will be outside the jurisdiction of the authorities of the country of importation. The use of the computed value method will generally be limited to those cases where the buyer and seller are related, and the producer is prepared to supply to the authorities of the country of importation the necessary costings and to provide facilities for any subsequent verification which may be necessary.

2. The 'cost or value' referred to in paragraph 1(a) of Article 6 is to be determined on the basis of information relating to the production of the goods being valued supplied by or on behalf of the producer. It is to be based upon the commercial accounts of the producer, provided that such accounts are consistent with the generally accepted accounting principles applied in the country where the goods are produced.

3. The 'cost or value' shall include the cost of elements specified in paragraphs 1(a)(ii) and (iii) of Article 8. It shall also include the value, apportioned as appropriate under the provisions of the relevant note to Article 8, of any element specified in paragraph 1(b) of Article 8 which has been supplied directly or indirectly by the buyer for use in connection with the production of the imported goods. The value of the elements specified in paragraph 1(b)(iv) of Article 8 which are undertaken in the country of importation shall be included only to the extent that such elements are charged to the producer. It is to be understood that no cost or value of the elements referred to in this paragraph shall be counted twice in determining the computed value.

4. The 'amount for profit and general expenses' referred to in paragraph 1(b) of Article 6 is to be determined on the basis of information supplied by or on behalf of the producer unless the producer's figures are inconsistent with those usually reflected in sales of goods of the same class or kind as the goods being valued which are made by producers in the country of exportation for export to the country of importation.

5. It should be noted in this context that the 'amount for profit and general expenses' has to be taken as a whole. It follows that if, in any particular case, the producer's profit figure is low and the producer's general expenses are high, the producer's profit and general expenses taken together may nevertheless be consistent with that usually reflected in sales of goods of the same class or kind. Such a situation might occur, for example, if a product were being launched in the country of importation and the producer accepted a nil or low profit to offset high general expenses associated with the launch. Where the producer can demonstrate a low profit on sales of the imported goods because of particular commercial circumstances, the producer's actual profit figures should be taken into account provided that the producer has valid commercial reasons to justify them and the producer's pricing policy reflects usual pricing policies in the branch of industry concerned. Such a

situation might occur, for example, where producers have been forced to lower prices temporarily because of an unforeseeable drop in demand, or where they sell goods to complement a range of goods being produced in the country of importation and accept a low profit to maintain competitivity. Where the producer's own figures for profit and general expenses are not consistent with those usually reflected in sales of goods of the same class or kind as the goods being valued which are made by producers in the country of exportation for export to the country of importation, the amount for profit and general expenses may be based upon relevant information other than that supplied by or on behalf of the producer of the goods.

6. Where information other than that supplied by or on behalf of the producer is used for the purposes of determining a computed value, the authorities of the importing country shall inform the importer, if the latter so requests, of the source of such information, the data used and the calculations based upon such data, subject to the provisions of Article 10.

7. The 'general expenses' referred to in paragraph 1(b) of Article 6 covers the direct and indirect costs of producing and selling the goods for export which are not included under paragraph 1(a) of Article 6.

8. Whether certain goods are 'of the same class or kind' as other goods must be determined on a case-by-case basis with reference to the circumstances involved. In determining the usual profits and general expenses under the provisions of Article 6, sales for export to the country of importation of the narrowest group or range of goods, which includes the goods being valued, for which the necessary information can be provided, should be examined. For the purposes of Article 6, 'goods of the same class or kind' must be from the same country as the goods being valued.

Note to Article 7

1. Customs values determined under the provisions of Article 7 should, to the greatest extent possible, be based on previously determined customs values.

2. The methods of valuation to be employed under Article 7 should be those laid down in Articles 1 through 6 but a reasonable flexibility in the application of such methods would be in conformity with the aims and provisions of Article 7.

3. Some examples of reasonable flexibility are as follows:

(a) *Identical goods* - the requirement that the identical goods should be exported at or about the same time as the goods being valued could be flexibly interpreted; identical imported goods produced in a country other than the country of exportation of the goods being valued could be the basis for customs valuation; customs values of identical imported goods already determined under the provisions of Articles 5 and 6 could be used.

(b) *Similar goods* - the requirement that the similar goods should be exported at or about the same time as the goods being valued could be flexibly interpreted; similar imported goods produced in a country other than the country of exportation of the goods being valued could be the basis for customs valuation; customs values of similar imported goods already determined under the provisions of Articles 5 and 6 could be used.

(c) *Deductive method* - the requirement that the goods shall have been sold in the 'condition as imported' in paragraph 1(a) of Article 5 could be flexibly interpreted; the '90 days' requirement could be administered flexibly.

Note to Article 8

Paragraph 1(a)(i)

The term 'buying commissions' means fees paid by an importer to the importer's agent for the service of representing the importer abroad in the purchase of the goods being valued.

Paragraph 1(b)(ii)

1. There are two factors involved in the apportionment of the elements specified in paragraph 1(b)(ii) of Article 8 to the imported goods - the value of the element itself and the way in which that value is to be apportioned to the imported goods. The apportionment of these elements should be made in a reasonable manner appropriate to the circumstances and in accordance with generally accepted accounting principles.

2. Concerning the value of the element, if the importer acquires the element from a seller not related to the importer at a given cost, the value of the element is that cost. If the element was produced by the importer or by a person related to the importer, its value would be the cost of producing it. If the element had been previously used by the importer, regardless of whether it had been acquired or produced by such importer, the original cost of acquisition or production would have to be adjusted downward to reflect its use in order to arrive at the value of the element.

3. Once a value has been determined for the element, it is necessary to apportion that value to the imported goods. Various possibilities exist. For example, the value might be apportioned to the first shipment if the importer wishes to pay duty on the entire value at one time. As another example, the importer may request that the value be apportioned over the number of units produced up to the time of the first shipment. As a further example, the importer may request that the value be apportioned over the entire anticipated production where contracts or firm commitments exist for that production. The method of apportionment used will depend upon the documentation provided by the importer.

4. As an illustration of the above, an importer provides the producer with a mould to be used in the production of the imported goods and contracts with the producer to buy 10,000 units. By the time of arrival of the first shipment of 1,000 units, the producer has already produced 4,000 units. The importer may request the customs administration to apportion the value of the mould over 1,000 units, 4,000 units or 10,000 units.

Paragraph 1(b)(iv)

1. Additions for the elements specified in paragraph 1(b)(iv) of Article 8 should be based on objective and quantifiable data. In order to

minimize the burden for both the importer and customs administration in determining the values to be added, data readily available in the buyer's commercial record system should be used in so far as possible.

2. For those elements supplied by the buyer which were purchased or leased by the buyer, the addition would be the cost of the purchase or the lease. No addition shall be made for those elements available in the public domain, other than the cost of obtaining copies of them.

3. The ease with which it may be possible to calculate the values to be added will depend on a particular firm's structure and management practice, as well as its accounting methods.

4. For example, it is possible that a firm which imports a variety of products from several countries maintains the records of its design centre outside the country of importation in such a way as to show accurately the costs attributable to a given product.

5. In such cases, a direct adjustment may appropriately be made under the provisions of Article 8. In another case, a firm may carry the cost of the design centre outside the country of importation as a general overhead expense without allocation to specific products. In this instance, an appropriate adjustment could be made under the provisions of Article 8 with respect to the imported goods by apportioning total design centre costs over total production benefiting from the design centre and adding such apportioned cost on a unit basis to imports.

6. Variations in the above circumstances will, of course, require different factors to be considered in determining the proper method of allocation.

7. In cases where the production of the element in question involves a number of countries and over a period of time, the adjustment should be limited to the value actually added to that element outside the country of importation.

Paragraph 1(c)

1. The royalties and licence fees referred to in paragraph 1(c) of Article 8 may include, among other things, payments in respect to patents, trade marks and copyrights. However, the charges for the right to reproduce the imported goods in the country of importation shall not be added to the price actually paid or payable for the imported goods in determining the customs value.

2. Payments made by the buyer for the right to distribute or resell the imported goods shall not be added to the price actually paid or payable for the imported goods if such payments are not a condition of the sale for export to the country of importation of the imported goods.

Paragraph 3

Where objective and quantifiable data do not exist with regard to the additions required to be made under the provisions of Article 8, the transaction value cannot be determined under the provisions of Article 1. As an illustration of this, a royalty is paid on the basis of the price in a sale in the importing country of a litre of a particular product that was imported by the kilogram and made up into a solution after importation. If the royalty is based partially on the imported goods and partially on other factors which have nothing to do with the imported goods (such as when the imported goods are mixed with domestic ingredients and are no longer separately identifiable, or when the royalty cannot be distinguished from special financial arrangements between the buyer and the seller), it would be inappropriate to attempt to make an addition for the royalty. However, if the amount of this royalty is based only on the imported goods and can be readily quantified, an addition to the price actually paid or payable can be made.

Note to Article 9

For the purposes of Article 9, 'time of importation' may include the time of entry for customs purposes.

Note to Article 11

1. Article 11 provides the importer with the right to appeal against a valuation determination made by the customs administration for the goods being valued. Appeal may first be to a higher level in the customs administration, but the importer shall have the right in the final instance to appeal to the judiciary.

2. 'Without penalty' means that the importer shall not be subject to a fine or threat of fine merely because the importer chose to exercise the right of appeal. Payment of normal court costs and lawyers' fees shall not be considered to be a fine.

3. However, nothing in Article 11 shall prevent a Member from requiring full payment of assessed customs duties prior to an appeal.

Note to Article 15

Paragraph 4

For the purposes of Article 15, the term 'persons' includes a legal person, where appropriate.

Paragraph 4(e)

For the purposes of this Agreement, one person shall be deemed to control another when the former is legally or operationally in a position to exercise restraint or direction over the latter.

ANNEX II

TECHNICAL COMMITTEE ON CUSTOMS VALUATION

1. In accordance with Article 18 of this Agreement, the Technical Committee shall be established under the auspices of the CCC with a view to ensuring, at the technical level, uniformity in interpretation and application of this Agreement.

2. The responsibilities of the Technical Committee shall include the following:

   (a) to examine specific technical problems arising in the day-to-day administration of the customs valuation system of Members and to give advisory opinions on appropriate solutions based upon the facts presented;

(b) to study, as requested, valuation laws, procedures and practices as they relate to this Agreement and to prepare reports on the results of such studies;

(c) to prepare and circulate annual reports on the technical aspects of the operation and status of this Agreement;

(d) to furnish such information and advice on any matters concerning the valuation of imported goods for customs purposes as may be requested by any Member or the Committee. Such information and advice may take the form of advisory opinions, commentaries or explanatory notes;

(e) to facilitate, as requested, technical assistance to Members with a view to furthering the international acceptance of this Agreement;

(f) to carry out an examination of a matter referred to it by a panel under Article 19 of this Agreement; and

(g) to exercise such other responsibilities as the Committee may assign to it.

General

3. The Technical Committee shall attempt to conclude its work on specific matters, especially those referred to it by Members, the Committee or a panel, in a reasonably short period of time. As provided in paragraph 4 of Article 19, a panel shall set a specific time period for receipt of a report of the Technical Committee and the Technical Committee shall provide its report within that period.

4. The Technical Committee shall be assisted as appropriate in its activities by the CCC Secretariat.

Representation

5. Each Member shall have the right to be represented on the Technical Committee. Each Member may nominate one delegate and one or more alternates to be its representatives on the Technical Committee. Such a Member so represented on the Technical Committee is referred to in this Annex as a 'member of the Technical Committee.' Representatives of members of the Technical Committee may be assisted by advisers. The WTO Secretariat may also attend such meetings with observer status.

6. Members of the CCC which are not Members of the WTO may be represented at meetings of the Technical Committee by one delegate and one or more alternates. Such representatives shall attend meetings of the Technical Committee as observers.

7. Subject to the approval of the Chairman of the Technical Committee, the Secretary-General of the CCC (referred to in this Annex as 'the Secretary-General') may invite representatives of governments which are neither Members of the WTO nor members of the CCC and representatives of international governmental and trade organizations to attend meetings of the Technical Committee as observers.

8. Nominations of delegates, alternates and advisers to meetings of the Technical Committee shall be made to the Secretary-General.

Technical Committee Meetings

9. The Technical Committee shall meet as necessary but at least two times a year. The date of each meeting shall be fixed by the Technical Committee at its preceding session. The date of the meeting may be varied either at the request of any member of the Technical Committee concurred in by a simple majority of the members of the Technical Committee or, in cases requiring urgent attention, at the request of the Chairman. Notwithstanding the provisions in sentence 1 of this paragraph, the Technical Committee shall meet as necessary to consider matters referred to it by a panel under the provisions of Article 19 of this Agreement.

10. The meetings of the Technical Committee shall be held at the headquarters of the CCC unless otherwise decided.

11. The Secretary-General shall inform all members of the Technical Committee and those included under paragraphs 6 and 7 at least 30 days in advance, except in urgent cases, of the opening date of each session of the Technical Committee.

Agenda

12. A provisional agenda for each session shall be drawn up by the Secretary-General and circulated to the members of the Technical Committee and to those included under paragraphs 6 and 7 at least 30 days in advance of the session, except in urgent cases. This agenda shall comprise all items whose inclusion has been approved by the Technical Committee during its preceding session, all items included by the Chairman on the Chairman's own initiative, and all items whose inclusion has been requested by the Secretary-General, by the Committee or by any member of the Technical Committee.

13. The Technical Committee shall determine its agenda at the opening of each session. During the session the agenda may be altered at any time by the Technical Committee.

Officers and Conduct of Business

14. The Technical Committee shall elect from among the delegates of its members a Chairman and one or more Vice-Chairmen. The Chairman and Vice-Chairmen shall each hold office for a period of one year. The retiring Chairman and Vice-Chairmen are eligible for re-election. The mandate of a Chairman or Vice-Chairman who no longer represents a member of the Technical Committee shall terminate automatically.

15. If the Chairman is absent from any meeting or part thereof, a Vice-Chairman shall preside. In that event, the latter shall have the same powers and duties as the Chairman.

16. The Chairman of the meeting shall participate in the proceedings of the Technical Committee as such and not as the representative of a member of the Technical Committee.

17. In addition to exercising the other powers conferred upon the Chairman by these rules, the Chairman shall declare the opening and closing of each meeting, direct the discussion, accord the right to speak, and, pursuant to these rules, have control of the proceedings. The Chairman may also call a

speaker to order if the speaker's remarks are not relevant.

18. During discussion of any matter a delegation may raise a point of order. In this event, the Chairman shall immediately state a ruling. If this ruling is challenged, the Chairman shall submit it to the meeting for decision and it shall stand unless overruled.

19. The Secretary-General, or officers of the CCC Secretariat designated by the Secretary-General, shall perform the secretarial work of meetings of the Technical Committee.

Quorum and Voting

20. Representatives of a simple majority of the members of the Technical Committee shall constitute a quorum.

21. Each member of the Technical Committee shall have one vote. A decision of the Technical Committee shall be taken by a majority comprising at least two thirds of the members present. Regardless of the outcome of the vote on a particular matter, the Technical Committee shall be free to make a full report to the Committee and to the CCC on that matter indicating the different views expressed in the relevant discussions. Notwithstanding the above provisions of this paragraph, on matters referred to it by a panel, the Technical Committee shall take decisions by consensus. Where no agreement is reached in the Technical Committee on the question referred to it by a panel, the Technical Committee shall provide a report detailing the facts of the matter and indicating the views of the members.

Languages and Records

22. The official languages of the Technical Committee shall be English, French and Spanish. Speeches or statements made in any of these three languages shall be immediately translated into the other official languages unless all delegations agree to dispense with translation. Speeches or statements made in any other language shall be translated into English, French and Spanish, subject to the same conditions, but in that event the delegation concerned shall provide the translation into English, French or Spanish. Only English, French and Spanish shall be used for the official documents of the Technical Committee. Memoranda and correspondence for the consideration of the Technical Committee must be presented in one of the official languages.

23. The Technical Committee shall draw up a report of all its sessions and, if the Chairman considers it necessary, minutes or summary records of its meetings. The Chairman or a designee of the Chairman shall report on the work of the Technical Committee at each meeting of the Committee and at each meeting of the CCC.

ANNEX III

1. The five-year delay in the application of the provisions of the Agreement by developing country Members provided for in paragraph 1 of Article 20 may, in practice, be insufficient for certain developing country Members. In such cases a developing country Member may request before the end of the period referred to in paragraph 1 of Article 20 an extension of such period, it being understood that the Members will give sympathetic

consideration to such a request in cases where the developing country Member in question can show good cause.

2. Developing countries which currently value goods on the basis of officially established minimum values may wish to make a reservation to enable them to retain such values on a limited and transitional basis under such terms and conditions as may be agreed to by the Members.

3. Developing countries which consider that the reversal of the sequential order at the request of the importer provided for in Article 4 of the Agreement may give rise to real difficulties for them may wish to make a reservation to Article 4 in the following terms:

> 'The Government of .... reserves the right to provide that the relevant provision of Article 4 of the Agreement shall apply only when the customs authorities agree to the request to reverse the order of Articles 5 and 6.'

If developing countries make such a reservation, the Members shall consent to it under Article 21 of the Agreement.

4. Developing countries may wish to make a reservation with respect to paragraph 2 of Article 5 of the Agreement in the following terms:

> 'The Government of .... reserves the right to provide that paragraph 2 of Article 5 of the Agreement shall be applied in accordance with the provisions of the relevant note thereto whether or not the importer so requests.'

If developing countries make such a reservation, the Members shall consent to it under Article 21 of the Agreement.

5. Certain developing countries may have problems in the implementation of Article 1 of the Agreement insofar as it relates to importations into their countries by sole agents, sole distributors and sole concessionaires. If such problems arise in practice in developing country Members applying the Agreement, a study of this question shall be made, at the request of such Members, with a view to finding appropriate solutions.

6. Article 17 recognizes that in applying the Agreement, customs administrations may need to make enquiries concerning the truth or accuracy of any statement, document or declaration presented to them for customs valuation purposes. The Article thus acknowledges that enquiries may be made which are, for example, aimed at verifying that the elements of value declared or presented to customs in connection with a determination of customs value are complete and correct. Members, subject to their national laws and procedures, have the right to expect the full cooperation of importers in these enquiries.

7. The price actually paid or payable includes all payments actually made or to be made as a condition of sale of the imported goods, by the buyer to the seller, or by the buyer to a third party to satisfy an obligation of the seller."

Decision Regarding Cases Where Customs Administrations Have Reasons to Doubt the Truth or Accuracy of the Declared Value—the Text

"DECISION REGARDING CASES WHERE CUSTOMS ADMINISTRATIONS HAVE REASONS TO DOUBT THE TRUTH OR ACCURACY OF THE DECLARED VALUE

Ministers invite the Committee on Customs Valuation established under the Agreement on Implementation of Article VII of GATT 1994 to take the following decision:

The Committee on Customs Valuation,

Reaffirming that the transaction value is the primary basis of valuation under the Agreement on Implementation of Article VII of GATT 1994 (hereinafter referred to as the 'Agreement');

Recognizing that the customs administration may have to address cases where it has reason to doubt the truth or accuracy of the particulars or of documents produced by traders in support of a declared value;

Emphasizing that in so doing the customs administration should not prejudice the legitimate commercial interests of traders;

Taking into account Article 17 of the Agreement, paragraph 6 of Annex III to the Agreement, and the relevant decisions of the Technical Committee on Customs Valuation;

Decides as follows:

1. When a declaration has been presented and where the customs administration has reason to doubt the truth or accuracy of the particulars or of documents produced in support of this declaration, the customs administration may ask the importer to provide further explanation, including documents or other evidence, that the declared value represents the total amount actually paid or payable for the imported goods, adjusted in accordance with the provisions of Article 8. If, after receiving further information, or in the absence of a response, the customs administration still has reasonable doubts about the truth or accuracy of the declared value, it may, bearing in mind the provisions of Article 11, be deemed that the customs value of the imported goods cannot be determined under the provisions of Article 1. Before taking a final decision, the customs administration shall communicate to the importer, in writing if requested, its grounds for doubting the truth or accuracy of the particulars or documents produced and the importer shall be given a reasonable opportunity to respond. When a final decision is made, the customs administration shall communicate to the importer in writing its decision and the grounds therefor.

2. It is entirely appropriate in applying the Agreement for one Member to assist another Member on mutually agreed terms."

Decision on Texts Relating to Minimum Values and Imports by Sole Agents, Sole Distributors and Sole Concessionaires—the Text

"DECISION ON TEXTS RELATING TO MINIMUM VALUES AND IMPORTS BY SOLE AGENTS, SOLE DISTRIBUTORS AND SOLE CONCESSIONAIRES

Ministers decide to refer the following texts to the Committee on Customs Valuation established under the Agreement on Implementation of Article VII of GATT 1994, for adoption.

Where a developing country makes a reservation to retain officially established minimum values within the terms of paragraph 2 of Annex III and shows good cause, the Committee shall give the request for the reservation sympathetic consideration.

Where a reservation is consented to, the terms and conditions referred to in paragraph 2 of Annex III shall take full account of the development, financial and trade needs of the developing country concerned.

II

1. A number of developing countries have a concern that problems may exist in the valuation of imports by sole agents, sole distributors and sole concessionaires. Under paragraph 1 of Article 20, developing country Members have a period of delay of up to five years prior to the application of the Agreement. In this context, developing country Members availing themselves of this provision could use the period to conduct appropriate studies and to take such other actions as are necessary to facilitate application.

2. In consideration of this, the Committee recommends that the Customs Co-operation Council assist developing country Members, in accordance with the provisions of Annex II, to formulate and conduct studies in areas identified as being of potential concern, including those relating to importations by sole agents, sole distributors and sole concessionaires."

CHAPTER IX: WTO/GATT Control of Non-Tariff Import Barriers

The Nature and History of Non-Tariff Import Barriers

The provisions of GATT 1947 contained only general references to technical regulations and standards in Articles III, XI, and XX. A GATT working group, set up to evaluate the impact of non-tariff barriers in international trade, concluded that technical barriers were the largest category of non-tariff measures faced by exporters. There is little point in dwelling at length on the bad old days, but it should be pointed out regarding non-tariff import barriers that, before the Tokyo Round Standards Code was created, all countries had a great many of them. Some were well-meaning but vaguely worded, unpublicized, or inefficiently administered. That was bad enough. Many were widely-recognized as existing purely for the purpose of preventing the importation of some foreign goods. They were protectionist measures operating under the pretext of serving some legitimate purpose and they were very effective as protectionist measures. Following adoption by most industrialized countries of the Standards Code, things got better —but only in relative terms.

The WTO Agreement on Technical Barriers to Trade has strengthened and clarified the provisions of the Tokyo Round Standards Code. The multilateral standards and non-tariff provisions of GATT subsequent to the conclusion of the Uruguay Round (largely an incorporation of the Tokyo Round Standards Code into GATT, but including other measures dealing with non-tariff barriers other technical ones) are a great step forward but are still largely exhortative rather than acting as enforceable proscriptions of abusive behavior. Even when non-tariff barriers are well drafted, well-administered, and legitimate in their purposes, they are still an impediment to trade and confusing to traders because traders may not quantify in monetary terms, as they may with tariffs, their effect on actual landed costs of importation of goods.

Technical regulations and industrial standards are necessary, but when they vary from country to country they impose huge compliance burdens on importers. Too many different standards also make life difficult for producers and exporters. Where standards are arbitrary, they are susceptible to abusive, protectionist uses.

Description of the Agreement on Technical Barriers to Trade

The Agreement on Technical Barriers to Trade is meant to ensure that regulations, standards, testing, and certification procedures do not create unnecessary obstacles. The agreement recognizes countries' rights to adopt the standards they consider appropriate. Countries are not prevented from taking measures necessary to ensure their standards are met. Nonetheless, the agreement encourages countries to use international standards where these are appropriate but does not require them to change their levels of protection as a result. The agreement sets out a code of good practice for the preparation, adoption, and application of standards by central government bodies. It also includes provisions describing how local government and non-governmental bodies should apply their own regulations. Normally they should use the same principles as apply to central governments. The agreement states that the procedures used to decide whether a product conforms with national standards must be fair and equitable and discourages any methods that would give domestically produced goods an unfair advantage. The agreement also encourages countries to recognize each other's testing procedures so a product can be assessed to see if it meets the importing country's standards through testing in the country where it is made.

Manufacturers and exporters need to know what the latest standards are in their prospective markets. To ensure that this information is made timely and conveniently available, all WTO member governments are required to establish national enquiry points from which this information may be obtained on a current basis.

The Code of Good Practice for the Preparation, Adoption, and Application of Standards lays down disciplines in respect of central government, local government, non-governmental, and regional standardizing bodies developing voluntary standards. The code is open for acceptance by any of these standardizing bodies. Central government standardizing bodies must accept and comply with the provisions of the code. A standardizing body wishing to adhere to, or withdraw from, the code must notify its acceptance of, or withdrawal from, the code using the appropriate notification format. Standardizing bodies that have accepted the code must notify the WTO at least twice a year of the existence of their work program and where details of this program can be obtained. Notifications are to be sent either directly to the International Standardization Organization ("ISO")/the International Electrotechnical Commission ("IEC") Information Centre in Geneva, Switzerland; to its national member of ISO/IEC; or, preferably, to the relevant national member or international affiliate of ISONET.

Transparency is also ensured through the existence of a Technical Barriers to Trade Committee. This allows members to consult together on any matters relating to the operation of the agreement or the furtherance of its objectives. The committee holds on average two to three meetings a year and, if necessary, can establish working parties to carry out specific functions.

The number of technical regulations and standards adopted by countries has grown significantly in recent years and continues to grow at an increasing pace. This may simply reflect increased consumer demand for safe and high-quality products and the growing problems of water, air, and soil pollution that have encouraged modern societies to explore environmentally-friendly products. The precise impact on international trade of the need to comply with different foreign technical regulations and standards is speculative but it certainly involves significant costs for producers and exporters. In general, these costs arise from the translation of foreign regulations, hiring of technical experts to explain foreign regulations, and adjustment of production facilities to comply with the requirements. In addition, there is the need to prove that the exported product meets the foreign regulations. These costs may discourage manufacturers from trying to sell abroad.

Technical regulations and standards set out specific characteristics of a product, such as size, shape, design, functions, and performance, or the way it is labeled or packaged before it is put on sale. In certain cases, the way a product is produced may affect these characteristics. In such cases, it is often more appropriate to draft technical regulations and standards in terms of a product's process and production methods rather than its characteristics *per se*. The Technical Barriers to Trade Agreement makes allowance for both approaches in the way it defines technical regulations and standards in its Annex 1.

The difference between a standard and a technical regulation lies in compliance. While conformity with standards is voluntary, technical regulations are by nature mandatory. They have different implications for international trade. If an imported product does not fulfil the requirements of a technical regulation, it will not be allowed to be put on sale. In case of standards, non-complying imported products will be allowed on the market, but then their market share may be affected if consumers' prefer products that meet local standards. Conformity assessment procedures are technical procedures—*e.g.*, testing, verification, inspection, and certification—which confirm that products fulfil the requirements laid down in regulations and standards. Exporters generally bear the cost, if any, of these procedures. Non-transparent and discriminatory conformity assessment procedures can become effective protectionist tools.

The largest number of technical regulations and standards are for protection of human safety or health. Regulations that protect animal and plant life or health are also very common. Increased environmental concerns among consumers have led many governments to adopt regulations aimed at protecting the environment. Most of these regulations protect consumers through information, mainly in the form of labeling requirements. Other regulations prescribe classification and definition, packaging requirements, and quantitative measurements to avoid deceptive practices. Other regulatory objectives may be quality, technical harmonization, or simply trade facilitation. Quality regulations are very common in certain developed countries. Regulations aimed at harmonizing certain sectors, for example that of telecommunications and terminal equipment, are widespread in economically integrated areas.

Adjusting production to comply with varying technical requirements in individual markets increases production costs per unit and is particularly onerous for small and medium enterprises. Compliance with technical regulations generally requires confirmation through testing, certification, or inspection by laboratories or certification bodies, almost always at the producer's expense. Information costs include the costs of evaluating the technical impact of foreign regulations, translating and disseminating product information, training of experts, etc. Exporters are normally at a cost disadvantage *vis-à-vis* domestic firms in the market of importation in being able to timely and efficiently adjust production in compliance with new regulations.

Technical barriers to trade generally result from the preparation, adoption, and application of different technical regulations and conformity assessment procedures. Differences between one country and another in their technical regulations and conformity assessment procedures may have legitimate origins based on history, happenstance, local tastes, or local financial and other conditions. The Technical Barriers to Trade Agreement accepts these legitimate differences and accords members a high degree of flexibility in the preparation, adoption, and application of their national technical regulations. Nonetheless, members' regulatory flexibility is limited by the requirement that technical regulations "are not prepared, adopted or applied with a view to, or with the effect of, creating unnecessary obstacles to trade" per Article 2.2.

Avoiding unnecessary obstacles to trade means that when a government is preparing a technical regulation to achieve a certain legitimate policy objective, compliance may not be more trade-restrictive than is necessary to fulfil the legitimate objective. Illegitimate policy objectives are *per se* unnecessary obstacles. Specifying, whenever appropriate, product regulations in terms of performance rather than design or descriptive characteristics helps in avoiding unnecessary obstacles to international trade according to Article 2.8. Avoidance of trade obstacles also means that if the circumstances that led a country to adopt a technical regulation no longer exist or have changed or if the policy objective may be achieved by an alternative and less trade-restrictive measure, that technical regulation should be eliminated or changed to conform with evolving requirements. A regulation is more restrictive than necessary when the objective pursued can be achieved through alternative measures which have less trade-restricting effects, taking into account the risks that failure to fulfil the objective would entail. Elements to be used in making a risk assessment are available technical and scientific information, technology, or end-uses of the products. Article 2.2 specifies that legitimate objectives include, *inter alia*, national security requirements, prevention of deceptive practices, protection of human health or safety, protection of animal and plant life or health, or the environment. The obligation to avoid unnecessary obstacles to trade applies also to conformity assessment procedures. An unnecessary obstacle to trade could result from stricter or more time-consuming procedures than are necessary to assess that a product complies with the domestic laws and regulations of the importing country. Information requirements should be no greater than needed and the siting of facilities to carry out conformity assessment and the selection of samples should not create unnecessary inconvenience to the agents per Articles 5.2.3 and 5.2.6.

Members must provide MFN and national treatment for other members' goods regarding technical barriers to trade, and these also apply to conformity assessment procedures. This means that imported products must be treated equally with respect to any fees charged to assess their conformity with regulations. Similarly, Members must respect the confidentiality of information about the results of conformity assessment procedures for imported products in the same way as for domestic products so that commercial interests are protected per Articles 5.2.4 and 5.2.5.

Harmonization of various countries' technical regulations is necessary for the connection and compatibility of parts of products, *i.e.*, telecommunications equipment or car parts. Lack of technical compatibility would generate barriers to international trade and costs of designing, manufacturing, and delivering the same product in various configurations would be high. Technical harmonization would benefit consumers by ensuring that consumers have a wide and economically attractive choice of products, assuming that technical regulations do not go beyond fulfilling their legitimate regulatory objective by unnecessarily stifling innovation or otherwise discouraging producers from introducing new products or product variants. Technical experts have worked towards the international harmonization of standards. An important role in these efforts is played by ISO, IEC, and the International Telecommunication Union ("ITU"). Their activities have had major impact on trade, especially in industrial products. For example, ISO has developed more than 9,600 international standards covering almost all technical fields. The agreement encourages members to use existing international standards for part or all of their national regulations unless "their use would be ineffective or inappropriate" to fulfil a given policy objective. Similar provisions apply to conformity assessment procedures to use international guides or recommendations issued by international standardizing bodies, or the relevant parts of them, barring some legitimate reasons that their use would be inappropriate.

The development, broad acceptance, and universal implementation of an international product standard does not come quickly. Consequently, the Technical Barriers to Trade Agreement introduced a complementary approach to technical harmonization, an idea known as "equivalence." Technical barriers to international trade could be quickly eliminated if members were to accept that technical regulations of other countries that are different from their own fulfil the same policy objectives, even if they do so through different means. This approach is articulated in Article 2.7. Requirements to demonstrate in each importing country compliance with technical regulations may also serve as a severe impediment to international trade. If products are to be exported to multiple markets, multiple testing would be required. Manufacturers may have difficulty in obtaining certification of their products for multiple foreign markets. Testing experts regularly disagree on optimal testing procedures. Bureaucratic inertia is always a concern. Protectionist and other groups antithetic to the manufacturer or the manufacturer's country, industry, or products may even successfully manipulate the testing process such as to deny accreditation to the product. Such impediments may be both daunting and costly. A major cause of high costs for the international trade in many products is the result of the requirement to essentially repeat the same tests again and again for each foreign market before it may sell the product in that foreign market. These costs would be drastically reduced if a product could be tested once and the testing results accepted in all markets.

Countries should agree to accept the results of one another's conformity assessment procedures, although these procedures might be different, assuming the country and assessment procedures under which certification would be determined are credible regarding their testing standards and results. Article 6.3 strongly encourages members to enter into negotiations with other members for the mutual acceptance of conformity assessment results. Since a high degree of confidence in testing and certification bodies is a prerequisite for the good functioning of an international system of mutual recognition of such assessments, Article 6.1 recognizes that prior consultations may be necessary to arrive at a mutually satisfactory understanding regarding the competence of the conformity assessment bodies and also points out that compliance by conformity assessment bodies with relevant guides or recommendations issued by international standardizing bodies can be regarded as an indication of adequate technical competence.

Members must notify the WTO when two conditions apply: (1) whenever a relevant international standard or guide or recommendation does not exist, or the technical content of a proposed or adopted technical regulation or procedure is not in accordance with the technical content of relevant international standards or guides of recommendations; and (2) if the technical regulation or conformity assessment procedure may have a significant effect on the trade of other members per Articles 2.9 and 5.6. Draft regulations are to be notified to the WTO Secretariat and this should be done, if possible, sixty days prior to their formal adoption so as to allow time for other members to make comments. Regulations may also be notified following their implementation whenever urgent problems of safety, health, or environmental protection arise per Articles 2.10 and 5.7. Local Governments at the level directly below central government are required to notify technical regulations and conformity assessment procedures that have not been previously notified by their central government authorities (Article 3.2 and 7.2).

Special provision is made in the agreement to assist underdeveloped countries in bringing their technical standards into compliance with the agreement and to give those countries special flexibility in the timing and manner of their compliance.

Each WTO member must, promptly after the Technical Barriers to Trade Agreement enters into force for it, notify all other members of the measures in existence or taken to ensure the implementation and administration of the agreement and of any subsequent changes to them per Article 15.2). This written statement must include, *inter alia*, all relevant laws, regulations, administrative orders, etc., to ensure that the provisions of the agreement are applied; the names of the publications where draft and final technical regulations, standards and conformity assessment procedures are published; the expected length of time for the presentation of written comments on technical regulations, standards, or conformity assessment procedures; and the name and address of the enquiry points established under Article 10. Under Article 10.7, a member who has reached an agreement with any other country or countries on issues related to technical regulations, standards, or conformity assessment procedures which may have a significant effect on trade must notify all other members through the WTO Secretariat of the products to be covered by the agreement and provide a brief description of the agreement with the other country or countries.

As a complement to the obligation to notify, each WTO member must set up a national enquiry point. This national inquiry point serves as the focus for other members inquiries for information and documentation on a member's technical regulations, standards, and test procedures—whether impending or adopted—as well as on participation in bilateral or plurilateral standard-related agreements, regional standardizing bodies, and conformity assessment systems. Enquiry points are generally governmental agencies but the relevant functions can also be assigned to private agencies. The obligation to set up enquiry points is particularly important for developing countries. It is not only the first step by a developing country member towards implementation of the agreement, but it is also the means by which developing countries may acquire information from other members' enquiry points regarding foreign regulations and standards affecting products in which they have a trade interest.

Although less widely used now than in the past, import licensing systems are subject to disciplines in the WTO. The Agreement on Import Licensing Procedures requires import licensing to be simple, transparent, and predictable. Governments must, for example, publish sufficient information for traders to know how and why the licenses are granted. The agreement also describes how countries must notify the WTO when they introduce new import licensing procedures or change existing procedures. The agreement offers guidance on how governments should assess applications for licenses. Some licenses are issued automatically if certain conditions are met. The agreement sets criteria for automatic licensing so that the procedures used do not restrict trade. Other licenses are not issued automatically. For these, the agreement tries to minimize the importers' burden in applying for licenses so that the administrative work does not in itself restrict or distort imports. The agreement says that the agencies handling licensing should not normally take more than 30 days to deal with an application or 60 days when all applications are considered at the same time. The revised agreement contains strengthened rules for the notification of the institution of import licensing procedures or changes to them and also offers guidance on the assessment of applications.

Preshipment inspection is the practice of employing specialized private companies to check shipment details, generally price, quantity, and quality, of goods ordered overseas at a point overseas before they are exported to the country requiring the inspection. This practice is usually used by governments of developing countries that seek to safeguard their national financial interests by preventing capital flight, commercial fraud, and customs duty evasion and to compensate for inadequacies—usually rampant corruption but sometimes (or also) gross inefficiencies—in customs administrative infrastructures. The Preshipment Inspection Agreement recognizes that GATT principles and obligations apply to the activities of preshipment inspection agencies that are performed under mandates from governments. Obligations imposed on governments adopting preshipment inspections include non-discrimination, transparency, protection of confidential business information, avoidance of unreasonable delay, the use of specific guidelines for conducting price verification, and the avoidance of conflicts of interest by the agencies performing the inspections. Exporting contracting parties' governments have obligations towards governments requiring preshipment inspections to not discriminate in the application of domestic laws and regulations, to promptly publish such laws and regulations, and to provide technical assistance where requested. The agreement established an independent review procedure administered jointly by an organization representing agencies performing preshipment inspections and an organization representing exporters to resolve disputes between an exporter and preshipment inspector.

The Agreement on Rules of Origin seeks the long-term harmonization of rules of origin, other than rules of origin relating to the granting of tariff preferences, and to ensure that such rules do not themselves create unnecessary obstacles to trade. The agreement sets up a harmonization program based upon a set of principles, including making rules of origin objective, understandable, and predictable, under the direction of a Committee on Rules of Origin in the GATT and a technical committee under the auspices of the CCC/WCO. Until the completion of the harmonization program, contracting parties are expected to ensure that their rules of origin are transparent; that they do not have restricting, distorting or disruptive effects on international trade; that they are administered in a consistent, uniform, impartial, and reasonable manner; and that they are based on a positive standard by asserting what confers origin status rather than asserting what fails to confer that status. An annex to the agreement sets out a "common declaration" with respect to the operation of rules of origin on goods which qualify for preferential treatment.

The Agreement on Sanitary and Phytosanitary Measures deals with measures intended to assure food safety and regulations concerning the health of animals and plants. The agreement recognizes that governments have the right to take such measures but that they should be applied only to the extent necessary to protect human, animal, or plant life or health and should not arbitrarily or unjustifiably discriminate between members where identical or similar conditions prevail. In order to harmonize sanitary and phytosanitary measures on as wide a basis as possible, members are encouraged to base their measures on international standards, guidelines, and recommendations where they exist. Nonetheless, members may maintain or introduce measures that result in higher standards if there is scientific justification or as a consequence of consistent risk decisions based on an appropriate risk assessment. The agreement spells out procedures and criteria for the assessment of risk and the determination of appropriate levels of sanitary or phytosanitary protection. Members are expected to accept the sanitary and phytosanitary measures of others as equivalent if the exporting country demonstrates to the importing country that its measures achieve the importing country's appropriate level of health protection. The agreement includes provisions on control, inspection and approval procedures.

The Agreement on Marks of Origin deals with what is virtually a universal requirement in each customs territory that entering goods be marked in a manner required by law to show the country of origin of such goods. Making such marking requirements consistent among WTO members would greatly ease the burden of compliance on manufacturers and traders. This was not explicitly encouraged by this agreement, but the agreement did require members to be accommodating in permitting importers to effect compliance at the time of importation when discrepancies are found, forbade them from penalizing those effecting such compliance at the time of importation through special taxes or fees, and encouraged them to make marking requirements such as to not result in damage to the goods so marked.

International Standard Making Organizations and Places to Find Information Regarding National Technical Regulations and Other Non-Tariff Barriers to Trade

Product standards may be prepared by governmental or non-governmental standardizing bodies. There are numerous private standardizing bodies. The Code of Good Practice, contained in Annex 3 of the Technical Barriers to Trade Agreement, provides disciplines—including those related to transparency—for the preparation, adoption and application of standards by all central governmental, local government, non-governmental and regional standardizing bodies. The code is open for acceptance to any standardizing bodies, whether central government, local government or non-governmental and regional standardizing bodies. The code seeks to bring all standards within its purview and provides for [and gives] transparency in the preparation, adoption, and application of standards.

Members are responsible for the acceptance and compliance with the code by their central government standardizing bodies. Furthermore, they are required to take such reasonable measures as may be available to them to ensure also that local government and non-governmental standardizing bodies within their territories, and regional standardizing bodies of which they are members, accept and comply with the code.

The WTO web site provides on line access to contact information regarding every WTO member's national point of enquiry regarding technical standards and provides all those technical standards/non-tariff barriers to trade that each WTO member has made as part of its bindings under WTO/GATT.

The US point of enquiry is the National Center for Standards and Certification Information, National Institute of Standards and Technology ("NIST"), Bldg. 820, Room 164, Gaithersburg, MD 20899, Telephone: (301) 975-4040, E-mail: ncsci@nist.gov, web site at http://www.nist.gov/public_affairs/standards.htm. NIST maintains a reference collection of standards, specifications, test methods, codes, and recommended practices. This reference material includes US government agencies' regulations and standards of US private standards-developing organizations and foreign national and international standardizing bodies. NIST is the source of copious information and assistance to US international traders seeking to understand and comply with non-US product standards and related importation requirements and procedures. The enquiry point responds to all enquiries for information concerning federal, state, and private regulations, standards, and conformity assessment procedures. Its telephone and e-mail inquiry point supplies information on US, foreign, and international voluntary standards; government regulations; and rules of conformity assessment for non-agricultural products. It also offers telephone hotlines that report standards-related developments in the WTO and in the EU. NIST also actively coordinates standards activities with those of the private sector, in particular the American National Standards Institute ("ANSI"). ANSI is not a standards developer but coordinates US activities, particularly with respect to ISO and IEC, and develops cross-sectoral policy positions within the United States. NIST and ANSI have signed a memorandum of understanding that mutually recognizes the particular responsibilities of each. WTO Standards

Notifications at http://www.mac.doc.gov/TCC/TCC2/monitor/index.html, a service of the US Trade Compliance Center, part of the US International Trade Administration, which in turn is part of the US Department of Commerce, posts WTO members' advance notifications of impending changes in standards requirements that could affect trade. Notices provide businesses and other organizations with the opportunity to comment.

ISO is generally considered to be the global standard-making and monitoring organization and the one through which specialized and national standard-making organizations coordinate their activities. Information regarding ISO may be obtained from its web site at http//www.iso.ch and its cooperative function with the WTO is specially dealt with at http://www.iso.ch/wtotbt/wtotbt.htm. Information regarding IEC is available from its web site at http://www.iec.ch. Information regarding ITU is available from its web site at http://www.itu.net. Information on the organizations mentioned in the sanitary and phytosanitary agreement may be found at their various web sites: the Codex Alimentarius Commission, www.fao.org/WAICENT/FAOINFO/ECONOMIC/ESN/codex/default.htm; the International Office of Epizootics, http://www.oie.int; and the International Plant Protection Convention Secretariat, http://www.fao.org/WAICENT/FAOINFO/AGRICULT/AGP/AGPP/PQ/Default.htm.

GATT 1947 Article IX—the Text

[***asterisks** below mark the portions of the text which should be read in conjunction with notes and supplementary provisions in Annex I to the Agreement.]

"Article IX
Marks of Origin

1. Each contracting party shall accord to the products of the territories of other contracting parties treatment with regard to marking requirements no less favourable than the treatment accorded to like products of any third country.

2. The contracting parties recognize that, in adopting and enforcing laws and regulations relating to marks of origin, the difficulties and inconveniences which such measures may cause to the commerce and industry of exporting countries should be reduced to a minimum, due regard being had to the necessity of protecting consumers against fraudulent or misleading indications.

3. Whenever it is administratively practicable to do so, contracting parties should permit required marks of origin to be affixed at the time of importation.

4. The laws and regulations of contracting parties relating to

the marking of imported products shall be such as to permit compliance without seriously damaging the products, or materially reducing their value, or unreasonably increasing their cost.

5. As a general rule, no special duty or penalty should be imposed by any contracting party for failure to comply with marking requirements prior to importation unless corrective marking is unreasonably delayed or deceptive marks have been affixed or the required marking has been intentionally omitted.

6. The contracting parties shall co-operate with each other with a view to preventing the use of trade names in such manner as to misrepresent the true origin of a product, to the detriment of such distinctive regional or geographical names of products of the territory of a contracting party as are protected by its legislation. Each contracting party shall accord full and sympathetic consideration to such requests or representations as may be made by any other contracting party regarding the application of the undertaking set forth in the preceding sentence to names of products which have been communicated to it by the other contracting party."

GATT 1947 Article XI and its Annex I Notes —the Texts

[***asterisks** below mark the portions of the text which should be read in conjunction with notes and supplementary provisions in Annex I to the Agreement.]

"Article XI*

General Elimination of Quantitative Restrictions

1. No prohibitions or restrictions other than duties, taxes or other charges, whether made effective through quotas, import or export licences or other measures, shall be instituted or maintained by any contracting party on the importation of any product of the territory of any other contracting party or on the exportation or sale for export of any product destined for the territory of any other contracting party.

2. The provisions of paragraph 1 of this Article shall not extend to the following:

(*a*) Export prohibitions or restrictions temporarily applied to prevent or relieve critical shortages of foodstuffs or other products essential to the exporting contracting party;

(*b*) Import and export prohibitions or restrictions necessary to the application of standards or regulations for the classification, grading or marketing of commodities in international trade;

(*c*) Import restrictions on any agricultural or fisheries product, imported in any form,* necessary to the enforcement of governmental measures which operate:

(*i*) to restrict the quantities of the like domestic product permitted to be marketed or produced, or, if there is no substantial domestic production of the like product, of a domestic product for which the imported product can be directly substituted; or

(ii) to remove a temporary surplus of the like domestic product, or, if there is no substantial domestic production of the like product, of a domestic product for which the imported product can be directly substituted, by making the surplus available to certain groups of domestic consumers free of charge or at prices below the current market level; or

(iii) to restrict the quantities permitted to be produced of any animal product the production of which is directly dependent, wholly or mainly, on the imported commodity, if the domestic production of that commodity is relatively negligible.

Any contracting party applying restrictions on the importation of any product pursuant to sub-paragraph (*c*) of this paragraph shall give public notice of the total quantity or value of the product permitted to be imported during a specified future period and of any change in such quantity or value. Moreover, any restrictions applied under (i) above shall not be such as will reduce the total of imports relative to the total of domestic production, as compared with the proportion which might reasonably be expected to rule between the two in the absence of restrictions. In determining this proportion, the contracting party shall pay due regard to the proportion prevailing during a previous representative period and to any special factors* which may have affected or may be affecting the trade in the product concerned."

"**Ad Articles XI, XII, XIII, XIV and XVIII**

Throughout Articles XI, XII, XIII, XIV and XVIII, the terms 'import restrictions' or 'export restrictions' include restrictions made effective through state-trading operations."

"**Ad Article XI**

Paragraph 2 (c)

The term 'in any form' in this paragraph covers the same products when in an early stage of processing and still perishable, which compete directly with the fresh product and if freely imported would tend to make the restriction on the fresh product ineffective.

Paragraph 2, last sub-paragraph

The term 'special factors' includes changes in relative productive efficiency as between domestic and foreign producers, or as between different foreign producers, but not changes artificially brought about by means not permitted under the Agreement."

Agreement on Sanitary and Phytosanitary Measures—the Text

"AGREEMENT ON THE APPLICATION OF SANITARY AND PHYTOSANITARY MEASURES

Members,

Reaffirming that no Member should be prevented from adopting or enforcing measures necessary to protect human, animal or plant life or health, subject to the requirement that these measures are not applied in a manner which would constitute a means of arbitrary or unjustifiable discrimination between Members where the same conditions prevail or a disguised restriction on international trade;

Desiring to improve the human health, animal health and phytosanitary situation in all Members;

Noting that sanitary and phytosanitary measures are often applied on the basis of bilateral agreements or protocols;

Desiring the establishment of a multilateral framework of rules and disciplines to guide the development, adoption and enforcement of sanitary and phytosanitary measures in order to minimize their negative effects on trade;

Recognizing the important contribution that international standards, guidelines and recommendations can make in this regard;

Desiring to further the use of harmonized sanitary and phytosanitary measures between Members, on the basis of international standards, guidelines and recommendations developed by the relevant international organizations, including the Codex Alimentarius Commission, the International Office of Epizootics, and the relevant international and regional organizations operating within the framework of the International Plant Protection Convention, without requiring Members to change their appropriate level of protection of human, animal or plant life or health;

Recognizing that developing country Members may encounter special difficulties in complying with the sanitary or phytosanitary measures of importing Members, and as a consequence in access to markets, and also in the formulation and application of sanitary or phytosanitary measures in their own territories, and desiring to assist them in their endeavours in this regard;

Desiring therefore to elaborate rules for the application of the provisions of GATT 1994 which relate to the use of sanitary or phytosanitary measures, in particular the provisions of Article XX(b) [IN THIS AGREEMENT, REFERENCE TO ARTICLE XX(B) INCLUDES ALSO THE CHAPEAU OF THAT ARTICLE.];

Hereby agree as follows:

Article 1
General Provisions

1. This Agreement applies to all sanitary and phytosanitary measures which may, directly or indirectly, affect international trade. Such measures shall be developed and applied in accordance with the provisions of this Agreement.

2. For the purposes of this Agreement, the definitions provided in Annex A shall apply.

3. The annexes are an integral part of this Agreement.

4. Nothing in this Agreement shall affect the rights of Members under the Agreement on Technical Barriers to Trade with respect to measures not within the scope of this Agreement.

Article 2
Basic Rights and Obligations

1. Members have the right to take sanitary and phytosanitary measures necessary for the protection of human, animal or plant life or health, provided that such measures are not inconsistent with the provisions of this Agreement.

2. Members shall ensure that any sanitary or phytosanitary measure is applied only to the extent necessary to protect human, animal or plant life or health, is based on scientific principles and is not maintained without sufficient scientific evidence, except as provided for in paragraph 7 of Article 5.

3. Members shall ensure that their sanitary and phytosanitary measures do not arbitrarily or unjustifiably discriminate between Members where identical or similar conditions prevail, including between their own territory and that of other Members. Sanitary and phytosanitary measures shall not be applied in a manner which would constitute a disguised restriction on international trade.

4. Sanitary or phytosanitary measures which conform to the relevant provisions of this Agreement shall be presumed to be in accordance with the obligations of the Members under the provisions of GATT 1994 which relate to the use of sanitary or phytosanitary measures, in particular the provisions of Article XX(b).

Article 3
Harmonization

1. To harmonize sanitary and phytosanitary measures on as wide a basis as possible, Members shall base their sanitary or phytosanitary measures on international standards, guidelines or recommendations, where they exist, except as otherwise provided for in this Agreement, and in particular in paragraph 3.

2. Sanitary or phytosanitary measures which conform to international standards, guidelines or recommendations shall be deemed to be necessary to protect human, animal or plant life or health, and presumed to be consistent with the relevant provisions of this Agreement and of GATT 1994.

3. Members may introduce or maintain sanitary or phytosanitary measures which result in a higher level of sanitary or phytosanitary protection than would be achieved by measures based on the relevant international standards, guidelines or recommendations, if there is a scientific justification, or as a consequence of the level of sanitary or phytosanitary protection a Member determines to be appropriate in accordance with the relevant provisions of paragraphs 1 through 8 of Article 5 [FOR THE PURPOSES OF PARAGRAPH

3 OF ARTICLE 3, THERE IS A SCIENTIFIC JUSTIFICATION IF, ON THE BASIS OF AN EXAMINATION AND EVALUATION OF AVAILABLE SCIENTIFIC INFORMATION IN CONFORMITY WITH THE RELEVANT PROVISIONS OF THIS AGREEMENT, A MEMBER DETERMINES THAT THE RELEVANT INTERNATIONAL STANDARDS, GUIDELINES OR RECOMMENDATIONS ARE NOT SUFFICIENT TO ACHIEVE ITS APPROPRIATE LEVEL OF SANITARY OR PHYTOSANITARY PROTECTION.]. Notwithstanding the above, all measures which result in a level of sanitary or phytosanitary protection different from that which would be achieved by measures based on international standards, guidelines or recommendations shall not be inconsistent with any other provision of this Agreement.

4. Members shall play a full part, within the limits of their resources, in the relevant international organizations and their subsidiary bodies, in particular the Codex Alimentarius Commission, the International Office of Epizootics, and the international and regional organizations operating within the framework of the International Plant Protection Convention, to promote within these organizations the development and periodic review of standards, guidelines and recommendations with respect to all aspects of sanitary and phytosanitary measures.

5. The Committee on Sanitary and Phytosanitary Measures provided for in paragraphs 1 and 4 of Article 12 (referred to in this Agreement as the 'Committee') shall develop a procedure to monitor the process of international harmonization and coordinate efforts in this regard with the relevant international organizations.

Article 4
Equivalence

1. Members shall accept the sanitary or phytosanitary measures of other Members as equivalent, even if these measures differ from their own or from those used by other Members trading in the same product, if the exporting Member objectively demonstrates to the importing Member that its measures achieve the importing Member's appropriate level of sanitary or phytosanitary protection. For this purpose, reasonable access shall be given, upon request, to the importing Member for inspection, testing and other relevant procedures.

2. Members shall, upon request, enter into consultations with the aim of achieving bilateral and multilateral agreements on recognition of the equivalence of specified sanitary or phytosanitary measures.

Article 5
Assessment of Risk and Determination of the Appropriate Level of Sanitary or Phytosanitary Protection

1. Members shall ensure that their sanitary or phytosanitary measures are based on an assessment, as appropriate to the circumstances, of the risks to human, animal or plant life or health, taking into account risk assessment techniques developed by the relevant international organizations.

2. In the assessment of risks, Members shall take into account available scientific evidence; relevant processes and production methods;

relevant inspection, sampling and testing methods; prevalence of specific diseases or pests; existence of pest- or disease-free areas; relevant ecological and environmental conditions; and quarantine or other treatment.

3. In assessing the risk to animal or plant life or health and determining the measure to be applied for achieving the appropriate level of sanitary or phytosanitary protection from such risk, Members shall take into account as relevant economic factors: the potential damage in terms of loss of production or sales in the event of the entry, establishment or spread of a pest or disease; the costs of control or eradication in the territory of the importing Member; and the relative cost-effectiveness of alternative approaches to limiting risks.

4. Members should, when determining the appropriate level of sanitary or phytosanitary protection, take into account the objective of minimizing negative trade effects.

5. With the objective of achieving consistency in the application of the concept of appropriate level of sanitary or phytosanitary protection against risks to human life or health, or to animal and plant life or health, each Member shall avoid arbitrary or unjustifiable distinctions in the levels it considers to be appropriate in different situations, if such distinctions result in discrimination or a disguised restriction on international trade. Members shall cooperate in the Committee, in accordance with paragraphs 1, 2 and 3 of Article 12, to develop guidelines to further the practical implementation of this provision. In developing the guidelines, the Committee shall take into account all relevant factors, including the exceptional character of human health risks to which people voluntarily expose themselves.

6. Without prejudice to paragraph 2 of Article 3, when establishing or maintaining sanitary or phytosanitary measures to achieve the appropriate level of sanitary or phytosanitary protection, Members shall ensure that such measures are not more trade-restrictive than required to achieve their appropriate level of sanitary or phytosanitary protection, taking into account technical and economic feasibility [FOR PURPOSES OF PARAGRAPH 6 OF ARTICLE 5, A MEASURE IS NOT MORE TRADE-RESTRICTIVE THAN REQUIRED UNLESS THERE IS ANOTHER MEASURE, REASONABLY AVAILABLE TAKING INTO ACCOUNT TECHNICAL AND ECONOMIC FEASIBILITY, THAT ACHIEVES THE APPROPRIATE LEVEL OF SANITARY OR PHYTOSANITARY PROTECTION AND IS SIGNIFICANTLY LESS RESTRICTIVE TO TRADE.].

7. In cases where relevant scientific evidence is insufficient, a Member may provisionally adopt sanitary or phytosanitary measures on the basis of available pertinent information, including that from the relevant international organizations as well as from sanitary or phytosanitary measures applied by other Members. In such circumstances, Members shall seek to obtain the additional information necessary for a more objective assessment of risk and review the sanitary or phytosanitary measure accordingly within a reasonable period of time.

8. When a Member has reason to believe that a specific sanitary or phytosanitary measure introduced or maintained by another Member is constraining, or has the potential to constrain, its exports and the measure is not based on the relevant international standards, guidelines or

recommendations, or such standards, guidelines or recommendations do not exist, an explanation of the reasons for such sanitary or phytosanitary measure may be requested and shall be provided by the Member maintaining the measure.

Article 6

Adaptation to Regional Conditions, Including Pest- or Disease-Free Areas and Areas of Low Pest or Disease Prevalence

1. Members shall ensure that their sanitary or phytosanitary measures are adapted to the sanitary or phytosanitary characteristics of the area - whether all of a country, part of a country, or all or parts of several countries - from which the product originated and to which the product is destined. In assessing the sanitary or phytosanitary characteristics of a region, Members shall take into account, *inter alia*, the level of prevalence of specific diseases or pests, the existence of eradication or control programmes, and appropriate criteria or guidelines which may be developed by the relevant international organizations.

2. Members shall, in particular, recognize the concepts of pest- or disease-free areas and areas of low pest or disease prevalence. Determination of such areas shall be based on factors such as geography, ecosystems, epidemiological surveillance, and the effectiveness of sanitary or phytosanitary controls.

3. Exporting Members claiming that areas within their territories are pest- or disease-free areas or areas of low pest or disease prevalence shall provide the necessary evidence thereof in order to objectively demonstrate to the importing Member that such areas are, and are likely to remain, pest- or disease-free areas or areas of low pest or disease prevalence, respectively. For this purpose, reasonable access shall be given, upon request, to the importing Member for inspection, testing and other relevant procedures.

Article 7

Transparency

Members shall notify changes in their sanitary or phytosanitary measures and shall provide information on their sanitary or phytosanitary measures in accordance with the provisions of Annex B.

Article 8

Control, Inspection and Approval Procedures

Members shall observe the provisions of Annex C in the operation of control, inspection and approval procedures, including national systems for approving the use of additives or for establishing tolerances for contaminants in foods, beverages or feedstuffs, and otherwise ensure that their procedures are not inconsistent with the provisions of this Agreement.

Article 9

Technical Assistance

1. Members agree to facilitate the provision of technical assistance to other Members, especially developing country Members, either

bilaterally or through the appropriate international organizations. Such assistance may be, *inter alia*, in the areas of processing technologies, research and infrastructure, including in the establishment of national regulatory bodies, and may take the form of advice, credits, donations and grants, including for the purpose of seeking technical expertise, training and equipment to allow such countries to adjust to, and comply with, sanitary or phytosanitary measures necessary to achieve the appropriate level of sanitary or phytosanitary protection in their export markets.

2. Where substantial investments are required in order for an exporting developing country Member to fulfil the sanitary or phytosanitary requirements of an importing Member, the latter shall consider providing such technical assistance as will permit the developing country Member to maintain and expand its market access opportunities for the product involved.

Article 10
Special and Differential Treatment

1. In the preparation and application of sanitary or phytosanitary measures, Members shall take account of the special needs of developing country Members, and in particular of the least-developed country Members.

2. Where the appropriate level of sanitary or phytosanitary protection allows scope for the phased introduction of new sanitary or phytosanitary measures, longer time-frames for compliance should be accorded on products of interest to developing country Members so as to maintain opportunities for their exports.

3. With a view to ensuring that developing country Members are able to comply with the provisions of this Agreement, the Committee is enabled to grant to such countries, upon request, specified, time-limited exceptions in whole or in part from obligations under this Agreement, taking into account their financial, trade and development needs.

4. Members should encourage and facilitate the active participation of developing country Members in the relevant international organizations.

Article 11
Consultations and Dispute Settlement

1. The provisions of Articles XXII and XXIII of GATT 1994 as elaborated and applied by the Dispute Settlement Understanding shall apply to consultations and the settlement of disputes under this Agreement, except as otherwise specifically provided herein.

2. In a dispute under this Agreement involving scientific or technical issues, a panel should seek advice from experts chosen by the panel in consultation with the parties to the dispute. To this end, the panel may, when it deems it appropriate, establish an advisory technical experts group, or consult the relevant international organizations, at the request of either party to the dispute or on its own initiative.

3. Nothing in this Agreement shall impair the rights of Members under other international agreements, including the right to resort to the good offices or dispute settlement mechanisms of other international organizations or established under any international agreement.

Article 12
Administration

1. A Committee on Sanitary and Phytosanitary Measures is hereby established to provide a regular forum for consultations. It shall carry out the functions necessary to implement the provisions of this Agreement and the furtherance of its objectives, in particular with respect to harmonization. The Committee shall reach its decisions by consensus.

2. The Committee shall encourage and facilitate ad hoc consultations or negotiations among Members on specific sanitary or phytosanitary issues. The Committee shall encourage the use of international standards, guidelines or recommendations by all Members and, in this regard, shall sponsor technical consultation and study with the objective of increasing coordination and integration between international and national systems and approaches for approving the use of food additives or for establishing tolerances for contaminants in foods, beverages or feedstuffs.

3. The Committee shall maintain close contact with the relevant international organizations in the field of sanitary and phytosanitary protection, especially with the Codex Alimentarius Commission, the International Office of Epizootics, and the Secretariat of the International Plant Protection Convention, with the objective of securing the best available scientific and technical advice for the administration of this Agreement and in order to ensure that unnecessary duplication of effort is avoided.

4. The Committee shall develop a procedure to monitor the process of international harmonization and the use of international standards, guidelines or recommendations. For this purpose, the Committee should, in conjunction with the relevant international organizations, establish a list of international standards, guidelines or recommendations relating to sanitary or phytosanitary measures which the Committee determines to have a major trade impact. The list should include an indication by Members of those international standards, guidelines or recommendations which they apply as conditions for import or on the basis of which imported products conforming to these standards can enjoy access to their markets. For those cases in which a Member does not apply an international standard, guideline or recommendation as a condition for import, the Member should provide an indication of the reason therefor, and, in particular, whether it considers that the standard is not stringent enough to provide the appropriate level of sanitary or phytosanitary protection. If a Member revises its position, following its indication of the use of a standard, guideline or recommendation as a condition for import, it should provide an explanation for its change and so inform the Secretariat as well as the relevant international organizations, unless such notification and explanation is given according to the procedures of Annex B.

5. In order to avoid unnecessary duplication, the Committee may decide, as appropriate, to use the information generated by the procedures, particularly for notification, which are in operation in the relevant international organizations.

6. The Committee may, on the basis of an initiative from one of the Members, through appropriate channels invite the relevant international organizations or their subsidiary bodies to examine specific matters with respect

to a particular standard, guideline or recommendation, including the basis of explanations for non-use given according to paragraph 4.

7. The Committee shall review the operation and implementation of this Agreement three years after the date of entry into force of the WTO Agreement, and thereafter as the need arises. Where appropriate, the Committee may submit to the Council for Trade in Goods proposals to amend the text of this Agreement having regard, *inter alia*, to the experience gained in its implementation.

Article 13

Implementation

Members are fully responsible under this Agreement for the observance of all obligations set forth herein. Members shall formulate and implement positive measures and mechanisms in support of the observance of the provisions of this Agreement by other than central government bodies. Members shall take such reasonable measures as may be available to them to ensure that non-governmental entities within their territories, as well as regional bodies in which relevant entities within their territories are members, comply with the relevant provisions of this Agreement. In addition, Members shall not take measures which have the effect of, directly or indirectly, requiring or encouraging such regional or non-governmental entities, or local governmental bodies, to act in a manner inconsistent with the provisions of this Agreement. Members shall ensure that they rely on the services of non-governmental entities for implementing sanitary or phytosanitary measures only if these entities comply with the provisions of this Agreement.

Article 14

Final Provisions

The least-developed country Members may delay application of the provisions of this Agreement for a period of five years following the date of entry into force of the WTO Agreement with respect to their sanitary or phytosanitary measures affecting importation or imported products. Other developing country Members may delay application of the provisions of this Agreement, other than paragraph 8 of Article 5 and Article 7, for two years following the date of entry into force of the WTO Agreement with respect to their existing sanitary or phytosanitary measures affecting importation or imported products, where such application is prevented by a lack of technical expertise, technical infrastructure or resources.

ANNEX A

DEFINITIONS [FOR THE PURPOSE OF THESE DEFINITIONS, 'ANIMAL' INCLUDES FISH AND WILD FAUNA; 'PLANT' INCLUDES FORESTS AND WILD FLORA; 'PESTS' INCLUDE WEEDS; AND 'CONTAMINANTS' INCLUDE PESTICIDE AND VETERINARY DRUG RESIDUES AND EXTRANEOUS MATTER.]

1. *Sanitary or phytosanitary measure* - Any measure applied:

(a) to protect animal or plant life or health within the territory of the Member from risks arising from the entry, establishment or spread of pests, diseases, disease-carrying organisms or disease-causing organisms;

(b) to protect human or animal life or health within the territory of the Member from risks arising from additives, contaminants, toxins or disease-causing organisms in foods, beverages or feedstuffs;

(c) to protect human life or health within the territory of the Member from risks arising from diseases carried by animals, plants or products thereof, or from the entry, establishment or spread of pests; or

(d) to prevent or limit other damage within the territory of the Member from the entry, establishment or spread of pests.

Sanitary or phytosanitary measures include all relevant laws, decrees, regulations, requirements and procedures including, *inter alia*, end product criteria; processes and production methods; testing, inspection, certification and approval procedures; quarantine treatments including relevant requirements associated with the transport of animals or plants, or with the materials necessary for their survival during transport; provisions on relevant statistical methods, sampling procedures and methods of risk assessment; and packaging and labelling requirements directly related to food safety.

2. *Harmonization* - The establishment, recognition and application of common sanitary and phytosanitary measures by different Members.

3. *International standards, guidelines and recommendations*

(a) for food safety, the standards, guidelines and recommendations established by the Codex Alimentarius Commission relating to food additives, veterinary drug and pesticide residues, contaminants, methods of analysis and sampling, and codes and guidelines of hygienic practice;

(b) for animal health and zoonoses, the standards, guidelines and recommendations developed under the auspices of the International Office of Epizootics;

(c) for plant health, the international standards, guidelines and recommendations developed under the auspices of the Secretariat of the International Plant Protection Convention in cooperation with regional organizations operating within the framework of the International Plant Protection Convention; and

(d) for matters not covered by the above organizations, appropriate standards, guidelines and recommendations promulgated by other relevant international organizations open for membership to all Members, as identified by the Committee.

4. *Risk assessment* - The evaluation of the likelihood of entry, establishment or spread of a pest or disease within the territory of an importing Member according to the sanitary or phytosanitary measures which might be applied, and of the associated potential biological and economic consequences; or the evaluation of the potential for adverse effects on human or animal health arising from the presence of additives, contaminants, toxins or disease-causing organisms in food, beverages or feedstuffs.

5. *Appropriate level of sanitary or phytosanitary protection* - The level of protection deemed appropriate by the Member establishing a sanitary or phytosanitary measure to protect human, animal or plant life or health within its territory.

NOTE: Many Members otherwise refer to this concept as the 'acceptable level of risk.'

6. *Pest- or disease-free area* - An area, whether all of a country,

part of a country, or all or parts of several countries, as identified by the competent authorities, in which a specific pest or disease does not occur.

NOTE: A pest- or disease-free area may surround, be surrounded by, or be adjacent to an area - whether within part of a country or in a geographic region which includes parts of or all of several countries - in which a specific pest or disease is known to occur but is subject to regional control measures such as the establishment of protection, surveillance and buffer zones which will confine or eradicate the pest or disease in question.

7. *Area of low pest or disease prevalence* - An area, whether all of a country, part of a country, or all or parts of several countries, as identified by the competent authorities, in which a specific pest or disease occurs at low levels and which is subject to effective surveillance, control or eradication measures.

ANNEX B

TRANSPARENCY OF SANITARY AND PHYTOSANITARY REGULATIONS

Publication of regulations

1. Members shall ensure that all sanitary and phytosanitary regulations [SANITARY AND PHYTOSANITARY MEASURES SUCH AS LAWS, DECREES OR ORDINANCES WHICH ARE APPLICABLE GENERALLY.] which have been adopted are published promptly in such a manner as to enable interested Members to become acquainted with them.

2. Except in urgent circumstances, Members shall allow a reasonable interval between the publication of a sanitary or phytosanitary regulation and its entry into force in order to allow time for producers in exporting Members, and particularly in developing country Members, to adapt their products and methods of production to the requirements of the importing Member.

Enquiry points

3. Each Member shall ensure that one enquiry point exists which is responsible for the provision of answers to all reasonable questions from interested Members as well as for the provision of relevant documents regarding:

(a) any sanitary or phytosanitary regulations adopted or proposed within its territory;

(b) any control and inspection procedures, production and quarantine treatment, pesticide tolerance and food additive approval procedures, which are operated within its territory;

(c) risk assessment procedures, factors taken into consideration, as well as the determination of the appropriate level of sanitary or phytosanitary protection;

(d) the membership and participation of the Member, or of relevant bodies within its territory, in international and regional sanitary and phytosanitary organizations and systems, as well as in bilateral and multilateral agreements and arrangements within the scope of this Agreement, and the texts of such agreements and arrangements.

4. Members shall ensure that where copies of documents are requested by interested Members, they are supplied at the same price (if any),

apart from the cost of delivery, as to the nationals [WHEN 'NATIONALS' ARE REFERRED TO IN THIS AGREEMENT, THE TERM SHALL BE DEEMED, IN THE CASE OF A SEPARATE CUSTOMS TERRITORY MEMBER OF THE WTO, TO MEAN PERSONS, NATURAL OR LEGAL, WHO ARE DOMICILED OR WHO HAVE A REAL AND EFFECTIVE INDUSTRIAL OR COMMERCIAL ESTABLISHMENT IN THAT CUSTOMS TERRITORY.] of the Member concerned.

Notification procedures

5. Whenever an international standard, guideline or recommendation does not exist or the content of a proposed sanitary or phytosanitary regulation is not substantially the same as the content of an international standard, guideline or recommendation, and if the regulation may have a significant effect on trade of other Members, Members shall:

(a) publish a notice at an early stage in such a manner as to enable interested Members to become acquainted with the proposal to introduce a particular regulation;

(b) notify other Members, through the Secretariat, of the products to be covered by the regulation together with a brief indication of the objective and rationale of the proposed regulation. Such notifications shall take place at an early stage, when amendments can still be introduced and comments taken into account;

(c) provide upon request to other Members copies of the proposed regulation and, whenever possible, identify the parts which in substance deviate from international standards, guidelines or recommendations;

(d) without discrimination, allow reasonable time for other Members to make comments in writing, discuss these comments upon request, and take the comments and the results of the discussions into account.

6. However, where urgent problems of health protection arise or threaten to arise for a Member, that Member may omit such of the steps enumerated in paragraph 5 of this Annex as it finds necessary, provided that the Member:

(a) immediately notifies other Members, through the Secretariat, of the particular regulation and the products covered, with a brief indication of the objective and the rationale of the regulation, including the nature of the urgent problem(s);

(b) provides, upon request, copies of the regulation to other Members;

(c) allows other Members to make comments in writing, discusses these comments upon request, and takes the comments and the results of the discussions into account.

7. Notifications to the Secretariat shall be in English, French or Spanish.

8. Developed country Members shall, if requested by other Members, provide copies of the documents or, in case of voluminous documents, summaries of the documents covered by a specific notification in English, French or Spanish.

9. The Secretariat shall promptly circulate copies of the notification to all Members and interested international organizations and draw the attention of developing country Members to any notifications relating to products of particular interest to them.

10. Members shall designate a single central government authority as responsible for the implementation, on the national level, of the provisions concerning notification procedures according to paragraphs 5, 6, 7 and 8 of this Annex.

General reservations

11. Nothing in this Agreement shall be construed as requiring:

(a) the provision of particulars or copies of drafts or the publication of texts other than in the language of the Member except as stated in paragraph 8 of this Annex; or

(b) Members to disclose confidential information which would impede enforcement of sanitary or phytosanitary legislation or which would prejudice the legitimate commercial interests of particular enterprises.

ANNEX C

CONTROL, INSPECTION AND APPROVAL PROCEDURES

[CONTROL, INSPECTION AND APPROVAL PROCEDURES INCLUDE, *INTER ALIA*, PROCEDURES FOR SAMPLING, TESTING AND CERTIFICATION.]

1. Members shall ensure, with respect to any procedure to check and ensure the fulfilment of sanitary or phytosanitary measures, that:

(a) such procedures are undertaken and completed without undue delay and in no less favourable manner for imported products than for like domestic products;

(b) the standard processing period of each procedure is published or that the anticipated processing period is communicated to the applicant upon request; when receiving an application, the competent body promptly examines the completeness of the documentation and informs the applicant in a precise and complete manner of all deficiencies; the competent body transmits as soon as possible the results of the procedure in a precise and complete manner to the applicant so that corrective action may be taken if necessary; even when the application has deficiencies, the competent body proceeds as far as practicable with the procedure if the applicant so requests; and that upon request, the applicant is informed of the stage of the procedure, with any delay being explained;

(c) information requirements are limited to what is necessary for appropriate control, inspection and approval procedures, including for approval of the use of additives or for the establishment of tolerances for contaminants in food, beverages or feedstuffs;

(d) the confidentiality of information about imported products arising from or supplied in connection with control, inspection and approval is respected in a way no less favourable than for domestic products and in such a manner that legitimate commercial interests are protected;

(e) any requirements for control, inspection and approval of individual specimens of a product are limited to what is reasonable and necessary;

(f) any fees imposed for the procedures on imported products are equitable in relation to any fees charged on like domestic products or products originating in any other Member and should be no higher than the actual cost of the service;

(g) the same criteria should be used in the siting of facilities used in the procedures and the selection of samples of imported products as for domestic products so as to minimize the inconvenience to applicants, importers, exporters or their agents;

(h) whenever specifications of a product are changed subsequent to its control and inspection in light of the applicable regulations, the procedure for the modified product is limited to what is necessary to determine whether adequate confidence exists that the product still meets the regulations concerned; and

(i) a procedure exists to review complaints concerning the operation of such procedures and to take corrective action when a complaint is justified.

Where an importing Member operates a system for the approval of the use of food additives or for the establishment of tolerances for contaminants in food, beverages or feedstuffs which prohibits or restricts access to its domestic markets for products based on the absence of an approval, the importing Member shall consider the use of a relevant international standard as the basis for access until a final determination is made.

2. Where a sanitary or phytosanitary measure specifies control at the level of production, the Member in whose territory the production takes place shall provide the necessary assistance to facilitate such control and the work of the controlling authorities.

3. Nothing in this Agreement shall prevent Members from carrying out reasonable inspection within their own territories."

Agreement on Technical Barriers to Trade—the Text

"AGREEMENT ON TECHNICAL BARRIERS TO TRADE

Members,

Having regard to the Uruguay Round of Multilateral Trade Negotiations;

Desiring to further the objectives of GATT 1994;

Recognizing the important contribution that international standards and conformity assessment systems can make in this regard by improving efficiency of production and facilitating the conduct of international trade;

Desiring therefore to encourage the development of such international standards and conformity assessment systems;

Desiring however to ensure that technical regulations and standards, including packaging, marking and labelling requirements, and procedures for assessment of conformity with technical regulations and standards do not create unnecessary obstacles to international trade;

Recognizing that no country should be prevented from taking measures necessary to ensure the quality of its exports, or for the protection of human, animal or plant life or health, of the environment, or for the prevention of deceptive practices, at the levels it considers appropriate, subject to the requirement that they are not applied in a manner which would constitute a means of arbitrary or unjustifiable discrimination between countries where the same conditions prevail or a disguised restriction on international trade, and are otherwise in accordance with the provisions of this Agreement;

Recognizing that no country should be prevented from taking measures necessary for the protection of its essential security interest;

Recognizing the contribution which international standardization can make to the transfer of technology from developed to developing countries;

Recognizing that developing countries may encounter special difficulties in the formulation and application of technical regulations and standards and procedures for assessment of conformity with technical regulations and standards, and desiring to assist them in their endeavours in this regard;

Hereby *agree* as follows:

Article 1
General Provisions

1.1 General terms for standardization and procedures for assessment of conformity shall normally have the meaning given to them by definitions adopted within the United Nations system and by international standardizing bodies taking into account their context and in the light of the object and purpose of this Agreement.

1.2 However, for the purposes of this Agreement the meaning of the terms given in Annex 1 applies.

1.3 All products, including industrial and agricultural products, shall be subject to the provisions of this Agreement.

1.4 Purchasing specifications prepared by governmental bodies for production or consumption requirements of governmental bodies are not subject to the provisions of this Agreement but are addressed in the Agreement on Government Procurement, according to its coverage.

1.5 The provisions of this Agreement do not apply to sanitary and phytosanitary measures as defined in Annex A of the Agreement on the Application of Sanitary and Phytosanitary Measures.

1.6 All references in this Agreement to technical regulations, standards and conformity assessment procedures shall be construed to include any amendments thereto and any additions to the rules or the product coverage thereof, except amendments and additions of an insignificant nature.

TECHNICAL REGULATIONS AND STANDARDS

Article 2

Preparation, Adoption and Application of Technical Regulations by Central Government Bodies

With respect to their central government bodies:

2.1 Members shall ensure that in respect of technical regulations, products imported from the territory of any Member shall be accorded treatment no less favourable than that accorded to like products of national origin and to like products originating in any other country.

2.2 Members shall ensure that technical regulations are not prepared, adopted or applied with a view to or with the effect of creating unnecessary obstacles to international trade. For this purpose, technical regulations shall not be more trade-restrictive than necessary to fulfil a legitimate objective, taking account of the risks non-fulfilment would create. Such legitimate objectives are, *inter alia:* national security requirements; the prevention of deceptive practices; protection of human health or safety, animal or plant life or health, or the environment. In assessing such risks, relevant elements of consideration are, *inter alia:* available scientific and technical information, related processing technology or intended end-uses of products.

2.3 Technical regulations shall not be maintained if the circumstances or objectives giving rise to their adoption no longer exist or if the changed circumstances or objectives can be addressed in a less trade-restrictive manner.

2.4 Where technical regulations are required and relevant international standards exist or their completion is imminent, Members shall use them, or the relevant parts of them, as a basis for their technical regulations except when such international standards or relevant parts would be an ineffective or inappropriate means for the fulfilment of the legitimate objectives pursued, for instance because of fundamental climatic or geographical factors or fundamental technological problems.

2.5 A Member preparing, adopting or applying a technical regulation which may have a significant effect on trade of other Members shall, upon the request of another Member, explain the justification for that technical regulation in terms of the provisions of paragraphs 2 to 4. Whenever a technical regulation is prepared, adopted or applied for one of the legitimate objectives explicitly mentioned in paragraph 2, and is in accordance with relevant international standards, it shall be rebuttably presumed not to create an unnecessary obstacle to international trade.

2.6 With a view to harmonizing technical regulations on as wide a basis as possible, Members shall play a full part, within the limits of their resources, in the preparation by appropriate international standardizing bodies of international standards for products for which they either have adopted, or expect to adopt, technical regulations.

2.7 Members shall give positive consideration to accepting as equivalent technical regulations of other Members, even if these regulations differ from their own, provided they are satisfied that these regulations adequately fulfil the objectives of their own regulations.

2.8 Wherever appropriate, Members shall specify technical

regulations based on product requirements in terms of performance rather than design or descriptive characteristics.

2.9 Whenever a relevant international standard does not exist or the technical content of a proposed technical regulation is not in accordance with the technical content of relevant international standards, and if the technical regulation may have a significant effect on trade of other Members, Members shall:

2.9.1 publish a notice in a publication at an early appropriate stage, in such a manner as to enable interested parties in other Members to become acquainted with it, that they propose to introduce a particular technical regulation;

2.9.2 notify other Members through the Secretariat of the products to be covered by the proposed technical regulation, together with a brief indication of its objective and rationale. Such notifications shall take place at an early appropriate stage, when amendments can still be introduced and comments taken into account;

2.9.3 upon request, provide to other Members particulars or copies of the proposed technical regulation and, whenever possible, identify the parts which in substance deviate from relevant international standards;

2.9.4 without discrimination, allow reasonable time for other Members to make comments in writing, discuss these comments upon request, and take these written comments and the results of these discussions into account.

2.10 Subject to the provisions in the lead-in to paragraph 9, where urgent problems of safety, health, environmental protection or national security arise or threaten to arise for a Member, that Member may omit such of the steps enumerated in paragraph 9 as it finds necessary, provided that the Member, upon adoption of a technical regulation, shall:

2.10.1 notify immediately other Members through the Secretariat of the particular technical regulation and the products covered, with a brief indication of the objective and the rationale of the technical regulation, including the nature of the urgent problems;

2.10.2 upon request, provide other Members with copies of the technical regulation;

2.10.3 without discrimination, allow other Members to present their comments in writing, discuss these comments upon request, and take these written comments and the results of these discussions into account.

2.11 Members shall ensure that all technical regulations which have been adopted are published promptly or otherwise made available in such a manner as to enable interested parties in other Members to become acquainted with them.

2.12 Except in those urgent circumstances referred to in paragraph 10, Members shall allow a reasonable interval between the publication of technical regulations and their entry into force in order to allow time for producers in exporting Members, and particularly in developing country Members, to adapt their products or methods of production to the requirements of the importing Member.

Article 3

Preparation, Adoption and Application of Technical Regulations by Local Government Bodies and Non-Governmental Bodies

With respect to their local government and non-governmental bodies within their territories:

3.1 Members shall take such reasonable measures as may be available to them to ensure compliance by such bodies with the provisions of Article 2, with the exception of the obligation to notify as referred to in paragraphs 9.2 and 10.1 of Article 2.

3.2 Members shall ensure that the technical regulations of local governments on the level directly below that of the central government in Members are notified in accordance with the provisions of paragraphs 9.2 and 10.1 of Article 2, noting that notification shall not be required for technical regulations the technical content of which is substantially the same as that of previously notified technical regulations of central government bodies of the Member concerned.

3.3 Members may require contact with other Members, including the notifications, provision of information, comments and discussions referred to in paragraphs 9 and 10 of Article 2, to take place through the central government.

3.4 Members shall not take measures which require or encourage local government bodies or non-governmental bodies within their territories to act in a manner inconsistent with the provisions of Article 2.

3.5 Members are fully responsible under this Agreement for the observance of all provisions of Article 2. Members shall formulate and implement positive measures and mechanisms in support of the observance of the provisions of Article 2 by other than central government bodies.

Article 4

Preparation, Adoption and Application of Standards

4.1 Members shall ensure that their central government standardizing bodies accept and comply with the Code of Good Practice for the Preparation, Adoption and Application of Standards in Annex 3 to this Agreement (referred to in this Agreement as the 'Code of Good Practice'). They shall take such reasonable measures as may be available to them to ensure that local government and non-governmental standardizing bodies within their territories, as well as regional standardizing bodies of which they or one or more bodies within their territories are members, accept and comply with this Code of Good Practice. In addition, Members shall not take measures which have the effect of, directly or indirectly, requiring or encouraging such standardizing bodies to act in a manner inconsistent with the Code of Good Practice. The obligations of Members with respect to compliance of standardizing bodies with the provisions of the Code of Good Practice shall apply irrespective of whether or not a standardizing body has accepted the Code of Good Practice.

4.2 Standardizing bodies that have accepted and are complying with the Code of Good Practice shall be acknowledged by the Members as complying with the principles of this Agreement.

CONFORMITY WITH TECHNICAL REGULATIONS AND STANDARDS

Article 5

Procedures for Assessment of Conformity by Central Government Bodies

5.1 Members shall ensure that, in cases where a positive assurance of conformity with technical regulations or standards is required, their central government bodies apply the following provisions to products originating in the territories of other Members:

5.1.1 conformity assessment procedures are prepared, adopted and applied so as to grant access for suppliers of like products originating in the territories of other Members under conditions no less favourable than those accorded to suppliers of like products of national origin or originating in any other country, in a comparable situation; access entails suppliers' right to an assessment of conformity under the rules of the procedure, including, when foreseen by this procedure, the possibility to have conformity assessment activities undertaken at the site of facilities and to receive the mark of the system;

5.1.2 conformity assessment procedures are not prepared, adopted or applied with a view to or with the effect of creating unnecessary obstacles to international trade. This means, *inter alia*, that conformity assessment procedures shall not be more strict or be applied more strictly than is necessary to give the importing Member adequate confidence that products conform with the applicable technical regulations or standards, taking account of the risks non-conformity would create.

5.2 When implementing the provisions of paragraph 1, Members shall ensure that:

5.2.1 conformity assessment procedures are undertaken and completed as expeditiously as possible and in a no less favourable order for products originating in the territories of other Members than for like domestic products;

5.2.2 the standard processing period of each conformity assessment procedure is published or that the anticipated processing period is communicated to the applicant upon request; when receiving an application, the competent body promptly examines the completeness of the documentation and informs the applicant in a precise and complete manner of all deficiencies; the competent body transmits as soon as possible the results of the assessment in a precise and complete manner to the applicant so that corrective action may be taken if necessary; even when the application has deficiencies, the competent body proceeds as far as practicable with the conformity assessment if the applicant so requests; and that, upon request, the applicant is informed of the stage of the procedure, with any delay being explained;

5.2.3 information requirements are limited to what is necessary to assess conformity and determine fees;

5.2.4 the confidentiality of information about products originating in the territories of other Members arising from or supplied in connection with such conformity assessment procedures is respected in the same way as for domestic products and in such a manner that legitimate commercial interests are protected;

5.2.5 any fees imposed for assessing the conformity of products originating in the territories of other Members are equitable in relation to any fees chargeable for assessing the conformity of like products of national origin or originating in any other country, taking into account communication, transportation and other costs arising from differences between location of facilities of the applicant and the conformity assessment body;

5.2.6 the siting of facilities used in conformity assessment procedures and the selection of samples are not such as to cause unnecessary inconvenience to applicants or their agents;

5.2.7 whenever specifications of a product are changed subsequent to the determination of its conformity to the applicable technical regulations or standards, the conformity assessment procedure for the modified product is limited to what is necessary to determine whether adequate confidence exists that the product still meets the technical regulations or standards concerned;

5.2.8 a procedure exists to review complaints concerning the operation of a conformity assessment procedure and to take corrective action when a complaint is justified.

5.3 Nothing in paragraphs 1 and 2 shall prevent Members from carrying out reasonable spot checks within their territories.

5.4 In cases where a positive assurance is required that products conform with technical regulations or standards, and relevant guides or recommendations issued by international standardizing bodies exist or their completion is imminent, Members shall ensure that central government bodies use them, or the relevant parts of them, as a basis for their conformity assessment procedures, except where, as duly explained upon request, such guides or recommendations or relevant parts are inappropriate for the Members concerned, for, *inter alia*, such reasons as: national security requirements; the prevention of deceptive practices; protection of human health or safety, animal or plant life or health, or the environment; fundamental climatic or other geographical factors; fundamental technological or infrastructural problems.

5.5 With a view to harmonizing conformity assessment procedures on as wide a basis as possible, Members shall play a full part, within the limits of their resources, in the preparation by appropriate international standardizing bodies of guides and recommendations for conformity assessment procedures.

5.6 Whenever a relevant guide or recommendation issued by an international standardizing body does not exist or the technical content of a proposed conformity assessment procedure is not in accordance with relevant guides and recommendations issued by international standardizing bodies, and if the conformity assessment procedure may have a significant effect on trade of other Members, Members shall:

5.6.1 publish a notice in a publication at an early appropriate stage, in such a manner as to enable interested parties in other Members to become acquainted with it, that they propose to introduce a particular conformity assessment procedure;

5.6.2 notify other Members through the Secretariat of the products to be covered by the proposed conformity assessment procedure, together with a brief indication of its objective and rationale. Such notifications shall take place at an early appropriate stage, when amendments can still be introduced and comments taken into account;

5.6.3 upon request, provide to other Members particulars or copies of the proposed procedure and, whenever possible, identify the parts which in substance deviate from relevant guides or recommendations issued by international standardizing bodies;

5.6.4 without discrimination, allow reasonable time for other Members to make comments in writing, discuss these comments upon request, and take these written comments and the results of these discussions into account.

5.7 Subject to the provisions in the lead-in to paragraph 6, where urgent problems of safety, health, environmental protection or national security arise or threaten to arise for a Member, that Member may omit such of the steps enumerated in paragraph 6 as it finds necessary, provided that the Member, upon adoption of the procedure, shall:

5.7.1 notify immediately other Members through the Secretariat of the particular procedure and the products covered, with a brief indication of the objective and the rationale of the procedure, including the nature of the urgent problems;

5.7.2 upon request, provide other Members with copies of the rules of the procedure;

5.7.3 without discrimination, allow other Members to present their comments in writing, discuss these comments upon request, and take these written comments and the results of these discussions into account.

5.8 Members shall ensure that all conformity assessment procedures which have been adopted are published promptly or otherwise made available in such a manner as to enable interested parties in other Members to become acquainted with them.

5.9 Except in those urgent circumstances referred to in paragraph 7, Members shall allow a reasonable interval between the publication of requirements concerning conformity assessment procedures and their entry into force in order to allow time for producers in exporting Members, and particularly in developing country Members, to adapt their products or methods of production to the requirements of the importing Member.

Article 6

Recognition of Conformity Assessment by Central Government Bodies

With respect to their central government bodies:

6.1 Without prejudice to the provisions of paragraphs 3 and 4, Members shall ensure, whenever possible, that results of conformity assessment procedures in other Members are accepted, even when those procedures differ from their own, provided they are satisfied that those procedures offer an assurance of conformity with applicable technical regulations or standards equivalent to their own procedures. It is recognized that prior consultations may be necessary in order to arrive at a mutually satisfactory understanding regarding, in particular:

6.1.1 adequate and enduring technical competence of the relevant conformity assessment bodies in the exporting Member, so that confidence in the continued reliability of their conformity assessment results can exist; in this regard, verified compliance, for instance through accreditation, with relevant guides or recommendations issued by international standardizing bodies shall be taken into account as an indication of adequate technical competence;

6.1.2 limitation of the acceptance of conformity assessment results to those produced by designated bodies in the exporting Member.

6.2 Members shall ensure that their conformity assessment procedures permit, as far as practicable, the implementation of the provisions in paragraph 1.

6.3 Members are encouraged, at the request of other Members, to be willing to enter into negotiations for the conclusion of agreements for the mutual recognition of results of each other's conformity assessment procedures. Members may require that such agreements fulfil the criteria of paragraph 1 and give mutual satisfaction regarding their potential for facilitating trade in the products concerned.

6.4 Members are encouraged to permit participation of conformity assessment bodies located in the territories of other Members in their conformity assessment procedures under conditions no less favourable than those accorded to bodies located within their territory or the territory of any other country.

Article 7
Procedures for Assessment of Conformity by Local Government Bodies

With respect to their local government bodies within their territories:

7.1 Members shall take such reasonable measures as may be available to them to ensure compliance by such bodies with the provisions of Articles 5 and 6, with the exception of the obligation to notify as referred to in paragraphs 6.2 and 7.1 of Article 5.

7.2 Members shall ensure that the conformity assessment procedures of local governments on the level directly below that of the central government in Members are notified in accordance with the provisions of paragraphs 6.2 and 7.1 of Article 5, noting that notifications shall not be required for conformity assessment procedures the technical content of which is substantially the same as that of previously notified conformity assessment procedures of central government bodies of the Members concerned.

7.3 Members may require contact with other Members, including the notifications, provision of information, comments and discussions referred to in paragraphs 6 and 7 of Article 5, to take place through the central government.

7.4 Members shall not take measures which require or encourage local government bodies within their territories to act in a manner inconsistent with the provisions of Articles 5 and 6.

7.5 Members are fully responsible under this Agreement for the observance of all provisions of Articles 5 and 6. Members shall formulate and implement positive measures and mechanisms in support of the observance of the provisions of Articles 5 and 6 by other than central government bodies.

Article 8
Procedures for Assessment of Conformity by Non-Governmental Bodies

8.1 Members shall take such reasonable measures as may be available to them to ensure that non-governmental bodies within their territories which operate conformity assessment procedures comply with the provisions of Articles 5 and 6, with the exception of the obligation to notify proposed conformity assessment procedures. In addition, Members shall not take measures which have the effect of, directly or indirectly, requiring or encouraging such bodies to act in a manner inconsistent with the provisions of Articles 5 and 6.

8.2 Members shall ensure that their central government bodies rely on conformity assessment procedures operated by non-governmental bodies only if these latter bodies comply with the provisions of Articles 5 and 6, with the exception of the obligation to notify proposed conformity assessment procedures.

Article 9
International and Regional Systems

9.1 Where a positive assurance of conformity with a technical regulation or standard is required, Members shall, wherever practicable, formulate and adopt international systems for conformity assessment and become members thereof or participate therein.

9.2 Members shall take such reasonable measures as may be available to them to ensure that international and regional systems for conformity assessment in which relevant bodies within their territories are members or participants comply with the provisions of Articles 5 and 6. In addition, Members shall not take any measures which have the effect of, directly or indirectly, requiring or encouraging such systems to act in a manner inconsistent with any of the provisions of Articles 5 and 6.

9.3 Members shall ensure that their central government bodies rely on international or regional conformity assessment systems only to the extent that these systems comply with the provisions of Articles 5 and 6, as applicable.

INFORMATION AND ASSISTANCE

Article 10
Information About Technical Regulations, Standards and Conformity Assessment Procedures

10.1 Each Member shall ensure that an enquiry point exists which is able to answer all reasonable enquiries from other Members and interested parties in other Members as well as to provide the relevant documents regarding:

10.1.1 any technical regulations adopted or proposed within its territory by central or local government bodies, by non-governmental bodies which have legal power to enforce a technical regulation, or by regional standardizing bodies of which such bodies are members or participants;

10.1.2 any standards adopted or proposed within its territory by central or local government bodies, or by regional standardizing bodies of which such bodies are members or participants;

10.1.3 any conformity assessment procedures, or proposed conformity assessment procedures, which are operated within its territory by central or local government bodies, or by non-governmental bodies which have legal power to enforce a technical regulation, or by regional bodies of which such bodies are members or participants;

10.1.4 the membership and participation of the Member, or of relevant central or local government bodies within its territory, in international and regional standardizing bodies and conformity assessment systems, as well as in bilateral and multilateral arrangements within the scope of this Agreement; it shall also be able to provide reasonable information on the provisions of such systems and arrangements;

10.1.5 the location of notices published pursuant to this Agreement, or the provision of information as to where such information can be obtained; and

10.1.6 the location of the enquiry points mentioned in paragraph 3.

10.2 If, however, for legal or administrative reasons more than one enquiry point is established by a Member, that Member shall provide to the other Members complete and unambiguous information on the scope of responsibility of each of these enquiry points. In addition, that Member shall ensure that any enquiries addressed to an incorrect enquiry point shall promptly be conveyed to the correct enquiry point.

10.3 Each Member shall take such reasonable measures as may be available to it to ensure that one or more enquiry points exist which are able to answer all reasonable enquiries from other Members and interested parties in other Members as well as to provide the relevant documents or information as to where they can be obtained regarding:

10.3.1 any standards adopted or proposed within its territory by non-governmental standardizing bodies, or by regional standardizing bodies of which such bodies are members or participants; and

10.3.2 any conformity assessment procedures, or proposed conformity assessment procedures, which are operated within its territory by non-governmental bodies, or by regional bodies of which such bodies are members or participants;

10.3.3 the membership and participation of relevant non-governmental bodies within its territory in international and regional standardizing bodies and conformity assessment systems, as well as in bilateral and multilateral arrangements within the scope of this Agreement; they shall also be able to provide reasonable information on the provisions of such systems and arrangements.

10.4 Members shall take such reasonable measures as may be

available to them to ensure that where copies of documents are requested by other Members or by interested parties in other Members, in accordance with the provisions of this Agreement, they are supplied at an equitable price (if any) which shall, apart from the real cost of delivery, be the same for the nationals ['NATIONALS' HERE SHALL BE DEEMED, IN THE CASE OF A SEPARATE CUSTOMS TERRITORY MEMBER OF THE WTO, TO MEAN PERSONS, NATURAL OR LEGAL, WHO ARE DOMICILED OR WHO HAVE A REAL AND EFFECTIVE INDUSTRIAL OR COMMERCIAL ESTABLISHMENT IN THAT CUSTOMS TERRITORY.] of the Member concerned or of any other Member.

10.5 Developed country Members shall, if requested by other Members, provide, in English, French or Spanish, translations of the documents covered by a specific notification or, in case of voluminous documents, of summaries of such documents.

10.6 The Secretariat shall, when it receives notifications in accordance with the provisions of this Agreement, circulate copies of the notifications to all Members and interested international standardizing and conformity assessment bodies, and draw the attention of developing country Members to any notifications relating to products of particular interest to them.

10.7 Whenever a Member has reached an agreement with any other country or countries on issues related to technical regulations, standards or conformity assessment procedures which may have a significant effect on trade, at least one Member party to the agreement shall notify other Members through the Secretariat of the products to be covered by the agreement and include a brief description of the agreement. Members concerned are encouraged to enter, upon request, into consultations with other Members for the purposes of concluding similar agreements or of arranging for their participation in such agreements.

10.8 Nothing in this Agreement shall be construed as requiring:

10.8.1 the publication of texts other than in the language of the Member;

10.8.2 the provision of particulars or copies of drafts other than in the language of the Member except as stated in paragraph 5; or

10.8.3 Members to furnish any information, the disclosure of which they consider contrary to their essential security interests.

10.9 Notifications to the Secretariat shall be in English, French or Spanish.

10.10 Members shall designate a single central government authority that is responsible for the implementation on the national level of the provisions concerning notification procedures under this Agreement except those included in Annex 3.

10.11 If, however, for legal or administrative reasons the responsibility for notification procedures is divided among two or more central government authorities, the Member concerned shall provide to the other Members complete and unambiguous information on the scope of responsibility of each of these authorities.

Article 11

Technical Assistance to Other Members

11.1 Members shall, if requested, advise other Members, especially the developing country Members, on the preparation of technical regulations.

11.2 Members shall, if requested, advise other Members, especially the developing country Members, and shall grant them technical assistance on mutually agreed terms and conditions regarding the establishment of national standardizing bodies, and participation in the international standardizing bodies, and shall encourage their national standardizing bodies to do likewise.

11.3 Members shall, if requested, take such reasonable measures as may be available to them to arrange for the regulatory bodies within their territories to advise other Members, especially the developing country Members, and shall grant them technical assistance on mutually agreed terms and conditions regarding:

11.3.1 the establishment of regulatory bodies, or bodies for the assessment of conformity with technical regulations; and

11.3.2 the methods by which their technical regulations can best be met.

11.4 Members shall, if requested, take such reasonable measures as may be available to them to arrange for advice to be given to other Members, especially the developing country Members, and shall grant them technical assistance on mutually agreed terms and conditions regarding the establishment of bodies for the assessment of conformity with standards adopted within the territory of the requesting Member.

11.5 Members shall, if requested, advise other Members, especially the developing country Members, and shall grant them technical assistance on mutually agreed terms and conditions regarding the steps that should be taken by their producers if they wish to have access to systems for conformity assessment operated by governmental or non-governmental bodies within the territory of the Member receiving the request.

11.6 Members which are members or participants of international or regional systems for conformity assessment shall, if requested, advise other Members, especially the developing country Members, and shall grant them technical assistance on mutually agreed terms and conditions regarding the establishment of the institutions and legal framework which would enable them to fulfil the obligations of membership or participation in such systems.

11.7 Members shall, if so requested, encourage bodies within their territories which are members or participants of international or regional systems for conformity assessment to advise other Members, especially the developing country Members, and should consider requests for technical assistance from them regarding the establishment of the institutions which would enable the relevant bodies within their territories to fulfil the obligations of membership or participation.

11.8 In providing advice and technical assistance to other Members in terms of paragraphs 1 to 7, Members shall give priority to the needs of the least-developed country Members.

Article 12

Special and Differential Treatment of Developing Country Members

12.1 Members shall provide differential and more favourable treatment to developing country Members to this Agreement, through the following provisions as well as through the relevant provisions of other Articles of this Agreement.

12.2 Members shall give particular attention to the provisions of this Agreement concerning developing country Members' rights and obligations and shall take into account the special development, financial and trade needs of developing country Members in the implementation of this Agreement, both nationally and in the operation of this Agreement's institutional arrangements.

12.3 Members shall, in the preparation and application of technical regulations, standards and conformity assessment procedures, take account of the special development, financial and trade needs of developing country Members, with a view to ensuring that such technical regulations, standards and conformity assessment procedures do not create unnecessary obstacles to exports from developing country Members.

12.4 Members recognize that, although international standards, guides or recommendations may exist, in their particular technological and socio-economic conditions, developing country Members adopt certain technical regulations, standards or conformity assessment procedures aimed at preserving indigenous technology and production methods and processes compatible with their development needs. Members therefore recognize that developing country Members should not be expected to use international standards as a basis for their technical regulations or standards, including test methods, which are not appropriate to their development, financial and trade needs.

12.5 Members shall take such reasonable measures as may be available to them to ensure that international standardizing bodies and international systems for conformity assessment are organized and operated in a way which facilitates active and representative participation of relevant bodies in all Members, taking into account the special problems of developing country Members.

12.6 Members shall take such reasonable measures as may be available to them to ensure that international standardizing bodies, upon request of developing country Members, examine the possibility of, and, if practicable, prepare international standards concerning products of special interest to developing country Members.

12.7 Members shall, in accordance with the provisions of Article 11, provide technical assistance to developing country Members to ensure that the preparation and application of technical regulations, standards and conformity assessment procedures do not create unnecessary obstacles to the expansion and diversification of exports from developing country Members. In determining the terms and conditions of the technical assistance, account shall be taken of the stage of development of the requesting Members and in particular of the least-developed country Members.

12.8 It is recognized that developing country Members may face special problems, including institutional and infrastructural problems, in the field of preparation and application of technical regulations, standards and conformity assessment procedures. It is further recognized that the special development and trade needs of developing country Members, as well as their stage of technological development, may hinder their ability to discharge fully their obligations under this Agreement. Members, therefore, shall take this fact fully into account. Accordingly, with a view to ensuring that developing country Members are able to comply with this Agreement, the Committee on Technical Barriers to Trade provided for in Article 13 (referred to in this Agreement as the 'Committee') is enabled to grant, upon request, specified, time-limited exceptions in whole or in part from obligations under this Agreement. When considering such requests the Committee shall take into account the special problems, in the field of preparation and application of technical regulations, standards and conformity assessment procedures, and the special development and trade needs of the developing country Member, as well as its stage of technological development, which may hinder its ability to discharge fully its obligations under this Agreement. The Committee shall, in particular, take into account the special problems of the least-developed country Members.

12.9 During consultations, developed country Members shall bear in mind the special difficulties experienced by developing country Members in formulating and implementing standards and technical regulations and conformity assessment procedures, and in their desire to assist developing country Members with their efforts in this direction, developed country Members shall take account of the special needs of the former in regard to financing, trade and development.

12.10 The Committee shall examine periodically the special and differential treatment, as laid down in this Agreement, granted to developing country Members on national and international levels.

INSTITUTIONS, CONSULTATION AND DISPUTE SETTLEMENT

Article 13

The Committee on Technical Barriers to Trade

13.1 A Committee on Technical Barriers to Trade is hereby established, and shall be composed of representatives from each of the Members. The Committee shall elect its own Chairman and shall meet as necessary, but no less than once a year, for the purpose of affording Members the opportunity of consulting on any matters relating to the operation of this Agreement or the furtherance of its objectives, and shall carry out such responsibilities as assigned to it under this Agreement or by the Members.

13.2 The Committee shall establish working parties or other bodies as may be appropriate, which shall carry out such responsibilities as may be assigned to them by the Committee in accordance with the relevant provisions of this Agreement.

13.3 It is understood that unnecessary duplication should be avoided between the work under this Agreement and that of governments in other technical bodies. The Committee shall examine this problem with a view to minimizing such duplication.

Article 14
Consultation and Dispute Settlement

14.1 Consultations and the settlement of disputes with respect to any matter affecting the operation of this Agreement shall take place under the auspices of the Dispute Settlement Body and shall follow, *mutatis mutandis*, the provisions of Articles XXII and XXIII of GATT 1994, as elaborated and applied by the Dispute Settlement Understanding.

14.2 At the request of a party to a dispute, or at its own initiative, a panel may establish a technical expert group to assist in questions of a technical nature, requiring detailed consideration by experts.

14.3 Technical expert groups shall be governed by the procedures of Annex 2.

14.4 The dispute settlement provisions set out above can be invoked in cases where a Member considers that another Member has not achieved satisfactory results under Articles 3, 4, 7, 8 and 9 and its trade interests are significantly affected. In this respect, such results shall be equivalent to those as if the body in question were a Member.

FINAL PROVISIONS

Article 15
Final Provisions

Reservations

15.1 Reservations may not be entered in respect of any of the provisions of this Agreement without the consent of the other Members.

Review

15.2 Each Member shall, promptly after the date on which the WTO Agreement enters into force for it, inform the Committee of measures in existence or taken to ensure the implementation and administration of this Agreement. Any changes of such measures thereafter shall also be notified to the Committee.

15.3 The Committee shall review annually the implementation and operation of this Agreement taking into account the objectives thereof.

15.4 Not later than the end of the third year from the date of entry into force of the WTO Agreement and at the end of each three-year period thereafter, the Committee shall review the operation and implementation of this Agreement, including the provisions relating to transparency, with a view to recommending an adjustment of the rights and obligations of this Agreement where necessary to ensure mutual economic advantage and balance of rights and obligations, without prejudice to the provisions of Article 12. Having regard, *inter alia,* to the experience gained in the implementation of the Agreement, the Committee shall, where appropriate, submit proposals for amendments to the text of this Agreement to the Council for Trade in Goods.

Annexes

15.5 The annexes to this Agreement constitute an integral part thereof.

ANNEX 1

TERMS AND THEIR DEFINITIONS FOR THE PURPOSE OF THIS AGREEMENT

The terms presented in the sixth edition of the ISO/IEC Guide 2: 1991, General Terms and Their Definitions Concerning Standardization and Related Activities, shall, when used in this Agreement, have the same meaning as given in the definitions in the said Guide taking into account that services are excluded from the coverage of this Agreement.

For the purpose of this Agreement, however, the following definitions shall apply:

1. *Technical regulation*

Document which lays down product characteristics or their related processes and production methods, including the applicable administrative provisions, with which compliance is mandatory. It may also include or deal exclusively with terminology, symbols, packaging, marking or labelling requirements as they apply to a product, process or production method.

Explanatory note

The definition in ISO/IEC Guide 2 is not self-contained, but based on the so-called 'building block' system.

2. *Standard*

Document approved by a recognized body, that provides, for common and repeated use, rules, guidelines or characteristics for products or related processes and production methods, with which compliance is not mandatory. It may also include or deal exclusively with terminology, symbols, packaging, marking or labelling requirements as they apply to a product, process or production method.

Explanatory note

The terms as defined in ISO/IEC Guide 2 cover products, processes and services. This Agreement deals only with technical regulations, standards and conformity assessment procedures related to products or processes and production methods. Standards as defined by ISO/IEC Guide 2 may be mandatory or voluntary. For the purpose of this Agreement standards are defined as voluntary and technical regulations as mandatory documents. Standards prepared by the international standardization community are based on consensus. This Agreement covers also documents that are not based on consensus.

3. *Conformity assessment procedures*

Any procedure used, directly or indirectly, to determine that relevant requirements in technical regulations or standards are fulfilled.

Explanatory note

Conformity assessment procedures include, *inter alia*, procedures for sampling, testing and inspection; evaluation, verification and assurance of conformity; registration, accreditation and approval as well as their combinations.

4. *International body or system*

Body or system whose membership is open to the relevant bodies of at least all Members.

5. *Regional body or system*

Body or system whose membership is open to the relevant bodies of only some of the Members.

6. *Central government body*

Central government, its ministries and departments or any body subject to the control of the central government in respect of the activity in question.

Explanatory note:

In the case of the European Communities the provisions governing central government bodies apply. However, regional bodies or conformity assessment systems may be established within the European Communities, and in such cases would be subject to the provisions of this Agreement on regional bodies or conformity assessment systems.

7. *Local government body*

Government other than a central government (e.g. states, provinces, Länder, cantons, municipalities, etc.), its ministries or departments or any body subject to the control of such a government in respect of the activity in question.

8. *Non-governmental body*

Body other than a central government body or a local government body, including a non-governmental body which has legal power to enforce a technical regulation.

ANNEX 2

TECHNICAL EXPERT GROUPS

The following procedures shall apply to technical expert groups established in accordance with the provisions of Article 14.

1. Technical expert groups are under the panel's authority. Their terms of reference and detailed working procedures shall be decided by the panel, and they shall report to the panel.

2. Participation in technical expert groups shall be restricted to persons of professional standing and experience in the field in question.

3. Citizens of parties to the dispute shall not serve on a technical expert group without the joint agreement of the parties to the dispute, except

in exceptional circumstances when the panel considers that the need for specialized scientific expertise cannot be fulfilled otherwise. Government officials of parties to the dispute shall not serve on a technical expert group. Members of technical expert groups shall serve in their individual capacities and not as government representatives, nor as representatives of any organization. Governments or organizations shall therefore not give them instructions with regard to matters before a technical expert group.

4. Technical expert groups may consult and seek information and technical advice from any source they deem appropriate. Before a technical expert group seeks such information or advice from a source within the jurisdiction of a Member, it shall inform the government of that Member. Any Member shall respond promptly and fully to any request by a technical expert group for such information as the technical expert group considers necessary and appropriate.

5. The parties to a dispute shall have access to all relevant information provided to a technical expert group, unless it is of a confidential nature. Confidential information provided to the technical expert group shall not be released without formal authorization from the government, organization or person providing the information. Where such information is requested from the technical expert group but release of such information by the technical expert group is not authorized, a non-confidential summary of the information will be provided by the government, organization or person supplying the information.

6. The technical expert group shall submit a draft report to the Members concerned with a view to obtaining their comments, and taking them into account, as appropriate, in the final report, which shall also be circulated to the Members concerned when it is submitted to the panel.

ANNEX 3

CODE OF GOOD PRACTICE FOR THE PREPARATION, ADOPTION AND APPLICATION OF STANDARDS

General Provisions

A. For the purposes of this Code the definitions in Annex 1 of this Agreement shall apply.

B. This Code is open to acceptance by any standardizing body within the territory of a Member of the WTO, whether a central government body, a local government body, or a non-governmental body; to any governmental regional standardizing body one or more members of which are Members of the WTO; and to any non-governmental regional standardizing body one or more members of which are situated within the territory of a Member of the WTO (referred to in this Code collectively as 'standardizing bodies' and individually as 'the standardizing body').

C. Standardizing bodies that have accepted or withdrawn from this Code shall notify this fact to the ISO/IEC Information Centre in Geneva. The notification shall include the name and address of the body concerned and the scope of its current and expected standardization activities. The notification may be sent either directly to the ISO/IEC Information Centre, or through the national member body of ISO/IEC or, preferably, through the relevant national member or international affiliate of ISONET, as appropriate.

Substantive Provisions

D. In respect of standards, the standardizing body shall accord treatment to products originating in the territory of any other Member of the WTO no less favourable than that accorded to like products of national origin and to like products originating in any other country.

E. The standardizing body shall ensure that standards are not prepared, adopted or applied with a view to, or with the effect of, creating unnecessary obstacles to international trade.

F. Where international standards exist or their completion is imminent, the standardizing body shall use them, or the relevant parts of them, as a basis for the standards it develops, except where such international standards or relevant parts would be ineffective or inappropriate, for instance, because of an insufficient level of protection or fundamental climatic or geographical factors or fundamental technological problems.

G. With a view to harmonizing standards on as wide a basis as possible, the standardizing body shall, in an appropriate way, play a full part, within the limits of its resources, in the preparation by relevant international standardizing bodies of international standards regarding subject matter for which it either has adopted, or expects to adopt, standards. For standardizing bodies within the territory of a Member, participation in a particular international standardization activity shall, whenever possible, take place through one delegation representing all standardizing bodies in the territory that have adopted, or expect to adopt, standards for the subject matter to which the international standardization activity relates.

H. The standardizing body within the territory of a Member shall make every effort to avoid duplication of, or overlap with, the work of other standardizing bodies in the national territory or with the work of relevant international or regional standardizing bodies. They shall also make every effort to achieve a national consensus on the standards they develop. Likewise the regional standardizing body shall make every effort to avoid duplication of, or overlap with, the work of relevant international standardizing bodies.

I. Wherever appropriate, the standardizing body shall specify standards based on product requirements in terms of performance rather than design or descriptive characteristics.

J. At least once every six months, the standardizing body shall publish a work programme containing its name and address, the standards it is currently preparing and the standards which it has adopted in the preceding period. A standard is under preparation from the moment a decision has been taken to develop a standard until that standard has been adopted. The titles of specific draft standards shall, upon request, be provided in English, French or Spanish. A notice of the existence of the work programme shall be published in a national or, as the case may be, regional publication of standardization activities.

The work programme shall for each standard indicate, in accordance with any ISONET rules, the classification relevant to the subject matter, the stage attained in the standard's development, and the references of any international standards taken as a basis. No later than at the time of publication of its work programme, the standardizing body shall notify the existence thereof to the ISO/IEC Information Centre in Geneva.

The notification shall contain the name and address of the standardizing body, the name and issue of the publication in which the work programme is published, the period to which the work programme applies, its price (if any), and how and where it can be obtained. The notification may be sent directly to the ISO/IEC Information Centre, or, preferably, through the relevant national member or international affiliate of ISONET, as appropriate.

K. The national member of ISO/IEC shall make every effort to become a member of ISONET or to appoint another body to become a member as well as to acquire the most advanced membership type possible for the ISONET member. Other standardizing bodies shall make every effort to associate themselves with the ISONET member.

L. Before adopting a standard, the standardizing body shall allow a period of at least 60 days for the submission of comments on the draft standard by interested parties within the territory of a Member of the WTO. This period may, however, be shortened in cases where urgent problems of safety, health or environment arise or threaten to arise. No later than at the start of the comment period, the standardizing body shall publish a notice announcing the period for commenting in the publication referred to in paragraph J. Such notification shall include, as far as practicable, whether the draft standard deviates from relevant international standards.

M. On the request of any interested party within the territory of a Member of the WTO, the standardizing body shall promptly provide, or arrange to provide, a copy of a draft standard which it has submitted for comments. Any fees charged for this service shall, apart from the real cost of delivery, be the same for foreign and domestic parties.

N. The standardizing body shall take into account, in the further processing of the standard, the comments received during the period for commenting. Comments received through standardizing bodies that have accepted this Code of Good Practice shall, if so requested, be replied to as promptly as possible. The reply shall include an explanation why a deviation from relevant international standards is necessary.

O. Once the standard has been adopted, it shall be promptly published.

P. On the request of any interested party within the territory of a Member of the WTO, the standardizing body shall promptly provide, or arrange to provide, a copy of its most recent work programme or of a standard which it produced. Any fees charged for this service shall, apart from the real cost of delivery, be the same for foreign and domestic parties.

Q. The standardizing body shall afford sympathetic consideration to, and adequate opportunity for, consultation regarding representations with respect to the operation of this Code presented by standardizing bodies that have accepted this Code of Good Practice. It shall make an objective effort to solve any complaints."

Agreement on Preshipment Inspection—the Text

"AGREEMENT ON PRESHIPMENT INSPECTION

Members,

Noting that Ministers on 20 September 1986 agreed that the Uruguay Round of Multilateral Trade Negotiations shall aim to 'bring about further liberalization and expansion of world trade,' 'strengthen the role of GATT' and 'increase the responsiveness of the GATT system to the evolving international economic environment';

Noting that a number of developing country Members have recourse to preshipment inspection;

Recognizing the need of developing countries to do so for as long and in so far as it is necessary to verify the quality, quantity or price of imported goods;

Mindful that such programmes must be carried out without giving rise to unnecessary delays or unequal treatment;

Noting that this inspection is by definition carried out on the territory of exporter Members;

Recognizing the need to establish an agreed international framework of rights and obligations of both user Members and exporter Members;

Recognizing that the principles and obligations of GATT 1994 apply to those activities of preshipment inspection entities that are mandated by governments that are Members of the WTO;

Recognizing that it is desirable to provide transparency of the operation of preshipment inspection entities and of laws and regulations relating to preshipment inspection;

Desiring to provide for the speedy, effective and equitable resolution of disputes between exporters and preshipment inspection entities arising under this Agreement;

Hereby *agree* as follows:

Article 1
Coverage - Definitions

1. This Agreement shall apply to all preshipment inspection activities carried out on the territory of Members, whether such activities are contracted or mandated by the government, or any government body, of a Member.

2. The term 'user Member' means a Member of which the government or any government body contracts for or mandates the use of preshipment inspection activities.

3. Preshipment inspection activities are all activities relating to the verification of the quality, the quantity, the price, including currency exchange rate and financial terms, and/or the customs classification of goods to be exported to the territory of the user Member.

4. The term 'preshipment inspection entity' is any entity contracted or mandated by a Member to carry out preshipment inspection activities [IT IS UNDERSTOOD THAT THIS PROVISION DOES NOT

OBLIGATE MEMBERS TO ALLOW GOVERNMENT ENTITIES OF OTHER MEMBERS TO CONDUCT PRESHIPMENT INSPECTION ACTIVITIES ON THEIR TERRITORY.].

Article 2
Obligations of User Members

Non-discrimination

1. User Members shall ensure that preshipment inspection activities are carried out in a non-discriminatory manner, and that the procedures and criteria employed in the conduct of these activities are objective and are applied on an equal basis to all exporters affected by such activities. They shall ensure uniform performance of inspection by all the inspectors of the preshipment inspection entities contracted or mandated by them.

Governmental Requirements

2. User Members shall ensure that in the course of preshipment inspection activities relating to their laws, regulations and requirements, the provisions of paragraph 4 of Article III of GATT 1994 are respected to the extent that these are relevant.

Site of Inspection

3. User Members shall ensure that all preshipment inspection activities, including the issuance of a Clean Report of Findings or a note of non-issuance, are performed in the customs territory from which the goods are exported or, if the inspection cannot be carried out in that customs territory given the complex nature of the products involved, or if both parties agree, in the customs territory in which the goods are manufactured.

Standards

4. User Members shall ensure that quantity and quality inspections are performed in accordance with the standards defined by the seller and the buyer in the purchase agreement and that, in the absence of such standards, relevant international standards [AN INTERNATIONAL STANDARD IS A STANDARD ADOPTED BY A GOVERNMENTAL OR NON-GOVERNMENTAL BODY WHOSE MEMBERSHIP IS OPEN TO ALL MEMBERS, ONE OF WHOSE RECOGNIZED ACTIVITIES IS IN THE FIELD OF STANDARDIZATION.] apply.

Transparency

5. User Members shall ensure that preshipment inspection activities are conducted in a transparent manner.

6. User Members shall ensure that, when initially contacted by exporters, preshipment inspection entities provide to the exporters a list of all the information which is necessary for the exporters to comply with inspection requirements. The preshipment inspection entities shall provide the actual information when so requested by exporters. This information shall include a reference to the laws and regulations of user Members relating to preshipment

inspection activities, and shall also include the procedures and criteria used for inspection and for price and currency exchange-rate verification purposes, the exporters' rights vis-à-vis the inspection entities, and the appeals procedures set up under paragraph 21. Additional procedural requirements or changes in existing procedures shall not be applied to a shipment unless the exporter concerned is informed of these changes at the time the inspection date is arranged. However, in emergency situations of the types addressed by Articles XX and XXI of GATT 1994, such additional requirements or changes may be applied to a shipment before the exporter has been informed. This assistance shall not, however, relieve exporters from their obligations in respect of compliance with the import regulations of the user Members.

7. User Members shall ensure that the information referred to in paragraph 6 is made available to exporters in a convenient manner, and that the preshipment inspection offices maintained by preshipment inspection entities serve as information points where this information is available.

8. User Members shall publish promptly all applicable laws and regulations relating to preshipment inspection activities in such a manner as to enable other governments and traders to become acquainted with them.

Protection of Confidential Business Information

9. User Members shall ensure that preshipment inspection entities treat all information received in the course of the preshipment inspection as business confidential to the extent that such information is not already published, generally available to third parties, or otherwise in the public domain. User Members shall ensure that preshipment inspection entities maintain procedures to this end.

10. User Members shall provide information to Members on request on the measures they are taking to give effect to paragraph 9. The provisions of this paragraph shall not require any Member to disclose confidential information the disclosure of which would jeopardize the effectiveness of the preshipment inspection programmes or would prejudice the legitimate commercial interest of particular enterprises, public or private.

11. User Members shall ensure that preshipment inspection entities do not divulge confidential business information to any third party, except that preshipment inspection entities may share this information with the government entities that have contracted or mandated them. User Members shall ensure that confidential business information which they receive from preshipment inspection entities contracted or mandated by them is adequately safeguarded. Preshipment inspection entities shall share confidential business information with the governments contracting or mandating them only to the extent that such information is customarily required for letters of credit or other forms of payment or for customs, import licensing or exchange control purposes.

12. User Members shall ensure that preshipment inspection entities do not request exporters to provide information regarding:

(a) manufacturing data related to patented, licensed or undisclosed processes, or to processes for which a patent is pending;

(b) unpublished technical data other than data necessary to demonstrate compliance with technical regulations or standards;

(c) internal pricing, including manufacturing costs;

(d) profit levels;

(e) the terms of contracts between exporters and their suppliers unless it is not otherwise possible for the entity to conduct the inspection in question. In such cases, the entity shall only request the information necessary for this purpose.

13. The information referred to in paragraph 12, which preshipment inspection entities shall not otherwise request, may be released voluntarily by the exporter to illustrate a specific case.

Conflicts of Interest

14. User Members shall ensure that preshipment inspection entities, bearing in mind also the provisions on protection of confidential business information in paragraphs 9 through 13, maintain procedures to avoid conflicts of interest:

(a) between preshipment inspection entities and any related entities of the preshipment inspection entities in question, including any entities in which the latter have a financial or commercial interest or any entities which have a financial interest in the preshipment inspection entities in question, and whose shipments the preshipment inspection entities are to inspect;

(b) between preshipment inspection entities and any other entities, including other entities subject to preshipment inspection, with the exception of the government entities contracting or mandating the inspections;

(c) with divisions of preshipment inspection entities engaged in activities other than those required to carry out the inspection process.

Delays

15. User Members shall ensure that preshipment inspection entities avoid unreasonable delays in inspection of shipments. User Members shall ensure that, once a preshipment inspection entity and an exporter agree on an inspection date, the preshipment inspection entity conducts the inspection on that date unless it is rescheduled on a mutually agreed basis between the exporter and the preshipment inspection entity, or the preshipment inspection entity is prevented from doing so by the exporter or by *force majeure* [IT IS UNDERSTOOD THAT, FOR PURPOSES OF THIS AGREEMENT, '*FORCE MAJEURE*' SHALL MEAN 'IRRESISTIBLE COMPULSION OR COERCION, UNFORESEEABLE COURSE OF EVENTS EXCUSING FROM FULFILLMENT OF CONTACT.'].

16. User Members shall ensure that, following receipt of the final documents and completion of the inspection, preshipment inspection entities, within five working days, either issue a Clean Report of Findings or provide a detailed written explanation specifying the reasons for non-issuance. User Members shall ensure that, in the latter case, preshipment inspection entities give exporters the opportunity to present their views in writing and, if exporters so request, arrange for re-inspection at the earliest mutually convenient date.

17. User Members shall ensure that, whenever so requested by the exporters, preshipment inspection entities undertake, prior to the date of

physical inspection, a preliminary verification of price and, where applicable, of currency exchange rate, on the basis of the contract between exporter and importer, the *pro forma* invoice and, where applicable, the application for import authorization. User Members shall ensure that a price or currency exchange rate that has been accepted by a preshipment inspection entity on the basis of such preliminary verification is not withdrawn, providing the goods conform to the import documentation and/or import licence. They shall ensure that, after a preliminary verification has taken place, preshipment inspection entities immediately inform exporters in writing either of their acceptance or of their detailed reasons for non-acceptance of the price and/or currency exchange rate.

18. User Members shall ensure that, in order to avoid delays in payment, preshipment inspection entities send to exporters or to designated representatives of the exporters a Clean Report of Findings as expeditiously as possible.

19. User Members shall ensure that, in the event of a clerical error in the Clean Report of Findings, preshipment inspection entities correct the error and forward the corrected information to the appropriate parties as expeditiously as possible.

Price Verification

20. User Members shall ensure that, in order to prevent over- and under-invoicing and fraud, preshipment inspection entities conduct price verification [THE OBLIGATIONS OF USER MEMBERS WITH RESPECT TO THE SERVICES OF PRESHIPMENT INSPECTION ENTITIES IN CONNECTION WITH CUSTOMS VALUATION SHALL BE THE OBLIGATIONS WHICH EHY HAVE ACCEPTED IN GATT 1994 AND THE OTHER MULTILATERAL TRADE AGREEMENTS INCLUDED IN ANNEX 1A OF THE WTO AGREEMENT.] according to the following guidelines:

(a) preshipment inspection entities shall only reject a contract price agreed between an exporter and an importer if they can demonstrate that their findings of an unsatisfactory price are based on a verification process which is in conformity with the criteria set out in subparagraphs (b) through (e);

(b) the preshipment inspection entity shall base its price comparison for the verification of the export price on the price(s) of identical or similar goods offered for export from the same country of exportation at or about the same time, under competitive and comparable conditions of sale, in conformity with customary commercial practices and net of any applicable standard discounts. Such comparison shall be based on the following:

(i) only prices providing a valid basis of comparison shall be used, taking into account the relevant economic factors pertaining to the country of importation and a country or countries used for price comparison;

(ii) the preshipment inspection entity shall not rely upon the price of goods offered for export to different countries of importation to arbitrarily impose the lowest price upon the shipment;

(iii) the preshipment inspection entity shall take into account the specific elements listed in subparagraph (c);

(iv) at any stage in the process described above, the preshipment inspection entity shall provide the exporter with an opportunity to explain the price;

(c) when conducting price verification, preshipment inspection entities shall make appropriate allowances for the terms of the sales contract and generally applicable adjusting factors pertaining to the transaction; these factors shall include but not be limited to the commercial level and quantity of the sale, delivery periods and conditions, price escalation clauses, quality specifications, special design features, special shipping or packing specifications, order size, spot sales, seasonal influences, licence or other intellectual property fees, and services rendered as part of the contract if these are not customarily invoiced separately; they shall also include certain elements relating to the exporter's price, such as the contractual relationship between the exporter and importer;

(d) the verification of transportation charges shall relate only to the agreed price of the mode of transport in the country of exportation as indicated in the sales contract;

(e) the following shall not be used for price verification purposes:

(i) the selling price in the country of importation of goods produced in such country;

(ii) the price of goods for export from a country other than the country of exportation;

(iii) the cost of production;

(iv) arbitrary or fictitious prices or values.

Appeals Procedures

21. User Members shall ensure that preshipment inspection entities establish procedures to receive, consider and render decisions concerning grievances raised by exporters, and that information concerning such procedures is made available to exporters in accordance with the provisions of paragraphs 6 and 7. User Members shall ensure that the procedures are developed and maintained in accordance with the following guidelines:

(a) preshipment inspection entities shall designate one or more officials who shall be available during normal business hours in each city or port in which they maintain a preshipment inspection administrative office to receive, consider and render decisions on exporters' appeals or grievances;

(b) exporters shall provide in writing to the designated official(s) the facts concerning the specific transaction in question, the nature of the grievance and a suggested solution;

(c) the designated official(s) shall afford sympathetic consideration to exporters' grievances and shall render a decision as soon as possible after receipt of the documentation referred to in subparagraph (b).

Derogation

22. By derogation to the provisions of Article 2, user Members shall provide that, with the exception of part shipments, shipments whose value is less than a minimum value applicable to such shipments as defined by

the user Member shall not be inspected, except in exceptional circumstances. This minimum value shall form part of the information furnished to exporters under the provisions of paragraph 6.

Article 3
Obligations of Exporter Members

Non-discrimination

1. Exporter Members shall ensure that their laws and regulations relating to preshipment inspection activities are applied in a non-discriminatory manner.

Transparency

2. Exporter Members shall publish promptly all applicable laws and regulations relating to preshipment inspection activities in such a manner as to enable other governments and traders to become acquainted with them.

Technical Assistance

3. Exporter Members shall offer to provide to user Members, if requested, technical assistance directed towards the achievement of the objectives of this Agreement on mutually agreed terms [IT IS UNDERSTOOD THAT SUCH TECHNICAL ASSISTANCE MAY BE GIVEN ON A BILATERAL, PLURILATERAL, OR MULTILATERAL BASIS].

Article 4
Independent Review Procedures

Members shall encourage preshipment inspection entities and exporters mutually to resolve their disputes. However, two working days after submission of the grievance in accordance with the provisions of paragraph 21 of Article 2, either party may refer the dispute to independent review. Members shall take such reasonable measures as may be available to them to ensure that the following procedures are established and maintained to this end:

(a) these procedures shall be administered by an independent entity constituted jointly by an organization representing preshipment inspection entities and an organization representing exporters for the purposes of this Agreement;

(b) the independent entity referred to in subparagraph (a) shall establish a list of experts as follows:

(i) a section of members nominated by an organization representing preshipment inspection entities;

(ii) a section of members nominated by an organization representing exporters;

(iii) a section of independent trade experts, nominated by the independent entity referred to in subparagraph (a).

The geographical distribution of the experts on this list shall be such as to enable any disputes raised under these procedures to be dealt with expeditiously. This list shall be drawn up within two months of the entry into force of the

WTO Agreement and shall be updated annually. The list shall be publicly available. It shall be notified to the Secretariat and circulated to all Members;

(c) an exporter or preshipment inspection entity wishing to raise a dispute shall contact the independent entity referred to in subparagraph (a) and request the formation of a panel. The independent entity shall be responsible for establishing a panel. This panel shall consist of three members. The members of the panel shall be chosen so as to avoid unnecessary costs and delays. The first member shall be chosen from section (i) of the above list by the preshipment inspection entity concerned, provided that this member is not affiliated to that entity. The second member shall be chosen from section (ii) of the above list by the exporter concerned, provided that this member is not affiliated to that exporter. The third member shall be chosen from section (iii) of the above list by the independent entity referred to in subparagraph (a). No objections shall be made to any independent trade expert drawn from section (iii) of the above list;

(d) the independent trade expert drawn from section (iii) of the above list shall serve as the chairman of the panel. The independent trade expert shall take the necessary decisions to ensure an expeditious settlement of the dispute by the panel, for instance, whether the facts of the case require the panelists to meet and, if so, where such a meeting shall take place, taking into account the site of the inspection in question;

(e) if the parties to the dispute so agree, one independent trade expert could be selected from section (iii) of the above list by the independent entity referred to in subparagraph (a) to review the dispute in question. This expert shall take the necessary decisions to ensure an expeditious settlement of the dispute, for instance taking into account the site of the inspection in question;

(f) the object of the review shall be to establish whether, in the course of the inspection in dispute, the parties to the dispute have complied with the provisions of this Agreement. The procedures shall be expeditious and provide the opportunity for both parties to present their views in person or in writing;

(g) decisions by a three-member panel shall be taken by majority vote. The decision on the dispute shall be rendered within eight working days of the request for independent review and be communicated to the parties to the dispute. This time-limit could be extended upon agreement by the parties to the dispute. The panel or independent trade expert shall apportion the costs, based on the merits of the case;

(h) the decision of the panel shall be binding upon the preshipment inspection entity and the exporter which are parties to the dispute.

Article 5
Notification

Members shall submit to the Secretariat copies of the laws and regulations by which they put this Agreement into force, as well as copies of any other laws and regulations relating to preshipment inspection, when the WTO Agreement enters into force with respect to the Member concerned. No changes in the laws and regulations relating to preshipment inspection shall be enforced before such changes have been officially published. They shall be notified to the Secretariat immediately after their publication. The Secretariat shall inform the Members of the availability of this information.

Article 6
Review

At the end of the second year from the date of entry into force of the WTO Agreement and every three years thereafter, the Ministerial Conference shall review the provisions, implementation and operation of this Agreement, taking into account the objectives thereof and experience gained in its operation. As a result of such review, the Ministerial Conference may amend the provisions of the Agreement.

Article 7
Consultation

Members shall consult with other Members upon request with respect to any matter affecting the operation of this Agreement. In such cases, the provisions of Article XXII of GATT 1994, as elaborated and applied by the Dispute Settlement Understanding, are applicable to this Agreement.

Article 8
Dispute Settlement

Any disputes among Members regarding the operation of this Agreement shall be subject to the provisions of Article XXIII of GATT 1994, as elaborated and applied by the Dispute Settlement Understanding.

Article 9
Final Provisions

1. Members shall take the necessary measures for the implementation of the present Agreement.
2. Members shall ensure that their laws and regulations shall not be contrary to the provisions of this Agreement."

Agreement on Rules of Origin—the Text

"AGREEMENT ON RULES OF ORIGIN

Members,

Noting that Ministers on 20 September 1986 agreed that the Uruguay Round of Multilateral Trade Negotiations shall aim to 'bring about further liberalization and expansion of world trade,' 'strengthen the role of GATT' and 'increase the responsiveness of the GATT system to the evolving international economic environment';

Desiring to further the objectives of GATT 1994;

Recognizing that clear and predictable rules of origin and their application facilitate the flow of international trade;

Desiring to ensure that rules of origin themselves do not create unnecessary obstacles to trade;

Desiring to ensure that rules of origin do not nullify or impair the rights of Members under GATT 1994;

Recognizing that it is desirable to provide transparency of laws, regulations, and practices regarding rules of origin;

Desiring to ensure that rules of origin are prepared and applied in an impartial, transparent, predictable, consistent and neutral manner;

Recognizing the availability of a consultation mechanism and procedures for the speedy, effective and equitable resolution of disputes arising under this Agreement;

Desiring to harmonize and clarify rules of origin;

Hereby *agree* as follows:

PART I

DEFINITIONS AND COVERAGE

Article 1
Rules of Origin

1. For the purposes of Parts I to IV of this Agreement, rules of origin shall be defined as those laws, regulations and administrative determinations of general application applied by any Member to determine the country of origin of goods provided such rules of origin are not related to contractual or autonomous trade regimes leading to the granting of tariff preferences going beyond the application of paragraph 1 of Article I of GATT 1994.

2. Rules of origin referred to in paragraph 1 shall include all rules of origin used in non-preferential commercial policy instruments, such as in the application of: most-favoured-nation treatment under Articles I, II, III, XI and XIII of GATT 1994; anti-dumping and countervailing duties under Article VI of GATT 1994; safeguard measures under Article XIX of GATT 1994; origin marking requirements under Article IX of GATT 1994; and any discriminatory quantitative restrictions or tariff quotas. They shall also include rules of origin used for government procurement and trade statistics [IT IS UNDERSTOOD THAT THIS PROVISION IS WITHOUT PREJUDICE TO THOSE DETERMINATIONS MADE FOR PURPOSES OF DEFINING "DOMESTIC INDUSTRY' OR 'LIKE PRODUCTS OF DOMESTIC INDUSTRY' OR SIMILAR TERMS WHEREVER THEY APPLY.].

PART II

DISCIPLINES TO GOVERN THE APPLICATION OF RULES OF ORIGIN

Article 2
Disciplines During the Transition Period

Until the work programme for the harmonization of rules of origin set out in Part IV is completed, Members shall ensure that:

(a) when they issue administrative determinations of general application, the requirements to be fulfilled are clearly defined. In particular:

(i) in cases where the criterion of change of tariff classification is applied, such a rule of origin, and any exceptions to the rule, must clearly specify the subheadings or headings within the tariff nomenclature that are addressed by the rule;

(ii) in cases where the *ad valorem* percentage criterion is applied, the method for calculating this percentage shall also be indicated in the rules of origin;

(iii) in cases where the criterion of manufacturing or processing operation is prescribed, the operation that confers origin on the good concerned shall be precisely specified;

(b) notwithstanding the measure or instrument of commercial policy to which they are linked, their rules of origin are not used as instruments to pursue trade objectives directly or indirectly;

(c) rules of origin shall not themselves create restrictive, distorting, or disruptive effects on international trade. They shall not pose unduly strict requirements or require the fulfilment of a certain condition not related to manufacturing or processing, as a prerequisite for the determination of the country of origin. However, costs not directly related to manufacturing or processing may be included for the purposes of the application of an *ad valorem* percentage criterion consistent with subparagraph (a);

(d) the rules of origin that they apply to imports and exports are not more stringent than the rules of origin they apply to determine whether or not a good is domestic and shall not discriminate between other Members, irrespective of the affiliation of the manufacturers of the good concerned [WITH RESPECT TO RULES OF ORIGIN APPLIED FOR THE PURPOSES OF GOVERNMENT PROCUREMENT, THIS PROVISION SHALL NOT CREATE OBLIGATIONS ADDITIONAL TO THOSE ALREADY ASSUMED BY MEMBERS UNDER GATT 1994.].

(e) their rules of origin are administered in a consistent, uniform, impartial and reasonable manner;

(f) their rules of origin are based on a positive standard. Rules of origin that state what does not confer origin (negative standard) are permissible as part of a clarification of a positive standard or in individual cases where a positive determination of origin is not necessary;

(g) their laws, regulations, judicial decisions and administrative rulings of general application relating to rules of origin are published as if they were subject to, and in accordance with, the provisions of paragraph 1 of Article X of GATT 1994;

(h) upon the request of an exporter, importer or any person with a justifiable cause, assessments of the origin they would accord to a good are issued as soon as possible but no later than 150 days [IN RESPECT OF REQUESTS MADE DURING THE FIRST YEAR FROM THE DATE OF ENTRY INTO FORCE OF THE WTO AGREEMENT,

MEMBERS SHALL ONLY BE REQUIRED TO ISSUE THESE ASSESSMENTS AS SOON AS POSSIBLE.] after a request for such an assessment provided that all necessary elements have been submitted. Requests for such assessments shall be accepted before trade in the good concerned begins and may be accepted at any later point in time. Such assessments shall remain valid for three years provided that the facts and conditions, including the rules of origin, under which they have been made remain comparable. Provided that the parties concerned are informed in advance, such assessments will no longer be valid when a decision contrary to the assessment is made in a review as referred to in subparagraph (j). Such assessments shall be made publicly available subject to the provisions of subparagraph (k);

(i) when introducing changes to their rules of origin or new rules of origin, they shall not apply such changes retroactively as defined in, and without prejudice to, their laws or regulations;

(j) any administrative action which they take in relation to the determination of origin is reviewable promptly by judicial, arbitral or administrative tribunals or procedures, independent of the authority issuing the determination, which can effect the modification or reversal of the determination;

(k) all information that is by nature confidential or that is provided on a confidential basis for the purpose of the application of rules of origin is treated as strictly confidential by the authorities concerned, which shall not disclose it without the specific permission of the person or government providing such information, except to the extent that it may be required to be disclosed in the context of judicial proceedings.

Article 3

Disciplines after the Transition Period

Taking into account the aim of all Members to achieve, as a result of the harmonization work programme set out in Part IV, the establishment of harmonized rules of origin, Members shall ensure, upon the implementation of the results of the harmonization work programme, that:

(a) they apply rules of origin equally for all purposes as set out in Article 1;

(b) under their rules of origin, the country to be determined as the origin of a particular good is either the country where the good has been wholly obtained or, when more than one country is concerned in the production of the good, the country where the last substantial transformation has been carried out;

(c) the rules of origin that they apply to imports and exports are not more stringent than the rules of origin they apply to determine whether or not a good is domestic and shall not discriminate between other Members, irrespective of the affiliation of the manufacturers of the good concerned;

(d) the rules of origin are administered in a consistent, uniform, impartial and reasonable manner;

(e) their laws, regulations, judicial decisions and administrative rulings of general application relating to rules of origin are published as if they were subject to, and in accordance with, the provisions of paragraph 1 of Article X of GATT 1994;

(f) upon the request of an exporter, importer or any person with a justifiable cause, assessments of the origin they would accord to a good are issued as soon as possible but no later than 150 days after a request for such an assessment provided that all necessary elements have been submitted. Requests for such assessments shall be accepted before trade in the good concerned begins and may be accepted at any later point in time. Such assessments shall remain valid for three years provided that the facts and conditions, including the rules of origin, under which they have been made remain comparable. Provided that the parties concerned are informed in advance, such assessments will no longer be valid when a decision contrary to the assessment is made in a review as referred to in subparagraph (h). Such assessments shall be made publicly available subject to the provisions of subparagraph (i);

(g) when introducing changes to their rules of origin or new rules of origin, they shall not apply such changes retroactively as defined in, and without prejudice to, their laws or regulations;

(h) any administrative action which they take in relation to the determination of origin is reviewable promptly by judicial, arbitral or administrative tribunals or procedures, independent of the authority issuing the determination, which can effect the modification or reversal of the determination;

(i) all information which is by nature confidential or which is provided on a confidential basis for the purpose of the application of rules of origin is treated as strictly confidential by the authorities concerned, which shall not disclose it without the specific permission of the person or government providing such information, except to the extent that it may be required to be disclosed in the context of judicial proceedings.

PART III

PROCEDURAL ARRANGEMENTS ON NOTIFICATION, REVIEW, CONSULTATION AND DISPUTE SETTLEMENT

Article 4
Institutions

1. There is hereby established a Committee on Rules of Origin (referred to in this Agreement as 'the Committee') composed of the representatives from each of the Members. The Committee shall elect its own Chairman and shall meet as necessary, but not less than once a year, for the purpose of affording Members the opportunity to consult on matters relating to the operation of Parts I, II, III and IV or the furtherance of the objectives set out in these Parts and to carry out such other responsibilities assigned to it under this Agreement or by the Council for Trade in Goods. Where appropriate, the Committee shall request information and advice from the Technical Committee referred to in paragraph 2 on matters related to this Agreement. The Committee may also request such other work from the Technical Committee

as it considers appropriate for the furtherance of the above-mentioned objectives of this Agreement. The WTO Secretariat shall act as the secretariat to the Committee.

2. There shall be established a Technical Committee on Rules of Origin (referred to in this Agreement as 'the Technical Committee') under the auspices of the Customs Co-operation Council (CCC) as set out in Annex I. The Technical Committee shall carry out the technical work called for in Part IV and prescribed in Annex I. Where appropriate, the Technical Committee shall request information and advice from the Committee on matters related to this Agreement. The Technical Committee may also request such other work from the Committee as it considers appropriate for the furtherance of the above-mentioned objectives of the Agreement. The CCC Secretariat shall act as the secretariat to the Technical Committee.

Article 5
Information and Procedures for Modification and Introduction of New Rules of Origin

1. Each Member shall provide to the Secretariat, within 90 days after the date of entry into force of the WTO Agreement for it, its rules of origin, judicial decisions, and administrative rulings of general application relating to rules of origin in effect on that date. If by inadvertence a rule of origin has not been provided, the Member concerned shall provide it immediately after this fact becomes known. Lists of information received and available with the Secretariat shall be circulated to the Members by the Secretariat.

2. During the period referred to in Article 2, Members introducing modifications, other than *de minimis* modifications, to their rules of origin or introducing new rules of origin, which, for the purpose of this Article, shall include any rule of origin referred to in paragraph 1 and not provided to the Secretariat, shall publish a notice to that effect at least 60 days before the entry into force of the modified or new rule in such a manner as to enable interested parties to become acquainted with the intention to modify a rule of origin or to introduce a new rule of origin, unless exceptional circumstances arise or threaten to arise for a Member. In these exceptional cases, the Member shall publish the modified or new rule as soon as possible.

Article 6
Review

1. The Committee shall review annually the implementation and operation of Parts II and III of this Agreement having regard to its objectives. The Committee shall annually inform the Council for Trade in Goods of developments during the period covered by such reviews.

2. The Committee shall review the provisions of Parts I, II and III and propose amendments as necessary to reflect the results of the harmonization work programme.

3. The Committee, in cooperation with the Technical Committee, shall set up a mechanism to consider and propose amendments to the results of the harmonization work programme, taking into account the objectives and principles set out in Article 9. This may include instances where the rules

need to be made more operational or need to be updated to take into account new production processes as affected by any technological change.

Article 7
Consultation

The provisions of Article XXII of GATT 1994, as elaborated and applied by the Dispute Settlement Understanding, are applicable to this Agreement.

Article 8
Dispute Settlement

The provisions of Article XXIII of GATT 1994, as elaborated and applied by the Dispute Settlement Understanding, are applicable to this Agreement.

PART IV

HARMONIZATION OF RULES OF ORIGIN

Article 9
Objectives and Principles

1. With the objectives of harmonizing rules of origin and, *inter alia*, providing more certainty in the conduct of world trade, the Ministerial Conference shall undertake the work programme set out below in conjunction with the CCC, on the basis of the following principles:

(a) rules of origin should be applied equally for all purposes as set out in Article 1;

(b) rules of origin should provide for the country to be determined as the origin of a particular good to be either the country where the good has been wholly obtained or, when more than one country is concerned in the production of the good, the country where the last substantial transformation has been carried out;

(c) rules of origin should be objective, understandable and predictable;

(d) notwithstanding the measure or instrument to which they may be linked, rules of origin should not be used as instruments to pursue trade objectives directly or indirectly. They should not themselves create restrictive, distorting or disruptive effects on international trade. They should not pose unduly strict requirements or require the fulfilment of a certain condition not relating to manufacturing or processing as a prerequisite for the determination of the country of origin. However, costs not directly related to manufacturing or processing may be included for purposes of the application of an *ad valorem* percentage criterion;

(e) rules of origin should be administrable in a consistent, uniform, impartial and reasonable manner;

(f) rules of origin should be coherent;

(g) rules of origin should be based on a positive standard. Negative standards may be used to clarify a positive standard.

Work Programme

2. (a) The work programme shall be initiated as soon after the entry into force of the WTO Agreement as possible and will be completed within three years of initiation.

(b) The Committee and the Technical Committee provided for in Article 4 shall be the appropriate bodies to conduct this work.

(c) To provide for detailed input by the CCC, the Committee shall request the Technical Committee to provide its interpretations and opinions resulting from the work described below on the basis of the principles listed in paragraph 1. To ensure timely completion of the work programme for harmonization, such work shall be conducted on a product sector basis, as represented by various chapters or sections of the Harmonized System (HS) nomenclature.

(i) *Wholly Obtained and Minimal Operations or Processes*
The Technical Committee shall develop harmonized definitions of:

— the goods that are to be considered as being wholly obtained in one country. This work shall be as detailed as possible;
— minimal operations or processes that do not by themselves confer origin to a good.

The results of this work shall be submitted to the Committee within three months of receipt of the request from the Committee.

(ii) *Substantial Transformation - Change in Tariff Classification*

— The Technical Committee shall consider and elaborate upon, on the basis of the criterion of substantial transformation, the use of change in tariff subheading or heading when developing rules of origin for particular products or a product sector and, if appropriate, the minimum change within the nomenclature that meets this criterion.
— The Technical Committee shall divide the above work on a product basis taking into account the chapters or sections of the HS nomenclature, so as to submit results of its work to the Committee at least on a quarterly basis. The Technical Committee shall complete the above work within one year and three months from receipt of the request of the Committee.

(iii) *Substantial Transformation - Supplementary Criteria*
Upon completion of the work under subparagraph (ii) for each product sector or individual product category where the exclusive use of the HS nomenclature does not allow for the expression of substantial transformation, the Technical Committee:

— shall consider and elaborate upon, on the basis of the criterion of substantial transformation, the use, in a supplementary or exclusive manner, of other requirements, including *ad valorem* percentages [IF THE AD VALOREM CRITERION IS PRESCRIBED, THE METHOD FOR CALCULATING THIS PERCENTAGE SHALL ALSO BE

INDICATED IN THE RULES OF ORIGIN] and/or manufacturing or processing operations [IF THE CRITERION OF MANUFACTURING OR PROCESSING OPERATION IS PRESCRIBED, THE OPERATION THAT CONFERS ORIGIN ON THE PRODUCT CONCERNED SHALL BE PRECISELY SPECIFIED.], when developing rules of origin for particular products or a product sector;

— may provide explanations for its proposals;

— shall divide the above work on a product basis taking into account the chapters or sections of the HS nomenclature, so as to submit results of its work to the Committee at least on a quarterly basis. The Technical Committee shall complete the above work within two years and three months of receipt of the request from the Committee.

Role of the Committee

3. On the basis of the principles listed in paragraph 1:

(a) the Committee shall consider the interpretations and opinions of the Technical Committee periodically in accordance with the time-frames provided in subparagraphs (i), (ii) and (iii) of paragraph 2(c) with a view to endorsing such interpretations and opinions. The Committee may request the Technical Committee to refine or elaborate its work and/or to develop new approaches. To assist the Technical Committee, the Committee should provide its reasons for requests for additional work and, as appropriate, suggest alternative approaches;

(b) upon completion of all the work identified in subparagraphs (i), (ii) and (iii) of paragraph 2(c), the Committee shall consider the results in terms of their overall coherence.

Results of the Harmonization Work Programme and Subsequent Work

4. The Ministerial Conference shall establish the results of the harmonization work programme in an annex as an integral part of this Agreement [AT THE SAME TIME, CONSIDERATION SHALL BE GIVEN TO ARRANGEMENTS CONCERNING THE SETTLEMENT OF DISPUTES RELATING TO CUSTOMS CLASSIFICATION.]. The Ministerial Conference shall establish a time-frame for the entry into force of this annex.

ANNEX I

TECHNICAL COMMITTEE ON RULES OF ORIGIN

Responsibilities

1. The ongoing responsibilities of the Technical Committee shall include the following:

(a) at the request of any member of the Technical Committee, to examine specific technical problems arising in the day-to-day administration of the rules of origin of Members and to give advisory opinions on appropriate solutions based upon the facts presented;

(b) to furnish information and advice on any matters concerning the origin determination of goods as may be requested by any Member or the Committee;

(c) to prepare and circulate periodic reports on the technical aspects of the operation and status of this Agreement; and

(d) to review annually the technical aspects of the implementation and operation of Parts II and III.

2. The Technical Committee shall exercise such other responsibilities as the Committee may request of it.

3. The Technical Committee shall attempt to conclude its work on specific matters, especially those referred to it by Members or the Committee, in a reasonably short period of time.

Representation

4. Each Member shall have the right to be represented on the Technical Committee. Each Member may nominate one delegate and one or more alternates to be its representatives on the Technical Committee. Such a Member so represented on the Technical Committee is hereinafter referred to as a 'member' of the Technical Committee. Representatives of members of the Technical Committee may be assisted by advisers at meetings of the Technical Committee. The WTO Secretariat may also attend such meetings with observer status.

5. Members of the CCC which are not Members of the WTO may be represented at meetings of the Technical Committee by one delegate and one or more alternates. Such representatives shall attend meetings of the Technical Committee as observers.

6. Subject to the approval of the Chairman of the Technical Committee, the Secretary-General of the CCC (referred to in this Annex as 'the Secretary-General') may invite representatives of governments which are neither Members of the WTO nor members of the CCC and representatives of international governmental and trade organizations to attend meetings of the Technical Committee as observers.

7. Nominations of delegates, alternates and advisers to meetings of the Technical Committee shall be made to the Secretary-General.

Meetings

8. The Technical Committee shall meet as necessary, but not less than once a year.

Procedures

9. The Technical Committee shall elect its own Chairman and shall establish its own procedures.

ANNEX II

COMMON DECLARATION WITH REGARD TO PREFERENTIAL RULES OF ORIGIN

1. Recognizing that some Members apply preferential rules of origin, distinct from non-preferential rules of origin, the Members hereby *agree*

as follows.

2. For the purposes of this Common Declaration, preferential rules of origin shall be defined as those laws, regulations and administrative determinations of general application applied by any Member to determine whether goods qualify for preferential treatment under contractual or autonomous trade regimes leading to the granting of tariff preferences going beyond the application of paragraph 1 of Article I of GATT 1994.

3. The Members *agree* to ensure that:

(a) when they issue administrative determinations of general application, the requirements to be fulfilled are clearly defined. In particular:

(i) in cases where the criterion of change of tariff classification is applied, such a preferential rule of origin, and any exceptions to the rule, must clearly specify the subheadings or headings within the tariff nomenclature that are addressed by the rule;

(ii) in cases where the *ad valorem* percentage criterion is applied, the method for calculating this percentage shall also be indicated in the preferential rules of origin;

(iii) in cases where the criterion of manufacturing or processing operation is prescribed, the operation that confers preferential origin shall be precisely specified;

(b) their preferential rules of origin are based on a positive standard. Preferential rules of origin that state what does not confer preferential origin (negative standard) are permissible as part of a clarification of a positive standard or in individual cases where a positive determination of preferential origin is not necessary;

(c) their laws, regulations, judicial decisions and administrative rulings of general application relating to preferential rules of origin are published as if they were subject to, and in accordance with, the provisions of paragraph 1 of Article X of GATT 1994;

(d) upon request of an exporter, importer or any person with a justifiable cause, assessments of the preferential origin they would accord to a good are issued as soon as possible but no later than 150 days [IN RESPECT OF REQUESTS MADE DURING THE FIRST YEAR FROM ENTRY INTO FORCE OF THE WTO AGREEMENT, MEMBERS SHALL ONLY BE REQUIRED TO ISSUE THESE ASSESSMENTS AS SOON AS POSSIBLE.] after a request for such an assessment provided that all necessary elements have been submitted. Requests for such assessments shall be accepted before trade in the good concerned begins and may be accepted at any later point in time. Such assessments shall remain valid for three years provided that the facts and conditions, including the preferential rules of origin, under which they have been made remain comparable. Provided that the parties concerned are informed in advance, such assessments will no longer be valid when a decision contrary to the assessment is made in a review as referred to in subparagraph (f). Such assessments shall be made publicly available subject to the provisions of subparagraph (g);

(e) when introducing changes to their preferential rules of origin or new preferential rules of origin, they shall not apply such changes retroactively as defined in, and without prejudice to, their laws or regulations;

(f) any administrative action which they take in relation to the determination of preferential origin is reviewable promptly by judicial, arbitral or administrative tribunals or procedures, independent of the authority issuing the determination, which can effect the modification or reversal of the determination;

(g) all information that is by nature confidential or that is provided on a confidential basis for the purpose of the application of preferential rules of origin is treated as strictly confidential by the authorities concerned, which shall not disclose it without the specific permission of the person or government providing such information, except to the extent that it may be required to be disclosed in the context of judicial proceedings.

4. Members *agree* to provide to the Secretariat promptly their preferential rules of origin, including a listing of the preferential arrangements to which they apply, judicial decisions, and administrative rulings of general application relating to their preferential rules of origin in effect on the date of entry into force of the WTO Agreement for the Member concerned. Furthermore, Members agree to provide any modifications to their preferential rules of origin or new preferential rules of origin as soon as possible to the Secretariat. Lists of information received and available with the Secretariat shall be circulated to the Members by the Secretariat."

Agreement on Import Licensing Procedures—the Text

"AGREEMENT ON IMPORT LICENSING PROCEDURES

Members,

Having regard to the Multilateral Trade Negotiations;

Desiring to further the objectives of GATT 1994;

Taking into account the particular trade, development and financial needs of developing country Members;

Recognizing the usefulness of automatic import licensing for certain purposes and that such licensing should not be used to restrict trade;

Recognizing that import licensing may be employed to administer measures such as those adopted pursuant to the relevant provisions of GATT 1994;

Recognizing the provisions of GATT 1994 as they apply to import licensing procedures;

Desiring to ensure that import licensing procedures are not utilized in a manner contrary to the principles and obligations of GATT 1994;

Recognizing that the flow of international trade could be impeded by the inappropriate use of import licensing procedures;

Convinced that import licensing, particularly non-automatic import licensing, should be implemented in a transparent and predictable manner;

Recognizing that non-automatic licensing procedures should be no more administratively burdensome than absolutely necessary to administer the relevant measure;

Desiring to simplify, and bring transparency to, the administrative procedures and practices used in international trade, and to ensure the fair and equitable application and administration of such procedures and practices;

Desiring to provide for a consultative mechanism and the speedy, effective and equitable resolution of disputes arising under this Agreement;

Hereby *agree* as follows:

Article 1

General Provisions

1. For the purpose of this Agreement, import licensing is defined as administrative procedures [THOSE PROCEDURES REFERRED TO AS 'LICENSING' AS WELL AS OTHER SIMILAR ADMINISTRATIVE PROCEDURES.] used for the operation of import licensing regimes requiring the submission of an application or other documentation (other than that required for customs purposes) to the relevant administrative body as a prior condition for importation into the customs territory of the importing Member.

2. Members shall ensure that the administrative procedures used to implement import licensing regimes are in conformity with the relevant provisions of GATT 1994 including its annexes and protocols, as interpreted by this Agreement, with a view to preventing trade distortions that may arise from an inappropriate operation of those procedures, taking into account the economic development purposes and financial and trade needs of developing country Members [NOTHING IN THIS AGREEMENT SHALL BE TAKEN AS IMPLYING THAT THE BASIS, SCOPE OR DURATION OF A MEASURE BEING IMPLEMENTED BY A LICENSING PROCEDURE IS SUBJECT TO QUESTION UNDER THIS AGREEMENT.].

3. The rules for import licensing procedures shall be neutral in application and administered in a fair and equitable manner.

(a) The rules and all information concerning procedures for the submission of applications, including the eligibility of persons, firms and institutions to make such applications, the administrative body(ies) to be approached, and the lists of products subject to the licensing requirement shall be published, in the sources notified to the Committee on Import Licensing provided for in Article 4 (referred to in this Agreement as 'the Committee'), in such a manner as to enable governments [FOR THE PURPOSE OF THIS AGREEMENT, THE TERM 'GOVERNMENTS' IS DEEMED TO INCLUDE THE COMPETENT AUTHORITIES OF THE EUROPEAN COMMUNITIES.] and traders to become acquainted with them. Such publication shall take place, whenever practicable, 21 days prior to the effective date of the requirement but in all events not later than such effective date. Any exception, derogations or changes in or from the rules concerning licensing procedures or the list of products subject to import licensing shall also be published in the same manner and within the same time periods as specified above. Copies of these publications shall also be made available to the Secretariat.

(b) Members which wish to make comments in writing shall be

provided the opportunity to discuss these comments upon request. The concerned Member shall give due consideration to these comments and results of discussion.

5. Application forms and, where applicable, renewal forms shall be as simple as possible. Such documents and information as are considered strictly necessary for the proper functioning of the licensing regime may be required on application.

6. Application procedures and, where applicable, renewal procedures shall be as simple as possible. Applicants shall be allowed a reasonable period for the submission of licence applications. Where there is a closing date, this period should be at least 21 days with provision for extension in circumstances where insufficient applications have been received within this period. Applicants shall have to approach only one administrative body in connection with an application. Where it is strictly indispensable to approach more than one administrative body, applicants shall not need to approach more than three administrative bodies.

7. No application shall be refused for minor documentation errors which do not alter basic data contained therein. No penalty greater than necessary to serve merely as a warning shall be imposed in respect of any omission or mistake in documentation or procedures which is obviously made without fraudulent intent or gross negligence.

8. Licensed imports shall not be refused for minor variations in value, quantity or weight from the amount designated on the licence due to differences occurring during shipment, differences incidental to bulk loading and other minor differences consistent with normal commercial practice.

9. The foreign exchange necessary to pay for licensed imports shall be made available to licence holders on the same basis as to importers of goods not requiring import licences.

10. With regard to security exceptions, the provisions of Article XXI of GATT 1994 apply.

11. The provisions of this Agreement shall not require any Member to disclose confidential information which would impede law enforcement or otherwise be contrary to the public interest or would prejudice the legitimate commercial interests of particular enterprises, public or private.

Article 2
Automatic Import Licensing

[THOSE IMPORT LICENSING PROCEDURES REQUIRING A SECURITY WHICH HAVE NO RESTRICTIVE EFFECTS ON IMPORTS ARE TO BE CONSIDERED AS FALLING WITHIN THE SCOPE OF PARAGRAPHS 1 AND 2.]

1. Automatic import licensing is defined as import licensing where approval of the application is granted in all cases, and which is in accordance with the requirements of paragraph 2(a).

2. The following provisions [A DEVELOPING COUNTRY MEMBER, OTHER THAN A DEVELOPING COUNTRY MEMBER WHICH WAS A PARTY TO THE AGREEMENT ON IMPORT LICENSING PROCEDURES DONE ON 12 APRIL 1979, WHICH HAS SPECIFIC DIFFICULTIES WITH THE REQUIREMENTS OF SUBPARAGRAPHS (A)(II)

AND (A)(III) MAY, UPON NOTIFICATION TO THE COMMITTEE, DELAY THE APPLICATION OF THESE SUBPARAGRAPHS BY NOT MORE THAN TWO YEARS FROM THE DATE OF ENTRY INTO FORCE OF THE WTO AGREEMENT FOR SUCH MEMBER.], in addition to those in paragraphs 1 through 11 of Article 1 and paragraph 1 of this Article, shall apply to automatic import licensing procedures:

(a) automatic licensing procedures shall not be administered in such a manner as to have restricting effects on imports subject to automatic licensing. Automatic licensing procedures shall be deemed to have trade-restricting effects unless, *inter alia*:

(i) any person, firm or institution which fulfils the legal requirements of the importing Member for engaging in import operations involving products subject to automatic licensing is equally eligible to apply for and to obtain import licences;

(ii) applications for licences may be submitted on any working day prior to the customs clearance of the goods;

(iii) applications for licences when submitted in appropriate and complete form are approved immediately on receipt, to the extent administratively feasible, but within a maximum of 10 working days;

(b) Members recognize that automatic import licensing may be necessary whenever other appropriate procedures are not available. Automatic import licensing may be maintained as long as the circumstances which gave rise to its introduction prevail and as long as its underlying administrative purposes cannot be achieved in a more appropriate way.

Article 3
Non-Automatic Import Licensing

1. The following provisions, in addition to those in paragraphs 1 through 11 of Article 1, shall apply to non-automatic import licensing procedures. Non-automatic import licensing procedures are defined as import licensing not falling within the definition contained in paragraph 1 of Article 2.

2. Non-automatic licensing shall not have trade-restrictive or -distortive effects on imports additional to those caused by the imposition of the restriction. Non-automatic licensing procedures shall correspond in scope and duration to the measure they are used to implement, and shall be no more administratively burdensome than absolutely necessary to administer the measure.

3. In the case of licensing requirements for purposes other than the implementation of quantitative restrictions, Members shall publish sufficient information for other Members and traders to know the basis for granting and/or allocating licences.

4. Where a Member provides the possibility for persons, firms or institutions to request exceptions or derogations from a licensing requirement, it shall include this fact in the information published under paragraph 4 of Article 1 as well as information on how to make such a request and, to the extent possible, an indication of the circumstances under which requests would be considered.

5. (a) Members shall provide, upon the request of any Member having an interest in the trade in the product concerned, all relevant information concerning:

(i) the administration of the restrictions;
(ii) the import licences granted over a recent period;
(iii) the distribution of such licences among supplying countries;
(iv) where practicable, import statistics (*i.e.* value and/or volume) with respect to the products subject to import licensing. Developing country Members would not be expected to take additional administrative or financial burdens on this account;

(b) Members administering quotas by means of licensing shall publish the overall amount of quotas to be applied by quantity and/or value, the opening and closing dates of quotas, and any change thereof, within the time periods specified in paragraph 4 of Article 1 and in such a manner as to enable governments and traders to become acquainted with them;

(c) in the case of quotas allocated among supplying countries, the Member applying the restrictions shall promptly inform all other Members having an interest in supplying the product concerned of the shares in the quota currently allocated, by quantity or value, to the various supplying countries and shall publish this information within the time periods specified in paragraph 4 of Article 1 and in such a manner as to enable governments and traders to become acquainted with them;

(d) where situations arise which make it necessary to provide for an early opening date of quotas, the information referred to in paragraph 4 of Article 1 should be published within the time-periods specified in paragraph 4 of Article 1 and in such a manner as to enable governments and traders to become acquainted with them;

(e) any person, firm or institution which fulfils the legal and administrative requirements of the importing Member shall be equally eligible to apply and to be considered for a licence. If the licence application is not approved, the applicant shall, on request, be given the reason therefor and shall have a right of appeal or review in accordance with the domestic legislation or procedures of the importing Member;

(f) the period for processing applications shall, except when not possible for reasons outside the control of the Member, not be longer than 30 days if applications are considered as and when received, *i.e.* on a first-come first-served basis, and no longer than 60 days if all applications are considered simultaneously. In the latter case, the period for processing applications shall be considered to begin on the day following the closing date of the announced application period;

(g) the period of licence validity shall be of reasonable duration and not be so short as to preclude imports. The period of licence validity shall not preclude imports from distant sources, except in special cases where imports are necessary to meet unforeseen short-term requirements;

(h) when administering quotas, Members shall not prevent importation from being effected in accordance with the issued licences, and shall not discourage the full utilization of quotas;

(i) when issuing licences, Members shall take into account the desirability of issuing licences for products in economic quantities;

(j) in allocating licences, the Member should consider the import performance of the applicant. In this regard, consideration should be given as to whether licences issued to applicants in the past have been fully utilized during a recent representative period. In cases where licences have not been fully utilized, the Member shall examine the reasons for this and take these reasons into consideration when allocating new licences. Consideration shall also be given to ensuring a reasonable distribution of licences to new importers, taking into account the desirability of issuing licences for products in economic quantities. In this regard, special consideration should be given to those importers importing products originating in developing country Members and, in particular, the least-developed country Members;

(k) in the case of quotas administered through licences which are not allocated among supplying countries, licence holders [SOMETIMES REFERRED TO AS 'QUOTA HOLDERS.'] shall be free to choose the sources of imports. In the case of quotas allocated among supplying countries, the licence shall clearly stipulate the country or countries;

(l) in applying paragraph 8 of Article 1, compensating adjustments may be made in future licence allocations where imports exceeded a previous licence level.

Article 4
Institutions

There is hereby established a Committee on Import Licensing composed of representatives from each of the Members. The Committee shall elect its own Chairman and Vice-Chairman and shall meet as necessary for the purpose of affording Members the opportunity of consulting on any matters relating to the operation of this Agreement or the furtherance of its objectives.

Article 5
Notification

1. Members which institute licensing procedures or changes in these procedures shall notify the Committee of such within 60 days of publication.

2. Notifications of the institution of import licensing procedures shall include the following information:

(a) list of products subject to licensing procedures;

(b) contact point for information on eligibility;

(c) administrative body(ies) for submission of applications;

(d) date and name of publication where licensing procedures are published;

(e) indication of whether the licensing procedure is automatic or non-automatic according to definitions contained in Articles 2 and 3;

(f) in the case of automatic import licensing procedures, their administrative purpose;

(g) in the case of non-automatic import licensing procedures, indication of the measure being implemented through the licensing procedure; and

(h) expected duration of the licensing procedure if this can be estimated with some probability, and if not, reason why this information cannot be provided.

3. Notifications of changes in import licensing procedures shall indicate the elements mentioned above, if changes in such occur.

4. Members shall notify the Committee of the publication(s) in which the information required in paragraph 4 of Article 1 will be published.

5. Any interested Member which considers that another Member has not notified the institution of a licensing procedure or changes therein in accordance with the provisions of paragraphs 1 through 3 may bring the matter to the attention of such other Member. If notification is not made promptly thereafter, such Member may itself notify the licensing procedure or changes therein, including all relevant and available information.

Article 6
Consultation and Dispute Settlement

Consultations and the settlement of disputes with respect to any matter affecting the operation of this Agreement shall be subject to the provisions of Articles XXII and XXIII of GATT 1994, as elaborated and applied by the Dispute Settlement Understanding.

Article 7
Review

1. The Committee shall review as necessary, but at least once every two years, the implementation and operation of this Agreement, taking into account the objectives thereof, and the rights and obligations contained therein.

2. As a basis for the Committee review, the Secretariat shall prepare a factual report based on information provided under Article 5, responses to the annual questionnaire on import licensing procedures [ORIGINALLY CIRCULATED AS GATT 1947 DOCUMENT L/3515 OF 23 MARCH 1971.] and other relevant reliable information which is available to it. This report shall provide a synopsis of the aforementioned information, in particular indicating any changes or developments during the period under review, and including any other information as agreed by the Committee.

3. Members undertake to complete the annual questionnaire on import licensing procedures promptly and in full.

4. The Committee shall inform the Council for Trade in Goods of developments during the period covered by such reviews.

Article 8
Final Provisions

Reservations

1. Reservations may not be entered in respect of any of the provisions of this Agreement without the consent of the other Members.

Domestic Legislation

2. (a) Each Member shall ensure, not later than the date of entry into force of the WTO Agreement for it, the conformity of its laws, regulations and administrative procedures with the provisions of this Agreement.

(b) Each Member shall inform the Committee of any changes in its laws and regulations relevant to this Agreement and in the administration of such laws and regulations."

Decision on Proposed Understanding on WTO-ISO Standards Information System—the Text

"DECISION ON PROPOSED UNDERSTANDING ON WTO-ISO STANDARDS INFORMATION SYSTEM

Ministers decide to recommend that the Secretariat of the World Trade Organization reach an understanding with the International Organization for Standardization ('ISO') to establish an information system under which:

1. ISONET members shall transmit to the ISO/IEC Information Centre in Geneva the notifications referred to in paragraphs C and J of the Code of Good Practice for the Preparation, Adoption and Application of Standards in Annex 3 to the Agreement on Technical Barriers to Trade, in the manner indicated there;

2. the following (alpha)numeric classification systems shall be used in the work programmes referred to in paragraph J:

(a) *a standards classification system* which would allow standardizing bodies to give for each standard mentioned in the work programme an (alpha)numeric indication of the subject matter;

(b) *a stage code system* which would allow standardizing bodies to give for each standard mentioned in the work programme an (alpha)numeric indication of the stage of development of the standard; for this purpose, at least five stages of development should be distinguished: (*1*) the stage at which the decision to develop a standard has been taken, but technical work has not yet begun; (*2*) the stage at which technical work has begun, but the period for the submission of comments has not yet started; (*3*) the stage at which the period for the submission of comments has started, but has not yet been completed; (*4*) the stage at which the period for the submission of comments has been completed, but the standard has not yet been adopted; and (*5*) the stage at which the standard has been adopted;

(c) *an identification system* covering all international standards which would allow standardizing bodies to give for each standard mentioned in the work programme an (alpha) numeric indication of the international standard(s) used as a basis;

3. the ISO/IEC Information Centre shall promptly convey to the Secretariat copies of any notifications referred to in paragraph C of the Code of Good Practice;

4. the ISO/IEC Information Centre shall regularly publish the information received in the notifications made to it under paragraphs C and J of the Code of Good Practice; this publication, for which a reasonable fee may be charged, shall be available to ISONET members and through the Secretariat to the Members of the WTO.

Decision on Review of the ISO/IEC Information Centre Publication—the Text

"DECISION ON REVIEW OF THE ISO/IEC INFORMATION CENTRE PUBLICATION

Ministers decide that in conformity with paragraph 1 of Article 13 of the Agreement on Technical Barriers to Trade in Annex 1A of the Agreement Establishing the World Trade Organization, the Committee on Technical Barriers to Trade established thereunder shall, without prejudice to provisions on consultation and dispute settlement, at least once a year review the publication provided by the ISO/IEC Information Centre on information received according to the Code of Good Practice for the Preparation, Adoption and Application of Standards in Annex 3 of the Agreement, for the purpose of affording Members opportunity of discussing any matters relating to the operation of that Code

In order to facilitate this discussion, the Secretariat shall provide a list by Member of all standardizing bodies that have accepted the Code, as well as a list of those standardizing bodies that have accepted or withdrawn from the Code since the previous review.

The Secretariat shall also distribute promptly to the Members copies of the notification it receives from the ISO/IEC Information Centre."

Chapter X: Other Import Duties, Fees, and Restrictions

The Purpose of This Chapter

The comment of an American football coach regarding when his team passed the football to the effect that when one passes, lots of things can happen and only one of them is good for your side, has its parallels in importing. In importing, as in throwing a football pass, lots of things can happen and only one of them— moving goods through customs expeditiously after paying the expected tariffs—is good for your side. Anything else that happens will be bad. This chapter is intended to describe a number of these untoward possibilities so that the reader may be alerted to them and may be able to timely avert them.

There are a great number of taxes, duties, fees, and restrictions that may be imposed on or enforced against goods imported into a country in addition to tariffs. A general enumeration of them will be provided below, but the ones treated in some detail will be additional taxes and the imposition of duties resulting from the results of trade remedies proceedings in the country of importation.

A Compendium of Importation Problems Other than Tariffs, Taxes, and Fees; Trade Remedies Duties; and Procedural Non-Tariff Trade Barriers

This section will consist of an enumeration, which is and could not be dispositive of all such possibilities, of some of the non-duty and other payment problems that may befall an importation of goods. The purpose of this listing is not to frighten or alarm—although there is value in doing so if it makes the importer act with greater prudence and forethought—but to induce the importer to consider in advance the possibility of such inadvertent occurrences and to take whatever preliminary measures that can be taken to avert their occurrence and/or to ameliorate their adverse consequences were they to occur. It is always best to get the most catastrophic of these out of the way by listing them first.

It has been reported recently that some recipients of imported goods in some countries have adopted the practice of refusing to pick up imported goods from the customs shed which were destined for them. It is suspected that these import recipients act in close collusion with national customs officials. The result is that such unclaimed goods are sold at public auction. The price paid is invariably far less than their real market value. When the intended recipient is able to obtain these goods at the lesser auction price and is not compelled to pay the exporter the contract price, this is obviously of great benefit to the recipient and a disastrous outcome for the exporter. Exporters may attempt to prevent this by ascertaining in advance of shipment the reputation, reliability, and past practices of the intended recipient; by shipping only to recipients which it is certain would place a high value on further repeated business with the exporter; by assuring payment under letters of credit of goods cleared for receipt by customs without regard to whether the recipient actually picks up the goods or pays the assessed tariffs and other fees; or by other means.

The imported goods may be subject to inspection by customs officials and other authorized parties. While this prospect should not be surprising, what could be upsetting to the importer is the latitude granted the inspecting officers. In the United States, for example, customs officers sometimes engage in inspections with brute force and heavy equipment, including chain saws. The most destructive of these inspections are often when drugs are suspected of being concealed in the imported goods. Most outrageous are the consequences of unfounded suspicions and unsuccessful searches. There have been reports of large and valuable wooden statues and other artifacts from primitive societies being "inspected" by slicing them into pieces and of yachts being "inspected" by ripping out all their wood decking and interiors with nothing untoward being found. When the customs officials are done, they walk away from the carnage without attempting to repair the damage. They are not required to, and do not, say "I'm sorry," "My mistake," or even "Oops" if they find nothing amiss nor does US Customs reimburse the owner of the "inspected" goods.

Proscribed items which enter the customs shed may not only be forbidden entry but may be seized and/or destroyed. Although some of these proscribed items may be ones which the importer should have known were at risk, such as drugs or pornography, there are others whose negative characterization in some countries may not be obvious to a foreign exporter, such as items bearing a cross, advocating or even mentioning a non-Islamic religion, containing pictorial representations deemed to be un-Koranically idolatrous, or containing pork products or other comestibles forbidden by local religious dietary laws in Islamic countries; materials deemed seditious or politically inflammatory in some unstable countries with only rudimentary—at best – democratic practices; or items said to be undermining the "national culture" —France and Canada are two countries most susceptible to desires to establish cultural cordons, primarily against US cultural influences —through their import laws.

Infringement of intellectual property rights may also lead not merely to a refusal to permit importation of infringing goods but to seizure and destruction of the goods themselves. The ways in which an exporter/importer may unwittingly and innocently run afoul of intellectual property rights are too numerous and complex to be fully described here, but three concepts will cover much of the subject: (a) intellectual property rights exist only as a matter of national law and often require a party to make timely application for them or lose them to the public generally or to another who successfully obtains them, (b) one party may own intellectual property rights to something in one country that is owned by another party in another country, setting the stage for two seemingly legitimate owners of intellectual property rights to face infringement proceedings when each attempts to sell its products into the domestic market of the other; and (c) even goods containing legitimate and authorized intellectual property may run into import problems if the owner of the intellectual property has not authorized transfer from the exporting to the importing country through so-called "gray market" transactions.

Some countries maintain sanctions and embargoes against goods originating in, shipped from, or in some other way associated with certain countries. This is seemingly a practice that is on the wane, but imports in violation of these rules may be denied entry upon importation or may, if the sanction is simply to place the products of a country in an unfavored category, be subject to higher than normal tariffs upon importation.

Transfer pricing has recently become a major national and international issue. What is involved is essentially the question of whether the declared price of an imported product for valuation purposes is an honest, fair-market value when the sale or transfer is between two related parties. A related issue concerns when an importer, manufacturer, or exporter has multiple occasions on which to declare the value of an imported good but where the declarer's self-interest may sometimes dictate declaration of the highest possible value and sometimes the declaration of the lowest possible value. Where there are multiple, different, and contradictory declarations of value, obviously numerous import valuation and legal issues arise. Finally, there are numerous instances in which false invoices, double invoicing, and similar deceptions occur in import transactions with culpability shared between importers and exporters but where the benefit is usually exclusively that of the importer and is often intended to evade local currency exchange laws and non-tariff taxes rather than a reduction in tariffs. Recently, there have been serious and sensational allegations made in national courts by foreign governments that local manufacturers—sometimes very large and prominent ones—collude with smugglers (particularly of tobacco and alcohol products) to evade the imposition of legitimate tariffs and processing through customs checkpoints upon importation.

A failure to comply with local product and labeling standards, such as electrical products being wired for the local voltage or comestible products bearing labels not bearing a list of ingredients as required by law in the country of importation, may bar the noncomplying goods from entry. There is often a requirement that labels, instructions, and other consumer information be in a prescribed language that is often not that of the country of exportation.

A variety of health and safety problems determined by the country of importation to afflict imported goods, including those concerning tainted food products, genetically-manipulated organisms or their products, or pharmaceuticals which are unsafe to use as directed, may prevent the importation of goods which are deemed both healthy and safe in their country of exportation.

If imported goods are not marked with their country of origin as required by local law or if a determination is made that a false country of origin has been indicated in order to avoid the imposition of quota restrictions—as is commonplace regarding textile imports—the goods may be delayed entry until the marking is rectified or may be seized as having been fraudulently entered.

Imported goods said to violate country of importation environmental requirements may be denied entry, as may those in violation of national or international programs to protect wild flora and fauna such as elephants, whales, sea turtles, or generally such as through the Convention on International Trade in Endangered Species of Wild Fauna and Flora of 1973 ("CITES").

Cultural property taken from the country of origin or exportation without the authorization of the government of the country of origin or exportation may be barred import entry and be seized from the owner in accordance with domestic law or international agreement, including the Convention on the Means of Prohibiting and Preventing the Illicit Import, Export, and Transfer of Ownership of Cultural Property and art work and similar properties that were at one time the subject of theft or were improperly expropriated by totalitarian governments may similarly be subject to seizure at the point of import entry. Although undoubtedly well-intended, the actual implementation of these programs often causes great difficulties for innocent importers with no reason to know of any irregularities in an items title and may be implemented in an idiosyncratic way which bars importation and seizes property in a patently unfair manner that is not in legitimate furtherance of the purposes of such measures.

Finally, should an importation be subject to a dispute between the importer and the importing country customs authority, the result is certain to be disastrous for the importer without regard to the ultimate disposition of the matter. The first recourse the importer is likely to have is an appeal to the customs authority itself and it is usually a requirement that such internal appeals be fully exhausted before appeals may be made to higher courts unassociated with the customs authority. When the customs authority is asked to rule on its own judgements, the situation is analogous to a panel of cats sitting in judgment on the treatment of a mouse by another cat. An outcome favorable to either the importer or the mouse is improbable in each case. When further appeals are made to the courts, the process will be slow and costly and the outcome will never be certain, no matter what the seeming facts and legal arguments the importer may argue.

Despite the dangers enumerated above, some reassurance is provided by the fact that such measures as are imposed by national customs authorities must be noticed to the public and provided to all WTO members per the WTO/GATT provision below.

GATT 1947 Article X—the Text

"**Article X**
Publication and Administration of Trade Regulations

1. Laws, regulations, judicial decisions and administrative rulings of general application, made effective by any contracting party, pertaining to the classification or the valuation of products for customs purposes, or to rates of duty, taxes or other charges, or to requirements, restrictions or prohibitions on imports or exports or on the transfer of payments therefor, or affecting their sale, distribution, transportation, insurance, warehousing inspection, exhibition, processing, mixing or other use, shall be published promptly in such a manner as to enable governments and traders to become acquainted with them. Agreements affecting international trade policy which are in force between the government or a governmental agency of any contracting party and the government or governmental agency of any other contracting party shall also be published. The provisions of this paragraph shall not require any contracting party to disclose confidential information which would impede law enforcement or otherwise be contrary to the public

interest or would prejudice the legitimate commercial interests of particular enterprises, public or private.

2. No measure of general application taken by any contracting party effecting an advance in a rate of duty or other charge on imports under an established and uniform practice, or imposing a new or more burdensome requirement, restriction or prohibition on imports, or on the transfer of payments therefor, shall be enforced before such measure has been officially published.

3.

(*a*) Each contracting party shall administer in a uniform, impartial and reasonable manner all its laws, regulations, decisions and rulings of the kind described in paragraph 1 of this Article.

(*b*) Each contracting party shall maintain, or institute as soon as practicable, judicial, arbitral or administrative tribunals or procedures for the purpose, *inter alia*, of the prompt review and correction of administrative action relating to customs matters. Such tribunals or procedures shall be independent of the agencies entrusted with administrative enforcement and their decisions shall be implemented by, and shall govern the practice of, such agencies unless an appeal is lodged with a court or tribunal of superior jurisdiction within the time prescribed for appeals to be lodged by importers; *Provided* that the central administration of such agency may take steps to obtain a review of the matter in another proceeding if there is good cause to believe that the decision is inconsistent with established principles of law or the actual facts.

(*c*) The provisions of sub-paragraph (*b*) of this paragraph shall not require the elimination or substitution of procedures in force in the territory of a contracting party on the date of this Agreement which in fact provide for an objective and impartial review of administrative action even though such procedures are not fully or formally independent of the agencies entrusted with administrative enforcement. Any contracting party employing such procedures shall, upon request, furnish the CONTRACTING PARTIES with full information thereon in order that they may determine whether such procedures conform to the requirements of this sub-paragraph."

Other Import Duties, Taxes, and Fees

Among taxes, tariffs, and fees that may be assessed against imported goods in addition to the customary tariff levied on the imported product are the following ones.

Surtaxes are taxes upon taxes or charges upon charges (for example, a 10% tax surcharge is the same as adding an additional 10% of the tax imposed on top of that tax). Tariff surcharges and other surtaxes on imported goods may be encountered.

A value added tax ("VAT") is a sort of sales tax under which a product is taxed at the VAT rate at every step in its production and sale until it reaches the ultimate consumer and then the proceeds are paid to the government which ultimately sorts out any reimbursements owing and keeps the rest. In order to bring taxation on imported goods into line with those on domestically-produced goods, VAT is generally levied on imported goods as they enter the country (and are repaid upon exported goods, which permits the equivalent of a sort of export subsidy).

Documentary taxes (usually paid as a percentage of the value of the transaction engaged in under the document being taxed) may come into play if the document underlying an import transaction has to be registered in a country where documentary taxes and fees are collected.

User fees, cost reimbursements, storage fees, and similar payments ostensibly to offset costs incurred by the importing government in order to service importation are sometimes assessed on imported goods.

Retaliatory tariffs may be imposed on imported goods in excess of the published tariffs if the imported goods are among those against which retaliatory tariffs have been placed by the country of importation on goods from the country of origin in retaliation for current WTO/GATT noncomformance by the country of origin to the detriment of the country of importation as permitted under the terms of GATT/WTO.

Fortunately, WTO/GATT provides the importer with some protection against the imposition of the type of charges described in this section by at least restricting the latitude with which a country may act in assessing those charges. The principal GATT/WTO provisions providing this protection are given in full text immediately below. Nonetheless, it should be borne in mind that those WTO/GATT provisions offer no help in countries not members of WTO and underdeveloped countries often will not be held to a strict standard of adherence to those obligatory protections.

GATT 1947 Article III and its Annex I Notes —the Texts

[***asterisks** below mark the portions of the text which should be read in conjunction with notes and supplementary provisions in Annex I to the Agreement.]

"PART II

Article III*
National Treatment on Internal Taxation and Regulation

1. The contracting parties recognize that internal taxes and other

internal charges, and laws, regulations and requirements affecting the internal sale, offering for sale, purchase, transportation, distribution or use of products, and internal quantitative regulations requiring the mixture, processing or use of products in specified amounts or proportions, should not be applied to imported or domestic products so as to afford protection to domestic production.*

2. The products of the territory of any contracting party imported into the territory of any other contracting party shall not be subject, directly or indirectly, to internal taxes or other internal charges of any kind in excess of those applied, directly or indirectly, to like domestic products. Moreover, no contracting party shall otherwise apply internal taxes or other internal charges to imported or domestic products in a manner contrary to the principles set forth in paragraph 1.*

3. With respect to any existing internal tax which is inconsistent with the provisions of paragraph 2, but which is specifically authorized under a trade agreement, in force on April 10, 1947, in which the import duty on the taxed product is bound against increase, the contracting party imposing the tax shall be free to postpone the application of the provisions of paragraph 2 to such tax until such time as it can obtain release from the obligations of such trade agreement in order to permit the increase of such duty to the extent necessary to compensate for the elimination of the protective element of the tax.

4. The products of the territory of any contracting party imported into the territory of any other contracting party shall be accorded treatment no less favourable than that accorded to like products of national origin in respect of all laws, regulations and requirements affecting their internal sale, offering for sale, purchase, transportation, distribution or use. The provisions of this paragraph shall not prevent the application of differential internal transportation charges which are based exclusively on the economic operation of the means of transport and not on the nationality of the product.

5. No contracting party shall establish or maintain any internal quantitative regulation relating to the mixture, processing or use of products in specified amounts or proportions which requires, directly or indirectly, that any specified amount or proportion of any product which is the subject of the regulation must be supplied from domestic sources. Moreover, no contracting party shall otherwise apply internal quantitative regulations in a manner contrary to the principles set forth in paragraph 1.*

6. The provisions of paragraph 5 shall not apply to any internal quantitative regulation in force in the territory of any contracting party on July 1, 1939, April 10, 1947, or March 24, 1948, at the option of that contracting party; *Provided* that any such regulation which is contrary to the provisions of paragraph 5 shall not be modified to the detriment of imports and shall be treated as a customs duty for the purpose of negotiation.

7. No internal quantitative regulation relating to the mixture, processing or use of products in specified amounts or proportions shall be applied in such a manner as to allocate any such amount or proportion among external sources of supply.

8.

(*a*) The provisions of this Article shall not apply to laws, regulations or requirements governing the procurement by governmental agencies of products purchased for governmental purposes and not with a view to commercial resale or with a view to use in the production of goods for commercial sale.

(*b*) The provisions of this Article shall not prevent the payment of subsidies exclusively to domestic producers, including payments to domestic producers derived from the proceeds of internal taxes or charges applied consistently with the provisions of this Article and subsidies effected through governmental purchases of domestic products.

9. The contracting parties recognize that internal maximum price control measures, even though conforming to the other provisions of this Article, can have effects prejudicial to the interests of contracting parties supplying imported products. Accordingly, contracting parties applying such measures shall take account of the interests of exporting contracting parties with a view to avoiding to the fullest practicable extent such prejudicial effects.

10. The provisions of this Article shall not prevent any contracting party from establishing or maintaining internal quantitative regulations relating to exposed cinematograph films and meeting the requirements of Article IV."

"Ad Article III

Any internal tax or other internal charge, or any law, regulation or requirement of the kind referred to in paragraph 1 which applies to an imported product and to the like domestic product and is collected or enforced in the case of the imported product at the time or point of importation, is nevertheless to be regarded as an internal tax or other internal charge, or a law, regulation or requirement of the kind referred to in paragraph 1, and is accordingly subject to the provisions of Article III.

Paragraph 1

The application of paragraph 1 to internal taxes imposed by local governments and authorities with the territory of a contracting party is subject to the provisions of the final paragraph of Article XXIV. The term 'reasonable measures' in the last-mentioned paragraph would not require, for example, the repeal of existing national legislation authorizing local governments to impose internal taxes which, although technically inconsistent with the letter of Article III, are not in fact inconsistent with its spirit, if such repeal would result in a serious financial hardship for the local governments or authorities concerned. With regard to taxation by local governments or authorities which is inconsistent with both the letter and spirit of Article III, the term 'reasonable measures' would permit a contracting party to eliminate the inconsistent taxation gradually over a transition period, if abrupt action would create serious administrative and financial difficulties.

Paragraph 2

A tax conforming to the requirements of the first sentence of paragraph 2 would be considered to be inconsistent with the provisions of the second sentence only in cases where competition was involved between, on the one hand, the taxed product and, on the other hand, a directly competitive or substitutable product which was not similarly taxed.

Paragraph 5

Regulations consistent with the provisions of the first sentence of paragraph 5 shall not be considered to be contrary to the provisions of the second sentence in any case in which all of the products subject to the regulations are produced domestically in substantial quantities. A regulation cannot be justified as being consistent with the provisions of the second sentence on the ground that the proportion or amount allocated to each of the products which are the subject of the regulation constitutes an equitable relationship between imported and domestic products."

GATT 1947 Article VIII and its Annex I Notes—the Texts

[***asterisks** below mark the portions of the text which should be read in conjunction with notes and supplementary provisions in Annex I to the Agreement.]

"**Article VIII**

*Fees and Formalities connected with Importation and Exportation**

1.

(*a*) All fees and charges of whatever character (other than import and export duties and other than taxes within the purview of Article III) imposed by contracting parties on or in connection with importation or exportation shall be limited in amount to the approximate cost of services rendered and shall not represent an indirect protection to domestic products or a taxation of imports or exports for fiscal purposes.

(*b*) The contracting parties recognize the need for reducing the number and diversity of fees and charges referred to in sub-paragraph (*a*).

(*c*) The contracting parties also recognize the need for minimizing the incidence and complexity of import and export formalities and for decreasing and simplifying import and export documentation requirements.*

2. A contracting party shall, upon request by another contracting party or by the CONTRACTING PARTIES, review the operation of its laws and regulations in the light of the provisions of this Article.

3. No contracting party shall impose substantial penalties for minor breaches of customs regulations or procedural requirements. In particular, no penalty in respect of any omission or mistake in customs documentation which is easily rectifiable and obviously made without fraudulent intent or gross negligence shall be greater than necessary to serve merely as a warning.

4. The provisions of this Article shall extend to fees, charges, formalities and requirements imposed by governmental authorities in connection with importation and exportation, including those relating to:

(*a*) consular transactions, such as consular invoices and certificates;
(*b*) quantitative restrictions;
(*c*) licensing;
(*d*) exchange control;
(*e*) statistical services;
(*f*) documents, documentation and certification;
(*g*) analysis and inspection; and
(*h*) quarantine, sanitation and fumigation."

"Ad Article VIII

1. While Article VIII does not cover the use of multiple rates of exchange as such, paragraphs 1 and 4 condemn the use of exchange taxes or fees as a device for implementing multiple currency practices; if, however, a contracting party is using multiple currency exchange fees for balance of payments reasons with the approval of the International Monetary Fund, the provisions of paragraph 9 (*a*) of Article XV fully safeguard its position.

2. It would be consistent with paragraph 1 if, on the importation of products from the territory of a contracting party into the territory of another contracting party, the production of certificates of origin should only be required to the extent that is strictly indispensable."

Understanding on GATT Article II:1(b) Interpretation—the Text

"UNDERSTANDING ON THE INTERPRETATION OF ARTICLE II:1(b) OF THE GENERAL AGREEMENT ON TARIFFS AND TRADE 1994

Members hereby *agree* as follows:

1. In order to ensure transparency of the legal rights and obligations deriving from paragraph 1(b) of Article II, the nature and level of any 'other duties or charges' levied on bound tariff items, as referred to in that provision, shall be recorded in the Schedules of concessions annexed to GATT 1994 against the tariff item to which they apply. It is understood that such recording does not change the legal character of 'other duties or charges.'

2. The date as of which 'other duties or charges' are bound, for the purposes of Article II, shall be 15 April 1994. 'Other duties or charges' shall therefore be recorded in the Schedules at the levels applying on this date. At each subsequent renegotiation of a concession or negotiation of a new concession the applicable date for the tariff item in question shall become the date of the incorporation of the new concession in the appropriate Schedule. However, the date of the instrument by which a concession on any particular tariff item was first incorporated into GATT 1947 or GATT 1994 shall also continue to be recorded in column 6 of the Loose-Leaf Schedules.

3. 'Other duties or charges' shall be recorded in respect of all tariff bindings.

4. Where a tariff item has previously been the subject of a concession, the level of 'other duties or charges' recorded in the appropriate

Schedule shall not be higher than the level obtaining at the time of the first incorporation of the concession in that Schedule. It will be open to any Member to challenge the existence of an 'other duty or charge,' on the ground that no such 'other duty or charge' existed at the time of the original binding of the item in question, as well as the consistency of the recorded level of any 'other duty or charge' with the previously bound level, for a period of three years after the date of entry into force of the WTO Agreement or three years after the date of deposit with the Director-General of the WTO of the instrument incorporating the Schedule in question into GATT 1994, if that is a later date.

5. The recording of 'other duties or charges' in the Schedules is without prejudice to their consistency with rights and obligations under GATT 1994 other than those affected by paragraph 4. All Members retain the right to challenge, at any time, the consistency of any 'other duty or charge' with such obligations.

6. For the purposes of this Understanding, the provisions of Articles XXII and XXIII of GATT 1994 as elaborated and applied by the Dispute Settlement Understanding shall apply.

7. 'Other duties or charges' omitted from a Schedule at the time of deposit of the instrument incorporating the Schedule in question into GATT 1994 with, until the date of entry into force of the WTO Agreement, the Director-General to the CONTRACTING PARTIES to GATT 1947 or, thereafter, with the Director-General of the WTO, shall not subsequently be added to it and any 'other duty or charge' recorded at a level lower than that prevailing on the applicable date shall not be restored to that level unless such additions or changes are made within six months of the date of deposit of the instrument.

8. The decision in paragraph 2 regarding the date applicable to each concession for the purposes of paragraph 1(b) of Article II of GATT 1994 supersedes the decision regarding the applicable date taken on 26 March 1980 (BISD 27S/24)."

Trade Remedies Duties

Perhaps the most important among the surprises that may lie in store for the importer and one that is—at least in some cases—explicitly endorsed by the WTO Agreement/GATT as currently written are so-called "trade remedies." Of course, domestic manufacturers under pressure from competition from imported goods view "trade remedies" as highly beneficial. It is one of the few overtly protectionist measures with official WTO/GATT endorsement. The most significant trade remedies are antidumping and countervailing duties.

"Trade remedies" is a term which is not in universal use but which, as used here, covers a long list of national statutory programs. Those programs are generally intended to rectify alleged abuses by a country's trading partners of the mutual trading relations among them that constitute an unbalanced and unfair condition. It is alleged that such abuses demand rectification in order to protect national markets and producers.

Antidumping cases allege that a product is being "dumped" (sold at a lesser price in its export market than in its home market). Countervailing duty cases allege that an imported product was exported with the benefit of a specially directed subsidy given by the exporter's country or one of its agencies or subdivisions. A distinction between the two is that the first involves the acts of individual exporters while the second involves the acts of the governments of exporting countries. Antidumping cases are much more common than are countervailing duty cases and the consequences of the former for those involved are generally more significant than for those affected by the latter. In order for a complainant to prevail in either case it is necessary for the complainant to also demonstrate that a domestic industry has been or is in danger of being materially injured as a result of the alleged dumping or subsidized exports.

It should be noted that WTO/GATT's recognition and acceptance of trade remedies may be challenged on at least four bases. There is much dissatisfaction by some WTO members with the current WTO position on trade remedies.

(A) Where a country determines, according to nothing but its self-designated standards of "fairness," that another country or that country's merchants are engaged in conduct forbidden neither by that other country's laws nor by any international agreement between the two countries and punishes or "counters" such conduct, that unilateral action is claimed by opponents of some trade remedies to be an act contrary to general standards of international law and comity.

(B) Where the above unilateral action is contrary to international agreements to which each country is a party, that action is an apparent direct violation of the acting country's duties under the agreements.

(C) Where the alleged harms countered by many national trade remedies do not exist in reality or are part of acceptable commercial practices (*e.g.*, dumping is claimed by some to not actually be economically harmful and to constitute fully-legal commercial practice when engaged in domestically) or, as alleged in the case of countervailed export assistance, are penalized in ways that do not properly gauge or measure the actual degree of harm, then the underlining premise which justifies the existence of trade remedies is false.

(D) Where, whatever the legitimacy and defensibility of the underlying rationales for trade remedies procedures, those procedures are regularly used by those bringing actions under them as impediments to trade and protectionist devices to frighten or impose significant additional costs on foreign competitors even when the claims made are ultimately dismissed wholly or in large part, trade remedies are subject to flagrant abuse.

Government export subsidies are universally recognized by economists as being a foolish transfer payment from the taxpayers of the exporting country to the consumers in the importing country. If consumer benefit were the only issue, or even an issue at all, any importing country would welcome export subsidies by other governments. Similarly, if the general well-being of its taxpaying citizenry were the primary issue, no country would provide export subsidies. Nonetheless, it is true that export subsidies distort rational trade patterns and create a climate in which each country's exporters demand export subsidies because "everyone else does it." Consequently, in the interest of rational markets and to avoid political pressure for misguided governmental competition subsidization, international efforts to eliminate export subsidies do provide a benefit to the global public.

Unlike export subsidies, virtually all economists would agree that, on selected occasions, dumping is a wise business practice. In domestic sales, the use of "loss leaders," "clearance sales," and similar discounts are common and legal retail marketing practice as long as low-priced sales do not constitute "predatory pricing" under antitrust laws. When there is excess production capacity within an industry, it is commercially beneficial to make and sell products at below their cost of production as long as the selling price for a product realizes income in excess of its variable cost of production, assuming the profitable market for the product ultimately revives, because fixed costs accrue whether or not goods are actually produced and sold. Nonetheless, if international traders were to make sales on similar terms and with similar justifications, their products would be subject to antidumping duties.

Companies dump goods internationally to get rid of excess production, to secure a foothold in a new market, or to drive competitors out of business. Sometimes "dumping" has been deemed to occur because changes in currency exchange rates generate an ostensible measured rate of dumping even when no dumping was intended by the exporter.

The alleged danger from dumping is that manufacturers in protected foreign domestic markets which extract high profits from high prices there or which are subsidized in those markets by governmental support will be able to quote unrealistically low prices for the same products when they are imported into a foreign market. These low prices will constitute unfair competition that may ultimately eliminate or suppress an otherwise viable domestic industry in the importing country and create monopolistic control over the domestic market by the foreign exporter. No credible case of where this has actually happened is offered in support of the alleged danger. Particularly in the case of free trade areas, such as that being created under NAFTA, the rationale for trade remedies—and particularly for antidumping duties—is very difficult to support logically. Nonetheless, antidumping and countervailing duties are still provided for in NAFTA—over the strenuous protests of Canada—at the insistence of the US .

It is also true that, no matter how theoretically justifiable the availability of antidumping, countervailing duty, or other trade remedies causes of action may be, national governments invariably adopt procedures and calculating methodologies that are patently intended to skew decision-making in such cases in favor of those bringing the actions and contrary to any objective demonstration or calculation of real dumping, subsidies, or injury. The adoption of such distorted methodologies is reflective of the impetus for such statutory causes of action: these are intended to be protectionist devices and the home town team is usually expected to win. This protectionist intention and effect is compounded when, as is virtually always the case, merely bringing the action is sufficient to depress the volume of imports complained of because the prospect of future but retroactive possible assessments of antidumping or countervailing duties on imported products is sufficient to deter importers from purchasing from those exporters or countries under such investigations.

However misguided they may be, at least some exporting countries or exporters do sometimes seem to actually intend to achieve the deleterious consequences that supporters of trade remedies use to justify antidumping and countervailing duties, and other trade remedies actions. Further, formulating appropriate methodologies to accurately measure countervailable subsidies and dumping is an immensely difficult, if not impossible, task. This is doubly true in the case of exports from nonmarket economies or of products with multiple national origins.

However unpersuasive the arguments in support of national trade remedies may be from an economic and legal standpoint, at least in the case of antidumping, countervailing duties, and some other trade remedies, the controversy has been resolved through their recognition and acceptance under WTO/GATT. GATT has, however, imposed some international standards for—and restrictions on the use and imposition of penalties under—some of those trade remedies.

Some Uruguay Round agreements significantly modified the Antidumping and Subsidies Codes and transferred most authority over agricultural subsidies to the AAg. The US and the EU were concerned about gaining GATT acceptance of the use of certain devices to prevent the circumvention of antidumping duties and in regulating more closely the procedures used in antidumping actions because of the increased use by developing countries of Antidumping measures. Countries commonly targeted under antidumping laws wanted substantive changes in the rules in order to reduce the use of Antidumping statutes as protectionist devices. A compromise was achieved. The procedural rules were tightened as were, although to a much lesser degree, the substantive rules. No agreement was reached, however, on anticircumvention measures.

Those issues dealt with by the WTO Agreement concerning trade remedies, particularly the modifications made to the Antidumping and Subsidies Codes under the Uruguay Round will necessarily be described here only in the broadest terms. Reference should be made to those agreements and to national legislation enacted to implement them. The Agreement on Implementation of Article VI provides greater clarity and more detailed rules concerning the method of determining that a product is dumped, the criteria to be considered in a determination that dumped imports cause injury to a domestic industry, the procedures to be followed in initiating and conducting antidumping investigations, and the implementation and duration of antidumping measures. Relatively specific provisions define such matters as the criteria for allocating costs when the export price is compared with a "constructed" normal value and rules to ensure that a fair comparison is made between the export price and the normal value of a product so as not to arbitrarily create of inflate the margins of dumping. The determination of "constructed normal value" based on the cost of production plus reasonable profit may not be calculated using arbitrary profit margins, and longer periods are permitted to exporters to amortize initial investments. Investigating authorities may compare either weighted averages or transaction-by-transaction calculations when comparing "normal" or fair market value and export price. Sales at a loss may be disregarded only if such sales are of sufficiently distorting magnitude. Short term fluctuations in exchange rates should be disregarded and exporters should be granted 60 days to adjust prices to conform to sustained currency movements. Injury may be assessed cumulatively (jointly for several exporting countries) in certain circumstances. The new antidumping agreement further prescribes the role of dispute settlement panels in disputes relating to antidumping actions taken by domestic authorities. A clear causal relationship between dumped imports and injury to the domestic industry is required. Procedures regarding the initiation and conduct of antidumping investigations, the participation by interested parties, the application of provisional measures, the use of price undertakings, and the duration (five years unless a determination is made that, in the event of termination of the measures, dumping and injury would be likely to continue or recur) of antidumping cases were mandated. New exporters unrelated to an export subject to duties entering a market after the investigation period must be granted a separate investigation by administering authorities although findings may be applied retroactively from the date such specific review was initiated and guarantees from importers of the payment of any retroactively assessed duties may be demanded. Immediate termination of an antidumping investigation is required where authorities determine that the margin of dumping is *de minimis* (less than 2%, expressed as a percentage of the export price of the product) or that the volume of dumped imports is negligible (in general, where the volume of dumped imports from an individual country accounts for less than 3% of the imports of the product in question into the importing country except where countries that individually have less than 3% of the volume collectively have over 7%). Prompt and detailed notification of all preliminary or final antidumping actions is required to a Committee on Antidumping Practices. Parties now have the opportunity to consult on matters relating to antidumping and may request the establishment of panels to examine disputes.

The ASCM defined three categories of subsidies: (1) prohibited subsidies (subject to new expedited dispute settlement procedures which may compel that they be withdrawn or may authorize the complaining member to take countermeasures) which are contingent in law or in fact upon export performance or are contingent, whether solely or as one of several other conditions, upon the use of domestic over imported goods; (2) actionable subsidies (subject to reference to the DSB which may compel the subsidizing member to withdraw the subsidy or remove the adverse effects if that member fails to meet its burden of proof by showing no cause of serious prejudice to another member) which cause adverse effects to the interests of other signatories (such as injury to their domestic industries or nullification or impairment of benefits accruing directly or indirectly to them under GATT, or serious prejudice presumed to exist for certain subsidies including when the total *ad valorem* subsidization of a product exceeds 5%); and (3) nonactionable subsidies (regarding which a member alleging serious adverse effects to a domestic industry may seek a determination and recommendation) which may be nonspecific or specific involving assistance to industrial research and precompetitive development activity, assistance to disadvantaged regions, or certain types of assistance for adapting existing facilities to new environmental requirements imposed by law and/or regulations. The AAg provided for a reduction in export subsidies (those "contingent upon export performance") by 21% from a base equal to the average annual subsidy granted during the 1986-1990 (1991-1992 in exceptional cases) base period and also to reduce budgetary outlays for export subsidies by 36% of the base. Export subsidies for any product not subsidized during the base period are prohibited. Specific product-specific reduction commitments are provided for. Subsidies subject to commitments include dumping on world markets of government surplus stocks, export payments financed from levies on the product, some subsidized marketing costs, internal transportation subsidies for exported goods, and subsidies on products contingent on their being incorporated into an exported product. Export subsidies on agriculture are otherwise exempt from countervailing duties and other constraints of Article XVI and ASCM. Developing countries, least-developed countries, and countries changing from centrally-planned to market economies were granted considerable special flexibility—largely a delay in the applicability to them of ASCM prohibitions—in their use of subsidies. Civil aircraft products are not subject to the presumption that subsidization in excess of 5% *ad valorem* causes serious prejudice to a member because of the expectation that special rules for the civil aircraft sector will be negotiated. Further, repayment of financing in the civil aircraft sector is dependent on the level of sales of a product. Consequently, when sales fall below expectations this does not in and of itself give rise to a presumption of serious prejudice. The US and EU will continue to apply existing rules regarding civil aircraft under a 1992 bilateral agreement.

There is a difference between (a) obligations restraining the use of subsidies and (b) rules governing the use of countervailing duties by an importing nation. Even where a subsidy is not prohibited by GATT 1994's rules, GATT 1994 may permit it to be offset by countervailing duties. Similarly, a subsidy against which countervailing duties are ineffective, *e.g.*, export subsidies for third-country markets, may still justify claims of GATT 1994 violations.

The ASCM contains a definition of subsidy and introduces the concept of a "specific" subsidy. The latter is generally a subsidy available only to an enterprise or industry or group of enterprises or industries within the jurisdiction of the authority granting the subsidy. Countervailing duties on subsidized imported goods were made the subject of disciplines on the initiation of cases, investigations by national authorities, and rules of evidence to assure that all interested parties could be heard. The calculation of the amount of a subsidy in terms of benefit to the recipients and the determination of the existence of a material injury to the domestic industry caused by subsidized imports were prescribed and made subject to certain rules. All relevant economic factors must be taken into account in assessing the state of the industry. A causal link must be established between the subsidized imports and the alleged injury. Countervailing duty investigations are to be terminated immediately in cases where the amount of a subsidy is *de minimis* (less than 1% *ad valorem*) or where the volume of subsidized imports, actual or potential, or the injury is negligible. Countervailing duty investigations must, except under exceptional circumstances, be concluded within one year after their initiation and must be concluded under any circumstances within 18 months. All countervailing duties must be terminated within 5 years of their imposition barring determination of the authorities, on the basis of a review, that the expiration of the countervailing duty would be likely to lead to continuation or recurrence of subsidization and injury.

The US imposes a number of trade remedies in addition to those explicitly permitted by WTO/GATT. Many nations have protested against the imposition of such trade remedies and have argued that some of them are incompatible with WTO/GATT. The principal organizations involved in the administration of all US trade remedy laws are the US Department of Commerce ("DOC"), the US International Trade Commission ("ITC"), and the Office of the US Trade Representative ("USTR"). Other entities and agencies may play special roles concerning particular types of trade remedies. Discretionary latitude regarding the timing and ultimate imposition of administratively determined trade remedy penalties is often vested in the US President, subject to limitations on that discretion as established by statutes. The actual practical imposition of trade remedy assessments and bans are usually made through US Customs. Determinations made in most trade remedy determinations are subject to the judicial review of the US Court of International Trade.

US trade remedy laws may generally be divided into (a) those that are directed at unfairly traded imports into the United States and are prescribed under international agreements to which the US is a party; (b) those that attempt to adjust trade flows between the United States and other countries, whether or not the products the subject of dispute are fairly traded, with the justification for the trade remedy being that major changes in international trade volumes threaten the existence of US industries or the integrity of a US government program unless a period of respite is given for adjustment, that US national security is threatened by some imports, or that balance of payments problems require a reduction in the value of imports; and (c) those that provide political and product-specific remedies outside normal international trading rules and conventions. Antidumping duties and countervailing duties were considered above. USCIFTA and NAFTA restricted the degree to which US trade remedies procedures may be applied to products from countries signatory to those agreements. The Uruguay Round Agreements Act ("URAA"), Pub. L. 103-465 of December 8, 1994, which implemented into US law the consequences of the completion in 1994 of the GATT/WTO Agreement revised some types of US trade remedies, including Section 201, Section 301, and Section 337 proceedings. Reference should be made to URAA regarding details of those revisions.

The principal other US trade remedy actions may not be described in detail but are listed below with a brief description provided for each of them.

TEMPORARY RELIEF UNDER "ESCAPE CLAUSE" OR "SAFEGUARDS" INVESTIGATIONS Commonly called Section 201 actions, they are undertaken under 19 U.S.C.S. §2251(b) and the authority of Article XIX of the GATT/WTO Agreement which allows a country to withdraw from its treaty obligations under GATT if imports seriously threaten a domestic industry.

"IMPORTS THREATENING NATIONAL SECURITY" INVESTIGATIONS Commonly called Section 232 actions, these are conducted by DOC after consultations with the US Department of Defense under 19 U.S.C.S. §1862 to determine whether to impose restrictions on imports which threaten to impair US national security.

"UNJUSTIFIABLE FOREIGN TRADE PRACTICE" INVESTIGATIONS Commonly called Section 301 actions, these are conducted by the USTR to determine if existing US rights under trade agreements are being violated by foreign governments or if the acts of foreign governments are unjustifiable, unreasonable, or discriminatory and burden or restrict US commerce (without regard to trade agreement obligations) such as to justify an American response under 19 U.S.C.S. §2411. Such proceedings are brought under Section 301 of the Trade Act of 1974, as amended by the Trade Agreements Act of 1979 (19 U.S.C.S. §§2411 *et seq.*). A Section 301 proceeding is the only major US trade remedy dealing with foreign unfair practices which is not subject to judicial review. Section 301 proceedings are directed at **foreign government** practices that restrict offshore markets to US goods and services or that artificially divert goods or services to the

United States. "Special 301" provisions principally address intellectual property issues and were designed to compel the President to self-initiate Section 301 proceedings against certain priority nations that engaged in resented practices.

"UNFAIR IMPORT PRACTICE" INVESTIGATIONS Commonly called Section 337 actions, these are conducted under 19 U.S.C.S. §1337 by the ITC which applies US statutory law and the common law of unfair competition to the importation of articles into the United States and to their sale in the United States. Almost all Section 337 cases are for patent infringement or regarding some other type of intellectual property. The US Government takes the position that Section 337 trade remedies are authorized by the exceptions of Article XX of GATT.

"MARKET DISRUPTION BY COMMUNIST IMPORTS" INVESTIGATIONS Commonly called Section 406 actions, these were modeled after Section 201 actions and are undertaken under the authority of 19 U.S.C.S. §2436(a). Rarely used, this trade remedy obviously has had limited utility since the collapse of the Soviet Union.

"AGRICULTURAL PRODUCT IMPORTATION" INVESTIGATIONS Commonly called Section 22 actions, these are undertaken under the authority of U.S.C.S. §624 and are initiated after the US Department of Agriculture advises the President that it believes agricultural commodities are being, or are practically certain to be, imported into the United States in such quantities as to render ineffective, or materially interfere with, US Department of Agriculture programs (including price support programs) or as to substantially reduce the amount of any product processed from a commodity covered by a US Department of Agriculture program.

BALANCE OF PAYMENTS TRADE REMEDY The President has the authority to impose a surcharge duty of up to 15% on all imports into the United States for a period of 150 days under 19 U.S.C.S. §2132. This authority may be asserted if the President finds that the United States is running a serious balance of payments deficit. Temporary balance of payment measures are permitted under GATT Article XII if they do not discriminate against particular countries.

OTHER US TRADE REMEDIES Some specific types of trade remedies include General Purpose Investigations by the ITC (commonly called Section 332 investigations), certain applications of US Customs fraud claims, denial of investment tax credits under Section 103 of the Revenue Act of 1971 [26 U.S.C.S. §48(a)(7)(D)], and retaliation for failure of a foreign government to prevent the exportation of strategic items or technologies to adversaries of the United States.

Additional actions like or equivalent to trade remedies, including retaliatory actions in response to closed foreign markets in telecommunications and government procurement, were created under the Omnibus Trade and Competitiveness Act of 1988.

GATT 1947 Article VI—the Text

[***asterisks** below mark the portions of the text which should be read in conjunction with notes and supplementary provisions in Annex I to the Agreement.]

"**Article VI**
Anti-dumping and Countervailing Duties

1. The contracting parties recognize that dumping, by which products of one country are introduced into the commerce of another country at less than the normal value of the products, is to be condemned if it causes or threatens material injury to an established industry in the territory of a contracting party or materially retards the establishment of a domestic industry. For the purposes of this Article, a product is to be considered as being introduced into the commerce of an importing country at less than its normal value, if the price of the product exported from one country to another

(*a*) is less than the comparable price, in the ordinary course of trade, for the like product when destined for consumption in the exporting country, or,

(*b*) in the absence of such domestic price, is less than either

(i) the highest comparable price for the like product for export to any third country in the ordinary course of trade, or

(ii) the cost of production of the product in the country of origin plus a reasonable addition for selling cost and profit.

Due allowance shall be made in each case for differences in conditions and terms of sale, for differences in taxation, and for other differences affecting price comparability.*

2. In order to offset or prevent dumping, a contracting party may levy on any dumped product an anti-dumping duty not greater in amount than the margin of dumping in respect of such product. For the purposes of this Article, the margin of dumping is the price difference determined in accordance with the provisions of paragraph 1.*

3. No countervailing duty shall be levied on any product of the territory of any contracting party imported into the territory of another contracting party in excess of an amount equal to the estimated bounty or subsidy determined to have been granted, directly or indirectly, on the manufacture, production or export of such product in the country of origin or exportation, including any special subsidy to the transportation of a particular product. The term 'countervailing duty' shall be understood to mean a special duty levied for the purpose of offsetting any bounty or subsidy bestowed, directly, or indirectly, upon the manufacture, production or export of any merchandise.*

4. No product of the territory of any contracting party imported

into the territory of any other contracting party shall be subject to anti-dumping or countervailing duty by reason of the exemption of such product from duties or taxes borne by the like product when destined for consumption in the country of origin or exportation, or by reason of the refund of such duties or taxes.

5. No product of the territory of any contracting party imported into the territory of any other contracting party shall be subject to both anti-dumping and countervailing duties to compensate for the same situation of dumping or export subsidization.

6.

(*a*) No contracting party shall levy any anti-dumping or countervailing duty on the importation of any product of the territory of another contracting party unless it determines that the effect of the dumping or subsidization, as the case may be, is such as to cause or threaten material injury to an established domestic industry, or is such as to retard materially the establishment of a domestic industry.

(*b*) The CONTRACTING PARTIES may waive the requirement of sub-paragraph (*a*) of this paragraph so as to permit a contracting party to levy an anti-dumping or countervailing duty on the importation of any product for the purpose of offsetting dumping or subsidization which causes or threatens material injury to an industry in the territory of another contracting party exporting the product concerned to the territory of the importing contracting party. The CONTRACTING PARTIES shall waive the requirements of sub-paragraph (*a*) of this paragraph, so as to permit the levying of a countervailing duty, in cases in which they find that a subsidy is causing or threatening material injury to an industry in the territory of another contracting party exporting the product concerned to the territory of the importing contracting party.*

(*c*) In exceptional circumstances, however, where delay might cause damage which would be difficult to repair, a contracting party may levy a countervailing duty for the purpose referred to in sub-paragraph (*b*) of this paragraph without the prior approval of the CONTRACTING PARTIES; *Provided* that such action shall be reported immediately to the CONTRACTING PARTIES and that the countervailing duty shall be withdrawn promptly if the CONTRACTING PARTIES disapprove.

7. A system for the stabilization of the domestic price or of the return to domestic producers of a primary commodity, independently of the movements of export prices, which results at times in the sale of the commodity for export at a price lower than the comparable price charged for the like commodity to buyers in the domestic market, shall be presumed not to result in material injury within the meaning of paragraph 6 if it is determined by consultation among the contracting parties substantially interested in the commodity concerned that:

(*a*) the system has also resulted in the sale of the commodity for export at a price higher than the comparable price charged for the like commodity to buyers in the domestic market, and

(*b*) the system is so operated, either because of the effective regulation of production, or otherwise, as not to stimulate exports unduly or otherwise seriously prejudice the interests of other contracting parties."

GATT 1947 Article XVI and its Annex I Notes—the Texts

[***asterisks** below mark the portions of the text which should be read in conjunction with notes and supplementary provisions in Annex I to the Agreement.]

"Article XVI*

Subsidies

Section A - Subsidies in General

1. If any contracting party grants or maintains any subsidy, including any form of income or price support, which operates directly or indirectly to increase exports of any product from, or to reduce imports of any product into, its territory, it shall notify the CONTRACTING PARTIES in writing of the extent and nature of the subsidization, of the estimated effect of the subsidization on the quantity of the affected product or products imported into or exported from its territory and of the circumstances making the subsidization necessary. In any case in which it is determined that serious prejudice to the interests of any other contracting party is caused or threatened by any such subsidization, the contracting party granting the subsidy shall, upon request, discuss with the other contracting party or parties concerned, or with the CONTRACTING PARTIES, the possibility of limiting the subsidization.

Section B - Additional Provisions on Export Subsidies*

2. The contracting parties recognize that the granting by a contracting party of a subsidy on the export of any product may have harmful effects for other contracting parties, both importing and exporting, may cause undue disturbance to their normal commercial interests, and may hinder the achievement of the objectives of this Agreement.

3. Accordingly, contracting parties should seek to avoid the use of subsidies on the export of primary products. If, however, a contracting party grants directly or indirectly any form of subsidy which operates to increase the export of any primary product from its territory, such subsidy shall not be applied in a manner which results in that contracting party having more than an equitable share of world export trade in that product, account being taken of the shares of the contracting parties in such trade in the product during a previous representative period, and any special factors which may have affected or may be affecting such trade in the product.*

4. Further, as from 1 January 1958 or the earliest practicable date thereafter, contracting parties shall cease to grant either directly or indirectly any form of subsidy on the export of any product other than a primary product which subsidy results in the sale of such product for export at a price lower than the comparable price charged for the like product to buyers in the domestic market. Until 31 December 1957 no contracting party shall extend the scope of any such subsidization beyond that existing on 1 January 1955 by the introduction of new, or the extension of existing, subsidies.*

5. The CONTRACTING PARTIES shall review the operation of the provisions of this Article from time to time with a view to examining its effectiveness, in the light of actual experience, in promoting the objectives of

this Agreement and avoiding subsidization seriously prejudicial to the trade or interests of contracting parties."

"**Ad Article XVI**

The exemption of an exported product from duties or taxes borne by the like product when destined for domestic consumption, or the remission of such duties or taxes in amounts not in excess of those which have accrued, shall not be deemed to be a subsidy.

Section B

1. Nothing in Section B shall preclude the use by a contracting party of multiple rates of exchange in accordance with the Articles of Agreement of the International Monetary Fund.

2. For the purposes of Section B, a 'primary product' is understood to be any product of farm, forest or fishery, or any mineral, in its natural form or which has undergone such processing as is customarily required to prepare it for marketing in substantial volume in international trade.

Paragraph 3

1. The fact that a contracting party has not exported the product in question during the previous representative period would not in itself preclude that contracting party from establishing its right to obtain a share of the trade in the product concerned.

2. A system for the stabilization of the domestic price or of the return to domestic producers of a primary product independently of the movements of export prices, which results at times in the sale of the product for export at a price lower than the comparable price charged for the like product to buyers in the domestic market, shall be considered not to involve a subsidy on exports within the meaning of paragraph 3 if the CONTRACTING PARTIES determine that:

(*a*) the system has also resulted, or is so designed as to result, in the sale of the product for export at a price higher than the comparable price charged for the like product to buyers in the domestic market; and

(*b*) the system is so operated, or is designed so to operate, either because of the effective regulation of production or otherwise, as not to stimulate exports unduly or otherwise seriously to prejudice the interests of other contracting parties.

Notwithstanding such determination by the CONTRACTING PARTIES, operations under such a system shall be subject to the provisions of paragraph 3 where they are wholly or partly financed out of government funds in addition to the funds collected from producers in respect of the product concerned.

Paragraph 4

The intention of paragraph 4 is that the contracting parties should seek before the end of 1957 to reach agreement to abolish all remaining subsidies as from 1 January 1958; or, failing this, to reach agreement to extend the application of the standstill until the earliest date thereafter by which they can expect to reach such agreement."

Agreement on Implementation of GATT Article VI—the Text

"AGREEMENT ON IMPLEMENTATION OF ARTICLE VI OF THE GENERAL AGREEMENT ON TARIFFS AND TRADE 1994

Members hereby *agree* as follows:

PART I

Article 1
Principles

An anti-dumping measure shall be applied only under the circumstances provided for in Article VI of GATT 1994 and pursuant to investigations initiated [THE TERM 'INITIATED' AS USED IN THIS AGREEMENT MEANS THE PROCEDURAL ACTION BY WHICH A MEMBER FORMALLY COMMENCES AN INVESTIGATION AS PROVIDED IN ARTICLE 5.] and conducted in accordance with the provisions of this Agreement. The following provisions govern the application of Article VI of GATT 1994 in so far as action is taken under anti-dumping legislation or regulations.

Article 2
Determination of Dumping

2.1 For the purpose of this Agreement, a product is to be considered as being dumped, *i.e.* introduced into the commerce of another country at less than its normal value, if the export price of the product exported from one country to another is less than the comparable price, in the ordinary course of trade, for the like product when destined for consumption in the exporting country.

2.2 When there are no sales of the like product in the ordinary course of trade in the domestic market of the exporting country or when, because of the particular market situation or the low volume of the sales in the domestic market of the exporting country [SALES OF THE LIKE PRODUCT DESTINED FOR CONSUMPTION IN THE DOMESTIC MARKET OF THE EXPORTING COUNTRY SHALL NORMALLY BE CONSIDERED A SUFFICIENT QUANTITY FOR THE DETERMINATION OF THE NORMAL VALUE IF SUCH SALES CONSTITUTE 5 PER CENT OR MORE OF THE SALES OF THE PRODUCT UNDER CONSIDERATION TO THE IMPORTING MEMBER, PROVIDED THAT A LOWER RATIO SHOULD BE ACCEPTABLE WHERE THE EVIDENCE DEMONSTRATES THAT DOMESTIC SALES AT SUCH LOWER RATIO ARE NONETHELESS OF SUFFICIENT MAGNITUDE TO PROVIDE FOR A PROPER COMPARISON.], such sales do not permit a proper comparison, the margin of dumping shall be determined by comparison with a comparable price of the like product when exported to an appropriate third country, provided that this price is representative, or with the cost of production in the country of origin plus a reasonable amount for administrative, selling and general costs and for profits.

2.2.1 Sales of the like product in the domestic market of the exporting country or sales to a third country at prices below per unit (fixed and variable) costs of production plus administrative, selling and general costs may be treated as not being in the ordinary course of trade by reason of price and may be disregarded in determining normal value only if the authorities [WHEN IN THIS AGREEMENT THE TERM 'AUTHORITIES' IS USED, IT SHALL BE INTERPRETED AS MEANING AUTHORITIES AT AN APPROPRIATE SENIOR LEVEL.] determine that such sales are made within an extended period of time [THE EXTENDED PERIOD OF TIME SHOULD NORMALLY BE ONE YEAR BUT SHALL IN NO CASE BE LESS THAN SIX MONTHS.] in substantial quantities [SALES BELOW PER UNIT COSTS ARE MADE IN SUBSTANTIAL QUANTITIES WHEN THE AUTHORITIES ESTABLISH THAT THE WEIGHTED AVERAGE SELLING PRICE OF THE TRANSACTIONS UNDER CONSIDERATION FOR THE DETERMINATION OF THE NORMAL VALUE IS BELOW THE WEIGHTED AVERAGE PER UNIT COSTS, OR THAT THE VOLUME OF SALES BELOW PER UNIT COSTS REPRESENTS NOT LESS THAN 20 PER CENT OF THE VOLUME SOLD IN TRANSACTIONS UNDER CONSIDERATION FOR THE DETERMINATION OF THE NORMAL VALUE.] and are at prices which do not provide for the recovery of all costs within a reasonable period of time. If prices which are below per unit costs at the time of sale are above weighted average per unit costs for the period of investigation, such prices shall be considered to provide for recovery of costs within a reasonable period of time.

2.2.1.1 For the purpose of paragraph 2, costs shall normally be calculated on the basis of records kept by the exporter or producer under investigation, provided that such records are in accordance with the generally accepted accounting principles of the exporting country and reasonably reflect the costs associated with the production and sale of the product under consideration. Authorities shall consider all available evidence on the proper allocation of costs, including that which is made available by the exporter or producer in the course of the investigation provided that such allocations have been historically utilized by the exporter or producer, in particular in relation to establishing appropriate amortization and depreciation periods and allowances for capital expenditures and other development costs. Unless already reflected in the cost allocations under this sub-paragraph, costs shall be adjusted appropriately for those non-recurring items of cost which benefit future and/or current production, or for circumstances in which costs during the period of investigation are affected by start-up operations [THE ADJUSTMENT MADE FOR START-UP OPERATIONS SHALL REFLECT THE COSTS AT THE END OF THE START-UP PERIOD OR, IF THAT PERIOD EXTENDS BEYOND THE PERIOD OF INVESTIGATION, THE MOST RECENT COSTS WHICH CAN REASONABLY BE TAKEN INTO ACCOUNT BY THE

AUTHORITIES DURING THE INVESTIGATION.].

2.2.2 For the purpose of paragraph 2, the amounts for administrative, selling and general costs and for profits shall be based on actual data pertaining to production and sales in the ordinary course of trade of the like product by the exporter or producer under investigation. When such amounts cannot be determined on this basis, the amounts may be determined on the basis of:

(i) the actual amounts incurred and realized by the exporter or producer in question in respect of production and sales in the domestic market of the country of origin of the same general category of products;

(ii) the weighted average of the actual amounts incurred and realized by other exporters or producers subject to investigation in respect of production and sales of the like product in the domestic market of the country of origin;

(iii) any other reasonable method, provided that the amount for profit so established shall not exceed the profit normally realized by other exporters or producers on sales of products of the same general category in the domestic market of the country of origin.

2.3 In cases where there is no export price or where it appears to the authorities concerned that the export price is unreliable because of association or a compensatory arrangement between the exporter and the importer or a third party, the export price may be constructed on the basis of the price at which the imported products are first resold to an independent buyer, or if the products are not resold to an independent buyer, or not resold in the condition as imported, on such reasonable basis as the authorities may determine.

2.4 A fair comparison shall be made between the export price and the normal value. This comparison shall be made at the same level of trade, normally at the ex-factory level, and in respect of sales made at as nearly as possible the same time. Due allowance shall be made in each case, on its merits, for differences which affect price comparability, including differences in conditions and terms of sale, taxation, levels of trade, quantities, physical characteristics, and any other differences which are also demonstrated to affect price comparability [IT IS UNDERSTOOD THAT SOME OF THE ABOVE FACTORS MAY OVERLAP, AND AUTHORITIES SHALL ENSURE THAT THEY DO NOT DUPLICATE ADJUSTMENTS THAT HAVE BEEN ALREADY MADE UNDER THIS PROVISION.]. In the cases referred to in paragraph 3, allowances for costs, including duties and taxes, incurred between importation and resale, and for profits accruing, should also be made. If in these cases price comparability has been affected, the authorities shall establish the normal value at a level of trade equivalent to the level of trade of the constructed export price, or shall make due allowance as warranted under this paragraph. The authorities shall indicate to the parties in question what information is necessary to ensure a fair comparison and shall not impose an unreasonable burden of proof on those parties.

2.4.1 When the comparison under paragraph 4 requires a conversion of currencies, such conversion should be made using the rate of exchange on the date of sale [NORMALLY, THE DATE OF SALE WOULD BE THE DATE OF CONTRACT, PURCHASE ORDER, ORDER CONFIRMATION, OR INVOICE, WHICHEVER ESTABLISHES THE MATERIAL TERMS OF SALE.], provided that when a sale of foreign currency on forward markets is directly linked to the export sale involved, the rate of exchange in the forward sale shall be used. Fluctuations in exchange rates shall be ignored and in an investigation the authorities shall allow exporters at least 60 days to have adjusted their export prices to reflect sustained movements in exchange rates during the period of investigation.

2.4.2 Subject to the provisions governing fair comparison in paragraph 4, the existence of margins of dumping during the investigation phase shall normally be established on the basis of a comparison of a weighted average normal value with a weighted average of prices of all comparable export transactions or by a comparison of normal value and export prices on a transaction-to-transaction basis. A normal value established on a weighted average basis may be compared to prices of individual export transactions if the authorities find a pattern of export prices which differ significantly among different purchasers, regions or time periods, and if an explanation is provided as to why such differences cannot be taken into account appropriately by the use of a weighted average-to-weighted average or transaction-to-transaction comparison.

2.5 In the case where products are not imported directly from the country of origin but are exported to the importing Member from an intermediate country, the price at which the products are sold from the country of export to the importing Member shall normally be compared with the comparable price in the country of export. However, comparison may be made with the price in the country of origin, if, for example, the products are merely transshipped through the country of export, or such products are not produced in the country of export, or there is no comparable price for them in the country of export.

2.6 Throughout this Agreement the term like product (*'produit similaire'*) shall be interpreted to mean a product which is identical, *i.e.* alike in all respects to the product under consideration, or in the absence of such a product, another product which, although not alike in all respects, has characteristics closely resembling those of the product under consideration.

2.7 This Article is without prejudice to the second Supplementary Provision to paragraph 1 of Article VI in Annex I to GATT 1994.

Article 3

Determination of Injury

[UNDER THIS AGREEMENT THE TERM 'INJURY' SHALL, UNLESS OTHERWISE SPECIFIED, BE TAKEN TO MEAN MATERIAL INJURY TO A DOMESTIC INDUSTRY, THREAT OF MATERIAL INJURY TO A DOMESTIC INDUSTRY OR MATERIAL RETARDATION OF THE ESTABLISHMENT OF SUCH AN INDUSTRY AND SHALL BE INTERPRETED IN ACCORDANCE WITH THE PROVISIONS OF THIS ARTICLE.]

3.1 A determination of injury for purposes of Article VI of GATT 1994 shall be based on positive evidence and involve an objective examination of both *(a)* the volume of the dumped imports and the effect of the dumped imports on prices in the domestic market for like products, and *(b)* the consequent impact of these imports on domestic producers of such products.

3.2 With regard to the volume of the dumped imports, the investigating authorities shall consider whether there has been a significant increase in dumped imports, either in absolute terms or relative to production or consumption in the importing Member. With regard to the effect of the dumped imports on prices, the investigating authorities shall consider whether there has been a significant price undercutting by the dumped imports as compared with the price of a like product of the importing Member, or whether the effect of such imports is otherwise to depress prices to a significant degree or prevent price increases, which otherwise would have occurred, to a significant degree. No one or several of these factors can necessarily give decisive guidance.

3.3 Where imports of a product from more than one country are simultaneously subject to anti-dumping investigations, the investigating authorities may cumulatively assess the effects of such imports only if they determine that *(a)* the margin of dumping established in relation to the imports from each country is more than *de minimis* as defined in paragraph 8 of Article 5 and the volume of imports from each country is not negligible and *(b)* a cumulative assessment of the effects of the imports is appropriate in light of the conditions of competition between the imported products and the conditions of competition between the imported products and the like domestic product.

3.4 The examination of the impact of the dumped imports on the domestic industry concerned shall include an evaluation of all relevant economic factors and indices having a bearing on the state of the industry, including actual and potential decline in sales, profits, output, market share, productivity, return on investments, or utilization of capacity; factors affecting domestic prices; the magnitude of the margin of dumping; actual and potential negative effects on cash flow, inventories, employment, wages, growth, ability to raise capital or investments. This list is not exhaustive, nor can one or several of these factors necessarily give decisive guidance.

3.5 It must be demonstrated that the dumped imports are, through the effects of dumping, as set forth in paragraphs 2 and 4, causing injury within the meaning of this Agreement. The demonstration of a causal relationship between the dumped imports and the injury to the domestic industry shall be based on an examination of all relevant evidence before the authorities. The authorities shall also examine any known factors other than the dumped imports which at the same time are injuring the domestic industry, and the injuries caused by these other factors must not be attributed to the dumped imports. Factors which may be relevant in this respect include, *inter alia*, the volume and prices of imports not sold at dumping prices, contraction in demand or changes in the patterns of consumption, trade restrictive practices of and competition between the foreign and domestic producers, developments in technology and the export performance and productivity of the domestic industry.

3.6 The effect of the dumped imports shall be assessed in relation to the domestic production of the like product when available data permit the separate identification of that production on the basis of such criteria as the production process, producers' sales and profits. If such separate identification of that production is not possible, the effects of the dumped imports shall be assessed by the examination of the production of the narrowest group or range of products, which includes the like product, for which the necessary information can be provided.

3.7 A determination of a threat of material injury shall be based on facts and not merely on allegation, conjecture or remote possibility. The change in circumstances which would create a situation in which the dumping would cause injury must be clearly foreseen and imminent [ONE EXAMPLE, THOUGH NOT AN EXCLUSIVE ONE, IS THAT THERE IS CONVINCING REASON TO BELIEVE THAT THERE WILL BE, IN THE NEAR FUTURE, SUBSTANTIALLY INCREASED IMPORTATION OF THE PRODUCT AT DUMPED PRICES.]. In making a determination regarding the existence of a threat of material injury, the authorities should consider, *inter alia*, such factors as:

- (i) a significant rate of increase of dumped imports into the domestic market indicating the likelihood of substantially increased importation;
- (ii) sufficient freely disposable, or an imminent, substantial increase in, capacity of the exporter indicating the likelihood of substantially increased dumped exports to the importing Member's market, taking into account the availability of other export markets to absorb any additional exports;
- (iii) whether imports are entering at prices that will have a significant depressing or suppressing effect on domestic prices, and would likely increase demand for further imports; and
- (iv) inventories of the product being investigated.

No one of these factors by itself can necessarily give decisive guidance but the totality of the factors considered must lead to the conclusion that further dumped exports are imminent and that, unless protective action is taken, material injury would occur.

3.8 With respect to cases where injury is threatened by dumped imports, the application of anti-dumping measures shall be considered and decided with special care.

Article 4
Definition of Domestic Industry

4.1 For the purposes of this Agreement, the term 'domestic industry' shall be interpreted as referring to the domestic producers as a whole of the like products or to those of them whose collective output of the products constitutes a major proportion of the total domestic production of those products, except that:

- (i) when producers are related [FOR THE PURPOSE OF THIS PARAGRAPH, PRODUCERS SHALL BE DEEMED TO BE RELATED TO EXPORTERS OR IMPORTERS ONLY IF *(A)* ONE OF THEM DIRECTLY OR INDIRECTLY CONTROLS THE OTHER; OR *(B)* BOTH OF THEM ARE DIRECTLY OR INDIRECTLY CONTROLLED BY A THIRD

PERSON; OR *(C)* TOGETHER THEY DIRECTLY OR INDIRECTLY CONTROL A THIRD PERSON, PROVIDED THAT THERE ARE GROUNDS FOR BELIEVING OR SUSPECTING THAT THE EFFECT OF THE RELATIONSHIP IS SUCH AS TO CAUSE THE PRODUCER CONCERNED TO BEHAVE DIFFERENTLY FROM NON-RELATED PRODUCERS. FOR THE PURPOSE OF THIS PARAGRAPH, ONE SHALL BE DEEMED TO CONTROL ANOTHER WHEN THE FORMER IS LEGALLY OR OPERATIONALLY IN A POSITION TO EXERCISE RESTRAINT OR DIRECTION OVER THE LATTER.] to the exporters or importers or are themselves importers of the allegedly dumped product, the term 'domestic industry' may be interpreted as referring to the rest of the producers;

(ii) in exceptional circumstances the territory of a Member may, for the production in question, be divided into two or more competitive markets and the producers within each market may be regarded as a separate industry if *(a)* the producers within such market sell all or almost all of their production of the product in question in that market, and *(b)* the demand in that market is not to any substantial degree supplied by producers of the product in question located elsewhere in the territory. In such circumstances, injury may be found to exist even where a major portion of the total domestic industry is not injured, provided there is a concentration of dumped imports into such an isolated market and provided further that the dumped imports are causing injury to the producers of all or almost all of the production within such market.

4.2 When the domestic industry has been interpreted as referring to the producers in a certain area, *i.e.* a market as defined in paragraph 1(ii), anti-dumping duties shall be levied [AS USED IN THIS AGREEMENT 'LEVY' SHALL MEAN THE DEFINITIVE OR FINAL LEGAL ASSESSMENT OR COLLECTION OF A DUTY OR TAX.] only on the products in question consigned for final consumption to that area. When the constitutional law of the importing Member does not permit the levying of anti-dumping duties on such a basis, the importing Member may levy the anti-dumping duties without limitation only if *(a)* the exporters shall have been given an opportunity to cease exporting at dumped prices to the area concerned or otherwise give assurances pursuant to Article 8 and adequate assurances in this regard have not been promptly given, and *(b)* such duties cannot be levied only on products of specific producers which supply the area in question.

4.3 Where two or more countries have reached under the provisions of paragraph 8(a) of Article XXIV of GATT 1994 such a level of integration that they have the characteristics of a single, unified market, the industry in the entire area of integration shall be taken to be the domestic industry referred to in paragraph 1.

4.4 The provisions of paragraph 6 of Article 3 shall be applicable to this Article.

Article 5

Initiation and Subsequent Investigation

5.1 Except as provided for in paragraph 6, an investigation to determine the existence, degree and effect of any alleged dumping shall be initiated upon a written application by or on behalf of the domestic industry.

5.2 An application under paragraph 1 shall include evidence of *(a)* dumping, *(b)* injury within the meaning of Article VI of GATT 1994 as interpreted by this Agreement and *(c)* a causal link between the dumped imports and the alleged injury. Simple assertion, unsubstantiated by relevant evidence, cannot be considered sufficient to meet the requirements of this paragraph. The application shall contain such information as is reasonably available to the applicant on the following:

(i) the identity of the applicant and a description of the volume and value of the domestic production of the like product by the applicant. Where a written application is made on behalf of the domestic industry, the application shall identify the industry on behalf of which the application is made by a list of all known domestic producers of the like product (or associations of domestic producers of the like product) and, to the extent possible, a description of the volume and value of domestic production of the like product accounted for by such producers;

(ii) a complete description of the allegedly dumped product, the names of the country or countries of origin or export in question, the identity of each known exporter or foreign producer and a list of known persons importing the product in question;

(iii) information on prices at which the product in question is sold when destined for consumption in the domestic markets of the country or countries of origin or export (or, where appropriate, information on the prices at which the product is sold from the country or countries of origin or export to a third country or countries, or on the constructed value of the product) and information on export prices or, where appropriate, on the prices at which the product is first resold to an independent buyer in the territory of the importing Member;

(iv) information on the evolution of the volume of the allegedly dumped imports, the effect of these imports on prices of the like product in the domestic market and the consequent impact of the imports on the domestic industry, as demonstrated by relevant factors and indices having a bearing on the state of the domestic industry, such as those listed in paragraphs 2 and 4 of Article 3.

5.3 The authorities shall examine the accuracy and adequacy of the evidence provided in the application to determine whether there is sufficient evidence to justify the initiation of an investigation.

5.4 An investigation shall not be initiated pursuant to paragraph 1 unless the authorities have determined, on the basis of an examination of the degree of support for, or opposition to, the application expressed [IN THE CASE OF FRAGMENTED INDUSTRIES INVOLVING AN EXCEPTIONALLY LARGE NUMBER OF PRODUCERS, AUTHORITIES MAY DETERMINE SUPPORT AND OPPOSITION BY USING STATISTICALLY VALID SAMPLING TECHNIQUES.] by domestic producers of the like product, that the application has been made by or on behalf of the domestic industry [MEMBERS ARE AWARE THAT IN THE TERRITORY OF CERTAIN MEMBERS EMPLOYEES OF DOMESTIC PRODUCERS OF THE LIKE PRODUCT OR REPRESENTATIVES OF THOSE EMPLOYEES MAY MAKE OR SUPPORT AN APPLICATION FOR AN INVESTIGATION UNDER PARAGRAPH 1.]. The application shall be considered to have been made 'by or on behalf of the domestic industry' if it is supported by those domestic producers whose collective output constitutes more than 50 per cent of the total production of the like product produced by that portion of the domestic industry expressing either support for or opposition to the application. However, no investigation shall be initiated when domestic producers expressly supporting the application account for less than 25 per cent of total production of the like product produced by the domestic industry.

5.5 The authorities shall avoid, unless a decision has been made to initiate an investigation, any publicizing of the application for the initiation of an investigation. However, after receipt of a properly documented application and before proceeding to initiate an investigation, the authorities shall notify the government of the exporting Member concerned.

5.6 If, in special circumstances, the authorities concerned decide to initiate an investigation without having received a written application by or on behalf of a domestic industry for the initiation of such investigation, they shall proceed only if they have sufficient evidence of dumping, injury and a causal link, as described in paragraph 2, to justify the initiation of an investigation.

5.7 The evidence of both dumping and injury shall be considered simultaneously *(a)* in the decision whether or not to initiate an investigation, and *(b)* thereafter, during the course of the investigation, starting on a date not later than the earliest date on which in accordance with the provisions of this Agreement provisional measures may be applied.

5.8 An application under paragraph 1 shall be rejected and an investigation shall be terminated promptly as soon as the authorities concerned are satisfied that there is not sufficient evidence of either dumping or of injury to justify proceeding with the case. There shall be immediate termination in cases where the authorities determine that the margin of dumping is *de minimis*, or that the volume of dumped imports, actual or potential, or the injury, is negligible. The margin of dumping shall be considered to be *de minimis* if this margin is less than 2 per cent, expressed as a percentage of the export price. The volume of dumped imports shall normally be regarded as negligible if the volume of dumped imports from a particular country is found to account for less than 3 per cent of imports of the like product in the importing Member, unless countries which individually account for less than 3 per cent of the imports of the like product in the importing Member collectively account for more than 7 per cent of imports of the like product in the importing Member.

5.9 An anti-dumping proceeding shall not hinder the procedures of customs clearance.

5.10 Investigations shall, except in special circumstances, be concluded within one year, and in no case more than 18 months, after their initiation.

Article 6
Evidence

6.1 All interested parties in an anti-dumping investigation shall be given notice of the information which the authorities require and ample opportunity to present in writing all evidence which they consider relevant in respect of the investigation in question.

6.1.1 Exporters or foreign producers receiving questionnaires used in an anti-dumping investigation shall be given at least 30 days for reply [AS A GENERAL RULE, THE TIME-LIMIT FOR EXPORTERS SHALL BE COUNTED FROM THE DATE OF RECEIPT OF THE QUESTIONNAIRE, WHICH FOR THIS PURPOSE SHALL BE DEEMED TO HAVE BEEN RECEIVED ONE WEEK FROM THE DATE ON WHICH IT WAS SENT TO THE RESPONDENT OR TRANSMITTED TO THE APPROPRIATE DIPLOMATIC REPRESENTATIVE OF THE EXPORTING MEMBER OR, IN THE CASE OF A SEPARATE CUSTOMS TERRITORY MEMBER OF THE WTO, AN OFFICIAL REPRESENTATIVE OF THE EXPORTING TERRITORY.]. Due consideration should be given to any request for an extension of the 30-day period and, upon cause shown, such an extension should be granted whenever practicable.

6.1.2 Subject to the requirement to protect confidential information, evidence presented in writing by one interested party shall be made available promptly to other interested parties participating in the investigation.

6.1.3 As soon as an investigation has been initiated, the authorities shall provide the full text of the written application received under paragraph 1 of Article 5 to the known exporters [IT BEING UNDERSTOOD THAT, WHERE THE NUMBER OF EXPORTERS INVOLVED IS PARTICULARLY HIGH, THE FULL TEXT OF THE WRITTEN APPLICATION SHOULD INSTEAD BE PROVIDED ONLY TO THE AUTHORITIES OF THE EXPORTING MEMBER OR TO THE RELEVANT TRADE ASSOCIATION.] and to the authorities of the exporting Member and shall make it available, upon request, to other interested parties involved. Due regard shall be paid to the requirement for the protection of confidential information, as provided for in paragraph 5.

6.2 Throughout the anti-dumping investigation all interested parties shall have a full opportunity for the defence of their interests. To this end, the authorities shall, on request, provide opportunities for all interested parties to meet those parties with adverse interests, so that opposing views may be presented and rebuttal arguments offered. Provision of such opportunities must take account of the need to preserve confidentiality and of the convenience to the parties. There shall be no obligation on any party to attend a meeting, and failure to do so shall not be prejudicial to that party's case. Interested parties shall also have the right, on justification, to present other information orally.

6.3 Oral information provided under paragraph 2 shall be taken into account by the authorities only in so far as it is subsequently reproduced in writing and made available to other interested parties, as provided for in subparagraph 1.2.

6.4 The authorities shall whenever practicable provide timely opportunities for all interested parties to see all information that is relevant to the presentation of their cases, that is not confidential as defined in paragraph 5, and that is used by the authorities in an anti-dumping investigation, and to prepare presentations on the basis of this information.

6.5 Any information which is by nature confidential (for example, because its disclosure would be of significant competitive advantage to a competitor or because its disclosure would have a significantly adverse effect upon a person supplying the information or upon a person from whom that person acquired the information), or which is provided on a confidential basis by parties to an investigation shall, upon good cause shown, be treated as such by the authorities. Such information shall not be disclosed without specific permission of the party submitting it [MEMBERS ARE AWARE THAT IN THE TERRITORY OF CERTAIN MEMBERS DISCLOSURE PURSUANT TO A NARROWLY-DRAWN PROTECTIVE ORDER MAY BE REQUIRED.].

6.5.1 The authorities shall require interested parties providing confidential information to furnish non-confidential summaries thereof. These summaries shall be in sufficient detail to permit a reasonable understanding of the substance of the information submitted in confidence. In exceptional circumstances, such parties may indicate that such information is not susceptible of summary. In such exceptional circumstances, a statement of the reasons why summarization is not possible must be provided.

6.5.2 If the authorities find that a request for confidentiality is not warranted and if the supplier of the information is either unwilling to make the information public or to authorize its disclosure in generalized or summary form, the authorities may disregard such information unless it can be demonstrated to their satisfaction from appropriate sources that the information is correct [MEMBERS AGREE THAT REQUESTS FOR CONFIDENTIALITY SHOULD NOT BE ARBITRARILY REJECTED.].

6.6 Except in circumstances provided for in paragraph 8, the authorities shall during the course of an investigation satisfy themselves as to the accuracy of the information supplied by interested parties upon which their findings are based.

6.7 In order to verify information provided or to obtain further details, the authorities may carry out investigations in the territory of other Members as required, provided they obtain the agreement of the firms concerned and notify the representatives of the government of the Member in question, and unless that Member objects to the investigation. The procedures described in Annex I shall apply to investigations carried out in the territory of other Members. Subject to the requirement to protect confidential information, the authorities shall make the results of any such investigations available, or shall provide disclosure thereof pursuant to paragraph 9, to the firms to which they pertain and may make such results available to the applicants.

6.8 In cases in which any interested party refuses access to, or otherwise does not provide, necessary information within a reasonable period or significantly impedes the investigation, preliminary and final determinations, affirmative or negative, may be made on the basis of the facts available. The provisions of Annex II shall be observed in the application of this paragraph.

6.9 The authorities shall, before a final determination is made, inform all interested parties of the essential facts under consideration which form the basis for the decision whether to apply definitive measures. Such disclosure should take place in sufficient time for the parties to defend their interests.

6.10 The authorities shall, as a rule, determine an individual margin of dumping for each known exporter or producer concerned of the product under investigation. In cases where the number of exporters, producers, importers or types of products involved is so large as to make such a determination impracticable, the authorities may limit their examination either to a reasonable number of interested parties or products by using samples which are statistically valid on the basis of information available to the authorities at the time of the selection, or to the largest percentage of the volume of the exports from the country in question which can reasonably be investigated.

6.10.1 Any selection of exporters, producers, importers or types of products made under this paragraph shall preferably be chosen in consultation with and with the consent of the exporters, producers or importers concerned.

6.10.2 In cases where the authorities have limited their examination, as provided for in this paragraph, they shall nevertheless determine an individual margin of dumping for any exporter or producer not initially selected who submits the necessary information in time for that information to be considered during the course of the investigation, except where the number of exporters or producers is so large that individual examinations would be unduly burdensome to the authorities and prevent the timely completion of the investigation. Voluntary responses shall not be discouraged.

6.11 For the purposes of this Agreement, 'interested parties' shall include:

(i) an exporter or foreign producer or the importer of a product subject to investigation, or a trade or business association a majority of the members of which are producers, exporters or importers of such product;

(ii) the government of the exporting Member; and

(iii) a producer of the like product in the importing Member or a trade and business association a majority of the members of which produce the like product in the territory of the importing Member.

This list shall not preclude Members from allowing domestic or foreign parties other than those mentioned above to be included as interested parties.

6.12 The authorities shall provide opportunities for industrial users of the product under investigation, and for representative consumer organizations in cases where the product is commonly sold at the retail level, to provide information which is relevant to the investigation regarding dumping, injury and causality.

6.13 The authorities shall take due account of any difficulties experienced by interested parties, in particular small companies, in supplying information requested, and shall provide any assistance practicable.

6.14 The procedures set out above are not intended to prevent the authorities of a Member from proceeding expeditiously with regard to initiating an investigation, reaching preliminary or final determinations, whether affirmative or negative, or from applying provisional or final measures, in accordance with relevant provisions of this Agreement.

Article 7

Provisional Measures

7.1 Provisional measures may be applied only if:

(i) an investigation has been initiated in accordance with the provisions of Article 5, a public notice has been given to that effect and interested parties have been given adequate opportunities to submit information and make comments;

(ii) a preliminary affirmative determination has been made of dumping and consequent injury to a domestic industry; and

(iii) the authorities concerned judge such measures necessary to prevent injury being caused during the investigation.

7.2 Provisional measures may take the form of a provisional duty or, preferably, a security - by cash deposit or bond - equal to the amount of the anti-dumping duty provisionally estimated, being not greater than the provisionally estimated margin of dumping. Withholding of appraisement is an appropriate provisional measure, provided that the normal duty and the estimated amount of the anti-dumping duty be indicated and as long as the withholding of appraisement is subject to the same conditions as other provisional measures.

7.3 Provisional measures shall not be applied sooner than 60 days from the date of initiation of the investigation.

7.4 The application of provisional measures shall be limited to as short a period as possible, not exceeding four months or, on decision of the authorities concerned, upon request by exporters representing a significant percentage of the trade involved, to a period not exceeding six months. When authorities, in the course of an investigation, examine whether a duty lower than the margin of dumping would be sufficient to remove injury, these periods may be six and nine months, respectively.

7.5 The relevant provisions of Article 9 shall be followed in the application of provisional measures.

Article 8
Price Undertakings

8.1 Proceedings may [THE WORD "MAY" SHALL NOT BE INTERPRETED TO ALLOW THE SIMULTANEOUS CONTINUATION OF PROCEEDINGS WITH THE IMPLEMENTATION OF PRICE UNDERTAKINGS EXCEPT AS PROVIDED IN PARAGRAPH 4.] be suspended or terminated without the imposition of provisional measures or anti-dumping duties upon receipt of satisfactory voluntary undertakings from any exporter to revise its prices or to cease exports to the area in question at dumped prices so that the authorities are satisfied that the injurious effect of the dumping is eliminated. Price increases under such undertakings shall not be higher than necessary to eliminate the margin of dumping. It is desirable that the price increases be less than the margin of dumping if such increases would be adequate to remove the injury to the domestic industry.

8.2 Price undertakings shall not be sought or accepted from exporters unless the authorities of the importing Member have made a preliminary affirmative determination of dumping and injury caused by such dumping.

8.3 Undertakings offered need not be accepted if the authorities consider their acceptance impractical, for example, if the number of actual or potential exporters is too great, or for other reasons, including reasons of general policy. Should the case arise and where practicable, the authorities shall provide to the exporter the reasons which have led them to consider acceptance of an undertaking as inappropriate, and shall, to the extent possible, give the exporter an opportunity to make comments thereon.

8.4 If an undertaking is accepted, the investigation of dumping and injury shall nevertheless be completed if the exporter so desires or the authorities so decide. In such a case, if a negative determination of dumping or injury is made, the undertaking shall automatically lapse, except in cases where such a determination is due in large part to the existence of a price undertaking. In such cases, the authorities may require that an undertaking be maintained for a reasonable period consistent with the provisions of this Agreement. In the event that an affirmative determination of dumping and injury is made, the undertaking shall continue consistent with its terms and the provisions of this Agreement.

8.5 Price undertakings may be suggested by the authorities of the importing Member, but no exporter shall be forced to enter into such undertakings. The fact that exporters do not offer such undertakings, or do not accept an invitation to do so, shall in no way prejudice the consideration of the case. However, the authorities are free to determine that a threat of injury is more likely to be realized if the dumped imports continue.

8.6 Authorities of an importing Member may require any exporter from whom an undertaking has been accepted to provide periodically information relevant to the fulfilment of such an undertaking and to permit verification of pertinent data. In case of violation of an undertaking, the authorities of the importing Member may take, under this Agreement in conformity with its provisions, expeditious actions which may constitute immediate application of provisional measures using the best information available. In such cases, definitive duties may be levied in accordance with this Agreement on products entered for consumption not more than 90 days before the application of such provisional measures, except that any such retroactive assessment shall not apply to imports entered before the violation of the undertaking.

Article 9

Imposition and Collection of Anti-Dumping Duties

9.1 The decision whether or not to impose an anti-dumping duty in cases where all requirements for the imposition have been fulfilled, and the decision whether the amount of the anti-dumping duty to be imposed shall be the full margin of dumping or less, are decisions to be made by the authorities of the importing Member. It is desirable that the imposition be permissive in the territory of all Members, and that the duty be less than the margin if such lesser duty would be adequate to remove the injury to the domestic industry.

9.2 When an anti-dumping duty is imposed in respect of any product, such anti-dumping duty shall be collected in the appropriate amounts in each case, on a non-discriminatory basis on imports of such product from all sources found to be dumped and causing injury, except as to imports from those sources from which price undertakings under the terms of this Agreement have been accepted. The authorities shall name the supplier or suppliers of the product concerned. If, however, several suppliers from the same country are involved, and it is impracticable to name all these suppliers, the authorities may name the supplying country concerned. If several suppliers from more than one country are involved, the authorities may name either all the suppliers involved, or, if this is impracticable, all the supplying countries involved.

9.3 The amount of the anti-dumping duty shall not exceed the margin of dumping as established under Article 2.

9.3.1 When the amount of the anti-dumping duty is assessed on a retrospective basis, the determination of the final liability for payment of anti-dumping duties shall take place as soon as possible, normally within 12 months, and in no case more than 18 months, after the date on which a request for a final assessment of the amount of the anti-dumping duty has been made. [It is understood that the observance of the time limits mentioned in this subparagraph and in subparagraph 3.2 may not be possible where the product in question is subject to judicial review proceedings.] Any refund shall be made promptly and normally in not more than 90 days following the determination of final liability made pursuant to this sub-paragraph. In any case, where a refund is not made within 90 days, the authorities shall provide an explanation if so requested.

9.3.2 When the amount of the anti-dumping duty is assessed on a prospective basis, provision shall be made for a prompt refund, upon request, of any duty paid in excess of the margin of dumping. A refund of any such duty paid in excess of the actual margin of dumping shall normally take place within 12 months, and in no case more than 18 months, after the date on which a request for a refund, duly supported by evidence, has been made by an importer of the product subject to the anti-dumping duty. The refund authorized should normally be made within 90 days of the above-noted decision.

9.3.3 In determining whether and to what extent a reimbursement should be made when the export price is constructed in accordance with paragraph 3 of Article 2, authorities should take account of any change in normal value, any change in costs incurred between importation and resale, and any movement in the resale price which is duly reflected in subsequent selling prices, and should calculate the export price with no deduction for the amount of anti-dumping duties paid when conclusive evidence of the above is provided.

9.4 When the authorities have limited their examination in accordance with the second sentence of paragraph 10 of Article 6, any anti-dumping duty applied to imports from exporters or producers not included in the examination shall not exceed:

(i) the weighted average margin of dumping established with respect to the selected exporters or producers or,

(ii) where the liability for payment of anti-dumping duties is calculated on the basis of a prospective normal value, the difference between the weighted average normal value of the selected exporters or producers and the export prices of exporters or producers not individually examined, provided that the authorities shall disregard for the purpose of this paragraph any zero and *de minimis* margins and margins established under the circumstances referred to in paragraph 8 of Article 6. The authorities shall apply individual duties or normal values to imports from any exporter or producer not included in the examination who has provided the necessary information during the course of the investigation, as provided for in subparagraph 10.2 of Article 6.

9.5 If a product is subject to anti-dumping duties in an importing Member, the authorities shall promptly carry out a review for the purpose of determining individual margins of dumping for any exporters or producers in the exporting country in question who have not exported the product to the importing Member during the period of investigation, provided that these exporters or producers can show that they are not related to any of the exporters or producers in the exporting country who are subject to the anti-dumping duties on the product. Such a review shall be initiated and carried out on an accelerated basis, compared to normal duty assessment and review proceedings in the importing Member. No anti-dumping duties shall be levied on imports from such exporters or producers while the review is being carried out. The authorities may, however, withhold appraisement and/or request guarantees to ensure that, should such a review result in a determination of dumping in respect of such producers or exporters, anti-dumping duties can be levied retroactively to the date of the initiation of the review.

Article 10
Retroactivity

10.1 Provisional measures and anti-dumping duties shall only be applied to products which enter for consumption after the time when the decision taken under paragraph 1 of Article 7 and paragraph 1 of Article 9, respectively, enters into force, subject to the exceptions set out in this Article.

10.2 Where a final determination of injury (but not of a threat thereof or of a material retardation of the establishment of an industry) is made or, in the case of a final determination of a threat of injury, where the effect of the dumped imports would, in the absence of the provisional measures, have led to a determination of injury, anti-dumping duties may be levied retroactively for the period for which provisional measures, if any, have been applied.

10.3 If the definitive anti-dumping duty is higher than the provisional duty paid or payable, or the amount estimated for the purpose of the security, the difference shall not be collected. If the definitive duty is lower than the provisional duty paid or payable, or the amount estimated for the purpose of the security, the difference shall be reimbursed or the duty recalculated, as the case may be.

10.4 Except as provided in paragraph 2, where a determination of threat of injury or material retardation is made (but no injury has yet occurred) a definitive anti-dumping duty may be imposed only from the date of the determination of threat of injury or material retardation, and any cash deposit made during the period of the application of provisional measures shall be refunded and any bonds released in an expeditious manner.

10.5 Where a final determination is negative, any cash deposit made during the period of the application of provisional measures shall be refunded and any bonds released in an expeditious manner.

10.6 A definitive anti-dumping duty may be levied on products which were entered for consumption not more than 90 days prior to the date of application of provisional measures, when the authorities determine for the dumped product in question that:

(i) there is a history of dumping which caused injury or that the importer was, or should have been, aware that the exporter practises dumping and that such dumping would cause injury, and

(ii) the injury is caused by massive dumped imports of a product in a relatively short time which in light of the timing and the volume of the dumped imports and other circumstances (such as a rapid build-up of inventories of the imported product) is likely to seriously undermine the remedial effect of the definitive anti-dumping duty to be applied, provided that the importers concerned have been given an opportunity to comment.

10.7 The authorities may, after initiating an investigation, take such measures as the withholding of appraisement or assessment as may be necessary to collect anti-dumping duties retroactively, as provided for in paragraph 6, once they have sufficient evidence that the conditions set forth in that paragraph are satisfied.

10.8 No duties shall be levied retroactively pursuant to paragraph 6 on products entered for consumption prior to the date of initiation of the investigation.

Article 11
Duration and Review of Anti-Dumping Duties and Price Undertakings

11.1 An anti-dumping duty shall remain in force only as long as and to the extent necessary to counteract dumping which is causing injury.

11.2 The authorities shall review the need for the continued imposition of the duty, where warranted, on their own initiative or, provided that a reasonable period of time has elapsed since the imposition of the definitive anti-dumping duty, upon request by any interested party which submits positive information substantiating the need for a review. [A DETERMINATION OF FINAL LIABILITY FOR PAYMENT OF ANTI-DUMPING DUTIES, AS PROVIDED IN PARAGRAPH 3 OF ARTICLE 9, DOES NOT BY ITSELF CONSTITUTE A REVIEW WITHIN THE MEANING OF THIS ARTICLE.] Interested parties shall have the right to request the authorities to examine whether the continued imposition of the duty is necessary to offset dumping, whether the injury would be likely to continue or recur if the duty were removed or varied, or both. If, as a result of the review under this paragraph, the authorities determine that the anti-dumping duty is no longer warranted, it shall be terminated immediately.

11.3 Notwithstanding the provisions of paragraphs 1 and 2, any definitive anti-dumping duty shall be terminated on a date not later than five years from its imposition (or from the date of the most recent review under paragraph 2 if that review has covered both dumping and injury, or under this paragraph), unless the authorities determine, in a review initiated before that date on their own initiative or upon a duly substantiated request made by or on behalf of the domestic industry within a reasonable period of time prior to that date, that the expiry of the duty would be likely to lead to continuation or recurrence of dumping and injury. [WHEN THE AMOUNT OF THE ANTI-DUMPING DUTY IS ASSESSED ON A RETROSPECTIVE BASIS, A FINDING IN THE MOST RECENT ASSESSMENT PROCEEDING UNDER PARAGRAPH 3.1 OF ARTICLE 9 THAT NO DUTY IS TO BE LEVIED SHALL NOT BY ITSELF REQUIRE THE AUTHORITIES TO TERMINATE THE DEFINITIVE DUTY.] The duty may remain in force pending the outcome of such a review.

11.4 The provisions of Article 6 regarding evidence and procedure shall apply to any review carried out under this Article. Any such review shall be carried out expeditiously and shall normally be concluded within 12 months of the date of initiation of the review.

11.5 The provisions of this Article shall apply *mutatis mutandis* to price undertakings accepted under Article 8.

Article 12
Public Notice and Explanation of Determinations

12.1 When the authorities are satisfied that there is sufficient evidence to justify the initiation of an anti-dumping investigation pursuant to Article 5, the Member or Members the products of which are subject to such investigation and other interested parties known to the investigating authorities to have an interest therein shall be notified and a public notice shall be given.

12.1.1 A public notice of the initiation of an investigation shall contain, or otherwise make available through a separate report [WHERE AUTHORITIES PROVIDE INFORMATION AND EXPLANATIONS UNDER THE PROVISIONS OF THIS ARTICLE IN A SEPARATE REPORT, THEY SHALL ASSURE THAT SUCH REPORT IS READILY AVAILABLE TO THE PUBLIC], adequate information on the following:

(i) the name of the exporting country or countries and the product involved;
(ii) the date of initiation of the investigation;
(iii) the basis on which dumping is alleged in the application;
(iv) a summary of the factors on which the allegation of injury is based;
(v) the address to which representations by interested parties should be directed;
(vi) the time-limits allowed to interested parties for making their views known.

12.2 Public notice shall be given of any preliminary or final determination, whether affirmative or negative, of any decision to accept an undertaking pursuant to Article 8, of the termination of such an undertaking, and of the termination of a definitive anti-dumping duty. Each such notice shall set forth, or otherwise make available through a separate report, in sufficient detail the findings and conclusions reached on all issues of fact and law considered material by the investigating authorities. All such notices and reports shall be forwarded to the Member or Members the products of which are subject to such determination or undertaking and to other interested parties known to have an interest therein.

12.2.1 A public notice of the imposition of provisional measures shall set forth, or otherwise make available through a separate report, sufficiently detailed explanations for the preliminary determinations on dumping and injury and shall refer to the matters of fact and law which have led to arguments being accepted or rejected. Such a notice or report shall, due regard being paid to the requirement for the protection of confidential information, contain in particular:

(i) the names of the suppliers, or when this is impracticable, the supplying countries involved;
(ii) a description of the product which is sufficient for customs purposes;
(iii) the margins of dumping established and a full explanation of the reasons for the methodology used in the establishment and comparison of the export price and the normal value under Article 2;
(iv) considerations relevant to the injury determination as set out in Article 3;
(v) the main reasons leading to the determination.

12.2.2 A public notice of conclusion or suspension of an investigation in the case of an affirmative determination providing for the imposition of a definitive duty or the acceptance of a price undertaking shall contain, or otherwise make available through a separate report separate report, all relevant information on the matters of fact and law and reasons which have led to the imposition of final measures or the acceptance of a price undertaking, due regard being paid to the requirement for the protection of confidential information. In particular, the notice or report shall contain the information described in subparagraph 2.1, as well as the reasons for the acceptance or rejection of relevant arguments or claims made by the exporters and importers, and the basis for any decision made under subparagraph 10.2 of Article 6.

12.2.3 A public notice of the termination or suspension of an investigation following the acceptance of an undertaking pursuant to Article 8 shall include, or otherwise make available through a separate report, the non-confidential part of this undertaking.

12.3 The provisions of this Article shall apply *mutatis mutandis* to the initiation and completion of reviews pursuant to Article 11 and to decisions under Article 10 to apply duties retroactively.

Article 13

Judicial Review

Each Member whose national legislation contains provisions on anti-dumping measures shall maintain judicial, arbitral or administrative tribunals or procedures for the purpose, *inter alia*, of the prompt review of administrative actions relating to final determinations and reviews of determinations within the meaning of Article 11. Such tribunals or procedures shall be independent of the authorities responsible for the determination or review in question.

Article 14

Anti-Dumping Action on Behalf of a Third Country

14.1 An application for anti-dumping action on behalf of a third country shall be made by the authorities of the third country requesting action.

14.2 Such an application shall be supported by price information to show that the imports are being dumped and by detailed information to show that the alleged dumping is causing injury to the domestic industry concerned in the third country. The government of the third country shall afford all assistance to the authorities of the importing country to obtain any further information which the latter may require.

14.3 In considering such an application, the authorities of the importing country shall consider the effects of the alleged dumping on the industry concerned as a whole in the third country; that is to say, the injury shall not be assessed in relation only to the effect of the alleged dumping on the industry's exports to the importing country or even on the industry's total exports.

14.4 The decision whether or not to proceed with a case shall rest with the importing country. If the importing country decides that it is prepared to take action, the initiation of the approach to the Council for Trade in Goods seeking its approval for such action shall rest with the importing country.

Article 15
Developing Country Members

It is recognized that special regard must be given by developed country Members to the special situation of developing country Members when considering the application of anti-dumping measures under this Agreement. Possibilities of constructive remedies provided for by this Agreement shall be explored before applying anti-dumping duties where they would affect the essential interests of developing country Members.

PART II

Article 16
Committee on Anti-Dumping Practices

16.1 There is hereby established a Committee on Anti-Dumping Practices (referred to in this Agreement as the 'Committee') composed of representatives from each of the Members. The Committee shall elect its own Chairman and shall meet not less than twice a year and otherwise as envisaged by relevant provisions of this Agreement at the request of any Member. The Committee shall carry out responsibilities as assigned to it under this Agreement or by the Members and it shall afford Members the opportunity of consulting on any matters relating to the operation of the Agreement or the furtherance of its objectives. The WTO Secretariat shall act as the secretariat to the Committee.

16.2 The Committee may set up subsidiary bodies as appropriate.

16.3 In carrying out their functions, the Committee and any subsidiary bodies may consult with and seek information from any source they deem appropriate. However, before the Committee or a subsidiary body seeks such information from a source within the jurisdiction of a Member, it shall inform the Member involved. It shall obtain the consent of the Member and any firm to be consulted.

16.4 Members shall report without delay to the Committee all preliminary or final anti-dumping actions taken. Such reports shall be available in the Secretariat for inspection by other Members. Members shall also submit, on a semi-annual basis, reports of any anti-dumping actions taken within the preceding six months. The semi-annual reports shall be submitted on an agreed standard form.

16.5 Each Member shall notify the Committee *(a)* which of its authorities are competent to initiate and conduct investigations referred to in Article 5 and *(b)* its domestic procedures governing the initiation and conduct of such investigations.

Article 17
Consultation and Dispute Settlement

17.1 Except as otherwise provided herein, the Dispute Settlement Understanding is applicable to consultations and the settlement of disputes under this Agreement.

17.2 Each Member shall afford sympathetic consideration to, and shall afford adequate opportunity for consultation regarding, representations made by another Member with respect to any matter affecting the operation of this Agreement.

17.3 If any Member considers that any benefit accruing to it, directly or indirectly, under this Agreement is being nullified or impaired, or that the achievement of any objective is being impeded, by another Member or Members, it may, with a view to reaching a mutually satisfactory resolution of the matter, request in writing consultations with the Member or Members in question. Each Member shall afford sympathetic consideration to any request from another Member for consultation.

17.4 If the Member that requested consultations considers that the consultations pursuant to paragraph 3 have failed to achieve a mutually agreed solution, and if final action has been taken by the administering authorities of the importing Member to levy definitive anti-dumping duties or to accept price undertakings, it may refer the matter to the Dispute Settlement Body ('DSB'). When a provisional measure has a significant impact and the Member that requested consultations considers that the measure was taken contrary to the provisions of paragraph 1 of Article 7, that Member may also refer such matter to the DSB.

17.5 The DSB shall, at the request of the complaining party, establish a panel to examine the matter based upon:

(i) a written statement of the Member making the request indicating how a benefit accruing to it, directly or indirectly, under this Agreement has been nullified or impaired, or that the achieving of the objectives of the Agreement is being impeded, and

(ii) the facts made available in conformity with appropriate domestic procedures to the authorities of the importing Member.

17.6 In examining the matter referred to in paragraph 5:

(i) in its assessment of the facts of the matter, the panel shall determine whether the authorities' establishment of the facts was proper and whether their evaluation of those facts was unbiased and objective. If the establishment of the facts was proper and the evaluation was unbiased and objective, even though the panel might have reached a different conclusion, the evaluation shall not be overturned;

(ii) the panel shall interpret the relevant provisions of the Agreement in accordance with customary rules of interpretation of public international law. Where the panel finds that a relevant provision of the Agreement admits of more than one permissible interpretation, the panel shall find the authorities' measure to be in conformity with the Agreement if it rests upon one of those permissible interpretations.

17.7 Confidential information provided to the panel shall not be disclosed without formal authorization from the person, body or authority providing such information. Where such information is requested from the panel but release of such information by the panel is not authorized, a non-confidential summary of the information, authorized by the person, body or authority providing the information, shall be provided.

PART III

Article 18
Final Provisions

18.1 No specific action against dumping of exports from another Member can be taken except in accordance with the provisions of GATT 1994, as interpreted by this Agreement. [THIS IS NOT INTENDED TO PRECLUDE ACTION UNDER OTHER RELEVANT PROVISIONS OF GATT 1994, AS APPROPRIATE].

18.2 Reservations may not be entered in respect of any of the provisions of this Agreement without the consent of the other Members.

18.3 Subject to subparagraphs 3.1 and 3.2, the provisions of this Agreement shall apply to investigations, and reviews of existing measures, initiated pursuant to applications which have been made on or after the date of entry into force for a Member of the WTO Agreement.

18.3.1 With respect to the calculation of margins of dumping in refund procedures under paragraph 3 of Article 9, the rules used in the most recent determination or review of dumping shall apply.

18.3.2 For the purposes of paragraph 3 of Article 11, existing anti-dumping measures shall be deemed to be imposed on a date not later than the date of entry into force for a Member of the WTO Agreement, except in cases in which the domestic legislation of a Member in force on that date already included a clause of the type provided for in that paragraph.

18.4 Each Member shall take all necessary steps, of a general or particular character, to ensure, not later than the date of entry into force of the WTO Agreement for it, the conformity of its laws, regulations and administrative procedures with the provisions of this Agreement as they may apply for the Member in question.

18.5 Each Member shall inform the Committee of any changes in its laws and regulations relevant to this Agreement and in the administration of such laws and regulations.

18.6 The Committee shall review annually the implementation and operation of this Agreement taking into account the objectives thereof. The Committee shall inform annually the Council for Trade in Goods of developments during the period covered by such reviews.

18.7 The Annexes to this Agreement constitute an integral part thereof.

ANNEX I

PROCEDURES FOR ON-THE-SPOT INVESTIGATIONS PURSUANT TO PARAGRAPH 7 OF ARTICLE 6

1. Upon initiation of an investigation, the authorities of the exporting Member and the firms known to be concerned should be informed of the intention to carry out on-the-spot investigations.

2. If in exceptional circumstances it is intended to include non-governmental experts in the investigating team, the firms and the authorities of the exporting Member should be so informed. Such

non-governmental experts should be subject to effective sanctions for breach of confidentiality requirements.

3. It should be standard practice to obtain explicit agreement of the firms concerned in the exporting Member before the visit is finally scheduled.

4. As soon as the agreement of the firms concerned has been obtained, the investigating authorities should notify the authorities of the exporting Member of the names and addresses of the firms to be visited and the dates agreed.

5. Sufficient advance notice should be given to the firms in question before the visit is made.

6. Visits to explain the questionnaire should only be made at the request of an exporting firm. Such a visit may only be made if *(a)* the authorities of the importing Member notify the representatives of the Member in question and *(b)* the latter do not object to the visit.

7. As the main purpose of the on-the-spot investigation is to verify information provided or to obtain further details, it should be carried out after the response to the questionnaire has been received unless the firm agrees to the contrary and the government of the exporting Member is informed by the investigating authorities of the anticipated visit and does not object to it; further, it should be standard practice prior to the visit to advise the firms concerned of the general nature of the information to be verified and of any further information which needs to be provided, though this should not preclude requests to be made on the spot for further details to be provided in the light of information obtained.

8. Enquiries or questions put by the authorities or firms of the exporting Members and essential to a successful on-the-spot investigation should, whenever possible, be answered before the visit is made.

ANNEX II

BEST INFORMATION AVAILABLE IN TERMS OF PARAGRAPH 8 OF ARTICLE 6

1. As soon as possible after the initiation of the investigation, the investigating authorities should specify in detail the information required from any interested party, and the manner in which that information should be structured by the interested party in its response. The authorities should also ensure that the party is aware that if information is not supplied within a reasonable time, the authorities will be free to make determinations on the basis of the facts available, including those contained in the application for the initiation of the investigation by the domestic industry.

2. The authorities may also request that an interested party provide its response in a particular medium (*e.g.* computer tape) or computer language. Where such a request is made, the authorities should consider the reasonable ability of the interested party to respond in the preferred medium or computer language, and should not request the party to use for its response a computer system other than that used by the party. The authority should not maintain a request for a computerized response if the interested party does not maintain computerized accounts and if presenting the response as requested would result in an unreasonable extra burden on the interested party,

e.g. it would entail unreasonable additional cost and trouble. The authorities should not maintain a request for a response in a particular medium or computer language if the interested party does not maintain its computerized accounts in such medium or computer language and if presenting the response as requested would result in an unreasonable extra burden on the interested party, *e.g.* it would entail unreasonable additional cost and trouble.

3. All information which is verifiable, which is appropriately submitted so that it can be used in the investigation without undue difficulties, which is supplied in a timely fashion, and, where applicable, which is supplied in a medium or computer language requested by the authorities, should be taken into account when determinations are made. If a party does not respond in the preferred medium or computer language but the authorities find that the circumstances set out in paragraph 2 have been satisfied, the failure to respond in the preferred medium or computer language should not be considered to significantly impede the investigation.

4. Where the authorities do not have the ability to process information if provided in a particular medium (*e.g.* computer tape), the information should be supplied in the form of written material or any other form acceptable to the authorities.

5. Even though the information provided may not be ideal in all respects, this should not justify the authorities from disregarding it, provided the interested party has acted to the best of its ability.

6. If evidence or information is not accepted, the supplying party should be informed forthwith of the reasons therefor, and should have an opportunity to provide further explanations within a reasonable period, due account being taken of the time-limits of the investigation. If the explanations are considered by the authorities as not being satisfactory, the reasons for the rejection of such evidence or information should be given in any published determinations.

7. If the authorities have to base their findings, including those with respect to normal value, on information from a secondary source, including the information supplied in the application for the initiation of the investigation, they should do so with special circumspection. In such cases, the authorities should, where practicable, check the information from other independent sources at their disposal, such as published price lists, official import statistics and customs returns, and from the information obtained from other interested parties during the investigation. It is clear, however, that if an interested party does not cooperate and thus relevant information is being withheld from the authorities, this situation could lead to a result which is less favourable to the party than if the party did cooperate."

Agreement on Subsidies and Countervailing Measures—the Text

"AGREEMENT ON SUBSIDIES AND COUNTERVAILING MEASURES

Members hereby *agree* as follows:

PART I: GENERAL PROVISIONS

Article 1
Definition of a Subsidy

1.1 For the purpose of this Agreement, a subsidy shall be deemed to exist if:

(a) (1) there is a financial contribution by a government or any public body within the territory of a Member (referred to in this Agreement as 'government'), *i.e.* where:

(i) a government practice involves a direct transfer of funds (*e.g.* grants, loans, and equity infusion), potential direct transfers of funds or liabilities (*e.g.* loan guarantees);

(ii) government revenue that is otherwise due is foregone or not collected (*e.g.* fiscal incentives such as tax credits) [IN ACCORDANCE WITH THE PROVISIONS OF ARTICLE XVI OF GATT 1994 (NOTE TO ARTICLE XVI) AND THE PROVISIONS OF ANNEXES I THROUGH III OF THIS AGREEMENT, THE EXEMPTION OF AN EXPORTED PRODUCT FROM DUTIES OR TAXES BORNE BY THE LIKE PRODUCT WHEN DESTINED FOR DOMESTIC CONSUMPTION, OR THE REMISSION OF SUCH DUTIES OR TAXES IN AMOUNTS NOT IN EXCESS OF THOSE WHICH HAVE ACCRUED, SHALL NOT BE DEEMED TO BE A SUBSIDY.];

(iii) a government provides goods or services other than general infrastructure, or purchases goods;

(iv) a government makes payments to a funding mechanism, or entrusts or directs a private body to carry out one or more of the type of functions illustrated in (i) to (iii) above which would normally be vested in the government and the practice, in no real sense, differs from practices normally followed by governments; or

(2) there is any form of income or price support in the sense of Article XVI of GATT 1994; and

(b) a benefit is thereby conferred.

1.2 A subsidy as defined in paragraph 1 shall be subject to the provisions of Part II or shall be subject to the provisions of Part III or V only if such a subsidy is specific in accordance with the provisions of Article 2.

Article 2
Specificity

2.1 In order to determine whether a subsidy, as defined in paragraph 1 of Article 1, is specific to an enterprise or industry or group of enterprises or industries (referred to in this Agreement as 'certain enterprises') within the jurisdiction of the granting authority, the following principles shall apply:

(a) Where the granting authority, or the legislation pursuant to which the granting authority operates, explicitly limits access to a subsidy to certain enterprises, such subsidy shall be specific.

(b) Where the granting authority, or the legislation pursuant to which the granting authority operates, establishes objective criteria or conditions [OBJECTIVE CRITERIA OR CONDITIONS, AS USED HEREIN, MEAN CRITERIA OR CONDITIONS WHICH ARE NEUTRAL, WHICH DO NOT FAVOUR CERTAIN ENTERPRISES OVER OTHERS, AND WHICH ARE ECONOMIC IN NATURE AND HORIZONTAL IN APPLICATION, SUCH AS NUMBER OF EMPLOYEES OR SIZE OF ENTERPRISE.] governing the eligibility for, and the amount of, a subsidy, specificity shall not exist, provided that the eligibility is automatic and that such criteria and conditions are strictly adhered to. The criteria or conditions must be clearly spelled out in law, regulation, or other official document, so as to be capable of verification.

(c) If, notwithstanding any appearance of non-specificity resulting from the application of the principles laid down in subparagraphs (a) and (b), there are reasons to believe that the subsidy may in fact be specific, other factors may be considered. Such factors are: use of a subsidy programme by a limited number of certain enterprises, predominant use by certain enterprises, the granting of disproportionately large amounts of subsidy to certain enterprises, and the manner in which discretion has been exercised by the granting authority in the decision to grant a subsidy [IN THIS REGARD, IN PARTICULAR, INFORMATION ON THE FREQUENCY WITH WHICH APPLICATIONS FOR A SUBSIDY ARE REFUSED OR APPROVED AND THE REASONS FOR SUCH DECISIONS SHALL BE CONSIDERED.]. In applying this subparagraph, account shall be taken of the extent of diversification of economic activities within the jurisdiction of the granting authority, as well as of the length of time during which the subsidy programme has been in operation.

2.2 A subsidy which is limited to certain enterprises located within a designated geographical region within the jurisdiction of the granting authority shall be specific. It is understood that the setting or change of generally applicable tax rates by all levels of government entitled to do so shall not be deemed to be a specific subsidy for the purposes of this Agreement.

2.3 Any subsidy falling under the provisions of Article 3 shall be deemed to be specific.

2.4 Any determination of specificity under the provisions of this Article shall be clearly substantiated on the basis of positive evidence.

PART II: PROHIBITED SUBSIDIES

Article 3
Prohibition

3.1 Except as provided in the Agreement on Agriculture, the following subsidies, within the meaning of Article 1, shall be prohibited:

(a) subsidies contingent, in law or in fact [THIS STANDARD IS MET WHEN THE FACTS DEMONSTRATE THAT THE GRANTING OF A SUBSIDY, WITHOUT HAVING BEEN MADE LEGALLY

CONTINGENT UPON EXPORT PERFORMANCE, IS IN FACT TIED TO ACTUAL OR ANTICIPATED EXPORTATION OR EXPORT EARNINGS. THE MERE FACT THAT A SUBSIDY IS GRANTED TO ENTERPRISES WHICH EXPORT SHALL NOT FOR THAT REASON ALONE BE CONSIDERED TO BE AN EXPORT SUBSIDY WITHIN THE MEANING OF THIS PROVISION.], whether solely or as one of several other conditions, upon export performance, including those illustrated in Annex I [MEASURES REFERRED TO IN ANNEX I AS NOT CONSTITUTING EXPORT SUBSIDIES SHALL NOT BE PROHIBITED UNDER THIS OR ANY OTHER PROVISION OF THIS AGREEMENT.];

(b) subsidies contingent, whether solely or as one of several other conditions, upon the use of domestic over imported goods.

3.2 A Member shall neither grant nor maintain subsidies referred to in paragraph 1.

Article 4
Remedies

4.1 Whenever a Member has reason to believe that a prohibited subsidy is being granted or maintained by another Member, such Member may request consultations with such other Member.

4.2 A request for consultations under paragraph 1 shall include a statement of available evidence with regard to the existence and nature of the subsidy in question.

4.3 Upon request for consultations under paragraph 1, the Member believed to be granting or maintaining the subsidy in question shall enter into such consultations as quickly as possible. The purpose of the consultations shall be to clarify the facts of the situation and to arrive at a mutually agreed solution.

4.4 If no mutually agreed solution has been reached within 30 days [ANY TIME-PERIODS MENTIONED IN THIS ARTICLE MAY BE EXTENDED BY MUTUAL AGREEMENT.] of the request for consultations, any Member party to such consultations may refer the matter to the Dispute Settlement Body ('DSB') for the immediate establishment of a panel, unless the DSB decides by consensus not to establish a panel.

4.5 Upon its establishment, the panel may request the assistance of the Permanent Group of Experts [AS ESTABLISHED IN ARTICLE 24.] (referred to in this Agreement as the 'PGE') with regard to whether the measure in question is a prohibited subsidy. If so requested, the PGE shall immediately review the evidence with regard to the existence and nature of the measure in question and shall provide an opportunity for the Member applying or maintaining the measure to demonstrate that the measure in question is not a prohibited subsidy. The PGE shall report its conclusions to the panel within a time-limit determined by the panel. The PGE's conclusions on the issue of whether or not the measure in question is a prohibited subsidy shall be accepted by the panel without modification.

4.6 The panel shall submit its final report to the parties to the dispute. The report shall be circulated to all Members within 90 days of the date of the composition and the establishment of the panel's terms of reference.

4.7 If the measure in question is found to be a prohibited subsidy, the panel shall recommend that the subsidizing Member withdraw the subsidy without delay. In this regard, the panel shall specify in its recommendation the time-period within which the measure must be withdrawn.

4.8 Within 30 days of the issuance of the panel's report to all Members, the report shall be adopted by the DSB unless one of the parties to the dispute formally notifies the DSB of its decision to appeal or the DSB decides by consensus not to adopt the report.

4.9 Where a panel report is appealed, the Appellate Body shall issue its decision within 30 days from the date when the party to the dispute formally notifies its intention to appeal. When the Appellate Body considers that it cannot provide its report within 30 days, it shall inform the DSB in writing of the reasons for the delay together with an estimate of the period within which it will submit its report. In no case shall the proceedings exceed 60 days. The appellate report shall be adopted by the DSB and unconditionally accepted by the parties to the dispute unless the DSB decides by consensus not to adopt the appellate report within 20 days following its issuance to the Members [IF A MEETING OF THE DSB IS NOT SCHEDULED DURING THIS PERIOD, SUCH A MEETING SHALL BE HELD FOR THIS PURPOSE.].

4.10 In the event the recommendation of the DSB is not followed within the time-period specified by the panel, which shall commence from the date of adoption of the panel's report or the Appellate Body's report, the DSB shall grant authorization to the complaining Member to take appropriate [THIS EXPRESSION IS NOT MEANT TO ALLOW COUNTERMEASURES THAT ARE DISPROPORTIONATE IN LIGHT OF THE FACT THAT THE SUBSIDIES DEALT WITH UNDER THESE PROVISIONS ARE PROHIBITED.] countermeasures, unless the DSB decides by consensus to reject the request.

4.11 In the event a party to the dispute requests arbitration under paragraph 6 of Article 22 of the Dispute Settlement Understanding ('DSU'), the arbitrator shall determine whether the countermeasures are appropriate [THIS EXPRESSION IS NOT MEANT TO ALLOW COUNTERMEASURES THAT ARE DISPROPORTIONATE IN LIGHT OF THE FACT THAT THE SUBSIDIES DEALT WITH UNDER THESE PROVISIONS ARE PROHIBITED.].

4.12 For purposes of disputes conducted pursuant to this Article, except for time-periods specifically prescribed in this Article, time-periods applicable under the DSU for the conduct of such disputes shall be half the time prescribed therein.

PART III: ACTIONABLE SUBSIDIES

Article 5
Adverse Effects

No Member should cause, through the use of any subsidy referred to in paragraphs 1 and 2 of Article 1, adverse effects to the interests of other Members, *i.e.*:

(a) injury to the domestic industry of another Member [THE TERM 'INJURY TO THE DOMESTIC INDUSTRY' IS USED HERE

IN THE SAME SENSE AS IT IS USED IN PART V.];

(b) nullification or impairment of benefits accruing directly or indirectly to other Members under GATT 1994 in particular the benefits of concessions bound under Article II of GATT 1994 [THE TERM 'NULLIFICATION OR IMPAIRMENT' IS USED IN THIS AGREEMENT IN THE SAME SENSE AS IT IS USED IN THE RELEVANT PROVISIONS OF GATT 1994, AND THE EXISTENCE OF SUCH NULLIFICATION OR IMPAIRMENT SHALL BE ESTABLISHED IN ACCORDANCE WITH THE PRACTICE OF APPLICATION OF THESE PROVISIONS.];

(c) serious prejudice to the interests of another Member [THE TERM 'SERIOUS PREJUDICE TO THE INTERESTS OF ANOTHER MEMBER' IS USED IN THIS AGREEMENT IN THE SAME SENSE AS IT IS USED IN PARAGRAPH 1 OF ARTICLE XVI OF GATT 1994, AND INCLUDES THREAT OF SERIOUS PREJUDICE.].

This Article does not apply to subsidies maintained on agricultural products as provided in Article 13 of the Agreement on Agriculture.

Article 6
Serious Prejudice

6.1 Serious prejudice in the sense of paragraph (c) of Article 5 shall be deemed to exist in the case of:

(a) the total *ad valorem* subsidization [THE TOTAL AD VALOREM SUBSIDIZATION SHALL BE CALCULATED IN ACCORDANCE WITH THE PROVISIONS OF ANNEX IV.] of a product exceeding 5 per cent [SINCE IT IS ANTICIPATED THAT CIVIL AIRCRAFT WILL BE SUBJECT TO SPECIFIC MULTILATERAL RULES, THE THRESHOLD IN THIS SUBPARAGRAPH DOES NOT APPLY TO CIVIL AIRCRAFT.];

(b) subsidies to cover operating losses sustained by an industry;

(c) subsidies to cover operating losses sustained by an enterprise, other than one-time measures which are non-recurrent and cannot be repeated for that enterprise and which are given merely to provide time for the development of long-term solutions and to avoid acute social problems;

(d) direct forgiveness of debt, *i.e.* forgiveness of government-held debt, and grants to cover debt repayment [MEMBERS RECOGNIZE THAT WHERE ROYALTY-BASED FINANCING FOR A CIVIL AIRCRAFT PROGRAMME IS NOT BEING FULLY REPAID DUE TO THE LEVEL OF ACTUAL SALES FALLING BELOW THE LEVEL OF FORECAST SALES, THIS DOES NOT IN ITSELF CONSTITUTE SERIOUS PREJUDICE FOR THE PURPOSES OF THIS SUBPARAGRAPH.].

6.2 Notwithstanding the provisions of paragraph 1, serious prejudice shall not be found if the subsidizing Member demonstrates that the subsidy in question has not resulted in any of the effects enumerated in paragraph 3.

6.3 Serious prejudice in the sense of paragraph (c) of Article 5 may arise in any case where one or several of the following apply:

(a) the effect of the subsidy is to displace or impede the imports of a like product of another Member into the market of the subsidizing Member;

(b) the effect of the subsidy is to displace or impede the exports of a like product of another Member from a third country market;

(c) the effect of the subsidy is a significant price undercutting by the subsidized product as compared with the price of a like product of another Member in the same market or significant price suppression, price depression or lost sales in the same market;

(d) the effect of the subsidy is an increase in the world market share of the subsidizing Member in a particular subsidized primary product or commodity [UNLESS OTHER MULTILATERALLY AGREED SPECIFIC RULES APPLY TO THE TRADE IN THE PRODUCT OR COMMODITY IN QUESTION.] as compared to the average share it had during the previous period of three years and this increase follows a consistent trend over a period when subsidies have been granted.

6.4 For the purpose of paragraph 3(b), the displacement or impeding of exports shall include any case in which, subject to the provisions of paragraph 7, it has been demonstrated that there has been a change in relative shares of the market to the disadvantage of the non-subsidized like product (over an appropriately representative period sufficient to demonstrate clear trends in the development of the market for the product concerned, which, in normal circumstances, shall be at least one year). 'Change in relative shares of the market' shall include any of the following situations: *(a)* there is an increase in the market share of the subsidized product; *(b)* the market share of the subsidized product remains constant in circumstances in which, in the absence of the subsidy, it would have declined; *(c)* the market share of the subsidized product declines, but at a slower rate than would have been the case in the absence of the subsidy.

6.5 For the purpose of paragraph 3(c), price undercutting shall include any case in which such price undercutting has been demonstrated through a comparison of prices of the subsidized product with prices of a non-subsidized like product supplied to the same market. The comparison shall be made at the same level of trade and at comparable times, due account being taken of any other factor affecting price comparability. However, if such a direct comparison is not possible, the existence of price undercutting may be demonstrated on the basis of export unit values.

6.6 Each Member in the market of which serious prejudice is alleged to have arisen shall, subject to the provisions of paragraph 3 of Annex V, make available to the parties to a dispute arising under Article 7, and to the panel established pursuant to paragraph 4 of Article 7, all relevant information that can be obtained as to the changes in market shares of the parties to the dispute as well as concerning prices of the products involved.

6.7 Displacement or impediment resulting in serious prejudice shall not arise under paragraph 3 where any of the following circumstances exist [THE FACT THAT CERTAIN CIRCUMSTANCES ARE REFERRED TO IN THIS PARAGRAPH DOES NOT, IN ITSELF, CONFER UPON THEM ANY LEGAL STATUS IN TERMS OF EITHER GATT 1994 OR THIS AGREEMENT.

THESE CIRCUMSTANCES MUST NOT BE ISOLATED, SPORADIC OR OTHERWISE INSIGNIFICANT.] during the relevant period:

(a) prohibition or restriction on exports of the like product from the complaining Member or on imports from the complaining Member into the third country market concerned;

(b) decision by an importing government operating a monopoly of trade or state trading in the product concerned to shift, for non-commercial reasons, imports from the complaining Member to another country or countries;

(c) natural disasters, strikes, transport disruptions or other *force majeure* substantially affecting production, qualities, quantities or prices of the product available for export from the complaining Member;

(d) existence of arrangements limiting exports from the complaining Member;

(e) voluntary decrease in the availability for export of the product concerned from the complaining Member (including, *inter alia*, a situation where firms in the complaining Member have been autonomously reallocating exports of this product to new markets);

(f) failure to conform to standards and other regulatory requirements in the importing country.

6.8 In the absence of circumstances referred to in paragraph 7, the existence of serious prejudice should be determined on the basis of the information submitted to or obtained by the panel, including information submitted in accordance with the provisions of Annex V.

6.9 This Article does not apply to subsidies maintained on agricultural products as provided in Article 13 of the Agreement on Agriculture.

Article 7
Remedies

7.1 Except as provided in Article 13 of the Agreement on Agriculture, whenever a Member has reason to believe that any subsidy referred to in Article 1, granted or maintained by another Member, results in injury to its domestic industry, nullification or impairment or serious prejudice, such Member may request consultations with such other Member.

7.2 A request for consultations under paragraph 1 shall include a statement of available evidence with regard to *(a)* the existence and nature of the subsidy in question, and *(b)* the injury caused to the domestic industry, or the nullification or impairment, or serious prejudice [IN THE EVENT THAT THE REQUEST RELATES TO A SUBSIDY DEEMED TO RESULT IN SERIOUS PREJUDICE IN TERMS OF PARAGRAPH 1 OF ARTICLE 6, THE AVAILABLE EVIDENCE OF SERIOUS PREJUDICE MAY BE LIMITED TO THE AVAILABLE EVIDENCE AS TO WHETHER THE CONDITIONS OF PARAGRAPH 1 OF ARTICLE 6 HAVE BEEN MET OR NOT.] caused to the interests of the Member requesting consultations.

7.3 Upon request for consultations under paragraph 1, the Member believed to be granting or maintaining the subsidy practice in question shall enter into such consultations as quickly as possible. The purpose of the consultations shall be to clarify the facts of the situation and to arrive at a mutually agreed solution.

7.4 If consultations do not result in a mutually agreed solution within 60 days [ANY TIME-PERIODS MENTIONED IN THIS ARTICLE MAY BE EXTENDED BY MUTUAL AGREEMENT.], any Member party to such consultations may refer the matter to the DSB for the establishment of a panel, unless the DSB decides by consensus not to establish a panel. The composition of the panel and its terms of reference shall be established within 15 days from the date when it is established.

7.5 The panel shall review the matter and shall submit its final report to the parties to the dispute. The report shall be circulated to all Members within 120 days of the date of the composition and establishment of the panel's terms of reference.

7.6 Within 30 days of the issuance of the panel's report to all Members, the report shall be adopted by the DSB [IF A MEETING OF THE DSB IS NOT SCHEDULED DURING THIS PERIOD, SUCH A MEETING SHALL BE HELD FOR THIS PURPOSE.] unless one of the parties to the dispute formally notifies the DSB of its decision to appeal or the DSB decides by consensus not to adopt the report.

7.7 Where a panel report is appealed, the Appellate Body shall issue its decision within 60 days from the date when the party to the dispute formally notifies its intention to appeal. When the Appellate Body considers that it cannot provide its report within 60 days, it shall inform the DSB in writing of the reasons for the delay together with an estimate of the period within which it will submit its report. In no case shall the proceedings exceed 90 days. The appellate report shall be adopted by the DSB and unconditionally accepted by the parties to the dispute unless the DSB decides by consensus not to adopt the appellate report within 20 days following its issuance to the Members [IF A MEETING OF THE DSB IS NOT SCHEDULED DURING THIS PERIOD, SUCH A MEETING SHALL BE HELD FOR THIS PURPOSE.].

7.8 Where a panel report or an Appellate Body report is adopted in which it is determined that any subsidy has resulted in adverse effects to the interests of another Member within the meaning of Article 5, the Member granting or maintaining such subsidy shall take appropriate steps to remove the adverse effects or shall withdraw the subsidy.

7.9 In the event the Member has not taken appropriate steps to remove the adverse effects of the subsidy or withdraw the subsidy within six months from the date when the DSB adopts the panel report or the Appellate Body report, and in the absence of agreement on compensation, the DSB shall grant authorization to the complaining Member to take countermeasures, commensurate with the degree and nature of the adverse effects determined to exist, unless the DSB decides by consensus to reject the request.

7.10 In the event that a party to the dispute requests arbitration under paragraph 6 of Article 22 of the DSU, the arbitrator shall determine whether the countermeasures are commensurate with the degree and nature of the adverse effects determined to exist.

PART IV: NON-ACTIONABLE SUBSIDIES

Article 8

Identification of Non-Actionable Subsidies

8.1 The following subsidies shall be considered as non-actionable [IT IS RECOGNIZED THAT GOVERNMENT ASSISTANCE FOR VARIOUS PURPOSES IS WIDELY PROVIDED BY MEMBERS AND THAT THE MERE FACT THAT SUCH ASSISTANCE MAY NOT QUALIFY FOR NON-ACTIONABLE TREATMENT UNDER THE PROVISIONS OF THIS ARTICLE DOES NOT IN ITSELF RESTRICT THE ABILITY OF MEMBERS TO PROVIDE SUCH ASSISTANCE.]:

(a) subsidies which are not specific within the meaning of Article 2;

(b) subsidies which are specific within the meaning of Article 2 but which meet all of the conditions provided for in paragraphs 2(a), 2(b) or 2(c) below.

8.2 Notwithstanding the provisions of Parts III and V, the following subsidies shall be non-actionable:

(a) assistance for research activities conducted by firms or by higher education or research establishments on a contract basis with firms if [SINCE IT IS ANTICIPATED THAT CIVIL AIRCRAFT WILL BE SUBJECT TO SPECIFIC MULTILATERAL RULES, THE PROVISIONS OF THIS SUBPARAGRAPH DO NOT APPLY TO THAT PRODUCT.] [NOT LATER THAN 18 MONTHS AFTER THE DATE OF ENTRY INTO FORCE OF THE WTO AGREEMENT, THE COMMITTEE ON SUBSIDIES AND COUNTERVAILING MEASURES PROVIDED FOR IN ARTICLE 24 (REFERRED TO IN THIS AGREEMENT AS 'THE COMMITTEE') SHALL REVIEW THE OPERATION OF THE PROVISIONS OF SUBPARAGRAPH 2(A) WITH A VIEW TO MAKING ALL NECESSARY MODIFICATIONS TO IMPROVE THE OPERATION OF THESE PROVISIONS. IN ITS CONSIDERATION OF POSSIBLE MODIFICATIONS, THE COMMITTEE SHALL CAREFULLY REVIEW THE DEFINITIONS OF THE CATEGORIES SET FORTH IN THIS SUBPARAGRAPH IN THE LIGHT OF THE EXPERIENCE OF MEMBERS IN THE OPERATION OF RESEARCH PROGRAMMES AND THE WORK IN OTHER RELEVANT INTERNATIONAL INSTITUTIONS.] [THE PROVISIONS OF THIS AGREEMENT DO NOT APPLY TO FUNDAMENTAL RESEARCH ACTIVITIES INDEPENDENTLY CONDUCTED BY HIGHER EDUCATION OR RESEARCH ESTABLISHMENTS. THE TERM 'FUNDAMENTAL RESEARCH' MEANS AN ENLARGEMENT OF GENERAL SCIENTIFIC AND TECHNICAL KNOWLEDGE NOT LINKED TO INDUSTRIAL OR COMMERCIAL OBJECTIVES.]:

the assistance covers [THE ALLOWABLE LEVELS OF NON-ACTIONABLE ASSISTANCE REFERRED TO IN THIS SUBPARAGRAPH SHALL BE ESTABLISHED BY REFERENCE TO THE TOTAL ELIGIBLE COSTS INCURRED OVER THE DURATION OF AN INDIVIDUAL PROJECT.] not more than 75 per cent of the costs of industrial research [THE TERM 'INDUSTRIAL RESEARCH'

MEANS PLANNED SEARCH OR CRITICAL INVESTIGATION AIMED AT DISCOVERY OF NEW KNOWLEDGE, WITH THE OBJECTIVE THAT SUCH KNOWLEDGE MAY BE USEFUL IN DEVELOPING NEW PRODUCTS, PROCESSES OR SERVICES, OR IN BRINGING ABOUT A SIGNIFICANT IMPROVEMENT TO EXISTING PRODUCTS, PROCESSES OR SERVICES.] or 50 per cent of the costs of pre-competitive development activity [THE TERM PRE-COMPETITIVE DEVELOPMENT ACTIVITY' MEANS THE TRANSLATION OF INDUSTRIAL RESEARCH FINDINGS INTO A PLAN, BLUEPRINT OR DESIGN FOR NEW, MODIFIED OR IMPROVED PRODUCTS, PROCESSES OR SERVICES WHETHER INTENDED FOR SALE OR USE, INCLUDING THE CREATION OF A FIRST PROTOTYPE WHICH WOULD NOT BE CAPABLE OF COMMERCIAL USE. IT MAY FURTHER INCLUDE THE CONCEPTUAL FORMULATION AND DESIGN OF PRODUCTS, PROCESSES OR SERVICES ALTERNATIVES AND INITIAL DEMONSTRATION OR PILOT PROJECTS, PROVIDED THAT THESE SAME PROJECTS CANNOT BE CONVERTED OR USED FOR INDUSTRIAL APPLICATION OR COMMERCIAL EXPLOITATION. IT DOES NOT INCLUDE ROUTINE OR PERIODIC ALTERATIONS TO EXISTING PRODUCTS, PRODUCTION LINES, MANUFACTURING PROCESSES, SERVICES, AND OTHER ON-GOING OPERATIONS EVEN THOUGH THOSE ALTERATIONS MAY REPRESENT IMPROVEMENTS.] [IN THE CASE OF PROGRAMMES WHICH SPAN INDUSTRIAL RESEARCH AND PRE-COMPETITIVE DEVELOPMENT ACTIVITY, THE ALLOWABLE LEVEL OF NON-ACTIONABLE ASSISTANCE SHALL NOT EXCEED THE SIMPLE AVERAGE OF THE ALLOWABLE LEVELS OF NON-ACTIONABLE ASSISTANCE APPLICABLE TO THE ABOVE TWO CATEGORIES, CALCULATED ON THE BASIS OF ALL ELIGIBLE COSTS AS SET FORTH IN ITEMS (I) TO (V) OF THIS SUBPARAGRAPH.];

and provided that such assistance is limited exclusively to:

(i) costs of personnel (researchers, technicians and other supporting staff employed exclusively in the research activity);

(ii) costs of instruments, equipment, land and buildings used exclusively and permanently (except when disposed of on a commercial basis) for the research activity;

(iii) costs of consultancy and equivalent services used exclusively for the research activity, including bought-in research, technical knowledge, patents, *etc.*;

(iv) additional overhead costs incurred directly as a result of the research activity;

(v) other running costs (such as those of materials, supplies and the like), incurred directly as a result of the research activity.

(b) assistance to disadvantaged regions within the territory of a Member given pursuant to a general framework of regional development [A 'GENERAL FRAMEWORK OF REGIONAL DEVELOPMENT' MEANS THAT REGIONAL SUBSIDY

PROGRAMMES ARE PART OF AN INTERNALLY CONSISTENT AND GENERALLY APPLICABLE REGIONAL DEVELOPMENT POLICY AND THAT REGIONAL DEVELOPMENT SUBSIDIES ARE NOT GRANTED IN ISOLATED GEOGRAPHICAL POINTS HAVING NO, OR VIRTUALLY NO, INFLUENCE ON THE DEVELOPMENT OF A REGION.] and non-specific (within the meaning of Article 2) within eligible regions provided that:

(i) each disadvantaged region must be a clearly designated contiguous geographical area with a definable economic and administrative identity;

(ii) the region is considered as disadvantaged on the basis of neutral and objective criteria ['NEUTRAL AND OBJECTIVE CRITERIA' MEANS CRITERIA WHICH DO NOT FAVOUR CERTAIN REGIONS BEYOND WHAT IS APPROPRIATE FOR THE ELIMINATION OR REDUCTION OF REGIONAL DISPARITIES WITHIN THE FRAMEWORK OF THE REGIONAL DEVELOPMENT POLICY. IN THIS REGARD, REGIONAL SUBSIDY PROGRAMMES SHALL INCLUDE CEILINGS ON THE AMOUNT OF ASSISTANCE WHICH CAN BE GRANTED TO EACH SUBSIDIZED PROJECT. SUCH CEILINGS MUST BE DIFFERENTIATED ACCORDING TO THE DIFFERENT LEVELS OF DEVELOPMENT OF ASSISTED REGIONS AND MUST BE EXPRESSED IN TERMS OF INVESTMENT COSTS OR COST OF JOB CREATION. WITHIN SUCH CEILINGS, THE DISTRIBUTION OF ASSISTANCE SHALL BE SUFFICIENTLY BROAD AND EVEN TO AVOID THE PREDOMINANT USE OF A SUBSIDY BY, OR THE GRANTING OF DISPROPORTIONATELY LARGE AMOUNTS OF SUBSIDY TO, CERTAIN ENTERPRISES AS PROVIDED FOR IN ARTICLE 2.], indicating that the region's difficulties arise out of more than temporary circumstances; such criteria must be clearly spelled out in law, regulation, or other official document, so as to be capable of verification;

(iii) the criteria shall include a measurement of economic development which shall be based on at least one of the following factors:

— one of either income per capita or household income per capita, or GDP per capita, which must not be above 85 per cent of the average for the territory concerned;

— unemployment rate, which must be at least 110 per cent of the average for the territory concerned;

as measured over a three-year period; such measurement, however, may be a composite one and may include other factors.

(c) assistance to promote adaptation of existing facilities [THE TERM 'EXISTING FACILITIES' MEANS FACILITIES WHICH HAVE BEEN IN OPERATION FOR AT LEAST TWO YEARS AT THE TIME WHEN NEW ENVIRONMENTAL REQUIREMENTS ARE

IMPOSED.] to new environmental requirements imposed by law and/ or regulations which result in greater constraints and financial burden on firms, provided that the assistance:

(i) is a one-time non-recurring measure; and
(ii) is limited to 20 per cent of the cost of adaptation; and
(iii) does not cover the cost of replacing and operating the assisted investment, which must be fully borne by firms; and
(iv) is directly linked to and proportionate to a firm's planned reduction of nuisances and pollution, and does not cover any manufacturing cost savings which may be achieved; and
(v) is available to all firms which can adopt the new equipment and/or production processes.

8.3 A subsidy programme for which the provisions of paragraph 2 are invoked shall be notified in advance of its implementation to the Committee in accordance with the provisions of Part VII. Any such notification shall be sufficiently precise to enable other Members to evaluate the consistency of the programme with the conditions and criteria provided for in the relevant provisions of paragraph 2. Members shall also provide the Committee with yearly updates of such notifications, in particular by supplying information on global expenditure for each programme, and on any modification of the programme. Other Members shall have the right to request information about individual cases of subsidization under a notified programme [IT IS RECOGNIZED THAT NOTHING IN THIS NOTIFICATION PROVISION REQUIRES THE PROVISION OF CONFIDENTIAL INFORMATION, INCLUDING CONFIDENTIAL BUSINESS INFORMATION.].

8.4 Upon request of a Member, the Secretariat shall review a notification made pursuant to paragraph 3 and, where necessary, may require additional information from the subsidizing Member concerning the notified programme under review. The Secretariat shall report its findings to the Committee. The Committee shall, upon request, promptly review the findings of the Secretariat (or, if a review by the Secretariat has not been requested, the notification itself), with a view to determining whether the conditions and criteria laid down in paragraph 2 have not been met. The procedure provided for in this paragraph shall be completed at the latest at the first regular meeting of the Committee following the notification of a subsidy programme, provided that at least two months have elapsed between such notification and the regular meeting of the Committee. The review procedure described in this paragraph shall also apply, upon request, to substantial modifications of a programme notified in the yearly updates referred to in paragraph 3.

8.5 Upon the request of a Member, the determination by the Committee referred to in paragraph 4, or a failure by the Committee to make such a determination, as well as the violation, in individual cases, of the conditions set out in a notified programme, shall be submitted to binding arbitration. The arbitration body shall present its conclusions to the Members within 120 days from the date when the matter was referred to the arbitration body. Except as otherwise provided in this paragraph, the DSU shall apply to arbitrations conducted under this paragraph.

Article 9
Consultations and Authorized Remedies

9.1 If, in the course of implementation of a programme referred to in paragraph 2 of Article 8, notwithstanding the fact that the programme is consistent with the criteria laid down in that paragraph, a Member has reasons to believe that this programme has resulted in serious adverse effects to the domestic industry of that Member, such as to cause damage which would be difficult to repair, such Member may request consultations with the Member granting or maintaining the subsidy.

9.2 Upon request for consultations under paragraph 1, the Member granting or maintaining the subsidy programme in question shall enter into such consultations as quickly as possible. The purpose of the consultations shall be to clarify the facts of the situation and to arrive at a mutually acceptable solution.

9.3 If no mutually acceptable solution has been reached in consultations under paragraph 2 within 60 days of the request for such consultations, the requesting Member may refer the matter to the Committee.

9.4 Where a matter is referred to the Committee, the Committee shall immediately review the facts involved and the evidence of the effects referred to in paragraph 1. If the Committee determines that such effects exist, it may recommend to the subsidizing Member to modify this programme in such a way as to remove these effects. The Committee shall present its conclusions within 120 days from the date when the matter is referred to it under paragraph 3. In the event the recommendation is not followed within six months, the Committee shall authorize the requesting Member to take appropriate countermeasures commensurate with the nature and degree of the effects determined to exist.

PART V: COUNTERVAILING MEASURES

Article 10
Application of Article VI of GATT 1994

[THE PROVISIONS OF PART II OR III MAY BE INVOKED IN PARALLEL WITH THE PROVISIONS OF PART V; HOWEVER, WITH REGARD TO THE EFFECTS OF A PARTICULAR SUBSIDY IN THE DOMESTIC MARKET OF THE IMPORTING MEMBER, ONLY ONE FORM OF RELIEF (EITHER A COUNTERVAILING DUTY, IF THE REQUIREMENTS OF PART V ARE MET, OR A COUNTERMEASURE UNDER ARTICLES 4 OR 7) SHALL BE AVAILABLE. THE PROVISIONS OF PARTS III AND V SHALL NOT BE INVOKED REGARDING MEASURES CONSIDERED NON-ACTIONABLE IN ACCORDANCE WITH THE PROVISIONS OF PART IV. HOWEVER, MEASURES REFERRED TO IN PARAGRAPH 1(A) OF ARTICLE 8 MAY BE INVESTIGATED IN ORDER TO DETERMINE WHETHER OR NOT THEY ARE SPECIFIC WITHIN THE MEANING OF ARTICLE 2. IN ADDITION, IN THE CASE OF A SUBSIDY REFERRED TO IN PARAGRAPH 2 OF ARTICLE 8 CONFERRED PURSUANT TO A PROGRAMME WHICH HAS NOT BEEN NOTIFIED IN ACCORDANCE WITH PARAGRAPH 3 OF ARTICLE 8, THE PROVISIONS OF PART III OR V MAY BE INVOKED, BUT

SUCH SUBSIDY SHALL BE TREATED AS NON-ACTIONABLE IF IT IS FOUND TO CONFORM TO THE STANDARDS SET FORTH IN PARAGRAPH 2 OF ARTICLE 8.]

Members shall take all necessary steps to ensure that the imposition of a countervailing duty [THE TERM 'COUNTERVAILING DUTY' SHALL BE UNDERSTOOD TO MEAN A SPECIAL DUTY LEVIED FOR THE PURPOSE OF OFFSETTING ANY SUBSIDY BESTOWED DIRECTLY OR INDIRECTLY UPON THE MANUFACTURE, PRODUCTION OR EXPORT OF ANY MERCHANDISE, AS PROVIDED FOR IN PARAGRAPH 3 OF ARTICLE VI OF GATT 1994.] on any product of the territory of any Member imported into the territory of another Member is in accordance with the provisions of Article VI of GATT 1994 and the terms of this Agreement. Countervailing duties may only be imposed pursuant to investigations initiated [THE TERM 'INITIATED' AS USED HEREINAFTER MEANS PROCEDURAL ACTION BY WHICH A MEMBER FORMALLY COMMENCES AN INVESTIGATION AS PROVIDED IN ARTICLE 11.] and conducted in accordance with the provisions of this Agreement and the Agreement on Agriculture.

Article 11

Initiation and Subsequent Investigation

11.1 Except as provided in paragraph 6, an investigation to determine the existence, degree and effect of any alleged subsidy shall be initiated upon a written application by or on behalf of the domestic industry.

11.2 An application under paragraph 1 shall include sufficient evidence of the existence of *(a)* a subsidy and, if possible, its amount, *(b)* injury within the meaning of Article VI of GATT 1994 as interpreted by this Agreement, and *(c)* a causal link between the subsidized imports and the alleged injury. Simple assertion, unsubstantiated by relevant evidence, cannot be considered sufficient to meet the requirements of this paragraph. The application shall contain such information as is reasonably available to the applicant on the following:

(i) the identity of the applicant and a description of the volume and value of the domestic production of the like product by the applicant. Where a written application is made on behalf of the domestic industry, the application shall identify the industry on behalf of which the application is made by a list of all known domestic producers of the like product (or associations of domestic producers of the like product) and, to the extent possible, a description of the volume and value of domestic production of the like product accounted for by such producers;

(ii) a complete description of the allegedly subsidized product, the names of the country or countries of origin or export in question, the identity of each known exporter or foreign producer and a list of known persons importing the product in question;

(iii) evidence with regard to the existence, amount and nature of the subsidy in question;

(iv) evidence that alleged injury to a domestic industry is caused by subsidized imports through the effects of the subsidies; this evidence includes information on the evolution of the volume of the allegedly subsidized imports, the effect of these imports on prices of the like product in the domestic market and the consequent impact of the imports on the domestic industry, as demonstrated by relevant factors and indices having a bearing on the state of the domestic industry, such as those listed in paragraphs 2 and 4 of Article 15.

11.3 The authorities shall review the accuracy and adequacy of the evidence provided in the application to determine whether the evidence is sufficient to justify the initiation of an investigation.

11.4 An investigation shall not be initiated pursuant to paragraph 1 unless the authorities have determined, on the basis of an examination of the degree of support for, or opposition to, the application expressed [IN THE CASE OF FRAGMENTED INDUSTRIES INVOLVING AN EXCEPTIONALLY LARGE NUMBER OF PRODUCERS, AUTHORITIES MAY DETERMINE SUPPORT AND OPPOSITION BY USING STATISTICALLY VALID SAMPLING TECHNIQUES.] by domestic producers of the like product, that the application has been made by or on behalf of the domestic industry [MEMBERS ARE AWARE THAT IN THE TERRITORY OF CERTAIN MEMBERS EMPLOYEES OF DOMESTIC PRODUCERS OF THE LIKE PRODUCT OR REPRESENTATIVES OF THOSE EMPLOYEES MAY MAKE OR SUPPORT AN APPLICATION FOR AN INVESTIGATION UNDER PARAGRAPH 1.]. The application shall be considered to have been made 'by or on behalf of the domestic industry' if it is supported by those domestic producers whose collective output constitutes more than 50 per cent of the total production of the like product produced by that portion of the domestic industry expressing either support for or opposition to the application. However, no investigation shall be initiated when domestic producers expressly supporting the application account for less than 25 per cent of total production of the like product produced by the domestic industry.

11.5 The authorities shall avoid, unless a decision has been made to initiate an investigation, any publicizing of the application for the initiation of an investigation.

11.6 If, in special circumstances, the authorities concerned decide to initiate an investigation without having received a written application by or on behalf of a domestic industry for the initiation of such investigation, they shall proceed only if they have sufficient evidence of the existence of a subsidy, injury and causal link, as described in paragraph 2, to justify the initiation of an investigation.

11.7 The evidence of both subsidy and injury shall be considered simultaneously *(a)* in the decision whether or not to initiate an investigation and *(b)* thereafter, during the course of the investigation, starting on a date not later than the earliest date on which in accordance with the provisions of this Agreement provisional measures may be applied.

11.8 In cases where products are not imported directly from the country of origin but are exported to the importing Member from an intermediate country, the provisions of this Agreement shall be fully applicable and the transaction or transactions shall, for the purposes of this Agreement, be regarded as having taken place between the country of origin and the importing Member.

11.9 An application under paragraph 1 shall be rejected and an investigation shall be terminated promptly as soon as the authorities concerned are satisfied that there is not sufficient evidence of either subsidization or of injury to justify proceeding with the case. There shall be immediate termination in cases where the amount of a subsidy is *de minimis*, or where the volume of subsidized imports, actual or potential, or the injury, is negligible. For the purpose of this paragraph, the amount of the subsidy shall be considered to be *de minimis* if the subsidy is less than 1 per cent *ad valorem*.

11.10 An investigation shall not hinder the procedures of customs clearance.

11.11 Investigations shall, except in special circumstances, be concluded within one year, and in no case more than 18 months, after their initiation.

Article 12
Evidence

12.1 Interested Members and all interested parties in a countervailing duty investigation shall be given notice of the information which the authorities require and ample opportunity to present in writing all evidence which they consider relevant in respect of the investigation in question.

12.1.1 Exporters, foreign producers or interested Members receiving questionnaires used in a countervailing duty investigation shall be given at least 30 days for reply [AS A GENERAL RULE, THE TIME-LIMIT FOR EXPORTERS SHALL BE COUNTED FROM THE DATE OF RECEIPT OF THE QUESTIONNAIRE, WHICH FOR THIS PURPOSE SHALL BE DEEMED TO HAVE BEEN RECEIVED ONE WEEK FROM THE DATE ON WHICH IT WAS SENT TO THE RESPONDENT OR TRANSMITTED TO THE APPROPRIATE DIPLOMATIC REPRESENTATIVES OF THE EXPORTING MEMBER OR, IN THE CASE OF A SEPARATE CUSTOMS TERRITORY MEMBER OF THE WTO, AN OFFICIAL REPRESENTATIVE OF THE EXPORTING TERRITORY]. Due consideration should be given to any request for an extension of the 30-day period and, upon cause shown, such an extension should be granted whenever practicable.

12.1.2 Subject to the requirement to protect confidential information, evidence presented in writing by one interested Member or interested party shall be made available promptly to other interested Members or interested parties participating in the investigation.

12.1.3 As soon as an investigation has been initiated, the authorities shall provide the full text of the written application received under paragraph 1 of Article 11 to the known exporters [IT BEING UNDERSTOOD THAT WHERE THE NUMBER OF EXPORTERS INVOLVED IS PARTICULARLY HIGH, THE FULL

TEXT OF THE APPLICATION SHOULD INSTEAD BE PROVIDED ONLY TO THE AUTHORITIES OF THE EXPORTING MEMBER OR TO THE RELEVANT TRADE ASSOCIATION WHO THEN SHOULD FORWARD COPIES TO THE EXPORTERS CONCERNED.] and to the authorities of the exporting Member and shall make it available, upon request, to other interested parties involved. Duc regard shall be paid to the protection of confidential information, as provided for in paragraph 4.

12.2. Interested Members and interested parties also shall have the right, upon justification, to present information orally. Where such information is provided orally, the interested Members and interested parties subsequently shall be required to reduce such submissions to writing. Any decision of the investigating authorities can only be based on such information and arguments as were on the written record of this authority and which were available to interested Members and interested parties participating in the investigation, due account having been given to the need to protect confidential information.

12.3 The authorities shall whenever practicable provide timely opportunities for all interested Members and interested parties to see all information that is relevant to the presentation of their cases, that is not confidential as defined in paragraph 4, and that is used by the authorities in a countervailing duty investigation, and to prepare presentations on the basis of this information.

12.4 Any information which is by nature confidential (for example, because its disclosure would be of significant competitive advantage to a competitor or because its disclosure would have a significantly adverse effect upon a person supplying the information or upon a person from whom the supplier acquired the information), or which is provided on a confidential basis by parties to an investigation shall, upon good cause shown, be treated as such by the authorities. Such information shall not be disclosed without specific permission of the party submitting it [MEMBERS ARE AWARE THAT IN THE TERRITORY OF CERTAIN MEMBERS DISCLOSURE PURSUANT TO A NARROWLY-DRAWN PROTECTIVE ORDER MAY BE REQUIRED.].

12.4.1 The authorities shall require interested Members or interested parties providing confidential information to furnish non-confidential summaries thereof. These summaries shall be in sufficient detail to permit a reasonable understanding of the substance of the information submitted in confidence. In exceptional circumstances, such Members or parties may indicate that such information is not susceptible of summary. In such exceptional circumstances, a statement of the reasons why summarization is not possible must be provided.

12.4.2 If the authorities find that a request for confidentiality is not warranted and if the supplier of the information is either unwilling to make the information public or to authorize its disclosure in generalized or summary form, the authorities may disregard such information unless it can be demonstrated to their satisfaction from appropriate sources that the information is correct [MEMBERS AGREE THAT REQUESTS FOR

CONFIDENTIALITY SHOULD NOT BE ARBITRARILY REJECTED. MEMBERS FURTHER AGREE THAT THE INVESTIGATING AUTHORITY MAY REQUEST THE WAIVING OF CONFIDENTIALITY ONLY REGARDING INFORMATION RELEVANT TO THE PROCEEDINGS.].

12.5 Except in circumstances provided for in paragraph 7, the authorities shall during the course of an investigation satisfy themselves as to the accuracy of the information supplied by interested Members or interested parties upon which their findings are based.

12.6 The investigating authorities may carry out investigations in the territory of other Members as required, provided that they have notified in good time the Member in question and unless that Member objects to the investigation. Further, the investigating authorities may carry out investigations on the premises of a firm and may examine the records of a firm if *(a)* the firm so agrees and *(b)* the Member in question is notified and does not object. The procedures set forth in Annex VI shall apply to investigations on the premises of a firm. Subject to the requirement to protect confidential information, the authorities shall make the results of any such investigations available, or shall provide disclosure thereof pursuant to paragraph 8, to the firms to which they pertain and may make such results available to the applicants.

12.7 In cases in which any interested Member or interested party refuses access to, or otherwise does not provide, necessary information within a reasonable period or significantly impedes the investigation, preliminary and final determinations, affirmative or negative, may be made on the basis of the facts available.

12.8 The authorities shall, before a final determination is made, inform all interested Members and interested parties of the essential facts under consideration which form the basis for the decision whether to apply definitive measures. Such disclosure should take place in sufficient time for the parties to defend their interests.

12.9 For the purposes of this Agreement, 'interested parties' shall include:

(i) an exporter or foreign producer or the importer of a product subject to investigation, or a trade or business association a majority of the members of which are producers, exporters or importers of such product; and

(ii) a producer of the like product in the importing Member or a trade and business association a majority of the members of which produce the like product in the territory of the importing Member.

This list shall not preclude Members from allowing domestic or foreign parties other than those mentioned above to be included as interested parties.

12.10 The authorities shall provide opportunities for industrial users of the product under investigation, and for representative consumer organizations in cases where the product is commonly sold at the retail level, to provide information which is relevant to the investigation regarding subsidization, injury and causality.

12.11 The authorities shall take due account of any difficulties experienced by interested parties, in particular small companies, in supplying information requested, and shall provide any assistance practicable.

12.12 The procedures set out above are not intended to prevent the authorities of a Member from proceeding expeditiously with regard to initiating an investigation, reaching preliminary or final determinations, whether affirmative or negative, or from applying provisional or final measures, in accordance with relevant provisions of this Agreement.

Article 13
Consultations

13.1 As soon as possible after an application under Article 11 is accepted, and in any event before the initiation of any investigation, Members the products of which may be subject to such investigation shall be invited for consultations with the aim of clarifying the situation as to the matters referred to in paragraph 2 of Article 11 and arriving at a mutually agreed solution.

13.2 Furthermore, throughout the period of investigation, Members the products of which are the subject of the investigation shall be afforded a reasonable opportunity to continue consultations, with a view to clarifying the factual situation and to arriving at a mutually agreed solution [IT IS PARTICULARLY IMPORTANT, IN ACCORDANCE WITH THE PROVISIONS OF THIS PARAGRAPH, THAT NO AFFIRMATIVE DETERMINATION WHETHER PRELIMINARY OR FINAL BE MADE WITHOUT REASONABLE OPPORTUNITY FOR CONSULTATIONS HAVING BEEN GIVEN. SUCH CONSULTATIONS MAY ESTABLISH THE BASIS FOR PROCEEDING UNDER THE PROVISIONS OF PART II, III OR X.].

13.3 Without prejudice to the obligation to afford reasonable opportunity for consultation, these provisions regarding consultations are not intended to prevent the authorities of a Member from proceeding expeditiously with regard to initiating the investigation, reaching preliminary or final determinations, whether affirmative or negative, or from applying provisional or final measures, in accordance with the provisions of this Agreement.

13.4 The Member which intends to initiate any investigation or is conducting such an investigation shall permit, upon request, the Member or Members the products of which are subject to such investigation access to non-confidential evidence, including the non-confidential summary of confidential data being used for initiating or conducting the investigation.

Article 14
Calculation of the Amount of a Subsidy in Terms of the Benefit to the Recipient

For the purpose of Part V, any method used by the investigating authority to calculate the benefit to the recipient conferred pursuant to paragraph 1 of Article 1 shall be provided for in the national legislation or implementing regulations of the Member concerned and its application to each particular case shall be transparent and adequately explained. Furthermore, any such method shall be consistent with the following guidelines:

(a) government provision of equity capital shall not be considered as conferring a benefit, unless the investment decision can be regarded as inconsistent with the usual investment practice (including for the provision of risk capital) of private investors in the territory of that Member;

(b) a loan by a government shall not be considered as conferring a benefit, unless there is a difference between the amount that the firm receiving the loan pays on the government loan and the amount the firm would pay on a comparable commercial loan which the firm could actually obtain on the market. In this case the benefit shall be the difference between these two amounts;

(c) a loan guarantee by a government shall not be considered as conferring a benefit, unless there is a difference between the amount that the firm receiving the guarantee pays on a loan guaranteed by the government and the amount that the firm would pay on a comparable commercial loan absent the government guarantee. In this case the benefit shall be the difference between these two amounts adjusted for any differences in fees;

(d) the provision of goods or services or purchase of goods by a government shall not be considered as conferring a benefit unless the provision is made for less than adequate remuneration, or the purchase is made for more than adequate remuneration. The adequacy of remuneration shall be determined in relation to prevailing market conditions for the good or service in question in the country of provision or purchase (including price, quality, availability, marketability, transportation and other conditions of purchase or sale).

Article 15
Determination of Injury

[UNDER THIS AGREEMENT THE TERM 'INJURY' SHALL, UNLESS OTHERWISE SPECIFIED, BE TAKEN TO MEAN MATERIAL INJURY TO A DOMESTIC INDUSTRY, THREAT OF MATERIAL INJURY TO A DOMESTIC INDUSTRY OR MATERIAL RETARDATION OF THE ESTABLISHMENT OF SUCH AN INDUSTRY AND SHALL BE INTERPRETED IN ACCORDANCE WITH THE PROVISIONS OF THIS ARTICLE.]

15.1 A determination of injury for purposes of Article VI of GATT 1994 shall be based on positive evidence and involve an objective examination of both *(a)* the volume of the subsidized imports and the effect of the subsidized imports on prices in the domestic market for like products [THROUGHOUT THIS AGREEMENT THE TERM 'LIKE PRODUCT' (*'PRODUIT SIMILAIRE'*) SHALL BE INTERPRETED TO MEAN A PRODUCT WHICH IS IDENTICAL, *I.E.* ALIKE IN ALL RESPECTS TO THE PRODUCT UNDER CONSIDERATION, OR IN THE ABSENCE OF SUCH A PRODUCT, ANOTHER PRODUCT WHICH, ALTHOUGH NOT ALIKE IN ALL RESPECTS, HAS CHARACTERISTICS CLOSELY RESEMBLING THOSE OF THE PRODUCT UNDER CONSIDERATION.] and *(b)* the consequent impact of these imports on the domestic producers of such products.

15.2 With regard to the volume of the subsidized imports, the investigating authorities shall consider whether there has been a significant increase in subsidized imports, either in absolute terms or relative to production or consumption in the importing Member. With regard to the effect of the subsidized imports on prices, the investigating authorities shall consider whether there has been a significant price undercutting by the subsidized imports as compared with the price of a like product of the importing Member, or whether the effect of such imports is otherwise to depress prices to a significant degree or to prevent price increases, which otherwise would have occurred, to a significant degree. No one or several of these factors can necessarily give decisive guidance.

15.3 Where imports of a product from more than one country are simultaneously subject to countervailing duty investigations, the investigating authorities may cumulatively assess the effects of such imports only if they determine that *(a)* the amount of subsidization established in relation to the imports from each country is more than *de minimis* as defined in paragraph 9 of Article 11 and the volume of imports from each country is not negligible and *(b)* a cumulative assessment of the effects of the imports is appropriate in light of the conditions of competition between the imported products and the conditions of competition between the imported products and the like domestic product.

15.4 The examination of the impact of the subsidized imports on the domestic industry shall include an evaluation of all relevant economic factors and indices having a bearing on the state of the industry, including actual and potential decline in output, sales, market share, profits, productivity, return on investments, or utilization of capacity; factors affecting domestic prices; actual and potential negative effects on cash flow, inventories, employment, wages, growth, ability to raise capital or investments and, in the case of agriculture, whether there has been an increased burden on government support programmes. This list is not exhaustive, nor can one or several of these factors necessarily give decisive guidance.

15.5 It must be demonstrated that the subsidized imports are, through the effects [AS SET FORTH IN PARAGRAPHS 2 AND 4.] of subsidies, causing injury within the meaning of this Agreement. The demonstration of a causal relationship between the subsidized imports and the injury to the domestic industry shall be based on an examination of all relevant evidence before the authorities. The authorities shall also examine any known factors other than the subsidized imports which at the same time are injuring the domestic industry, and the injuries caused by these other factors must not be attributed to the subsidized imports. Factors which may be relevant in this respect include, *inter alia*, the volumes and prices of non-subsidized imports of the product in question, contraction in demand or changes in the patterns of consumption, trade restrictive practices of and competition between the foreign and domestic producers, developments in technology and the export performance and productivity of the domestic industry.

15.6 The effect of the subsidized imports shall be assessed in relation to the domestic production of the like product when available data permit the separate identification of that production on the basis of such criteria as the production process, producers' sales and profits. If such separate identification of that production is not possible, the effects of the subsidized imports shall be assessed by the examination of the production of the narrowest group or range of products, which includes the like product, for which the necessary information can be provided.

15.7 A determination of a threat of material injury shall be based on facts and not merely on allegation, conjecture or remote possibility. The change in circumstances which would create a situation in which the subsidy would cause injury must be clearly foreseen and imminent. In making a determination regarding the existence of a threat of material injury, the investigating authorities should consider, *inter alia*, such factors as:

(i) nature of the subsidy or subsidies in question and the trade effects likely to arise therefrom;

(ii) a significant rate of increase of subsidized imports into the domestic market indicating the likelihood of substantially increased importation;

(iii) sufficient freely disposable, or an imminent, substantial increase in, capacity of the exporter indicating the likelihood of substantially increased subsidized exports to the importing Member's market, taking into account the availability of other export markets to absorb any additional exports;

(iv) whether imports are entering at prices that will have a significant depressing or suppressing effect on domestic prices, and would likely increase demand for further imports; and

(v) inventories of the product being investigated.

No one of these factors by itself can necessarily give decisive guidance but the totality of the factors considered must lead to the conclusion that further subsidized exports are imminent and that, unless protective action is taken, material injury would occur.

15.8 With respect to cases where injury is threatened by subsidized imports, the application of countervailing measures shall be considered and decided with special care.

Article 16
Definition of Domestic Industry

16.1 For the purposes of this Agreement, the term 'domestic industry' shall, except as provided in paragraph 2, be interpreted as referring to the domestic producers as a whole of the like products or to those of them whose collective output of the products constitutes a major proportion of the total domestic production of those products, except that when producers are related [FOR THE PURPOSE OF THIS PARAGRAPH, PRODUCERS SHALL BE DEEMED TO BE RELATED TO EXPORTERS OR IMPORTERS ONLY IF *(A)* ONE OF THEM DIRECTLY OR INDIRECTLY CONTROLS THE OTHER; OR *(B)* BOTH OF THEM ARE DIRECTLY OR INDIRECTLY CONTROLLED BY A THIRD PERSON; OR *(C)* TOGETHER THEY DIRECTLY OR INDIRECTLY CONTROL A THIRD PERSON, PROVIDED THAT THERE ARE GROUNDS FOR BELIEVING OR SUSPECTING THAT THE EFFECT OF THE RELATIONSHIP IS SUCH AS TO CAUSE THE PRODUCER CONCERNED TO BEHAVE DIFFERENTLY FROM NON-RELATED PRODUCERS. FOR THE PURPOSE OF THIS PARAGRAPH, ONE SHALL

BE DEEMED TO CONTROL ANOTHER WHEN THE FORMER IS LEGALLY OR OPERATIONALLY IN A POSITION TO EXERCISE RESTRAINT OR DIRECTION OVER THE LATTER.] to the exporters or importers or are themselves importers of the allegedly subsidized product or a like product from other countries, the term 'domestic industry' may be interpreted as referring to the rest of the producers.

16.2. In exceptional circumstances, the territory of a Member may, for the production in question, be divided into two or more competitive markets and the producers within each market may be regarded as a separate industry if *(a)* the producers within such market sell all or almost all of their production of the product in question in that market, and *(b)* the demand in that market is not to any substantial degree supplied by producers of the product in question located elsewhere in the territory. In such circumstances, injury may be found to exist even where a major portion of the total domestic industry is not injured, provided there is a concentration of subsidized imports into such an isolated market and provided further that the subsidized imports are causing injury to the producers of all or almost all of the production within such market.

16.3 When the domestic industry has been interpreted as referring to the producers in a certain area, *i.e.* a market as defined in paragraph 2, countervailing duties shall be levied only on the products in question consigned for final consumption to that area. When the constitutional law of the importing Member does not permit the levying of countervailing duties on such a basis, the importing Member may levy the countervailing duties without limitation only if *(a)* the exporters shall have been given an opportunity to cease exporting at subsidized prices to the area concerned or otherwise give assurances pursuant to Article 18, and adequate assurances in this regard have not been promptly given, and *(b)* such duties cannot be levied only on products of specific producers which supply the area in question.

16.4 Where two or more countries have reached under the provisions of paragraph 8(a) of Article XXIV of GATT 1994 such a level of integration that they have the characteristics of a single, unified market, the industry in the entire area of integration shall be taken to be the domestic industry referred to in paragraphs 1 and 2.

16.5 The provisions of paragraph 6 of Article 15 shall be applicable to this Article.

Article 17

Provisional Measures

17.1 Provisional measures may be applied only if:

(a) an investigation has been initiated in accordance with the provisions of Article 11, a public notice has been given to that effect and interested Members and interested parties have been given adequate opportunities to submit information and make comments;

(b) a preliminary affirmative determination has been made that a subsidy exists and that there is injury to a domestic industry caused by subsidized imports; and

(c) the authorities concerned judge such measures necessary to prevent injury being caused during the investigation.

17.2 Provisional measures may take the form of provisional

countervailing duties guaranteed by cash deposits or bonds equal to the amount of the provisionally calculated amount of subsidization.

17.3 Provisional measures shall not be applied sooner than 60 days from the date of initiation of the investigation.

17.4 The application of provisional measures shall be limited to as short a period as possible, not exceeding four months.

17.5 The relevant provisions of Article 19 shall be followed in the application of provisional measures.

Article 18
Undertakings

18.1 Proceedings may [THE WORD 'MAY' SHALL NOT BE INTERPRETED TO ALLOW THE SIMULTANEOUS CONTINUATION OF PROCEEDINGS WITH THE IMPLEMENTATION OF UNDERTAKINGS, EXCEPT AS PROVIDED IN PARAGRAPH 4.] be suspended or terminated without the imposition of provisional measures or countervailing duties upon receipt of satisfactory voluntary undertakings under which:

(a) the government of the exporting Member agrees to eliminate or limit the subsidy or take other measures concerning its effects; or

(b) the exporter agrees to revise its prices so that the investigating authorities are satisfied that the injurious effect of the subsidy is eliminated. Price increases under such undertakings shall not be higher than necessary to eliminate the amount of the subsidy. It is desirable that the price increases be less than the amount of the subsidy if such increases would be adequate to remove the injury to the domestic industry.

18.2 Undertakings shall not be sought or accepted unless the authorities of the importing Member have made a preliminary affirmative determination of subsidization and injury caused by such subsidization and, in case of undertakings from exporters, have obtained the consent of the exporting Member.

18.3 Undertakings offered need not be accepted if the authorities of the importing Member consider their acceptance impractical, for example if the number of actual or potential exporters is too great, or for other reasons, including reasons of general policy. Should the case arise and where practicable, the authorities shall provide to the exporter the reasons which have led them to consider acceptance of an undertaking as inappropriate, and shall, to the extent possible, give the exporter an opportunity to make comments thereon.

18.4 If an undertaking is accepted, the investigation of subsidization and injury shall nevertheless be completed if the exporting Member so desires or the importing Member so decides. In such a case, if a negative determination of subsidization or injury is made, the undertaking shall automatically lapse, except in cases where such a determination is due in large part to the existence of an undertaking. In such cases, the authorities concerned may require that an undertaking be maintained for a reasonable period consistent with the provisions of this Agreement. In the event that an affirmative determination of subsidization and injury is made, the undertaking shall continue consistent with its terms and the provisions of this Agreement.

18.5 Price undertakings may be suggested by the authorities of the importing Member, but no exporter shall be forced to enter into such undertakings. The fact that governments or exporters do not offer such undertakings, or do not accept an invitation to do so, shall in no way prejudice the consideration of the case. However, the authorities are free to determine that a threat of injury is more likely to be realized if the subsidized imports continue.

18.6 Authorities of an importing Member may require any government or exporter from whom an undertaking has been accepted to provide periodically information relevant to the fulfilment of such an undertaking, and to permit verification of pertinent data. In case of violation of an undertaking, the authorities of the importing Member may take, under this Agreement in conformity with its provisions, expeditious actions which may constitute immediate application of provisional measures using the best information available. In such cases, definitive duties may be levied in accordance with this Agreement on products entered for consumption not more than 90 days before the application of such provisional measures, except that any such retroactive assessment shall not apply to imports entered before the violation of the undertaking.

Article 19
Imposition and Collection of Countervailing Duties

19.1 If, after reasonable efforts have been made to complete consultations, a Member makes a final determination of the existence and amount of the subsidy and that, through the effects of the subsidy, the subsidized imports are causing injury, it may impose a countervailing duty in accordance with the provisions of this Article unless the subsidy or subsidies are withdrawn.

19.2 The decision whether or not to impose a countervailing duty in cases where all requirements for the imposition have been fulfilled, and the decision whether the amount of the countervailing duty to be imposed shall be the full amount of the subsidy or less, are decisions to be made by the authorities of the importing Member. It is desirable that the imposition should be permissive in the territory of all Members, that the duty should be less than the total amount of the subsidy if such lesser duty would be adequate to remove the injury to the domestic industry, and that procedures should be established which would allow the authorities concerned to take due account of representations made by domestic interested parties [FOR THE PURPOSE OF THIS PARAGRAPH, THE TERM 'DOMESTIC INTERESTED PARTIES' SHALL INCLUDE CONSUMERS AND INDUSTRIAL USERS OF THE IMPORTED PRODUCT SUBJECT TO INVESTIGATION.] whose interests might be adversely affected by the imposition of a countervailing duty.

19.3 When a countervailing duty is imposed in respect of any product, such countervailing duty shall be levied, in the appropriate amounts in each case, on a non-discriminatory basis on imports of such product from all sources found to be subsidized and causing injury, except as to imports from those sources which have renounced any subsidies in question or from which undertakings under the terms of this Agreement have been accepted. Any exporter whose exports are subject to a definitive countervailing duty but who was not actually investigated for reasons other than a refusal to cooperate, shall be entitled to an expedited review in order that the investigating authorities promptly establish an individual countervailing duty rate for that exporter.

19.4 No countervailing duty shall be levied [AS USED IN THIS AGREEMENT 'LEVY' SHALL MEAN THE DEFINITIVE OR FINAL LEGAL ASSESSMENT OR COLLECTION OF A DUTY OR TAX.] on any imported product in excess of the amount of the subsidy found to exist, calculated in terms of subsidization per unit of the subsidized and exported product.

Article 20
Retroactivity

20.1 Provisional measures and countervailing duties shall only be applied to products which enter for consumption after the time when the decision under paragraph 1 of Article 17 and paragraph 1 of Article 19, respectively, enters into force, subject to the exceptions set out in this Article.

20.2 Where a final determination of injury (but not of a threat thereof or of a material retardation of the establishment of an industry) is made or, in the case of a final determination of a threat of injury, where the effect of the subsidized imports would, in the absence of the provisional measures, have led to a determination of injury, countervailing duties may be levied retroactively for the period for which provisional measures, if any, have been applied.

20.3 If the definitive countervailing duty is higher than the amount guaranteed by the cash deposit or bond, the difference shall not be collected. If the definitive duty is less than the amount guaranteed by the cash deposit or bond, the excess amount shall be reimbursed or the bond released in an expeditious manner.

20.4 Except as provided in paragraph 2, where a determination of threat of injury or material retardation is made (but no injury has yet occurred) a definitive countervailing duty may be imposed only from the date of the determination of threat of injury or material retardation, and any cash deposit made during the period of the application of provisional measures shall be refunded and any bonds released in an expeditious manner.

20.5 Where a final determination is negative, any cash deposit made during the period of the application of provisional measures shall be refunded and any bonds released in an expeditious manner.

20.6 In critical circumstances where for the subsidized product in question the authorities find that injury which is difficult to repair is caused by massive imports in a relatively short period of a product benefiting from subsidies paid or bestowed inconsistently with the provisions of GATT 1994 and of this Agreement and where it is deemed necessary, in order to preclude the recurrence of such injury, to assess countervailing duties retroactively on those imports, the definitive countervailing duties may be assessed on imports which were entered for consumption not more than 90 days prior to the date of application of provisional measures.

Article 21
Duration and Review of Countervailing Duties and Undertakings

21.1 A countervailing duty shall remain in force only as long as and to the extent necessary to counteract subsidization which is causing injury.

21.2 The authorities shall review the need for the continued imposition of the duty, where warranted, on their own initiative or, provided that a reasonable period of time has elapsed since the imposition of the definitive countervailing duty, upon request by any interested party which submits positive information substantiating the need for a review. Interested parties shall have the right to request the authorities to examine whether the continued imposition of the duty is necessary to offset subsidization, whether the injury would be likely to continue or recur if the duty were removed or varied, or both. If, as a result of the review under this paragraph, the authorities determine that the countervailing duty is no longer warranted, it shall be terminated immediately.

21.3 Notwithstanding the provisions of paragraphs 1 and 2, any definitive countervailing duty shall be terminated on a date not later than five years from its imposition (or from the date of the most recent review under paragraph 2 if that review has covered both subsidization and injury, or under this paragraph), unless the authorities determine, in a review initiated before that date on their own initiative or upon a duly substantiated request made by or on behalf of the domestic industry within a reasonable period of time prior to that date, that the expiry of the duty would be likely to lead to continuation or recurrence of subsidization and injury [WHEN THE AMOUNT OF THE COUNTERVAILING DUTY IS ASSESSED ON A RETROSPECTIVE BASIS, A FINDING IN THE MOST RECENT ASSESSMENT PROCEEDING THAT NO DUTY IS TO BE LEVIED SHALL NOT BY ITSELF REQUIRE THE AUTHORITIES TO TERMINATE THE DEFINITIVE DUTY.]. The duty may remain in force pending the outcome of such a review.

21.4 The provisions of Article 12 regarding evidence and procedure shall apply to any review carried out under this Article. Any such review shall be carried out expeditiously and shall normally be concluded within 12 months of the date of initiation of the review.

21.5 The provisions of this Article shall apply *mutatis mutandis* to undertakings accepted under Article 18.

Article 22
Public Notice and Explanation of Determinations

22.1 When the authorities are satisfied that there is sufficient evidence to justify the initiation of an investigation pursuant to Article 11, the Member or Members the products of which are subject to such investigation and other interested parties known to the investigating authorities to have an interest therein shall be notified and a public notice shall be given.

22.2 A public notice of the initiation of an investigation shall contain, or otherwise make available through a separate report [WHERE AUTHORITIES PROVIDE INFORMATION AND EXPLANATIONS UNDER THE PROVISIONS OF THIS ARTICLE IN A SEPARATE REPORT, THEY SHALL ENSURE THAT SUCH REPORT IS READILY AVAILABLE TO THE PUBLIC.], adequate information on the following:

(i) the name of the exporting country or countries and the product involved;

(ii) the date of initiation of the investigation;

(iii) a description of the subsidy practice or practices to be investigated;
(iv) a summary of the factors on which the allegation of injury is based;
(v) the address to which representations by interested Members and interested parties should be directed; and
(vi) the time-limits allowed to interested Members and interested parties for making their views known.

22.3 Public notice shall be given of any preliminary or final determination, whether affirmative or negative, of any decision to accept an undertaking pursuant to Article 18, of the termination of such an undertaking, and of the termination of a definitive countervailing duty. Each such notice shall set forth, or otherwise make available through a separate report, in sufficient detail the findings and conclusions reached on all issues of fact and law considered material by the investigating authorities. All such notices and reports shall be forwarded to the Member or Members the products of which are subject to such determination or undertaking and to other interested parties known to have an interest therein.

22.4 A public notice of the imposition of provisional measures shall set forth, or otherwise make available through a separate report, sufficiently detailed explanations for the preliminary determinations on the existence of a subsidy and injury and shall refer to the matters of fact and law which have led to arguments being accepted or rejected. Such a notice or report shall, due regard being paid to the requirement for the protection of confidential information, contain in particular:

(i) the names of the suppliers or, when this is impracticable, the supplying countries involved;
(ii) a description of the product which is sufficient for customs purposes;
(iii) the amount of subsidy established and the basis on which the existence of a subsidy has been determined;
(iv) considerations relevant to the injury determination as set out in Article 15;
(v) the main reasons leading to the determination.

22.5 A public notice of conclusion or suspension of an investigation in the case of an affirmative determination providing for the imposition of a definitive duty or the acceptance of an undertaking shall contain, or otherwise make available through a separate report, all relevant information on the matters of fact and law and reasons which have led to the imposition of final measures or the acceptance of an undertaking, due regard being paid to the requirement for the protection of confidential information. In particular, the notice or report shall contain the information described in paragraph 4, as well as the reasons for the acceptance or rejection of relevant arguments or claims made by interested Members and by the exporters and importers.

22.6 A public notice of the termination or suspension of an investigation following the acceptance of an undertaking pursuant to Article 18 shall include, or otherwise make available through a separate report, the non-confidential part of this undertaking.

22.7 The provisions of this Article shall apply *mutatis mutandis* to the initiation and completion of reviews pursuant to Article 21 and to decisions under Article 20 to apply duties retroactively.

Article 23
Judicial Review

Each Member whose national legislation contains provisions on countervailing duty measures shall maintain judicial, arbitral or administrative tribunals or procedures for the purpose, *inter alia*, of the prompt review of administrative actions relating to final determinations and reviews of determinations within the meaning of Article 21. Such tribunals or procedures shall be independent of the authorities responsible for the determination or review in question, and shall provide all interested parties who participated in the administrative proceeding and are directly and individually affected by the administrative actions with access to review.

PART VI: INSTITUTIONS

Article 24
Committee on Subsidies and Countervailing Measures and Subsidiary Bodies

24.1 There is hereby established a Committee on Subsidies and Countervailing Measures composed of representatives from each of the Members. The Committee shall elect its own Chairman and shall meet not less than twice a year and otherwise as envisaged by relevant provisions of this Agreement at the request of any Member. The Committee shall carry out responsibilities as assigned to it under this Agreement or by the Members and it shall afford Members the opportunity of consulting on any matter relating to the operation of the Agreement or the furtherance of its objectives. The WTO Secretariat shall act as the secretariat to the Committee.

24.2 The Committee may set up subsidiary bodies as appropriate.

24.3 The Committee shall establish a Permanent Group of Experts composed of five independent persons, highly qualified in the fields of subsidies and trade relations. The experts will be elected by the Committee and one of them will be replaced every year. The PGE may be requested to assist a panel, as provided for in paragraph 5 of Article 4. The Committee may also seek an advisory opinion on the existence and nature of any subsidy.

24.4 The PGE may be consulted by any Member and may give advisory opinions on the nature of any subsidy proposed to be introduced or currently maintained by that Member. Such advisory opinions will be confidential and may not be invoked in proceedings under Article 7.

24.5 In carrying out their functions, the Committee and any subsidiary bodies may consult with and seek information from any source they deem appropriate. However, before the Committee or a subsidiary body seeks such information from a source within the jurisdiction of a Member, it shall inform the Member involved.

PART VII: NOTIFICATION AND SURVEILLANCE

Article 25
Notifications

25.1 Members agree that, without prejudice to the provisions of paragraph 1 of Article XVI of GATT 1994, their notifications of subsidies shall be submitted not later than 30 June of each year and shall conform to the provisions of paragraphs 2 through 6.

25.2 Members shall notify any subsidy as defined in paragraph 1 of Article 1, which is specific within the meaning of Article 2, granted or maintained within their territories.

25.3 The content of notifications should be sufficiently specific to enable other Members to evaluate the trade effects and to understand the operation of notified subsidy programmes. In this connection, and without prejudice to the contents and form of the questionnaire on subsidies [THE COMMITTEE SHALL ESTABLISH A WORKING PARTY TO REVIEW THE CONTENTS AND FORM OF THE QUESTIONNAIRE AS CONTAINED IN BISD 9S/193-194.], Members shall ensure that their notifications contain the following information:

(i) form of a subsidy (*i.e.* grant, loan, tax concession, *etc.*);
(ii) subsidy per unit or, in cases where this is not possible, the total amount or the annual amount budgeted for that subsidy (indicating, if possible, the average subsidy per unit in the previous year);
(iii) policy objective and/or purpose of a subsidy;
(iv) duration of a subsidy and/or any other time-limits attached to it;
(v) statistical data permitting an assessment of the trade effects of a subsidy.

25.4 Where specific points in paragraph 3 have not been addressed in a notification, an explanation shall be provided in the notification itself.

25.5 If subsidies are granted to specific products or sectors, the notifications should be organized by product or sector.

25.6 Members which consider that there are no measures in their territories requiring notification under paragraph 1 of Article XVI of GATT 1994 and this Agreement shall so inform the Secretariat in writing.

25.7 Members recognize that notification of a measure does not prejudge either its legal status under GATT 1994 and this Agreement, the effects under this Agreement, or the nature of the measure itself.

25.8 Any Member may, at any time, make a written request for information on the nature and extent of any subsidy granted or maintained by another Member (including any subsidy referred to in Part IV), or for an explanation of the reasons for which a specific measure has been considered as not subject to the requirement of notification.

25.9 Members so requested shall provide such information as quickly as possible and in a comprehensive manner, and shall be ready, upon request, to provide additional information to the requesting Member. In particular, they shall provide sufficient details to enable the other Member to assess their compliance with the terms of this Agreement. Any Member which considers that such information has not been provided may bring the matter to the attention of the Committee.

25.10 Any Member which considers that any measure of another Member having the effects of a subsidy has not been notified in accordance with the provisions of paragraph 1 of Article XVI of GATT 1994 and this Article may bring the matter to the attention of such other Member. If the alleged subsidy is not thereafter notified promptly, such Member may itself bring the alleged subsidy in question to the notice of the Committee.

25.11 Members shall report without delay to the Committee all preliminary or final actions taken with respect to countervailing duties. Such reports shall be available in the Secretariat for inspection by other Members. Members shall also submit, on a semi-annual basis, reports on any countervailing duty actions taken within the preceding six months. The semi-annual reports shall be submitted on an agreed standard form.

25.12 Each Member shall notify the Committee *(a)* which of its authorities are competent to initiate and conduct investigations referred to in Article 11 and *(b)* its domestic procedures governing the initiation and conduct of such investigations.

Article 26
Surveillance

26.1 The Committee shall examine new and full notifications submitted under paragraph 1 of Article XVI of GATT 1994 and paragraph 1 of Article 25 of this Agreement at special sessions held every third year. Notifications submitted in the intervening years (updating notifications) shall be examined at each regular meeting of the Committee.

26.2 The Committee shall examine reports submitted under paragraph 11 of Article 25 at each regular meeting of the Committee.

PART VIII: DEVELOPING COUNTRY MEMBERS

Article 27
Special and Differential Treatment of Developing Country Members

27.1 Members recognize that subsidies may play an important role in economic development programmes of developing country Members.

27.2 The prohibition of paragraph 1(a) of Article 3 shall not apply to:

(a) developing country Members referred to in Annex VII.

(b) other developing country Members for a period of eight years from the date of entry into force of the WTO Agreement, subject to compliance with the provisions in paragraph 4.

27.3 The prohibition of paragraph 1(b) of Article 3 shall not apply to developing country Members for a period of five years, and shall not apply to least developed country Members for a period of eight years, from the date of entry into force of the WTO Agreement.

27.4 Any developing country Member referred to in paragraph 2(b) shall phase out its export subsidies within the eight-year period, preferably in a progressive manner. However, a developing country Member shall not increase the level of its export subsidies [FOR A DEVELOPING COUNTRY

MEMBER NOT GRANTING EXPORT SUBSIDIES AS OF THE DATE OF ENTRY INTO FORCE OF THE WTO AGREEMENT, THIS PARAGRAPH SHALL APPLY ON THE BASIS OF THE LEVEL OF EXPORT SUBSIDIES GRANTED IN 1986.], and shall eliminate them within a period shorter than that provided for in this paragraph when the use of such export subsidies is inconsistent with its development needs. If a developing country Member deems it necessary to apply such subsidies beyond the 8-year period, it shall not later than one year before the expiry of this period enter into consultation with the Committee, which will determine whether an extension of this period is justified, after examining all the relevant economic, financial and development needs of the developing country Member in question. If the Committee determines that the extension is justified, the developing country Member concerned shall hold annual consultations with the Committee to determine the necessity of maintaining the subsidies. If no such determination is made by the Committee, the developing country Member shall phase out the remaining export subsidies within two years from the end of the last authorized period.

27.5 A developing country Member which has reached export competitiveness in any given product shall phase out its export subsidies for such product(s) over a period of two years. However, for a developing country Member which is referred to in Annex VII and which has reached export competitiveness in one or more products, export subsidies on such products shall be gradually phased out over a period of eight years.

27.6 Export competitiveness in a product exists if a developing country Member's exports of that product have reached a share of at least 3.25 per cent in world trade of that product for two consecutive calendar years. Export competitiveness shall exist either *(a)* on the basis of notification by the developing country Member having reached export competitiveness, or *(b)* on the basis of a computation undertaken by the Secretariat at the request of any Member. For the purpose of this paragraph, a product is defined as a section heading of the Harmonized System Nomenclature. The Committee shall review the operation of this provision five years from the date of the entry into force of the WTO Agreement.

27.7 The provisions of Article 4 shall not apply to a developing country Member in the case of export subsidies which are in conformity with the provisions of paragraphs 2 through 5. The relevant provisions in such a case shall be those of Article 7.

27.8 There shall be no presumption in terms of paragraph 1 of Article 6 that a subsidy granted by a developing country Member results in serious prejudice, as defined in this Agreement. Such serious prejudice, where applicable under the terms of paragraph 9, shall be demonstrated by positive evidence, in accordance with the provisions of paragraphs 3 through 8 of Article 6.

27.9 Regarding actionable subsidies granted or maintained by a developing country Member other than those referred to in paragraph 1 of Article 6, action may not be authorized or taken under Article 7 unless nullification or impairment of tariff concessions or other obligations under GATT 1994 is found to exist as a result of such a subsidy, in such a way as to displace or impede imports of a like product of another Member into the market of the subsidizing developing country Member or unless injury to a domestic industry in the market of an importing Member occurs.

27.10 Any countervailing duty investigation of a product originating in a developing country Member shall be terminated as soon as the authorities concerned determine that:

(a) the overall level of subsidies granted upon the product in question does not exceed 2 per cent of its value calculated on a per unit basis; or

(b) the volume of the subsidized imports represents less than 4 per cent of the total imports of the like product in the importing Member, unless imports from developing country Members whose individual shares of total imports represent less than 4 per cent collectively account for more than 9 per cent of the total imports of the like product in the importing Member.

27.11 For those developing country Members within the scope of paragraph 2(b) which have eliminated export subsidies prior to the expiry of the period of eight years from the date of entry into force of the WTO Agreement, and for those developing country Members referred to in Annex VII, the number in paragraph 10(a) shall be 3 per cent rather than 2 per cent. This provision shall apply from the date that the elimination of export subsidies is notified to the Committee, and for so long as export subsidies are not granted by the notifying developing country Member. This provision shall expire eight years from the date of entry into force of the WTO Agreement.

27.12 The provisions of paragraphs 10 and 11 shall govern any determination of *de minimis* under paragraph 3 of Article 15.

27.13 The provisions of Part III shall not apply to direct forgiveness of debts, subsidies to cover social costs, in whatever form, including relinquishment of government revenue and other transfer of liabilities when such subsidies are granted within and directly linked to a privatization programme of a developing country Member, provided that both such programme and the subsidies involved are granted for a limited period and notified to the Committee and that the programme results in eventual privatization of the enterprise concerned.

27.14 The Committee shall, upon request by an interested Member, undertake a review of a specific export subsidy practice of a developing country Member to examine whether the practice is in conformity with its development needs.

27.15 The Committee shall, upon request by an interested developing country Member, undertake a review of a specific countervailing measure to examine whether it is consistent with the provisions of paragraphs 10 and 11 as applicable to the developing country Member in question.

PART IX: TRANSITIONAL ARRANGEMENTS

Article 28
Existing Programmes

28.1 Subsidy programmes which have been established within the territory of any Member before the date on which such a Member signed the WTO Agreement and which are inconsistent with the provisions of this Agreement shall be:

(a) notified to the Committee not later than 90 days after the date of entry into force of the WTO Agreement for such Member; and

(b) brought into conformity with the provisions of this Agreement within three years of the date of entry into force of the WTO Agreement for such Member and until then shall not be subject to Part II.

28.2 No Member shall extend the scope of any such programme, nor shall such a programme be renewed upon its expiry.

Article 29

Transformation into a Market Economy

29.1 Members in the process of transformation from a centrally-planned into a market, free-enterprise economy may apply programmes and measures necessary for such a transformation.

29.2 For such Members, subsidy programmes falling within the scope of Article 3, and notified according to paragraph 3, shall be phased out or brought into conformity with Article 3 within a period of seven years from the date of entry into force of the WTO Agreement. In such a case, Article 4 shall not apply. In addition during the same period:

(a) Subsidy programmes falling within the scope of paragraph 1(d) of Article 6 shall not be actionable under Article 7;

(b) With respect to other actionable subsidies, the provisions of paragraph 9 of Article 27 shall apply.

29.3 Subsidy programmes falling within the scope of Article 3 shall be notified to the Committee by the earliest practicable date after the date of entry into force of the WTO Agreement. Further notifications of such subsidies may be made up to two years after the date of entry into force of the WTO Agreement.

29.4 In exceptional circumstances Members referred to in paragraph 1 may be given departures from their notified programmes and measures and their time-frame by the Committee if such departures are deemed necessary for the process of transformation.

PART X: DISPUTE SETTLEMENT

Article 30

The provisions of Articles XXII and XXIII of GATT 1994 as elaborated and applied by the Dispute Settlement Understanding shall apply to consultations and the settlement of disputes under this Agreement, except as otherwise specifically provided herein.

PART XI: FINAL PROVISIONS

Article 31

Provisional Application

The provisions of paragraph 1 of Article 6 and the provisions of Article 8 and Article 9 shall apply for a period of five years, beginning with the date of entry into force of the WTO Agreement. Not later than 180 days before the end of this period, the Committee shall review the operation of those provisions, with a view to determining whether to extend their application, either as presently drafted or in a modified form, for a further period.

Article 32

Other Final Provisions

32.1 No specific action against a subsidy of another Member can be taken except in accordance with the provisions of GATT 1994, as interpreted by this Agreement [THIS PARAGRAPH IS NOT INTENDED TO PRECLUDE ACTION UNDER OTHER RELEVANT PROVISIONS OF GATT 1994, WHERE APPROPRIATE.].

32.2 Reservations may not be entered in respect of any of the provisions of this Agreement without the consent of the other Members.

32.3 Subject to paragraph 4, the provisions of this Agreement shall apply to investigations, and reviews of existing measures, initiated pursuant to applications which have been made on or after the date of entry into force for a Member of the WTO Agreement.

32.4 For the purposes of paragraph 3 of Article 21, existing countervailing measures shall be deemed to be imposed on a date not later than the date of entry into force for a Member of the WTO Agreement, except in cases in which the domestic legislation of a Member in force at that date already included a clause of the type provided for in that paragraph.

32.5 Each Member shall take all necessary steps, of a general or particular character, to ensure, not later than the date of entry into force of the WTO Agreement for it, the conformity of its laws, regulations and administrative procedures with the provisions of this Agreement as they may apply to the Member in question.

32.6 Each Member shall inform the Committee of any changes in its laws and regulations relevant to this Agreement and in the administration of such laws and regulations.

32.7 The Committee shall review annually the implementation and operation of this Agreement, taking into account the objectives thereof. The Committee shall inform annually the Council for Trade in Goods of developments during the period covered by such reviews.

32.8 The Annexes to this Agreement constitute an integral part thereof.

ANNEX I

ILLUSTRATIVE LIST OF EXPORT SUBSIDIES

(a) The provision by governments of direct subsidies to a firm or an industry contingent upon export performance.

(b) Currency retention schemes or any similar practices which involve a bonus on exports.

(c) Internal transport and freight charges on export shipments, provided or mandated by governments, on terms more favourable than for domestic shipments.

(d) The provision by governments or their agencies either directly or indirectly through government-mandated schemes, of imported or domestic products or services for use in the production of exported goods, on terms or conditions more favourable than for provision of like or directly competitive products or services for use in the production of goods for domestic consumption, if (in the case of products) such terms or conditions are more favourable than those commercially available [THE TERM 'COMMERCIALLY AVAILABLE' MEANS THAT THE CHOICE BETWEEN DOMESTIC AND IMPORTED PRODUCTS IS UNRESTRICTED AND DEPENDS ONLY ON COMMERCIAL CONSIDERATIONS.] on world markets to their exporters.

(e) The full or partial exemption remission, or deferral specifically related to exports, of direct taxes [FOR THE PURPOSE OF THIS AGREEMENT: THE TERM 'DIRECT TAXES' SHALL MEAN TAXES ON WAGES, PROFITS, INTERESTS, RENTS, ROYALTIES, AND ALL OTHER FORMS OF INCOME, AND TAXES ON THE OWNERSHIP OF REAL PROPERTY; THE TERM 'IMPORT CHARGES' SHALL MEAN TARIFFS, DUTIES, AND OTHER FISCAL CHARGES NOT ELSEWHERE ENUMERATED IN THIS NOTE THAT ARE LEVIED ON IMPORTS; THE TERM 'INDIRECT TAXES' SHALL MEAN SALES, EXCISE, TURNOVER, VALUE ADDED, FRANCHISE, STAMP, TRANSFER, INVENTORY AND EQUIPMENT TAXES, BORDER TAXES AND ALL TAXES OTHER THAN DIRECT TAXES AND IMPORT CHARGES; 'PRIOR-STAGE' INDIRECT TAXES ARE THOSE LEVIED ON GOODS OR SERVICES USED DIRECTLY OR INDIRECTLY IN MAKING THE PRODUCT; 'CUMULATIVE' INDIRECT TAXES ARE MULTI-STAGED TAXES LEVIED WHERE THERE IS NO MECHANISM FOR SUBSEQUENT CREDITING OF THE TAX IF THE GOODS OR SERVICES SUBJECT TO TAX AT ONE STAGE OF PRODUCTION ARE USED IN A SUCCEEDING STAGE OF PRODUCTION; 'REMISSION' OF TAXES INCLUDES THE REFUND OR REBATE OF TAXES; 'REMISSION OR DRAWBACK' INCLUDES THE FULL OR PARTIAL EXEMPTION OR DEFERRAL OF IMPORT CHARGES.] or social welfare charges paid or payable by industrial or commercial enterprises [THE MEMBERS RECOGNIZE THAT DEFERRAL NEED NOT AMOUNT TO AN EXPORT SUBSIDY WHERE, FOR EXAMPLE, APPROPRIATE INTEREST CHARGES ARE COLLECTED. THE MEMBERS REAFFIRM THE PRINCIPLE THAT PRICES FOR GOODS IN TRANSACTIONS BETWEEN EXPORTING ENTERPRISES AND FOREIGN BUYERS UNDER THEIR OR UNDER THE SAME CONTROL SHOULD FOR TAX PURPOSES BE THE PRICES WHICH WOULD BE CHARGED BETWEEN INDEPENDENT ENTERPRISES ACTING AT ARM'S LENGTH. ANY MEMBER MAY DRAW THE ATTENTION OF ANOTHER MEMBER TO ADMINISTRATIVE OR OTHER PRACTICES WHICH MAY CONTRAVENE THIS PRINCIPLE AND WHICH RESULT IN A SIGNIFICANT SAVING OF DIRECT TAXES IN EXPORT TRANSACTIONS. IN SUCH CIRCUMSTANCES THE MEMBERS SHALL NORMALLY ATTEMPT TO RESOLVE THEIR DIFFERENCES USING THE FACILITIES OF EXISTING

BILATERAL TAX TREATIES OR OTHER SPECIFIC INTERNATIONAL MECHANISMS, WITHOUT PREJUDICE TO THE RIGHTS AND OBLIGATIONS OF MEMBERS UNDER GATT 1994, INCLUDING THE RIGHT OF CONSULTATION CREATED IN THE PRECEDING SENTENCE. PARAGRAPH (E) IS NOT INTENDED TO LIMIT A MEMBER FROM TAKING MEASURES TO AVOID THE DOUBLE TAXATION OF FOREIGN-SOURCE INCOME EARNED BY ITS ENTERPRISES OR THE ENTERPRISES OF ANOTHER MEMBER.].

(f) The allowance of special deductions directly related to exports or export performance, over and above those granted in respect to production for domestic consumption, in the calculation of the base on which direct taxes are charged.

(g) The exemption or remission, in respect of the production and distribution of exported products, of indirect taxes [PARAGRAPH (H) DOES NOT APPLY TO VALUE-ADDED TAX SYSTEMS AND BORDER-TAX ADJUSTMENT IN LIEU THEREOF; THE PROBLEM OF THE EXCESSIVE REMISSION OF VALUE-ADDED TAXES IS EXCLUSIVELY COVERED BY PARAGRAPH (G).] in excess of those levied in respect of the production and distribution of like products when sold for domestic consumption.

(h) The exemption, remission or deferral of prior-stage cumulative indirect taxes [PARAGRAPH (H) DOES NOT APPLY TO VALUE-ADDED TAX SYSTEMS AND BORDER-TAX ADJUSTMENT IN LIEU THEREOF; THE PROBLEM OF THE EXCESSIVE REMISSION OF VALUE-ADDED TAXES IS EXCLUSIVELY COVERED BY PARAGRAPH (G).] on goods or services used in the production of exported products in excess of the exemption, remission or deferral of like prior-stage cumulative indirect taxes on goods or services used in the production of like products when sold for domestic consumption; provided, however, that prior-stage cumulative indirect taxes may be exempted, remitted or deferred on exported products even when not exempted, remitted or deferred on like products when sold for domestic consumption, if the prior-stage cumulative indirect taxes are levied on inputs that are consumed in the production of the exported product (making normal allowance for waste) [PARAGRAPH (H) DOES NOT APPLY TO VALUE-ADDED TAX SYSTEMS AND BORDER-TAX ADJUSTMENT IN LIEU THEREOF; THE PROBLEM OF THE EXCESSIVE REMISSION OF VALUE-ADDED TAXES IS EXCLUSIVELY COVERED BY PARAGRAPH (G).]. This item shall be interpreted in accordance with the guidelines on consumption of inputs in the production process contained in Annex II.

(i) The remission or drawback of import charges [PARAGRAPH (H) DOES NOT APPLY TO VALUE-ADDED TAX SYSTEMS AND BORDER-TAX ADJUSTMENT IN LIEU THEREOF; THE PROBLEM OF THE EXCESSIVE REMISSION OF VALUE-ADDED TAXES IS EXCLUSIVELY COVERED BY PARAGRAPH (G).] in excess of those levied on imported inputs that are consumed in the production of the exported product (making normal allowance for waste); provided, however, that in particular cases a firm may use a quantity of home market inputs equal to, and having the same quality and characteristics as, the imported inputs as a substitute for them in order to benefit from this provision if the import and the corresponding export operations both occur within a reasonable time period, not to exceed two years. This item shall be interpreted in accordance with the guidelines on consumption of inputs in the production process contained in Annex II and the guidelines in the determination of substitution drawback systems as export subsidies contained in Annex III.

(j) The provision by governments (or special institutions controlled by governments) of export credit guarantee or insurance programmes, of insurance or guarantee programmes against increases in the cost of exported products or of exchange risk programmes, at premium rates which are inadequate to cover the long-term operating costs and losses of the programmes.

(k) The grant by governments (or special institutions controlled by and/or acting under the authority of governments) of export credits at rates below those which they actually have to pay for the funds so employed (or would have to pay if they borrowed on international capital markets in order to obtain funds of the same maturity and other credit terms and denominated in the same currency as the export credit), or the payment by them of all or part of the costs incurred by exporters or financial institutions in obtaining credits, in so far as they are used to secure a material advantage in the field of export credit terms.

Provided, however, that if a Member is a party to an international undertaking on official export credits to which at least twelve original Members to this Agreement are parties as of 1 January 1979 (or a successor undertaking which has been adopted by those original Members), or if in practice a Member applies the interest rates provisions of the relevant undertaking, an export credit practice which is in conformity with those provisions shall not be considered an export subsidy prohibited by this Agreement.

(l) Any other charge on the public account constituting an export subsidy in the sense of Article XVI of GATT 1994.

ANNEX II

GUIDELINES ON CONSUMPTION OF INPUTS IN THE PRODUCTION PROCESS

[INPUTS CONSUMED IN THE PRODUCTION PROCESS ARE INPUTS PHYSICALLY INCORPORATED, ENERGY, FUELS AND OIL USED IN THE PRODUCTION PROCESS AND CATALYSTS WHICH ARE CONSUMED IN THE COURSE OF THEIR USE TO OBTAIN THE EXPORTED PRODUCT.]

I

1. Indirect tax rebate schemes can allow for exemption, remission or deferral of prior-stage cumulative indirect taxes levied on inputs that are consumed in the production of the exported product (making normal allowance for waste). Similarly, drawback schemes can allow for the remission or

drawback of import charges levied on inputs that are consumed in the production of the exported product (making normal allowance for waste).

2. The Illustrative List of Export Subsidies in Annex I of this Agreement makes reference to the term 'inputs that are consumed in the production of the exported product' in paragraphs (h) and (i). Pursuant to paragraph (h), indirect tax rebate schemes can constitute an export subsidy to the extent that they result in exemption, remission or deferral of prior-stage cumulative indirect taxes in excess of the amount of such taxes actually levied on inputs that are consumed in the production of the exported product. Pursuant to paragraph (i), drawback schemes can constitute an export subsidy to the extent that they result in a remission or drawback of import charges in excess of those actually levied on inputs that are consumed in the production of the exported product. Both paragraphs stipulate that normal allowance for waste must be made in findings regarding consumption of inputs in the production of the exported product. Paragraph (i) also provides for substitution, where appropriate.

II

In examining whether inputs are consumed in the production of the exported product, as part of a countervailing duty investigation pursuant to this Agreement, investigating authorities should proceed on the following basis:

1. Where it is alleged that an indirect tax rebate scheme, or a drawback scheme, conveys a subsidy by reason of over-rebate or excess drawback of indirect taxes or import charges on inputs consumed in the production of the exported product, the investigating authorities should first determine whether the government of the exporting Member has in place and applies a system or procedure to confirm which inputs are consumed in the production of the exported product and in what amounts. Where such a system or procedure is determined to be applied, the investigating authorities should then examine the system or procedure to see whether it is reasonable, effective for the purpose intended, and based on generally accepted commercial practices in the country of export. The investigating authorities may deem it necessary to carry out, in accordance with paragraph 6 of Article 12, certain practical tests in order to verify information or to satisfy themselves that the system or procedure is being effectively applied.

2. Where there is no such system or procedure, where it is not reasonable, or where it is instituted and considered reasonable but is found not to be applied or not to be applied effectively, a further examination by the exporting Member based on the actual inputs involved would need to be carried out in the context of determining whether an excess payment occurred. If the investigating authorities deemed it necessary, a further examination would be carried out in accordance with paragraph 1.

3. Investigating authorities should treat inputs as physically incorporated if such inputs are used in the production process and are physically present in the product exported. The Members note that an input need not be present in the final product in the same form in which it entered the production process.

4. In determining the amount of a particular input that is consumed in the production of the exported product, a 'normal allowance for

waste' should be taken into account, and such waste should be treated as consumed in the production of the exported product. The term 'waste' refers to that portion of a given input which does not serve an independent function in the production process, is not consumed in the production of the exported product (for reasons such as inefficiencies) and is not recovered, used or sold by the same manufacturer.

5. The investigating authority's determination of whether the claimed allowance for waste is 'normal' should take into account the production process, the average experience of the industry in the country of export, and other technical factors, as appropriate. The investigating authority should bear in mind that an important question is whether the authorities in the exporting Member have reasonably calculated the amount of waste, when such an amount is intended to be included in the tax or duty rebate or remission.

ANNEX III

GUIDELINES IN THE DETERMINATION OF SUBSTITUTION DRAWBACK SYSTEMS AS EXPORT SUBSIDIES

I

Drawback systems can allow for the refund or drawback of import charges on inputs which are consumed in the production process of another product and where the export of this latter product contains domestic inputs having the same quality and characteristics as those substituted for the imported inputs. Pursuant to paragraph (i) of the Illustrative List of Export Subsidies in Annex I, substitution drawback systems can constitute an export subsidy to the extent that they result in an excess drawback of the import charges levied initially on the imported inputs for which drawback is being claimed.

II

In examining any substitution drawback system as part of a countervailing duty investigation pursuant to this Agreement, investigating authorities should proceed on the following basis:

1. Paragraph (i) of the Illustrative List stipulates that home market inputs may be substituted for imported inputs in the production of a product for export provided such inputs are equal in quantity to, and have the same quality and characteristics as, the imported inputs being substituted. The existence of a verification system or procedure is important because it enables the government of the exporting Member to ensure and demonstrate that the quantity of inputs for which drawback is claimed does not exceed the quantity of similar products exported, in whatever form, and that there is not drawback of import charges in excess of those originally levied on the imported inputs in question.

2. Where it is alleged that a substitution drawback system conveys a subsidy, the investigating authorities should first proceed to determine whether the government of the exporting Member has in place and applies a verification system or procedure. Where such a system or procedure is determined to be applied, the investigating authorities should then examine

the verification procedures to see whether they are reasonable, effective for the purpose intended, and based on generally accepted commercial practices in the country of export. To the extent that the procedures are determined to meet this test and are effectively applied, no subsidy should be presumed to exist. It may be deemed necessary by the investigating authorities to carry out, in accordance with paragraph 6 of Article 12, certain practical tests in order to verify information or to satisfy themselves that the verification procedures are being effectively applied.

3. Where there are no verification procedures, where they are not reasonable, or where such procedures are instituted and considered reasonable but are found not to be actually applied or not applied effectively, there may be a subsidy. In such cases a further examination by the exporting Member based on the actual transactions involved would need to be carried out to determine whether an excess payment occurred. If the investigating authorities deemed it necessary, a further examination would be carried out in accordance with paragraph 2.

4. The existence of a substitution drawback provision under which exporters are allowed to select particular import shipments on which drawback is claimed should not of itself be considered to convey a subsidy.

5. An excess drawback of import charges in the sense of paragraph (i) would be deemed to exist where governments paid interest on any monies refunded under their drawback schemes, to the extent of the interest actually paid or payable.

ANNEX IV

CALCULATION OF THE TOTAL AD VALOREM SUBSIDIZATION (PARAGRAPH 1(A) OF ARTICLE 6)

[AN UNDERSTANDING AMONG MEMBERS SHOULD BE DEVELOPED, AS NECESSARY, ON MATTERS WHICH ARE NOT SPECIFIED IN THIS ANNEX OR WHICH NEED FURTHER CLARIFICATION FOR THE PURPOSES OF PARAGRAPH 1(A) OF ARTICLE 6.]

1. Any calculation of the amount of a subsidy for the purpose of paragraph 1(a) of Article 6 shall be done in terms of the cost to the granting government.

2. Except as provided in paragraphs 3 through 5, in determining whether the overall rate of subsidization exceeds 5 per cent of the value of the product, the value of the product shall be calculated as the total value of the recipient firm's [THE RECIPIENT FIRM IS A FIRM IN THE TERRITORY OF THE SUBSIDIZING MEMBER.] sales in the most recent 12-month period, for which sales data is available, preceding the period in which the subsidy is granted [IN THE CASE OF TAX-RELATED SUBSIDIES THE VALUE OF THE PRODUCT SHALL BE CALCULATED AS THE TOTAL VALUE OF THE RECIPIENT FIRM'S SALES IN THE FISCAL YEAR IN WHICH THE TAX-RELATED MEASURE WAS EARNED.].

3. Where the subsidy is tied to the production or sale of a given product, the value of the product shall be calculated as the total value of the recipient firm's sales of that product in the most recent 12-month period, for which sales data is available, preceding the period in which the subsidy is

granted.

4. Where the recipient firm is in a start-up situation, serious prejudice shall be deemed to exist if the overall rate of subsidization exceeds 15 per cent of the total funds invested. For purposes of this paragraph, a start-up period will not extend beyond the first year of production [START-UP SITUATIONS INCLUDE INSTANCES WHERE FINANCIAL COMMITMENTS FOR PRODUCT DEVELOPMENT OR CONSTRUCTION OF FACILITIES TO MANUFACTURE PRODUCTS BENEFITING FROM THE SUBSIDY HAVE BEEN MADE, EVEN THOUGH PRODUCTION HAS NOT BEGUN.].

5. Where the recipient firm is located in an inflationary economy country, the value of the product shall be calculated as the recipient firm's total sales (or sales of the relevant product, if the subsidy is tied) in the preceding calendar year indexed by the rate of inflation experienced in the 12 months preceding the month in which the subsidy is to be given.

6. In determining the overall rate of subsidization in a given year, subsidies given under different programmes and by different authorities in the territory of a Member shall be aggregated.

7. Subsidies granted prior to the date of entry into force of the WTO Agreement, the benefits of which are allocated to future production, shall be included in the overall rate of subsidization.

8. Subsidies which are non-actionable under relevant provisions of this Agreement shall not be included in the calculation of the amount of a subsidy for the purpose of paragraph 1(a) of Article 6.

ANNEX V

PROCEDURES FOR DEVELOPING INFORMATION CONCERNING SERIOUS PREJUDICE

1. Every Member shall cooperate in the development of evidence to be examined by a panel in procedures under paragraphs 4 through 6 of Article 7. The parties to the dispute and any third-country Member concerned shall notify to the DSB, as soon as the provisions of paragraph 4 of Article 7 have been invoked, the organization responsible for administration of this provision within its territory and the procedures to be used to comply with requests for information.

2. In cases where matters are referred to the DSB under paragraph 4 of Article 7, the DSB shall, upon request, initiate the procedure to obtain such information from the government of the subsidizing Member as necessary to establish the existence and amount of subsidization, the value of total sales of the subsidized firms, as well as information necessary to analyze the adverse effects caused by the subsidized product [IN CASES WHERE THE EXISTENCE OF SERIOUS PREJUDICE HAS TO BE DEMONSTRATED.]. This process may include, where appropriate, presentation of questions to the government of the subsidizing Member and of the complaining Member to collect information, as well as to clarify and obtain elaboration of information available to the parties to a dispute through the notification procedures set forth in Part VII [THE INFORMATION-GATHERING PROCESS BY THE DSB SHALL TAKE INTO ACCOUNT THE NEED TO PROTECT INFORMATION

WHICH IS BY NATURE CONFIDENTIAL OR WHICH IS PROVIDED ON A CONFIDENTIAL BASIS BY ANY MEMBER INVOLVED IN THIS PROCESS.].

3. In the case of effects in third-country markets, a party to a dispute may collect information, including through the use of questions to the government of the third-country Member, necessary to analyse adverse effects, which is not otherwise reasonably available from the complaining Member or the subsidizing Member. This requirement should be administered in such a way as not to impose an unreasonable burden on the third-country Member. In particular, such a Member is not expected to make a market or price analysis specially for that purpose. The information to be supplied is that which is already available or can be readily obtained by this Member (*e.g.* most recent statistics which have already been gathered by relevant statistical services but which have not yet been published, customs data concerning imports and declared values of the products concerned, *etc.*). However, if a party to a dispute undertakes a detailed market analysis at its own expense, the task of the person or firm conducting such an analysis shall be facilitated by the authorities of the third-country Member and such a person or firm shall be given access to all information which is not normally maintained confidential by the government.

4. The DSB shall designate a representative to serve the function of facilitating the information-gathering process. The sole purpose of the representative shall be to ensure the timely development of the information necessary to facilitate expeditious subsequent multilateral review of the dispute. In particular, the representative may suggest ways to most efficiently solicit necessary information as well as encourage the cooperation of the parties.

5. The information-gathering process outlined in paragraphs 2 through 4 shall be completed within 60 days of the date on which the matter has been referred to the DSB under paragraph 4 of Article 7. The information obtained during this process shall be submitted to the panel established by the DSB in accordance with the provisions of Part X. This information should include, *inter alia*, data concerning the amount of the subsidy in question (and, where appropriate, the value of total sales of the subsidized firms), prices of the subsidized product, prices of the non-subsidized product, prices of other suppliers to the market, changes in the supply of the subsidized product to the market in question and changes in market shares. It should also include rebuttal evidence, as well as such supplemental information as the panel deems relevant in the course of reaching its conclusions.

6. If the subsidizing and/or third-country Member fail to cooperate in the information-gathering process, the complaining Member will present its case of serious prejudice, based on evidence available to it, together with facts and circumstances of the non-cooperation of the subsidizing and/or third-country Member. Where information is unavailable due to non-cooperation by the subsidizing and/or third-country Member, the panel may complete the record as necessary relying on best information otherwise available.

7. In making its determination, the panel should draw adverse inferences from instances of non- cooperation by any party involved in the information-gathering process.

8. In making a determination to use either best information

available or adverse inferences, the panel shall consider the advice of the DSB representative nominated under paragraph 4 as to the reasonableness of any requests for information and the efforts made by parties to comply with these requests in a cooperative and timely manner.

9. Nothing in the information-gathering process shall limit the ability of the panel to seek such additional information it deems essential to a proper resolution to the dispute, and which was not adequately sought or developed during that process. However, ordinarily the panel should not request additional information to complete the record where the information would support a particular party's position and the absence of that information in the record is the result of unreasonable non-cooperation by that party in the information-gathering process.

ANNEX VI

PROCEDURES FOR ON-THE-SPOT INVESTIGATIONS PURSUANT TO PARAGRAPH 6 OF ARTICLE 12

1. Upon initiation of an investigation, the authorities of the exporting Member and the firms known to be concerned should be informed of the intention to carry out on-the-spot investigations.

2. If in exceptional circumstances it is intended to include non-governmental experts in the investigating team, the firms and the authorities of the exporting Member should be so informed. Such non-governmental experts should be subject to effective sanctions for breach of confidentiality requirements.

3. It should be standard practice to obtain explicit agreement of the firms concerned in the exporting Member before the visit is finally scheduled.

4. As soon as the agreement of the firms concerned has been obtained, the investigating authorities should notify the authorities of the exporting Member of the names and addresses of the firms to be visited and the dates agreed.

5. Sufficient advance notice should be given to the firms in question before the visit is made.

6. Visits to explain the questionnaire should only be made at the request of an exporting firm. In case of such a request the investigating authorities may place themselves at the disposal of the firm; such a visit may only be made if *(a)* the authorities of the importing Member notify the representatives of the government of the Member in question and *(b)* the latter do not object to the visit.

7. As the main purpose of the on-the-spot investigation is to verify information provided or to obtain further details, it should be carried out after the response to the questionnaire has been received unless the firm agrees to the contrary and the government of the exporting Member is informed by the investigating authorities of the anticipated visit and does not object to it; further, it should be standard practice prior to the visit to advise the firms concerned of the general nature of the information to be verified and of any further information which needs to be provided, though this should not preclude requests to be made on the spot for further details to be provided in the light of information obtained.

8. Enquiries or questions put by the authorities or firms of the exporting Members and essential to a successful on-the-spot investigation should, whenever possible, be answered before the visit is made.

ANNEX VII

DEVELOPING COUNTRY MEMBERS REFERRED TO IN PARAGRAPH 2(A) OF ARTICLE 27

The developing country Members not subject to the provisions of paragraph 1(a) of Article 3 under the terms of paragraph 2(a) of Article 27 are:

(a) Least-developed countries designated as such by the United Nations which are Members of the WTO.

(b) Each of the following developing countries which are Members of the WTO shall be subject to the provisions which are applicable to other developing country Members according to paragraph 2(b) of Article 27 when GNP per capita has reached $1,000 per annum [THE INCLUSION OF DEVELOPING COUNTRY MEMBERS IN THE LIST IN PARAGRAPH (B) IS BASED ON THE MOST RECENT DATA FROM THE WORLD BANK ON GNP PER CAPITA.]: Bolivia, Cameroon, Congo, Côte d'Ivoire, Dominican Republic, Egypt, Ghana, Guatemala, Guyana, India, Indonesia, Kenya, Morocco, Nicaragua, Nigeria, Pakistan, Philippines, Senegal, Sri Lanka and Zimbabwe."

Decision on Anti-Circumvention—the Text

"DECISION ON ANTI-CIRCUMVENTION

Ministers,

Noting that while the problem of circumvention of anti-dumping duty measures formed part of the negotiations which preceded the Agreement on Implementation of Article VI of GATT 1994, negotiators were unable to agree on specific text,

Mindful of the desirability of the applicability of uniform rules in this area as soon as possible,

Decide to refer this matter to the Committee on Anti-Dumping Practices established under that Agreement for resolution."

Decision on Review of Article 17.6 of the Agreement on Implementation of GATT's Article VI – the Text

"DECISION ON REVIEW OF ARTICLE 17.6 OF THE AGREEMENT ON IMPLEMENTATION OF ARTICLE VI OF THE GENERAL AGREEMENT ON TARIFFS AND TRADE 1994

Ministers decide as follows:

The standard of review in paragraph 6 of Article 17 of the Agreement on Implementation of Article VI of GATT 1994 shall be reviewed after a period of three years with a view to considering the question of whether it is capable of general application."

1 The word "may" shall not be interpreted to allow the simultaneous continuation of proceedings with the implementation of price undertakings except as provided in paragraph 4.

2 It is understood that the observance of the time-limits mentioned in this subparagraph and in subparagraph 3.2 may not be possible where the product in question is subject to judicial review proceedings.

3A determination of final liability for payment of anti-dumping duties, as provided for in paragraph 3 of Article 9, does not by itself constitute a review within the meaning of this Article.

4 When the amount of the anti-dumping duty is assessed on a retrospective basis, a finding in the most recent assessment proceeding under subparagraph 3.1 of Article 9 that no duty is to be levied shall not by itself require the authorities to terminate the definitive duty.

5 Where authorities provide information and explanations under the provisions of this Article in a separate report, they shall ensure that such report is readily available to the public.

6 This is not intended to preclude action under other relevant provisions of GATT 1994, as appropriate."

INDEX

www.ingramcontent.com/pod-product-compliance
Ingram Content Group UK Ltd.
Pitfield, Milton Keynes, MK11 3LW, UK
UKHW041143300926
15471UKWH00011B/110

9 781571 052223